Contents

iii

4. BIOLOGICAL ARCHITECTURE: TISSUES, ORGANS, AND ORGANISMS 85

5. THE LIVING COMMUNITY 117

6. ENERGY 175

7. SUPPORTING PROCESSES OF LIFE 203

v

Credits for Chapter Opening Photographs

1 Honeybees surrounding queen. (Courtesy of Carolina Biological Supply Company.)

2 Bull sea lion guarding his harem in the Galápagos Islands. (George H. Harrison, from Grant Heilman.)

3 *Elodea* leaf showing cells, chloroplasts, and nucleus (X 1000). (Runk/Schoenberger, from Grant Heilman.)

4 Mushroom cluster. (California Academy of Sciences.)

5 Tidepool showing sea anemones, starfish, and coralline algae. (California Academy of Sciences.)

6 Sun—the source of energy. (Alan Pitcairn, from Grant Heilman.)

7 Scanning electron micrograph of a red blood corpuscle enmeshed in fibrin. (Courtesy of Emil Bernstein and Eila Kairinen, Gillette Company Research Institute, Rockville, Md.)

8 *Elodea* leaf cells showing plasmolysis, by addition of salt (X 450). (Runk/Schoenberger, from Grant Heilman.)

9 Blue-footed booby shielding its egg. (Maggie Cavagnaro; California Academy of Sciences.)

10 Forty-day-old human embryo within intact fluid sac. (Chester F. Reather, RBP, FBPA, Carnegie Institution of Washington.)

11 Mixed cattle. (Grant Heilman.)

12 Fossil of shell in stone fence post on a prairie in Kansas. (Grant Heilman.)

Appendix Milk snake. (Jack Dermid.)

Preface

One of the most exciting and relevant experiences of education can be the study of life—what it is, how it functions, and how knowledge of it can affect our everyday existence. The discoveries of modern science have enabled us to make successful organ transplants, consider genetic manipulation, vastly improve crop yields, and even send man to the moon. But our very existence may be threatened by the activities of life itself. For example, the side effects of some insecticides may cancel the benefits, imprudent use of technology often pollutes the environment, and the increasing human population strains our basic resources. A study of biology thus is necessary for a rational and intelligent consideration of the many medical and ecological issues of our day.

It is important that students have an understanding of all fields of biology, not just the areas in which exciting developments are occurring today. In this book, therefore, we have attempted to present a balance between the classical aspects of the biological sciences and the areas of recent research. Historical perspective often helps in the understanding of certain biological concepts. Thus, for topics like the cell, photosynthesis, genetics, and evolution, historical development is judiciously traced. And since it is also important for students to appreciate the nature of science, scientific methodology, and the analysis of data, these are stressed throughout the book.

This book presents the important principles of biology through the use of selected examples and requires no previous knowledge of biology or related sciences. It is organized into twelve chapters, or modular units, which represent the major areas of biology: (1) the study of science and biology; (2) chemistry and life; (3) cells; (4) tissues, organs, and organisms; (5) ecology and environment; (6) energy relationships; (7) metabolism and supporting processes; (8) control mechanisms; (9) behavior; (10) reproduction; (11) genetics; and (12) evolution. This organization follows a logical sequence of subject matter; but since each chapter is a complete topic, the sequence can be changed to fit a preferred course of study. For example, the chapters on reproduction and genetics could readily follow the chapters on chemistry and cells. It is recommended, however, that the first three chapters, which contain fundamental information, be studied early in the course.

Each chapter concludes with summarizing statements outlining the major points in the chapter. Thought-provoking review questions are also provided at the end of each chapter. And an up-to-date list of supplementary readings encourages the student to study a particular subject in more detail. The classification and major characteristics of organisms appear in an appendix for use throughout the course. An extensive glossary is also available and should be consulted.

It is a rare textbook that cannot be significantly improved in subsequent editions. Acting on this premise, the authors consulted students and instructors across the nation who used the first edition, as well as specialists in the subdisciplines of biology. The second edition reflects the results of this scrutiny, scrubbing, updating, and polishing. For example, a chapter on behavior has been added. Human reproduction, protein synthesis, development, and evolution have received special attention. Finally, more emphasis has been placed on environmental and human biology throughout the second edition of *Living Systems*.

1

Science and Biology: Perspective

Most of us at some time have been irresistibly drawn to investigate a bee hive or a wasp nest; this attraction no doubt stems from the living activity around these insect homes. Often our observations lead to further investigation and, eventually, inspection of the contents of the hive, exposing the inhabitants and their way of life. What were these activities that stimulated our curiosity? First of all we saw the movement and the characteristic structure of these animals. We could see bees collecting nectar from flowers to make honey, and if we looked closer we saw eggs and various growth and developmental stages. More subtle than these obvious characteristics are the social structure and the communication among members of the society. The well-developed communication system employed by these organisms permits the exchange of important information on the location and source of food. All the characteristics of life—movement, responsiveness, reproduction, growth and development, structure and organization, and metabolism and adaptation—can be observed in a bee hive.

Through curiosity and experimentation with nature, man has been able to modify much of his environment to suit his needs. For example, man has derived great benefit from the discovery of better medical techniques and better agricultural practices. Man's eagerness to investigate and manipulate his environment, however, has produced some damaging results to the balance of nature. Some of these, such as air and water pollution, are among the most serious problems in biology today.

Around 1940, DDT, a compound which belongs to a group of chemicals known as chlorinated hydrocarbons, was heralded for its great usefulness to humanity. It was used to destroy many of the insects affecting man and his economy. Mosquitoes, flies, tree moths, bark beetles, and a host of agricultural insect pests became the targets of this pesticide, and as a result man and his crops and various trees benefited. But then certain problems connected with the use of DDT arose. After a few years of spraying, mosquitoes and other insects became immune to the pesticide; by 1960 over 65 insects which infect crops developed resistance. More seriously, DDT was demonstrated to be a cancer producer. The chemical was also directly linked with the death of many birds; this often occurred through a sequence of food steps beginning from the leaves of sprayed trees which dropped and decayed, to the earthworms which lived in the decaying material, and leading finally to the birds which ate the worms. Fish-eating birds and animals were also affected by DDT. The chemical was carried into lakes and oceans where it was ingested by small organisms which in turn were eaten by fish or clams. And since sea birds eat many fish and clams, the DDT became more concentrated in their bodies through the process of *magnification*. Fat soluble DDT is stored with fats and oils and concentrated when these materials are eaten and digested. Clams may show a body concentration of only 0.09 parts per million whereas a seagull may contain 25 parts per million, principally in body fat.

In Borneo, where DDT was used to kill malaria-carrying mosquitoes, cockroaches also absorbed the chemical and were eaten by small rodents which were then eaten by cats. DDT was picked up by the cockroaches, concentrated by the rodents, and finally concentrated again by the cats to an amount sufficient to kill them. The rat population thrived with the decrease in cats and soon a new problem emerged—numerous rats carrying another disease, bubonic plague. A world-wide problem resulted from what was earlier considered to be an advantage of using DDT as a pesticide—that is, its relative stability. DDT degrades very slowly; approximately half of a given amount will still be around in the environment 15 to 20 years later. After another 15 to 20 years, only half of the remaining amount will have been broken down. In 1962, the book *Silent Spring*, by Rachel Carson, forcefully pointed out the dangers of using DDT and other pesticides.

It is well documented now that many populations of birds have been affected by DDT and are decreasing in number, especially those birds which eat fish or small mammals. It has been demonstrated that the eggshells of birds which have ingested DDT contain less calcium and are consequently thinner. After this discovery was made, biologists began to search for the mechanism of DDT action on bird eggs. D. B. Peakall of Cornell University has studied the effects of DDE (a product of DDT breakdown) on reproduction in ringdoves. His experiments demonstrated that DDE lowered estrogen levels and also depressed the activity of an enzyme essential for the incorporation of calcium into eggshells in the oviducts of the birds. Lowered estrogen levels affect breeding behavior, and if mating is delayed, the reproduction cycle may not be completed within the breeding season. More information is needed, however, for a full understanding of how low levels of DDT affect birds and other animals. We know that in some parts of the country today brown pelicans (Figure 1-1) and bald eagles can crush their eggs merely by sitting on them, thereby killing the developing young. Even man is now known to contain about 12 parts per million of DDT in his fatty tissues.

At the present time the use of DDT in the United States is almost completely banned even though other countries continue its use. But there are many who feel that DDT must be used again since it is the only pesticide known to be effective on certain agricultural

Figure 1–1 Brown pelican, a species endangered by the use of DDT. (Grant Heilman.)

THE NATURAL SCIENCES

When the term *science* is used, we frequently think of one of the natural sciences. The natural sciences (physics, chemistry, and biology) deal with matter, energy, and their interactions. Most fields of study are interdisciplinary—that is, understanding them involves knowledge of more than one of these general areas. For example, geology, the study of the earth, must utilize knowledge and concepts from both chemistry and physics. Oceanography is an excellent example of interdisciplinary study, since its subject matter spans every area of the sciences. It is concerned not only with the physical structure and chemical composition of the oceans but also with the life found there. Biochemistry, a relatively new interdisciplinary field, concerns the chemistry of organisms, and biophysics deals with the physics of life. In fact, all of modern biology requires some background in physics and chemistry. Science, as we will use the term, seeks to investigate matter and its properties and to explain nature. Stated another way, the goal of science is to derive meaningful concepts about nature.

THE METHODS OF SCIENCE

Most scientists agree that no single method really exists for scientific investigation, and some contend that there are perhaps as many methods as there are problems in science. What is characteristic of science, however, is an attitude and a general approach to problems. This logical, systematic approach might really be used by anyone in problem solving. A person contemplating the purchase of an automobile, a homeowner attempting to discover why the light doesn't burn when he flips the switch, or a mechanic trying to figure out why your automobile won't start are all approaching their problems in a general systematic manner. But each is using specific methods unique to his field or to the solution of his

insects and moths that infest fir trees. One possibility for increasing man's effectiveness against pests is to modify the molecular structure of DDT or to find new pesticides which will degrade at a faster rate. The use of DDT and other pesticides has become an important political issue—an issue which can potentially involve every world inhabitant. The DDT story is typical of the many problems that will face mankind in the years ahead. It is therefore important that everyone have some knowledge of the sciences, especially of biology, in order to understand the complex issues of the future. Decisions must be made wisely, and they will be made in the political arena using information gained from scientific studies and experimentation.

problem. Objectivity, maintaining an open mind, hard work, honesty, and critical thinking are all characteristics of a scientific attitude. What we have in science then, rather than a rigid "scientific method," is a general scheme of inquiry or approach. This general scheme can be outlined as follows:

1 An unexplained situation exists.

2 A tentative explanation, or *hypothesis*, is selected to be tested.

3 Experiments designed to test the hypothesis are set up and data are collected.

4 These data are analyzed.

5 The hypothesis is either supported by the data or it is not. If it is, then further experimentation determines the *probability* or degree of certainty to which the hypothesis explains the phenomenon.

6 If the probability is high, the hypothesis can be considered to be a reliable explanation. It then becomes a *theory*.

7 If the hypothesis turns out to have a low probability, then a new hypothesis is sought and tested by experimentation.

Figure 1–2 illustrates a test of the hypothesis that light is necessary for the making of food, in the form of starch, in plants. Two plants that were taken as cuttings from the same plant were used in the experiment. Both plants were given equal amounts of water and the same exposure to air (oxygen, carbon dioxide, etc.). Their treatment was varied, however, in one respect only—exposure to light. The diagrams in Figure 1–2 illustrate the experimental procedure. Thus the original hypothesis that light is necessary for food production in plants appears to be true; that is, it has high probability. This experiment could lead to further questions and hypotheses about the light factor involved in the food-making process. For example, is all the light that falls on the plant necessary for food making? In what part of the food-production process is light required? (These questions will be considered later in Chapter 6.)

The use of a control was introduced in this experiment. A control is a standard against which the effects of the experimental condi-

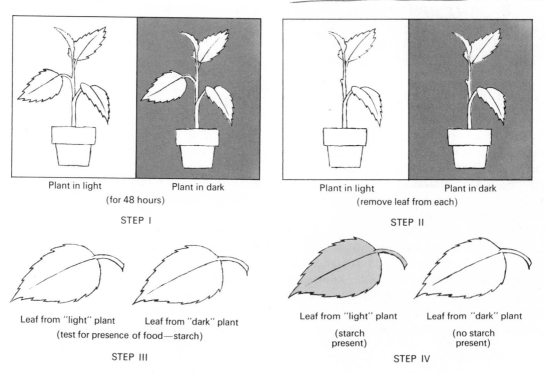

Plant in light   Plant in dark
(for 48 hours)

STEP I

Plant in light   Plant in dark
(remove leaf from each)

STEP II

Leaf from "light" plant   Leaf from "dark" plant
(test for presence of food—starch)

STEP III

Leaf from "light" plant   Leaf from "dark" plant
(starch present)   (no starch present)

STEP IV

Figure 1–2 Example of how scientific procedure can be employed to test a hypothesis.

4

tions are compared and indicates how much change was produced by the experiment and how much would have happened without experimental treatment. Since exposure to periods of light is a normal condition for plants, the light-exposed plant served as a control.

Another example of the use of controls in experimentation can be shown in studies on air pollution. When plants are grown in polluted air, their growth and yield are severely reduced. This effect is quite evident when these plants are compared with control plants grown in filtered air (Figure 1-3).

Probability, Hypothesis, Theory, Law

Note that the solution to the foregoing problem was stated in terms of *probability*. The suggested hypothesis may not be correct 100

Figure 1–3 Example of a controlled experiment on the effects of air pollution. The potato plant on the right was grown in city air, while the plant on the left grew in filtered air. (Courtesy of U.S. Department of Agriculture.)

percent of the time (few answers or explanations hold true in all cases), but it may be correct 90 percent of the time. Modern science therefore seeks the answers and explanations to natural phenomena in terms of probability. The greater the probability of a solution to a problem, the greater its value to scientific prediction.

Besides the term *hypothesis*, you have no doubt also heard the terms *theory* and *law* and wonder where they fit into this scheme. In order of importance they can be defined as follows. A *hypothesis* implies present insufficiency of evidence and therefore is only a tentative explanation. A *theory* implies a greater range of evidence and greater likelihood of truth. And, finally, a *law* implies a statement of order and relation in nature that has been found to be invariable under the same conditions.

Any explanation or interpretation of natural phenomena must be viewed in light of the available evidence. New evidence may be obtained through the use of new instruments and techniques, and we may find that the old explanation does not hold true. Even the use of the term *law* therefore should be regarded as somewhat tentative, since new evidence may show the relations explained by that law to be variable under different conditions.

Models

When scientists seek an explanation of some natural process or event they often use a physical *model*. This model may be very tentative at first until it is tested further; thus models serve as working hypotheses with varying degrees of probability. One biological model, proposed by Watson and Crick to explain the structure of the hereditary material DNA, will be presented in Chapter 2. We will encounter other models in our study of biology, such as the one currently used to explain the structure of the cell membrane.

SCIENCE AS A SELF-CORRECTING SYSTEM

Since science deals with the material world and involves experimentation, any theory pro-

5

posed by one scientist can be tested by others. A scientist is forced to report his findings honestly, since it is possible for another scientist to check his results. Thus science is characterized as a *self-correcting system*.

This self-correcting characteristic is unique to science, and the same principle cannot be applied to problems in the humanities or philosophy. This of course does not mean that a scientist cannot make a mistake. They are as vulnerable to human error as anyone. A scientist may approach his work with the same deep feelings and emotions that any other professional individual may have. In fact, a researcher may select a hypothesis on the basis of a "hunch" that it might be the right solution to a problem. In doing so, the scientist is drawing on his background and experience in his field.

THE MECHANISTIC NATURE OF SCIENCE AND ITS LIMITATIONS

The attitude of science is often referred to as *mechanistic*. The concept of mechanism holds that natural phenomena are due to the properties of matter; that is, all events can be explained in physical and chemical terms. An alternative to the mechanistic viewpoint is the doctrine of *vitalism*, which relies on supernatural explanations. Vitalists often refer to a "vital force" as causing natural events or processes.

Just as vitalism impedes the progress of science, so does *teleology*, the belief that all natural phenomena have a definite purpose and thus are in some way preordained. Teleology is actually a form of vitalism, since it suggests a "divine plan" in nature. Statements such as "some plants have developed thorns to protect themselves" or "some worms have light-sensitive cells so that they can orient themselves to light" suggests that these organisms have consciously developed these structures for a purpose. It would be more scientifically correct to state that "some plants have thorns and as a result they have some protection" and "some worms have light-

sensitive cells and as a result they can orient themselves to light."

Science is limited, however, to the study of the properties and interactions of matter and therefore cannot be effective in certain areas such as philosophy, theology, and politics. It is presently impossible to test certain questions and problems that arise in these fields. Social scientists, working in the fields of psychology and sociology, have utilized the methods of science in their work. Since these researchers are dealing with total human beings, the application of scientific methods has been helpful in limiting and controlling many variable factors. The use of experimentation in the fields of learning and memory has been noteworthy, but the complexity of living material and especially the complex structure of the human brain make it extremely difficult to isolate individual aspects of human behavior for study and experimentation.

BIOLOGY AS A SCIENCE

Biology encompasses all aspects of the study of life. If biological knowledge is to be acquired and recorded in a usable manner and if meaningful concepts are to be synthesized about the living world, organized studies must be conducted. In most studies of organisms it is possible to apply the methods of science.

It should be quite evident that science must seek its explanations in the material substance. Advances have been made in medicine and agriculture, for example, because research has followed mechanistic procedure. A patient would have little faith in modern medicine if it attributed his diseased condition to a vital spirit or demon. Although science cannot yet explain the causes of all natural phenomena, such as specific diseases or how certain minerals are taken in by plants, it cannot simply ascribe such unexplained phenomena to some mysterious force.

Knowledge in biology has grown tremendously in the past thirty years and this "knowledge explosion" is likely to continue.

6

At the same time, discoveries that were made a hundred years ago are still important to our understanding of certain concepts. To understand the growth of biology we will look at some of the important developments that have led to the existing study we call the modern biological sciences. Like the other sciences, biology has a long history during which many false starts were made and progress was slow. A brief review of this history will illustrate the problems faced by the early researchers and to a great extent by their modern counterparts. Although we often give credit to one or two individuals for a major discovery, their achievement would not have been possible without the contributions of earlier researchers. It does require ingenuity and imagination, however, to tie isolated and often seemingly unrelated bits of knowledge together into a meaningful concept.

EARLY DEVELOPMENTS IN BIOLOGY

THE GREEKS

We might say that man first showed interest in biology when he learned to identify the plants and animals that supplied his food. His descendants no doubt later practiced selective breedings and crossings of certain plant groups in an effort to obtain better crops. The historical records of this activity are fragmentary, and we can only conclude that the biological activity was essentially practical. Since the Greeks left some of the earliest records of their activity, discussions of biological history usually begin with them. The speculations and interpretations of nature that the Greeks recorded show that they did attempt to see relationships in the natural world.

Although there were several distinct periods of Greek civilization dating back to around 3000 B.C., perhaps the greatest contributions to science were made during the Hellenic and Hellenistic periods (about 750–31 B.C.). Driven by an insatiable curiosity, the desire to observe nature carefully, and the ability to reason both inductively and deductively, Greek scholars formulated many concepts about their natural environment. *Inductive* reasoning involves the formulation of general conclusions from individual facts; *deductive* reasoning is the process of utilizing a general premise to explain a specific case. Both types of reasoning are useful to scientific thought. The Greeks were good observers but they were primarily philosophers and often arrived at philosophical explanations for natural phenomena. It was Hippocrates, known today as the "father of medicine," who stressed the importance of careful observation. In his school, which he founded in 420 B.C., the notion originated that all diseases have natural causes and that "divine diseases" do not exist.

Aristotle

No doubt the greatest Greek scientist was Aristotle (384–322 B.C.), a student of Plato. Aristotle was a truly great natural historian who obviously possessed a very keen power of observation. Many of his descriptions of certain animals, their characteristics, and their behavior, were accurate even by modern standards. For example, Aristotle recognized that mammals (animals that are "hair-coated," as he referred to them) gave birth to young that were attached to the mother by an umbilical cord. He also realized that although most fish lay eggs from which the young hatch, others (the shark group) released live offspring. He knew, however, that these young were not attached to an umbilical cord except in the case of the dogfish shark, in which the young carry a yolk sac for some time after birth. The remarkable thing here is that zoologists paid little attention to this account until it was confirmed about 1850. Aristotle was shown to be correct even though the cord has a different origin in the dogfish than in mammals.

On the organization and complexity of life, Aristotle placed plants as the "lowest form" of life, animals higher, and man, since he possessed a "rational soul," as the most complex organism. The Aristotelian system of classification, often known as the "scala

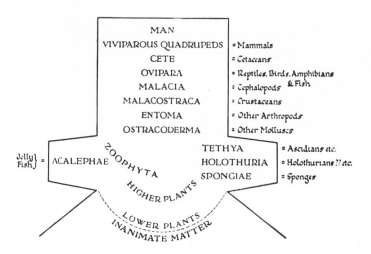

Figure 1-4 *Scala naturae*, or "ladder of life," by Aristotle (384–322 B.C.), Greek philosopher often called the "father of natural history." (Reproduced from Charles Singer, *A History of Biology*, Third and Revised Edition, Abelard-Schuman, 1959.)

naturae," was utilized for approximately 2,000 years (Figure 1–4). In matters concerning the complexity and the nature of life we would term Aristotle a vitalist.

Although Aristotle was a good observer, he unfortunately relied heavily on second-hand information, much of which was faulty. Thus many of his interpretations and pronouncements were incorrect, but most of these were accepted as facts long into the 1800s merely because Aristotle had stated them. For example, he claimed that plants did not have sexual organs. Aristotle's ideas on sex determination in humans were nonsensical, since he taught that if the father were weak, his child would be a girl, whereas a strong father would produce a son. His teachings on the human circulatory system also showed a lack of close observation or experimentation. Aristotle believed that the heart was the center of intelligence and sensations and that the arteries contained blood and air while the veins carried only blood.

THE ROMANS AND THE MIDDLE AGES

Science under the Romans did not flourish as it had in Grecian times. The Greeks were curious about their natural environment, but the Romans showed little concern except in matters that pertained directly to the practical aspects of life, such as government, engineering, and warfare. Two scientists of this era are often referred to—Pliny (23–79 A.D.) and Galen (ca. 130–200 A.D.). The former was a natural historian and the latter, a Greek anatomist and physician. Many of Pliny's works were not original but rather collections of tales he had heard and recounted in his books.

Galen

Although Galen was considered a great physician of his time, it is doubtful that he went so far as to perform dissections on the human body. Many of his interpretations of the function of organs, such as the heart and the lungs, were wrong, and these were perpetuated for many centuries because of the respect in which he was held. Most of Galen's writings were based on his dissections of the Barbary ape, and he seemed to be preoccupied with the spiritual nature of the blood. For example, he wrote that the forming blood receives "natural" spirits in the liver, "vital" spirits in the

8

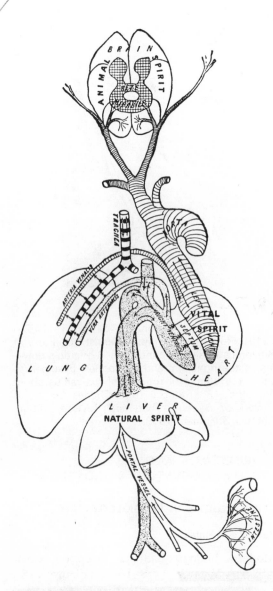

Figure 1–5 Physiological system according to Galen (130–200 A.D.), Greek physician and anatomist. (Reproduced from Charles Singer, *A Short History of Anatomy and Physiology from the Greeks to Harvey.* Copyright © 1957 by Dover Publications, Inc.)

in the heart passed from the right side to the left side through tiny pores in the ventricular septum.

Although some chemical elements and compounds were discovered by alchemists in the period we call the Middle Ages, substantial advances in biology did not take place. New concepts and discoveries in science were to come later in a period that embraced new philosophies.

THE RENAISSANCE

The general climate of this era can be characterized by two important developments. First, there was a great resurgence of interest in the Greeks and their intellectual accomplishments; and second, and perhaps more important, a new spirit developed embracing a questioning attitude. The social and religious systems of medieval Europe were questioned, and the freedom of the individual was proclaimed. This then offered an atmosphere in which science could again flourish.

Art also blossomed along with the natural sciences during the Renaissance. The most famous artist-naturalist was Leonardo da Vinci (1452–1519) (Figure 1–6a). He was interested in both how the human body worked and how it should be drawn and painted. His interest in science certainly went beyond biology as is evident from his engineering accomplishments. Another important scientist of this era was the anatomist Andreas Vesalius (1514–1564) who, as a most careful dissector (Figure 1–7), challenged much of the work of Galen, who was still the accepted authority.

Perhaps the most characteristic feature of da Vinci and Vesalius, and other scientists of this time, was their insistence on the importance of first-hand observations in the study of nature. Certainly, it was this factor plus the general spirit of the Renaissance that led to the development of important concepts about the living world.

left ventricle of the heart, and "animal" spirits in the brain (Figure 1–5). Another erroneous belief concerning the blood was that it ebbed and flowed through the body (rather than circulated). He also supposed that the blood

(a)

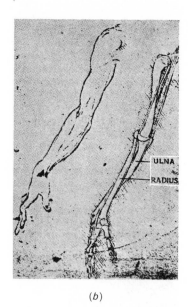

(b)

Figure 1–6 (*a*) Leonardo da Vinci (1452–1519), Florentine artist and scientist. (Courtesy of Biblioteca Reale di Torino.) (*b*) Leonardo's drawing of the right arm and arm bones, designed to show the effects of rotation of the radius about the ulna. (Reproduced from Charles Singer, *A History of Biology*, Third and Revised Edition, Abelard-Schuman, 1959.)

SEVENTEENTH- AND EIGHTEENTH-CENTURY DISCOVERIES

EARLY STUDIES IN PHYSIOLOGY

Harvey and Hales

Modern biology had its inception when William Harvey (1578–1657) (Figure 1–8), an English physician and physiologist, traced the pattern of the circulation of blood in man. Aristotle's and Galen's incorrect theories on the mechanism of blood circulation were still respected when Harvey set out to solve the problem in an experimental manner. He realized, as his calculations showed, that the blood had to travel through the arteries and veins in a circular pattern in one direction. Moreover, Harvey was a careful observer and he studied the heart cavities, the valves between the cavities, and the vessels entering and leaving the heart. Where Galen had believed that the blood passed from the

Figure 1–7 Andreas Vesalius (1514–1564), Belgian anatomist, with one of his dissections. (The Bettmann Archive, Inc.)

10

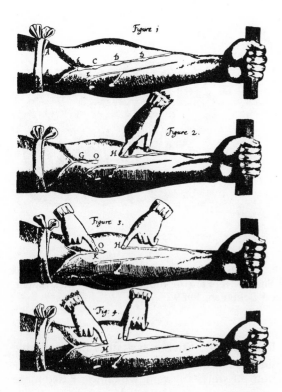

Figure 1–8 Experiments by William Harvey (1578–1657) on a bandaged arm. By applying pressure on arteries and veins, he was able to trace the direction of blood flow. (Reproduced from Charles Singer, *A Short History of Anatomy and Physiology from the Greeks to Harvey*. Copyright © 1957 by Dover Publications, Inc.)

right side of the heart through the wall to the left side, Harvey concluded that the blood moved from the right side of the heart, to the lungs, and then to the left side, to be circulated through the body. Harvey did not fully understand how the blood passed from arteries to veins. This discovery was to be made later by those who had access to microscopes.

Another pioneer in physiology of the next generation was the Reverend Stephen Hales (1677–1761) of England. He conducted many experiments on plants and demonstrated such basic functions as water intake and its loss by transpiration. Hales was also interested in animal physiology and he successfully measured blood pressure in mammals. His work was always characterized by his concern for quantitative measurements. This was a new

concept in science at this time, but its importance was soon to be recognized.

THE DEVELOPMENT OF THE MICROSCOPE

About 1590 the Dutch lens maker Zacharias Janssens developed the first compound microscope by placing a lens at each end of a long tube. In this same manner, Galileo Galilei (1564–1642), the great Italian scientist and philosopher, constructed a telescope with which he studied the planets and stars. Later more efficient microscopes were produced when lenses were ground to provide shorter focal lengths. The microscope made possible the observation of cellular structure in larger organisms as well as the study of minute living organisms such as protozoa and bacteria.

Hooke and Leeuwenhoek

Two men, Robert Hooke (1635–1703), an Englishman, and Anton van Leeuwenhoek (1632–1723), a Dutchman, pioneered the field of microscopy. It was Hooke who used the word *cell* to describe the "honeycomb" appearance of a thin section of cork he observed under his microscope (Figure 1–9a). Hooke's many studies and drawings of varied subjects certainly demonstrated the great usefulness of the microscope to biology. Leeuwenhoek (Figure 1–10) made excellent microscopes for his day and vigorously observed almost anything that suited his fancy. Several of his discoveries were outstanding. He discovered bacteria, differentiated them from other single-celled forms, and described spermatozoa. Another contribution was his detailed description of the capillary bed between arteries and veins. This filled in the remaining information to complete Harvey's partial description of the pattern of circulation.

THE DEVELOPMENT OF CLASSIFICATION SYSTEMS

Ray and Linnaeus

A major accomplishment of this period was the recognition of the need for some classification schemes to deal with the diversity of

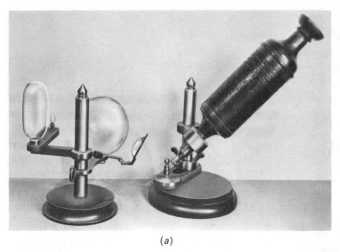
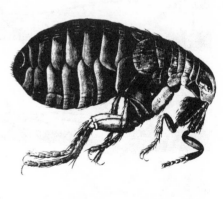

(a)   (b)

Figure 1–9 (a) Microscope used by Robert Hooke (1635–1703), English experimental scientist. (Courtesy of Bausch & Lomb, Inc.) (b) Drawing of a flea by Hooke. (Reproduced from Charles Singer, *A History of Biology*, Third and Revised Edition, Abelard-Schuman, 1959.)

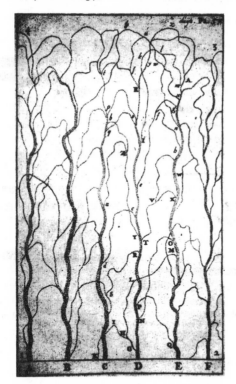

Figure 1–10 Illustration of capillaries connecting arteries and veins, as drawn by Anton van Leeuwenhoek (1632–1723), the Dutch microscopist. (Reproduced from Marius J. Sirks and Conway Zirkle, *The Evolution of Biology*, copyright © 1964, The Ronald Press Company, New York.)

living things. Such a system is indispensable both for an orderly study and for communication. Aristotle's system, which was based more on function and reproduction than on structure, was essentially too simple to handle the many different kinds of organisms known today. John Ray (1627–1705), an English naturalist, devised a classification scheme for both plants and animals, based on structure, and he classified the plants as herbs, shrubs, and trees. Later in his study of animals, Ray differentiated between vertebrates and invertebrates.

In the eighteenth century, classification was further developed by the work of Carolus Linnaeus (1707–1778), who laid the basic foundation for the system we use today. Linnaeus, a Swede, attempted to classify every known plant and animal, assigning a *genus* and *species* name to each (Figure 1–11). Thus every living organism is known by two names, the genus and the species. (For example, the dog is called *Canis familiaris*.) Furthermore these names are in Latin or Greek and therefore are the same in any country regardless of the spoken language.

Linnaeus used the sexual organs of flowers to classify them and this method is still used

12

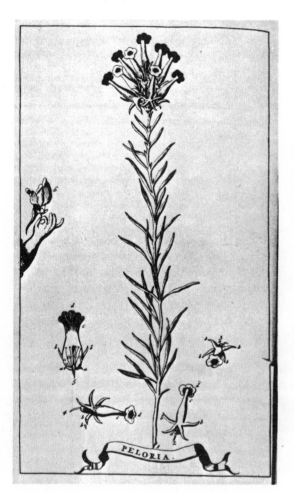

Figure 1–11 Drawing of the *Peloria* by the Swedish botanist Carolus Linnaeus (1707–1778), for his dissertation in 1774. (Reproduced from James L. Larson, *Reason and Experience: The Representation of Natural Order in the Work of Carl von Linné*. Copyright © 1971 by the Regents of the University of California. Originally published by the University of California Press; reprinted by permission of The Regents of the University of California.)

today. Perhaps his greatest single contribution was his *Systema Naturae*, published in 1735. Linnaeus used the concept of the species as the basis for classification and at first felt that a species was a fixed, unchanging unit created in nature. He apparently questioned this concept of the permanency of a species later in his work.

THE SYNTHESES OF THE NINETEENTH CENTURY

The 1800s can be regarded as one of the most important periods in the history of biology when some of the most significant concepts of biology were developed. These significant concepts were made possible no doubt through specialized studies in such fields as embryology, the study of development, and cytology, the study of cells. Even though specialization was an important aspect of nineteenth-century biology, many unifying themes that span the entire field of biology were formulated.

THE CELL THEORY

The idea that the cell is the structural and functional unit of life gained acceptance at this time. Cells were first observed in the 1600s and 1700s when microscopes became available. As improvements in microscope construction advanced, cellular studies also advanced and a great deal of information about cells was gradually accumulated. Based on these observations, M. J. Schleiden and Theodor Schwann, in 1838 and 1839, were able to formulate a "cell theory" for the structure of living things—that is, all organisms are composed of cells.

HEREDITY

The nineteenth century also saw remarkable accomplishments in the study of *heredity*. Most significant were the findings of Gregor Mendel in 1866, which dealt with the basic mechanisms of inheritance. These events are described in Chapter 11.

EMBRYOLOGY

Many important concepts in embryology emerged during this period. At the same time, however, many erroneous ideas were formulated as biologists sought to explain how an individual organism develops from a single cell into a mature adult. The idea of *pre-*

formation, which supposed that all adult structures were present in the egg and merely grew larger and developed to produce an adult individual, was widely held. Those biologists who believed these structures to be present in the egg were called "ovists," while others, known as "spermists," contended that the immature structures were all present in the sperm. A controversy thus developed between the two schools. Some spermists even claimed that they could see in sperm cells a tiny, undeveloped individual whom they called a "homunculus" (Figure 1–12). The idea of preformation was dealt a severe blow late in the eighteenth century by C. F. Wolff who proposed the concept of *epigenesis* based on his research on developing root and shoot tips in plants. Epigenesis refers to the formation of completely new parts as an organism grows and develops. Karl von Baer's "germ layer theory" in the 1800s strengthened the idea of epigenesis over preformation. It was von Baer who followed the development of the fertilized egg into three distinct germ layers and the subsequent development of tissues and organs from these germ layers. Another important discovery in embryology was made by Oscar Hertwig, who in 1875 proved that one nucleus in the fertilized egg came from the egg and the other nucleus from the sperm.

SPONTANEOUS GENERATION

The idea of "spontaneous generation" was a very controversial topic. Proponents of this concept believed that life could arise from putrifying or decaying organic matter. Francesco Redi in 1668 and Lazzaro Spallanzani in 1766 demonstrated that spontaneous generation did not occur under their experimental conditions. Other experimenters had arrived at an opposite conclusion and so the controversy continued into the nineteenth century. Louis Pasteur (Figure 1–13), the great French chemist, performed the conclusive experiments to adequately prove to the scientific world that spontaneous generation does not take place if existing life such as spores, eggs, and bacteria are excluded from a growth medium (Figure 1–14).

EVOLUTION

An outstanding step in the 1800s was the introduction of the concept of *evolution*, the theory that all existing types of animals and plants are derived from preexisting types. The Darwin and Wallace theory proposed around 1859 provided a fundamental framework and unifying theme for the study of biology. This theory, based on *natural selection*, also provided for the first time a logical explanation of how the diversity of life arose on our planet. Natural selection explains how some organisms survive and reproduce better than others because of favorable hereditary characteristics that occur by chance. Although evolution will be discussed in detail in a later chapter, it will be referred to in many places throughout this book.

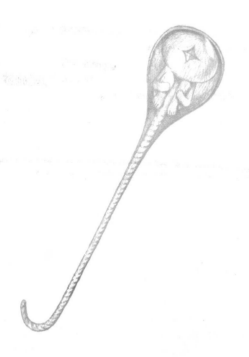

Figure 1–12 The homunculus, a tiny, fully formed individual supposedly found in sperm cells.

Figure 1–13 Louis Pasteur (1822–1895), the French chemist. (The Bettmann Archive, Inc.)

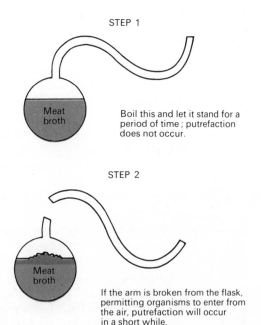

STEP 1

Meat broth

Boil this and let it stand for a period of time; putrefaction does not occur.

STEP 2

Meat broth

If the arm is broken from the flask, permitting organisms to enter from the air, putrefaction will occur in a short while.

Figure 1–14 Pasteur's experiment showing that putrefaction is caused by organisms from the air.

TWENTIETH-CENTURY BIOLOGY

With the development of new chemical and physical techniques, more refined studies on the chemical composition of life have become possible. New, more powerful electron microscopes have revealed parts of the cell hitherto unknown. Modern genetics is no longer concerned only with the transmission of heredity from generation to generation but also with the structure and function of the hereditary material. Embryologists are devising experiments to determine how cells differentiate in the development of an organism—that is, why one cell becomes a muscle cell and another, a nerve cell. The term *molecular biology* has been applied to some of the newer aspects of the biological sciences which are concerned with structure and function at the level of molecules. Learning and memory are being approached from this viewpoint today. In addition to the great emphasis on molecular biology an acute awareness of *environmental biology* has emerged, and we are turning to the use of scientific knowledge to cope with environmental problems. Many of the new findings will be discussed in this book and woven in with the important knowledge gained in earlier times in an attempt to present a clear picture of biology.

SUMMARIZING STATEMENTS

Science is an organized study of the material world; the methods of science provide an orderly and systematic approach to problems dealing with matter; since any proposed theory can be subjected to experimentation, science is a self-correcting system.

Science is based on the mechanistic concept that all natural phenomena can be explained in terms of physics and chemistry; biology therefore is mechanistic in its approach.

Most concepts in the biological sciences have been developed over a long period of time; recent discoveries generally have been made possible through observations and experiments of earlier workers.

Because of their ability to observe and reason, the Greeks made many discoveries in the biological sciences; most important among the Greeks was Aristotle.

Under the Romans and during the Middle Ages science did not progress as it had with the Greeks; Galen was an outstanding physician and anatomist of this era, but he made many errors concerning the functioning of certain parts of the body.

The Renaissance was a period when observation was again stressed and a time when the status quo was questioned; this attitude provided an atmosphere in which science could advance.

During the seventeenth and eighteenth centuries important foundations were laid in many fields of biology: in physiology, William Harvey traced the circulation of blood; Hooke and Leeuwenhoek developed microscopy; a classification scheme for the living world was worked out by Ray and Linnaeus.

The nineteenth century was a period when important concepts in biology were clearly synthesized. The cell theory by Schleiden and Schwann was prominent among these concepts; Mendel's studies were extremely important in understanding the mechanism involved in inheritance; in embryology the theory of epigenesis replaced the old idea of preformation; the principle of spontaneous generation was disproved by Pasteur's experiments; perhaps the greatest synthesis of this period was the theory of evolution proposed by Darwin and Wallace.

Provided with such tools as the electron microscope, chemical analyses, and electronic instrumentation, twentieth-century biologists are able to study life at finer dimensions—the cellular and molecular levels.

REVIEW QUESTIONS

1 A dead osprey, a type of hawk, contained 33 parts per million DDT in its tissues, but the nearby lake water where it caught fish had less than 1 part per million DDT. What is the probable explanation for the large concentration of DDT in the hawk?

2 Using the scientific approach, design an experiment to test the hypothesis that:
   (a) light is necessary for the production of green pigment (chlorophyll) in plants.
   (b) moths are attracted to specific wavelengths of light.

3 What is the importance of a "control" in each experiment above?

4 It has been argued that religion has impeded the progress of science through the ages. List reasons why this might be true.

5 List some examples of explanations that show elements of vitalism in our modern thought.

6 What is your personal viewpoint on the role of scientists in modern society? Must they assume responsibility for the use of their discoveries?

7 How did the work of Galen, Vesalius, and Harvey contribute to the ability of modern medicine to transplant human organs?

8   In what ways can chemistry, physics, and social science contribute to the study of biology?

9   We often speak of the great syntheses of biology in the nineteenth century. What were some of the major ideas formulated during this period?

10   What were some of the attitudes and technological advances that led to the resurgence of scientific study during the Renaissance?

11   Is it reasonable to assume that one can apply scientific methods in the selection of a mate? Discuss the advantages and limitations.

12   How can knowledge of scientific methodology and the history of biology assist us in the solution of problems facing modern society?

SUPPLEMENTARY READINGS

Asimov, Isaac, *View from a Height*, Garden City, N.Y., Doubleday, 1963.

Bradbury, S., *The Evolution of the Microscope*, New York, Pergamon, 1967.

Bronowski, J., *Science and Human Values*, New York, Harper & Row, 1959.

Brooks, Harvey, and Raymond Bowers, "The Assessment of Technology," *Scientific American*, February, 1970.

Cartwright, F. F., *Disease and History*, New York, Crowell, 1972.

Eiseley, Loren, *The Firmament of Time*, New York, Atheneum, 1962.

Grobstein, C., *The Strategy of Life*, San Francisco, Freeman, 1965.

Hoyle, Fred, *Of Men and Galaxies*, Seattle, University of Washington Press, 1964.

Huxley, T. H., *On a Piece of Chalk*, New York, Charles Scribner's Sons, 1967.

Lenhoff, E. S., *Tools of Biology*, New York, Macmillan, 1966.

McCain, G., and E. M. Segal, *The Game of Science*, Belmont, Brooks/Cole, 1969.

Peakall, D. B., "Pesticides and the Reproduction of Birds," *Scientific American*, April, 1970.

Platt, J. R., *The Excitement of Science*, Boston, Houghton Mifflin, 1962.

Sarton, G., *The Life of Science*, Bloomington, Indiana University Press, 1960.

Shapley, H., *The View from a Distant Star*, New York, Basic Books, 1963.

Singer, Charles, *A History of Biology*, New York, Abelard-Schuman, 1959.

Stent, Gunther S., "Prematurity and Uniqueness in Scientific Discovery," *Scientific American*, December, 1972.

The following collections of readings about the principles and ideas of biology will enrich your study of life.

Asimov, Isaac, *Asimov's Guide to Science*, New York, Basic Books, 1972.

Bonner, John T., *The Ideas of Biology*, New York, Harper & Row, 1962.

Farago, Peter, and John Lagnado, *Life in Action*, New York, Knopf, 1972.

Gabriel, M., and S. Fogel, eds., *Great Experiments in Biology*, Englewood Cliffs, N.J., Prentice-Hall, 1955.

Johnson, W., and W. Steere, eds., *This is Life*, New York, Holt, Rinehart and Winston, 1962.

Moment, G., ed., *Frontiers of Modern Biology*, Boston, Houghton Mifflin, 1962.

Rapport, S., and H. Wright, eds., *Biology*, New York, New York University Press, 1969.

Waddington, C. H., *The Nature of Life*, New York, Atheneum, 1962.

2

Chemistry and Life

The sight of hundreds of fireflies on a summer evening is an experience not easily forgotten. A curious observer undoubtedly wonders how this light is produced. It is now known that the glow is the result of a complex series of chemical reactions that transform chemical energy into light energy. But before we can thoroughly understand this and other biological processes, some knowledge of chemistry is necessary.

Since living things are composed of matter and involve the interactions of matter, we should first attempt to answer the questions: what is matter and where does it come from? This will ultimately lead us to the bigger question of the possible origin of the earth and the universe.

Throughout this study we will be concerned with the structure of chemical compounds and how they react in living systems.

MATTER AND ELEMENTS

The first philosophical thoughts on the origin and structure of matter are attributed to the early Greeks. In the sixth century B.C., Thales of Miletus reasoned that water must be the "mother element" of all matter, whereas Anaximenes of Miletus, later in the same century, proposed that it was air. Heraclitus of Ephesus, about 500 B.C., considered change to be the only reality and fire the primary substance. Finally, Empedocles of Agrigentum, about 450 B.C., summarized the primary substances as water, air, fire, and earth. A different materialistic approach to the universe was taken by a group generally referred to as the atomists. Democritus (460–370 B.C.) felt that matter consisted of small, indivisible particles which he called *atomos.* Further, he considered these atomos, or *atoms* as we would call them, to be different for each kind of matter. These differences, he thought, were the cause of the different physical properties of matter.

During the period of the first century A.D. through the seventeenth century, much of the scientific activity was devoted to alchemy— the transmutation of elements such as iron and lead into gold and silver. Many basic elements and compounds were discovered and named by these sometimes mystic experimenters. Among these were mercury, sulfur, lead acetate, zinc, acetic acid, nitric acid, sulfuric acid, and hydrochloric acid.

Following a renewed interest in chemistry, the Englishman Robert Boyle, in 1661, defined the known chemical elements as substances that could not be further broken down by chemical means. In 1808, another English chemist, John Dalton, proposed a modern atomic theory and used the term *atom* after the earlier atomos of Democritus. This theory

gave rise to the concept that atoms were tiny, indivisible spheres that could not be destroyed. (We now know, however, that atoms can be broken into subparts.)

We will have more to say about the developments that lead to the modern atomic theory in the next section. For the present only a brief description of atomic structure will be presented in order to discuss some of the theories of cosmic evolution.

ATOMS AND MOLECULES

The smallest building blocks of nature that can be practically studied are the components of atoms, and we refer to these as subatomic particles, electrons, protons, and neutrons. Actually, other subatomic particles are known, but they are not essential to a basic understanding of the atom. The three particles we have named are organized into atoms as shown in Figure 2–1.

The protons and neutrons form a compact nucleus around which the electrons move in specific energy levels. A collection of one type of atoms is known as an *element*; therefore we speak of the elements hydrogen, helium, carbon, oxygen, etc. Although over a hundred such elements are known, only about eleven of these are present in abundance and are important to life. Elements range in complexity from hydrogen with one proton and one electron to lawrencium with 103 protons, 154 neutrons, and 103 electrons. When atoms of two or more elements unite, a *compound* is

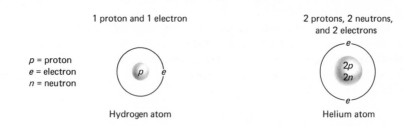

Figure 2–1   Subatomic components of hydrogen atom and helium atom.

formed and the fundamental unit of this compound is called a *molecule*. For example, when four hydrogen atoms combine with one carbon atom, the compound methane (CH_4) is formed. Thus a molecule of methane is composed of five atoms, four hydrogen and one carbon.

THE ORIGIN OF THE UNIVERSE

EXPLOSION THEORY

One popular theory on the origin of the universe holds that an original concentration of matter exploded about ten billion years ago. This theory is often referred to as the "explosion" or "big bang" theory. This theory assumes that, in the original concentration of matter, there were protons, neutrons, and electrons (or perhaps only neutrons, from which protons and electrons were derived). These subatomic particles rather randomly formed atoms of the chemical elements we know today. Since hydrogen is the simplest element and probably would have formed first, it is considered the parent element by those who accept this theory. That is, hydrogen came first and through subsequent additions of subatomic particles the other elements were formed. This process would require a vast amount of energy, which could have been furnished in the interior of stars, where element formation may be still going on. Some credence is granted to the explosion theory because several of the known elements have been artificially produced by the addition of subatomic particles to existing atoms.

STEADY-STATE THEORY

Another popular theory, the "steady-state theory," of the origin of the universe states that the universe has no beginning and no end. Matter is constantly being formed and converted from one form to another and energy—in other words, creative forces are continuously at work.

STARS, GALAXIES, AND OUR SOLAR SYSTEM

Whichever theory of the universe we accept, it is apparent that matter became organized into masses called *stars*. The star, then, becomes the fundamental unit in the universe. In addition, stars are found in large clusters called *galaxies* of which approximately 260 million are visible from the Mount Palomar telescope in California. Each galaxy is composed of approximately ten billion stars, and all galaxies are similar in appearance. The distances between galaxies are continuously increasing, indicating that they are swiftly moving farther apart and expanding into space.

Stars apparently are born when cosmic dust and gases concentrate into large masses within a galactic formation. Matter does exist between stars and galaxies as dust and gases, but it is very minute when compared to the density of a star, being on the order of about one atom per cubic centimeter. At sea level on our planet the atmosphere is composed of about ten million million million atoms per cubic centimeter.

OUR SOLAR SYSTEM

Our sun, with its solar system, is part of the Milky Way galaxy (Figures 2–2 and 2–3). Evidence indicates that our solar system was formed seven to ten billion years ago, and, according to the "explosion theory," this would also be the time of the formation of the other galactic systems in the universe. Various theories have also been proposed to account for the origin of our solar system. One of the first, which is quite plausible, was put forth by the philosopher-astronomer Laplace in 1796. According to his theory, the solar system was formed from a hot, swirling ball of gases that condensed, with the core forming the sun. Circling this mass was a belt of gases in which centers of condensation also occurred and the centers became solid bodies which are now the planets. Since Laplace a more refined

Figure 2–2 View of the rising earth as it greeted the Apollo 8 astronauts. On the earth, 240,000 miles away, the sunset terminator bisects Africa. (Courtesy of NASA.)

theory has been advanced by several modern astronomers. This theory incorporates some features of the Laplace theory but differs radically by suggesting that the gaseous atomic mixture was cold rather than hot. This theory proposes that cosmic dust and gases came together in a swirling mass to form the sun while secondary condensations occurred outside of this mass to form the planets. The planets then were held in orbits by the gravitational influence of the sun. Elements were formed during the origin of the planets, and molecules later formed from these elements. We have evidence from the decay of radioactive elements that the earth originated about five billion years ago.

This completes a brief sketch of cosmic evolution, and we should now turn our attention to a more detailed discussion of matter. The concept of how atoms unite to form molecules will be important when we consider the diverse chemical compounds and chemical reactions that occur in life.

ATOMIC STRUCTURE OF MATTER

SOME EARLY STUDIES

Experiments by Englishmen Davy and Faraday about 1800 demonstrated that certain compounds in solution could be separated into their component elements when an electric current was passed through them. If atoms and electricity could interact, then atoms must possess electrical charges. In 1897, J. J. Thompson working with high-voltage electrical discharge tubes (cathode ray tubes) correctly identified the charge and mass of tiny particles of matter known as electrons.

About 1911, Rutherford, Geiger, and Marsden performed a unique and valuable series of experiments. Using a radioactive element that emitted heavy particles, known as alpha particles (helium nuclei), the researchers bombarded a thin piece of gold foil. To their surprise, most of the particles passed straight through the foil, but a few were diverted from their normal course into angular paths. Ruther-

Figure 2–3 Great Spiral Galaxy in the constellation Andromeda. This galaxy, about two billion light years away, is the nearest one to our galaxy. (Courtesy of the Hale Observatories.)

ford decided that the individual atoms in the gold foil must contain areas of unequal mass. He therefore proposed that most of the mass of the atom is squeezed into a small, dense central nucleus that carries a positive charge. Thompson's negatively charged particles or electrons were believed to be distributed throughout the remaining atomic space. Since Rutherford knew that like charges repel each other, he assumed that the positively charged alpha particles had come into close association with positively charged gold atomic nuclei and were repulsed into new paths.

PROTONS AND NEUTRONS

Further research showed that the nuclei of atoms of all elements except hydrogen are composed of positively charged protons and uncharged neutrons (hydrogen has only a single proton). Protons and neutrons possess nearly equal mass, and thus each is assigned a mass unit of one. Hydrogen, with its single proton, is the simplest element, and the single proton has an atomic mass of one, whereas helium, which has two protons and two neutrons, has an atomic mass of four.

The number of protons (positive charges) in the nucleus of an atom determines the characteristic number of electrons (negative charges) for that atom, and in a neutral atom there are an equal number of negative and positive charges. Neutrons contribute only to the mass of the atom. Since the mass of a proton or a neutron is about 1,840 times greater than that of an electron, the total mass of the atom, for all intents and purposes, is determined by the number of protons and neutrons in the nucleus. This mass is also called the *atomic weight* of the atom. In addition, the atom is assigned an *atomic number*, which is simply the number of protons in the nucleus.

THE PERIODIC TABLE

For easy reference in scientific work, chemical elements are arranged in a *periodic table* on the basis of their atomic number and chemical properties. The first listing of the elements according to their relative weights, using hydrogen as the base 1, was proposed by John Dalton in 1803. The forerunner of the modern periodic chart of the elements (Figure 2–4) was developed in 1869 by the Russian chemist Mendeleev, who realized that the elements could be arranged in order of increasing atomic weights and related chemical properties.

The vertical columns in the table are called *groups* and represent elements that react similarly. For example, group Ia elements (the alkali metals) all react violently with water, and the degree of reaction increases with increased atomic weight. Therefore the order of the elements within a group also provides important information that can be used to predict chemical reactions.

The horizontal rows on the chart are called *periods*. Each period shows a range of properties, beginning with metals on the left, changing to nonmetals, and ending in inert gases. For example, sodium, magnesium, and aluminum are metals; silicon, phosphorous, sulfur, and chlorine are nonmetals; and argon is an inert gas.

If we examine the periodic chart, we notice that the atomic weights given underneath each chemical symbol are not whole numbers as might be expected. In order to understand this we must realize that the atomic weights are relative weights and not actual weights such as one might obtain by weighing. That is, one element has been assigned a certain weight arbitrarily, and all other elements are compared with this reference weight. It is known that not all atoms of an element have exactly the same weight. These variations are caused by varying numbers of neutrons above and below the number in most atoms of that element. Remember that the type of atom (element) is determined by the atomic number, which is the number of protons contained in the nucleus. It thus makes no difference to an atom's identity whether it has more or fewer neutrons, although it does change the atomic weight. Elements having the same

Handwritten margin notes (rotated): Top numbers are the atomic number — Bottom numbers are the atomic weights

Periodic table of the elements:

Ia	IIa	IIIb	IVb	Vb	VIb	VIIb	VIIIb			IB	IIB	IIIa	IVa	Va	VIa	VIIa	VIII / O
1 H 1.008																	2 He 4.00
3 Li 6.94	4 Be 9.01											5 B 10.81	6 C 12.01	7 N 14.00	8 O 15.99	9 F 18.99	10 Ne 20.18
11 Na 22.99	12 Mg 24.31											13 Al 26.98	14 Si 28.09	15 P 30.97	16 S 32.06	17 Cl 35.45	18 Ar 39.95
19 K 39.10	20 Ca 40.08	21 Sc 44.96	22 Ti 47.90	23 V 50.94	24 Cr 51.99	25 Mn 54.94	26 Fe 55.85	27 Co 58.93	28 Ni 58.71	29 Cu 63.54	30 Zn 65.37	31 Ga 69.72	32 Ge 72.59	33 As 74.92	34 Se 78.96	35 Br 79.91	36 Kr 83.80
37 Rb 85.47	38 Sr 87.62	39 Y 88.91	40 Zr 91.22	41 Nb 92.91	42 Mo 95.94	43 Tc (99)	44 Ru 101.07	45 Rh 102.91	46 Pd 106.4	47 Ag 107.87	48 Cd 112.40	49 In 114.82	50 Sn 118.69	51 Sb 121.75	52 Te 127.60	53 I 126.90	54 Xe 131.30
55 Cs 132.91	56 Ba 137.34	see below 57–71	72 Hf 178.49	73 Ta 180.95	74 W 183.85	75 Re 186.2	76 Os 190.2	77 Ir 192.2	78 Pt 195.09	79 Au 196.97	80 Hg 200.59	81 Tl 204.37	82 Pb 207.19	83 Bi 208.98	84 Po (210)	85 At (210)	86 Rn (222)
87 Fr (223)	88 Ra (226)	see below 89–103	104 Rf (261)	105 Ha (260)													

57 La 138.91	58 Ce 140.12	59 Pr 140.91	60 Nd 144.24	61 Pm (147)	62 Sm 150.35	63 Eu 151.96	64 Gd 157.25	65 Tb 158.92	66 Dy 162.50	67 Ho 164.93	68 Er 167.26	69 Tm 168.93	70 Yb 173.04	71 Lu 174.97
89 Ac (227)	90 Th 232.04	91 Pa (231)	92 U 238.03	93 Np (237)	94 Pu (242)	95 Am (243)	96 Cm (247)	97 Bk (247)	98 Cf (251)	99 Es (254)	100 Fm (253)	101 Md (256)	102 No (254)	103 Lw (257)

Figure 2–4 The periodic table of the elements. The elements which are most important for living systems are shown in the dark color, and trace elements are shown in the light color.

24

number of protons but varying numbers of neutrons are termed *isotopes*. For example, there are four isotopes of the element carbon —carbon-12, 13, 14, and 15—all of which have six protons and six electrons but differ in the number of neutrons (Figure 2–5). The reason then that the atomic weights given in the chart are not whole numbers is that these weights are averages of the weights of all the isotopes of a given element. Many isotopes are unstable, and may be in the process of breaking down into a more stable state—that is, they may give up a neutron by emitting it in the form of energetic particles. Isotopes of this type are said to be *radioactive*. Originally all atomic weights were based on oxygen-16 as the reference weight, but in 1963 the most abundant isotope of carbon, carbon-12, became the new standard.

ELECTRON DISTRIBUTION IN THE ATOM

A good approximation to atomic structure, and one that we will use in our discussion of atoms, is the so-called "planetary" or *Bohr model*. Niels Bohr, the Danish physicist, proposed this atomic model in which the electrons move around the nucleus in orbits corresponding to specific energies possessed by the particular electrons. Each orbit, also called a "shell" or "energy level," can accommodate only a certain number of electrons. Today we know that the electrons do not actually travel around the nucleus in specific orbits but are located in certain probable areas called *clouds*. Reported distances of an electron from the nucleus are based on the highest probability of finding the electron in that position.

To keep this discussion brief, we will give the arrangement of electrons for only a few elements, namely those for the first eleven elements in the periodic chart (Figure 2–6). There are seven principal energy levels or shells labeled 1, 2, 3, 4, 5, 6, 7. Although each of these is further divided into sublevels, we need not concern ourselves with that refinement. Again, each of the principal levels can accommodate only a certain number of electrons. The stable number of electrons in the outer shell of an element appears to be eight except in the case of helium which is stable with two. One clue to this stable configuration is that all of the chemically unreactive elements have eight outermost electrons (the inert gases).

An atom that has fewer than eight electrons in its outer shell may transfer or take up or share electrons with another atom to complete its electron shell. Either way, both atoms achieve a stable configuration which provides a strong force of attraction between the atoms.

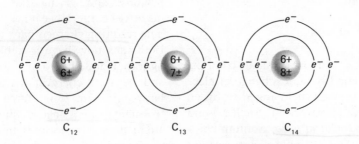

Figure 2–5 Three isotopes of carbon. Note that only the number of neutrons changes. Each neutron represents one mass unit.

Element	Symbol	Atomic Number	Electron Distribution in Shells		
			1	2	3
Hydrogen	H	1	1		
Helium	He	2	2		
Lithium	Li	3	2	1	
Beryllium	Be	4	2	2	
Boron	B	5	2	3	
Carbon	C	6	2	4	
Nitrogen	N	7	2	5	
Oxygen	O	8	2	6	
Fluorine	F	9	2	7	
Neon	Ne	10	2	8	
Sodium	Na	11	2	8	1

Figure 2–6 Electron distribution of the first eleven elements in the periodic table.

CHEMICAL BONDING

Whenever two or more atoms combine they are held together by a chemical bond. There are several kinds of chemical bonds, and they all depend on the electron distribution of the atoms. We will discuss three of the most important types of bonds—electrovalent, covalent, and hydrogen.

ELECTROVALENT BONDS

When atoms of two or more elements combine to form a compound by an exchange of electrons, they are strongly held together by an electrostatic force of attraction. Such a bond is termed an *electrovalent bond*. Sodium chloride offers an excellent example of electrovalent bonding (Figure 2–7). The atomic number of sodium is 11, and thus it has eleven electrons. When these are distributed in the shells we see that the outer, or *valence*, shell contains only one electron. Chlorine, atomic number 17, has seven electrons in its valence shell—one less than required for a complete shell. When sodium and chlorine come into close contact, one electron is transferred from sodium to chlorine, leaving sodium positively charged, since it now has one less electron than protons, and giving the chlorine atom a negative charge, since it has gained an electron. The resulting charged particles are called *ions*. Both ions now have a stable electronic configuration and, due to the formation of positive and negative charges, there is an attraction between them. This force forms the electrovalent or *ionic bond*. It should be noted that atoms possessing more than four valence electrons tend to take up electrons, whereas atoms with fewer than four outermost electrons generally transfer those electrons in bonding reactions. Therefore the number of electrons

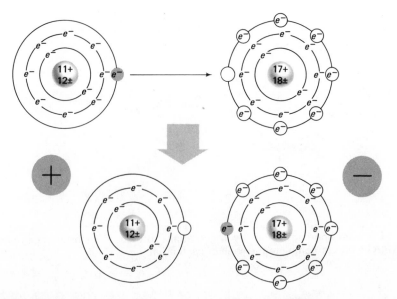

Figure 2–7 Electrovalent bond of sodium and chlorine. When the lone electron from the outer shell of sodium is transferred to the outer shell of chlorine, each has eight electrons, or a stable number, in its outer shell. The result is the compound sodium chloride (NaCl). Sodium, which has lost an electron, now has one more proton than it has electrons; thus it has a positive (+) charge. Chlorine, which received the electron, now has an additional electron; thus it possesses a negative (−) charge.

in the valence shells determines which atoms will react with one another.

COVALENT BONDS

If we examine the atomic structure of the element carbon, we note that its valence shell contains four electrons and this number of electrons is just one-half the number required for completion. In addition to electron transfer it is also possible for electrons to be shared between atoms, and the resulting bond when this occurs is called *covalent*. For example, it is possible for carbon to share its four electrons with the four electrons of four hydrogen atoms to form methane, CH_4 (Figure 2–8). In fact, many atoms, other than hydrogen, are capable of sharing electrons with carbon: oxygen, phosphorus, nitrogen, chlorine, and calcium are among the most common. Perhaps the most important characteristic of carbon is its ability to share electrons with other carbon atoms. In this manner, carbon atoms may form long chains or complicated ring structures. Later in this chapter we will discuss the structure of several types of carbon molecules.

The four valence electrons of a carbon atom are located at an equidistant 109.5° from each other. The resulting structure is similar to a regular tetrahedron (Figure 2–9.) We stated earlier that it is impossible to locate the exact position of an electron at any given instant, but in order to locate the electrons, it is necessary to conceive of the electron moving in a cloud rather than in precise orbits. It is possible, however, to calculate the density of the cloud and find out where the electron is most likely to be in terms of its distance from the nucleus. All bonds in carbon compounds must closely conform to the angles formed by the electron distribution whether they are in long chains or rings (Figure 2–10).

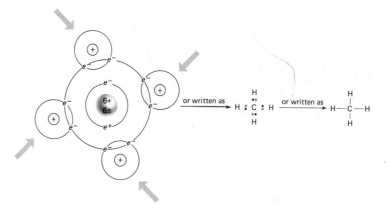

Figure 2–8 Covalent bonding of four hydrogen atoms to carbon. Each hydrogen atom shares a pair of electrons with carbon to complete the shell of each atom.

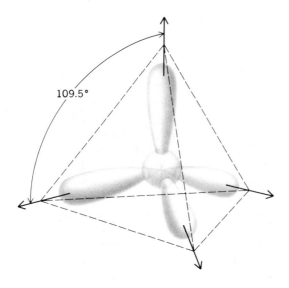

Figure 2–9 Tetrahedral configuration of the valence electrons of carbon. The long axis of each of the four electron clouds is oriented toward one corner of the tetrahedron, thus forming the bond angles.

Between two carbon atoms two pairs of electrons may be shared, and when this occurs it is termed a *double covalent bond* (Figure 2–10*b*). Covalent bonds are the most common bonds found in the molecules of living organisms.

HYDROGEN BONDS

A bond weaker than either ionic or covalent is formed when hydrogen is bonded simultaneously between two other atoms. This results when the positively charged proton of an already bonded hydrogen atom attracts a negatively charged atom such as oxygen or nitrogen. This attraction is known as a *hydrogen bond* and is demonstrated in the association of water molecules (Figure 2–11). Hydrogen bonding helps explain some of the unique properties of water, such as its resistance to temperature change and its ability to exist in three states—liquid, steam, or ice.

28

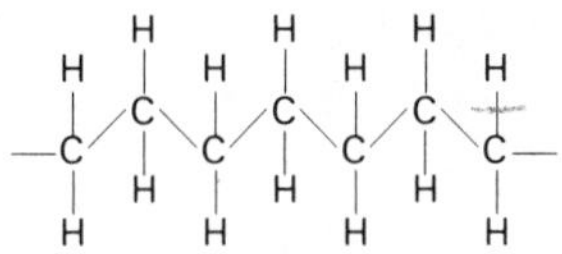

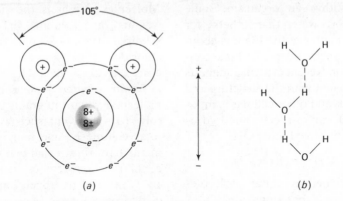

Carbon-to-carbon chain

(a)

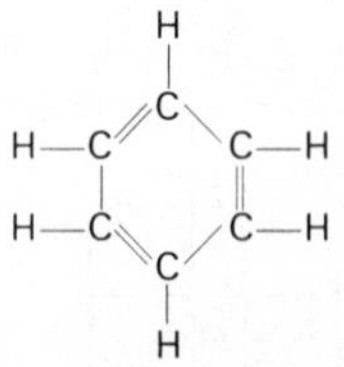

Carbon-to-carbon ring (benzene ring)

(b)

Figure 2–10 Two common types of carbon-to-carbon bonding. (a) A straight chain. (b) A six-carbon ring, the benzene ring.

ELECTROLYTES AND NONELECTROLYTES

Ionically bonded compounds, such as sodium chloride, that readily separate into charged particles in water are called *electrolytes* because, as charged particles, they will conduct an electric current (Figure 2–12). Generally, covalently bonded compounds, such as sucrose (table sugar, $C_{12}H_{22}O_{11}$), do not dissociate in water to any appreciable degree. Sucrose therefore is a *nonelectrolyte*.

COMPOUNDS IN NATURE

Chemical compounds that contain the element carbon are called *organic,* and all other compounds are classified as *inorganic.* The early chemists were convinced that carbon compounds could be produced only by living organisms, yet today we know that organic compounds can be synthesized. For example, all of our modern synthetic fabrics and plastics are organic compounds.

INORGANIC COMPOUNDS

Water, Acids, Bases, Salts, and Buffers

Water Water is an important component in all living organisms. The exact content varies

(a)

(b)

Figure 2–11 Water molecules. (a) The molecular structure of a water molecule. Because the electrons of hydrogen are primarily associated with the oxygen atom, this produces a dipolar molecule with negative and positive ends. (b) The hydrogen bonding found between water molecules. The dashed lines represent the hydrogen bonds. Since the electrons of hydrogen are associated with the oxygen valence shell, the positive charge of the proton attracts the negatively charged region of other water molecules, thus forming the hydrogen bond.

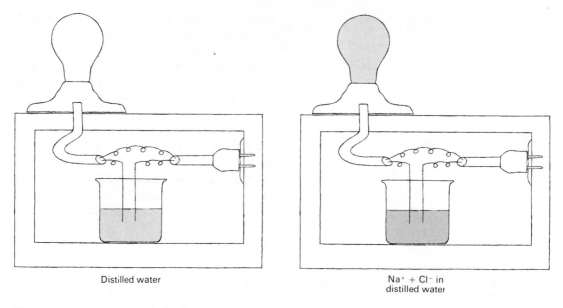

Distilled water

Na⁺ + Cl⁻ in
distilled water

Figure 2–12 Experiment showing the ability of dissociated ions (Na⁺Cl⁻) to conduct electricity. Sucrose is a nonelectrolyte. The bulb in the NaCl solution is the only one which lights.

greatly from one organism to another. Jellyfish are made up of nearly 99 percent water, whereas the human body is composed of about 65 percent water. Within an organism, some tissues contain more water than others; for example, the gray matter of the brain is about 80 percent water, whereas compact bone contains only 25 percent. Recent evidence suggests that water is associated with the structure and function of proteins and other cellular components. Water (H_2O) can dissociate into hydrogen ions, H^+, and hydroxyl ions, OH^-:

$$H_2O \leftrightharpoons H^+ + OH^-$$

Only a small number of water molecules actually dissociate into these ions.

Ionic concentrations may be expressed in terms of the *gram-atomic weight* of the ions present in one liter of solution. (One liter equals 1,000 cubic centimeters.) A gram-atomic weight is simply the atomic weight of the substance measured in grams. Another useful unit for expressing the amount of a substance is the *mole*. One mole is the amount of a substance equal to its *molecular weight* in grams. Molecular weight is the sum of the atomic weights of all atoms in a molecule. For example, the molecular weight of sodium chloride is 58 (Na = 23 + Cl = 35); of glucose, 180 ($C_6 = 72 + H_{12} = 12 + O_6 = 96$). A *molar solution* is one that contains the molecular weight in grams of a substance dissolved in a solvent such as water to yield a total volume of one liter. Careful measurements have shown that one liter of pure water contains 0.0000007 (or in scientific notation 10^{-7}) mole of hydrogen ions. Since the ratio of hydrogen ions to hydroxyl ions in water is one to one, there is also 10^{-7} mole of hydroxyl ions in the same water. Since pure water has an equal number of hydrogen and hydroxyl ions, it is considered neutral. If a solution contains more H^+ than OH^-, it is *acidic*; if more OH^-, it is basic or *alkaline*.

30

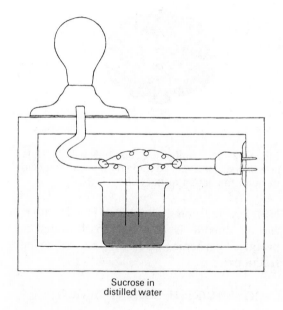

Sucrose in
distilled water

$$pH = \log \frac{1}{[H^+]} = -\log [H^+]$$

Since pH is a *reciprocal* number (a number divided into one), lower pH values stand for greater H^+ concentration. The acid range is then located between 0 and 7 on the pH scale (Figure 2–13). For example, if the H^+ concentration of a solution is 10^{-4} gram per liter, the pH is 4. Since pH is expressed on a logarithmic scale the numerical values are based on powers of ten and pH 3 represents ten times more H^+ than pH 4, and pH 2 represents a hundred times more than pH 4. Alkalinity or base range is between 7 and 14 on the pH scale. The neutral point, pH 7, represents the H^+ concentration of pure water.

The "strength" of an *acid* or *base* is proportional to the amount of its dissociation. In comparison to the strong inorganic acids, such as sulfuric acid (H_2SO_4) and hydrochloric acid (HCl), the organic acid, acetic acid (CH_3-COOH), is quite weak. The hydrogen covalently bonded to oxygen in the COOH part of the molecule does not dissociate as freely as the H^+ in hydrochloric or sulfuric acid.

There are also compounds that show basic

Acids and Bases To describe the acidity or alkalinity of a solution, it is sufficient to state only the hydrogen-ion concentration, $[H^+]$. This concentration is commonly expressed in terms of pH, which is defined as:

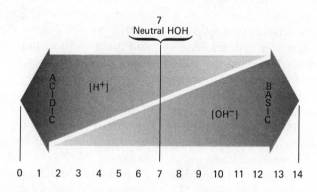

Figure 2–13 The pH scale. Equal concentrations of $[H^+]$ and $[OH^-]$ are considered to be neutral and are represented by pH 7.

properties even though they contain no hydroxyl ions. One example is NH_3, which accepts a proton to form NH_4. This fact led to a slightly different definition for both acids and bases. An acid is said to be any compound that can *donate* protons (H^+) to a solution, conversely, a base is any compound that can *accept* protons. The OH^- group is a very strong proton acceptor, and the addition of a single proton to an OH^- ion forms neutral HOH. This reaction is called a *neutralization reaction*.

Salts A salt is a compound containing a positive ion other than H^+ and a negative ion other than OH^-. The reaction between a strong acid and a strong base produces a *salt* and water.

$$HCl + NaOH \longrightarrow NaCl + H_2O$$
$$Acid + base \longrightarrow Salt + water$$

Buffers In living systems the pH value must be maintained within strict limits (pH balance is also discussed in Chapter 8). If the blood becomes too acidic, for instance, certain chemical reactions in the cells will cease to take place and the equilibrium of the body will be upset. Compounds known as *buffers* are found in the animal bloodstream which help to combat a sudden increase in acidity or alkalinity. Buffers, as implied in their name, act as a cushion for.pH changes. One of the most common buffering compounds is sodium bicarbonate ($NaHCO_3$), which dissociates into Na^+ and HCO_3^-. Excess hydrogen ions (H^+) in the blood plasma readily combine with bicarbonate ions to form a weak acid, carbonic acid (H_2CO_3). Through the buffering action of the bicarbonate ion on hydrochloric acid, a strong acid is converted into a weak acid and a salt (Figure 2–14). Under conditions of excessive hydroxyl ions, OH^-, buffers can release H^+ to help neutralize the solution.

The formation of carbonic acid in the blood

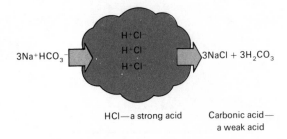

HCl—a strong acid   Carbonic acid—
                              a weak acid

Figure 2–14 Buffering action of $NaHCO_3$. Note how a weak acid can be formed from a strong acid through the action of the buffer $NaHCO_3$.

is a key reaction in biology. For example, carbon dioxide is combined with water to produce carbonic acid in the following reactions:

$$CO_2 + H_2O \rightleftharpoons H_2CO_3 \rightleftharpoons H^+ + HCO_3^-$$

This simple reaction which provides a source for the bicarbonate ion is involved in many important biological processes such as gas exchange and photosynthesis.

ORGANIC COMPOUNDS

Carbon compounds such as sugars, amino acids, fatty acids, and glycerine are all essential to the organism. Each of these basic molecules may combine with similar or other molecules to form more complex structures. In this section we will discuss the chemical structure and function of carbohydrates, fats, proteins, nucleic acids, and porphyrins.

Carbohydrates

This important class of organic compounds includes the various types of sugars. Sugars are compounds that contain from three to as many as twelve carbon atoms. Glucose, a *monosaccharide* and a major biological energy source, contains six carbon atoms arranged with hydrogen and oxygen in the following way:

If we add the components of this structure, we obtain the formula $C_6H_{12}O_6$. In this structural formula, the heavy lines are used to help us visualize a three-dimensional model. Ribose, a five-carbon sugar, $C_5H_{10}O_5$, may be written similarly:

Ribose is a very important structural component of compounds involved in energy processes (ATP) and heredity (DNA). Both ATP and DNA will be discussed at length later in the book. It should be noted that whereas six-carbon sugars are commonly utilized as fuel molecules, the five-carbon sugars are involved in the structure of molecules such as the nucleic acids.

Two monosaccharides linked together are called a *disaccharide* and more than two linked monosaccharides are known as *polysaccharide* compounds. Maltose is one example of a disaccharide, and it is formed by the union of two glucose molecules (Figure 2–15).

In this *synthesis* reaction of joining two molecules of glucose to form maltose, one molecule of water is lost. Since water is given off in this reaction it is known as a *dehydration* synthesis and the resulting formula for maltose is $C_{12}H_{22}O_{11}$. The linkage between the number 1 carbon of one molecule and the number 4 carbon of the other is simply an oxygen bridge (C—O—C) and the specific linkage described for maltose is an *alpha 1,4 glucoside*. Alpha is used here to indicate that the two hydrogen atoms attached to the oxygen bridge are in the same plane. Many glucose units linked in this manner into a long chain compose the polysaccharide, *starch* (Figure 2–16). In the liver a glucose storage product, *glycogen*, is formed which is structurally similar to starch in that it is linked by alpha 1,4 glucosides. It differs, however, in also having alpha 1,6 glucoside linkages that give a branched structure to the molecule. Glycogen, which provides a ready source of glucose for the blood, is also stored in the muscles.

Another important polysaccharide found in plant cell walls is *cellulose*, in which the 1,4 glucoside linkage is formed in a slightly different manner. Alternate glucose molecules are rotated 180° to form a "twisted" configuration, the *beta linkage* (Figure 2–16). One important result of this different linkage is that digestive juices, which split starch into glucose units, will not work on beta glucosides. Some organisms, such as bacteria, however, have the ability to digest cellulose. When starch and cellulose are broken down into glucose molecules during digestion, water is added at the linkage. This hydration reaction, often called *hydrolytic cleavage*, is the opposite of synthesis. We will return to this process in Chapter 7 when digestion is discussed.

Fats

Fats, often referred to as *lipids*, are important compounds since they store energy, provide

33

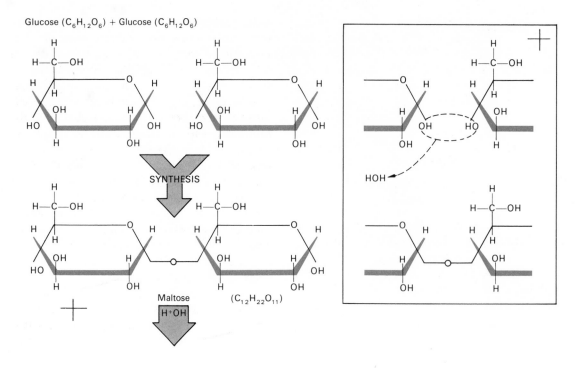

Glucose ($C_6H_{12}O_6$) + Glucose ($C_6H_{12}O_6$)

SYNTHESIS

Maltose   ($C_{12}H_{22}O_{11}$)

H^+OH

HOH

Figure 2–15   Synthesis of the disaccharide maltose from two glucose molecules. The linkage formed is an alpha 1,4 glucoside. The inset on the right shows the formation of the water molecule.

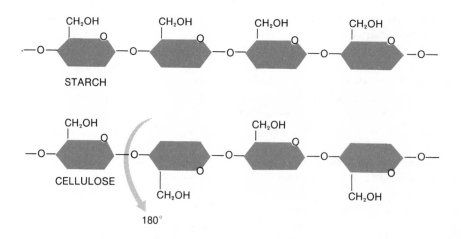

STARCH

CELLULOSE

180°

Figure 2–16   Comparison of the alpha glucoside linkages of starch with the beta glucoside linkages of cellulose. Note the alternate 180° rotation of the glucose molecules in cellulose.

protection for the internal organs, and are essential constituents of more complex molecules. The two components of a fat molecule are glycerine and fatty acids. Glycerine is a three-carbon molecule that contains three hydroxyl groups (OH). In this case the hydroxyl group is simply an oxygen atom that shares one pair of electrons with carbon and another pair with hydrogen (Figure 2–17).

Fatty acids are straight chains of carbon which have most of their bonding sites occupied by hydrogen. If some of the hydrogens of the fatty acid are removed, the carbon atoms may share two or even three pairs of electrons to form —C = C— or —C ≡ C— bonds (double and triple bonds). A fatty acid in which all available bonding sites are occupied by hydrogen is said to be *saturated* with hydrogen and when some hydrogen is removed, usually forming double bonds,

unsaturation is produced. You may be familiar with certain brands of vegetable oil that are advertised as *polyunsaturated*, which means that the carbons share most of the available bonds and very few hydrogen atoms occur along the chain. There is presently good evidence that the ingestion of saturated fats (animal fat) causes increased production of cholesterol in humans. In *arteriosclerosis*, or "hardening of the arteries," deposits of cholesterol are formed along arterial walls. Therefore, in many health diets, margarine (which contains vegetable, or unsaturated, fat) is recommended instead of butter.

One end of the fatty-acid molecule contains an acid or *carboxyl* group which is formed when carbon shares two pairs of electrons with oxygen to form a double bond and one pair of electrons with a hydroxyl. The carboxyl group is an acid because the hydrogen of the hydroxyl will dissociate to donate a proton to a solution. When it occurs as part of an organic acid group, the carboxyl end of the fatty acid may be linked to one of the hydroxyls of glycerine to form an *ester* linkage (Figure 2–17).

In this synthesis water is removed in much the same way as it is in the formation of maltose and starch. Three fatty acids attached to a glycerine molecule form a fat.

Proteins

Proteins are produced in every living cell in many sizes and shapes. Moreover, each cellular protein fulfills a specific function and is specifically synthesized according to the heredity of the cell. A protein, regardless of its size, is composed of smaller units called *amino acids* which are carbon compounds that possess a carboxyl group at one end and a nitrogen-containing amino group on the same carbon. The two simplest amino acids are glycine and alanine (Figure 2–18). Histidine and tryptophane, which incorporate ring structures, are more complex amino acids than glycine and alanine (Figure 2–19), but the amino and carboxyl groups are still present. Some amino

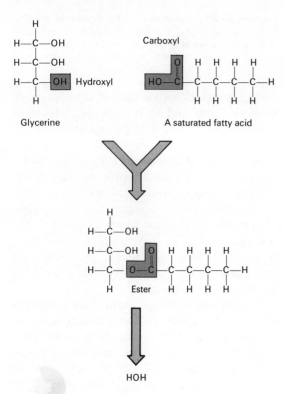

Figure 2–17 Formation of an ester linkage between a fatty acid and glycerine.

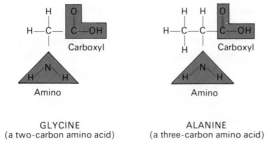

GLYCINE
(a two-carbon amino acid)

ALANINE
(a three-carbon amino acid)

Figure 2–18 The two simplest amino acids—glycine and alanine.

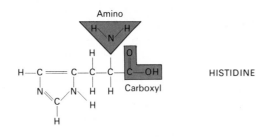

HISTIDINE

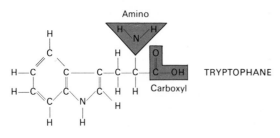

TRYPTOPHANE

Figure 2–19 Two more complex amino acids—histidine and tryptophane.

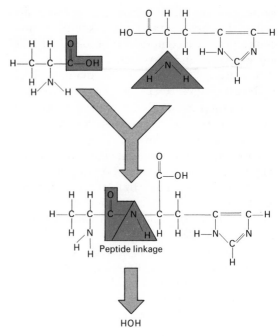

Figure 2–20 Synthesis of the dipeptide alanyl-histidine. Note that the structure of histidine here is reversed from that shown in Figure 2–19.

acids also contain sulfur. There are approximately 20 different types of amino acids.

When amino acids are linked together, the resulting linkage is a *peptide*. Two amino acids linked by one peptide is called a *dipeptide*; more than two linked amino acids produce a *polypeptide*. The peptide linkage is formed in an interaction between the amino group of one amino acid and the carboxyl group of another (Figure 2–20). The nitrogen unites with the carboxyl carbon, with the resultant loss of one water molecule.

Simple proteins are composed of only amino acids. In nature proteins can combine with other substances such as carbohydrates, fats, or inorganic ions and such proteins are said to be *conjugated*. Rather large amounts of conjugated proteins may be found in brain and nerve tissues, mucous secretions, egg white, and in all cells. In the cell, proteins provide the fundamental structure for all major structural components. One important class of proteins, vital to life, are *enzymes* which speed up chemical reactions in an organism. Tendons, hair, fingernails, blood globulins, and skin are other examples of structures in which proteins are the major component.

The primary linkage group in a protein is the peptide, which holds the amino acids in specific polypeptide chains. Since most proteins are made up of more than one polypeptide, other secondary bonds must also be present to maintain a spiral structure of the complex molecule. Hydrogen bonds are the most common in this secondary role, and these hydrogen bonds usually occur between adjacent peptide linkages. In addition, disulfide bridges (—S—S—) formed between certain sulfur-containing amino acids can maintain the protein in a folded pattern (Figure 2–21). Owing to these various types of bonds, proteins may occur in many structural forms, such as globular, sheetlike, or long spiraled fibers. The ability of protein molecules to function as enzymes is related to the fact that they can be structured into many specific configurations.

Nucleic Acids

Nucleic acids are macromolecules that are essential to all living things because they are indispensable to the heredity and the protein synthesis of every cell. Two types of nucleic acids are known, *ribonucleic acid* (RNA) and *deoxyribonucleic acid* (DNA). Each of these molecules is made up of subunits called *nucleotides* which are strung together (polymerized) to form long chains. Nucleotides are

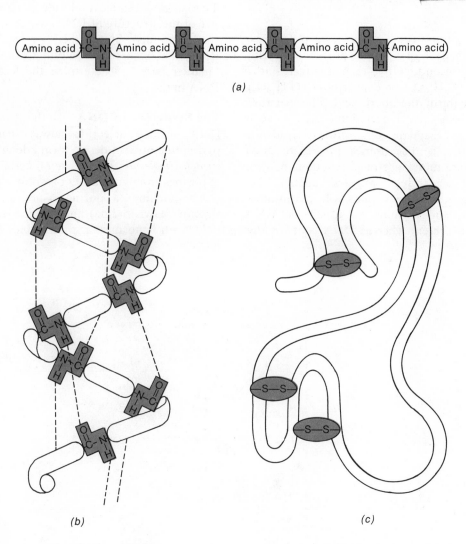

(a)

(b)   (c)

Figure 2–21 The three structural levels found in proteins. (*a*) Primary: peptide linkages between amino acids in a chain. (*b*) Secondary: hydrogen bonds hold the spiraled chain in an alpha helix (broken lines). (*c*) Tertiary: disulfide bonds maintain the complex three-dimensional shape of a protein.

37

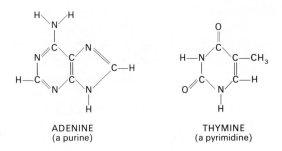

ADENINE
(a purine)

THYMINE
(a pyrimidine)

Figure 2–22 Two nitrogen bases—adenine and thymine—illustrating purine and pyrimidine structures.

always composed of three basic parts: first, nitrogenous bases (either purine or pyrimidine); second, a five-carbon sugar [either ribose ($C_5H_{10}O_5$) or deoxyribose ($C_5H_{10}O_4$)]; and the third, phosphoric acid. The structures of a purine and a pyrimidine are shown in Figure 2–22, and the composition of an adenine nucleotide is diagrammed in Figure 2–23. There are four kinds of nitrogenous bases in nucleic acids: two purines, adenine and guanine; and two kinds of pyrimidines, cytosine and thymine, or uracil. In RNA, uracil is present whereas DNA contains thymine.

The nucleotides of DNA always contain deoxyribose sugar (similar to ribose but having one less oxygen atom), one of the nitrogen bases mentioned above, and phosphoric acid. This means there are four kinds of DNA nucleotides. For example, the deoxyribose sugar and phosphoric acid may unite with adenine, guanine, cytosine, or thymine.

Simple phosphate ester linkages can hook the sugars and their attached nitrogen bases into a long nucleotide chain (Figure 2–24). This single-stranded molecule is representative of the structure of RNA, which is usually single stranded. Since uracil is found only in RNA, it is sometimes helpful to use it as a "marker base" to determine the location of RNA in the cell.

The Structure of DNA   In the structure of DNA purine nucleotides always pair with pyrimidine nucleotides to form a long *double-stranded molecule*. Furthermore, certain types of purines and pyrimidines pair only with each other: adenine (a purine) pairs only with thymine (a pyrimidine), and guanine (a purine) only with cytosine (a pyrimidine) (Figure 2–25).

PHOSPHATE | SUGAR | NITROGENOUS BASE

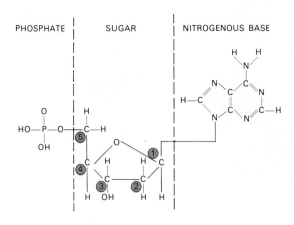

Figure 2–23 Structural diagram of an adenine nucleotide showing the three basic components: adenine, deoxyribose sugar, and phosphate.

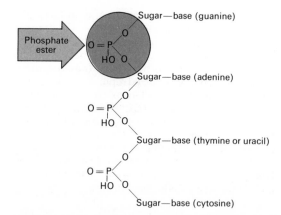

Figure 2–24 The phosphate ester linkages that link sugars and nitrogen bases into nucleic-acid chains.

In 1953, F. H. C. Crick of Cambridge University and the American molecular biologist, J. D. Watson (Figure 2–26), proposed a model to account for the structure of the DNA molecule. This model, based on chemical analyses and x-ray diffraction studies, also accounts for the unique activities of DNA such as reproduction and coding of hereditary in-information. The double-stranded DNA mol-

Figure 2–26 James D. Watson, recipient of the Nobel Prize in 1962 for his role in the discovery of the molecular structure of DNA. (Courtesy of Dr. Watson.)

ecule is believed to be twisted into a spiral or helical shape (Figure 2–27). If it were not twisted the molecule would look something

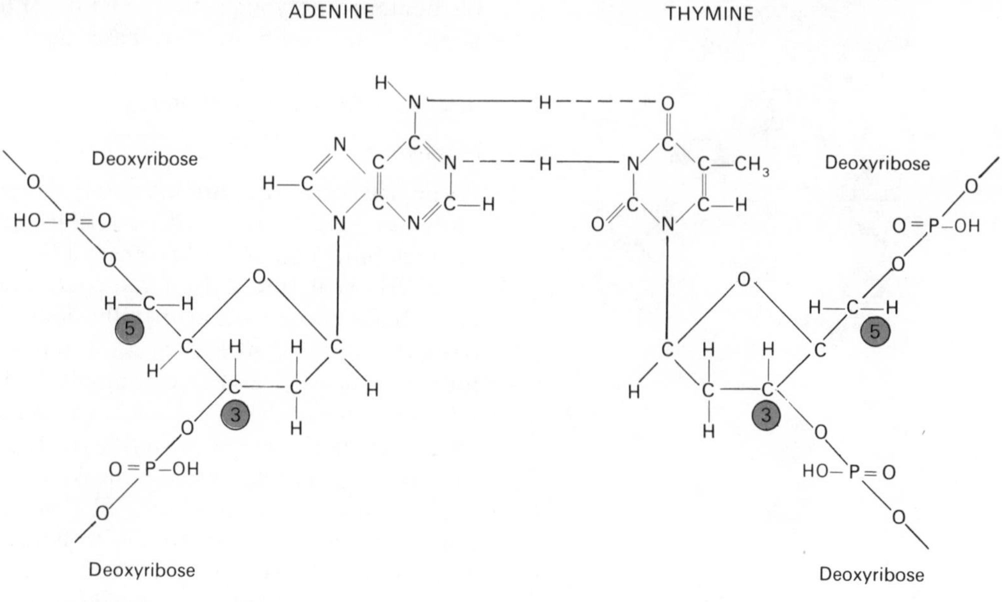

ADENINE   THYMINE

Figure 2–25 Structure of an adenine-thymine base pair. Note the hydrogen bonds (dashed lines) and the 3-5 phosphate esters that link the sugars into a polymeric chain.

39

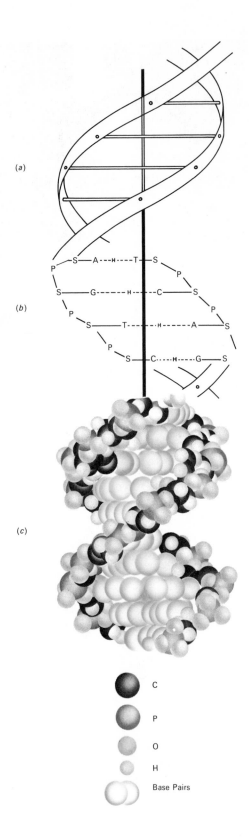

(a)

(b)

(c)

C

P

O

H

Base Pairs

Figure 2–27 The helix of DNA, with three different ways of representing the molecular arrangement. (*a*) General picture of the double helix, with the phosphate-sugar combinations making up the outside spirals and the base pairs the cross-bars. (*b*) Somewhat more detailed representation: phosphate (B), sugar (S), adenine (A), thymine (T), guanine (G), cytosine (C), and hydrogen (H). (*c*) Detailed structure showing how the space is filled with atoms: carbon (C), oxygen (O), hydrogen (H), phosphorus (P), and the base pairs. (Redrawn from Carl P. Swanson, *The Cell*, Second Edition, © 1964. By permission of Prentice-Hall, Inc., Englewood Cliffs, New Jersey.)

like a ladder, in which the rails of the ladder correspond to the sugar and phosphate and the steps to the sequence of paired nitrogenous bases.

One of the important characteristics of DNA is its ability to replicate itself and produce an exact duplicate. When the hydrogen bonds which hold the two strands together are broken, two distinct halves result. Since adenine pairs only with thymine and guanine pairs only with cytosine, each original strand contains the pattern for producing a new half exactly like the separated half. Therefore, each half of the molecule reproduces a new complementary polynucleotide chain (Figure 2–28). The significance of base pairing in genetic coding and protein synthesis will be discussed further in Chapter 3.

Porphyrins

Porphyrins are the fundamental structural units in pigments such as chlorophyll, hemoglobin, and cytochromes. The basic porphyrin structure is a unique configuration of carbon, nitrogen, and metallic ions. This basic structure (Figure 2–29), is composed of four *pyrrole rings* and is commonly called a *tetrapyrrole-ring compound*. Each carbon atom around the periphery of the tetrapyrrole structure may be bonded to specific side chains such as alcohols or proteins. The most important aspect of the molecule, to living systems, is its ability through its metallic ions (magnesium in chlorophyll and iron in cytochromes) to gain or lose electrons. Chlorophyll and cytochromes, in the process of trapping

40

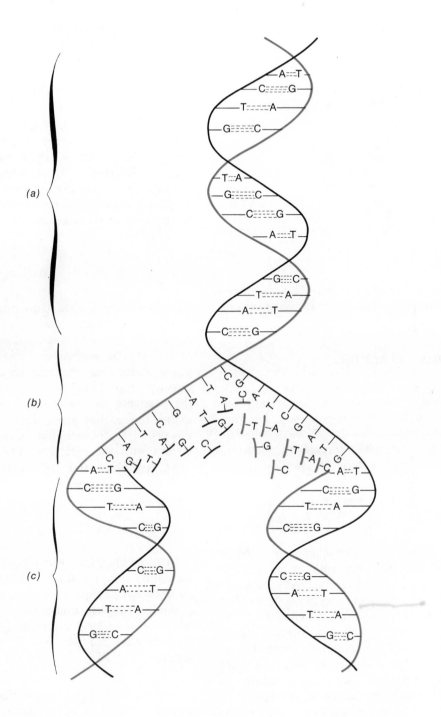

Figure 2–28 The process of replication in the DNA molecule. (*a*) Portion of original DNA molecule in the process of replication. (*b*) Area of uncoiling and breaking of hydrogen bonds between nitrogen bases. (*c*) Area of synthesis of two identical DNA molecules by pairing of complementary nucleotides and formation of hydrogen bonds.

41

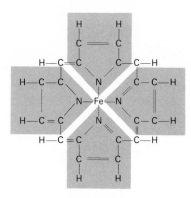

Figure 2–29 Basic structure of an iron-containing porphyrin. The colored areas represent pyrrole rings.

and transfer of energy, provide a mechanism for the transfer of electrons in living systems.

CHEMICAL REACTIONS

Chemical compounds may react with one another to form new compounds. For these new compounds to be formed, chemical bonds must be broken and reformed, and this rearrangement of bonds always involves energy changes.

ENERGY

Some chemicals react spontaneously—that is, the reaction proceeds without an external energy source. Such spontaneous reactions are called _exergonic,_ and they generally produce heat. One such reaction is the violent one that occurs when metallic sodium comes in contact with water. This is a rapidly completed reaction that produces both heat and light. Reactions that require external energy for their activation are known as _endergonic._ (It should also be noted that some exergonic reactions require energy to get them started.) Light, heat, and pressure are possible sources of the _activation energy_ needed to start a chemical reaction. Once started, a reaction

may or may not be self-sustaining. If it is not, small amounts of _continuation energy_ may be needed to keep it going.

CONCENTRATION AND MASS ACTION

In many instances where chemical reactions, for one reason or another, do not go to completion, the products formed may react in a reverse direction as their concentration increases. This is known as a _reversible chemical reaction_ and may be stated generally in terms of the ratio of the reactants to the products:

$$A + B \rightleftharpoons C + D$$

Reactants   Products

As the reactants are gradually used up and the products accumulate, the rate of the reaction to the right is slowed down and an equilibrium may finally be established. The _law of mass action_ states that the rate of a reaction is directly proportional to the concentration of the reactants. In the case of hydrogen and iodine, the reaction proceeds to the right until the product concentration reaches an equilibrium with the reactants. The addition of more hydrogen and iodine, however, will increase the reaction to the right to produce more HI.

$$H_2 + I_2 \rightleftharpoons 2HI$$

In some chemical reactions the product is constantly removed through the formation of an insoluble precipitate or a volatile gas. For example, in the reaction between silver nitrate and sodium chloride, the precipitated silver chloride does not take part in a reverse reaction:

$$AgNO_3 + NaCl \xrightarrow{H_2O} \overset{\text{Precipitate}}{AgCl} + NaNO_3$$

| Silver nitrate | Sodium chloride | Silver chloride | Sodium nitrate |

The law of mass action then enables us to predict not only the rate of a reaction but also its direction and duration.

ENZYME ACTION

The energy requirement in chemical reactions is chiefly needed to increase the thermal agitation of the atoms. With higher temperature and consequently greater movement, the atoms bump into each other with greater force and greater frequency. The probability of reactions among these atoms is therefore greatly increased. Organisms must sustain a large number of chemical reactions, and most of them require energy. For instance, how is it that, in cells, chemical reactions can occur that ordinarily would require enough heat to literally burn up the cells. Clearly some mechanism is needed, and it is provided by biological catalysts called *enzymes*. Although all enzymes are composed primarily of protein, the polypeptide chains are linked together in various ways to form specific structures that are specialized for catalyzing a certain reaction. That is, the enzyme appears to actually "fit" the reactants into its structure in order to bring them close together and thus increase the probability of the reaction. The function of enzymes thus is similar to that of heat— namely, to get the reactants together.

Active Sites

The catalytic action of enzyme molecules is located at specific *active sites*, which can react with specific regions of the reactant molecules. The specific geometry of the active site therefore is important, and any change in the molecule that alters the active site structure will change or possibly inactivate the enzyme. A hypothetical synthesis catalyzed by an enzyme is illustrated in Figure 2–30. Note that the enzyme does not appear in the product and thus is capable of participating in further reactions.

Ribonuclease, an enzyme capable of catalyzing the hydrolysis of nucleic acids, was the first enzyme for which the amino-acid sequence was determined (Figure 2–31). Ribonuclease is structured in a long, folded chain of 124 amino acids of 19 different types. At four spots along the folded molecule disulfide linkages hold the molecule in its specific shape. Recently scientists at Rockefeller University and Merck, Sharp and Dohme Research Laboratories have synthesized active forms of ribonuclease. Not only is this the first enzyme to be synthesized but it is also the largest protein thus far assembled outside of a living system.

Entirely different techniques were utilized by the two research teams to accomplish

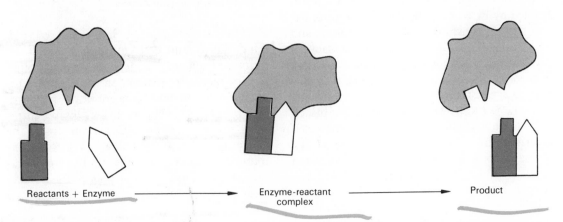

Reactants + Enzyme → Enzyme-reactant complex → Product

Figure 2–30 Proposed model for the action of an enzyme in a synthesis reaction. The reactants form a complex with the active sites of the enzyme, complete their reaction, and are released as product.

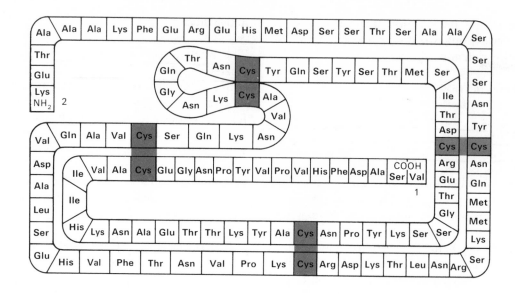

THE BUILDING BLOCKS—19 AMINO ACIDS

Ala —Alanine	Gln —Glutamine	Leu —Leucine	Ser —Serine
Arg—Arginine	Glu —Glutamic acid	Lys —Lysine	Thr —Threonine
Asn—Asparagine	Gly —Glycine	Met —Methionine	Tyr —Tyrosine
Asp—Aspartic Acid	His —Histidine	Phe —Phenylalanine	Val —Valine
Cys —Cysteine	Ile —Isoleucine	Pro —Proline	

COOH—Carboxy group   NH₂—Amino group

Figure 2–31   The amino-acid sequence of ribonuclease. In the synthesis of this enzyme by Merrifield and Gutte, reported in 1969, the carboxy-terminal amino-acid valine (1) was attached to a solid polymer resin. Then the residual 123 amino acids were coupled one at a time, the last one being the amino-terminal lysine (2). (Courtesy of Bernd Gutte.)

ribonuclease synthesis. The Rockefeller team, headed by R. B. Merrifield and B. Gutte, began with the terminal amino acid, valine, and added the remaining 123 amino acids in a process much like coupling a string of railroad cars together one at a time. The chain assemblage was constructed on a solid resin support; after the 124 units were coupled, it was placed in solution and allowed to fold into the characteristic three-dimensional structure of the active enzyme. It is also possible to construct small peptide groups composed of approximately three to twenty amino acids each and join these together to form the enzyme. This was the approach utilized by the Merck group led by R. G. Denkewalter and R. F. Hirschmann. They assembled an active ribonuclease from twenty different fragments.

Influences on Enzyme Action

Enzyme action may be influenced by pH, temperature, and concentration; optimal activity for each enzyme depends on a combination of these. In general, an increase in temperature or enzyme concentration increases reaction rates, whereas lower temperatures slow down reactions. Deviation from the optimum pH will also slow a reaction. Extreme deviation from the normal temperature or pH causes *denaturation* of the protein structure and inactivation of the enzyme. Denaturation refers to a structural change produced in a protein and will be further considered in Chapter 3.

A summary of our discussion on chemical compounds and reactions might well be done by returning to the firefly example given at the beginning of this chapter. Light, or bioluminescence, is produced in a series of chemical reactions involving at least three organic compounds—ATP, luciferin, and luciferase. It should be noted that ATP is involved in all energy reactions in all living forms. Luciferin is an organic compound produced by the firefly (and many other bioluminescent organisms) and luciferase is the principal enzyme involved in the reaction. The first reaction in this process apparently links luciferin and ATP. Light energy then can be released when a solution of luciferase and some inorganic ion, such as Mg^{++} in the presence of oxygen, is added to the luciferin-ATP complex. The final reaction in the process may be summarized as:

$$\text{Luciferin-ATP} \xrightarrow[\substack{Mg^{++},\,O_2 \\ H_2O}]{\text{luciferase}} \text{light} + \text{luciferin} + \text{ADP}$$

(Note that ATP is changed to ADP in this reaction and the reason for this will be given in Chapter 6 when energy is discussed.) In this process we can see a chemical change that releases light energy and occurs in the presence of an enzyme.

ENTROPY

Living systems require energy to perform work and to maintain their highly ordered structures and chemical reactions. In our universe, as we know it, all processes are moving toward disorganization and a state of complete disorder. This concept is known as the second law of thermodynamics.

The extent of disorder in a system may be measured and expressed mathematically as *entropy*. A high entropy value indicates a high level of disorganization whereas lower entropy values represent relatively more order in a system. The energy used by living organisms to do work is known as *free energy*, and it is important to note that free energy and entropy are closely related. For example, a highly organized system has more potential free energy and less entropy than does a poorly organized system.

The organized system therefore has the ability to perform more work. In physical terms, free energy changes in a system are inversely related to changes in entropy.

Since living systems reproduce and maintain an orderly state, they appear to defy the second law of thermodynamics. Living things, however, are not closed systems; they require large amounts of fuel either from the sun and photosynthesis or energy-rich molecules from other organisms. Life, in its ordered state, possesses low entropy and thus has the energy necessary to perform biological work. It might be said that an increase in entropy actually drives the energy-requiring reactions of life. In the total picture, then, entropy is increasing in the universe, and the living system is only a brief interlude along the course to disorder.

CHEMICAL DEVELOPMENT AND THE ORIGIN OF LIFE

Before we begin our discussion of the structure and function of living systems, a most fundamental question should be explored—the problem of the origin of life on our planet. Since all organisms are composed of chemical compounds, we must first look at some of the basic chemical principles involved. It is perhaps more realistic to think of the origin of life as a twofold process: first, the development or formation of very large molecules whose special duplicating and coding features are characteristic of life; and second, the organization of these molecules into cells.

SMALL MOLECULES TO LARGE MOLECULES

As the earth formed and heavy elements such as iron and nickel sank to the center of the earth, the lighter gases collected in the atmosphere. The Russian scientist Oparin suggested that this primitive atmosphere contained little or no oxygen but was composed mainly of hydrogen and nitrogen. Most of the oxygen probably escaped into space or was tied up in oxides of metals in the earth's crust (iron oxide, for example). The primitive atmosphere also probably contained methane (CH_4), ammonia (NH_3), hydrogen cyanide (HCN), and some water vapor (H_2O).

The fundamental problem in explaining the origin of life in a mechanistic manner lies in the interesting fact that the organic molecules we know today are essentially synthesized by living organisms. We must show that these molecules could have been produced outside of living systems under conditions which are believed to have existed in the early development of our planet.

We know that energy is required to form molecules from atoms and energy is also necessary to construct larger molecules from smaller ones. Sources of energy probably available on the primitive earth were ultraviolet light, electric discharges (lightning), cosmic radiation, shock waves (thunder and meteors entering the atmosphere), and heat (from volcanoes). It has been postulated that the molecules of this early atmosphere, under the stimulation of a source of energy, could have formed many of the simpler organic molecules such as amino acids (Figure 2–32).

In 1953, at the University of Chicago, Stanley Miller performed an experiment to test this hypothesis (Figure 2–33). Essentially he circulated the gases NH_3, CH_4, H_2, and H_2O past an electric discharge and examined the resulting mixture. Among the products were amino acids, a fatty acid, and formic acid! The study of the origin of organic molecules with electric discharge apparatus continues. One experimenter in this field is Dr. Cyril A. Ponnamperuma of Ames Research Center (Figure 2–34). This experiment proved that the process proposed by Oparin and others was possible, and experiments by other investigators have yielded similar results. An interesting report in 1970 by Sidney W. Fox and Charles Windsor showed that seven different amino acids could be synthesized from the heating of ammonia and formaldehyde. This is especially significant since these two simple molecules are present in galactic space and could certainly be precursors of amino acids. Configurations such as carbon chains, carbon rings, NH_2 groups, $-C=O$, and $-\overset{|}{\underset{|}{C}}-OH$ are important parts of molecules associated with life.

LARGE MOLECULES TO LARGER MOLECULES

The next logical step in the formation of molecules required for life would be the production of still larger molecules such as proteins. Proteins are large molecules that result when many amino acids combine. Sidney W. Fox and several of his coworkers at Florida State University have shown that such a process is possible. By subjecting a mixture of amino acids (including an abundance of glutamic and aspartic acids) to intense heat (160–200° C) for several hours they were able to produce proteinlike compounds which they called *proteinoids.* Other experiments have produced similar polymerizations.

By pouring water over a mixture of hot proteinoids, Fox produced tiny spherical bodies which he termed "microspheres (Figure 2–35). These can be seen under the light microscope and, when observed with the

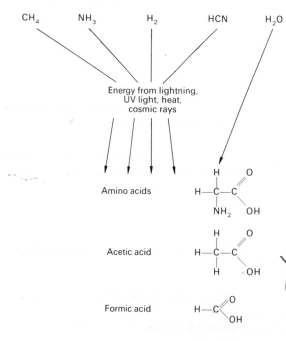

Figure 2–32 Formation of simple organic molecules from a hypothetical primitive atmosphere.

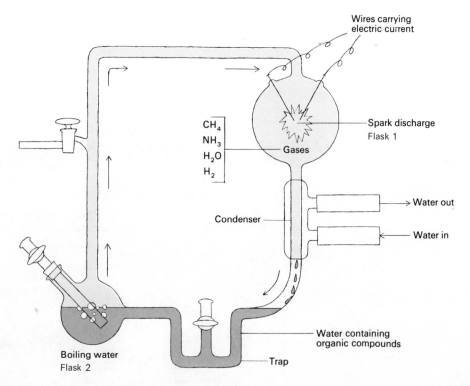

Figure 2-33 Laboratory apparatus set up by Stanley Miller to simulate the chemical and physical conditions on the primitive earth. Water vapor produced in Flask 2 is mixed with the gases in Flask 1, passed through an electric discharge, and condensed in the U tube at the bottom. After the gases had circulated for one week, samples of the water were analyzed for organic compounds and several amino acids were found. (Redrawn from *Early Evolution of Life*, BSCS Pamphlet No. 11, 1964, by permission of D. C. Heath and Company and Biological Sciences Curriculum Study.)

electron microscope, a double-walled membrane, typical of living cells, is apparent. These microspheres, however, cannot be considered cells, but this experiment demonstrated that proteinoids could form membranelike structures that are characteristic of cells.

Certainly, compounds other than proteins are necessary for life, and among these are sugars, purines, pyrimidines, and fatty acids. It seems quite likely that molecules of these compounds could have been produced early in the total series of events leading up to life.

Figure 2-34 Working with the electric-discharge apparatus for the study of the origin of organic molecules is Cyril A. Ponnamperuma, chief of the Chemical Evolution Branch at NASA's Ames Research Center. (Courtesy of NASA.)

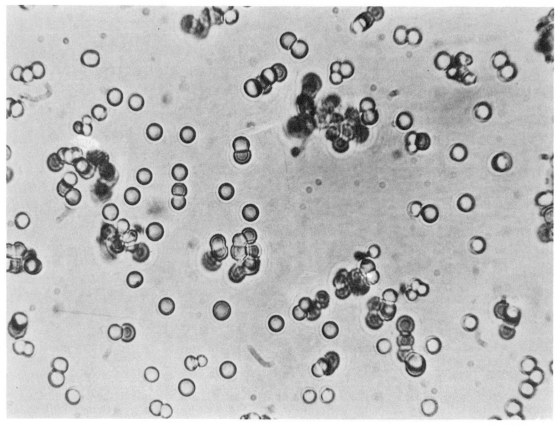

Figure 2–35 Microspheres produced by combining water with hot proteinoids. The spheres range in size from 1 to 3 microns. (Courtesy of Institute of Molecular Evolution, University of Miami.)

Simple sugars have been produced by irradiating solutions of formaldehyde ($H_2C = O$) with ultraviolet or gamma rays, and larger sugar molecules have also been produced by heating mixtures of simple sugars. Fats, as we learned earlier, are formed from one glycerine molecule and three molecules of fatty acids. The glycerine molecule is a rather simple three-carbon structure, whereas fatty acids may be long carbon chains. It is conceivable that these molecules could have come together in the presence of an energy source to produce large fat molecules. Purines and pyrimidines are ring compounds of carbon and nitrogen which are necessary for the heredity and reproductive processes in all organisms (Figure 2–22). The purine adenine has been synthesized in several different ways, and in one experiment it was produced when HCN and NH_3 were heated

together at 100°C. In other experiments purines and pyrimidines were produced from mixtures of methane, ammonia, hydrogen, and water.

Compounds such as purines and sugars frequently combine to form even larger molecules. This combination has also been duplicated in laboratory conditions paralleling those of the primitive earth. Recently at Ames Research Center, a large molecule known as a nucleotide was produced when a solution of ribose sugar, adenine, and phosphoric acid was irradiated with ultraviolet light. This was an important step in the confirmation of the theory of the origin of life as outlined here, since nucleotides are inseparably linked with life's functions. The nucleotide synthesized at Ames was adenosine triphosphate, commonly known as ATP, which

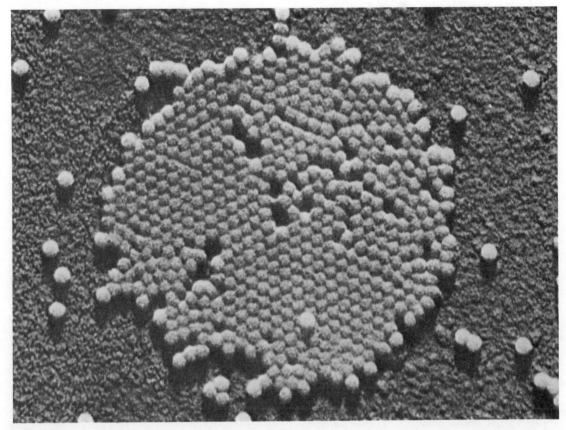

Figure 2—36   Electron micrograph of the polio virus, a polyhedral type (× 230,000). (Courtesy of Virus Laboratory, University of California at Berkeley.)

functions as the basic energy carrier for all life. (See diagram of ATP shown in Chapter 6.)

SELF-DUPLICATING, CODING MOLECULES

Life requires even larger molecules than the nucleotide structure, and further polymerization or construction of larger molecules from smaller units must have occurred. We know that nucleotides can unite in living systems in the presence of an enzyme to form some of the largest natural molecules known, the nucleic acids. As was noted earlier in this chapter, ribonucleic acid (RNA) is a long single chain of nucleotides, and deoxyribonucleic acid (DNA) is a long double chain of nucleotides. Efforts to synthesize these nucleic acids under the hypothetical primitive earth conditions have not been completely successful. Large nucleic-

acid structures have been approximated, however, by mixing high concentrations of nucleotides at temperatures of around 60°C.

The chromosomes of living cells, to be discussed in detail later, are composed of nucleic acids (essentially DNA) and protein. Viruses (Figures 2–36 and 2–37) have a similar composition—that is, either RNA or DNA, and protein—and it is tempting to speculate that they are similar to the early structures formed when nucleic acid and protein molecules first evolved. This is only one hypothesis, however, to explain the existence of viruses. Some biologists believe that viruses have evolved to an extreme state of parasitism, with the gradual loss of all cellular structures except nucleic acid and protein. Since viruses do not possess the necessary cell parts for reproduction and other life processes, they must invade living cells and

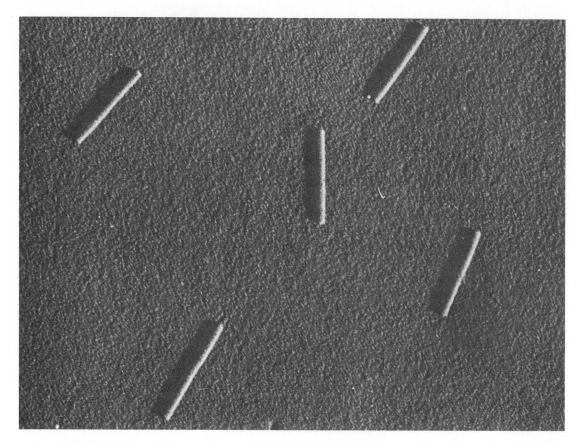

Figure 2–37 Electron micrograph of the tobacco mosaic virus, a rod-shaped type (× 100,000). (Courtesy of Virus Laboratory, University of California at Berkeley.)

utilize the host's cellular machinery. Recently small, lightweight RNA molecules, called "viroids" (like a virus), have been identified from diseased plants, such as stunt disease of chrysanthemums. These infectious RNA molecules are much smaller than any known virus, yet are capable of reproducing themselves after entering a host.

The important point to note at this stage of our discussion is that DNA is a molecule that can divide and produce two molecules exactly like itself. In addition, it provides a code system of information for the cell. These are two basic requirements for living systems. In reproduction a DNA molecule splits down the middle, and each half constructs another half exactly like the one it lost (Figure 2–28).

The code, which results from the linear sequence of nitrogen bases, can be organized in a variety of combinations and controls the cellular synthesis of proteins. We will discuss the information code of DNA in greater detail in Chapter 3.

Following the introduction in 1953 of the three-dimensional model of DNA by Watson and Crick, many scientists turned to the task of synthesizing DNA. In 1958 Arthur Kornberg (Figure 2–38) succeeded in isolating the enzyme DNA polymerase which links individual nucleotides into long DNA molecules if a strand of "natural" DNA is added as a template. This test-tube synthesis constituted a great advance in biochemistry for which Kornberg was awarded the Nobel Prize in Medicine in 1959.

The synthetic DNA produced by Kornberg

Figure 2–38 Arthur Kornberg, recipient of the Nobel Prize in 1959 for his work in DNA synthesis. (Courtesy of Dr. Kornberg and Stanford University Photographic Department.)

was not, however, exactly like "normal" DNA. The new chains were branched and exhibited no biological activity. If a biologically active DNA could be produced, it would prove that a molecule could be synthesized which could perform the essential functions of life. In 1967 Kornberg announced a new synthesis. In his laboratory at Stanford University he and his associates had synthesized a viral DNA that was capable of invading bacterial cells to produce a new generation of normal viruses. Kornberg used the virus ΦX174, which is unique because its DNA is single stranded and circular. He was able to isolate the viral DNA, copy it in a test tube, and finally copy the copy (Figure 2–39). A photograph of the duplicating DNA of step 3 is shown in Figure 2–40. This amounted to a completely extracellular synthesis of DNA. When the artificial

DNA was introduced into a specially prepared culture of *Escherichia coli* bacteria, the copy DNA entered the cells and produced normal viruses. Although the DNA in this case was single stranded, the biological activity demonstrated indicates that scientists have moved a step nearer to an understanding of the origin of life and genetic mechanisms.

Later, in 1970, H. G. Khorana of the University of Wisconsin successfully synthesized the basic code unit for the production of an important type of yeast RNA. In this experiment he joined 77 nucleotides into double-stranded DNA, which constitutes the laboratory synthesis of a unit of heredity, the *gene*.

CELLULAR DEVELOPMENT

Most of the basic molecules necessary for life have been discussed in this chapter, but we know that these molecules must be enclosed in cells. How then were the first cells formed? Fox's experiments demonstrated a possible way in which cells could have been formed with protein membranes. Other possibilities have been suggested, however, and the truth is that, at this stage, we do not really know how the first cells were formed. We do know that cells have membranes composed of protein and fat and possess chromosomes containing DNA which seem to control the activities of the cell. Perhaps the first cells utilized proteins as their informational molecules which controlled important chemical reactions. But nucleic acids with their coding and self-duplicating capabilities provide for greater control and diversity (Figure 2–41). Perhaps the fundamental problem in understanding the origin of life is to explain how nucleic acids became associated with cellular structures, and how the vital nucleic acid–protein relationship developed. With the development of additional cell structures, the processes of *respiration* (which provide energy to the cell) and *photosynthesis* (food making) could have evolved. In cellular respiration, carbon dioxide is given off while oxygen is

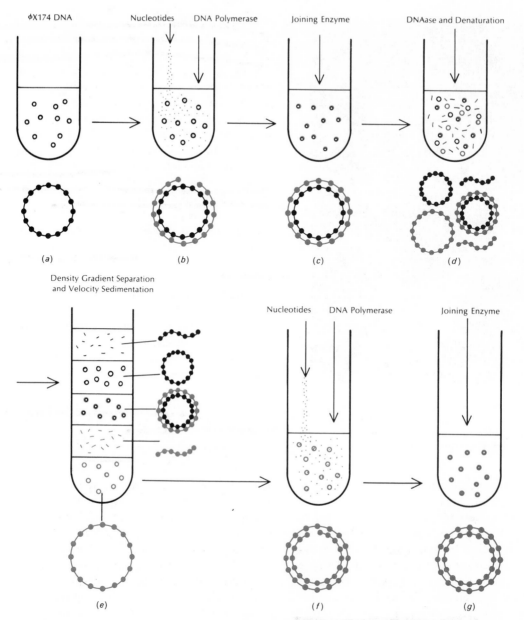

Figure 2–39 Steps in the synthesis of complete, biologically active, viral DNA. (*a*) The circular DNA of $\phi \times 174$ virus is used as a template. (*b*) Nucleotides containing adenine, thymine, guanine, and cytosine are then added, along with DNA polymerase. The enzyme causes formation of a synthetic polypeptide circle complementary to the template DNA. However, the synthetic circle is incomplete and therefore not biologically active. (*c*) Completion of the complementary circle is accomplished by the polynucleotide-joining enzyme, and a semisynthetic covalent duplex circle is formed. (*d*) DNAase treatment and denaturation permit separation of the two circles and of linear forms of both template and synthetic origin. (*e*) Various techniques have been employed along the way to create density differences and exploit shape differences so that the template and synthetic linears, the template and synthetic circles, and the semisynthetic duplexes can be segregated. (*f*), (*g*) The synthetic circles can then be employed as templates for the formation of a second complementary synthetic circle, using the same procedures as before. The result is a completely synthetic viral DNA in its biologically active replicating form. (Reproduced by permission from "The Synthesis of Infective DNA and Its Implications" by Arthur Kornberg, *Hospital Practice*, April 1968.)

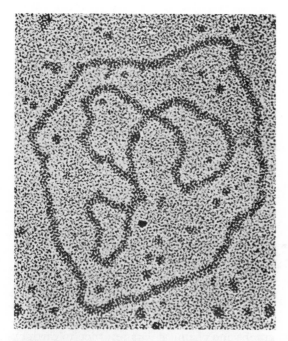

Figure 2–40 Electron micrograph of two duplex circles of partially synthetic $\phi \times$ DNA ($\times$ 310,000). One duplex happens to lie inside the other. Each consists of a template of natural virus with a complete synthetic complementary circle. (Reproduced by permission from "The Synthesis of Infective DNA and Its Implications" by Arthur Kornberg, *Hospital Practice*, April 1968.)

used. In food making the reverse is true—that is, oxygen is released and carbon dioxide is used. These processes probably played a significant role in the conversion of the primitive reducing atmosphere to the present one which contains a considerable amount of oxygen. In fact, most of the oxygen in our modern atmosphere is believed to be the result of oxygen produced by photosynthesis.

WHAT IS LIFE?

Perhaps the best summarizing statements about life involve cellular structure and the chemical compounds contained within the cell. That is, life can be simply defined as "cells containing nucleic acids." Inherent in this definition is the ability of life to reproduce, code messages, and change (mutate), since nucleic acids can perform these three functions.

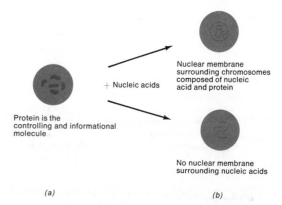

Figure 2–41 Probable scheme for the origin of modern cell types from a primitive cell. (*a*) Primitive cell type. (*b*) Modern cell types.

Usually life is defined in terms of the characteristics of the living material (sometimes known as *protoplasm*). All living material exhibits *sensitivity* and living things respond to their environment. *Movement* is yet another characteristic of the living substance. Further, all life must constantly undergo chemical reactions for nourishment and the construction of new protoplasm. In this process, *ingestion* of food, *secretion*, and *excretion* of wastes occur. All of the chemical reactions necessary for life are often summarized with the term *metabolism*. Living cells and organisms must also *reproduce* and undergo an orderly process of *growth*. Each living organism must ultimately die, decay, and decompose returning the living substance to nonliving material. Finally, the important characteristic of *adaptation* is exhibited by all forms of life, and all of the other functions certainly contribute to the ability of an organism to adapt. Actually, these fundamental characteristics form the framework for the rest of this book.

WHERE IS LIFE GOING?

NATURAL SELECTION

The explanation for the diversity of life found on our planet is based on the concept of *natural selection*. In its simplest form natural selection is the effect of the environment upon the different coding combinations of DNA. We can assume that various code arrangements (A-T, G-C, etc.) developed and environments must have varied in the early days of our earth just as they do today. Certain codes then could produce cells varying in their abilities to cope with the various environments. Perhaps many different coded cells were produced in a specific environment but only those suited to that environment could live there. These "favored" cells could divide and produce others like themselves.

Natural selection is a fundamental concept that should be kept in mind throughout your study of biology, for it is a mechanism that can explain the diversity of life. Natural selection therefore is considered to be the force that determines the type of life that inhabits the earth.

DOES LIFE EXIST ON OTHER PLANETS?

Several investigators have reported the presence of amino acids and purines and pyrimidines in pieces of meteorites. It is easy for meteorites to become contaminated once they have arrived on earth especially if the meteorites are old. But Cyril Ponnamperuma was able to obtain and analyze essentially uncontaminated samples from the Murchison meteorite which fell near Victoria, Australia in September, 1969. In addition to six amino acids common to organisms on earth (glycine, alanine, glutamic acid, valine, proline, and serine), two amino acids ordinarily not found here (2-methylalanine and sarcosine) were identified. Amino acids, like many other molecules, exist as either "right- or left-handed" molecules, and most of the amino acids on earth are of the "left-handed" form. In the samples from this meteorite, both configurations of the amino acids were found in almost equal amounts making it highly unlikely that these amino acids came from contamination on the earth or in the atmosphere. It seems then that amino acids and other organic molecules exist in other parts of the universe. And if these important building blocks are available, it is possible that life may have originated on other planets as it did on earth.

Following this line of reasoning and utilizing our space-travel capabilities, we are now studying Mars. Although some scientists believe that life already exists on Mars, recent photographs and chemical data returned to earth by Mariner 9 indicate that Mars may be undergoing events similar to those of our primitive earth. Volcanic activity may be starting; if the polar caps are frozen water, they may melt and produce atmospheric and surface water necessary for the origin of life. We now know that the Martian atmosphere contains *ozone* (O_3), and this could serve as a protective filter, as it does for earth, against harmful ultraviolet rays from the sun. Certainly future space explorations will have significant impact in the field of *exobiology*, the study of evidence of extraterrestrial life.

SUMMARIZING STATEMENTS

All material substance of the universe is known as matter, and each element is a substance composed of one kind of atom. The fundamental unit of matter is the atom, which is composed principally of protons, neutrons, and electrons.

Theories of the origin of the universe include: (1) the explosion theory which proposes that the universe was formed by the explosion of a concentration of matter some seven to ten billion years ago; and (2) the steady-state theory which holds that the universe has always existed and thus has no beginning and no end.

One of the most useful models of the structure of the atom is the Bohr model which depicts the electrons moving about a central nucleus in shells corresponding to the specific energies of the electrons.

The forces that hold atoms together to form molecules are chemical bonds;

the most common bonds are electrovalent or ionic, covalent, and hydrogen.

Compounds may be divided into two groups, organic and inorganic. Organic compounds always contain the element carbon; common organic compounds of life are carbohydrates, fats or lipids, proteins, and nucleic acids.

Chemical reactions occur when atoms or compounds interact to form other compounds, called products. These reactions always involve energy changes and rearrangement of bonds. The rate, duration, and direction of a chemical reaction is directly proportional to the concentration of the reactants; practically all biological reactions are accelerated by enzymes.

The proposed chemical events leading to the development of life are summarized as follows:

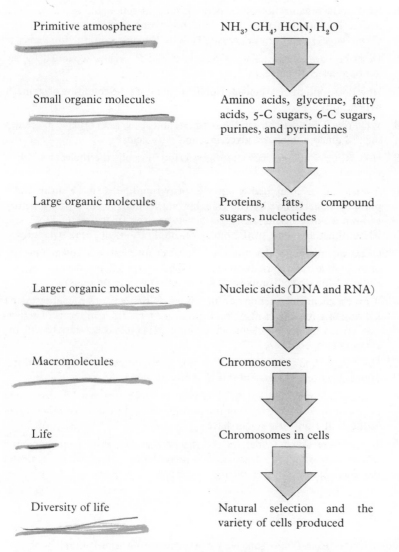

Primitive atmosphere	NH_3, CH_4, HCN, H_2O
Small organic molecules	Amino acids, glycerine, fatty acids, 5-C sugars, 6-C sugars, purines, and pyrimidines
Large organic molecules	Proteins, fats, compound sugars, nucleotides
Larger organic molecules	Nucleic acids (DNA and RNA)
Macromolecules	Chromosomes
Life	Chromosomes in cells
Diversity of life	Natural selection and the variety of cells produced

Life may be defined essentially as "cells containing nucleic acids." The characteristics of living organisms include: sensitivity, movement, metabolism,

55

reproduction, growth, and adaptation. The most plausible explanation for the direction of the development of life lies in the concept of natural selection.

REVIEW QUESTIONS

1 Why is this unit, which contains principles of matter and chemistry, necessary for a study of life?

2 Outline the development of the modern concept of atomic structure. How does atomic structure relate to bonding potential?

3 Name and illustrate the basic structures of five different organic compounds and explain how each might be utilized in living systems.

4 Why is hydrochloric acid a stronger acid than acetic acid?

5 Explain the organization of the periodic table as you would to a nonscience major. In your explanation include the terms *groups*, *periods*, *isotopes*, *atomic number*, and *atomic weight*. How is this chart useful to chemists?

6 Describe how electrovalent or ionic compounds can be separated by the use of an electric current.

7 How does sodium bicarbonate ($NaHCO_3$) alleviate the condition of stomach hyperacidity?

8 What role does water play in the synthesis and cleavage of organic molecules such as glucose, maltose, glycerine, and fatty acids?

9 How is it possible for cows to digest cellulose (split the molecules) while human beings cannot?

10 A nucleotide is composed of a purine or pyrimidine, a ribose sugar, and a phosphate ester. Show by a diagram how nucleotides can be strung together to form a nucleic acid. Distinguish between the structures of DNA and RNA. What are some of the biological implications of these structures?

11 Of the organic molecules discussed in this chapter, protein can assume the most complex and varied structures. What is the chemical basis for this ability? Why do you suppose all known enzymes are proteins?

12 Why do chemical reactions occur? What is the activation energy in the lighting of a match? How do biological reactions differ in terms of activation energy? Why do chemical reactions generally occur faster with increasing temperature?

13 How do we know that all living systems are tending toward disorder and disorganization? How could this be demonstrated?

14 Someday we may find life on other planets which may not be exactly like life on earth. What are some of the possible characteristics that other forms of life in the universe might have?

15 If you were asked to defend the theory that life arose from nonliving matter, how would you organize your presentation? Note any experimental evidence that would strengthen your case.

SUPPLEMENTARY READINGS

Alder, Irving, *How Life Began*, New York, New American Library, 1957.

Bernal, J. D., *The Origin of Life*, New York, World, 1967.

Bok, Bart J., "The Birth of Stars," *Scientific American*, August, 1972.

Borek, E., *The Atoms Within Us,* New York, Columbia University Press, 1961.

Calvin, M., and J. A. Bassham, *The Photosynthesis of Carbon Compounds,* New York, Benjamin, 1962.

Crick, F. H. C., "Nucleic Acids," *Scientific American,* September, 1957.

Eglinton, G., and M. Calvin, "Chemical Fossils," *Scientific American,* January, 1967.

Frieden, Earl, "The Chemical Elements of Life," *Scientific American,* July, 1972.

Haensel, Vladimir, and R. L. Burwell, Jr., "Catalysis," *Scientific American,* December, 1971.

Hodge, Paul W., *Concepts of the Universe,* New York, McGraw-Hill, 1969.

Hoyle, Fred, "The Steady-State Universe," *Scientific American,* September, 1956.

Kendall, Henry W., and W. Panofsky, "The Structure of the Proton and the Neutron," *Scientific American,* June, 1971.

Keosian, John, *The Origin of Life,* New York, Reinhold, 1964.

Kornberg, Arthur, "The Synthesis of DNA," *Scientific American,* October, 1968.

Lawless, J. G., C. E. Folsome, and K. A. Kvenvolden, "Organic Matter in Meteorites," *Scientific American,* June, 1972.

Locke, David, M., *Enzymes—The Agents of Life,* New York, Crown, 1969.

Merrifield, R. B., "The Automatic Synthesis of Proteins," *Scientific American,* March, 1968.

Miller, Stanley L., "The Origin of Life," in W. Johnson and W. Steere, eds., *This Is Life,* New York, Holt, Rinehart and Winston, 1962.

Mirsky, Alfred E., "The Discovery of DNA," *Scientific American,* June, 1968.

Moore, Ruth, *Niels Bohr: The Man, His Science, and the World They Changed,* New York, Knopf, 1966.

Murray, Bruce C., "Mars from Mariner 9," *Scientific American,* January, 1973.

Oparin, A. I., *Origin of Life,* New York, Dover, 1953.

Ovenden, Michael W., *Life in the Universe,* Garden City, N.Y., Doubleday (Anchor Books), 1962.

Patton, Stuart, "Milk," *Scientific American,* July, 1969.

Pryor, William A., "Free Radicals in Biological Systems," *Scientific American,* August, 1970.

Schrödinger, Erwin, *What Is Life?,* London, Cambridge University Press, 1944.

Schrödinger, Erwin, "What Is Matter?" *Scientific American,* September, 1953.

Shklovskii, I. S., and Carl Sagan, *Intelligent Life in the Universe,* San Francisco, Holden-Day, 1966.

Sinsheimer, R. L., "Single-Stranded DNA," *Scientific American,* July, 1962.

Stein, William H., and Stanford Moore, "The Chemical Structure of Proteins," *Scientific American,* February, 1961.

Sullivan, Walter, *We Are Not Alone,* New York, McGraw-Hill, 1964.

Wald, George, "The Origin of Life," *Scientific American,* August, 1954.

Young, R. S., and Cyril Ponnamperuma, *Early Evolution of Life,* BSCS Pamphlet No. 11, American Institute of Biological Sciences, Boston, Heath, 1964.

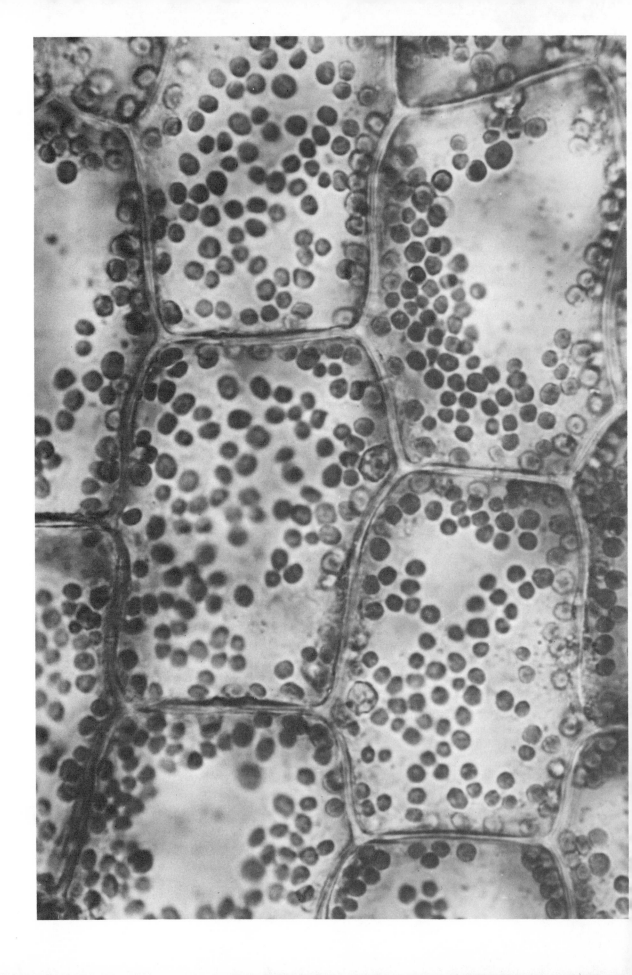

3

Biological Architecture: Cells

Cells have sometimes been compared with architectural bricks. The various sizes, shapes, and strengths of bricks permit the design of many different functional structures, and although the bricks differ, still they are easily recognized as bricks. This is also true of living cells. For decades now biologists have labored to understand life and its processes primarily by studying the structure and function of cells.

Consider the mushrooms in their multitude of sizes, shapes, and colors. What are they, where did they come from, and what are they made of? Perhaps you know the answer to most of these questions. A dictionary might say mushrooms are the fruiting bodies of certain fungi that arise from the soil each year to produce reproductive spores, but a microscopic examination reveals much more. All parts of the mushroom are composed of small cells, but these remarkably similar cells give rise to strikingly different structures such as a stalk, gill filaments, and a cap. Furthermore, different fungi produce structurally unique mushrooms.

The term *cell* was first used by Robert Hooke in 1665 to describe the small chambers he had observed in cork. Much later, in 1838, the German botanist M. J. Schleiden recognized the aggregation of cells in *tissues* of plants. This observation was extended to animals and developed more fully about a year later by Theodor Schwann, a German zoologist. The cell theory proposed by Schleiden and Schwann became a basic concept in biology and is one of the most significant generalizations ever made in the field. According to this theory all living organisms are composed of cells, and the cell may be considered to be the fundamental unit of all life.

THE CELL AND ITS PARTS

The discoveries of the various parts of the cell were made over a period of 300 years by many men. In 1835 Dujardin described the contents of cells from his studies on certain protozoa as a "perfectly homogeneous, elastic, contractile, diaphanous, gelatinous substance, insoluble in water and without traces of organization." In 1839 Purkinje and von Mohl adopted the term *protoplasm* for this substance so articulately described by Dujardin. But today, owing to our finer microscopes, we know more about the organization and structure of cells. Consequently the term protoplasm is used currently only as a generalized description of living materials. Cytoplasm is another general term used to describe the living material between the outer limits of the cell (the cell membrane) and the nucleus.

By 1900 the structures shown in Figure 3–1 had been observed and described. Robert Brown discovered the nucleus in 1831 while examining the cells of orchids. He described

it as an opaque spot and demonstrated its presence in most of the plant's cells. The original observation of the nucleus and a smaller body within it called the *nucleolus* had been made by Fontana in 1781. It was Brown, however, who proposed that they were characteristic structures of all cells. Flemming and Strasburger (1882) showed that the nuclear material produced long threads which split lengthwise and passed into the daughter cells during cell division. In 1888 Waldeyer named these threads *chromosomes* because they became much more visible when dyes were added to the cell, a technique called *staining*.

Altmann, in 1886, suggested that the long filaments he observed in the cytoplasm under a light microscope might have something to do with the energy production in cells. We call these filaments *mitochondria*. Biochemists have now proved that mitochondria produce most molecules for storing and delivering energy. In 1898 Camillo Golgi reported a network of material in nerve-cell cytoplasm which stained heavily with silver nitrate. The *Golgi apparatus* was hotly disputed by many biologists to be a product resulting from the staining techniques. After many years of controversy, the validity of Golgi's observations was confirmed, and today we know that these structures perform an important function in cellular secretion.

The cytoplasm of all animal and some protist cells contains two small structures that function in cell division. Boveri in 1888 referred to these as "central bodies," but they are now known as *centrioles*. The role of the centrioles in cell division will be discussed later in this chapter.

As improved lenses became available, it was found that the limiting factor in light microscopy was the wavelength of light itself. The most important aspect of microscopy is the capability to clearly separate the images of two structures. This characteristic is termed *resolution*. The greatest practical resolution with a light microscope is about 0.25 micron. (A micron is 1/1000 of a mm.)

In 1940 a revolutionary type of microscope

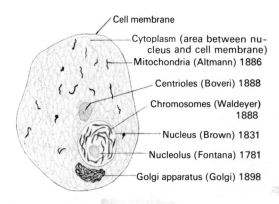

Cell membrane

Cytoplasm (area between nucleus and cell membrane)

Mitochondria (Altmann) 1886

Centrioles (Boveri) 1888

Chromosomes (Waldeyer) 1888

Nucleus (Brown) 1831

Nucleolus (Fontana) 1781

Golgi apparatus (Golgi) 1898

Figure 3–1 Summary of cell structure before the introduction of the electron microscope.

60

was produced. It utilized a beam of high-speed electrons of extremely short wavelength and electromagnetic "lenses" to focus the electrons onto a photographic plate. Today, through perfected electron microscopes, resolution is routinely possible to less than 10 angstrom units (1 Å = 1/10,000 micron), and magnification may approach 300,000 times (Figure 3–2). With the advantages of this greater resolution, many cellular components have been discovered in recent years. Moreover, a more thorough investigation of the structure of all parts of cells is now possible.

In electron micrographs (Figures 3–3 and 3–4), several new structures such as the endo-

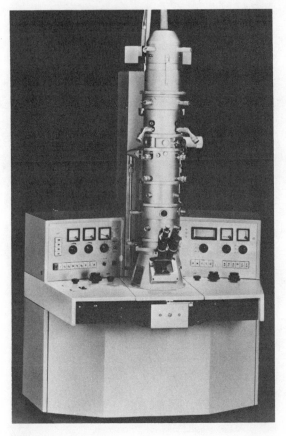

Figure 3–2 Modern electron microscope. This Elmiskop 101, with a point resolution of 3.5 Angstrom units and a magnification range of ×285 to 280,000, provides excellent high-resolution microscopy. (Courtesy of Siemens America, Inc.)

plasmic reticulum, ribosomes, and lysosomes can be seen in addition to the previously known components. Since it is generally believed that structure and function are closely related, the ability to observe subcellular components in almost molecular detail has enabled scientists to formulate theories about the function of each part in the cell. We shall now turn to a detailed discussion of the structure and function of these subcellular components.

THE CELL MEMBRANE

One structure common to all living cells is the cell membrane (often called plasma membrane), the molecular boundary between the cell and its immediate environment. This living membrane not only provides a physical containment for the cell but also produces a large surface area on which many chemical reactions occur. The Danielli model of these cell membranes (Figure 3–5) represents a theoretical molecular arrangement of proteins and lipids that agrees with biochemical and electron-microscope observations. Essentially, the structure is a sandwich of proteins and lipids with two protein layers enclosing a double layer of lipids. One end of the lipid molecules found in the membrane is water soluble and associates with the protein layer (Figure 3–5).

If the cell is so securely bounded by a structural membrane, one might ask how water and nutrients get inside. All living cells require that water and minerals be able to enter through the membrane. Membrane permeability therefore is of extreme interest.

THE MOVEMENT OF MATERIALS INTO CELLS

It is highly probable that cell membranes contain pores that allow the passage of water and certain ions into and out of the cell. It is also probable that these pores are protein lined (Figure 3–5). Since the free amino and carboxyl groups of the amino acids of the protein can take either a negative or positive charge and since like charges repel, it would be possible for specific charged ions to be attracted

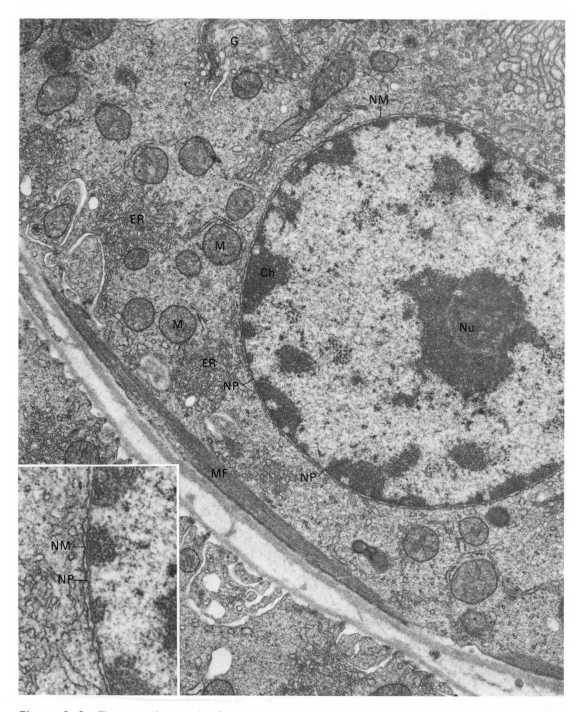

Figure 3–3 Electron micrograph of a rat-kidney tubule cell (× 22,800): nucleolus (Nu), nuclear membrane (NM), chromosome (Ch), mitochondria (M), endoplasmic reticulum (ER), nuclear pore (NP), microfilaments (MF), Golgi apparatus (G). The inset is an enlargement of the nuclear membrane showing nuclear pores (× 50,000). (Courtesy of James D. Newstead.)

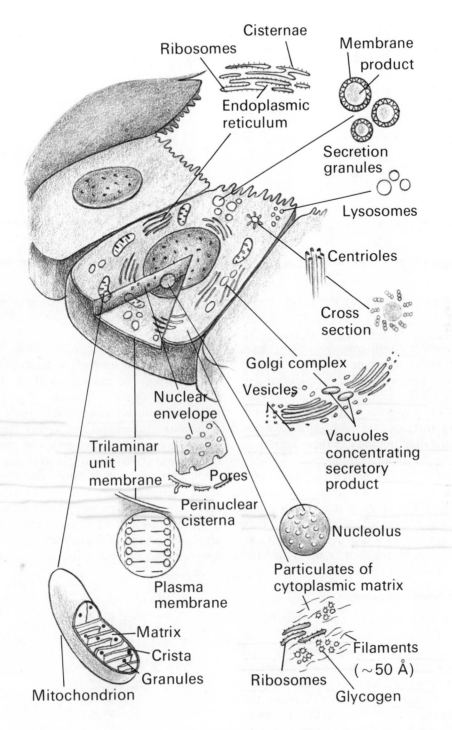

Figure 3–4 Three-dimensional diagram of a generalized animal cell based on electron micrographs. The structures of the organelles and inclusions are emphasized. (Redrawn from Fig. 2–1, p. 24, in *Cell Biology* by Robert M. Dowben, Harper & Row, 1971.)

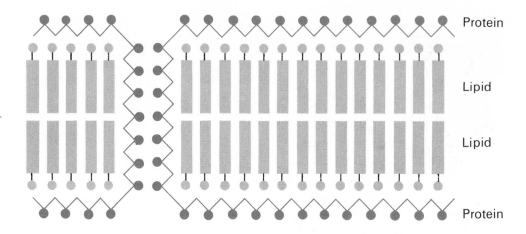

Figure 3–5 Molecular structure of a membrane; sometimes called the Danielli model.

or rejected according to the immediate physiological state of the cell. This hypothesis also helps to explain the high degree of selectivity shown by these semipermeable membranes for certain ions even when others may exist in greater concentrations. A semipermeable membrane allows certain materials to pass through, but excludes others. Most membranes, for instance, are permeable to water in either direction but vary in their degrees of permeability for other substances.

A second possibility is that the ability of a substance to penetrate a cell depends largely on its solubility in lipids. For instance, many large molecules having high fat solubility pass relatively easily into a cell. Apparently these molecules penetrate the membrane on the basis of their solubility in lipids.

Phagocytosis and Pinocytosis

Like the amoeba, most cells can actively ingest nutrients. The engulfment of solid materials is known as *phagocytosis*—a process employed by human white blood cells to rid the body of bacteria and waste. Another process is *pinocytosis* or "cell drinking." In either case the cell membrane encircles the particle or droplet and forms a small membranous pouch. Once inside the cell the droplet is pinched off to become a pinocytotic vesicle or, as it is commonly known, a *vacuole* (Figure 3–6).

However, all vacuoles observed in cells are not produced in this manner.

Diffusion and Osmosis

From a chemical standpoint, fluids containing particles may be classed in three systems: simple suspension or mixture, *colloidal suspension*, and true solution. Larger particles that settle out of a mixture in a very short time illustrate a simple suspension. The suspension of fine sand grains in water is an example. Very small particles such as table salt or sugar remain suspended in water almost indefinitely and form a true solution. One must consider, however, that 100 ml of cold water holds only about 36 grams of NaCl; after this amount has been added, the solution becomes satu-

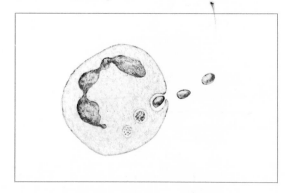

Figure 3–6 Phagocytosis: white blood cell engulfing bacteria.

rated and salt crystals form on the bottom of the container. A colloidal suspension is formed when relatively large particles remain suspended in a medium over long periods. In colloidal suspensions the fluid part of the system (which is commonly water) is termed the *dispersion phase*, and the suspended particles are collectively termed the *dispersed phase*. In a solution, the terms that correspond to these phases are *solvent* and *solute*, respectively. The most important factor determining dispersions is simply the size of the suspended particles. Droplets of water suspended in air to form clouds are a common example. Homogenized milk in which the fat droplets are extremely small is also a type of colloidal suspension.

One method used to distinguish between a colloidal suspension and a true solution is simply passing a strong beam of light through the liquid. In a true solution the light passes invisibly through the liquid; in a colloidal suspension, however, the particles are large enough to scatter the light and form a cloudy cone known as a *Tyndall beam*. This is similar to the beam produced by automobile headlamps in fog (Figure 3–7).

Colloidal suspensions may exist in two forms—the watery, fluid state or sol, and the more solid state known as a gel (Figure 3–8). In some cells temporary reversible changes occur frequently and naturally. Sometimes the change in state from sol to gel is irreversible, as with the boiling of egg white. When this occurs in a protein suspension, the permanent change is known as *denaturation*.

In 1827 Robert Brown noted that tiny particles suspended in water collide with one another and move in random zigzag patterns. Although Brown thought that the plant spores he had observed under the microscope were capable of independent movement, it was soon demonstrated by other scientists that a similar movement occurred with nonliving particles in liquid or gas. This phenomenon, known as *Brownian motion*, has been observed in all states of matter—solid, liquid, and gas. The theory that all matter is in constant motion is known as the *kinetic theory*. Heat is the measurable result of this bombardment among atoms and molecules.

Traditionally the study of the interchange of substances between the cell and its environment was approached as some aspect of diffusion or osmosis. It must be noted, however, that these processes are not specifically cellular mechanisms and do not explain how materials get into and out of cells. Diffusion is often defined as the movement of particles through a medium from a greater concentration toward a lesser concentration. For example, if a bottle of ammonia is opened in a classroom, the first

Figure 3–7 The beam of light in the bottle on the left is bright because of scattering in the colloidal particles of egg white. The bottle on the right is a sodium chloride solution in which the beam is barely visible. This is known as the Tyndall effect.

Sol state   Gel state

Figure 3–8 Dispersed and dispersion phases of a colloid in sol and gel states. Protein molecules are represented by irregular blocks, and water by shading.

students to detect the odoriferous molecules are those seated nearest the demonstration. Within a short time, however, the molecules distribute themselves so that even those in the back row can detect the smell of ammonia in the air.

It is possible for particles in a water medium to diffuse through a membrane if they are small enough to pass through the membrane pores. The particles on the left side of the membrane represented in Figure 3–9 are in constant motion and move through the membrane pores from a greater to a lesser concentration until an equilibrium is reached—that is, after equilibrium is reached particles will continue to move in equal numbers back and forth across the membrane.

The term *osmosis* is used to denote the passage of water across a semipermeable membrane from a region of greater concentration of water to a region of lesser concentration of water. The side of the membrane that has the greatest number of dissolved particles bordering it is the side that has proportionally less water. Thus the passage of water may be controlled by the concentration of particles dissolved on either side of the membrane.

Figure 3–10 illustrates three conditions that affect the osmotic process. In this demonstra-

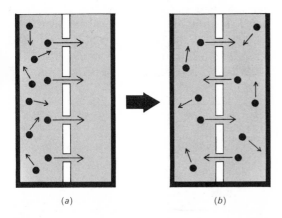

(a)   *(b)*

Figure 3–9 Diffusion of particles through a membrane. In (*a*), particles move from a greater to a lesser concentration, until an equal number of particles is present on each side of the membrane as shown in (*b*). The short arrows indicate random movement.

tion, cellulose sausage skins were used for the semipermeable membrane, since cellulose contains many small holes that permit water to pass through the membrane but block the passage of large particles such as sucrose. Three such bags were prepared and filled with the following solutions: (1) 1 M NaCl, (2) distilled water, and (3) 1 M sucrose. Each bag then was tied tightly to a 1/10 ml pipette that extended into the bag. The pipettes were secured to a holder and the bags were immersed in three beakers of distilled water. Within a few minutes it was noted that the solution in pipette number 1 (NaCl) was rising rapidly. After about 25 minutes, however, the sucrose solution in pipette number 3 equaled that of number 1 and gradually surpassed number 1 until it spilled over the top of the pipette.

Since NaCl ionizes in solution, nearly twice as many particles were present in the NaCl bag as were in the sucrose bag. For this reason water moved into the NaCl bag faster than into the sucrose bag. In this simple experiment, however, particles of dissociated Na^+Cl^- eventually will pass through the holes and the solutions will attain equilibrium —that is, an equal number of particles will be found on each side. Because the sucrose molecules are too large to move through the bag, equilibrium cannot be reached. In the bag containing distilled water, equilibrium was present from the beginning with an equal number of water molecules moving into and out of the bag. The distilled water bag thus represents a "control" in this experiment.

Active Transport

It has been found that the movement of materials into certain cells does not always follow the principles of diffusion or osmosis. The absorptive cells of the small intestine, for example, are capable of taking in large amounts of glucose liberated by the digestive process. Even though the bloodstream may contain many more glucose molecules than are found inside the intestine, glucose is still moved into the bloodstream. Since this violates the principle of diffusion, we refer to it as an absorption

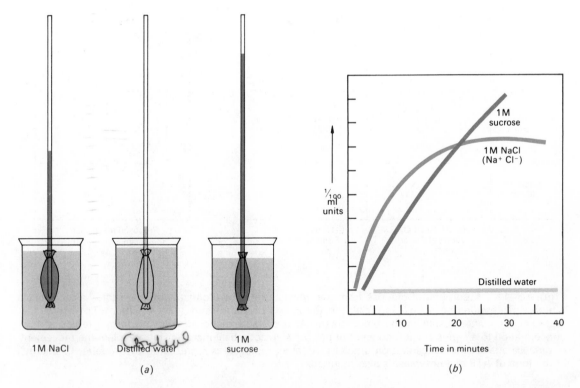

Figure 3–10 Demonstration of osmosis across semipermeable membrane using sausage-skin bags. (*a*) The bag at the left contains 1M NaCl; the center bag, distilled water; the right bag, 1M sucrose. (*b*) Graph of the results.

against a concentration gradient, concentration gradient being that tendency for molecules to move from higher to lower concentration. This very necessary and important process is called *active transport* and requires the expenditure of energy by the cell. For some substances it is the only means of entering a cell. At this time the exact details of the process are not understood, but experiments have shown that a carrier molecule and energy (ATP) are probably involved. Figure 3–11 illustrates the movement of glucose across the intestinal cells into the bloodstream against a high concentration gradient. Figure 3–11c presents a hypothetical mechanism to account for this movement which involves the expenditure of energy and the use of a carrier. The carrier molecule is released when the glucose is "delivered" to the bloodstream. A detailed discussion of ATP will be presented in Chapter 6. At this point it is only necessary to note that

ATP (a complex organic molecule) stores and delivers the energy utilized by living organisms. In all cases of active transport that have been studied, the addition of a poison, to stop the production of ATP, inhibits the transport mechanism.

Large molecules like glucose are not the only materials that may be taken into cells against a concentration gradient. Ions such as sodium (Na^+), potassium (K^+), calcium (Ca^{++}), chloride (Cl^-), and sulfate ($SO_4^=$) are also transported by many cells. The cells that form the tubules of the kidneys actively reclaim ions and glucose from the forming urine. The freshwater alga *Nitella* concentrates large amounts of certain ions in its sap. A comparison of the ionic concentration in the sap and in pond water is shown in Figure 3–12. Note particularly that the concentration of chloride ion (Cl^-) in the cell sap is a hundred times greater than in pond water.

67

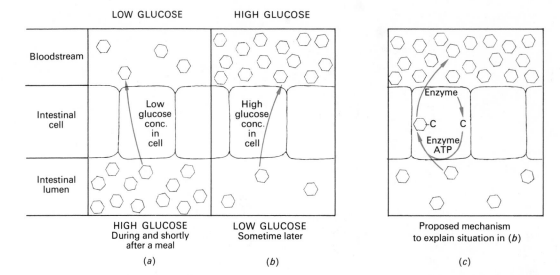

LOW GLUCOSE   HIGH GLUCOSE

Bloodstream

Intestinal cell

Intestinal lumen

Low glucose conc. in cell

High glucose conc. in cell

Enzyme

C   C

Enzyme ATP

HIGH GLUCOSE
During and shortly
after a meal

(a)

LOW GLUCOSE
Sometime later

(b)

Proposed mechanism
to explain situation in (b)

(c)

Figure 3–11 Absorption of glucose from the intestine into the bloodstream. (a) Shortly after a meal, a high concentration of glucose is present in the lumen of the intestine. (b) As glucose is absorbed, a higher concentration results in the bloodstream. At this stage, glucose is moving from a region of low concentration to a region of high concentration. (c) A hypothetical mechanism to explain the movement of glucose against the concentration gradient. A carrier molecule is represented by the letter C. Energy, in the form of ATP and enzymes, is also required.

STRUCTURE OF THE CYTOPLASM

The term *protoplasm,* once used to define living substance, is obviously inadequate in the light of modern biochemical and electron micrographic studies. The fluid portion of the cell between the nuclear envelope and the cell membrane is known as the *cytoplasmic matrix* and contains many different dissolved and colloidal substances. Of special interest among these inclusions are the fibrillar proteins. Since DeRobertis and Franchi reported the occurrence of long, unbranched microtubules in the cytoplasm of nerve cells in 1953, microtubules and smaller, nontubular microfilaments have been observed in many cell types. It is now known that these tubules and filaments have contractile properties and play important roles in cell division, cytoplasmic streaming, amoeboid movement, and muscle contraction. Apparently the movement of pseudopods in amoebae is due to the contraction of and association between microfilaments. During the process of movement these filaments are con-

stantly forming, breaking up, and reforming (Figure 3–13).

It has been suggested that the small membranous structures, known as organelles, lo-

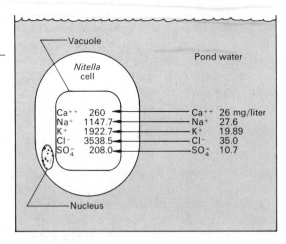

Figure 3–12 Comparison of the ionic concentration in the vacuolar sap of *Nitella* and the pond water in which it lives. The higher concentration of ions in the cell sap is a result of active transport. The data are expressed in milligrams per liter.

68

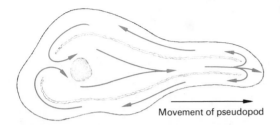

Movement of pseudopod

Figure 3–13 Fountain-streaming of amoeboid movement. At the tip of the advancing pseudopod, the sol turns to gel. The streaming movement is caused by the contraction of protein microfilaments.

cated in the cytoplasm may have derived from the cell membrane through an evolutionary process of infolding and adaptation to specific functions. This suggestion is supported by evidence that mitochondria and the nuclear membrane are essentially double membrane structures. If the cell membrane is considered to be a single-unit membrane (Figure 3–5), these organelles should then be thought of as double-unit membrane structures.

ENDOPLASMIC RETICULUM AND RIBOSOMES

Early electron micrographs clearly showed that an extensive system of tubules and membranous plates extend throughout the supposedly homogeneous area called cytoplasm. These structures, known as the *endoplasmic reticulum* (ER), generally have small particles called *ribosomes* attached to their surfaces. If the ER has no ribosomes, it is called *smooth ER*. Ribosomes were discovered by George Palade of the Rockefeller Institute, who also found that they contain protein and RNA. Ribosomes, as we shall see later, are the sites of protein synthesis.

GOLGI APPARATUS

The basketlike system of silver-stained fibers observed by Camillo Golgi is actually a series of membranous, laminar tubules very closely related to the endoplasmic reticulum. There are, however, no ribosome particles on their surfaces. The function of the Golgi apparatus appears to be the storage and release of cellular

secretions. Cells that are very active in producing secretions always contain large amounts of Golgi structure (Figure 3–14). The larger lamellae appear to break up into smaller vesicles that eventually reach the cell membrane to be expelled as secretion droplets. Cells of the pancreas, which secrete digestive enzymes, are an excellent example of this process. Since enzymes are composed of protein, studies using radioactive-labeled amino acids such as leucine have enabled scientists to trace the formation, storage, and release of cellular secretions.

MITOCHONDRIA

When Richard Altmann observed tiny thread-like bodies in the cytoplasm of stained cells, he named them "bioblasts," thinking that they might be the elementary living particles. The name *mitochondrion*, suggested by Benda in 1897, corresponds to the two principal shapes he had observed (*mito*, meaning "thread" and *chondrion*, meaning "granule").

Through biochemical studies and electron

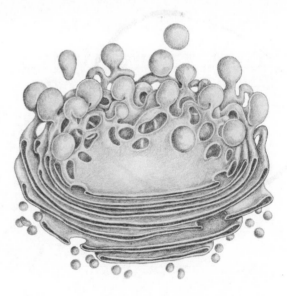

Figure 3–14 Three-dimensional drawing of a Golgi apparatus showing the formation of secretory vesicles. (Redrawn, courtesy of Dr. C. P. Leblond.)

microscopy, we know today that the mitochondrion is an essential organelle and is not caused by chemical treatment, a bacterium, or a parasite within the cell. It is the principal site of energy production in every cell and often has been called the "powerhouse of the cell." A look at an electron micrograph (Figure 3–3) shows that the mitochondrion is made up of two membranes: an outer membrane and a greatly folded inner membrane. The folds of the inner membrane are called *cristae*, and the increased surface area provided by the cristae folds is believed to permit the attachment of extensive enzyme systems.

Energy-rich compounds are produced within the mitochondrion through two enzyme-catalyzed processes. The enzymes for the first series of reactions (the Krebs cycle, Chapter 6) are located in the mitochondrial fluid between the cristae; the enzymes for the second series are attached to the crista membrane itself (Figure 3–15).

Even when the mitochondria are removed from cells by centrifugation, the energy-producing reactions still operate. Indeed, if the mitochondria are broken up into small fragments, certain fragments are still capable of producing energy, if incubated in the proper medium. The cristae, therefore, must contain many functional areas along their surfaces. A detailed study of these enzyme reactions will be presented in Chapter 6.

Recently it was discovered that mitochondria contain a small amount of DNA and ribosomal RNA and therefore have the system necessary for the production of specific proteins. Mitochondrial DNA occurs as naked fibers—that is, the DNA is not associated with protein as it is in a nucleus. Although the information necessary for the synthesis of most of the mitochondrial enzymes is probably contained in nuclear DNA, the nucleic acid system of mitochondria is apparently responsible for the synthesis of some proteins necessary for the structure and function of mitochondrial membranes. It has long been known that mitochondria are capable of dividing but the discovery of DNA has also raised the question of their origin. One hypothesis suggests their possible origin from once free-living organisms similar to modern bacteria. These entered other cells and subsequently became part of the host cell's machinery in a *symbiotic* relationship.

CENTRIOLES

The area that includes the centrioles was described and named the *centrosome* by Walther Flemming in 1875. Through the light microscope the centrioles appear as two dark granules embedded in a heterogeneous matrix, but electron micrographs show their structure in much greater detail. They are cylindrical and contain numerous microtubules arranged in a very precise pattern. Nine sets of three tubules are spaced around the periphery of the cylinder. It has been observed that the basal part of *flagella* and *cilia*, which are organelles specialized for locomotion, have a similar structure. This similarity in structure suggests that centrioles may have given rise to both flagella and cilia. Figure 3–16*a* shows the centriole microtubule arrangement in a longitudinal and cross section. In cilia and flagella

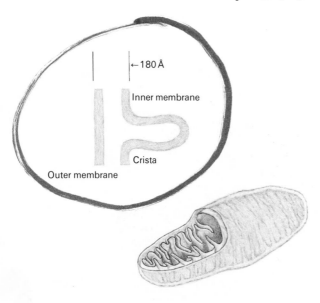

Figure 3–15 Cutaway view of a mitochondrion showing the relationship between the inner cristae membrane and the outer membrane. An enlargement of these membranes is shown upper left.

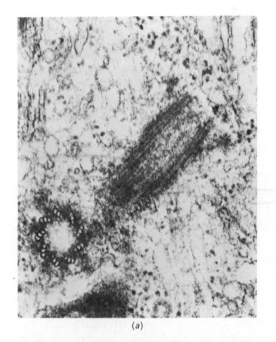

(a)

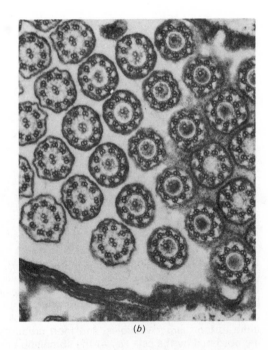

(b)

Figure 3–16 Electron micrographs of centrioles from rat kidney. (a) Longitudinal and cross section (× 73,000). Note the nine sets of microtubules in the cross section. (b) Cross section of cilia from the ciliate *Trichodina* (× 35,000). (Courtesy of James D. Newstead.)

two additional tubules appear in the center, known as the 9 + 2 tubular arrangement (Figure 3–16b). The centriole pattern is described as 9 + 0.

During cell division, centrioles split away from the centrosome area and move to positions on opposite sides of the nucleus. By this time many protein fibers have radiated from each centriole to form an aster, and other fibers have connected centrioles to the chromosomes. It is believed that these contractile microtubules or spindle fibers (as they are commonly known) play a major role in the separation of the chromosomes and the formation of daughter cells.

The centrioles are capable of reproduction, and a duplication occurs before cell division. It is interesting, however, that the centrioles do not occur in many algae and seldom in higher plants. In these species the spindle fibers form just before the separation of the chromosomes. Since spindle fibers may form in the absence of centrioles, the relationship between the two is still uncertain.

LYSOSOMES

Contained in a single membrane, the lysosome (splitting body) appears in electron micrographs as a nearly homogeneous vacuole. The name *lysosome* describes the great hydrolytic power of the enzymes contained within its structure. Among the enzymes present are those that digest protein, polysaccharides, nucleic acids, and those that permit the release of energy from ATP. These enzymes could be very destructive to the cell if released into the cytoplasm; for this reason they have sometimes been called "suicide bags." We do not yet know how the enzymes are retained within the membrane. It has been successfully demonstrated that the lysosomes have an important function in the digestion of materials taken into individual cells through the cell membrane (Figure 3–17). It is also likely that the lysosomes normally digest dead structures within the cell, thus ridding the cell of waste and nonfunctional organelles. One interesting example of how lysosomes function is the absorption of

71

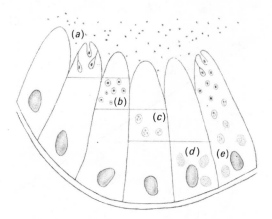

Figure 3–17 Functional stages of lysosome digestion found in the digestive gland cells of snails. (*a*) Small granules of food are taken into the cell by pinocytosis at the free end. (*b*) Enzyme action occurs within the vacuoles. (*c*) Small vacuoles unite to form larger vacuoles, and food products are absorbed by the cell. (*d*) At the completion of enzyme digestion, large vacuoles are formed near the base of the cell and are finally excreted from the cell. (*e*) The entire process is shown as it occurs in one cell.

the tadpole tail in frog development. In this case entire cells are digested by the lysosomes in a controlled manner until the tail disappears. The products of this digestion will be translocated to other areas and used to fabricate new tissue in the developing frog.

PLASTIDS

In plant and algae cells there are three types of cytoplasmic bodies known generally as *plastids*. These three types of plastids are *leucoplasts*, which contain no pigments but are generally the site of starch formation and storage; *chromoplasts*, which contain pigments other than chlorophyll; and *chloroplasts*, which are complex laminar structures and contain chlorophyll. Chloroplasts are highly specialized for photosynthesis and will be described in detail in Chapter 6.

Up to this point we have discussed only the membranes and membranous organelles of the cytoplasm. The nucleus, with its inclusions, is also extremely important to the functions of the cell. Of course, not all cells contain a well-defined nucleus with surrounding membranes, but even such cells as bacteria and blue-green algae do have DNA that functions similar to the organized nucleus of more complex organisms.

Many experiments have shown that the nucleus is necessary for the continuation of life activities in a cell. With a very fine glass needle mounted on a microscope, it is possible to remove the nucleus from an amoeba. The resulting enucleate cell is incapable of reproduction or digestion and can make only sluggish movements. An enucleate amoeba usually will die within three weeks. If a new nucleus from the same species is transplanted back into the cell within a few days, however, normal functions will return.

One interesting aspect of this enucleate amoeba is its inability to digest foods. Digestion is accomplished by enzymes, which are specific proteins, and when these important proteins are lacking, digestion cannot take place. This supports the theory that the nucleus contains the information necessary for the cell to synthesize specific proteins.

The nuclear membrane actually contains many small pores (Figure 3–3) which are passageways for the exchange of materials between the nuclear and cytoplasmic regions. These pores are roughly 400 Å in diameter and appear to be evenly distributed over the membrane.

CHROMOSOMES

The nucleus contains a fluid (nucleoplasm) similar to the watery, nonmembranous cytoplasm. Long, threadlike chromosomes composed of DNA and protein are suspended in this nuclear sap. When observed under a light microscope, the chromosomes appear to be a network of fibers; the original term "chromatin network" was based on this observation. This term is still used occasionally, but we know today that the DNA-protein threads are simple uncoiled chromosomes of quite definite individual structure.

The chromosomes contain the genetic information necessary for the development and maintenance of each cell in the organism. Chapter 11 will deal specifically with the genetic mechanism of inheritance. At this point it is important to know only that the DNA in the chromosomes contains coded information that assures the proper organization and continuation of life processes.

NUCLEOLUS

In addition to the chromosomes, the nucleus of most cells contains one or more smaller bodies called nucleoli. Each nucleolus is produced by a specific chromosome after cell division and contains a large amount of RNA. The function of the nucleolus was not understood for over a hundred years after its discovery. We know today, however, that the nucleolus is directly involved in the conversion of precursor ribosomal RNA into ribosomal subunits which are transported to the cytoplasm where they function in the synthesis of specific proteins.

DNA AND THE CODE

DNA is a molecule composed of repeating pairs of nucleotides. It is believed that nitrogen base pairs are arranged in some meaningful code that can be transcribed by the cell at the time of protein synthesis. It is further hypothesized that a linear sequence of nucleotides provides protein synthesis information. The question then is how many nucleotides are involved in each "unit" of information. Since

proteins are made up of different combinations of about 20 different amino acids, a workable code must be capable of "recognizing" each of these amino acids. If the code were "one nucleotide—one amino acid," only four amino acids could be coded, because there are only four different DNA nucleotides. If a sequence of two nucleotides were used, 16 amino acids could be recognized ($4^2 = 16$). Sequences of three nucleotides could handle the operation ($4^3 = 64$) with some to spare. If the code were analogous to a language of letters and words, it would not be unreasonable to have some *triplet nucleotides* for use as synonyms and punctuation. The unit of genetic information, known as a *codon*, is composed of three nucleotides and specifies one particular amino acid. This is referred to as *triplet coding*, and has been verified in the laboratory using the nucleic acids of bacteria. Since the pioneering work of Ochoa and Nirenberg in the early 1960s, we know most of the triplet codons for the 20 amino acids (Figure 3–18). A specific amino acid may be coded for by more than one codon combination.

Amino Acid	RNA Codon	Amino Acid	RNA Codon
Phenylalanine	UUU	Aspartic Acid	GAU GAC
Threonine	ACU ACC ACA AGA	Alanine	GCU GCC GCA GCG
Serine	UCU UCC UCA UCG	Methionine	AUG GUG
Leucine	CUU CUC CUA CUG	Glycine	GGU GGC GGA GGG
Tryptophan	UAU UAC		

Figure 3–18 Messenger RNA triplet codons for some selected amino acids.

The synthesis of proteins, one of the more exciting areas of cell research, illustrates one of the important relationships between the nucleus and the cytoplasm. Protein synthesis involves the chromosomes (DNA) and three types of RNA: messenger (mRNA), ribosomal (rRNA), and transfer (tRNA). Essentially, the process involves the transfering of a DNA code sequence to mRNA and the interaction of mRNA with ribosomes and tRNA to produce a polypeptide chain of amino acids. The ribosomes appear to move along the mRNA as the polypeptide is synthesized. Finally, the end of the mRNA is reached and the newly formed polypeptide is released to become a functional protein (Figure 3–19).

The production of a specific protein begins with chromosomal DNA which contains the "master blueprint" or code discussed in the previous section. Messenger RNA is synthesized along a segment of chromosomal DNA, and its nucleotides are ordered into the specific base sequence which is complementary to that portion of the DNA molecule (transcription) (Figure 3–20). Thus the coded message contained in the nitrogen base sequence of DNA is transcribed to mRNA as a complementary sequence of nucleotides. The coded mRNA now leaves the nucleus through a nuclear pore and combines with one or more ribosomes in the cytoplasm (Figure 3–21). Ribosomes occur as two parts of unequal size, and each part is composed of RNA and protein. The largest particle is known as the 50s and the smaller one

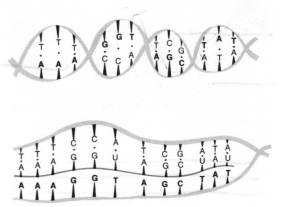

Figure 3–20 DNA passing code to mRNA. A segment of DNA opens between the hydrogen-bonded nitrogen bases, and mRNA is synthesized along one strand according to complementary nitrogen bases. Note that the base uracil is found in RNA, whereas thymine is present in DNA.

as 30s, where the *s* designations refer to their respective rates of separation in an ultracentrifuge. Ribosomal RNA is synthesized in the nucleus and may be stored in the nucleolus for some time before its incorporation into ribosomes (Figure 3–22). In order to function, the two parts come together to clamp the coded mRNA molecule between them. When several ribosomes attach to mRNA the resulting complex is a *polyribosome* (Figure 3–23).

At this point another form of RNA, transfer RNA, becomes involved. Although tRNA is synthesized by the chromosomes in the nucleus, recent evidence shows that this molecule has a very different structure than mRNA. The tRNA takes the form of a folded chain containing several areas of paired bases as well as at

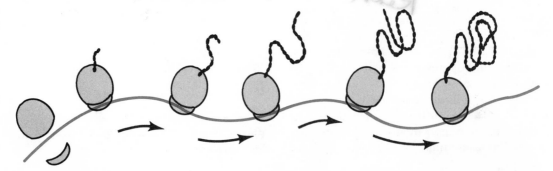

Figure 3–19 Simplified scheme of protein synthesis. The polypeptide chain (protein) is formed as the ribosome moves along the mRNA molecule (colored), which is attached to the ribosome. Each dark unit of the chain represents an amino acid.

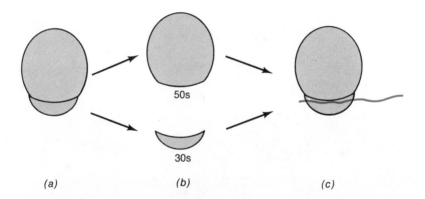

Figure 3–21 The three phases of ribosomes. (*a*) Nonfunctional. (*b*) Separate 50s and 30s particles. (*c*) Functional, when attached to messenger RNA (colored).

least three areas of unpaired bases. Most of the models of the structure of tRNA are based on the "cloverleaf" design proposed by R. W. Holley in 1965. The chains of approximately 80 nucleotides are folded into a series of three major loops with one open end (Figure 3–24*a*). In addition, a helical spiraling of the entire molecule has also been reported. An amino acid is attached by an ester linkage to one strand at the open end which terminates in the unpaired bases C—C—A. Specific enzymes and ATP are required to attach the amino acids to the tRNA molecules. Opposite to this amino acid end is the *anticodon* loop which contains three unpaired bases which complement a specific mRNA triplet codon. There are one or more tRNA molecules for each of the 20 amino acids and each type of tRNA must possess the particular amino acid specified by the anticodon so that a specific amino acid can be brought into sequential order along the mRNA (Figure 3–25). In this manner the tRNA molecules are able to "read" the message contained in the mRNA and construct a protein dictated by the code which came originally from the DNA molecule.

The 30s portion of the ribosome appears to have specific attachment sites for messenger RNA. The 50s subunit is thought to contain two functional areas, one for an incoming tRNA and its specific amino acid and another for the synthesis of peptide bonds. The entire ribosome appears to move along the messenger RNA as tRNAs bring in their amino acids and

peptide bonds are formed. After donating an amino acid to the growing polypeptide chain, the tRNAs are released to the cytoplasm where they may pick up another amino acid. When the end of the mRNA molecule is reached, the completed polypeptide chain is released and the ribosome splits into its original subunits. Hydrogen and disulfide bonds form to complete the secondary and tertiary protein structure. Finally, messenger RNA dissociates into unreadable fragments and returns to the cytoplasmic pool of nucleotides. The following summary of the step-by-step process of protein synthesis is correlated with the numbered segments in Figure 3–26.

1   Double-stranded DNA having hydrogen-bonded nitrogen base pairs contains the information for the synthesis of a specific protein.

2   Strands of DNA separate in a specific area and messenger RNA (mRNA) is synthesized along one strand of DNA according to complementary base pairing. Note that uracil is present in RNA but not in DNA.

3   Messenger RNA containing triplet nucleotide code sequences (codons) enters the cell cytoplasm where one or more ribosomes attach to the mRNA molecule.

4   Transfer RNA molecules (tRNA) are synthesized by DNA in the nucleus, leave the nucleus and pick up a specific amino acid in the cytoplasm; ATP is required to form this linkage.

5   The anticodon loop of the tRNA molecule contains three unpaired bases which "rec-

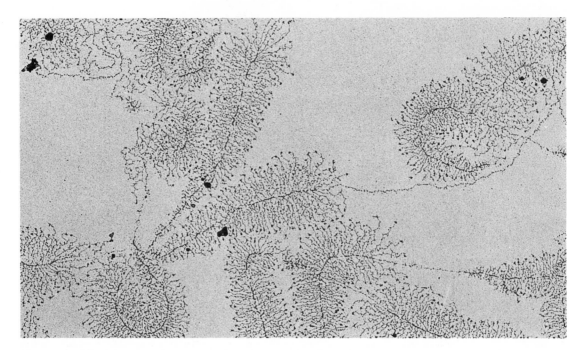

Figure 3–22 Electron micrograph of nucleolar DNA from a salamander egg synthesizing precursor molecules of ribosomal RNA (× 25,000). The long axial filaments are composed of DNA, and the lateral fibrils are RNA molecules coated with protein. This is apparently the first photograph of DNA-directed synthesis of RNA and protein. (Courtesy of O. L. Miller, Jr., and Barbara R. Beatty, Biology Division, Oak Ridge National Laboratory.)

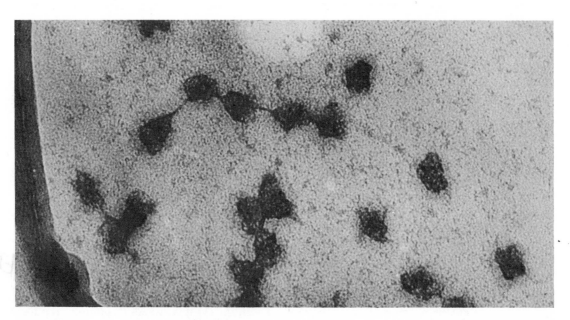

Figure 3–23 Electron micrograph of polyribosomes (the dark bodies), each consisting of several ribosomes (× 400,000). The connecting strand between the polyribosomes is probably messenger RNA. (Courtesy of Alexander Rich, Massachusetts Institute of Technology.)

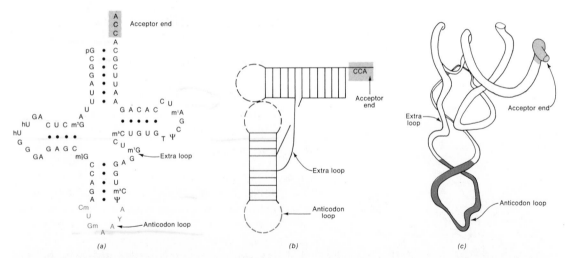

Figure 3–24 Three representations of tRNA structure. (*a*) Cloverleaf model of yeast phenylalanine tRNA. (*b*) Diagrammatic modification of cloverleaf twisted into L shape. (*c*) Perspective diagram showing the helical loops of the L-shaped model. The unfamiliar symbols represent nitrogen bases of slightly different structure. (Redrawn from "Three-Dimensional Structure of Yeast Phenylalanine Transfer RNA: Folding of the Polynucleotide Chain" by Sung-Hou Kim *et al.*, *Science*, Vol. 179, pp. 285–288, January, 1973. Copyright © 1973 by the American Association for the Advancement of Science.)

ognize" the mRNA codon and the appropriate amino acid is brought into the mRNA–ribosome complex.

6 The ribosome now moves to the next codon, and the next specified amino acid is brought into position by another tRNA; a peptide linkage is formed between the first and second amino acids; the first tRNA is released and may pick up a new amino acid from the cytoplasm.

7 The ribosome continues its movement along the mRNA molecule until all the necessary amino acids for the protein being synthesized are brought into position and peptide linkages are formed between the amino-acid molecules.

8 When the ribosome reaches the end of the mRNA, it separates into its 50s and 30s components. The mRNA breaks up, and the specifically ordered polypeptide is released and assumes its secondary and tertiary structure.

TYPES OF CELLS—
PROCARYOTIC AND EUCARYOTIC

In the foregoing description of cell structure and function we were concerned with a general understanding of living cells. Actually there is no such thing as a typical cell. Generalizations

have been made, however, by many biologists in order to classify all cells as either plant or animal. Perhaps the most fundamental separation that can be made among living cells is on the basis of the *procaryotic* or *eucaryotic* condition. (Eucaryotic derives from the Greek *eu*, meaning true, and *karyon*, meaning nucleus. *Eucaryotic* therefore refers to cells having true nuclei, and *procaryotic* indicates a more primitive condition.) Many differences exist between procaryotic and eucaryotic cells. Essentially the discussion so far in this chapter has been on eucaryotic cells; procaryotic cells will be described in the next section under Moneran cells. It should be noted however that procaryotic and eucaryotic cells do share some similarities. Both have cell membranes; both utilize DNA and RNA as informational molecules; and apparently both have a similar genetic code. As you will see, the issue of categorizing cell types can be clarified somewhat by the consideration of four main types of cells and, consequently, four main groups of organisms.

MONERAN CELLS

Bacteria and blue-green algae are procaryotic organisms which differ markedly from all other

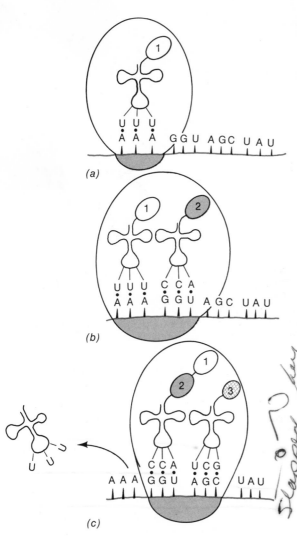

(a)

(b)

(c)

Figure 3–25 Translation of mRNA by tRNA in the ribosome. (*a*) The 50s and 30s particles clamp onto one end of mRNA, and a tRNA anticodon pairs with the first codon of mRNA. (*b*) The ribosome complex shifts to the next codon, and a second tRNA comes into position. (*c*) A peptide linkage forms between the first two amino acids, and the ribosome shifts to the next codon as a third amino acid is brought in. The first tRNA is now released to the cytoplasm, where it can combine with another amino acid.

organisms. For one, their genetic material is composed only of nucleic acid, whereas the genetic material of eucaryotic cells is contained in chromosomes that are composed of nucleic acids and protein. Further, procaryotic organisms have no nuclear membranes, and photosynthetic procaryotes never contain chlorophyll *a* or chloroplasts. Mitochondria, Golgi

apparatus, lysosomes, and centrioles are also lacking in these cells. The flagella of procaryotes are not related to the 9 + 2 microtubule pattern of cilia and flagella of nucleated cells.

The procaryotes are often classified in the kingdom *Monera*, whereas all eucaryotic organisms are placed in three kingdoms—*Protista*, *Metaphyta* (plants), and *Metazoa* (animals).

PROTISTAN CELLS

Many eucaryotic organisms exist in nature as single cells (*Euglena*, Appendix). Some organisms are simply aggregations of similar cells —that is, a cellular colony (*Volvox*, Appendix) —and many organisms are constructed of a body of rather similar cells (fungi; and brown, red, and green algae, Appendix). The cells in all these examples often have a mixture of the characteristics we generally associate with either plant or animal cells. In other words, a large group of living forms cannot be called true plants or animals. For convenience, and for a clearer understanding of evolution, these organisms can be classified as Protista (from the Greek *protistos*, meaning "first").

A good example of a protist is the green unicellular *Euglena*. It moves with a whiplike flagellum and sometimes ingests food like an animal cell. But, since *Euglena* contains chlorophyll, it has the ability to synthesize food like a typical green plant cell. Most authorities agree that the flagellate protistans are living examples of some of the earliest forms of life. It is thought that the ancestors of cells which possess both animal and plant characteristics probably gave rise to plant and animal groups.

PLANT AND ANIMAL CELLS

On higher levels of development organisms are commonly classified either as plant or animal. Plant cells generally have cell walls, large central vacuoles, and contain chlorophyll but lack centrioles. Animals, on the other hand, have cells that contain centrioles, lack cell walls and chlorophyll, but are capable of locomotion. It can be assumed that animal cells have lost chlorophyll and thus the ability to make their own food. Plant cells, on the other hand, have lost centrioles and, generally, the ability to move. A summary of the characteristics of the cells of organisms is presented

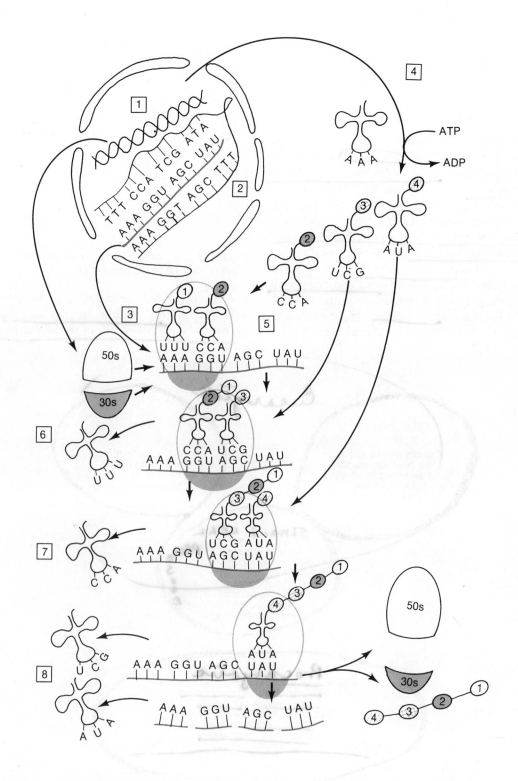

Figure 3–26 Summary of protein synthesis. The numbers within squares correspond to the numbered steps of the summary in the text. The structure of bases in anticodons can vary (Figure 3–24). For simplicity, U, A, C, G are used here.

in Figure 3–27. This method of grouping organisms into four kingdoms is also used in the classification section in the Appendix.

The Plant Cell

The plant cell commonly has an outer wall that is hardened and nonliving. Unlike the cell membrane, plant walls have no selective permeability. Any substance that can pass through the cell wall approaches the cell membrane which lies just inside the wall. Since the cell wall is nonliving, most substances pass through it. It is composed of two layers, an outer primary wall, which is the first to be formed, and an inner secondary wall (Figure 3–28). The major structural component of these walls is cellulose (1,4 beta-linked glucose units, Chapter 2). An additional layer

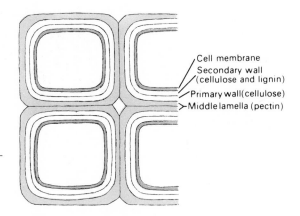

Cell membrane
Secondary wall (cellulose and lignin)
Primary wall(cellulose)
Middle lamella (pectin)

Figure 3–28 Microscopic structure of the cell walls of four adjacent plant cells.

may be produced when two cells lie closely adjacent. A thin middle lamella is formed between the primary walls of the two cells and

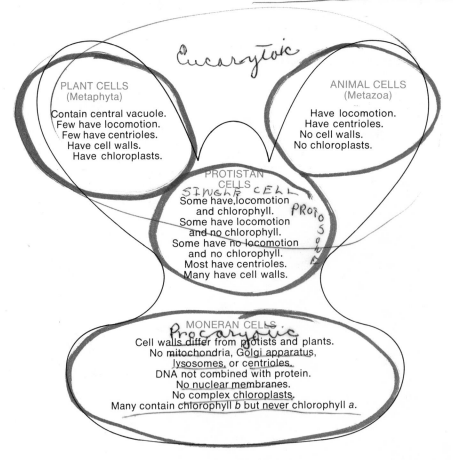

Eucaryotic

PLANT CELLS
(Metaphyta)

Contain central vacuole.
Few have locomotion.
Few have centrioles.
Have cell walls.
Have chloroplasts.

ANIMAL CELLS
(Metazoa)

Have locomotion.
Have centrioles.
No cell walls.
No chloroplasts.

PROTISTAN CELLS

SINGLE CELL
Some have locomotion and chlorophyll.
Some have locomotion and no chlorophyll.
Some have no locomotion and no chlorophyll.
Most have centrioles.
Many have cell walls.

PROTOS.....

MONERAN CELLS
Procaryotic
Cell walls differ from protists and plants.
No mitochondria, Golgi apparatus, lysosomes, or centrioles.
DNA not combined with protein.
No nuclear membranes.
No complex chloroplasts.
Many contain chlorophyll *b* but never chlorophyll *a*.

Figure 3–27 Summary of the characteristics of the cells of the four kingdoms of organisms and their possible evolutionary relationships.

80

contains a colloidal substance called pectin (polymers of the six-carbon sugar galactose). Powdered pectin is the familiar substance added to fruits to make jellies. In older tissues the soft pectin may become hardened by the accumulation of calcium to form calcium pectate. Evidently the middle lamella is important in holding cells together. In woody plants a tough, gluelike substance called lignin is impregnated in the cellulose walls. Lignin helps to bind the wood-fiber cells together to form a solid material.

A central vacuole is very common in plant cells and is functional in the cell's water balance. Since the nonliving cell wall produces a rigid framework for the cell's contents, the cell is unable to swell to accommodate changes in osmotic conditions. The central vacuole therefore is important in regulating the osmotic pressure balance by losing or gaining water. The vacuole contains a slightly viscous colloid which may include salts, mineral ions, proteins, sugars, and pigments. The typical

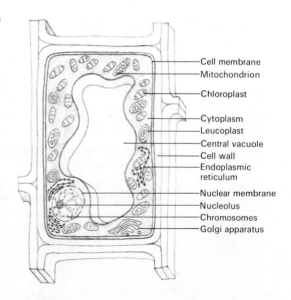

Cell membrane
Mitochondrion
Chloroplast
Cytoplasm
Leucoplast
Central vacuole
Cell wall
Endoplasmic reticulum
Nuclear membrane
Nucleolus
Chromosomes
Golgi apparatus

Figure 3–29 Leaf cell of *Elodea*, a common aquarium plant, showing the major structural components.

structure of a plant cell is shown in Figure 3–29.

SUMMARIZING STATEMENTS

All organisms are composed of individual units called cells. A cell is divided into two regions—the cytoplasm and the nucleus. Cytoplasmic cell parts include: cell membrane, centrioles, golgi apparatus, mitochondria, endoplasmic reticulum, lysosomes, and ribosomes. The nucleus includes the nuclear membrane, chromosomes, and nucleoli.

The movement of materials into cells may occur in the following ways: phagocytosis, pinocytosis, diffusion, osmosis, and active transport.

The nucleus is the functional control center for all cell activities. The DNA of the chromosomes provides the information necessary for the production of specific proteins, some of which function as enzymes. The actual synthesis of proteins occurs in the cytoplasm on the ribosomes. The transcription of the DNA code into specific proteins involves mRNA and tRNA.

Two fundamental cell types occur—procaryotic and eucaryotic. Further, cells (and consequently organisms) can be categorized into four groups: Monera (procaryotes), Protista, Metaphyta (plants), and Metazoa (animals). All groups have cells containing DNA and RNA, cell membranes, and the same genetic code. Moneran cells lack a nuclear membrane, chlorophyll *a*, chloroplasts, mitochondria, Golgi apparatus, lysosomes, and centrioles; the nucleic acids are not organized into chromosomes with protein.

Plant and animal cells can be compared in the following ways. Plant cells have cell walls, large central vacuoles, generally contain chlorophyll, and lack centrioles. Animal cells contain centrioles and lack cell walls and chlorophyll. Many protistan cells show combinations and variations of these characteristics.

81

REVIEW QUESTIONS

1 Compare and contrast our knowledge of a cell (*a*) as viewed under a light microscope, and (*b*) as seen under an electron microscope.

2 How has the electron microscope assisted biologists in determining the construction and function of cells? What advantages does the electron microscope offer over the light microscope? What advantages does the light microscope provide?

3 The cells of the pancreas contain large numbers of Golgi apparatus. What might you conclude about the function of these cells?

4 Describe the structural features of the cell membrane or the process which might account for each of the following:
   (*a*) glucose molecules pass into intestinal cells
   (*b*) alcohol molecules pass quickly into cells lining the stomach
   (*c*) positively or negatively charged particles may be selectively taken into certain cells
   (*d*) white blood cells engulf and destroy bacteria

5 When sea urchin eggs are placed in distilled water they swell and burst. Explain why.

6 Centrioles, cilia, and flagella show a similar structural organization. What evolutionary or developmental relationships does this suggest?

7 Why don't the large molecules and organelles within a living cell settle out in response to gravity?

8 When the nucleus is removed from a cell it survives only a short time. Discounting its inability to reproduce, why does the cell die?

9 Sketch an original diagram which shows the relationship between DNA and RNA in the synthesis of specific proteins. Include the roles of mRNA, tRNA, and rRNA and indicate their location in the cell.

10 Construct the messenger RNA codon sequence for a polypeptide composed of alanine, phenylalanine, serine, glycine, and leucine.

11 In humans wide variations occur in the types and amounts of blood plasma proteins among individuals. From your knowledge of the total process of protein synthesis explain why this is so.

12 Bacteria cells are procaryotic, and muscle cells are eucaryotic. Describe some differences you would expect to find between these two types of cells.

13 Summarize the structural differences found in cells of organisms from the four kingdoms: Monera, Protista, Metaphyta, and Metazoa.

14 Even though differences exist among cells in the four kingdoms, there are also similarities. What are these common features?

SUPPLEMENTARY READINGS

Allison, Anthony, "Lysosomes and Disease," *Scientific American*, November, 1967.

Brachet, Jean, "The Living Cell," *Scientific American*, September, 1961.

Child, Graham, *The New Biology*, New York, Basic Books, 1972.

Clowes, Royston, *The Structure of Life*, Baltimore, Penguin, 1967.

Crewe, Albert V., "A High-Resolution Scanning Electron Microscope," *Scientific American*, April, 1971.

Crick, F. H. C., "The Genetic Code," *Scientific American*, October, 1962.

Crick, F. H. C., "The Genetic Code: III," *Scientific American*, October, 1966.

Dippell, Ruth V., "Ultrastructure and Function," in W. H. Johnson and W. C. Steere, eds., *This Is Life*, New York, Holt, Rinehart and Winston, 1962.

Everhart, T. E., and Thomas L. Hayes, "The Scanning Electron Microscope," *Scientific American*, January, 1972.

Fox, C. F., "The Structure of Cell Membranes," *Scientific American*, February, 1972.

Goodenough, U. W., and R. P. Levine, "The Genetic Activity of Mitochondria and Chloroplasts," *Scientific American*, November, 1970.

Gorini, Luigi, "Antibiotics and the Genetic Code," *Scientific American*, April, 1966.

Grimstone, A. V., *The Electron Microscope in Biology*, New York, St. Martin's Press, 1968.

Hayflick, Leonard, "Human Cells and Aging," *Scientific American*, March, 1968.

Hokin, Lowell E., and Mabel R. Hokin, "The Chemistry of Cell Membranes," *Scientific American*, October, 1965.

Hurwitz, Jerard, and J. J. Furth, "Messenger RNA," *Scientific American*, February, 1962.

Mercer, E. A., *Cells, Their Structure and Function*, New York, Natural History Press, 1962.

Miller, O. L., Jr., "The Visualization of Genes in Action," *Scientific American*, March, 1973.

Mosbach, Klaus, "Enzymes Bound to Artificial Matrixes," *Scientific American*, March, 1971.

Neutra, Marian, and C. P. Leblond, "The Golgi Apparatus," *Scientific American*, February, 1969.

Nomura, Masayasu, "Ribosomes," *Scientific American*, October, 1969.

Paul, John, *Cell Biology*, Stanford, Calif., Stanford University Press, 1966.

Rich, Alexander, "Polyribosomes," *Scientific American*, December, 1963.

Satir, Peter, "Cilia," *Scientific American*, February, 1961.

Sharon, Nathan, "The Bacterial Cell Wall," *Scientific American*, May, 1969.

Siekevitz, Philip, "Powerhouse of the Cell," *Scientific American*, July, 1957.

Solomon, Arthur K., "Pores in the Cell Membrane," *Scientific American*, December, 1960.

Stent, Gunther S., "Cellular Communication," *Scientific American*, September, 1972.

Swanson, C. P., *The Cell*, 2nd ed., Englewood Cliffs, N.J., Prentice-Hall, 1964.

Temin, Howard M., "RNA-Directed DNA Synthesis," *Scientific American*, January, 1972.

Wessells, Norman K., "How Living Cells Change Shape," *Scientific American*, October, 1971.

83

4

Biological Architecture: Tissues, Organs, and Organisms

In the preceding chapter an analogy was drawn between cells and bricks as building blocks. Like individual bricks, cells are ultimately organized into functional structures such as walls. Groups of similar cells working together to perform specific functions are called *tissues*. Since there are several different types of tissues, it is necessary to discuss the major types in order to understand their function. With tissues, as with cells, scientists frequently distinguish between plant and animal. Even though each group has developed tissues to serve common functions, the differences are sufficient to warrant separate discussion. Some of the common functions of tissues include (1) protection, (2) support, (3) circulation, (4) growth, and (5) reproduction.

PLANT TISSUES

Plant tissues are identified and named primarily according to their location and function. The four basic types of plant tissues are meristematic (growth), vascular (conduction), fundamental (storage and support), and epidermal (protection).

Before discussing specific examples of plant tissues, we should consider briefly their general

85

organization and evolutionary pattern. The classification system used today is an attempt to demonstrate the probable evolutionary relationships among organisms (see Appendix). In plants these evolutionary relationships are most evident in the cellular structure and reproductive cycles.

Although mosses do not possess roots, stems, or leaves homologous to the higher plants, they do have simple tissue organizations that perform functions similar to those of the higher plants. For example, small hair-like *rhizoids* serve to anchor the plant and absorb water, and the "stem" provides the rigidity necessary for erect growth. The leafy outgrowths contain chloroplasts for making food and the areas at the tips of stems form sex organs. The complexity in tissue organization increases from the mosses through the ferns to the conifers and flowering plants. Since the distribution of the basic tissues varies greatly throughout the plant kingdom, we will limit our observations to the more familiar seed plants that possess true roots, stems, and leaves—the *gymnosperms* (conifers) and the *angiosperms* (flowering plants).

Angiosperms may be divided into the orders Dicotyledonae and Monocotyledonae. Dicots are characterized by having (1) two "seed leaves" or *cotyledons* upon germination, (2) net-veined leaves, (3) flower parts in fours or fives, and (4) fibrovascular tissue arranged in concentric rings. Dicots may be herbaceous (they generally lack lignin) like the pansy or they may be woody like the apple tree. Monocots, on the other hand, possess (1) a single cotyledon, (2) parallel-veined leaves, (3) flower parts in threes, and (4) scattered fibrovascular bundles. Typical examples are the lily and corn plants.

MERISTEMATIC TISSUE

These tissues provide for growth in plants. All tissues of seed plants differentiate from a rapidly dividing group of cells known as the *apical meristem*. The subsequent development and growth of a maturing plant is due primarily

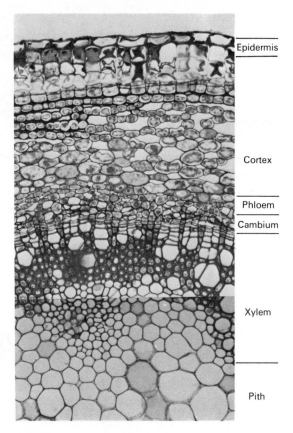

Figure 4-1 Location of tissues in a mature stem of elderberry, a woody angiosperm. (Courtesy of Eliott Weier.)

to these apical meristems, stem and root tip, and the lateral cambiums, vascular and cork. The vascular cambium is one of several tissue types found in a gymnosperm or a woody dicot stem (Figure 4-1). The cellular regions of a growing root tip and an apical meristem are illustrated in Figure 4-2.

The cambium layer, which is present as a complete ring of tissue in gymnosperms and woody dicots, gives rise to the vascular tissues. This complete cambium sheath is sometimes absent in herbaceous dicots and is always absent in monocots.

VASCULAR TISSUE

The vascular tissues of plants are *xylem* and *phloem*. The structure of the monocot stem,

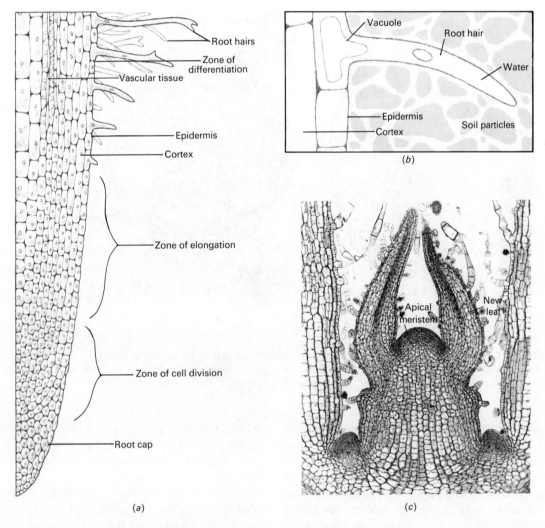

Figure 4-2 Cellular regions of a growing root and an apical meristem. (*a*) Longitudinal section of a growing root. Note the proliferation of cells that forms the root cap. (*b*) Root hair in soil. (*c*) Growing stem tip of *Coleus* showing meristematic tissue. (Courtesy of Triarch, Inc., Ripon, Wisconsin.)

such as corn, is perhaps the most graphic example of the location of the xylem and phloem. The vascular bundles, which are groups of xylem and phloem, are scattered throughout the supportive tissue of the stem. The arrangement of the vascular bundles resembles a monkey face. The brow is composed of thin-walled phloem cells (sieve tubes) and companion cells, and the eyes and nose are vessel tubes of xylem. What appears as the mouth is a ruptured xylem vessel, resulting

from stem growth that forms an air space (Figure 4-3).

In woody plants the cambium produces at its inner surface, xylem cells, which conduct water and minerals, and toward the outside, the cambium produces phloem, the food-transporting tissue (Figure 4-1). Each year following spring and summer growth, the old phloem layer dies and is pushed outward by new spring phloem where it remains as bark. The xylem layers are left on the inside

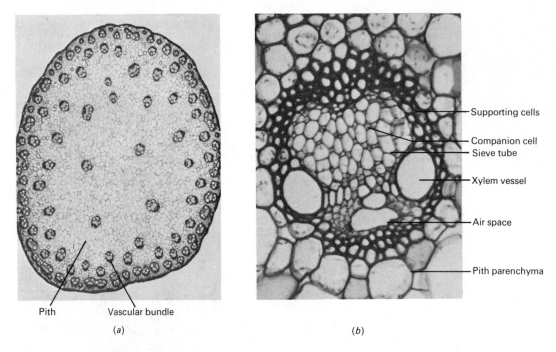

Pith   Vascular bundle

Supporting cells

Companion cell
Sieve tube

Xylem vessel

Air space

Pith parenchyma

(a)   (b)

Figure 4–3 (a) Cross section of a corn stem showing scattered vascular bundles (× 20). Note that the "monkey faces" all look toward the center of the stem; therefore, the phloem is external to the xylem. (b) A single vascular bundle similar to those in (a) (× 350). (Courtesy of Eliott Weier.)

as wood. Thus the rings of xylem present in a stem indicate the age of the plant. It must be noted, however, that a year's growth of xylem shows two bands—an inner band of large vessels known as spring wood and an adjacent outer band of smaller vessels of summer wood. The greater availability of water in the spring allows faster growth and the formation of larger cells than during the summer.

Xylem

Water and minerals are conducted upward through the xylem from the roots. The leaves thus receive raw materials to use in photosynthesis. Sugar-laden sap moves primarily downward in the phloem to the actively absorbing and growing roots. In early spring, sap also may rise in the plant to nourish developing buds and flowers.

Xylem tissues in general are composed of two types of conducting tubes: tracheids and vessels. Gymnosperms possess only tracheids, whereas angiosperms contain both tracheids and vessels. The tracheids are elongate cells and somewhat narrowed at the ends. At maturity, in some cells, the nucleus and the cell contents die leaving a large lumen. Thin spots, called pits, along the cell walls allow water and minerals to pass from cell to cell. Thickenings of lignified cellulose along the secondary cell walls form annular reticulated or spiral rings (Figure 4–4).

Although vessel cells found in flowering plants also contain pits, small openings or pores occur at the ends to form a continuous open tube. Vessels have a larger diameter than tracheids, thus allowing easier passage of fluids. Not all the cells in the xylem are dead. Living xylem parenchyma cells are located in rays throughout the wood and function in food storage and lateral conduction.

Phloem

Living phloem tissue is easily observed as the slick, glistening layer just beneath the bark of

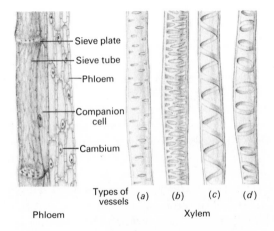

Sieve plate
Sieve tube
Phloem
Companion cell
Cambium

Types of vessels (a) (b) (c) (d)

Phloem   Xylem

Figure 4–4 Conducting structures of angiosperms. *Left:* longitudinal section of phloem and cambium. *Right:* longitudinal section of xylem vessels. (*a*) Pitted. (*b*) Reticulated. (*c*) Spiral. (*d*) Annular.

a tree. The cells of these food-transporting tissues are unique in that they possess end walls that are perforated with many small pores (Figure 4–4). These end walls are called *sieve plates*. Phloem cells are stacked end to end like xylem cells. Unlike xylem cells, however, phloem cells contain slimy strands of protoplasm that appear to stretch from cell to cell through the pores of the sieve plates. It is believed that a phloem cell which has no nucleus at maturity is controlled by adjacent, nucleated companion cells through cytoplasmic connections.

FUNDAMENTAL TISSUE

The regions of the plant stem that are utilized specifically for support and storage are the *pith* and *cortex*. Although xylem is obviously an important supporting tissue in wood plants, its primary function is that of conduction. The three tissues that are collectively termed *fundamental* include *parenchyma, collenchyma,* and *sclerenchyma*.

Parenchyma

This is a thin-walled, living tissue found in unspecialized regions of all parts of a plant. Parenchyma cells vary in shape, generally contain a central vacuole, and retain their capacity for cell division. These cells function in various ways such as food making, storage, and support.

Collenchyma

Collenchyma is a living tissue that has tough cell walls and often contains chloroplasts in the cytoplasm. The pectin compounds in the cell walls give this tissue strength and elasticity. The cortex cylinder of growing stems and roots often contains this special support tissue.

Sclerenchyma

Sclerenchyma is much less flexible than collenchyma. The secondary cell walls in these tissues become very hard at maturity, and the cells always die at maturity and lose their cytoplasm. Both collenchyma and sclerenchyma may occur in long bundles or sheaths in the cortex and pith. The hard shells of nuts and the gritty texture of pears are due to sclerenchyma cells.

EPIDERMAL TISSUE

The protective outer covering of plant structures is termed *epidermis* (outer skin). The cells of this tissue are generally one layer and organized into a thin sheath. The shape of epidermal cells is generally polyhedral—having more than four sides.

The epidermis of plants, especially leaves, shows several functional adaptations. The upper and lower epidermis of a leaf usually has a secreted cuticle of a waxy substance known as *cutin* which helps the leaf retain water. Many stems and leaves possess tiny hairs which also reduce evaporation. Perhaps the most unique epidermal structures are the tiny openings principally on the underside of leaves that regulate the exchange of water and gases. These openings, called *stomata*, are actively controlled by the swelling or shrinking of two adjacent *guard cells* (Figure 4–5). The action of guard cells appears to be controlled by osmotic pressure. When osmotic pressure is high and more water moves into guard cells, the stomata open. The loss of water to ad-

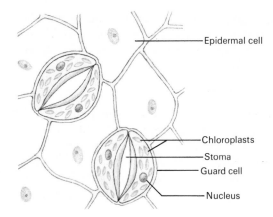

Figure 4–5　Stomata in the epidermis of a leaf.

jacent epidermal cells causes the guard cells to become limp and the openings to close. In general, the production of sugar by guard-cell chloroplasts during daylight causes increased osmotic pressure and swelling. At night osmotic pressure decreases due to the utilization of sugar for energy and its conversion to larger starch molecules. Recall that osmotic conditions are determined by the number of dissolved particles. In mature woody stems, the original epidermis has been destroyed by the developing bark, which is continuously being pushed outward and eroded.

We have seen that plants possess tissues which are related to their particular needs: epidermal for protection, meristematic for growth, fundamental for support, and vascular for conduction. Not all plants contain all these tissues and certainly not in the same ratio. For example, the most simple land plants, such as mosses and liverworts, do not contain vascular tissues at all.

ANIMAL TISSUES

The ability of animals to move and to communicate with the environment is based on several unique tissues. As in the case of plants these tissues can be organized in a functional manner. The basic animal tissues include epithelial (protection), connective (support), muscle (locomotion), nerve (communication), and blood (circulation).

EPITHELIAL TISSUE

These tissues cover the structures of the body or line cavities. At this point we should add that the cells of epithelial tissues may also function in secretion or absorption. Certain glands such as intestinal glands, which lie beneath the inner intestinal lining, empty secretions into the gut through special ducts. Nutrients provided through the action of digestive enzymes are actively absorbed into the circulatory system through the intestinal lining. The primary function of the epithelial tissues, however, is protection. The shapes of epithelial cells may be *squamous, cuboidal,* or *columnar* (Figure 4–6).

Squamous Cells

Squamous or "pavement" epithelium is composed of extremely thin cells. In most cases, the cells are so thin that the nucleus bulges out when viewed from the edge. This type of tissue lines the inside of the mouth, the body cavity, and also covers the body as skin epidermis. In the skin, these cells are stacked in thick layers called stratified squamous epithelium (Figure 4–7).

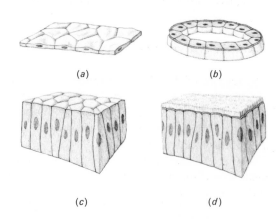

(a)　　　　　　　　　(b)

(c)　　　　　　　　　(d)

Figure 4–6　Examples of epithelial types. (*a*) Squamous. (*b*) Cuboidal. (*c*) Columnar. (*d*) Ciliated columnar.

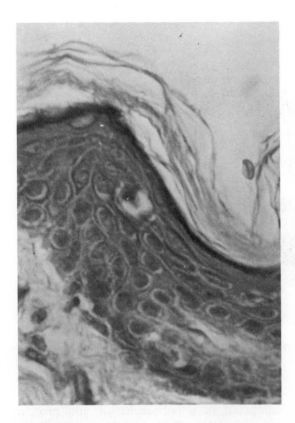

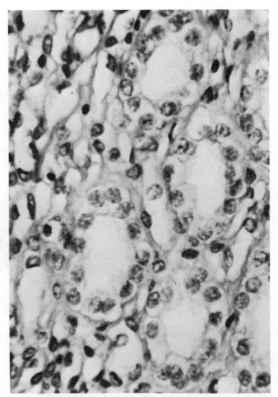

Figure 4–7 Stratified squamous epithelium of the human hand (×500). Note the sloughing of dead cells.

Figure 4–8 Cuboidal epithelium of the collecting tubules of the mammalian kidney (×450).

Cuboidal Cells

Cuboidal epithelium cells, as the name indicates, are cube-shaped and make up the tissues found as the lining of special ducts. Particularly important are the urine-collecting tubules in the kidneys (Figure 4–8).

Columnar Cells

Columnar cells are taller than cuboidal and form the lining tissue of many organs. The most common example is the lining of the small intestine (Figure 4–9). Both columnar and cuboidal cells can possess tiny hairlike structures called *cilia* (Figure 4–6). Cilia have the ability to move in a whiplike, rhythmical motion. Ducts that require a continuous clearing of foreign particles, such as the nasal passages or trachea, contain many ciliated

cells. Recent research suggests that the movement of a cilium is due to contractile proteins in the cilium itself. It is not yet clear just how the contraction is initiated or how the regular rhythm is coordinated.

CONNECTIVE TISSUE

The tissues responsible for support in animal bodies fall into several categories: loose or areolar connective tissue, tendon, cartilage, bone, and fat-storing or adipose tissue. The connective tissues contain tough white fibers of a protein called *collagen* and sometimes yellow elastic fibers also made of protein. Depending on the location and function of these tissues, the arrangement may be loose as in the mesenteries which support internal

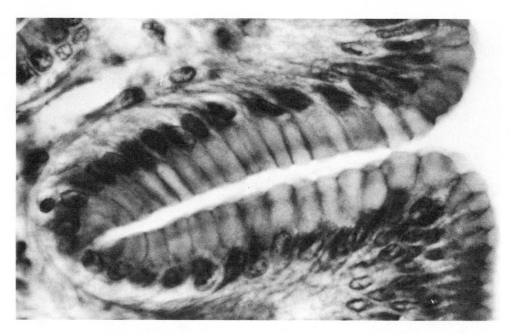

Figure 4–9 Columnar epithelium lining the small intestine of the cat (× 450).

organs (Figure 4–10) or more compact as in the underlying layers of the skin. Loose connective tissue allows for movement and pliability in an organ. This is especially important in the digestive tract, since food must be moved through the tube by rhythmic muscular contractions (peristalsis). Dense connective tissues such as tendon, cartilage, and bone are found where structural strength is required.

Loose or Areolar Tissue

This type of tissue forms the *mesentery* membranes that hold the organs of the body cavities in place, and through its elastic properties it also helps hold the skin to the muscles. Undifferentiated cells called *fibroblasts* are the most common in this tissue, and next in number are large phagocytic cells known as *macrophages*. The fibroblasts synthesize collagenous and elastic fibers and the macrophages ingest foreign substances. Figure 4–10 is a photograph of cat mesentery.

Cartilage

The function of cartilage is to give firm support without rigidity. Basically, the various types of cartilage are similar in cellular detail. The

living cartilage cells, or *chondrocytes,* secrete a matrix material around themselves that is composed of a polysaccharide and protein material. All cartilage contains protein fibrils

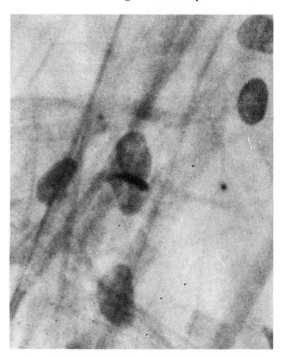

Figure 4–10 Loose areolar connective tissue from the mesentery of a cat (× 1000).

92

to a greater or lesser degree and thus is classified as a fibrous connective tissue. The hyaline cartilage in the end of the nose, lining the joints between bones and forming tracheal rings, is tough but flexible, whereas the outer ear cartilage, elastic cartilage, contains springy elastic fibers. Figure 4–11 is a photograph of hyaline cartilage from a tracheal ring. A very strong cartilage, fibrocartilage, contains a dense network of protein fibers and is found between the vertebrae as intervertebral discs.

Adipose Tissue

Adipose tissue is composed of special cells that store fat. The nuclei of the mature cells are always pushed up against one side of the cell membrane by the accumulation of fats in the cytoplasm (Figure 4–12). Adipose tissues function in support (packing), protection (overlying organs), and food storage.

Bone

We are all familiar with bone and its function of structural support. A thin section of bone shows a complicated pattern of cells and

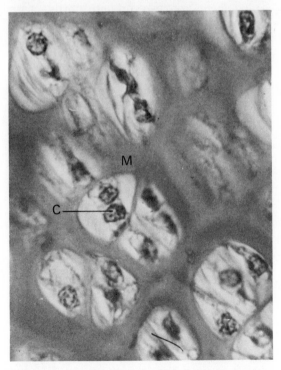

Figure 4–11 Hyaline cartilage from the trachea of a cat (× 1000): matrix (M), chondrocyte (C).

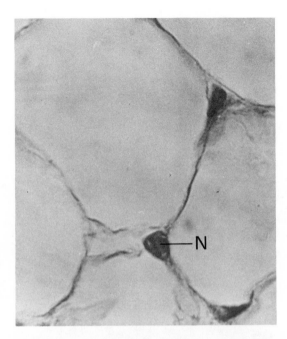

Figure 4–12 Adipose (fat) tissue (× 1000). The central portion of the cell is filled with fat, which forces the nucleus (N) to the periphery of the cells.

canals (Figure 4–13). The living bone cells or *osteocytes* are located in tiny chambers called *lacunae* in the compact, calcified bone. The cells are interconnected and also are connected to the central marrow cavity by a network of tiny canals called *canaliculi*. All the nutrients that reach these cells must pass through these tiny channels by way of the main nutrient canal, known as the *Haversian canal*, which brings blood and nerves into the compact bone from the outer covering.

Essentially there are two types of bone tissue, that which develops from an original cartilage "model" (endochondrial ossification) and that which replaces a membrane (intramembranous ossification). The long bones of the arms and legs, for example, develop slowly from cartilage whereas some bones of the cranium form within a special membrane.

MUSCLE TISSUE

Three types of muscle tissue may be recognized: smooth, striated, and cardiac. Although all of these have a contractile function, each is highly specialized.

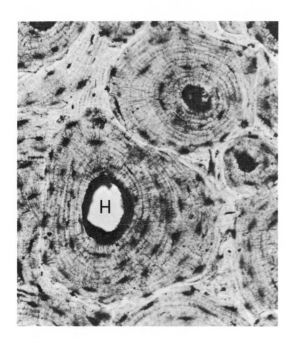

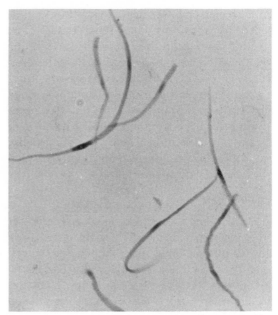

Figure 4–13 Photomicrograph of a thin section of ground bond (×1000): Haversian canal (H). (Courtesy of Triarch, Inc., Ripon, Wisconsin.)

Figure 4–14 Smooth muscle fibers teased from the intestinal wall (×450). These fibers are generally spindle-shaped and have no striations.

Smooth Muscle

These muscle tissues have the simplest cells of the three types. An individual muscle cell is called a *fiber* and is capable of independent contraction. The muscle cytoplasm, or *sarcoplasm*, of each spindle-shaped cell contains contractile protein fibers called *myofibrils*. A smooth muscle is composed of many cells grouped into a bundle (Figure 4–14). Smooth muscles are sometimes called *involuntary* muscles because their action is not directly under conscious control. They are located in the visceral organs and are responsible for such movements as *peristalsis*. Smooth muscle fibers are also found in the walls of blood vessels and the uterus.

Striated Muscle

Movement of striated or skeletal muscle tissues is primarily under conscious direction. The term *striated* comes from the observation of large numbers of crossbands along the fibers under the microscope. Careful observation with the electron microscope coupled with chemical analysis has demonstrated that the

striation patterns are produced by specific arrangements of two protein fibrils—actin and myosin. As in smooth muscle the myofibrils compose the contractile elements of the muscle fiber. A striated muscle fiber (cell) contains several nuclei, all of which are located near the membrane, and therefore is termed *multinucleate* (Figure 4–15). The contractile myofibrils within each fiber show a definite banded pattern or striations, which are set off by dark-staining bands called Z lines (Figure 4–16). The banded area between the Z lines is termed a *sarcomere*. The overlapping arrangement of myosin (thick filament) and actin (thin filament) proteins produces the bands of differing density within the sarcomere. In cross section, the filaments are arranged in hexagonal patterns. The area marked A is the pattern formed along the entire myosin length, including the dark end regions, where myosin and actin interdigitate.

The picture of the muscle we have presented so far is that of the tissue at rest. What happens when the muscle contracts? A nerve impulse or mild electric shock will cause a certain number of muscle fibers to contract depending

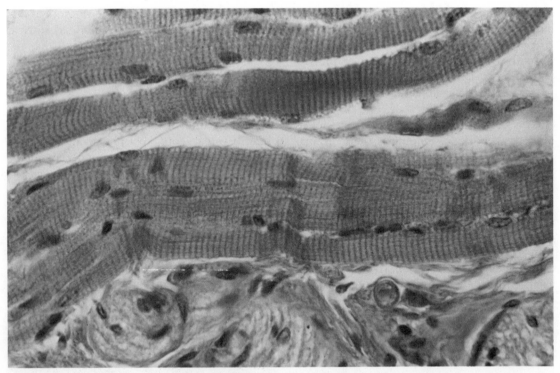

Figure 4–15   Striated muscle fibers from the tongue of a rat (× 450). The banded pattern is due to the arrangement of the actin and myosin protein fibrils.

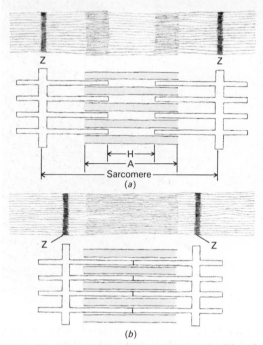

Figure 4–16   Model of striated muscle. Myosin is shown in color. (*a*) The regions of crossbanding are lettered as they appear in relaxed muscle. (*b*) The contracted state.

on the strength of the stimulus. Physiological studies have shown that increasing the strength of the stimulus causes a corresponding increase in the strength of muscle contraction. In vertebrate muscle, each fiber contracts to its greatest extent when it is stimulated; thus muscle contractions of varied strengths depend on the number of fibers that are stimulated.

At the moment of contraction, the actin filaments move together in a horizontal sliding action. This action changes the pattern (Figure 4–16) as follows: the Z bands are brought closer together, since the actin filaments are anchored to these bands, and the H zones, which represent the spaces between the actin filaments, disappear. Because this shortening occurs throughout the entire muscle, a great contraction can be accomplished. Following the contraction phase, the actin filaments return to their original relaxed condition.

The thick filaments have projections called cross bridges which extend to touch the thin filaments. Each cross bridge ends in an enlargement (the head of the cross bridge) where it touches a thin filament. During contraction the action is primarily in this head region, and it is here that ATP is hydrolyzed to provide the energy for contraction. The exact mechanism which provides ATP energy to cause the sets of interdigitating filaments to slide with respect to one another is a subject of intense research at the present time. Although we have some clues about this process, more information is needed for an understanding of the molecular mechanism.

We know that contraction of a muscle is initiated by changes in the permeability of the muscle-cell membrane to calcium following the arrival of a nerve impulse. The small amount of calcium which enters the muscle fiber reacts with a special regulatory protein located on the thin filaments called *troponin*. In the absence of calcium, troponin inhibits the interaction of thin and thick filaments, but in the presence of calcium, interaction between the filaments occurs and contraction results.

Cardiac Muscle

Cardiac or heart muscle is a unique tissue that begins regular rhythmic contractions during embryonic development and continues to beat throughout the lifetime of an organism. In vertebrates the control of the heartbeat rhythm is principally through nerve impulses originating in the *medulla* of the brain. The contractility of the muscle itself, however, appears to be inherent in the tissue. The fine structure of the myofibrils of cardiac muscle is similar to that described for skeletal muscle. The nucleus of a cardiac-muscle cell, however, is located in the center of the fiber rather than along the outer membrane. Each cardiac-muscle fiber contains only one nucleus.

Cardiac muscle is oriented in flat, overlapping sheets and surrounds the heart cavities. The individual fibers are broad and many-sided in shape—that is, the cell membranes are irregular and branching. Early investigators observed dark-staining transverse bands in the muscle. It was once thought that these bands were in some way related to the heartbeat and apparent tirelessness of the muscle. The bands were called *intercalated discs* but are now known to be only the thickened, adjacent cell membranes of individual muscle cells (Figure 4–17).

NERVE TISSUE

The tissues that provide for communication and integration in animals are found in the brain, spinal cord, peripheral nerves, and nerve endings. The fundamental element of nerve tissue is the nerve cell or *neuron.* Although several other specialized cell types are also found in this tissue, the neuron is the "functional unit."

A typical neuron is composed of a cell body and filamentous extensions. These extensions associate with similar ones from other neurons to form a communication "chain" (Figure 4–18). The cytoplasm of a neuron contains a nucleus, nucleolus, mitochondria, Golgi apparatus, and many small particles of RNA and

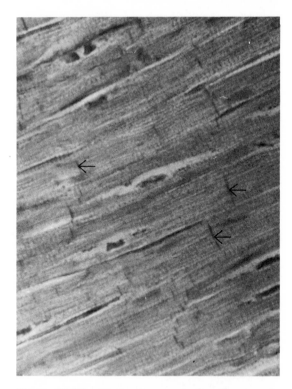

Figure 4–17 Photomicrograph of cardiac muscle of a dog showing intercalated discs (arrows) (× 500).

96

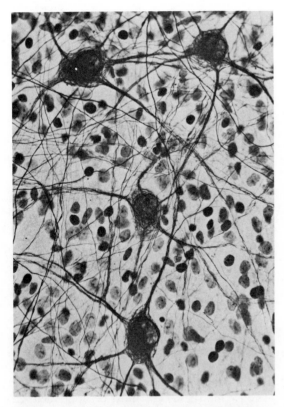

Figure 4–18 Multipolar neurons from the cerebellum of a rat (×350). (Reproduced from Walther J. Hild, "Cell Types and Neuronal Connections in Cultures of Mammalian Central Nervous Tissue," *Zeitschrift für Zellforschung und mikroskopische Anatomie*, Bd. 69, S. 155–188, Berlin-Heidelberg-New York: Springer 1966.)

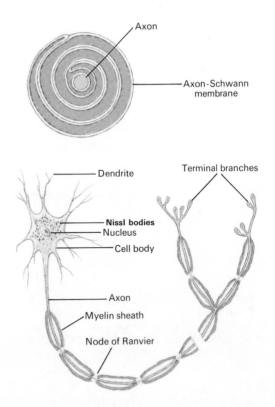

Figure 4–19 Myelinated neuron. At upper left is an enlarged view of a cross section of an axon and the myelin sheath.

protein known as Nissl bodies (Figure 4–19). Cellular structures, *axons* and *dendrites*, extend from the cell body. In some cases these extensions may reach over a meter in length. A nerve impulse travels along the cell membrane from a dendrite toward the axon. In this manner the axon of one cell excites one or several dendrites of the next cell and the impulse is carried the length of the neuron "chain." (The formation and propagation of the nerve impulse will be explained in detail in Chapter 8.) In other words, the nerve impulse travels toward the cell body along the dendrites and away from the cell body along the axon. Where the axon connects with a dendrite, small bulbous structures are found which are known as

synaptic knobs (Figure 4–20). A small space of approximately 200 Å, called a *synaptic cleft*, lies between these endings. The terminal portion of an axon (see Figure 4–19) is referred to as a presynaptic component. The region of a dendrite which is adjacent to the end of the axon is the postsynaptic component (see Figure 4–20). The traveling nerve impulse triggers tiny vesicles in the synaptic knob to secrete *acetylcholine*, which in turn excites the adjacent dendrites. The chemical reactions at the synapse keep nerve impulses flowing in a specific direction (axons to dendrites). This is possible, since only the dendrite membrane has chemically sensitive receptor sites. Immediately following the production of acetylcholine, an enzyme, *cholinesterase*, splits the chemical into nonreactive components. The synapse thus is prepared to transfer a new impulse. The apparent function of acetylcholine is to

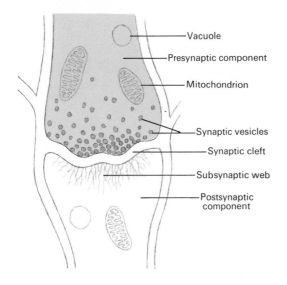

Vacuole
Presynaptic component
Mitochondrion
Synaptic vesicles
Synaptic cleft
Subsynaptic web
Postsynaptic component

Figure 4–20 Synaptic region between a dendrite and an axon showing a synaptic cleft and a synaptic knob. (Redrawn from Eduardo DeRobertis *et al.*, *Cell Biology*, Fourth Edition, Philadelphia, W. B. Saunders Co., 1965.)

increase the ionic permeability of the postsynaptic membrane. The importance of this permeability and the details of the nerve impulse will be discussed in Chapter 8.

The Nissl bodies, first described in 1876, were thought to be related to the nuclear material, since they were stained by nuclear dyes. It was supposed that the Nissl substance somehow supplemented the nuclear function during nerve activity. Using modern techniques, however, it has been learned that the Nissl substance corresponds to the ribosomal parts of other cells. It is understandable, then, that a concentrated complex of protein-producing organelles are needed for these cells that contain such large amounts of cytoplasm and undergo intense activity.

The central area of the spinal cord of vertebrates is gray in color, shaped like a butterfly, and is composed of nerve cell bodies. The peripheral areas of the cord, however, are composed of white, glistening nerve tracts known as the white matter. The white appearance is due to myelin sheaths that surround axons (Figure 4–19). Gaps which expose axon membranes occur at intervals along the myelin sheath and are called *nodes of Ranvier*. This special fatty sheath is formed around an axon by nearby Schwann cells. During development, these cells actually wrap themselves around an axon to form a spiral layer of membrane and myelin. It has been discovered that the speed of impulse transmission in myelinated nerves is about four times as great as in nonmyelinated nerves. At first it was thought that the fatty sheath only protected the cell membrane like the insulation on an electric wire, but it was later theorized that the impulse jumps along the axon from node to node. In this event, impulses would not have to pass through the entire length of the axon membrane, and the time required to reach the synapse would be greatly shortened. Gray-matter neurons have no myelin sheaths and are sometimes referred to as "naked."

BLOOD TISSUE

Tissues, then, are made up of various kinds of cells, and these cells must be nourished. In vertebrates and most higher animals the blood, within a circulating system, serves many important functions such as transportation for nutrients, oxygen, carbon dioxide, metabolic wastes, hormones, and proteins. Blood is composed of several cell types carried in a fluid matrix or *plasma*. Oxygen-transporting pigments may be dissolved in the plasma, as in the earthworm, or they may be contained in cells.

In man, the cellular components make up about 45 percent of the blood, and all that remains is plasma. Noncellular plasma contains water, dissolved salts and nutrients, hormones, gases, and antibodies. In addition, certain proteins such as serum albumin, serum globulin, *complement*, and fibrinogen (necessary for clotting) are also present. Complement works with antibodies to destroy foreign cells.

The cells found in the blood are derived from the same cells that form bone, muscle, and cartilage. This process of the differentiation of early cells into basic tissues will be discussed in Chapter 10.

Red Blood Cells

In vertebrates the oxygen-carrying cells are called red blood cells (RBCs) or *erythrocytes*, due to the presence of the pigment *hemoglobin* which is red. Not all erythrocytes are the same size or shape. For example, the nucleated erythrocytes of amphibian blood are very large and elongated when compared to those of a mammal (24 microns for a frog to 7.7 microns for man). The red blood cells of man, produced in the red bone marrow, are small, biconcave discs which lose their nuclei at maturity (Figure 4–21). The average life span of an enucleate RBC is about 120 days, after which destruction occurs in the spleen or liver. The red blood cells of all vertebrates, except mammals, possess nuclei.

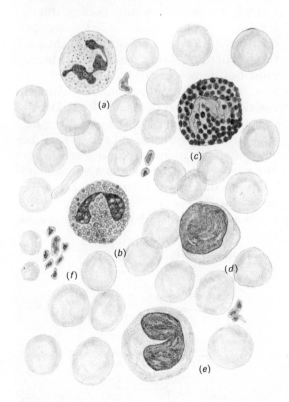

Figure 4–21 Cellular components of human blood. (*a*) Neutrophils with multilobed nuclei. (*b*) Eosinophils with large red granules. (*c*) Basophils with large purple-staining granules. (*d*) Lymphocytes with large nuclei. (*e*) Monocytes. (*f*) Platelets. The numerous enucleate corpuscles in each plate are erythrocytes.

White Blood Cells

The blood of man and other vertebrates also contains colorless white blood cells (WBCs), or *leucocytes*. The leucocytes are larger than the erythrocytes (10–12 microns) and can be identified by their characteristically shaped nuclei. The function of the leucocytes is primarily the ingestion (phagocytosis) of bacteria and particulate wastes in the bloodstream and tissue fluids. The number of white cells can therefore vary; a marked increase may temporarily occur during times of infection. Leukemia, a malignant disease of the blood, occurs when certain white cells are formed at an extremely rapid rate. It is currently believed that this uncontrolled, abnormal growth is caused by viruses.

Classification of WBCs

Leucocytes, most of which are produced in the red bone marrow (Figure 4–21), are classified in two general groups, granular and agranular, depending on the presence or absence of stainable granules in the cytoplasm.

1 Granular
   (*a*) *Neutrophils* (about 65 percent of all WBCs) possess fine cytoplasmic granules and a multilobed nucleus. These are phagocytic cells which may pass in and out of capillaries to ingest foreign particles.
   (*b*) *Eosinophils* (about 3 percent of all WBCs) contain very large red-staining cytoplasmic granules and possibly function in antigen-antibody immune reactions (asthma, hayfever, and parasite infections). The nucleus is usually bilobed at maturity.
   (*c*) *Basophils* (about 1 percent of all WBCs resemble eosinophils in having large cytoplasmic granules. However, the granules stain dark purple and the nucleus may have several lobes. Their function is unknown.

2 Agranular
   (*a*) *Lymphocytes* (25 percent of all WBCs) have a large nucleus that occupies almost the entire cell. Lymphocytes are produced in lymphoid tissue (lymph nodes and spleen) and function in the production of antibodies.
   (*b*) *Monocytes* (6 percent of all WBCs)

also possess a large nucleus which is kidney shaped. They function in phagocytosis and some enter the connective tissues to become giant macrophage cells that ingest foreign substances.

Platelets

Platelets are fragments of large cells, megakaryocytes, which are produced in the bone marrow. These fragments contain the enzyme *thromboplastin*, which is essential for initiating blood clotting (Figure 4–22). A blood clot is essentially a meshwork of insoluble fibrin that traps all the nearby blood cells and platelets. The remaining fluid is called blood serum.

PROTECTION AND IMMUNITY

We should not leave the topic of blood without discussing the aspects of immunity and protection against germs (especially bacteria and viruses). Although the skin and certain cell secretions may act as a first barrier to the entrance of germs or other foreign particles, the ability of white blood cells to engulf and destroy foreign particles is one of the primary defenses against infection in vertebrate animals. Another defense mechanism involves the production of *interferon*, a protein produced by an individual's cells in response to the invasion of a virus. When interferon is released from infected cells, nearby, uninfected cells gain resistance to the viruses. Apparently this is accomplished by the production of proteins in the uninfected cells which prevent the replication of the viruses. A specific chemical system also exists in vertebrate organisms which combats invading molecules once they have gained entrance. This *immunity* system is founded in the chemical uniqueness of the cells of each individual. Understanding of immunity came partially from observing the fact that individuals who had certain diseases would develop a resistance to those diseases which could last for many years.

ANTIGENS AND ANTIBODIES

When foreign substances enter a vertebrate system, a reaction usually occurs wherein special molecules called *antibodies* are produced. The foreign substances which cause this reaction are called *antigens* and are usually proteins. (Some carbohydrates and lipids are also capable of acting as antigens.) Antigens entering a body may be viruses, bacterial cells, poisonous compounds (toxins) from the bacteria, or foreign proteins, and all may stimulate antibody production. Moreover, each antigen brings about the formation of a specific antibody and thus many different antibodies can be produced. The reaction which occurs between antigen and antibody is highly specific

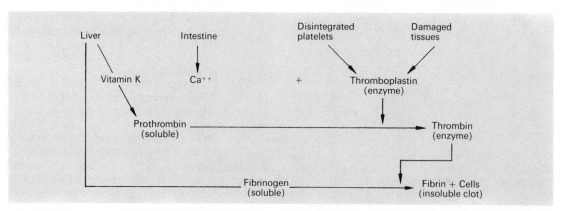

Figure 4–22 Interacting substances and their sources in blood clotting. Prothrombin and fibrinogen are soluble blood proteins produced in the liver. Vitamin K is necessary for the synthesis of prothrombin. A deficiency of vitamin K will produce symptoms similar to bleeder's disease.

and results in the neutralization of the antigen by the antibody. This can happen in any one of a variety of ways, such as covering the active sites of the antigen, clumping, precipitating, breaking up of cells, or assisting in the phagocytosis of bacteria. Invading germs or foreign molecules are thus rendered inactive by the antibodies.

But what are antibodies, and what is their chemical structure? The 1972 Nobel Prize for Physiology and Medicine was awarded to two biologists, R. R. Porter of the University of Oxford and G. M. Edelman of Rockefeller University (Figure 4–23), for their research on the chemical structure of antibodies. Their work, dating back to the 1950s and 1960s, indicated that antibody molecules were composed of two light polypeptide chains (L chains) and two larger chains (H chains) held together by disulfide bonds (Figure 4–24). The structure throughout most of the four chains is apparently similar for all antibodies; the variability in structure occurs at the amino (NH_2) ends of the chains. This variability seems to determine the specificity of the antibody to its antigen.

How and where are antibodies formed?

Antibodies are globulin proteins in the blood which have been produced by special lymphocytes known as *plasma cells*. Several theories have been proposed to account for their production. One theory, proposed in the 1940s, assumed that antigens were templates against which antibodies could be formed in a shape which matched the antigen. This is often known as the Instructive Theory, since the antigen supposedly provides the information for the manufacture of the antibody. A more recent theory, the Selective Theory, suggests that many antibodies can be synthesized like other proteins and that the information for this synthesis is contained in the plasma cells. A specific invading antigen then "selects" a specific plasma cell and antibody production is stimulated. The Clonal Theory, a modification of the Selective Theory put forth about 1960, holds that plasma cells can form *clones* (a group of cells produced from one cell type) when stimulated by an antigen; these clones then form antibodies against the antigen (Figure 4–25). There are apparent flaws in all of these theories at the present time, although the Clonal Theory is the most probable in light of current evidence. One of the active areas of

Figure 4–23   (*a*) R. R. Porter of the University of Oxford and (*b*) G. M. Edelman of Rockefeller University, recipients of the Nobel Prize in Physiology or Medicine in 1972 for their research on the chemical structure of antibodies. (Courtesy of Dr. Porter and University of Oxford; Dr. Edelman and Rockefeller University.)

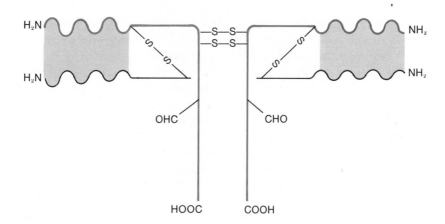

Figure 4-24 Four-chain structure of an antibody. The colored bars represent the heavy polypeptide chains. The wavy lines indicate areas of variable amino-acid sequences which provide specific antigen-combining sites (shaded). CHO refers to carbohydrate molecules.

immunological research is the search for a clearer explanation of how antibodies are produced. Only recently have we learned that the *thymus* gland of the embryo is a primary source of lymphocytes with antibody-forming capability. This gland, the function of which was a mystery to biologists for a long time, is found in most vertebrates especially in the early stages of life. In man, the thymus lies in the upper chest region, is prominent until puberty, and diminishes in size and function thereafter. Lymphocytes from the thymus migrate to the spleen and lymph nodes to provide a large portion of the primary supply of antibody-producing cells.

The principles of immunology have actually been used since the late eighteenth century when Edward Jenner discovered that people exposed to cowpox developed only a mild case of smallpox if they caught it at all. From this observation came the principle of *vaccination* —the introduction of dead or weakened (attenuated) viruses or bacteria which cause an individual to develop specific antibodies. Vaccinations are possible today for smallpox, polio, rabies, and cholera. It is also possible, in the process of *immunization*, to inject the antigenic toxin, as in diphtheria and tetanus, and permit the development of antibodies against these diseases.

ALLERGY

This important, protective antigen-antibody system can also be a source of painful problems. A relatively harmless germ or foreign substance, such as pollen or wasp poison, may cause little trouble when first encountered even though antibodies are produced. When the antigen is introduced another time, however, a violent reaction may occur between the antigen and the antibodies previously formed. The damage in this case is not primarily from the antigen, but from the immunological response of the individual, and may result in an *allergy*. In fact there is now strong evidence to indicate that in many cases of disease it is this immune response which causes damage to the cells, rather than the reproducing virus. It now looks as though the initial breakdown of cells in measles and influenza is due to antibodies and blood complement which is then followed by tissue destruction from reproducing viruses. Thus, some disease symptoms are the collective result of the virus and the immunological response of the host.

ORGAN TRANSPLANTS

Although the immunological system can help to ward off invading organisms or foreign

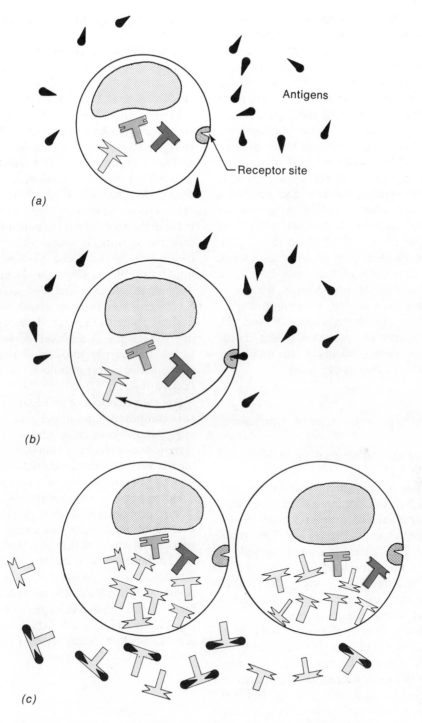

Figure 4–25 Stages in the Clonal Theory of antibody production. (*a*) Antigens surround a plasma cell which has the potential for producing antibodies. (*b*) Antigen combines with a receptor site. (*c*) This stimulation causes the production of specific antibodies and cell division to form a clone; inactivation of antigens is also shown.

molecules, it has some drawbacks. And these drawbacks become even more serious when surgeons attempt to transplant tissues or organs from one organism to another. In many instances, the antigen-antibody reactions occurring between two organisms are too great to permit transplants. Obviously, greater success can be achieved if the donor and recipient can be matched very closely in terms of their body chemistries. Radiation and drugs have assisted transplant processes by suppressing the immune system, but this also interferes with other cell functions, often to the point of making the recipient highly susceptible to infection and disease. With these techniques, kidney transplants have been fairly successful, however, transplants of heart and lung have resulted in a high rate of mortality. The positive and negative aspects of immunological responses are still being explored, and the knowledge gained in this area of biology holds promise for future advances in medicine, including the treatment of cancer.

GROUPING OF TISSUES INTO ORGANS

To continue our earlier analogy of biological structure to architecture, we must now turn our attention to the specific structures that are formed by the association of various types of tissues. Functional structures made up of different tissues are called *organs*. The small intestine of a vertebrate is a good example of an organ. A photograph of a cross section of the small intestine of a monkey shows four major regions: mucosa, submucosa, muscularis, and serosa (Figure 4–26).

The mucosa consists of a columnar epithelial lining, some glands, and loose connective tissues that support the villi (fingerlike projections on the inner surface of the intestine). Immediately beneath the mucosa lies the submucosa, a region of more closely packed connective tissues, intestinal glands, arterioles and venules, lymphatic vessels, and nerve fibers. The muscularis is composed of an inner layer of circular smooth muscle and a thinner external band of longitudinal fibers, and the organ is covered externally with a

thin layer of squamous epithelium called the serosa.

The skin or integument of a mammal is composed of several tissue types and also contains elements of the blood vascular organs (Figure 4–27). The outer layer of skin is the epidermis and is composed of many layers of stratified squamous epithelium. The squamous cells are formed at the base of the epidermis and are constantly pushed toward the surface where they become hardened, die, and are finally sloughed off. Cells in the deep layer of the epidermis produce pigments which give color to the skin. The layer beneath the epidermis, the dermis, is composed principally of connective tissue. Blood vessels, nerve endings, hair follicles, sweat glands, and oil glands (sebaceous glands) are also common here. Sweat glands, sebaceous glands, and hairs are derived from the epidermis as invaginations into the dermis. A relatively loose attachment to the underlying muscles is provided by a subcutaneous layer composed of fat and connective tissues.

Another example of an organ is a plant leaf. It is composed of an upper and lower epidermis, parenchyma cells, and vascular tissues (xylem and phloem). Together these tissues form a very efficient food-making organ. The structural relationships of a leaf are shown in Chapter 6 where photosynthesis is discussed.

The principle of *division of labor* is clearly illustrated in an organ since each tissue has a specific function in that organ. For example, the epithelial cells of the mucosa layer of the intestine form a lining, whereas the muscle tissue of the muscularis provides for movement of the organ. An organ consequently is capable of doing a job which could not be accomplished by each tissue functioning independently.

THE ORGANISM

To complete our concept of biological architecture we must recognize that all organs are finally organized into functional *systems*. For example, the mouth, esophagus, stomach, small intestine, and large intestine form the

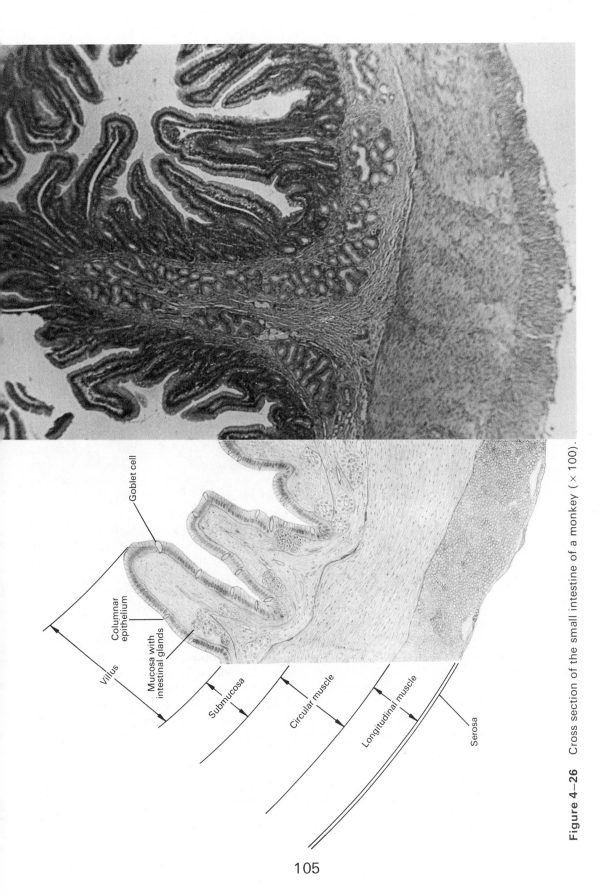

Goblet cell

Columnar epithelium

Mucosa with intestinal glands

Villus

Submucosa

Circular muscle

Longitudinal muscle

Serosa

Figure 4–26 Cross section of the small intestine of a monkey (×100).

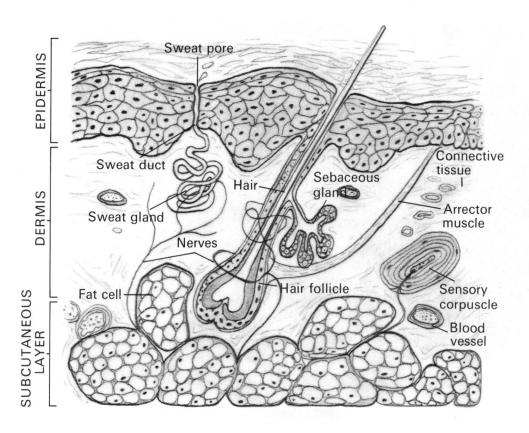

Figure 4–27 Cross section of skin.

digestive system in higher animals. Other systems include the respiratory, circulatory, reproductive, excretory, muscular, skeletal, endocrine, and nervous systems. Some organs actually contribute to more than one system. The liver, for example, participates in digestion, excretion, and circulation. All systems are organized into a functional *organism* by nervous and hormonal control. The success of an organism therefore depends on the orderly coordination and organization of all organs as they function together to meet the demands of the environment.

THE SPECIES CONCEPT

An organism constitutes a living unit in nature, and many different types of organisms exist. Similarities within the diversity are evident, however, and organisms can be placed in specific groups. This grouping, which is generally based on external characteristics (though others are often needed), forms a classification system. One category of organisms, for instance, is known as sparrows. Within this general group of sparrows is a distinct subgroup known as English sparrows which are identified by their coloration and song. A group of similar organisms is called a *species* and forms the fundamental category of classification. For example, one variety of clams, the butter clam, lives in the gravel and sand along certain regions of the West Coast (Figure 4–28). These clams live in close association, and potentially the sperm cells of any male butter clam can fertilize the eggs of

Figure 4–28 *Saxidomus giganteus*, the butter (or Washington) clam.

any female butter clam; thus, we say that they can interbreed. The definition of a species then should include the principle of reproduction, and species definitions always include interbreeding groups. Ernst Mayr, in 1942, very aptly defined the species as "a group of actually or potentially interbreeding populations that are reproductively isolated from other such groups." The species name for the butter clam is *giganteus*. It is always stated with the genus name, however, and the total specific designation for the organism is *Saxidomus giganteus*. The term species is both singular and plural.

The concept of a species, however, has much greater significance than merely a classification group. The fact that sexual reproduction is involved in the definition implies that organisms can be formed which differ from the parents. Consequently, species can change. Although regarded as a fixed unit in nature,

for the purpose of classification we must treat them as variable, dynamic, and alterable groups. As a result of changes, some members of the once interbreeding group would be incapable of mating with other members of the original species. The process by which a species may change and become two species is discussed under "speciation" in Chapter 12.

CLASSIFICATION OF ORGANISMS

Since there are many different organisms on our planet, some type of organizational system is required to deal with this diversity. Authorities seldom agree on every detail of classification, and various schemes have been proposed. Any system of classification should be as natural as possible—that is, it should reflect the way organisms have developed and, as far as possible, their relationships to one another. We have used a system of four *kingdoms* in this book, and although it may not represent the exact pattern by which life evolved, it seems more natural than a system that recognizes only plant and animal categories. It should be noted, however, that any system of classification is man-made and represents man's attempts to categorize nature into specific groups.

Organisms were at first classified on the basis of the only characteristics available—their gross visible features. With the development of the microscope and other instruments, it has been possible to use other characteristics such as microscopic structures, chromosome comparisons (Figure 4–29), and protein comparisons (serum analyses). The use of these additional techniques should help biologists arrive at a more accurate classification system —that is, one that more closely parallels nature. We often refer to the field of biology that employs these techniques in classification as *biosystematics*.

The kingdoms are divided into *phyla* (singular = phylum). Additional subclassification categories are used, and these are noted in the Appendix. The general characteristics of the kingdoms are given below, and some of the

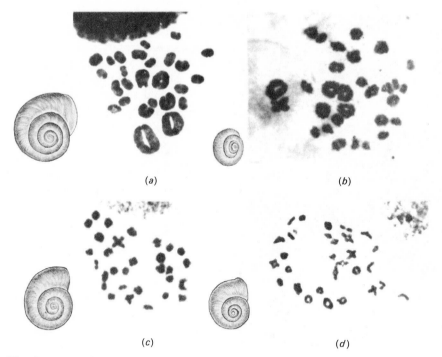

Figure 4–29 Four sets of chromosomes from four closely related pulmonate snails. (*a*) and (*b*) Same family, Polygyridae, but two different genera. (*c*) and (*d*) Family Haplotrematidae and members of the same genus. (*c*) *Haplotrema vancouverense* (*n* = 30). (*d*) *Haplotrema sportella* (*n* = 29).

important phyla in each kingdom are presented with a brief summary of their characteristics. For a more complete classification scheme of the living world, see the Appendix.

KINGDOM MONERA

In relationship to other organisms this kingdom shows a lack of specialized cell structures. Monerans do not have a well-defined nucleus —that is, the genetic material is not organized into chromosomes with protein—and a nuclear membrane is absent. Furthermore, their cells do not contain mitochondria, Golgi apparatus, lysosomes, or centrioles. Flagella, when present, are composed of a single fibril which differs from the 9 + 2 microtubule arrangement of other flagellated organisms. Bacteria and blue-green algae are classified as monerans and are found in most environments where some moisture is present.

PHYLUM SCHIZOPHYTA (BACTERIA)

These tiny organisms (the smallest cells known) occur in a variety of shapes and patterns. Many bacteria have a tough cell wall, and some are covered by a gelatinous capsule in addition. Flagella provide locomotion in some bacteria, but they differ structurally from the flagella of other organisms. Bacteria are capable of walling off a portion of their contents to produce dormant endospores which enable them to withstand conditions that would otherwise destroy them. Although many bacteria produce diseases in man and other organisms, they are necessary for life on our planet because they play a vital role in nitrogen metabolism and the decay process. These processes will be discussed in the next chapter.

PHYLUM CYANOPHYTA (BLUE-GREEN ALGAE)

Although this group is known as the blue-green algae, many species are red, blue, green, yellow, or mixtures of these colors; they often give the characteristic color to a body of water. These organisms, like the bacteria, can live under extreme temperature conditions, from ice water to nearly boiling water. The blue-greens do not possess flagella but may move by gliding or oscillating movements.

KINGDOM PROTISTA

This large and diverse kingdom includes organisms with varying characteristics. Many of the members that do not immediately seem to be related to each other represent rather specialized groups. The criteria for this kingdom often vary among biologists and thus the boundaries are not clear-cut. For example, algae and fungi may or may not be placed in this kingdom depending on the specific characteristics used. The general characteristics that differentiate protists from plants and animals are (1) unicellular or a simple, undifferentiated body (except in some algae); (2) unicellular reproductive structures; (3) mostly aquatic; and (4) some have chlorophyll (plantlike) while others do not (animallike).

PHYLUM CHLOROPHYTA (GREEN ALGAE)

Green algae are widespread and can be found in most bodies of water and on moist soils. These organisms contain the two types of chlorophyll found in plants, chlorophyll a and b. For this reason, as well as others, it is believed the members of the plant kingdom have evolved from the green algae.

Although members of this phylum do not show a high degree of differentiation, three basic structural plans are evident, namely the single cell, filamentous colonies, and non-filamentous colonies. Within the colonies it is important to note the specialization of some cells as reproductive cells.

PHYLUM MASTIGOPHORA

This large and varied phylum consists of unicellular or colonial organisms that possess one to several flagella. The group is often divided into three classes: (1) photosynthetic flagellates that contain chlorophyll, (2) dinoflagellates that also contain chlorophyll and have two flagella; these are important as one of the primary food sources in the ocean and some species can produce the toxic condition known as "red tide"; and (3) animallike flagellates, many of which are parasitic and cause diseases in vertebrates such as sleeping sickness in man.

PHYLUM EUMYCOPHYTA (FUNGI)

Since these organisms lack chlorophyll, they cannot manufacture their own food and consequently must obtain nutrients from sources of already synthesized foodstuffs, such as decaying matter or another living organism. These generally multicellular organisms show little differentiation and are usually composed of filaments. The fungi probably represent a specialized sideline in the evolutionary process.

PHYLA SARCODINA, SPOROZOA, CILIOPHORA

These single-celled forms do not contain chlorophyll and are sometimes grouped into the single phylum Protozoa. Many of the members of these phyla exhibit a high degree of specialization within a single cell and possess organelles specialized for feeding, excretion, water balance, and protection. Locomotion is accomplished in Sarcodina by extensions of the cell cytoplasm known as "pseudopodia," whereas ciliophorans move by cilia. Sporozoans are all parasitic in the blood or tissues of animals (some cause malaria) and produce spores at some stage of their life cycles.

KINGDOM METAPHYTA

These are the organisms commonly known as plants. It seems quite certain that metaphytes have evolved from protistan origins, which is evidenced by their similarity in cell structure. The plant body is generally more complex than protists, and their tissues may be organized into organs. Chlorophyll *a* and *b* and other pigments similar to those found in some protista are present. One of the most characteristic aspects of all metaphytes is the pattern of the life cycle which alternates between gamete-forming and spore-forming generations. (This will be explained in detail in Chapter 10.) The members of this group are the mosses and liverworts and the common vascular plants.

PHYLUM BRYOPHYTA (MOSSES AND LIVERWORTS)

Bryophytes are land plants that can live only under moist conditions, since water is required for completion of one stage of their life cycle. They contain chlorophyll but lack true leaves, stems, and roots. Vascular tissue (xylem and phloem), necessary in tall plants for the conduction of water and food, is also absent in the bryophytes.

PHYLUM TRACHEOPHYTA (VASCULAR PLANTS)

These organisms are the familiar land plants and have the typical plant plan of leaves, stems, and roots. The possession of vascular tissue has permitted many of these plants to grow tall and inhabit most environments on the earth. The ferns are primitive members of this group but probably the most familiar are the seed-producing tracheophytes—the gymnosperms and the angiosperms.

KINGDOM METAZOA

Many structural features of animals are determined by the fact that animals cannot manufacture food. The muscle tissue provides locomotion, and nervous tissue permits the coordination of muscle action and senses to aid in obtaining food.

One method of discussing and differentiating the several body plans that have evolved in animals is to consider the presence or absence of a body cavity between the internal organs and the body wall. Those animals without such a cavity have a rather solid type of body construction. Some of the advantages of having a body cavity are:

1 More space and freer movement is provided for coiled and folded internal organs.
2 A certain degree of protection is afforded for internal organs that are not connected directly to the body wall.
3 Fluid is present in the cavity and can assist in the circulation of gases and foods as well as help remove wastes.
4 Overall increase in size of animals would probably not have been possible without a body cavity to facilitate the physiological and anatomical adaptations necessary for larger animals.

These body cavities are of two types—*coelom* and *pseudocoelom*. A coelom is a cavity in which the internal organs and the inside surface of the body wall are lined with an epithelial tissue. This tissue is known as the *peritoneum* and, in addition to serving as a lining, it forms part of the mesenteries that hold the internal organs in place. This lining forms from the embryonic tissue called the mesoderm, which will be discussed in Chapter 10. A cavity which is not completely lined with a mesodermal tissue is a pseudocoelom. Figure 4–30 compares the major coelomic conditions.

It is possible to use this distinguishing characteristic as a basis for classification. Thus we find animals without body cavity or coelom, the *Acoelomata*; animals with a body cavity but without a true coelom, the *Pseudocoelomata*; and animals with a coelom, the *Coelomata*. Coelomic animals can be further divided on the basis of the manner in which the coelom develops from the mesoderm. In some animals, notably the earthworms, molluscs, and arthropods, a group of mesoderm cells separate with one group forming a lining for internal organs and the other a lining for the body wall. These animals are in the subgroup *schizocoelomates* (*schizo* referring to the splitting of the group of mesodermal cells). In other animals, among these are the chordates and echinoderms, the coelom develops as a pouch with one side of the pouch

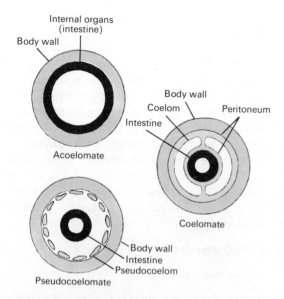

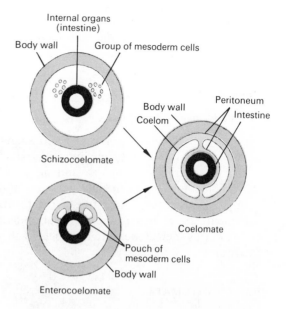

Figure 4–30 The three major coelomic conditions—acoelomate, pseudocoelomate, and coelomate. The diagrams represent cross sections of generalized animal bodies.

Figure 4–31 Schizocoelomate and enterocoelomate development of the coelomate body plan. The diagrams represent cross sections of generalized animal bodies.

lining the internal organs and the other side lining the body wall. This group of animals is referred to as the *enterocoelomates* (*entero* denoting the formation of the pouches from the enteron which is the developing intestine). These two types (schizo and entero) of coelom development are shown in Figure 4–31. The metazoans or animals therefore can be divided into four subgroups—Acoelomata, Pseudocoelomata, Schizocoelomata, and Enterocoelomata.

The acoelomate condition is believed to be most primitive. Although the pseudocoelomates do have the advantage of a body cavity, the organs are free within the cavity and are not lined with a peritoneum. The coelomate body plan is considered to be the highest level of development.

Another important characteristic in the animal kingdom is that of body symmetry. Some animals such as amoebae and certain sponges have no definite body shape and are classified as *asymmetrical*. Body plans that appear to radiate from a central area like the spokes of a wheel are termed *radially symmetrical* (jellyfish are a good example). Most

animals are *bilaterally symmetrical*, which means that the body may be cut into two halves along one plane only so that the halves are mirror images.

ACOELOMATA

Phylum Coelenterata

This is a large group of chiefly marine animals constructed of essentially two layers of tissues. A *gastrovascular* cavity with only one opening, a mouth, provides for digestion and circulation. Tentacles, with stinging cells that assist in the capturing of food, surround the mouth in some forms. The characteristics stated above can be manifested into two basic types of body plans: (1) the *polyp*, a usually sedentary form; or (2) the *medusa*, a free-swimming or floating form. Freshwater hydras, jellyfish, and sea anemones are members of this group.

Phylum Platyhelminthes (Flatworms)

Some organ development is shown in the members of this phylum, but a gastrovascular cavity with only one opening still exists. The small, freshwater planaria, for instance, shows

111

characteristics of the flatworms. Many parasitic forms, among them the flukes and tapeworms, are in this phylum.

PSEUDOCOELOMATA

Phylum Aschelminthes

This phylum shows a significant evolutionary advancement in its complete intestinal tract with two openings—a mouth and an anus. The body form is generally slender and tubular. Both parasitic and free-living forms are members of this group. The abundant roundworms (nematodes) are members of this phylum.

SCHIZOCOELOMATA

Phylum Mollusca

This large group of animals has a general body plan of the following characteristics: (1) a muscular foot, (2) a soft body, and (3) usually a shell around the soft body secreted by a *mantle*. Common members of this phylum are snails, clams, and octopuses. Many mollusks are important as food for man.

Phylum Annelida (Segmented Worms)

The members of this phylum are wormlike and have a body composed of a series of segments. Although the segments may appear similar externally, considerable differentiation and specialization occurs internally. For example, the intestinal tract has many specialized regions. Annelids, like the animals already mentioned, still depend on an aquatic environment even though it may be only moist soil. The earthworm is the most familiar example

of this phylum. Leeches and many marine worms are also annelids.

Phylum Arthropoda

The arthropods are the largest and most successful (biologically speaking) phylum. It is a very diverse group including insects, crustaceans, spiders, millipedes, and centipedes. Among the characteristics of this phylum are a hard skeleton on the outside of the body; paired, jointed appendages; body usually divided into a head, thorax, and abdomen. The insects make up the largest group of animals known.

ENTEROCOELOMATA

Phylum Echinodermata

Echinoderms possess an internal skeleton of calcium plates embedded in their skin. A unique characteristic of this group is tube feet, which are operated by a water vascular system. These animals show a closer relationship to the chordates (the most highly developed phylum) than any other group. Starfish, sea cucumbers, and sea urchins are members of this phylum.

Phylum Chordata

Although this phylum contains some relatively primitive-appearing forms, it also contains some of the most highly developed animals, including man. Characteristics such as similarity in early development (embryological development) and the possession of a hollow nerve cord down the back are reasons for placing these diverse-appearing animals in this phylum. A large subphylum, Vertebrata, includes animals with backbones, such as fish, frogs, snakes, birds, and mammals.

SUMMARIZING STATEMENTS

Groups of cells which perform specific functions are known as tissues and may be identified according to their structure and function. Functions common to both plants and animals include protection, support, circulation, growth, and reproduction.

The principal plant tissues are: meristematic (cambium), vascular (xylem and phloem), fundamental (parenchyma, collenchyma, and sclerenchyma), and epidermal (epidermis).

The principal animal tissues are: epithelial (squamous, cuboidal, and columnar), connective (areolar, cartilage, adipose, and bone), muscle (smooth, striated, and cardiac), nerve, and blood. Blood cells originate from the same cells that produce cartilage and bone and therefore may be considered to be a connective tissue. Immunity against foreign substances, or antigens, is provided by white blood cells through the production of antibodies.

Functional structures composed of more than one tissue are known as organs. Examples of organs in man include the heart, lungs, pancreas, stomach, and intestines. Each of these organs contains structural components of nearly all tissue types. The principle of division of labor is evidenced in organs since each tissue performs specific functions.

Organs are interrelated in functional organ systems which comprise the organism. Examples include respiratory, circulatory, digestive, excretory, reproductive, muscular, skeletal, nervous, and endocrine systems.

The living unit in nature is the organism and each unique type is referred to as a species. Usually, individual species may be identified by their different structures. Technically, however, the definition must include the fact that species are interbreeding groups.

In order to handle the many diverse species, all organisms are placed into broad categories called kingdoms. Several classification systems are generally recognized, and a four-kingdom approach is used in this book—Monera, Protista, Metaphyta, and Metazoa. Each kingdom is further subdivided into more and more specific groups including phylum, class, order, family, genus, and species.

Animals which possess a body cavity (coelom) show adaptive advantages over those without a cavity (acoelomates). The type and development of the body cavity is helpful in classification.

REVIEW QUESTIONS

1 If an amoeba and a single cell from the intestinal lining of a frog are placed in pond water, the frog cell will soon die. What are some reasons for this?

2 What are some of the advantages of cellular construction to life? What are some advantages of tissue construction?

3 What structural characteristics would you use to identify microscopic sections of the following plant tissues: meristematic, xylem, phloem, and epidermal.

4 How does the arrangement of vascular tissue differ in monocot, dicot, and gymnosperm stems?

5 What structural and functional characteristics are common to all animal connective tissues?

6 Skeletal muscles show striated patterns which change when the muscle contracts and relaxes. How can these pattern changes be explained?

7 What are the unique characteristics of nerve cells? How is the nerve impulse passed from neuron to neuron?

113

8 Compare the cellular components of human blood with respect to size, shape, nucleus, relative numbers, and function.

9 In transplanting organs, why must surgeons consider the immune reaction?

10 How has man made use of his knowledge of antigens and antibodies?

11 In an organ such as the small intestine several tissue types are present. Describe the specific functions of each of the following: serosa layer, smooth muscle, nerve fibers, and epithelial lining.

12 What is the value of the term species? Why must reproduction be considered in a definition of a species?

13 How has the concept and use of the kingdom Protista facilitated the classification of the living world? Can you see how this kingdom could be further divided into additional kingdoms?

14 How are the structural variations of the animal body cavity, or coelom, of value in classifying animals? Define acoelomate, pseudocoelomate, schizocoelomate, and enterocoelomate.

15 Some people who have previously taken penicillin have a violent reaction to a later shot and cannot take this drug. What is the probable mechanism for this reaction?

SUPPLEMENTARY READINGS

Bevelander, Gerrit, *Essentials of Histology*, St. Louis, C. V. Mosby, 1970.

Bold, H. C., *The Plant Kingdom*, Englewood Cliffs, N.J., Prentice-Hall, 1960.

Burnet, Sir Macfarlane, "The Mechanism of Immunity," *Scientific American*, January, 1961.

Eccles, Sir John, "The Synapse," *Scientific American*, January, 1965.

Echlin, Patrick, "The Blue-Green Algae," *Scientific American*, June, 1966.

Edelman, Gerald M., "The Structure and Function of Antibodies," *Scientific American*, August, 1970.

Epstein, Emanuel, "Roots," *Scientific American*, May, 1973.

Fritts, Harold C., "Tree Rings and Climate," *Scientific American*, May, 1972.

Gross, Jerome, "Collagen," *Scientific American*, May, 1961.

Harris, M. C., and Norman Shure, *All About Allergy*, Englewood Cliffs, N.J., Prentice-Hall, 1969.

Hilleman, M. R., and A. A. Tytell, "The Induction of Interferon," *Scientific American*, July, 1971.

Huxley, H. E., "The Mechanism of Muscular Contraction," *Scientific American*, December, 1965.

Jaques, H. E., *Living Things, How to Know Them*, Dubuque, Iowa, Wm. C. Brown, 1960.

Jerne, Niels K., "The Immune System," *Scientific American*, July, 1973.

Laki, K., "The Clotting of Fibrinogen," *Scientific American*, March, 1962.

Lerner, Richard A., and Frank J. Dixon, "The Human Lymphocyte as an Experimental Animal," *Scientific American*, June, 1973.

Notkins, Abner L., and H. Koprowski, "How the Immune Response to a Virus Can Cause Disease," *Scientific American*, January, 1973.

Patt, Donald I., and Gail R. Patt, *Comparative Vertebrate Histology*, New York, Harper & Row, 1969.

Reisfeld, R. A., and B. A. Kahan, "Markers of Biological Individuality," *Scientific American*, June, 1972.

Ross, Russell, and Paul Bornstein, "Elastic Fibers in the Body," *Scientific American*, June, 1971.

Solomon, Arthur K., "The State of Water in Red Cells," *Scientific American*, February, 1971.

Szent-Györgyi, A., "Muscle Research," *Scientific American*, June, 1949.

Wilkie, D. R., *Muscle*, New York, St. Martin's Press, 1968.

Zucker, M. B., "Blood Platelets," *Scientific American*, February, 1961.

5

The Living Community

An individual organism does not live alone. Each living thing is part of a *biotic community*, a group of organisms inhabiting a common environment and interacting with each other. Each species, moreover, fits into its community in a unique functional way—it has a specific *niche*. The specific part of a biotic community in which each organism lives is called a *habitat*. Between the seashore and high mountain peaks, we can observe many different communities such as ponds, forests, lakes, and deserts.

One example of a biotic community is a quiet ocean tidepool. Although a casual observation frequently will permit us to identify specific organisms, it will not help us to understand the interactions of these organisms or their relationships and contributions to their environment. This understanding comes only with close study and time. Usually an obvious member of the tidepool is the sea anemone. Patient observation might show the anemone devouring a fish, which had probably just eaten tiny microcrustaceans. The microcrustaceans might have just fed on certain algae cells that manufacture their food by trapping sunlight and using raw materials from the environment. We might see a chiton rasping algae from a rock or mussels passively filtering water over their gills to remove tiny food particles. Any barnacles in the water would show rhythmical beating of their appendages as they capture food. Some worms and crabs would find temporary homes under rocks and in crevices, while others were sheltered under large filaments of algae.

If newcomers, say a particular species of snails, join this community, we might see the *population* of this species undergo a specific growth pattern over a period of time. If the tide is out for quite a while and the sun is bright, the water becomes several degrees warmer. This condition is most unfavorable for study; in fact, activity may virtually cease. When the tide flows again, however, it brings cooler water, oxygen, chemical nutrients, and provides transportation into and out of the community for certain organisms. If we were to microscopically examine the water periodically, we could detect special sex cells from some of the organisms, such as the anemones. These appear at approximately the same time each year, and some of the sex cells unite for fertilization, thus producing new organisms.

All members of the community ultimately, of course, will die and even though parts of their bodies may be eaten by scavengers such as crabs, bacteria will also assist in the decomposition process. Thus the tidepool, like all communities, shows a definite organization with each organism contributing in an indispensable way. Cyclical patterns are also evident even though many of the individual chemical cycles, such as nitrogen and phosphorus, are not as obvious as those of the salinity and tide.

Although many relationships have been discussed in this brief account of the tidepool community, it is much more complex. A better understanding of a community can be gained by examining some of the associations and processes in detail. The area of science concerned with the relationships of organisms to one another and to their environments is known as *ecology*. Recently man has become acutely aware of the consequences of his activities for natural environments, and this awareness has led to an increased concern for *human ecology*. But before we consider the impact of human beings on nature, we must have some background in the general principles of ecology.

ENERGY FLOW AND CHEMICAL CYCLING

THE ECOSYSTEM

Each living community depends on energy for its structure and function, and these energy relationships follow a similar pattern in each community. The flow of energy is always in one direction, whereas the chemical materials involved circulate in cycles. Energy flows from organism to organism whereas the cycling of chemicals involves not only living forms (the biotic) but also the nonliving (the abiotic) environment. The biotic and the abiotic together form an *ecosystem*, and through this integrated system of energy flow and the cycling of materials the ecosystem is maintained.

ENERGY FLOW

In any ecosystem chemicals must be converted into living matter and energy storage

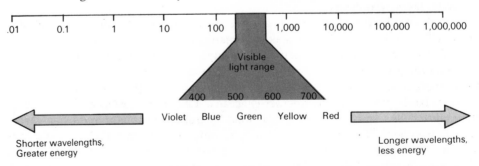

Figure 5–1   The electromagnetic spectrum. Wavelengths are given in millimicrons (1/1000 of a micron). Visible light is used in photosynthesis; thus only a small part of the sun's energy (about 2 percent) can be used by producers.

118

products. In general, large molecules, such as $C_6H_{12}O_6$, are synthesized from smaller molecules found in soil, air, and water. Organisms capable of performing these syntheses are referred to as *producers*—such as plants on land and plants and algae in aquatic environments. Although the flow of energy is not cyclical in a community, the sun provides a continuing source of energy (Figure 5-1). Producers or *autotrophs* (self-feeding) always contain chlorophyll and/or other light-trapping compounds that permit the utilization of the sun's energy. Simply stated, the basic process called *photosynthesis* (Figure 5-2) is one in which solar energy is converted to chemical energy in the form of simple carbohydrates. After photosynthesis takes place, metabolic processes convert these simple sugars into more complex sugars, proteins, and fats. In these forms, energy and material stored by producers are then transferred to *consumers*—first to the plant-eating herbivores and through them to the carnivores. These *heterotrophs* (other-feeding) are also known as primary and secondary consumers.

Although we have a constant source of energy from the sun, the chemical elements are not in such constant supply. Therefore a

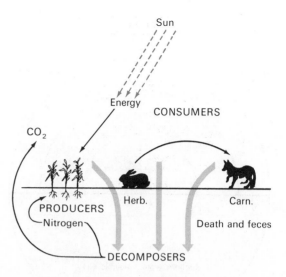

Figure 5-3 Relationships among members of an ecosystem.

very important element of any ecosystem is the group of bacteria and fungi, known as *decomposers*, that break down and decompose dead organisms. It is through decomposition that the necessary chemical nutrients are returned to the environment, and without it all life would eventually cease to exist. The important decomposers are found in the organic layer of the soil and at the bottom of ponds and lakes.

Thus we see a structural and functional organization within an ecosystem that begins with the producers, which provide food (and energy) for the consumers. The consumers, as well as many producers, are broken down by decomposers which return raw materials to the producers. Each group of organisms in the community derives energy from the group preceding it in this chain of events (Figure 5-3), and these represent *trophic levels*. The principal trophic levels in two ecosystems, a fresh water lake and a deciduous forest illustrate trophic levels and their relationship to the abiotic (Figure 5-4). A pyramid is frequently used to show the relative masses of the various components of an ecosystem (Figure 5-5). In the movement from one trophic level to another, 100 percent efficiency is not achieved and energy is lost from the system along the way. For example, a specific

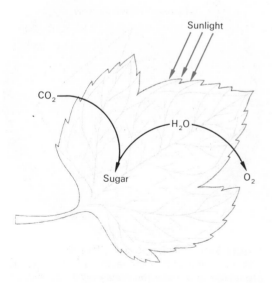

Figure 5-2 Basic scheme of photosynthesis.

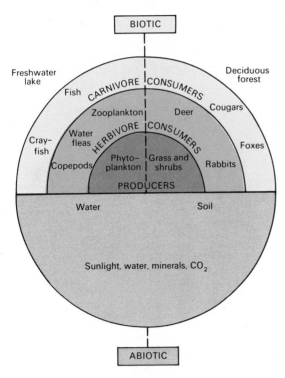

Figure 5–4 Principal trophic levels in two eco-systems—freshwater and terrestrial.

mass of plants will support a group of herbi-vores much smaller in mass than the plants and fewer carnivores in turn will be supported by the herbivores.

A specific structural organization as de-scribed here can be observed in a forest where the trees and shrubs are the primary pro-ducers. Plants supply food to deer and other herbivores who in turn are eaten by the carnivores such as cougars, wolves, and coyotes.

FOOD CHAINS AND WEBS

The flow of energy from one trophic level to another is called a *food chain*. For example, the following food relationship is important to game-management experts:

Plants → Deer → Cougars

To farmers in some areas the following food chain is recognized:

Crops → Field mice → Hawks and/or coyotes

Serious results can occur when one element of a food chain is disturbed. If bounties permit excessive cougar hunting, a deer population in a specific area may increase to the point where insufficient food is available to sustain the herd. Nutritional problems and crowding result so that a large herd of deer is produced which contains mostly weak and emaciated members. If the coyotes around a farming area are poisoned because they have killed a few sheep, the field mice population may increase to the point where they severely damage the grain crop, which may cause the death of many more sheep.

Many instances are known in which man has imported a predator to control nuisance animals such as rats. Soon the predator may destroy the pests to the point that he must feed on some of the more desirable animals. Man must be very careful when he interferes with a natural order and must realize that it is possible to change the entire ecological re-lationship by tampering with one element of a particular ecosystem. It is often necessary to correct a situation in which the activities of man and some of his domesticated animals have disturbed what were once natural con-ditions.

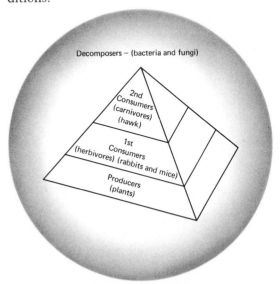

Figure 5–5 The biomass relationships in an eco-system. Fungi and bacteria decompose all dead organisms and make the decay products available for reuse.

120

Most animals do not rely on one species for their food source but usually feed on several different organisms. A hawk, for example, will eat squirrels, mice, rabbits, and large insects. Because consumers do not rely solely on one plant or animal for food, there are many interrelated food chains. These make up a *food web* which can be very complex (Figure 5–6).

CHEMICAL CYCLES

In addition to the one-way flow of energy through the ecosystem (from producers through consumers to decomposers), life also depends on nutrients and other chemical compounds that are cycled from the soil, through atmosphere and living organisms, and back to the soil. Perhaps the best known and most studied of these are water, oxygen, carbon, nitrogen, phosphorus, sulfur, and calcium. Some of these will be discussed here to show how they are made available to living organisms.

Oxygen

Oxygen is important not only as a structural component of sugar, fat, and protein molecules

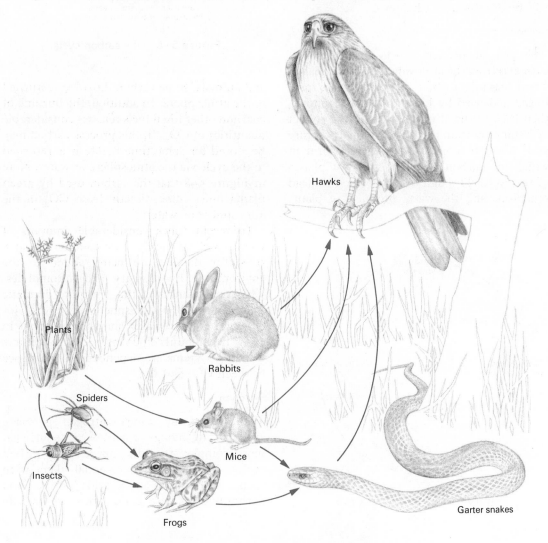

Figure 5–6 Part of a food web in a forest community.

121

but also as a necessary agent for the process, called oxidation, by which energy is released from foods. We know that oxygen is released as green plants manufacture food. It can be demonstrated that this oxygen comes from water taken in by the plant. Oxygen from the atmosphere (or from water in the case of aquatic forms) is used in the process of respiration by living organisms. Within cells the oxygen unites with hydrogen from sugar molecules to produce water. This water can be used again by green plants in photosynthesis and the cycle continues (Figure 5–7). The details of photosynthesis and respiration will be discussed in Chapter 6.

Carbon

The general pattern of the movement of carbon is from the atmosphere to green plants, where organic carbon compounds are produced and used by both plants and animals, then back to the atmosphere as a by-product of respiration from plants and animals (Figure 5–8). Carbon dioxide (CO_2) is the form in which the carbon circulates in most phases of the cycle. Through decomposition of dead organisms and the waste products of plants

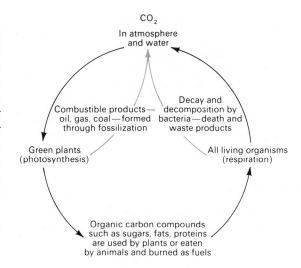

Figure 5–8 The carbon cycle.

and animals, some carbon dioxide is returned to the atmosphere. In addition, the burning of coal and other fossil fuels releases considerable quantities of CO_2. In this process carbon may be stored for some time before it is returned to the cycle via the atmosphere or water. Note in Figure 5–8 that the carbon used by green plants must come directly from CO_2 in the atmosphere or water.

In recent times considerable amounts of CO_2 as well as highly toxic compounds such as sulfur dioxide are being added to the environment by industry and automobiles. The consequences of this are quite dramatic in the smog-filled atmospheres of most major cities. In fact, even CO_2 may be hazardous in excessive amounts since many control centers in living systems are dependent on a balance between CO_2 and O_2.

Nitrogen

The process by which nitrogen is made available to living organisms is somewhat more complex than the oxygen and carbon cycles. Nitrogen is an essential element in such compounds as amino acids, purines, and pyrimidines. These compounds are usually

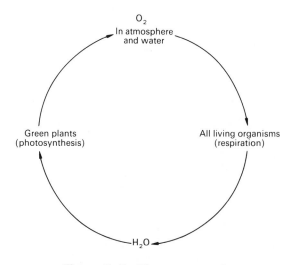

Figure 5–7 The oxygen cycle.

produced first in green plants and then made available to animals. Although nitrogen makes up 78 percent of the atmosphere, it is not directly available to the majority of living organisms since much of the nitrogen used by green plants must be in the form of nitrates. A slight amount of direct *nitrogen fixing* does take place, however, in a small number of organisms in some groups of bacteria, blue-green algae, and fungi. Lightning can also fix a small amount of nitrogen. Most of the nitrogen made available to living organisms originates through two principal routes—(1) through the production of *nitrate* and (2) through the action of *nodule bacteria* on the roots of certain plants (Figure 5–9).

Some free-living microorganisms in the soil and water can convert atmospheric nitrogen to ammonia (NH_3). This ammonia is either used by these organisms or given off to the environment. Another group of bacteria can convert the ammonia to *nitrite* (NO_2), and a third group can convert the nitrite to *nitrate* (NO_3). In the form of nitrates, nitrogen can be used by green plants. The ammonia, nitrites, and nitrates are usually present as ions (NH_4^+, NO_2^-, NO_3^-) which can unite with other ions of opposite charges to produce salts. Other sources of ammonia are also available to nitrite-forming bacteria such as the ammonia produced in animal wastes (urine) and in decomposition. This sequence may be summarized as follows:

Decomposing organisms
N$_2$-fixing bacteria ⟶ NH$_3$ → NO$_2$ → NO$_3$
Waste products ⟶
(available to green plants)

Certain plants, such as members of the pea family (legumes) and alder trees, have bacteria attached to nodules on the root structure which can take free nitrogen directly from the soil and convert it into organic nitrogen (Figure 5–9). This nitrogen, in the form of amino

Figure 5–9 Roots of birdsfoot trefoil, a legume, with nodules containing bacteria. (Courtesy of Nitragin Co., Inc., Milwaukee.)

acids, can be passed directly into the plants possessing these nodules. Thus legumes and alders can grow in soil that lacks usable nitrogen.

Although some bacteria are required for supplying nitrogen in usable form to living organisms, others are responsible for an opposite process known as *denitrification*. These bacteria can convert ammonia, nitrites, and nitrates to free nitrogen which is released to the atmosphere. Although it is unnecessary for nitrogen to return to the atmosphere to complete its cycle (as in the carbon cycle), some, nevertheless, is released as free nitrogen. Figure 5–10 is an attempt to summarize the complex details involved in the circulation of nitrogen in an ecosystem.

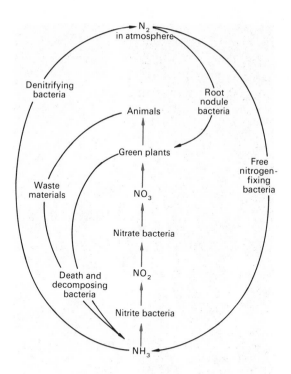

Figure 5–10 The nitrogen cycle.

Phosphorus

The major reservoirs of phosphorus are the rock formations of the earth's crust. Slowly, through the processes of weathering and leaching, phosphates are returned to the soil and the sea. Dissolved phosphate can be incorporated into living organisms, usually into plants and then into animals (Figure 5–11).

Phosphorus, in this form, is essential to the functioning of the metabolic processes that convert food to usable energy, energy transfer, and the structure of the hereditary material. In addition it is a major component of bones and teeth. In some aquatic environments, phosphates may be the "limiting factor" for growth and reproduction at certain times of the year. Since phosphorus is eroded away, phosphates are often added to lawns and farmland when the soil has become depleted.

When organisms excrete or decompose,

phosphates are put back into circulation. Some phosphate, however, is deposited in sediments, and the deep, rather insoluble sediments are lost to living organisms until an upheaval occurs. Eventually these will be returned to the cycle, although some concern has been expressed that gradually we are permanently losing more phosphates to the deep sediments. Shallow sediments often redissolve and may be brought up by the currents and waves of the oceans. Land-dwelling organisms contribute to the terrestrial phosphate deposits and thereby assist in maintaining the cycle. Fish eaten by man and birds help to return phosphorus from the sea to the land.

CHANGES IN A COMMUNITY— SUCCESSION

All environments change constantly. In addition to the many daily and yearly changes, every ecosystem undergoes a definite series of biological changes related to climate, parent soil material, and organisms living in adjacent areas. The home gardener, for instance, knows that weeds will soon overtake his garden if it is left unattended. A familiar sight in certain regions of the western United States is the swath cut through the evergeen forests for power lines (Figure 5–12). In this process all vegetation is removed from a strip that is 50 to 100 feet wide and may extend for miles in length. Within a short time herbaceous plants, such as grasses and fireweed, cover the strip and are soon followed by blackberry, salmon berry, currant, and other shrubs. Mingling with these plants and even replacing them in time are the deciduous alder and willow trees. But after a few years these trees will be crowded out by evergreen species such as Douglas fir, western hemlock, or western red cedar, which occupied these areas before the clearing was done. Over a

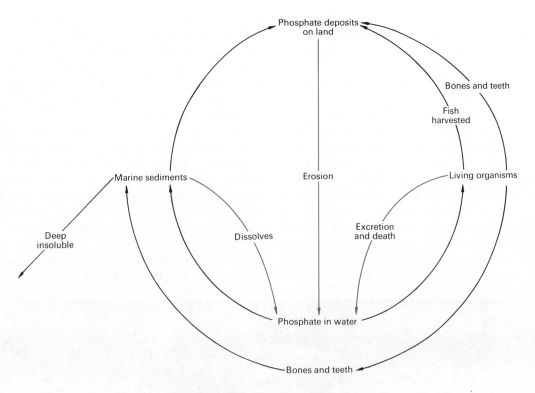

Figure 5–11 The phosphorus cycle.

Figure 5–12 Illustration of the successive reforestation of an area. The right of way beneath this power line was cleared of all vegetation. (Grant Heilman.)

period of years, therefore, one community will replace another until a relatively stable community, the evergreen forest, again inhabits these strips.

Analysis shows these events to be an orderly and sequential pattern that would repeat itself if the trees were again removed. Such a series of uniform vegetational changes through these several stages is known as ecological *succession*. The final occupants of an area make up a stable, essentially self-reproducing community called the *climax*. One group of plants prepares the way, chemically and physically, for the next group until this climax is attained. The series of changes that occurred in the cleared forest areas is an example of *secondary* succession since the land was previously occupied by plants. Succession in a new environment or on any area devoid of organisms is called *primary* succession. Although we are concerned here mostly with the plants involved in succession, we should note that the animal population in a particular area is determined in part by the plants.

One primary succession site is on bare rock, and this is generally a slow process depending on the hardness of the rock and the water available. The first occupants of the area are usually lichens and mosses, which contribute to the actual breakdown of the rock and the preparation of the area for later colonization (Figure 5–13). Soil collects in crevices permitting seeds from nearby herbaceous plants to gain a foothold, and the estab-

Figure 5–13 Early stage of primary succession in which rock is broken into soil by plants. The plants are primarily lichens and mosses. (Russell K. LeBarron; courtesy of U.S. Department of Agriculture, Forest Service.)

126

lishment of a rather specific type of vegetation begins (Figure 5–14). Grasses then can move in, followed by small shrubs, then larger shrubs, and eventually trees. When this process occurs along the western coast of the United States, deciduous, broad-leaved trees usually move in first to be succeeded later by evergreen, cone-bearing trees. In the Mid-west, on the East Coast, and in other parts of the United States, the climax vegetation will be different, depending on the soil, the climate, and the specific plants in the various areas. These climax communities will be discussed later in this section.

Another succession pattern is shown by a lake or pond. All lakes theoretically are in the process of being converted to land and the time required for this conversion will vary. As streams carry soil into a lake, the bottom begins to build up and change. Also plants, such as tussock sedges, cattails, rushes, or sphagnum moss, may grow out from the shore over the water's edge to form a mat. All of these plants, through the intertwining of their roots, can collect soil and hold humus material in place. Soon the way is prepared for other plants such as shrubs of the heath family to gain a foothold. At the same time a buildup is occurring from the bottom as the deposition of soil and dead plants and animals continues. After a time, larger shrubs and trees can move into this newly formed land area (Figure 5–15). Peat bogs in the northern United States and Canada are the result of this type of succession (Figure 5–16). If you have never done so, you should visit a peat bog to witness this striking example of succession. The quaking, resilient floating border of the bog presents a unique environment. Owing to the incomplete decay of organic matter, nitrogen in a usable form is insufficient. A variety of insectivorous plants such as the sundew, pitcher plant, and Venus's-flytrap inhabit bog communities. These plants trap insects to obtain nitrogen from the animal's proteins (Figure 5–17).

Although the basic patterns of succession are similar, different plant species are involved in different geographical areas. Certain stages may be accelerated or arrested in a successional series when man interferes or pollutes the environment. For example, mining, farming, and logging may seriously alter the environment from the natural state.

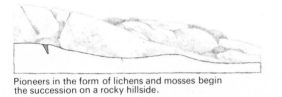

Pioneers in the form of lichens and mosses begin the succession on a rocky hillside.

More soil is produced and larger plants (herbs) can move in.

Next, shrubs requiring more soil can grow here.

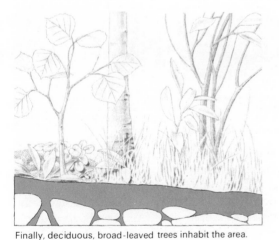

Finally, deciduous, broad-leaved trees inhabit the area.

Figure 5–14 Ecological succession on a rocky hillside.

127

Deposition begins and encroachment from the edges by sphagnum moss, the pioneer.

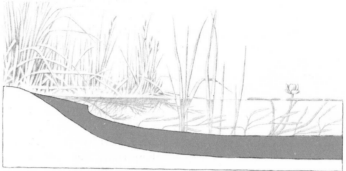

Deposition continues and a mat of mutual support from the moss, sedges, and trailing heaths forms.

The lake has been completely succeeded and a bog remains in the middle; soon this will be succeeded by shrubs and trees.

Figure 5–15   Succession of a lake by land.

THE MAJOR COMMUNITIES OF THE WORLD

BIOMES

The terrestrial regions of the earth are sometimes classified according to the dominant plant and animal life inhabiting them. Each area, with a unique group of climax plants and related animal species, is termed a *biome*. Generally, six principal biomes may be recognized: tundra, northern coniferous forest, deciduous forest, tropical forest, grassland, and desert (Figure 5–18). An overall view of the major biomes is presented in Figure 5–19.

Tundra

This biome stretches across the continents generally above 60 degrees north latitude.

128

Figure 5-16 A sphagnum, tamarack, and spruce bog in the northern United States. (Grant Heilman.)

Figure 5-17 The pitcher plant from a peat bog. These plants trap insects.

Since it is characterized by snow, ice, and frozen soil most of the year, the plants and animals that live here must have high resistance to cold. The tundra is virtually treeless and consists primarily of lichens, mosses, sedges, heaths, dwarfed willows, and a few grasses. Seasonal thawing of the permafrost is of considerable importance to plant distribution in the arctic tundra. In general, the frozen soil will thaw from only a few inches to a few feet; therefore, only shallow-rooted plants can survive. Moreover, the flat terrain with a frozen subsoil produces excessive surface water and shallow summer bogs. Caribou, arctic hares, foxes, lemmings, and migratory birds are common (Figure 5-20).

Northern Coniferous Forest

Characterized by coniferous trees this region forms a band across North America and Eurasia below the tundra. It also extends into the Cascade, Rocky, and Appalachian Mountains of the United States. These evergreen trees consist of pine, fir, cedar, hemlock, and

Figure 5–18 Climax vegetation zones of North America. Note that a specific type of vegetation develops in a specific climatic zone. (Map by Robert Winter.)

Legend:
- Tundra
- Boreal Forest
- Coastal Forest
- Rocky Mountain Forest
- Grasslands
- Hemlock–Hardwood Forest
- Desert Grass and Scrub
- Deciduous Forest
- S. E. Evergreen Forest
- Wet and Dry Tropical Forest
- Desert

spruce. In some areas these trees grow so dense that little light reaches the forest floor, and few shrubs are found. However, several shade resistant, broadleaf species such as vine maple and spring wild flowers are common. Another characteristic feature of northern forests is the numerous lakes and sphagnum peat bogs (Figure 5–16). Although temperatures and

precipitation vary throughout this biome, the plants must be able to withstand some freezing temperatures and often heavy snowfall. In addition the length of the growing season varies from a few months in the coldest areas to almost the full year along the Pacific Coast where the climate is moderated by the ocean. The coniferous forest is an excellent habitat

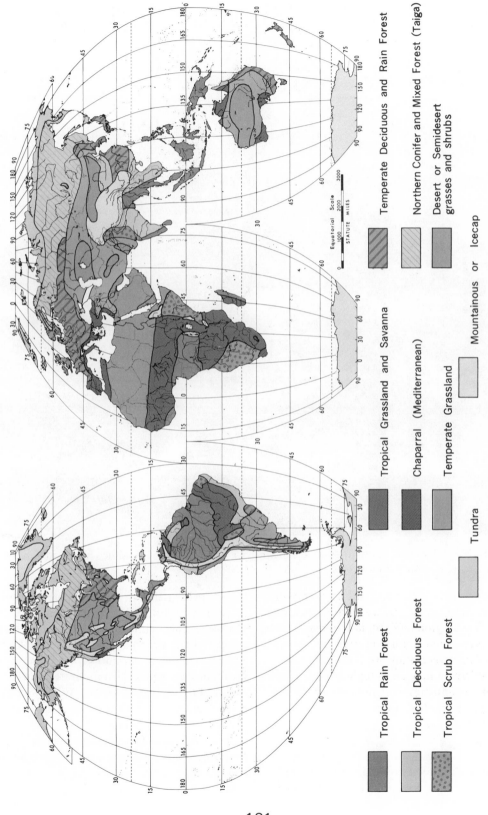

Figure 5–19 Major biomes of the world. (Map by Robert Winter.)

Tropical Rain Forest

Tropical Deciduous Forest

Tropical Scrub Forest

Tropical Grassland and Savanna

Chaparral (Mediterranean)

Temperate Grassland

Tundra

Temperate Deciduous and Rain Forest

Northern Conifer and Mixed Forest (Taiga)

Desert or Semidesert grasses and shrubs

Mountainous or Icecap

Equatorial Scale
0   1000   2000   3000
STATUTE MILES

Figure 5–20 Tundra of northern Alaska showing an isolated stand of spruce trees growing on a protected slope. (Steve McCutcheon.)

for elk, deer, grouse, rabbits, squirrels, mountain lions, and birds (Figure 5–21). In areas such as Washington's Olympic Peninsula and eastern Asia, high annual rainfall allows the growth of lush vegetation. In these *rain forests* the precipitation may be as high as 140 inches per year, producing the humid conditions necessary for the lush growth of mosses and ferns (Figure 5–22).

Deciduous Forest

Deciduous hardwood trees are the dominant vegetation in this biome. These forests are found principally in north central Europe, eastern Asia, and the eastern United States. Hickory, oak, elm, beech, and maple are typical of the broadleaf species in the United States. Annual precipitation between 30 and 60 inches as well as a temperate climate are critical factors in this biome. When temperatures drop in the autumn, most of the trees and shrubs shed their leaves.

The deciduous forests of the eastern United States are quite complex since varying altitudes, rainfall patterns, and soil types allow the establishment of many different trees and

Figure 5–21 Northern coniferous forest in Idaho: alpine fir, Engelmann spruce, and whitebark pine. (A. T. Boisen; courtesy of U.S. Department of Agriculture, Forest Service.)

shrubs. In the Appalachian and Great Smoky Mountains, for example, northern hardwoods may be closely bordered by and mixed with hemlock, oak, and spruce-fir stands. Southern pine forests extend to the southeast at lower elevations. The open stands of southern pine are actually subclimax forests and must be maintained by selective cutting and burning, or they will be succeeded by live oak and magnolia trees.

In the northern reaches of this biome, on the North American continent, temperatures range from 109°F to below −20°F, and annual precipitation averages about 30 inches. The common trees of this region are spruce, hem-

Figure 5–22 Rain forest in Olympic National Park. Note the lush moss growth on the vine maple. Spruce and hemlock are in the background. (National Park Service; courtesy of U.S. Department of the Interior.)

lock, white pine, sugar maple, basswood, oak, and birch. Also characteristic of this area are numerous sphagnum peat bogs. Frogs, salamanders, turtles, many snakes, lizards, squirrels, foxes, songbirds, rabbits, deer, and raccoons are representative animals (Figure 5-23).

Tropical Forest

The tropical forest is characterized by high rainfall during most of the year (up to 100 inches). The major regions include central Africa, southern Asia, and northern Central America. The warm, humid climate supports broadleaf evergreen plants, and we generally refer to this area as a *jungle*. A distinctive feature of a jungle is its stratification into an overstory and generally two understory levels. The tallest trees (about 120 feet) form an open canopy, but the second and third crown levels cut out most of the available light to the jungle floor. Ferns and herbaceous plants are common on the jungle floor, along with saplings of the upper strata. The animals may include monkeys, various snakes, anteaters, tropical birds, and large carnivores such as lions, tigers, and leopards (Figure 5–24).

Grassland

Grassland covers much of the world extending through north central Eurasia, north central and southern Africa, central United States, central South America, and the northern half of Australia. The irregular rainfall of this region averages between 10 and 30 inches annually (Figure 5–25). Strong winds, common throughout the grasslands, help to increase dryness and discourage the establishment of trees. The western border of the Great Plains has much less annual precipitation than the southern and eastern. Because of this difference in rainfall, short grasses dominate in the western regions, and longer grass species are found in the east. Large herds of bison and antelope once roamed the grasslands. With the arrival of man, however, the herds were restricted and destroyed by hunters. Early efforts at farming left much of the prairie

devastated due to the loss of topsoil through erosion by wind and water. Modern farmers using contour plowing and crop-rotation methods now have most of the prairie under cultivation or used for grazing. Grazing animals dominate in this biome; other common species include jack rabbits, antelope, and prairie dogs. The grasslands of Africa, commonly known as *savannah*, undergo a period of high rainfall, but several months of severe drought limit the establishment of trees. A variety of animals is characteristic of the African grassland.

Desert

Deserts are geographic regions characterized by extremely low rainfall, generally less than 10 inches per year. Rainfall is not only sparse but uneven in most deserts, and average rainfall figures are often misleading due to spring and summer flash floods. Although more than an inch of rain may fall in a short period, most of the water is unavailable to plants because of rapid runoff or high evaporation rates. The major deserts are found in North Africa, southern Europe, the interior of Australia, the southwestern United States, and Mexico. A strip of desert is also located along the ocean borders of Chile and Peru in South America, and another is found in the interior of Argentina (Figure 5–19).

The deserts of North America are often classified as cool or hot (Figure 5–26). The Great Basin Desert located in parts of Washington, Oregon, Idaho, Wyoming, Utah, and Nevada is essentially above 3,000 feet elevation. The annual rainfall of this cool, high desert varies between 8 and 15 inches, maximum temperatures average about 105°F, and early morning dew is not uncommon. Winter low temperatures may drop to −30°F in many areas. Sagebrush, cheatgrass, and saltbrush are the major plants. Many deserts such as the Washington and Oregon Great Basin areas are the result of a "rain shadow." The high mountain ranges bordering these deserts cause the cool, moist air to drop much of its water load on the west side, thereby creating an area of low

Figure 5-23 Deciduous oak-hickory forest in Virginia. (E. S. Shipp; courtesy of U.S. Department of Agriculture, Forest Service.)

Figure 5-24 Tropical forest in Hawaii. (R. E. Nelson; courtesy of U.S. Department of Agriculture, Forest Service.)

Figure 5–25 Mixed-grass prairie in Nebraska. (Bluford W. Muir; courtesy of U.S. Department of Agriculture, Forest Service.)

Figure 5–26 The deserts of North America. (*a*) Sagebrush community of a cool, high desert in eastern Oregon. (Courtesy of Matt Brown.)

136

(*b*) Mojave yucca and some sagebrush in Joshua Tree National Monument desert in Colorado. (Richard Weymouth Brooks.)

(*c*) Saguaro cactus in the Tucson mountain area of the Arizona desert. (Richard Weymouth Brooks.)

137

rainfall on the other side (see Figure 5–27).

The Mohave Desert in southern Nevada, eastern California, and the northwest quarter of Arizona is hotter than the great Basin Desert, sometimes reaching 115°F; the annual rainfall is lower and more uneven (4 to 8 inches). Common plants of this region include creosote bush, yucca, joshua trees, and various small cacti. Two more hot desert areas occur to the south of the Mohave—the Sonoran, principally in southern Arizona and California, Baja California, and Sonora, Mexico; and the

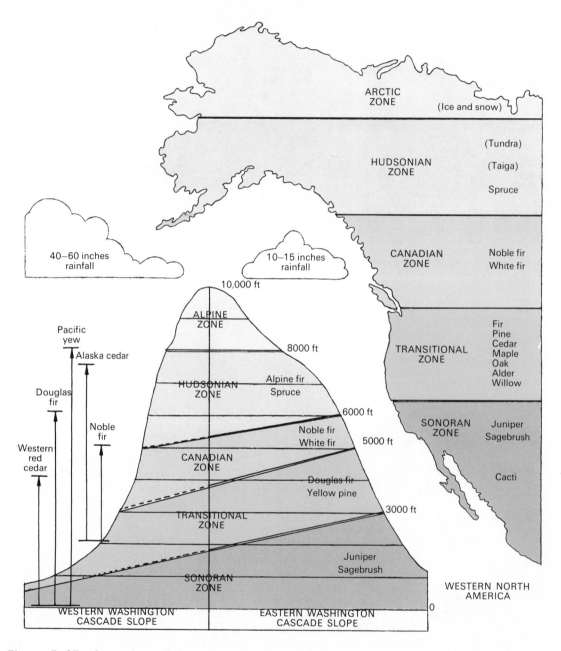

Figure 5–27 Comparison of the vegetation zones of the eastern and western slopes of the North Cascade Mountains. The eastern slope is further compared to the continental north-south distribution.

Chihuahuan (chi-wa'wan) of central New Mexico and the Mexican Plateau. Here the temperatures may soar to 125°F; there is a very low annual rainfall, except in some areas near the Mexican border where 10 to 16 inches are common. A cactus common to the southern Mohave and Sonoran Deserts is the giant saguaro, which often attains heights of 20 to 40 feet and a weight of nearly 10 tons. The hot deserts also support green-barked paloverde trees; creosote bush; mesquite; smaller cacti such as pincushion, prickly pear, and barrel; and a few hardy grasses and flowers.

Of particular interest are the adaptations of both plants and animals to these rather hostile conditions. Some plants (paloverde) lose their leaves during the hottest months, whereas others have small, waxy, or hairy leaves which retard evaporation. Most flowers are perennial and can withstand seed losses due to drought. Deep taproots and extensive, spreading root systems are common. Some animals such as the kangaroo rat have such efficient kidneys that they never need to drink water. Animals typically found in the desert biome include insects, rabbits, quail, doves, rattlesnakes, scorpions, lizards, and coyotes.

LIFE ZONES

In addition to the biomes another classification system for the distribution of plants and animals is sometimes used. This system is especially useful in the mountainous regions of western North America. In the 1890s, C. Hart Merriam, working in the San Francisco Peaks area of northern Arizona, recognized a definite distribution range according to altitude among the plants and animals. He further recognized the correlation between the altitudinal pattern and the north-south distribution of similar species according to latitude. For example, Merriam recognized the similarities between plant species living in the alpine mountain regions and those in the Arctic. Using North America as a model, he designated the Arctic-Alpine, Hudsonian, Canadian, transitional, and upper and lower Sonoran (Mexico) *life zones*. Merriam was convinced that the major

factor in this distribution was temperature. Although most ecologists today feel that temperature alone is not a sufficient basis for the stratigraphy of plants and animals, the Merriam life zones are still useful in the western, mountainous states.

A comparison can be made between the vegetation on the eastern and western slopes of the North Cascade Range and the vegetation distributed according to north latitude (Figure 5-27). On the western slopes, which receive 40 to 60 inches of annual precipitation, the typical life-zone pattern is not as distinct as on the eastern side. Although certain species of conifers show definite altitudinal preferences —western red cedar (0–4000 feet), noble fir (2000–5000 feet), Douglas fir (0–6000 feet), and Alaska cedar (2000–7500 feet)—the Pacific yew occurs from 0–8000 feet (treeline). This coastal slope distribution is apparently produced by high rainfall, generally cooler temperatures, and an ability to withstand "snow load." The distribution of plants on the eastern slopes, however, shows a definite correlation with the north-south plant distribution on the continent in accordance with Merriam's scheme.

THE FRESHWATER ENVIRONMENT— LAKES AND PONDS

Lakes and ponds are familiar features of the landscape and occur in practically every biome (Figure 5-28). They vary in size from less than an acre to many miles, and in depth from several feet to almost a mile. The origins of lakes are varied. Many are the direct or indirect result of glaciers, whereas natural or man-made dams may cause depressions to fill with water. Parts of meandering rivers, cut off from the main stream, can also result in lakes. Lakes are often classified on the basis of the amount of organic matter they contain. *Eutrophic* lakes are relatively shallow with a rich accumulation of organic products. *Oligotrophic* lakes, on the other hand, are generally deep and often have rocky, steep sides. The supply of circulating nutrients, such as phosphates, is often low in these lakes, and the ratio of organic

Figure 5–28 Crater Lake in southern Oregon, an example of a deep, oligotrophic lake. (Alan Pitcairn, from Grant Heilman.)

materials to the volume of water is also very low. Additional characteristics of these two types of lakes will be given in the following topical discussions on lakes.

Almost every biology class has access to a body of fresh water which can be observed, and a considerable amount of fundamental biology can be learned from the study of a lake. Moreover, such an ecosystem provides an excellent opportunity to correlate biological information with physical and chemical data.

LIGHT IN LAKES

The degree to which producers (algae) can photosynthesize depends on the amount of light entering the lake and the depth to which it penetrates. Several methods have been devised to determine the depth of the penetration of light in a body of water. Photoelectric cells and light-sensitive film are two of the

more refined methods. A rather simple method from which comparative data can be obtained is to determine the greatest depth at which the observer can see a round, black and white disc. This disc, known as a *Secchi disc*, provides only a rough estimate of visibility, however, and does not give an actual measurement of light penetration. The amount of organic particles in a lake affects the depth to which the disc can be seen. On the same day, under similar weather conditions, the light penetration in an oligotrophic lake and a eutrophic lake was studied; the Secchi disc was visible to 14 meters in the first lake but could be seen only to 1.5 meters in the second.

TEMPERATURE OF LAKES

The temperature of a lake is affected by solar radiation, thus every temperate lake, whether it is deep or shallow, undergoes a definite cycle of events during a year. In the late winter or early spring when conditions become warmer, the ice, if present that year, melts and the upper waters warm slightly. The water warms to about 4°C and produces a rather uniform temperature situation from the top to the bottom of the lake. Since water reaches its maximum density at 4°C, the water on the bottom of the lake would be 4°C; ice, at 0°C, is lighter and floats on top. Moreover, the water at the bottom of any deep lake is generally 4°C throughout the year. Currents and waves generated by the wind can bring about a thorough mixing of the water, the spring turnover, since the body of water is generally unstable. Soon the warmth of summer produces a warm layer of water on the surface while the lower water remains colder. A sharp drop in temperature often develops at a particular depth in many lakes during the summer period. This region of rapid temperature drop with depth is known as the *thermocline*. In the deep lake mentioned previously, the thermocline was found to lie between 30 and 45 meters, whereas in the shallower lake it occurred between 3.5 and 4.5 meters (Figure 5-29). The body of water above the thermocline is known as the *epilimnion* and that below, the *hypolimnion*. The formation of a thermocline, which produces layering, prevents mixing of these two

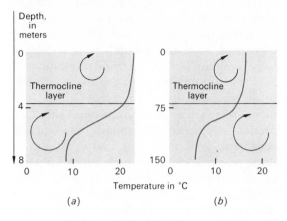

Figure 5–29 Summer temperature structures in two different lakes in Washington. (*a*) Cranberry Lake. (*b*) Lake Chelan.

bodies of water, thereby causing a summer stagnation.

The autumn of the year brings cooler temperatures and the surface waters begin to cool, thus bringing about a uniform temperature structure again. At this time mixing can again take place through the currents and waves produced by the wind, causing an autumn turnover. As winter begins, an ice layer may form to produce a winter stagnation period. If ice does not form, some mixing of the water may continue throughout the winter since the temperature remains fairly uniform from the top to the bottom of the lake. The general sequence of temperature changes throughout the year is summarized in Figure 5-30. If movement of the water from top to bottom of a lake did not occur, materials could not be circulated and interchanged within the total body of water. Seasonal turnovers provide the opportunity for mixing so that nutrients can be moved up from the bottom while oxygen can be transported to the lower layers. In addition, certain organisms can be distributed about the lake through overturning.

OXYGEN IN LAKES

The oxygen content at the various depths in a lake provides some indication of the *productivity* of that lake. Productivity here refers to the ability of the lake to produce organic material from inorganic substances. The upper part of a lake is usually the region for autotrophism, while heterotrophism occurs in the lower part (where light does not penetrate). Systematic oxygen determinations often reveal this, especially in eutrophic lakes.

Oxygen content in lakes can be determined readily by taking samples from different depths and subjecting them to chemical analyses such as the Hach or Winkler method. Oxygen levels are usually given in terms of milliliters or milligrams of oxygen per liter of water (ml/l or mg/l). The temperature structure may have a great deal to do with the amount of oxygen in certain parts of a lake especially during the summer when the hypo-

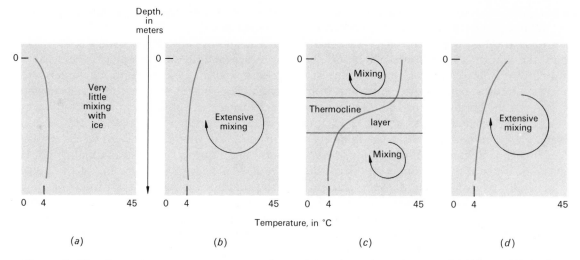

Figure 5–30 General temperature structure of most lakes throughout the year. (*a*) Winter. (*b*) Spring. (*c*) Summer. (*d*) Fall.

limnion is not in circulation with the epilimnion. Whether a lake is oligotrophic or eutrophic (high rate of photosynthesis) also determines how much oxygen is available and how it is distributed (Figure 5-31).

Dissolved oxygen in bodies of water comes essentially from two sources—(1) the atmosphere, by mixing when surface disturbances occur; and (2) from photosynthesis, by producers (algae). Anything that enhances mixing, such as winds, will increase the oxygen content of a lake. The temperature of the water is

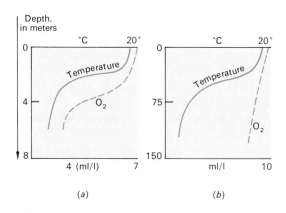

Figure 5–31 Summer temperatures and oxygen levels in two different lakes in Washington. (*a*) Cranberry Lake is eutrophic. (*b*) Lake Chelan is oligotrophic.

also involved since cold water can hold more oxygen than warm water.

OTHER CHEMICAL COMPOUNDS IN A LAKE

Some of the carbon dioxide in a lake is present as the bicarbonate ion since CO_2 readily unites with water. The entire relationship is:

$$CO_2 + H_2O \rightleftharpoons H_2CO_3 \rightleftharpoons HCO_3^- + H^+$$

Large amounts of CO_2 thus can increase the acidity of a body of water. This can happen at certain times of the year when consumer organisms increase in numbers and release large amounts of CO_2 through respiration.

Nitrates and phosphates are also important to the productivity of any ecosystem as was mentioned earlier. Since ammonia is the chief product of protein decomposition in plants and animals, it can be the source of nitrates if the proper bacteria are present. Phosphates, on the other hand, can be a limiting factor especially in oligotrophic lakes where they may be insoluble and unavailable. Some algae can concentrate phosphorus in their systems by the active-transport process even when its concentration is extremely low in the water.

FOOD RELATIONSHIPS

The same food relationships exist in an aquatic community as in a terrestrial system:

Producers → Consumers → Decomposers

A special group of organisms found in aquatic environments is the *plankton*, a large and varied group of mostly small, free-floating organisms. Some plankton, the *phytoplankton*, contain chlorophyll and therefore are capable of synthesizing food. Other types of plankton, the *zooplankton*, must depend on the phytoplankton as their food source. The plankton are essential members of all aquatic food chains since they are the producers and primary consumers. One common chain found in many lakes is:

Phytoplankton → Zooplankton →
Small fish → Large fish

Diatoms are one of the important members of the phytoplankton group, and it can be said that all animal life in the sea depends ultimately on diatoms. Although the statement probably exaggerates this dependency, it does stress the importance of these producers to the overall system. Some of the common plankton members found in lakes are shown in Figures 5–32, 5–33, and 5–34.

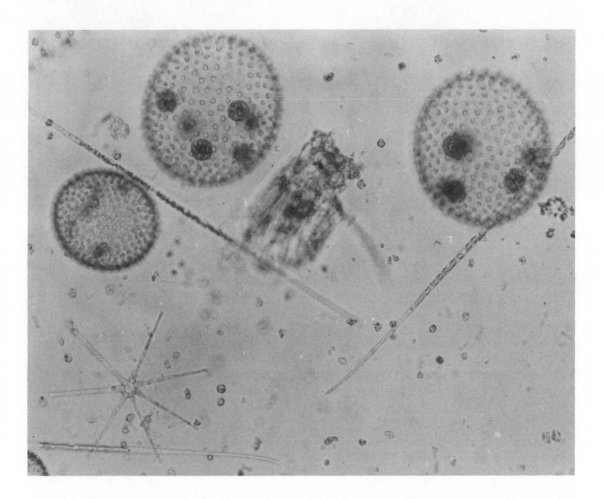

Figure 5–32   Common freshwater plankton: *Volvox*, a rotifer, and diatoms (X 400).

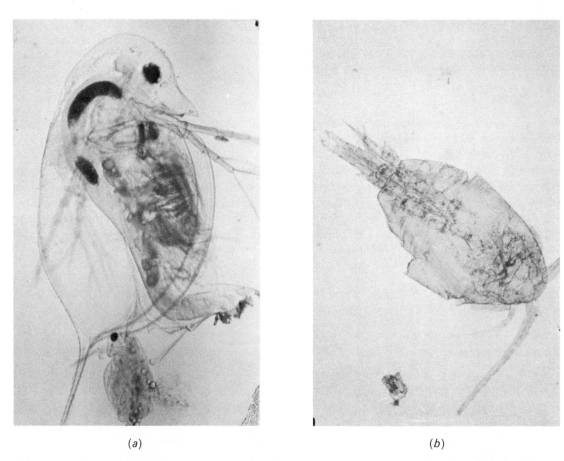

(a) (b)

Figure 5–33 Common freshwater plankton, microcrustaceans (X 50) : (*a*) *Daphnia*. (*b*) *Diaptomus*.

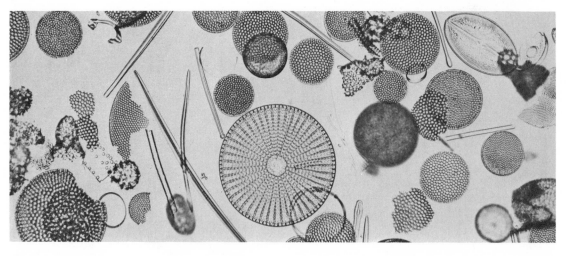

Figure 5–34 Diatoms, important members of the phytoplankton (X 250). (Philip Feinberg, Fellow, New York Microscopical Society.)

144

THE MARINE ENVIRONMENT

Today more and more attention is being focused on the sea, not only as a biome of interesting plants and animals but also as a source of food, minerals, petroleum, and even as a habitat for mankind's booming population. The study of the sea is known as *oceanography* and draws upon all branches of science.

Perhaps the most well-known characteristic of the ocean is its high concentration of salt and mineral ions. The most abundant ions in seawater are sodium and chlorine followed by sulfur, magnesium, and calcium. In addition, all the naturally occurring elements known to man are found in the sea.

The most common ions occurring in seawater, expressed as grams per kilogram, are listed below.

		grams/kilogram
Chloride	Cl^-	19.4
Sodium	Na^+	10.7
Sulfate	$SO_4^=$	2.7
Magnesium	Mg^{++}	1.3
Calcium	Ca^{++}	0.4
Potassium	K^+	0.39
Bicarbonate	HCO_3^-	0.14
Bromide	Br^-	0.065

The dissolved ions in seawater occur in very stable proportions, and the total salinity often is calculated from the determination of the amount of chloride ion. The total salt concentration or salinity is considered to be the total grams of solids, excluding organic material, found in one kilogram of seawater. Salinity of the oceans averages 35 parts per thousand (g/kg). Salinity varies the most in surface water which is affected by land run-off, precipitation, evaporation, and melting polar ice. Salinity is highest in the tropical regions owing to the greater rate of evaporation.

The five major oceans of the earth are the Pacific, Atlantic, Indian, Arctic, and the Antarctic. The oceans are shaped generally like a wash basin in which the rim of the basin represents the continental shelf or the edge of the continents. A relatively shallow area of water, the *neritic province*, covers the continental shelf. The *oceanic province*, the deeper region of the sea, lies off the continental shelf (the major portion of the wash basin in our analogy). The continental shelves extend from the shore an average of 100 miles and form the continental slope, a gradual slope downward to the ocean bottom. The profiles of the Pacific and Atlantic show an irregular topography of ridges, basins, and deep trenches. The Mariana trench, believed to be the deepest, is located east of the Philippine Islands in the Pacific. In 1960 the manned bathyscaph Trieste II descended to a depth of 35,802 feet, man's deepest penetration. Although there are several deep trenches, the average depth of the oceans is two and a half miles (12,000 feet).

Since the amount of photosynthesis is determined by the availability of light, the ocean is often zoned according to light penetration (Figure 5-35). The upper 600 feet, the lighted open-water or *photic* zone, contains the largest number of organisms, and plankton are especially abundant in this zone. The phytoplankton are essentially algal organisms with diatoms, dinoflagellates, blue-green algae, and green algae as the important groups. Although zooplankton species contain representatives from many animal phyla, the crustaceans are easily the most predominant in both total numbers and species. Another category of organisms, the *necton*, are free-swimming organisms such as fish, squid, and whales which live not only in the photic zone but in all parts of the ocean. Below the depth of photosynthetic activity, the rate of food utilization is greater than food production and consequently more oxygen is consumed than is produced by photosynthesis. The depth at which the respiratory and photosynthetic rates are equal is termed the *compensation depth*.

Although the upper 600 feet of the ocean is generally referred to as the photic zone, some light does penetrate to 1,200 feet. The light

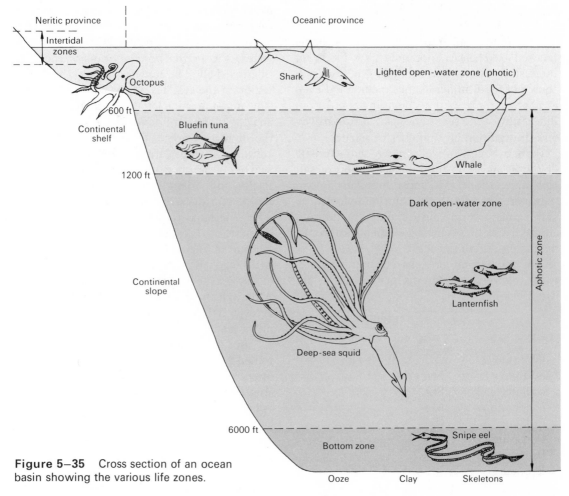

Figure 5–35 Cross section of an ocean basin showing the various life zones.

between 600 and 1,200 feet is insufficient for photosynthesis, however, and thus the area below 600 feet is generally called *aphotic*. Below 1,200 feet is the dark open-water zone which is a region of perpetual darkness. The animals living here are primarily predators that feed on smaller forms and exhibit interesting adaptations. Some, such as the viperfish and pelican fish, possess enormous jaws and sharp teeth, whereas others utilize luminescent organs to attract prey. Below 6,000 feet is the bottom or *benthic* zone. Samples brought to the surface by dredging and net trawling from this depth include such organisms as bacteria, silicious sponges, sea cucumbers, bivalves, polychaete worms, various crustaceans, and brittle stars. Perhaps the newest and most

efficient method of surveying benthic life is that of closed-circuit television (Figure 5-36).

Temperature in the ocean also limits the growth and respiration of both plants and animals. Many organisms are distributed according to their ability to withstand extreme temperatures. In general, however, the necessity for adaptation to great fluctuations in temperature is small when compared to that required in the land environment.

The major temperature variations in the ocean occur in the upper 3,000 feet. The Arctic and Antarctic regions are always near 0°C, the Antarctic being somewhat colder. Although certain seas such as the Red Sea reach surface temperatures above 30°C, the major expanse of ocean surface is 15 to 27°C.

146

Figure 5–36 Modern methods utilized in the study of life at the ocean's bottom. Woods Hole oceanographers lowering a deep-sea camera from the research vessel *Atlantis*. (Courtesy of R. G. Munns and David Owen.)

Since seawater freezes at −1.9°C, the range of surface water is approximately −1.9°C to 30°C. The deeper water below 6,000 feet between the two poles varies only 2 to 3 degrees throughout the seasons of the year. These temperature relationships are illustrated in Figure 5-37, which represents a section of the Atlantic Ocean between the Arctic and Antarctic poles.

A seasonal thermocline also can exist in the oceans, but it is less pronounced than that in freshwater lakes. Several factors that may contribute to this include: (1) the influence of warm or cold currents; (2) the geographical location—tropical, temperate, or polar; and (3) the amount of mixing produced by wave action and upwelling. Because the surface water of the tropical regions is consistently warm, little mixing occurs and a thermocline persists there throughout the year. In temperate and northern latitudes where surface cooling does occur, cyclic temperature profiles

may be established similar to those of freshwater lakes. Vertical mixing and upwelling allows a recirculation of minerals necessary to maintain the phytoplankton. Consequently the greatest amount of plankton and therefore the best fishing are found in the higher northern and southern latitudes.

THE INTERTIDAL ZONES

Tide refers to the vertical rise and fall of coastal waters resulting primarily from the gravitational effects of the moon and sun. The horizontal movements of water, the currents, are a consequence of tide, wind, temperature, and salinity. Plants and animals that live in the intertidal zones are repeatedly covered and uncovered by the cyclical tides. In general, four intertidal life zones may be recognized: (1) spray zone, (2) high-tide zone, (3) mid-tide zone, and (4) low-tide zone (Figure 5-38). (Tides are designated from a

147

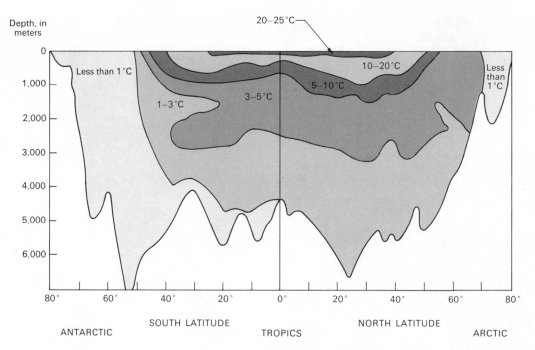

Depth, in meters

20–25 °C

Less than 1 °C

10–20 °C

Less than 1 °C

5–10 °C

1–3 °C

3–5 °C

80° 60° 40° 20° 0° 20° 40° 60° 80°

ANTARCTIC SOUTH LATITUDE TROPICS NORTH LATITUDE ARCTIC

Figure 5–37 Generalized temperature profile of the Atlantic Ocean.

zero point that is calculated as the average of the low tides. This average is indicated as zero on a tide table and consequently a range occurs on each side of this zero reference. Fluctuations above zero are plus tides and those below are minus tides.) The spray zone is never covered by water except during severe storms. The high-tide zone is above tide table zero, mid-tide zone represents the normal zero range, and the low-tide zone is uncovered only by minus tides (0 to −3).

The physical nature of the beach is significant in determining which species of plants and animals can survive there. The most common beach types are rocky, sandy, and mud flat (Figures 5–39, 5–40, and 5–41). In many areas, nearby freshwater sources may produce brackish or estuarine conditions. Organisms living in the estuarine habitat must be able to withstand extreme fluctuations in salinity. Several mechanisms exist in the organism for the regulation of internal salt concentration when the salt concentration changes in the environment. Some specific examples will be discussed in Chapter 7 under the topic of osmoregulation. Other determining factors of

the population of a beach include the amount of protection available from the pounding surf and the length of tidal exposure.

The animals living in the tide zones show definite zone preferences and often specific physiological adaptions for living in these particular zones. On the rocky, unprotected beaches of the Pacific Northwest, for example, the air-breathing isopod (*Ligyda*) and the small periwinkle snail (*Littorina*) live on the rocks and in the crevices in the spray zone; the acorn barnacle (*Balanus*) and the shore crab (*Hemigrapsus*) inhabit the high-tide zone; the purple and green sea urchins (*Strongylocentrotus*), green anemone (*Anthopleura*), and the black turban snail (*Tegula*) are common in the mid-tide zone; the giant red sea urchin (*Strongylocentrotus franciscanus*) and the gum boot chiton (*Cryptochiton*) live in the low-tide zone (Figure 5–42a). By far the greatest number and variety of plants and animals are found on the rocky beaches. Fragile organisms such as worms and sea cucumbers find shelter in crevices and under large rocks. Some animals, such as the sea urchins and piddock clams, actually burrow into hard sandstone in the numerous

148

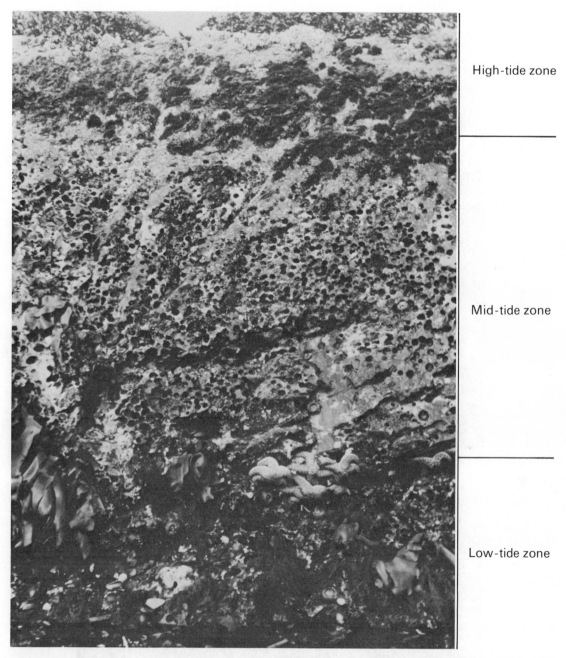

High-tide zone

Mid-tide zone

Low-tide zone

Figure 5–38 Zonation on a rocky beach. Note the vertical rock, which shows the tide zones and some of the typical organisms found there. The holes in the rock were bored by piddock clams. (Courtesy of Helen Dillon.)

tide pools left by the receding tide. Other hardy individuals such as barnacles, mussels, starfish, chitons, snails, and anemones cling to the rocks under the full force of the surf.

Sandy beaches may abound with clams, worms, sand dollars, and certain crabs (Figure 5–42b). Since distribution of life on the sandy beach is limited principally by the lack of shelter, attachment sites, and permanent tide pools, the burrowing animals are best suited to this

(a)

(b)

Figure 5–39 East Coast rocky reef. (a) This rocky reef is exposed only at very low tides. It abounds with both algal and animal life. (Grant Heilman.) (b) Close-up view showing various algae. (Runk/Schoenberger, from Grant Heilman.)

Figure 5–40 West Coast beach showing rocky headlands and sandy beach. (Alan Pitcairn, from Grant Heilman.)

environment. Zonation is also evident. On the Atlantic and Gulf Coasts, the ghost shrimp and ghost crab can live quite high on the beach with their burrows reaching down to the low-tide level. The entire beach usually abounds with the small variable clam (*Donax*). Other common species include the edible venus clam (*Mercenaria*), the cockle (*Dinocardium*), arc shells (*Arca*), jackknife clams (*Ensis*), scallops (*Aequipecten*), and the edible blue crab (*Callinectes*). On the West Coast, the sandy beaches support such edible varieties as the razor clam (*Siliqua*), butter clam (*Saxidomus*), steamer or little-neck clam (*Protothaca*), and the scallop (*Pecten*).

In the mud-flat habitat large expanses of mud and green eel grass may be exposed by even minor tidal fluctuations. Clams, worms, snails, crabs, shrimps, and isopods are the most common organisms. The muddy bottom is characteristic of shallow, protected bays that lack circulation and wave action. A rotten-egg stench of hydrogen sulfide gas from de-caying organic matter is quite common when the tide is out. The mud is mixed with fine organic debris which provides excellent food for burrowing filter feeders and scavengers. On West Coast sand and mud flats, the large, edible geoduck clam (*Panope*) sometimes reaches a weight of six pounds. The Dungeness crab (*Cancer*), important for its food value, also thrives here.

POPULATIONS

POPULATION GROWTH

The members of a species form a *population* in a community. All populations possess certain characteristics such as birth rate, relative age structure, numbers (density), distribution pattern, and death rate. Once a population is established, it undergoes a rather specific growth pattern if conditions remain favorable and the habitat is not occupied by a competitor

151

(a)

(b)

Figure 5–41 East Coast mud flat. (a) Tide in. (b) Tide out. Oysters and mud snails are easily observed when the tide is out. (Jack Dermid.)

152

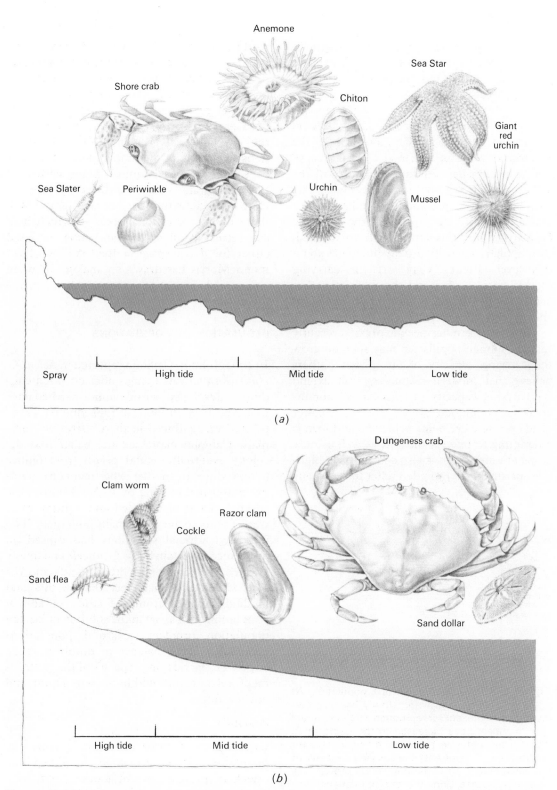

Figure 5–42 Representative animals found in tide zones on the West Coast. (*a*) Rocky beach. (*b*) Sandy beach.

153

(Figure 5-43). Although population growth may be slow at first, it soon increases as more individuals mature and reproduce. Expansion is geometrical and fairly steady, until a population reaches *carrying capacity*. This capacity of any particular habitat depends not only on the amount of food available but also on the nutritional value of the food (Figure 5-44), which in turn depends on the nature of the soil and adequate amounts of water. The shelter or cover provided by a habitat for animals is also an aspect of the carrying capacity. When this limit has been reached, the population density usually fluctuates about this level (Figure 5-43). If the carrying capacity is exceeded and the population becomes too dense, many harmful physiological and psychological effects may occur.

Much concern has been expressed recently that the human population may soon outgrow the carrying capacity of our planet. Others believe that modern technology can extend the carrying capacity to take care of our increasing population. It is true that better yields per acre are being achieved, and man is attempting to harvest the seas as well as raise crops in water. Man is also constructing high-rise apartments to provide shelter for the many

world inhabitants. It is hoped, however, that man can adequately control the environmental pollution that results from the increased population. Even if man can solve the technological problems of providing basic needs for a greater world population, there are still the psychological and emotional considerations. The bulk of the human population now lives in cities. Can a human being withstand the stresses and strains produced by constant close contacts with other human beings? Will there be no recreational areas to which man can retreat if all of the land must be used either for living space or food supply? Desmond Morris has drawn an analogy between cities and zoos to more accurately define man's life in the "concrete jungle."

REGULATION OF POPULATIONS

In 1962, John B. Calhoun reported in *Scientific American* that rats living under crowded conditions developed serious abnormal behavior patterns. In addition, the reproductive capabilities were reduced in these "stressed" animals. Calhoun expressed the belief that the colony eventually would perish from failure to reproduce. In another experiment on crowding, published in 1964 by F. H. Bronson, the adrenal glands of crowded and fighting mice were found to be abnormally enlarged. The increased adrenal secretions had caused an imbalance of certain body chemicals and finally affected the function of other glands and organs. Most ecologists feel that results and methods learned from the study of animal populations will assist in the solution of human population problems. Natural populations generally reach a balance of numbers based largely on the carrying capacity of the environment, relationships within the population, and outside forces.

Predation

One important force operating outside the population can be *predation*, in which one organism (prey) is eaten by another (predator). In some forest communities, for example, deer are specific prey for cougars or dogs

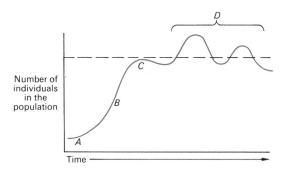

Figure 5-43 Growth curve of a population. At *A* the population is growing slowly because few members are present for reproduction. Soon, however, numbers have increased to the point, at *B*, where many mates are present and a rapid increase occurs. Line *C* represents the carrying capacity of the environment. At *D* the population growth has reached a plateau since the carrying capacity has been exceeded; food and shelter are lacking to support any further increase in population.

Figure 5–44 A deer browsing. The quality and availability of food determine the success of the population in an area. (Nick Drakos; courtesy of New York State Department of Conservation.)

(Figure 5–45), and the size of the population of one species is affected by the population size of the other species. The snowshoe hare on the tundra is preyed upon by the lynx and its population cycles reflect this relationship; the lynx population increases as the snowshoe hare population decreases and vice versa. The general fluctuations in population density that exist between a predator and its prey are shown in Figure 5–46. The situation is usually more complicated than the simple relationships shown in this graph, since most organisms are part of a complex food web.

One well-known example of herbivore-predator imbalance is that of the deer population of the north rim of Arizona's Grand Canyon. The north-rim area is a large plateau of approximately 10,000 square miles. This plateau, known as the Kaibab Plateau, is bounded on all sides by deep canyons that effectively isolate the animal populations.

In 1906, when the Grand Canyon was declared a national park, special attention was given to the preservation of the existing deer herd. Professional hunters and trappers were brought in to trap and kill the natural predators. By 1931, over 9,000 predators had been removed including cougars, coyotes, bobcats, and wolves. The virtual absence of natural predators allowed the deer to flourish, and the herd increased by about 20 percent each year. Although the Kaibab Plateau was rich in meadows, aspen groves, and ponderosa pine forest, it became apparent by 1920 that the area was overgrazed. By 1924 the deer population was estimated to be 100,000, over three times the carrying capacity (Figure 5–47).

During the next five years the Forest Service issued hunting permits, but only 5,000 animals were taken. Meanwhile, over 60 percent of the population died of starvation. By 1930 the herd had been lowered by hunting

155

Figure 5–45 Dogs have replaced cougars as predators of deer in some areas. (Courtesy of Michigan State Department of Natural Resources.)

and starvation to about 20,000. Further hunting and deaths finally brought the herd back into a balance with the environment, and by 1940 the herd numbered approximately 10,000.

Migration

Immigration and emigration of individual members of a population also may regulate

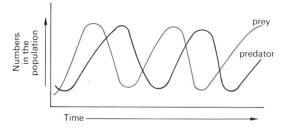

Figure 5–46 Fluctuations in population density of a predator and its prey. Note that the predator population reaches a peak after the prey population attains its peak.

the density of that population. An interesting example of this is a population of lemmings, mouselike rodents, living in the Scandinavian countries. The lemming species has a peculiar cyclic increase and decrease in population. In most lemming groups, fluctuations occur every three to four years. Apparently ample food and increased litter size cause the increased population.

During the peak of the population cycle, however, large numbers of these small animals leave their home ground in mass migrations. For many years these "suicide marches" (so-called because many drown in streams and in the sea) were believed to be simply a quest for food. The leading proponent of this theory is Dr. Olavi Kalela of Finland. Independent studies by Garrett Clough and J. J. Christian of the United States indicate that there may be additional causes for these migrations. Christian has proposed the theory that increases in population density cause social

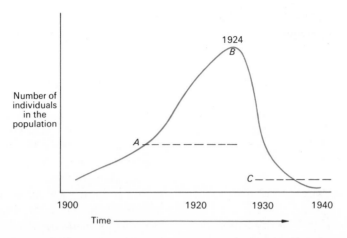

Figure 5–47 Increased deer population on Kaibab Plateau after the removal of natural predators. Line *A* is normal carrying capacity, *B* is peak population, and *C* represents decreased carrying capacity caused by overgrazing. (Redrawn from Raymond F. Dasmann, *Wildlife Biology*, John Wiley & Sons, Inc., 1964.)

stresses that result in lower birth rates. Earlier in our discussion it was mentioned that stress could bring about increased adrenal-gland secretion which influenced other organs. In this case, the control of egg production by the ovary and normal maternal functions could be altered.

Field observations by Clough in 1963 and 1964 indicate that lemmings show unusual intolerance for others of their species. As the population and social stresses increase, fighting and avoidance may trigger the migrations (Figure 5–48). According to Clough, the middle-sized lemmings leave the home territory first, leaving the older breeding population and the young behind. Many move into

Figure 5–48 Early stage in a lemming fight. (Courtesy of Garrett C. Clough.)

157

less favorable marsh and field areas and usually perish during the first winter. The very aggressive lemmings also appear to move away from high-density areas. Some scientists believe that this reaction to social stress is an innate mechanism that keeps these rodents from eating all the available food in an area and thus destroying the entire species through starvation.

RELATIONSHIPS AMONG SPECIES

In most communities very close relationships may exist between two or more species. These intimate associations, *symbiosis* (living together), can be discussed under three categories: *commensalism, mutualism,* and *parasitism.*

Commensalism is a relationship between two organisms in which one member of the pair receives direct benefit while the other is neither benefited nor harmed (Figure 5–49). When certain species of barnacles attach to whales,

they are transported to new feeding grounds and are also geographically dispersed. In the tropics some plant species, such as orchids, grow on trees, gaining only a base for attachment. Another example is a tropical fish that lives in the intestine of a sea cucumber. Apparently, the sea cucumber is not affected but the fish gains a safe home.

Mutualism is the relationship in which two organisms benefit from each other (Figure 5–50). Many of these associations are found in nature and often the situation is not clear as to how much benefit each obtains. A lichen, for example, is made up of an alga and a fungus living in a mutualistic relationship, wherein the alga produces food for both while the fungus obtains and holds water (Figure 5–51). Protozoans capable of digesting cellulose from wood live in the gut of termites. The termites provide shelter and food for the protozoans which assist the termite in the digestion of its food.

Parasitism is the relationship in which one member derives benefit while the other is harmed (Figure 5–52). Parasites that inhabit

Figure 5–49 Commensalism. As insects are stirred up by grazing cattle, egrets follow and feed on the insects. (Walter Dawn; National Audubon Society.)

Figure 5–50 Example of mutualism. The small birds on the back of this African Cape elk obtain food by eating insect parasites. The obvious benefit to the elk is the removal of parasites. (Grant Heilman.)

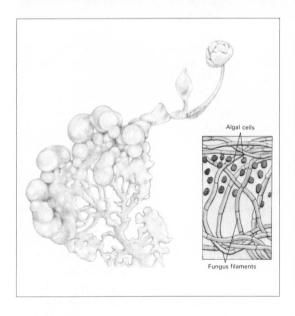

Algal cells

Fungus filaments

Figure 5–51 Mutualism in a lichen. The inset shows algal cells among the fungus filaments.

Figure 5–52 An ectoparasite, a sea lamprey attached to a fish. (Courtesy of Ontario Department of Lands and Services.)

the outer surfaces of their hosts are ectoparasites; those that live within the host organism are endoparasites. External forms include fleas and ticks which suck blood from their hosts. Internal parasites, such as tapeworms or liver flukes, show interesting structural and physiological adaptations. The tapeworm, for example, has evolved attachment devices such as hooks and suckers on its anterior end to prevent dislocation from the host's intestine (Figure 5–53). During the course of the human tapeworm life cycle (Figure 5–54), a cow eats grass infected with tapeworm eggs from human feces. Upon entering the cow's intestine, the eggs rupture and release many six-hooked larvae. These larvae bore through the intestinal wall into the blood or lymph where they are carried to the skeletal muscles. Here they encyst in an inactive bladder until they are eaten by man. When man eats rare beef infested with these, the bladders turn inside

out to expose the head which attaches by suckers to the intestinal wall. Sexual segments, known as proglottids, produced by the young worm mature and break off at the posterior end to release fertilized eggs which are distributed in feces. In this case man is the primary host since this is the phase of the life cycle where sexual reproduction occurs. The cow is the intermediate host which harbors the larval forms. The Chinese liver fluke undergoes a more complicated life cycle in which the larvae develop in a snail and later encyst in fish muscle before becoming sexually mature adults in the human liver. Another parasitic adaptation of tapeworms and flukes is the capacity for laying large numbers of eggs.

There are also parasitic plants. Mistletoe, which lives on oak and juniper trees (Figure 5–55), is a common example of a plant parasite. It actually sends rootlike structures into the vascular tissue of the tree and taps its nutrient supply. In order for a parasite to be successful, however, the host must not be destroyed, and although well-adapted parasites may weaken their hosts, they seldom cause immediate death. A plant parasite more serious than mistletoe is the fungus which causes *late blight* of potatoes. This disease produced the serious famine in Ireland, which lasted from 1843 to 1846, and led to starvation, death, and a mass migration to the United States. Spores, part of a rather complex life cycle, attack both the leaves and tubers of the potato, killing the leaves and rotting the tubers. Tomatoes are also susceptible to this fungus, and epidemics of late blight have occurred in the United States.

The three symbiotic groups listed here are somewhat arbitrary and open to interpretation. Not all biologists agree on the placement of a particular association into a category. Perhaps one symbiotic relationship is evolving toward another type of relationship—a commensalistic toward a parasitic association. It is easy to visualize how a harmless commensal could eventually become a parasite. Perhaps the mistletoe once used the oak tree only for an attachment, much like the commensalism

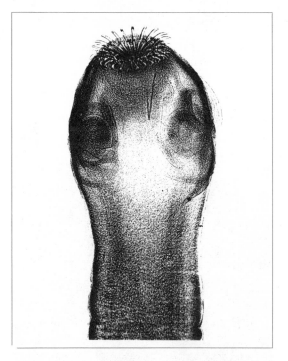

Figure 5–53 The anterior hooks and suckers of a mature dog tapeworm. These devices attach the tapeworm to the intestinal lining. (Courtesy of Carolina Biological Supply Company.)

160

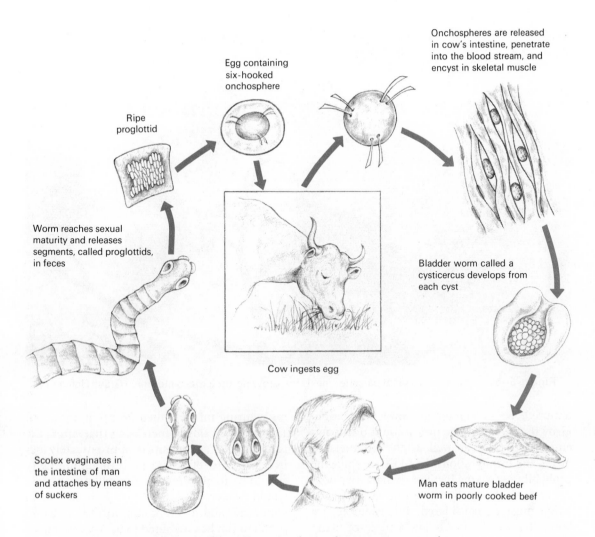

Egg containing
six-hooked
onchosphere

Ripe
proglottid

Onchospheres are released
in cow's intestine, penetrate
into the blood stream, and
encyst in skeletal muscle

Worm reaches sexual
maturity and releases
segments, called proglottids,
in feces

Bladder worm called a
cysticercus develops from
each cyst

Cow ingests egg

Scolex evaginates in
the intestine of man
and attaches by means
of suckers

Man eats mature bladder
worm in poorly cooked beef

Figure 5–54   Life cycle of a beef tapeworm, a parasite.

between some tropical plants, but as parts evolved permitting complete penetration into the vascular system, a parasitic relationship was established.

EFFECT OF MAN ON NATURAL COMMUNITIES—CONSERVATION

Some of the biggest problems confronting the human species today involve the relationship of man to his environment and therefore are ecological in nature. These environmental problems result from two factors: (1) man's increasing population density which places a tremendous burden on the carrying capacity of the total world ecosystem (Figure 5–56), and (2) man's ability to control the ecology of other organisms and to intentionally alter the natural environment.

HUMAN POPULATION

The first problem, the increasing human population, was pointed out in the discussion on population. Man's ability to ultimately provide adequate food and shelter and to withstand the psychological and sociological effects of overcrowding was questioned. When an analysis of human population trends is at-

161

Figure 5-55 Example of a plant parasite : mistletoe growing on a mesquite tree. (Grant Heilman.)

tempted, we encounter a complex situation. Growth rate must take into account death and emigration rates as well as the numbers of births and immigrations. In addition, since the probability of giving birth or dying varies with age and sex, the age-sex distribution of a population must be considered. For example, we know that death rates follow a trend of being

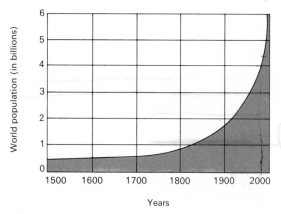

Figure 5-56 With more knowledge about, and concern for, human population growth, the increase may not be as steep as predicted here.

high during infancy, then dropping for about 12 years, and slowly increasing thereafter; the reproductive age group is approximately between the ages of 16 and 45. If infant mortality should be significantly decreased, more people would reach reproductive age. This has in fact happened, and much of our world population problem can be attributed to it. Another factor which increases the population is the overall decrease in death rates. Birth rates of course affect population growth, but these have been declining in many countries over the past 100 years or so. In 1930 the birth rate in Europe dropped to 15 per 1,000. Presently in the United States, where the birth rate was about 30 per 1,000 in the early 1900s, it has dropped to about 16.8 per 1,000. By comparison, the birth rates in Asia, Latin America, and Africa have remained at over 40 per 1,000. These countries have also experienced a declining death rate. It is apparent that a population will continue to increase if death rates decrease and birth rates do not.

What are the population projections for the

162

United States? According to the U.S. Census Bureau, by the year 2000, we should have from 251 to 300 million people, the variation depending primarily on the birth rate. If the typical family averages 2.8 children, then the upper population limit will be realized; if the average is 1.8, however, the population will hit 251 million.

POLLUTION

Although the population explosion poses great dilemmas to man (especially in underdeveloped countries), perhaps a problem of even greater magnitude is pollution of the total environment. The pollution problem has arisen mainly because of population increase. In the future the human race must be more concerned with adequate waste-disposal systems and control of air pollution, water pollution, and even noise pollution (Figures 5–57 and 5–58).

Air pollution continues to increase in importance as an environmental problem, and this can be expected to continue until such time as our primary fuels are changed. The fact that air pollution could occur from coal smoke must have been evident as early as the fourteenth century, although little concern was expressed until conditions became worse in the 1940s and 1950s. As industrialization increases and automobiles become more abundant (both utilize primarily petroleum products for energy), air-pollution problems also increase. The waste products from these energy processes are chiefly sulfur, nitrogen, and organic and oxygen compounds. Sulfur oxides (SO_2 and SO_3), some of the most harmful pollutants, result when sulfur, which is present in coal and oil, unites with oxygen upon burning. Auto exhausts contribute to the nitrogen oxides (NO and NO_2) produced by combustion where atmospheric nitrogen is available. Organic products are hydrocarbons

(a)

(b)

Figure 5–57 Downtown Los Angeles (a) A smoggy day in 1968. Heavy smog limits visibility so that mountains seen easily on a clear day, in (b), are completely invisible. (Courtesy of Los Angeles County Air Pollution Control District.)

Figure 5–58 Example of water pollution: detergent foam on the Mississippi River. (John H. Gerard; National Audubon Society.)

usually released upon the incomplete burning of fossil fuels. Although these pollutants are generally in the vapor form, they also occur as solid particles. Carbon monoxide and carbon dioxide also belong to this group. Ozone and other oxidizing compounds result from reactions of nitrogen oxides and hydrocarbons in sunlight and produce some of the greatest problems in sunny, polluted areas.

The effects of air pollution can range from causing a reduction in visibility to causing death. A large amount of the damage to agricultural and other plants is in the form of lowered yields, stunted growth, and poisoned tissues. Perhaps the most significant effect on man and some animals is the damage done to the lungs and other respiratory organs as a result of breathing polluted air. We know that

many of the pollutants found in air are cancer producing and capable of poisoning enzyme systems. These facts were significantly impressed upon us in the late 1940s during the smog occurrences in Los Angeles, California and Donora, Pennsylvania. The most disastrous occurrence, however, was the London smog of 1952 which claimed over 3,000 lives. We are now fully aware that as the population increases, more pure air will be needed; it is a priceless commodity which will ultimately require strict controls and cooperation on a world-wide basis.

PESTICIDES

The use of pesticides has been practiced extensively over the last 30 years in the United

164

States in an attempt to protect crops from insects and fungi. Serious concern about the effects of these chemicals on other organisms has been expressed in the last 15 years, and this point was stressed in the discussion of DDT in Chapter 1. As noted, Rachel Carson in her book, *Silent Spring*, discussed the problem of pesticides at great length and related many instances where pesticides used to control undesirable insects also annihilated desirable organisms such as birds, crops, and trees. The following quotation from her work indicates that mankind should certainly scrutinize this practice:

> For as long as man has dwelt on this planet, spring has been the season of rebirth, and the singing of birds. Now in some parts of America spring is strangely silent, for many of the birds are dead—incidental victims of our reckless attempt to control our environment by the use of chemicals that poison not only the insects against which they are directed but the birds in the air, the fish in the rivers, the earth which supplies our food, and, inevitably (to what degree is still unknown), man himself.*

But the fact remains that man is in competition with insects for food and that insects carry diseases. We also know that millions of human lives have been saved from starvation, disease, and death through the use of pesticides. Man must therefore continue to control insect populations but through means other than the use of DDT and highly stable chemicals. Some of the organic phosphates which decompose in a week or so could be of some value, but as is true of DDT, resistance may be built up against them. Another drawback to the use of chemicals is that pesticides often kill organisms other than the intended pests. Sterilization of male screwworm flies to reduce the population has been attempted with some success, since nonviable eggs are produced when female flies mate with sterilized males.

*Rachel Carson, *Silent Spring* (Boston: Houghton Mifflin, 1962), jacket copy.

In some cases natural enemies are employed to control pests. For example, viruses which kill tussock moths (a menace to fir trees) could be used as a control measure. Certain wasps feed on the larvae of some beetle pests, and importing these wasps into areas where the beetles are not wanted has helped.

RADIOACTIVITY

The use of radioactive isotopes and the testing of nuclear weaponry is also a cause for concern. Although the total harm that radiation can produce in living organisms is still not known, we are aware of certain metabolic disorders and general genetic changes that it can produce. The increases in background radiation, to which organisms are susceptible, are due chiefly to fallout and, to some extent, to the disposal of radioactive waste materials.

ENERGY

Another problem of exceptional magnitude is the energy crisis. We must now consider the prospect of running out of some of our present common fuel resources. The demand for energy use is nevertheless increasing at a rapid rate, and this accelerating demand will probably continue. It has been predicted, for example, that at least 90 percent of all oil and natural gas resources will be depleted by the year 2035. This means that man must ultimately find new energy sources. And we must search for energy sources which do not pollute. Nuclear power is a good prospect, but here the problem of contaminating the world with radioactivity must be considered. Certainly one of the most probable means of supplying sufficient energy in the future is the fusion process which occurs in the sun. This process of fusing hydrogen atoms into helium atoms is the basis for the hydrogen bomb. However, the details involved in producing and transporting this type of energy under controlled conditions must be worked out before this source can be tapped. Another possibility involving hydrogen is the use of liquid hydrogen to replace our hydrocarbon fuels. This has many advantages, not the least of which is its pollution-free quality.

NATURAL BALANCE

In most natural ecosystems a balance is generally achieved between the living populations and the environment, with certain limits providing the pivotal points for this balance. Although these balances can be upset and shifted by natural forces such as storms and fires, they can also be disrupted by man. In fact, farming methods, and to a certain extent forest management, are based on a disturbance of natural conditions in which man clears the land and replants with his desired crop or uses the cleared land for grazing. Improper farming techniques or overgrazing may lead to a decrease in vegetational cover which in turn leads to erosion of the soil. A greater and uneven runoff of water usually flows from an eroded area, and this increase of water plus the added soil and rocks can affect aquatic ecosystems at some distance from the overgrazed site.

Of equal concern is the introduction of new plant and animal species into areas that are in relative balance. For example, the accidental introduction of the chestnut blight fungus from China virtually eliminated the American chestnut. In the early 1900s the Belgian hare was introduced as a commercial enterprise on San Juan Island in Puget Sound. Many rabbits, however, escaped the breeding farm, reproduced rapidly, and soon overran the island. It was practically impossible to raise a home garden and the pea farms suffered severe damage during the cyclic peaks of the population. In 1962 the red fox was introduced as a predator and the rabbit population has dropped appreciably. A similar situation has occurred in Europe and parts of Asia where the American muskrat has been introduced and is spreading throughout these countries.

Earlier in this chapter the Kaibab deer story revealed how man can also upset an ecological balance through the removal of specific members from a community. Many serious problems have developed as a result of man's interference, either deliberately or accidentally, with natural, balanced ecosystems. The ecology of an area should be carefully studied and the relationships between all members of that area should be known before new species are added or existing ones removed.

CONSERVATION AND SOLUTIONS

Some aspects of human interference with natural ecosystems may not seem as important as the items just discussed—that is, they may not be considered "life or death" issues. These are aspects dealing with the preservation of natural areas and certain species such as the bison or American buffalo which are important to man's aesthetic and recreational needs.

Before mankind realized just how much he could influence natural systems and how much destruction he could produce through his interference, serious imbalances in nature occurred. Therefore man's imprudent exercise of his power, as well as his inability to efficiently use all natural resources, has caused many of the basic problems facing the human race. But many people now realize the importance of natural resources and the concept of *conservation*, the wise management of natural resources. In the United States, man's first conservational concern was for the forests that were heavily, and indiscriminately, logged in the 1800s. A relationship between logged-off lands, water runoff, and soil erosion was soon noted. Man cannot afford to exhaust resources such as soil and certain minerals which cannot be replaced. Although water and air are quantitatively inexhaustible, the quality of these resources must be guarded carefully. Man is beginning to realize that not all environmental problems are unsolvable. Public awareness and political pressure groups have prompted governmental agencies and private industry to respond by utilizing modern technology in both prevention and clean-up operations. The major oil companies are becoming more concerned with environmental problems such as oil spills and are working cooperatively to protect against these dangers (Figure 5–59). Another process holding much hope for the future is the *recycling* of materials such as metals and paper (Figure 5–60). Man's success on this planet will be determined chiefly by the extent to which he is progressively concerned with his effect upon nature, even to the point of being responsible for an unlittered environment (Figure 5–61). Man must show this concern as he constantly attempts to meet the needs of all people living on the planet Earth.

Figure 5–59 Two vessels towing a boom and skimmer into an oil slick. The oil is collected by the skimmer and stored in the support vessel towed behind. This system can handle up to 2,200 gallons per minute. (Courtesy of Clean Seas Incorporated.)

Figure 5–60 Metal-recycling processes. (Herb Williams; courtesy of Electric League of the Pacific Northwest.) (*a*) Junk cars and other scrap metal enter a shredder.

(*b*) After shredding, the metal is ready for reprocessing.

(c) Aluminum cans are also shredded for reuse.

Figure 5–61 Man's lack of concern for his environment results in water pollution and spoiled recreation areas as well as unfit habitats for many forms of aquatic life. (Courtesy of Ward's Natural Science Establishment, Inc., Rochester, N.Y.)

SUMMARIZING STATEMENTS

All the organisms living and interacting within a particular area constitute a biotic community; when the nonliving components of an area are considered with the living, it is called an ecosystem.

The energy flow through a community is in one direction, from the producers to the consumers to the decomposers; and the materials, such as water, oxygen, carbon, nitrogen, and phosphorus, move in a cyclic pattern.

Every community undergoes a series of changes, succession, until a group of organisms, the climax, are established which can live and reproduce most successfully in that area; the major terrestrial regions of the earth are tundra, northern coniferous forest, deciduous forest, tropical forest, grassland, and desert.

Physiological and biological aspects of freshwater and marine environments include: light, temperature, oxygen, chemical compounds, and food relationships.

The members of a particular species in a community form a population and only a limited number can be adequately supported by the environment, the carrying capacity of any area; certain regulating mechanisms exist in all populations such as predation and migration.

In most communities very close relationships often exist between two or more species; these relationships are known as symbiosis.

Mankind faces many environmental problems because of his increasing population density and his interference with natural ecosystems. One of the most important problems is pollution; in the future, man must be vitally concerned with conservation, the wise management of natural resources, and a less polluted environment.

REVIEW QUESTIONS

1   Describe a living community near your college or home, listing the organisms and any relationships between them which you may have observed. (This could be a garden, a pond, or a grove of trees.)

2   Define the terms ecology, biotic community, niche, habitat, population, ecosystem, producers, consumers, and decomposers.

3   Distinguish between autotrophs and heterotrophs and identify their roles in the energy flow of the ecosystem. What is meant by trophic levels?

4   Game laws in most states protect such birds as sea gulls, hawks and owls. Why is this important?

5   Control of hunting and predators has had little effect on the decreasing caribou population of British Columbia. Logging and forest fires, however, have proved to be the major causes of this population decline. From this information can you explain why this is happening?

6   Legumes such as peas and beans contain large amounts of protein even though they may grow on nitrogen-poor soil. Explain.

7   Construct a diagram that will show the interrelationship of the carbon and oxygen cycles.

8   What are some of the major characteristics of biomes? Compare the characteristics of a desert biome to those of an eastern hardwood forest.

9   Find out what the climax vegetation is in your area. Next, find a piece of land that has been cleared or altered by man. Describe the changes that will probably take place in reestablishing the climax.

10 On San Francisco Peaks near Flagstaff, Arizona, alpine fir grows at about 12,000 feet. In the Cascade Mountains of western Washington this same species may grow at 5,000 feet. How can you explain this distribution difference?

11 What could be some of the consequences of a late summer "bloom" (explosive growth) of phytoplankton in a lake? Consider temperature, oxygen, and zooplankton interrelationships.

12 Compare the physical and biological characteristics of the benthic and intertidal oceanic zones.

13 In about 1830, when England was colonizing India, the Indian population, which had probably been stable for a long period of time, increased rapidly. Explain the reason for this population growth.

14 In the 1870s starlings were introduced to the United States from Europe and gradually spread throughout the country. Construct a population curve, based on your knowledge of population dynamics, that will predict the growth rate and survival of this species in the United States.

15 Certain crabs have large colonies of sponges on their backs. What do you think is the symbiotic relationship between these two organisms and give your reasons.

16 List five major environmental problems facing mankind today and suggest two solutions for each.

17 What are some of the positive steps man is taking to avoid pollution and make better use of his resources?

SUPPLEMENTARY READINGS

Bormann, F. H., and G. E. Likens, "The Nutrient Cycles of an Ecosystem," *Scientific American*, October, 1970.

Brower, Lincoln P., "Ecological Chemistry," *Scientific American*, February, 1969.

Carson, Rachel, *Silent Spring*, Boston, Houghton Mifflin, 1962.

Clark, John R., "Thermal Pollution and Aquatic Life," *Scientific American*, March, 1969.

Deevey, Jr., Edward S., "The Human Population," *Scientific American*, September, 1960.

Denison, William C., "Life in Tall Trees," *Scientific American*, June, 1973.

de Nevers, Noel, "Enforcing the Clean Air Act of 1970," *Scientific American*, June, 1973.

Dewey, E. S., "Bogs," *Scientific American*, October, 1958.

Dorst, Jean, *Before Nature Dies*, Boston, Houghton Mifflin, 1970.

Editors of Ramparts, *Eco-Catastrophe*, San Francisco, Canfield Press, 1970.

Ehrlich, Paul R., *The Population Bomb*, New York, Ballantine Books, 1968.

Emery, K. O., *A Coastal Pond*, New York, American Elsevier, 1969.

Errington, Paul L., *Of Predation and Life*, Ames, Iowa State University Press, 1967.

Farb, Peter, *Face of North America: The Natural History of a Continent*, New York, Harper and Row, 1963.

Frejka, Tomas, "The Prospects for a Stationary World Population," *Scientific American*, March, 1973.

Gates, David M., "The Flow of Energy in the Biosphere," *Scientific American*, September, 1971.

Giddings, J. C., and M. B. Monroe, eds., *Our Chemical Environment*, San Francisco, Canfield Press, 1972.

Goldwater, Leonard J., "Mercury in the Environment," *Scientific American*, May, 1971.

Gotto, R. V., *Marine Animals: Partnerships and Other Associations*, New York, American Elsevier, 1969.

Graham, Frank, Jr., *Since Silent Spring*, Boston, Houghton Mifflin, 1970.

Hauser, Philip M., "The Census of 1970," *Scientific American*, July, 1971.

Heinrich, Bernd, "The Energetics of the Bumblebee," *Scientific American*, April, 1973.

Henry, Mark S., ed., *Symbiosis* (Vols. 1 and 2), New York, Academic Press, 1966.

Hubbert, M. K., "The Energy Resources of the Earth," *Scientific American*, September, 1971.

Idyll, C. P., "The Anchovy Crisis," *Scientific American*, June, 1973.

Isaacs, John D., "The Nature of Oceanic Life," *Scientific American*, September, 1969.

Kormandy, Edward J., ed., *Readings in Ecology*, Englewood Cliffs, N.J., Prentice-Hall, 1965.

Kormandy, Edward J., *Organisms, Populations, and Ecosystems*, Dubuque, Iowa, Wm. C. Brown, 1966.

Krutch, Joseph W., *The Desert Year*, New York, William Sloane Associates, 1952.

Langer, William L., "Checks on Population Growth: 1750–1850," *Scientific American*, February, 1972.

Limbaugh, Conrad, "Cleaning Symbiosis," *Scientific American*, August, 1961.

Marples, Mary J., "Life on the Human Skin," *Scientific American*, January, 1969.

Morse, Roger A., "Environmental Control in the Beehive," *Scientific American*, April, 1972.

172

Mudd, Stuart, *The Population Crisis and the Use of World Resources*, Bloomington, Indiana University Press, 1964.

Newell, N. D., "The Evolution of Reefs," *Scientific American*, June, 1972.

Peixoto, José P., and M. Ali Kettani, "The Control of the Water Cycle," *Scientific American*, April, 1973.

Revelle, Roger, "The Ocean," *Scientific American*, September, 1969.

Southward, A. J., *Life on the Sea Shore*, Cambridge, Harvard University Press, 1967.

Squires, Arthur M., "Clean Power from Dirty Fuels," *Scientific American*, October, 1972.

Starr, Chauncey, "Energy and Power," *Scientific American*, September, 1971.

Storer, John H., *Man in the Web of Life*, New York, Signet Science Library, 1968.

Woodwell, George M., "Toxic Substances and Ecological Cycles," *Scientific American*, March, 1967.

Wynne-Edwards, V. C., "Population Control in Animals," *Scientific American*, August, 1964.

6

Energy

Most of us have learned at some time or another that the source of all energy on earth is radiant energy from the sun. This is true for the great majority of living things; certain bacteria, however, have evolved mechanisms by which they can utilize energy from inorganic substances such as iron and sulfur. In our discussion of the origin of life in Chapter 2, it was noted that all forms of life would probably have died if some organisms had not acquired the ability to transform energy from sunlight into food molecules such as glucose.

The ability of biological organisms to trap, store, and utilize energy from their environment is one of the most intriguing aspects of modern biology. The exact mechanisms of energy transfer from one compound to another, without the use of heat as an intermediate form, are yet unknown, but certain chemical relationships are known that can help us understand the basic process.

ATP AND HIGH-ENERGY BONDS

First of all, it has been discovered that one compound capable of storing large amounts of energy in its chemical bonds is found universally in living organisms. This chemical compound has been identified as ATP (adenosine triphosphate). The structure of ATP is very similar to that of the nucleotide subunits found in nucleic acids (DNA and RNA) and is composed of adenine (nitrogen base), ribose (sugar), and three phosphate groups. It differs from a nucleotide of nucleic acid principally in that it contains two extra phosphates.

In organic compounds there are two major classes of phosphate groups: (1) simple phosphate esters and (2) high-energy phosphates. These organic phosphate groups differ in the amount of energy released upon hydrolysis. When glucose is phosphorylated on the sixth carbon to form glucose-6-phosphate, this simple ester contains a relatively small amount of energy. The high-energy phosphates located on ATP, however, are easily hydrolyzed to release large amounts of energy (Figure 6–1).

It is interesting that the basic nucleotide structure which might have been important in the origin of life is involved not only with reproduction and heredity but also in storing and supplying energy. Alterations in the basic structure adapt the molecule for the different jobs to be accomplished within living organisms. This example of a fundamental compound serving different vital functions is one of several such versatile compounds that are encountered in the study of biology.

How does the ATP molecule trap and store energy? Experiments have demonstrated that the energy is trapped in the last two phosphates that make up the "tail" of the molecule. Once trapped, however, the energy is not equally distributed among the three phosphates—the last phosphate group contains the greatest energy, the middle one a lesser amount, and the first the least.

The last two phosphate groups, which contain the greatest energy, may be designated with the symbol $O \sim P$ to show that they possess high energy. Upon hydrolysis in the laboratory, this group will release as much as 15,000 calories (Figure 6–2). It is important to note that this energy is not a property of the $O \sim P$ bond alone but involves the entire structure of the phosphate group. When the high-energy ($\sim$) bond of ATP is broken, only one phosphate is lost. The remaining portion of the molecule then becomes ADP (adenosine diphosphate). It is also possible to extract additional energy (more than that from a simple phosphate ester) from the middle phosphate. Thus ADP may be hydrolyzed to AMP (adenosine monophosphate) with the release of about 7,000 calories.

The high energy of ATP is obtained indirectly from the potential energy of electrons which spin in energy shells around the nuclei of all atoms. Each electron contains a specific amount of energy which is relative to its distance from the attracting nucleus. If an electron at a specific energy level is raised to a higher, but unstable, energy level and then

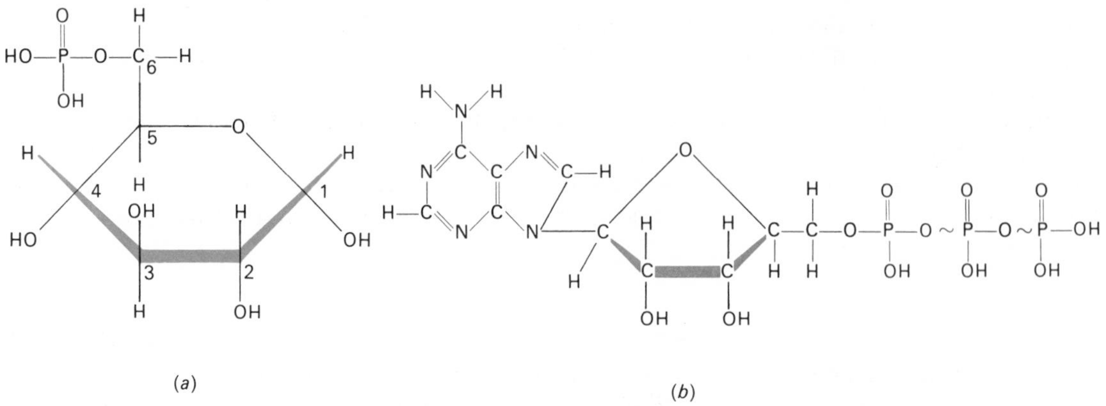

(a)

(b)

Figure 6–1 Two types of phosphate ester linkages. (a) Glucose-6-phosphate, an example of a low-energy phosphate. (b) ATP showing the high-energy phosphate groups that contain more energy.

176

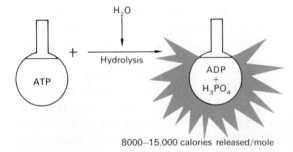

Figure 6–2 Results of a typical laboratory hydrolysis of ATP.

returns to its original level, energy may be released in the form of heat or light (Figure 6–3). It is not the release of energy that is biologically important, however; it is transfer, and that is the unique role of ATP. It acts as an intermediary between higher- and lower-energy compounds.

OXIDATION AND REDUCTION

The two chemical processes that provide energy for all living systems are oxidation and reduction reactions. The taking of oxygen into the structure of a compound is termed *oxidation*; a classic example of this process is the rusting of iron. In a strict chemical sense, however, it is necessary to define oxidation and its counterpart, *reduction*, in terms of the

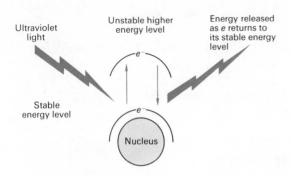

Figure 6–3 How an electron can be excited by ultraviolet light to a higher energy level. Since the higher state is unstable, energy, in the form of light or heat, is released when the electron returns to its normal energy level.

electron structure of the atoms. A compound is *oxidized* when it *loses* electrons and *reduced* when it *gains* electrons. Therefore oxidation is the removal of electrons from a substance and usually involves oxygen but may involve other elements such as sodium. Oxidation-reduction reactions usually occur simultaneously and therefore are called *coupled reactions*. One good example of a coupled reaction is that between calcium and zinc in which calcium loses electrons and zinc gains electrons (Figure 6–4). Calcium, then, is the electron donor and zinc is the electron acceptor. Organic oxidation-reduction reactions are somewhat more complex than this example. The electrons that we will be concerned with in our discussion of biological energy come from the carbon-carbon and carbon-hydrogen bonds produced in photosynthesis.

THE ROLE AND TRANSPORT OF HYDROGEN

In general, it is correct to equate the uptake of hydrogen with the uptake of an electron. Hydrogen will dissociate into its component

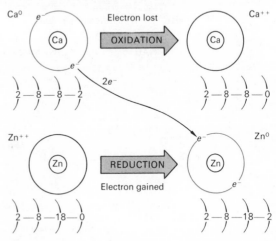

Figure 6–4 Simultaneous oxidation-reduction reaction between calcium and zinc. When two electrons are transferred from Ca^0 to Zn^{++}, the Zn^{++} is reduced to Zn^0 and Ca^0 is oxidized to Ca^{++}. Although this reaction is not typical of biological systems, it serves to illustrate electron transfer.

proton and electron as $H \rightleftharpoons H^+ + e^-$ and the electron thus becomes a potential reducing agent. If the hydrogen-accepting dye, methylene blue, is exposed to hydrogen, it will take the hydrogen electrons into its structure and turn colorless as shown in the following reaction:

Oxidized Form		Reduced Form
Methylene blue	$\xrightarrow{\text{2H}}$	Methylene blue
(blue color)		(colorless)

In the nutrition of an animal, certain foods must be digested and absorbed into the cells to provide energy. One exception to this is glucose (or dextrose), which is frequently called "quick energy." The quickness comes primarily because it does not require digestion

and can be absorbed directly into the blood-stream to be transported to cells. The glucose molecule contains energy in the electrons which form bonds between hydrogen and carbon. In every living cell there are special enzyme systems to remove these hydrogens and make the released energy available for the production of ATP within the mitochondria. When hydrogen is removed by these *dehydrogenase* enzymes, it is done in association with a *coenzyme*. Coenzymes are small organic molecules which are necessary for the activity of certain enzymes. The coenzyme may then transport the hydrogen to other compounds. Two coenzymes, very active in the uptake and transport of hydrogen, are NAD and FAD (Figure 6–5). The relationship between potential food energy, a three-carbon sugar, and the hydrogen-carrying coenzymes is summarized in Figure 6–6.

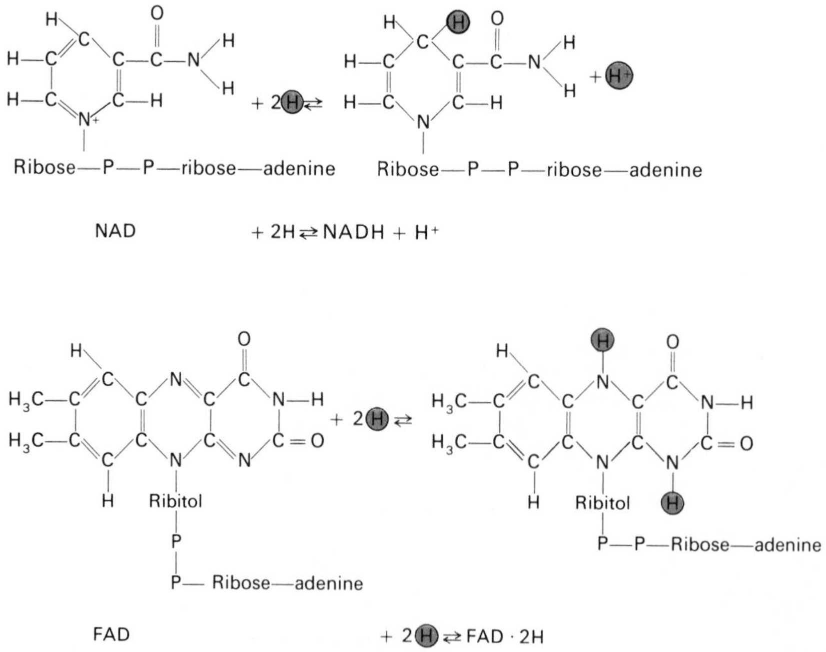

Figure 6–5 Structure of two hydrogen-transporting coenzymes—nicotinamide adenine dinucleotide (NAD) and flavin-adenine dinucleotide (FAD). The oxidized forms are shown on the left, and the reduced forms on the right. The reduced form of NAD is NADH + H$^+$ and will be referred to as NAD · 2H.

178

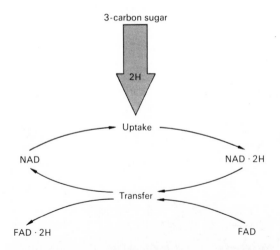

3-carbon sugar

2H

Uptake

NAD

NAD · 2H

Transfer

FAD · 2H

FAD

Figure 6–6 Oxidation-reduction reactions occurring between a three-carbon sugar and two coenzymes. Glucose is oxidized while NAD is being reduced. FAD is then reduced by hydrogen transfer from NAD · 2H, which then returns to its oxidized state.

MITOCHONDRIA AND THE ELECTRON-TRANSPORT SERIES

In the description of the cell given in Chapter 3, the cytoplasmic organelles called mitochondria were introduced as the "powerhouses" of the cell. Biochemical research has demonstrated conclusively that ATP is actively produced in these bodies and made available for energy-requiring reactions throughout the organism.

In recent years, biochemists have succeeded in breaking the mitochondrion into small fragments. When enzymes and other compounds contained within the mitochondrion were identified, they were not surprised to find that many of the enzymes were actually attached to the cristae membranes. Thorough study of the fragments and their enzymes revealed that there was a definite pattern of hydrogen transfer through a series of alternate oxidation-reduction reactions. The first hydrogen acceptor is NAD which passes its 2H along to FAD as shown in Figure 6–6 and Figure 6–7(a).

Cytochromes

The next compounds involved in the transfer of hydrogen are called *cytochromes* (Figure 6–7b). Cytochromes are complex molecules that contain an atom of iron within a nitrogen ring structure (Figure 6–8). This nitrogen structure consists of carbon rings, known as

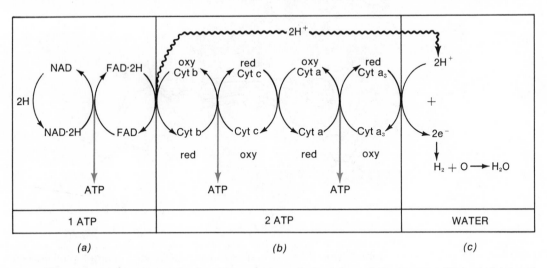

Figure 6–7 Electron-transport series. The compounds in (a) are coenzymes; (b) and (c) involve cytochromes $b, c, a,$ and a_3. Note in these coupled reactions that one compound is reduced as another is oxidized. For example, NAD · 2H is oxidized to NAD, while FAD is reduced to FAD · 2H; next, FAD · 2H is oxidized to FAD, while Cyt b (oxy) is reduced to Cyt b (red), and so on.

179

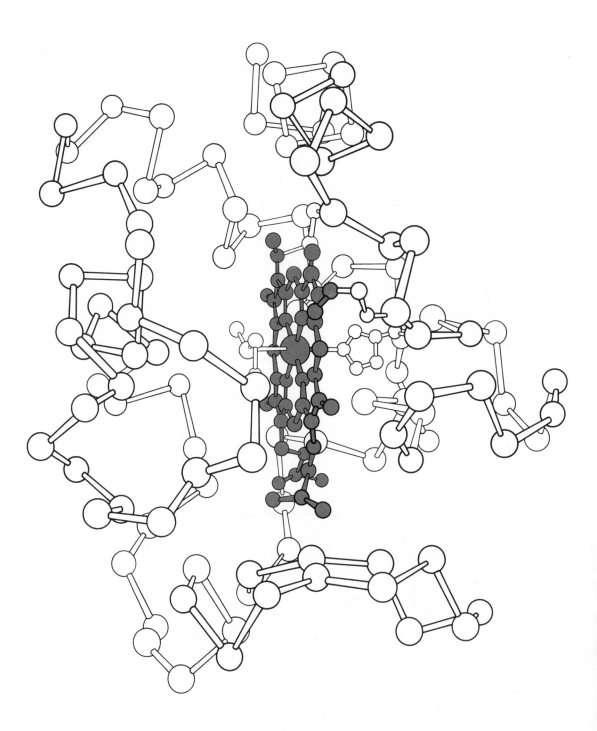

Figure 6–8 Skeleton of cytochrome *c* molecule. The tetrapyrrole, or porphyrin, portion of the molecule is shown in color. (Redrawn from "The Structure and History of an Ancient Protein" by Richard E. Dickerson, *Scientific American,* April 1972. Copyright © 1972 by R. E. Dickerson and J. Geis.)

pyrrole rings, and is called a *tetrapyrrole* compound. The name *cytochrome* (*cyto* = cell, *chrome* = color) refers to the fact that the basic tetrapyrrole ring structure is a colored compound or pigment found within the cell. The tetrapyrrole compound is an essential component of many important substances found throughout the living world. In fact, the tetrapyrrole structure of chlorophyll (the pigment of green plants) and the hemoglobin of blood are similar to cytochromes.

The iron (Fe) is bonded to the nitrogens in such a manner that it can alternately pick up or lose electrons somewhat like the calcium in Figure 6–4. The cytochromes in this sequence, which have been studied primarily in beef heart muscle mitochondria, are named b, c, a, and a_3 (Figure 6–7). These cytochrome molecules differ only slightly in structure, and they

all transport electrons along the folded inner membrane of the mitochondrion (Figure 6–9).

As electrons are passed along the *electron-transport series* (from $NAD \cdot 2H$ to cytochrome a_3), enabled by the action of enzymes known as reductases, enough energy is released at three points to complete the enzymatic phosphorylation of ADP to ATP. Although the exact mechanism is not fully understood, it is probable that electron energy is utilized to synthesize energy-rich phosphorylated intermediate compounds. These compounds then transfer phosphate to ADP to form ATP. For every 2H made available to the transport series, three molecules of ATP are synthesized (Figure 6–7).

At the point where $FAD \cdot 2H$ gives up its hydrogens to the cytochromes (Figure 6–7, segment b), it is important to note that the

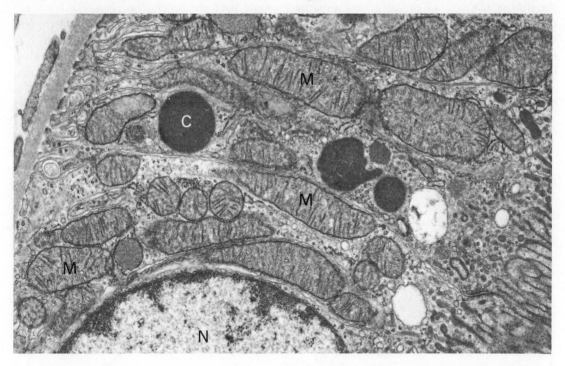

Figure 6–9 Electron micrograph of a rat-kidney tubule cell showing mitochondria (M) with inner cristae membranes, nucleus (N), and cytoplasmic inclusions containing lipids (C) (X 13,800). (Courtesy of James D. Newstead.)

181

protons $(2H^+)$ are not directly transferred, since the iron accepts only the electrons. While the electrons are being transported along the cytochrome series, the protons are released in the mitochondrial fluid and, at the very end of the chain, protons are united with electrons with the help of cytochrome a_3 (Figure 6–7, segment c). At this point, cytochrome a_3 also catalyzes the addition of oxygen to the two hydrogen atoms to form the oxidation by-product, water. Oxygen thus acts as the final hydrogen acceptor, and this is the vital role that oxygen plays in respiration.

HARNESSING AND RELEASING ENERGY

We have now formed a concept of biological energy, but it is still necessary to understand the *autotrophic* process by which energy from the sun is trapped to produce new organic molecules. When hydrogen is removed from these molecules in a stepwise process, energy is obtained for the synthesis of ATP. This process is called *cellular respiration*.

The processes of energy trapping and energy release can be illustrated as an "energy hill"

in which the greatest potential energy is in the molecules at the summit (Figure 6–10). Note the cyclic movement of carbon dioxide and water. This schematic diagram summarizes the energy picture as we will discuss it—that is, the harnessing or trapping of energy from the sunlight by *photosynthesis* and the subsequent release of this energy through the process of respiration in every living cell. Both photosynthesis and respiration are rigidly controlled and we need now to direct our attention to the detailed mechanics of these two processes.

PHOTOSYNTHESIS

"On this planet we are all guests of the green plants" is an expression used by some botanists to dramatize the fact that all organisms except some bacteria depend on photosynthesis as a direct or indirect source of food and oxygen. You may have experimented with goldfish or guppies and green aquarium plants to produce a "balanced aquarium." If you have, you may also have learned that it is a difficult task to "balance nature" in a closed container. In such

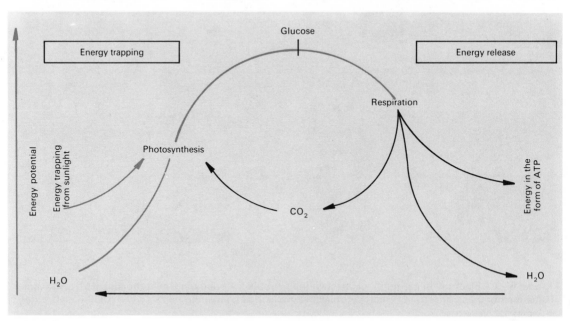

Figure 6–10 Summary of the energy concept showing the relationship between photosynthesis and respiration.

a closed system many factors must be balanced between the plants and animals including gas exchange and assimilation of waste products. Three possible experimental approaches with some sprigs of *Elodea* and a goldfish are shown in Figure 6–11. Although this coexistence can actually persist for only a short period of time, because all aspects such as growth and reproduction rates have not been considered, it does illustrate the important interdependence of plants and animals.

Before proceeding with the details of this important process, we should consider some of the more important historical developments that led to man's present understanding of photosynthesis.

GAS EXCHANGE

The English scientist Joseph Priestley, in 1771, performed an experiment similar to our balanced aquarium in which he discovered that "plants purified the air for animals." Placing a green plant and a mouse in a sealed container, he observed that the organisms lived together much longer than either could exist alone (Figure 6–12). Although he did not understand the exact nature of the "purification" of air by plants, his experiments led ultimately to the discovery of the following interrelationship:

$$CO_2 + H_2O \xrightarrow[\text{Green plant}]{\text{Light}} \text{Organic molecules} + O_2$$

(from animal) (used by animals)

Our balanced aquarium was a simple example of gas exchange and food supply. It is necessary to add, however, that the utilization of oxygen and release of CO_2 do not result only from the animal. Even though the green plant is capable of producing organic food, it must also convert this food to carbon dioxide, water, and ATP energy in order to continue its growth and function. Note the use of double arrows in Figure 6–13 to illustrate this respiration requirement.

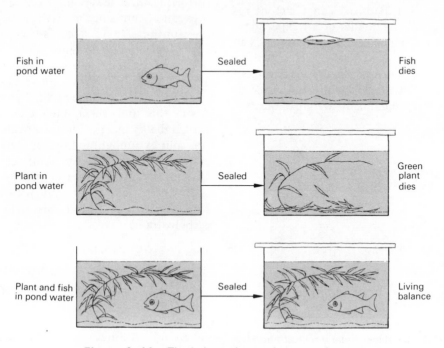

Figure 6–11 The balanced-aquarium experiment.

183

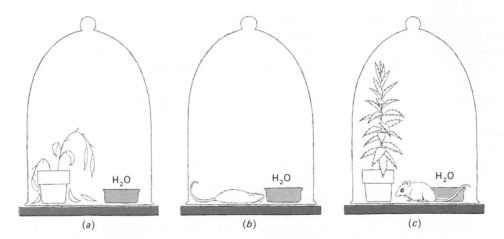

Figure 6–12 Three experiments designed to show the interdependence of gas exchange between plants and animals. (*a*) Plant dies. (*b*) Mouse dies. (*c*) Plant and mouse live.

RAW MATERIALS AND THE ROLE OF LIGHT

About 1450, Cardinal P. Nicolai Cusa was convinced that the mass of a green plant resulted from the interaction of water and sunlight and not from roots "eating" the soil as had been believed from the time of Aristotle. Much later, Jean-Baptiste Van Helmont reported in 1748 the results of an experiment that confirmed much of Cusa's thought. Van Helmont simply planted a five-pound willow shoot in 200 pounds of dried earth, watered this shoot for five years with rain water or distilled water, and finally weighed the two

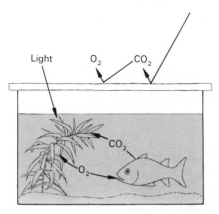

Figure 6–13 Balanced aquarium illustrating the relationships of light, oxygen, and carbon dioxide.

again. The willow had gained over 164 pounds while the soil had lost only two ounces. Van Helmont reasoned that 164 pounds of plant material had arisen from the water alone!

John Ingenhousz in 1779 recognized the role of light energy in photosynthesis. Ingenhousz wrote: "All plants possess a power of correcting, in a few hours, foul air unfit for respiration; but only in clear daylight, or in the sunshine." By 1804 advancements in chemistry allowed de Saussure to show that the photosynthetic process involved the uptake of carbon dioxide, the production of organic material, and the production of oxygen. About this time Ingenhousz offered the incorrect theory that the carbon dioxide molecule was split by sunlight to provide carbon for the nourishment of the plant (and releasing the oxygen). If this were true, reasoned other scientists, the carbon must then be combined with the two hydrogens of water to form simple carbohydrates:

$$CO_2 + H_2O \xrightarrow{\text{Light}} \underset{\text{(carbohydrate)}}{CH_2O} + \underset{\text{(from } CO_2)}{O_2}$$

It was not until the 1930s that this idea was successfully refuted by C. B. Van Niel of Stanford University working with purple sulfur bacteria. Van Niel proposed that light somehow split (ionized) the water molecules and not the carbon-dioxide molecules. Since Van Niel had found that these bacteria could photosynthesize without evolving oxygen, the splitting of carbon dioxide was seriously doubted. This new theory postulated that light energy split water into H^+ and OH^- radicals. The hydrogen could then be used to reduce CO_2 to carbohydrate (CH_2O) and the oxygen from the water could be given off as oxygen gas.

In 1939, a Cambridge University botanist, Robert Hill, published the results of a series of his experiments with isolated chloroplasts. In these classic experiments, dried leaves were ground with mortar and pestle and suspended in water. He then filtered this solution through glass wool to isolate the chloroplasts. By adding the known hydrogen acceptor ferric oxalate and the oxygen acceptor hemoglobin, Hill demonstrated that oxygen was liberated as iron was reduced. Hemoglobin, the oxygen-carrying pigment found in red blood cells, was a particularly good indicator since the oxyhemoglobin turns a bright red and could be easily distinguised in a colorimeter (Figure 6–14). Although Hill was not certain that the oxygen was being liberated from water, new techniques were soon to provide the answer to this question.

THE CONTRIBUTION OF OXYGEN-18

When isotopes of certain elements first became available in 1941, chemists at the University of California were able to incorporate oxygen-18 (heavy oxygen) into water to produce H_2O^{18}. Scientists were quick to recognize that oxygen-18 could be useful in clarifying the mystery surrounding the source of the oxygen liberated during photosynthesis. It should be explained here that oxygen-18 is not a typical radioactive element—that is, it does not emit radioactive waves or particles. With the use of a mass spectrograph, however, it can be identified by the difference in weight between it and oxygen-16. If the hypotheses of Van

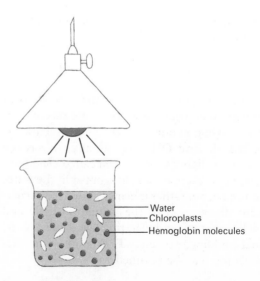

Water
Chloroplasts
Hemoglobin molecules

Figure 6–14 Hill's classic experiment. The chloroplasts were obtained from ground leaves and suspended in water. Hemoglobin was added as an oxygen acceptor. The chloroplasts reacted with the light to release oxygen from the water. When the hemoglobin accepted the oxygen, it turned bright red.

Niel and Hill were correct, green plants should take up this water and release oxygen-18 to the atmosphere. In experiments with the green alga *Chlorella*, it was determined not only that the oxygen released during photosynthesis contained oxygen-18 but also that no oxygen-18 could be detected in the plant carbohydrate. Although this experiment proved that oxygen was being released from ionized water, it did not prove that CO_2 was not contributing to the released oxygen. In order to confirm this, additional experiments were performed using CO_2^{18} with the results that all the oxygen-18 was found incorporated into carbohydrate and no oxygen-18 was released. The experiments with oxygen-18 proved conclusively that the oxygen liberated in the Hill reaction was specifically that contained in the water molecule.

In nature, water is always partially dissociated. As you recall from Chapter 2, most of the water on our planet is in the molecular form, but one liter of pure water contains 10^{-7} gram of hydrogen ion (H^+). This is a very small amount. The dissociation can be expressed as:

$$2H_2O \rightleftharpoons 2H^+ + 2\ OH^-$$

If water is to contribute to the formation of organic fuel, there must be some mechanism for bringing about the permanent separation of the H^+ and OH^-. Essentially, this is the role of the light reaction often called *photolysis*. The light reaction then does not split the water molecule, but rather it brings about the permanent dissociation of the water molecule and makes protons and electrons available for the fuel-building process. This photolytic dissociation may be outlined as:

$$2H_2O \xrightarrow{\text{Light}} 2e^- + 2H^+ + 2OH$$

(molecular state) (in the chloroplast) (ionized state)

THE CONTRIBUTION OF CARBON-14

Following the oxygen-18 experiments, many investigators became concerned with the chain of events in the photosynthetic process. Notable among these was Melvin Calvin (Figure 6–15) of the University of California at Berkeley who utilized carbon-14, a radioactive isotope of carbon, to trace the sequence of carbon compounds in the formation of glucose. Calvin was able to demonstrate the exact steps in this process by introducing $C^{14}O_2$ into green algae and determining the incorporation of C^{14} into the intermediate compounds produced during the synthesis of glucose. In this manner Calvin and his coworkers were able not only to identify the carbon compounds involved but also their sequence in the photosynthetic pathway.

In recent years many new schemes have been postulated to explain the actual mechanism of photosynthesis. These ideas have been formulated primarily through the use of modern biochemical techniques. The discovery and isolation of several new compounds in the chloroplast have led to the verification of their function in oxidation-reduction re-

Figure 6–15 Melvin Calvin, recipient of the Nobel Prize in 1961 for his work in tracing the pathway of carbon in photosynthesis. (Courtesy of Dr. Calvin and Lawrence Radiation Laboratory.)

actions. Most scientists now explain the process of photosynthesis in two interrelated stages: (1) the light reaction, in which radiant energy is trapped and utilized to produce excited electrons from chlorophyll, and (2) the dark reaction, in which hydrogen is used to reduce carbon dioxide to simple sugars.

THE LIGHT REACTION

The physical problems of raising the electrons to sufficiently high-energy levels and transporting them into carbon compounds are only partially understood. As was stated earlier, some newly discovered electron-acceptor compounds are helping to clarify these problems.

There is now strong evidence to suggest that the light reaction consists of two phases called systems which work in tandem (Figure 6–16). In System 1, chlorophyll *a* is excited by light energy causing electrons to be raised to a higher energy level. A very strong electron acceptor, an iron-containing protein called *ferredoxin*, now takes up the electrons from chlorophyll *a* leaving it in an oxidized state. In a subsequent transfer, ferredoxin passes the electrons to NADP (nicotine amide adenine dinucleotide phosphate). In this reduced

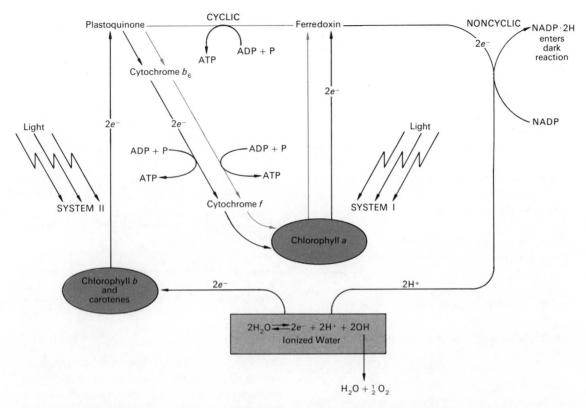

Figure 6–16 Two steps (systems) of hydrogen transfer in photolysis. Note that electrons lost in System I are replaced by electrons gained from ionized water in System II. It should be noted that the electrons from ferredoxin may be passed to NADP to form hydrogen or be cycled back to plastoquinone, the cytochromes, and chlorophyll *a* to produce ATP.

state NADP has the negative charges necessary to attract two protons (H^+) into its structure from ionized water. The final result of this phase of light reaction is the formation of the reduced coenzyme $NADP \cdot 2H$. It is also possible for the electrons captured by ferredoxin to be returned to chlorophyll *a* in a cyclic series of events. These reactions, often called *cyclic electron transfer*, yield the major portion of the ATP produced in the light reaction. This ATP can be used in the life activities of the plant the same as the ATP that results from respiration.

In the second phase of the light reaction, known as System II, excited electrons are passed from other pigments such as chlorophyll *b* and carotenes to a carbon-ring compound known as *plastoquinone*. Vitamin K, which has a similar structure, may also function at this energy level. The electrons are next passed to cytochromes b_6 and *f*. Since these

electrons are passed to a lower energy level, electron energy may be used in this downhill reaction to phosphorylate ADP to ATP. The difference in potential energy between plastoquinone and cytochrome *f* supplies the energy which is utilized to produce ATP. This is another example of a coupled reaction in which the simultaneous release and uptake of energy occurs.

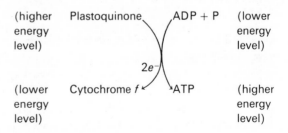

The electrons available from System II are finally passed to chlorophyll *a* to replace the electrons lost to ferredoxin. The electrons lost in System II are replaced from ionized water through the action of a yet unknown carrier substance.

Light reaction ends with the formation of NADP·2H and the release of oxygen. The process has taken hydrogen from ionized water and converted it to a usable form—that is, it may now be transferred to another compound by the coenzyme NADP·2H for the formation of carbohydrate.

THE DARK REACTION

Remember that the source of carbon for photosynthesis is atmospheric carbon dioxide. The conversion of CO_2 into carbohydrate is sometimes called "carbon fixation" and it occurs through a complicated series of enzymatic steps. For our purposes, we need to understand only the major steps involved at this point.

Calvin learned, by working with $C^{14}O_2$, that although carbon fixation occurred in systematic steps, it was not a true cycle, because some products were released as the reactions took place.

Since some reaction sequences in the dark reactions are cyclic, we must pick a point to begin our study. If we choose ribulose diphosphate (RDP), a five-carbon sugar having two phosphate groups, it can be shown how this substance is reformed (Figure 6–17).

Three molecules of the C5 compound, RDP, contain fifteen carbons. The addition of three CO_2 molecules will produce a total of eighteen carbons. When this is accomplished, three six-carbon, double-phosphate molecules are formed.

$$3 \enspace \text{(P)} - \boxed{\text{C5}} - \text{(P)} + 3CO_2 \longrightarrow 3 \enspace \text{(P)} - \boxed{\text{C6}} - \text{(P)}$$

This diphospho, six-carbon intermediate is very unstable and is quickly split into six C3 acids known as *phosphoglyceric acid*, abbreviated PGA. Calvin and his associates showed

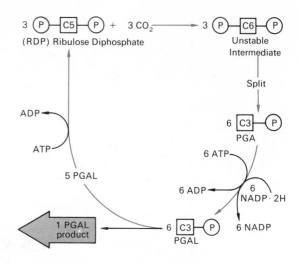

Figure 6–17 Major steps involved in carbon fixation. The six PGAL molecules are produced by the enzymatic splitting of the three C_6 compounds. Five PGAL's are converted back to RDP, while one PGAL represents the net gain.

that PGA is a very important intermediate step in CO_2 fixation. At this point, NADP·2H reduces the PGA to the aldehyde form, *phosphoglyceraldehyde*, commonly known as PGAL.

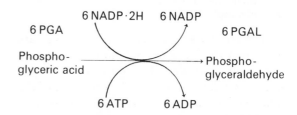

It should be noted that in the formation of PGAL, the light reaction and the dark reaction have merged to produce the end product of photosynthesis. We now know that photosynthesis ends with the formation of PGAL. In the case of RDP, five of the resulting six PGAL's must be phosphorylated and rearranged to replace the original three RDP's to keep the process going.

188

This leaves only one PGAL as net product. If the cycle is repeated, enough carbon is produced to synthesize the organic compound glucose.

We will see in the next section of this chapter how the cell can burn PGAL directly for energy. If the immediate energy requirements are satisfied, then PGAL is synthesized into glucose and finally into starch which is stored. PGAL is also used in the synthesis of other compounds in the cell such as glycerin, fatty acids, and amino acids.

THE SITE OF PHOTOSYNTHESIS

Although most of us think of photosynthesis as occurring in the leaves of green plants, it is also accomplished in some of the protists such as bacteria and algae. The organisms making up green scum of ponds and lakes, for instance, and the minute pigmented organisms that form the plankton of the seas are extremely important in supplying nutrients on our planet. These photosynthetic organisms that form the basis for the food chains in the sea are primary producers of organic compounds and are presently under intensive study by biological oceanographers.

Until 1901, it was believed that the entire leaf was the organ of photosynthesis. Friedel refuted this concept by showing that suspensions of powdered leaves gave off oxygen when illuminated. Hill's work on isolated chloroplasts pinpointed the major source of photosynthetic activity. A schematic breakdown to show the relationship of the chloroplast to the gross leaf structure is presented in Figure 6–18.

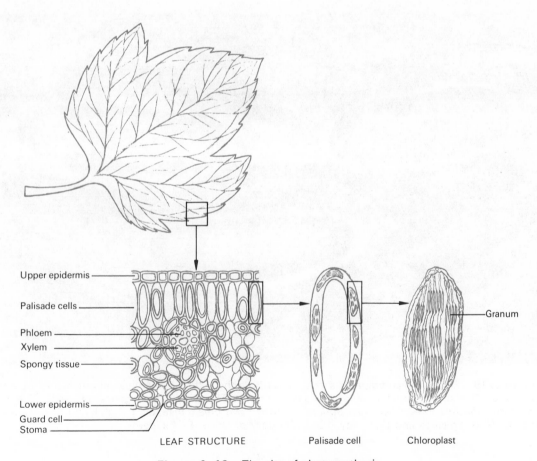

Upper epidermis
Palisade cells
Phloem
Xylem
Spongy tissue
Lower epidermis
Guard cell
Stoma

LEAF STRUCTURE   Palisade cell   Chloroplast

Granum

Figure 6–18   The site of photosynthesis.

189

Leaves, Chloroplasts, and Grana

A cross section of a green leaf has a functional arrangement of tissues (Figure 6–18). Apart from being necessary in the basic structure of the leaf, the palisade cells, which lie just beneath the upper epidermis, contain the functional photosynthetic units, the chloroplasts. Other leaf cells such as the spongy tissue and guard cells are also capable of photosynthesis.

The chloroplast is composed internally of a parallel array of platelike membranes called *lamellae*. Electron micrographs show that the lamellae are not uniform in thickness (Figures 6–19 and 6–20). At various points along the plates, the membrane is expanded into thickened, disk-shaped areas. These disks are closely packed within the chloroplast, resembling a stack of poker chips; each stack is called a *granum*. These double protein-lipid membrane structures contain all the pigments and enzymes necessary for photosynthesis.

Many researchers have attempted to describe the internal arrangement of molecules within the grana disks. The present model indicates that the essential pigments and enzymes are situated in definite patterns along the inner membrane surfaces, similar to the arrangement of the cytochromes and related enzymes along the cristae of the mitochondrion (Figure 6–21). The importance of the membrane surface in the cell is again indicated as a site for chemical reactions. We know that the grana contain the pigments chlorophyll, carotene, and xanthophyll, and recent evidence shows the presence of small amounts of DNA. These simple strands of DNA are somewhat similar in structure and function to the DNA of mitochondria (discussed in Chapter 3).

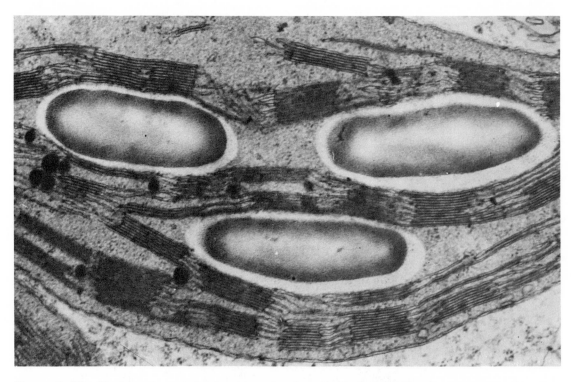

Figure 6–19 Electron micrograph of a chloroplast from the leaf of *Peperomia,* an ornamental pepper (X 72,000). The lamellar structure of the grana can be noted. Three large starch grains are visible. (Reproduced from *Plastids: Their Chemistry, Structure, Growth and Inheritance,* by J. T. Kirk and R. A. Tilney-Bassett, W. H. Freeman and Company, 1967. Courtesy of Dr. B. E. Juniper.)

190

Figure 6–20 Electron micrograph of a granum from a chloroplast of a spinach leaf. The small subunits in the exposed area contain chlorophyll and are known as quantasomes. (Courtesy of Roderic B. Park.)

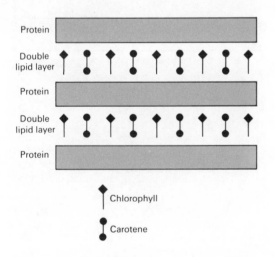

Figure 6–21 Hypothetical arrangement of the photosynthetic pigments in the chloroplast membrane. Note that the chlorophyll and carotene lie in the double lipid layer of the granum.

Pigments

Finally, we are led to the molecular level in our discussion of the site and structural elements involved in photosynthesis. The structure of chlorophyll was mentioned earlier in this chapter, and a diagram of the molecule is shown in Figure 6–22. Note particularly the similarities between the tetrapyrrol configuration of the main part of the molecule and the cytochromes. The metallic atom in the structure of chlorophyll, however, is magnesium rather than iron.

The essential role of the chlorophylls and the other pigments located within the leaf is to trap light for the photosynthetic process. In Chapter 5, it was indicated that visible light from the electromagnetic spectrum is the energy source for photosynthesis. The portions of the visible light spectrum that are absorbed by the photosynthetic pigments of green plants are shown in Figure 6–23a. Chlorophyll a has widely separated absorption peaks in the blue and red wavelengths, whereas chlorophyll b has highest absorbency in the blue-green and, to a lesser degree, red.

The characteristic action spectrum for photosynthesis, rate of photosynthesis plotted against wavelengths of light (Figure 6–23b), results from the combined absorption spectra for all three pigments. The excited electrons released from chlorophyll b and β-carotene are passed to chlorophyll a for the production of NADP·2H as outlined earlier in this chapter.

RESPIRATION

The story of the breakdown of organic molecules into usable energy is somewhat complex. All classes of foods, carbohydrates, fats, and proteins may be utilized for energy by most organisms. For example, the polysaccharide starch may be split into many glucose units by the action of several digestive enzymes. In vertebrates these enzymes are secreted in the mouth, pancreas, and small intestine. After the starch is hydrolyzed into glucose, the cells

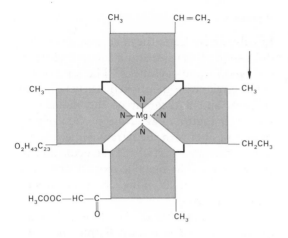

Figure 6–22 Molecular structure of chlorophyll *a* and *b*. The broken lines represent the possible valence bonds of magnesium. Note that chloro-

$$\overset{O}{\underset{\|}{}}$$

phyll *b* differs in having a —C—H group instead of CH_3 at the arrow. (For the structure of the shaded areas, see Figure 2–29.)

lining the intestine absorb the glucose into the blood where it is transported to all the cells of the body. Every living cell has the enzymes necessary to convert the potential energy of glucose into usable high-energy bonds in ATP.

The conversion of the energy in glucose into high-energy bonds may be described as a stepwise process. Each step along the route is catalyzed by a specific enzyme and can be summarized as follows:

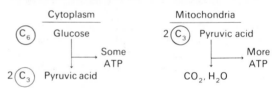

This conversion of glucose into CO_2, water, and energy can be separated into two major phases: (1) the cytoplasmic phase and (2) the mitochondrial phase.

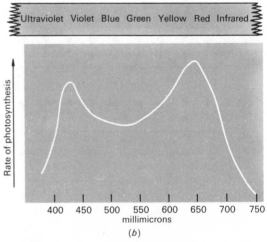

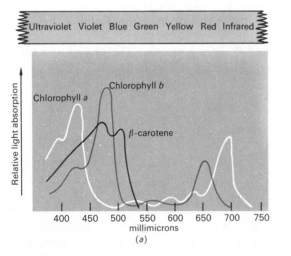

Figure 6–23 (*a*) *Absorption spectrum.* The relationship between the absorption of chlorophyll *a, b,* and β-carotene and the relative light absorption resulting from the light-trapping ability of these three pigments. Note the regions of the visible light spectrum which are most effective in photosynthesis. (*b*) *Action spectrum.* The rate of photosynthesis plotted against the wavelengths of light effective in photosynthesis produces an action spectrum. This spectrum results from the combined absorption of all pigments involved in photosynthesis.

192

Both of these phases produce ATP, but the most energy by far is liberated in the mitochondrial phase. The enzyme action in the cytoplasm breaks the six-carbon glucose molecule into two three-carbon fragments called pyruvic acid. The biochemical term for the series of reactions that break down glucose or glycogen is *glycolysis*. Figure 6–24 should be consulted frequently in the study of the next section.

GLYCOLYSIS

The first step in glycolysis involves getting glucose ready for the process, sometimes called a priming reaction. To accomplish this a phosphate group is placed on the sixth carbon by the enzymatic transfer of phosphate from ATP (the 6 in glucose-6-phosphate refers to the carbon on which the phosphate is attached).

$$\text{Glucose} \xrightarrow[\substack{\text{ATP} \quad \text{ADP}}]{\text{Mg}^{++}} \text{Glucose-6-phosphate}$$

In many enzyme reactions, an additional metallic ion is necessary, such as the magnesium ion in the foregoing example.

Glycogen, the polysaccharide storage form of carbohydrates found in liver and muscle, can also enter the glycolytic pathway by the addition of a phosphate group to one of its glucose units. It is interesting, however, that it does *not* require an ATP to accomplish this phosphorylation—instead, inorganic phosphate (Pi) can be used. This is very economical for the cell because ATP is conserved:

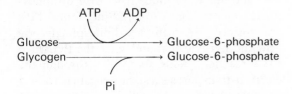

The discovery that a phosphate was added to the glucose molecule in this process was one of the first indications of the importance of the phosphorylation mechanism. Glucose is now prepared for the second step, which in-

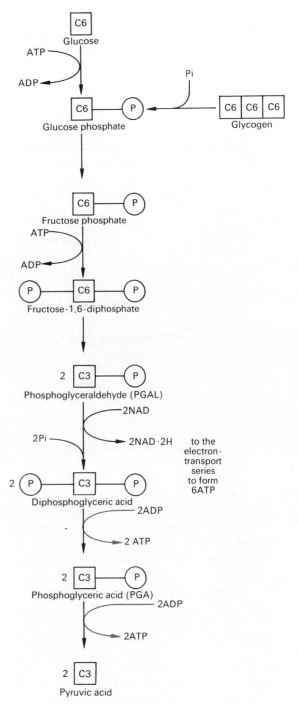

Figure 6–24 Summary of the chemical reactions in glycolysis. Pi indicates inorganic phosphate.

193

volves a complete rearrangement of the carbon-ring structure. In this step, glucose is changed to form another type of sugar, fructose.

$$\text{Glucose-6-phosphate} \xrightarrow{\text{isomerase}} \text{Fructose-6-phosphate}$$

This newly formed fructose-6-phosphate is next phosphorylated on its first carbon by the expenditure of another ATP:

$$\text{Fructose-6-phosphate} \xrightarrow{\text{ATP} \quad \text{ADP}} \text{Fructose-1,6-diphosphate}$$

We now have a six-carbon sugar with a phosphate group on each end. At this point, a very significant event occurs—the fructose-1,6-diphosphate is split into two molecules, each having three carbons and each bearing a phosphate group on one end. For our purposes here, these three-carbon compounds can be considered to be PGAL. (Remember that PGAL is also the end product in photosynthesis.)

$$\text{Fructose-1,6-diphosphate} \longrightarrow \text{2PGAL}$$

Actually, it is not possible to split fructose-1,6-diphosphate into two molecules of exactly the same structure, but it is not necessary to go into the chemical reactions that are required to convert the two compounds to PGAL's. At this point PGAL gives off hydrogen to the electron-transport series. When this happens PGAL becomes phosphoglyceric acid. It is important to note that this reaction, which is catalyzed by an enzyme called a dehydrogenase, involves the removal of hydrogen and is therefore an oxidation. Remember that oxidation is the loss of hydrogen and reduction is the gain of hydrogen. As the hydrogen is lost, an additional phosphate group is attached to the number 1 carbon. Thus a glyceric-acid molecule is formed with phosphorus at the one- and three-carbon positions. The overall reaction is:

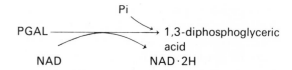

Two things are very important at this point: hydrogen has been given off to the electron-transport series and the 1,3-diphosphoglyceric acid now contains energy in the form of two high-energy phosphate groups. There is enough energy in this compound to allow the direct enzymatic conversion of ADP to ATP in essentially a two-step process.

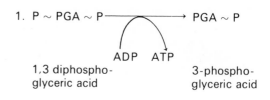

In the foregoing dephosphorylations of diphosphoglyceric acid, two ATP's are formed from each three-carbon molecule; however, since we started with glucose (a six-carbon molecule), the ATP production will be doubled to four for each glucose molecule entering glycolysis.

Recall that if we started with glucose, two ATP molecules were used to prime the glycolysis process; one to phosphorylate glucose and one to produce fructose-1,6-diphosphate (refer to Figure 6–24). Since four ATP's are formed between 1,3-diphosphoglyceric acid and pyruvic acid and since the PGAL to PGA reaction yields six ATP's through the electron-transport series, the net gain is 10 − 2 or eight ATP's. The cell is getting a good return for its original two-ATP investment.

Pyruvic Acid

When the pyruvic-acid stage is reached, the phosphate bond energy is spent. All that is left is the potential energy of the C—C and C—H bonds, yet we will see that this constitutes a tremendous amount of energy. Pyruvic acid is a three-carbon compound that marks the end of anaerobic glycolysis. Anaerobic simply means that this process which produces pyruvic acid and energy *can* operate in the cytoplasm in the absence of oxygen. The further conversion of pyruvic acid into energy and carbon dioxide in the mitochondrion, however, requires oxygen and ceases to function if oxygen is not supplied. The final breakdown of pyruvic acid is accomplished through a cyclic series of reactions discovered by the Englishman Hans Krebs and named for him (Figure 6–25). The *Krebs cycle* (also called the citric-acid cycle) is summarized in Figure 6–27.

Concerning the fate of pyruvic acid, we find that there are three possible routes for the breakdown of this compound in living organisms (Figure 6–26). If oxygen is available in

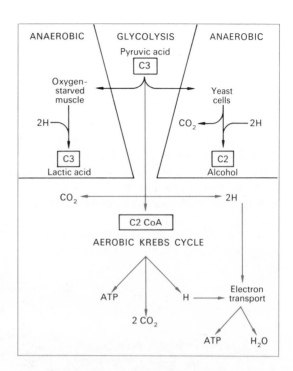

Figure 6–26 The three possible fates of pyruvic acid under anaerobic or aerobic conditions.

Figure 6–25 Hans Krebs, recipient of the Nobel Prize in 1953 for outlining the series of chemical reactions involved in the oxidation of pyruvic action in the citric-acid cycle. (Courtesy of Dr. Krebs.)

the cell, the route is directly into the Krebs cycle and the electron-transport series to produce CO_2 and energy. If no oxygen is available, as might be the case in greatly exercised muscle cells, the electron-transport series cannot operate and lactic acid is formed. Note that it requires 2H to make this conversion from pyruvic acid to lactic acid. The result of this is a loss of six ATP's which would have been made under aerobic conditions because the hydrogen produced in the conversion of PGAL to PGA in glycolysis is now used to convert pyruvic acid to lactic acid. When lactic acid is formed in the oxygen-starved cells, most of it is carried by the blood to the liver and converted to glycogen when aerobic conditions return. This process, however, requires both time and energy and about 20 percent of the original energy value of pyruvic acid is lost. Thus the formation of lactic acid under anerobic conditions is very inefficient in energy production. The same thing is true in the yeast organism where alcohol and CO_2 are the end products.

THE KREBS CYCLE

Under aerobic conditions the pyruvic acid enters the Krebs cycle. For our purposes it is necessary only to note the names of the intermediate compounds in the Krebs cycle. It is very important, however, to keep track of the loss of carbon dioxide as the three-carbon pyruvic acid molecule is completely converted to CO_2 and energy. The first step is to get pyruvic acid introduced into the cycle; to accomplish this, a sort of "key" compound is added. This key is a complicated coenzyme called *coenzyme A*, usually abbreviated CoA. With the loss of CO_2 and the addition of CoA, the molecule of pyruvic acid becomes a two-carbon structure known as acetyl CoA (Figure 6–27). In the next step, acetyl-CoA (or "active acetate" as it is sometimes called) is condensed with the four-carbon compound oxaloacetic acid (OAA) to form a six-carbon acid known as citric acid. It is important to see that the 2H fragments are transported into the electron-transport series by the coenzymes NAD and FAD. At one point, between C5 ketoglutaric acid and C4 succinic acid, ADP is converted to ATP without the use of the cytochromes.

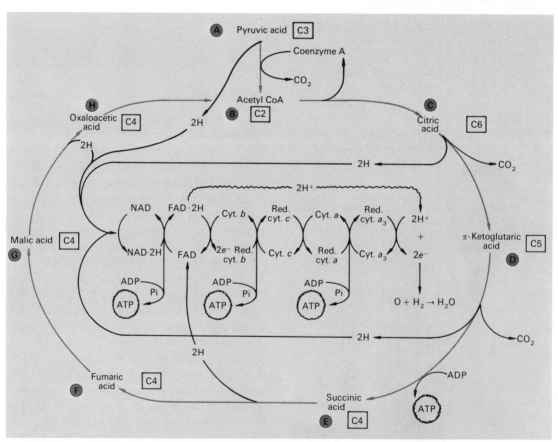

Figure 6–27 Summary of the interrelated events of the Krebs cycle and the electron-transport series occurring in the mitochondrion. Water enters the cycle between D and E and F and G.

Since the electron-transport series is not involved, the yield is only two ATP's per glucose molecule. Another unique reaction is the direct transfer of 2H to FAD between C4 succinic acid and C4 fumaric acid, with the result that the production of ATP between NAD and FAD is skipped, thus producing only four ATP's. The important events shown by the lettered segments in Figure 6–27 are summarized in Figure 6–28. The oxidative breakdown of one molecule of glucose into CO_2, energy, and water usually yields 38 molecules of ATP. One exception is with the compound glycogen where an additional ATP occurs as net gain from using inorganic phosphate to produce glucose-6-phosphate.

So far we have been concerned only with the metabolism of carbohydrates. Can other foodstuffs enter into this scheme? The answer is yes, and such energy-rich compounds as glycerol, fatty acids, and amino acids may enter into the carbohydrate pathway at various steps and be oxidized as fuels (Figure 6–29).

Other possible fuels	Glycerol	Fatty acids	Amino acids
Steps of respiration where non-carbohydrate fuels may enter	Pyruvic PGAL	Acetyl CoA Ketoglutaric acid	Acetyl CoA Pyruvic acid Ketoglutaric acid Fumaric acid Oxaloacetic acid

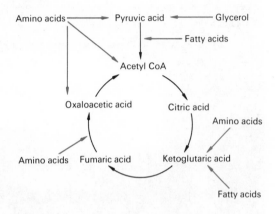

Figure 6–29   Key steps in respiration where non-carbohydrate substances may enter the respiration process (fuel breakdown).

Segment			Lose	Gain
A–B	2 pyruvic acid	2 acetyl CoA	2 CO_2, 4H	6 ATP
B–C	2 acetyl CoA	2 citric acid	2 CoA	
C–D	2 citric acid	2 ketoglutaric acid	2 CO_2, 4H	6 ATP
D–E	2 ketoglutaric acid	2 succinic acid	2 CO_2, 4H	6 ATP 2 ATP
E–F	2 succinic acid	2 fumaric acid	4H to FAD	4 ATP
F–G	2 fumaric acid	2 malic acid		
G–H	2 malic acid	2 oxaloacetic acid	4H	6 ATP
			6 CO_2, 20H	30 ATP's

Figure 6–28   Table showing ATP energy released from one molecule of glucose oxidized in the Krebs or citric-acid cycle. Note that the excess hydrogen and oxygen is from water molecules added in several enzyme steps. It should be remembered that eight additional ATP's were produced in glycolysis.

197

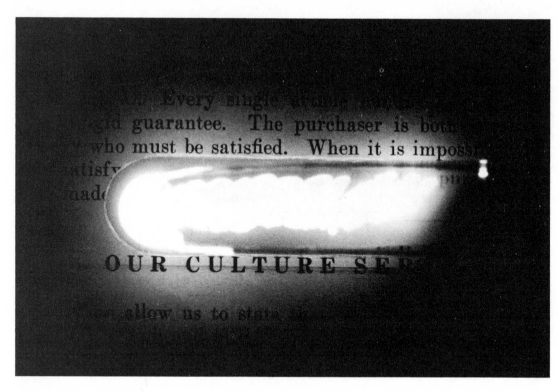

Figure 6–30 Utilization of ATP in the production of light by bioluminescent bacteria. The bacteria in this culture provided the necessary light for the photograph. (Courtesy of Carolina Biological Supply Company.)

At this stage you may wonder just what use can be made of all the ATP that is produced in cellular respiration. You will recall that ATP is necessary in the dark-reaction stage of photosynthesis, and also that some ATP is used to "prime" the early stages of glycolysis. In addition to these requirements, all biological work, such as muscle movement, biolumines-cence, and active transport, requires energy, and in practically every case, ATP is the energy supplier (Figure 6–30). One of the first investigators to demonstrate that ATP is necessary for muscle contraction was Dr. Albert Szent-Györgyi (Figure 6–31).

The energy events discussed in this chapter are summarized in Figure 6–32.

Figure 6–31 Albert Szent-Györgyi, recipient of the Nobel Prize in 1937 for his work with vitamin C. (C. Felker; courtesy of Dr. Szent-Györgyi.)

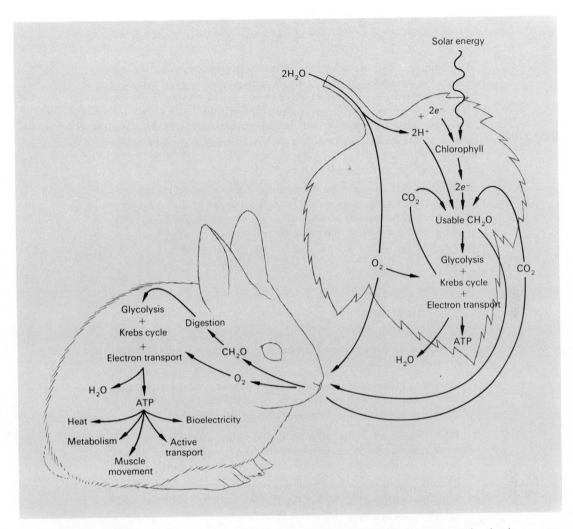

Figure 6–32 Summary of the nutrient and energy relationships in plants and animals.

SUMMARIZING STATEMENTS

Energy is required to perform the chemical reactions necessary for life. The principal source of biological energy is the terminal phosphate group of ATP; the unique role of ATP is as an intermediary between higher and lower energy compounds.

Most chemical reactions involve the breaking and reformation of chemical bonds; the electrons that participate in bonding therefore are exchanged in a reaction—uptake of electrons is reduction and release of electrons is oxidation.

The electron is the basic source of energy in all cells; the energy-making reactions in the cell trap the energy of the hydrogen electron for the production of ATP.

The ultimate source of energy for most organisms comes from the sun; the process of converting light energy to chemical energy in the form of carbohydrate (photosynthesis) is accomplished in plants with the aid of chlorophyll. Photosynthesis can be considered as a two-step process: (1) the light reaction in which light and chlorophyll separate hydrogen from water and make it available in the form of reduced coenzyme NADP (NADP·2H); (2) the dark reaction or carbon fixation in which a five-carbon sugar, RDP, is combined with CO_2 and NADP·2H to form the usable fuel PGAL.

Respiration is the process occurring in all cells to release energy from the C—H bonds in organic molecules; this energy is transferred to ATP for use in biological work; the phases of respiration are glycolysis, which occurs in the cytoplasm, and the Krebs cycle and electron-transport series located in the mitochondria.

REVIEW QUESTIONS

1   In what way does the ATP molecule trap energy? How is this energy released for use by the cell?

2   The action of cyanide poisoning is to inhibit the enzyme cytochrome oxidase from transferring electrons. Describe the effects that cyanide would have on energy production in the electron-transport series.

3   When organic materials are burned, the principal products are CO_2 and water, and energy is released. Sketch the chemical reaction that occurs between glucose and oxygen. Which compound is oxidized and which is reduced?

4   What are the roles of the following compounds in photosynthesis: ferredoxin, plastoquinone, NADP, and RDP?

5   How would you set up an experiment to demonstrate the source of the oxygen given off by green plants?

6   Explain the importance of PGAL in photosynthesis and respiration.

7   What is the role and importance of water in photosynthesis and respiration?

8   Essentially, what are the important chemical changes that occur in the Krebs cycle? What does this cycle accomplish?

9   Sometimes during strenuous exercise an individual cannot take in enough oxygen to meet his energy requirements. What happens in this case?

10   The burning or oxidation of glucose gives the same end products as the burning of any organic fuel such as wood or coal. How is this accomplished in the cell without the release of excessive amounts of heat?

11   Describe the possible routes for the breakdown of pyruvic acid under anaerobic and aerobic conditions. Why does the presence of oxygen make a difference?

12 Compare photosynthesis and respiration in terms of (*a*) raw materials, (*b*) end products, (*c*) site of occurrence, (*d*) energy relationships in the cell.

13 Compare the structural formulas of chlorophyll and cytochrome. How do they differ in structure and function?

14 A green leaf containing glucose is eaten by a rabbit. Outline the major events in the breakdown of a glucose molecule in the process of releasing energy.

SUPPLEMENTARY READINGS

Ackley, M. E., and P. B. Whitford, *The Chemistry of Photosynthesis* (a programmed text), New York, Appleton-Century-Crofts, 1965.

Bassham, J. A., "The Path of Carbon in Photosynthesis," *Scientific American*, June, 1962.

Calvin, Melvin, and J. A. Bassham, *The Photosynthesis of Carbon Compounds*, New York, Benjamin, 1962.

Giese, Arthur C., "Energy Release and Utilization," in W. Johnson and W. Steere, eds., *This Is Life*, New York, Holt, Rinehart and Winston, 1962.

Goldsby, Richard A., *Cells and Energy*, New York, Macmillan, 1967.

Goodenough, U. W., and R. P. Levine, "The Genetic Activity of Mitochondria and Chloroplasts," *Scientific American*, November, 1970.

Heath, O. V. S., *The Physiological Aspects of Photosynthesis*, Stanford, Stanford University Press, 1969.

Lehninger, Albert L., "Energy Transformation in the Cell," *Scientific American*, May, 1960.

Lehninger, Albert L., *Bioenergetics* (2nd ed.), New York, Benjamin, 1971.

Levine, R. P., "The Mechanism of Photosynthesis," *Scientific American*, December, 1969.

Margaria, Rodolfo, "The Sources of Muscular Energy," *Scientific American*, March, 1972.

McElroy, William D., and Howard H. Seliger, "Biological Luminescence," *Scientific American*, December, 1962.

Racker, Efraim, "The Membrane of the Mitochondrion," *Scientific American*, February, 1968.

Rosenberg, Jerome L., *Photosynthesis*, New York, Holt, Rinehart and Winston, 1965.

Siekevitz, P., "Powerhouse of the Cell," *Scientific American*, July, 1957.

Stumpf, Paul K., "ATP," *Scientific American*, April, 1953.

Tucker, Vance A., "The Energetics of Bird Flight," *Scientific American*, May, 1969.

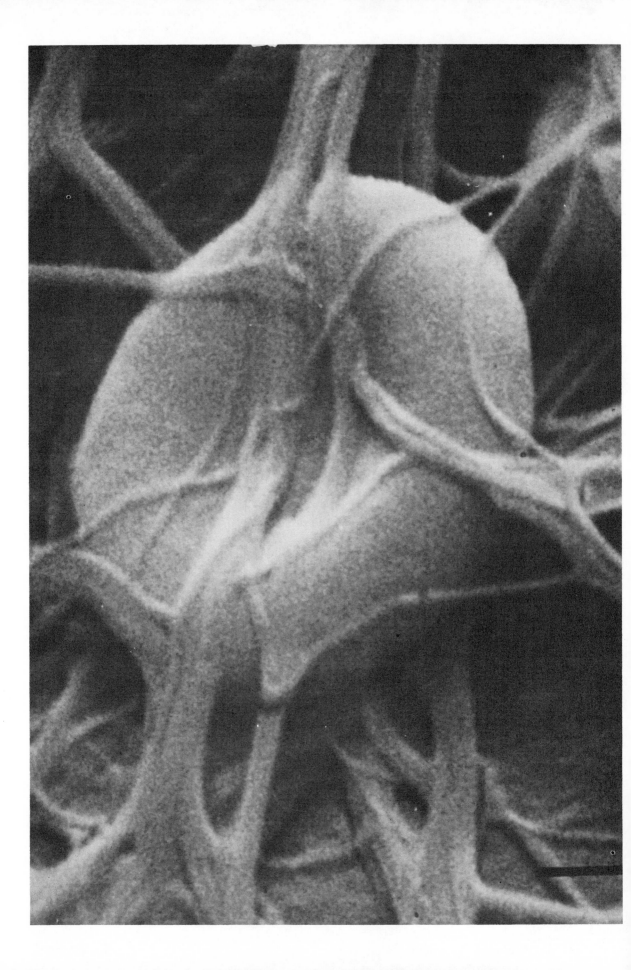

7

Supporting Processes of Life

The preceding chapter focused on the chemical energy pathways in cells—that is, the photosynthetic process and the various steps of respiration. To be sure, these are essential for life, but they are not the only chemical reactions that occur in living systems. For example, food must be broken down into small molecules that can enter cells and be used as fuels; gases must be exchanged with the external medium; and waste materials must be eliminated. The mechanisms for transporting nutrients, gases, and other chemical compounds in a living organism may be referred to as "supporting processes of life" since they essentially serve to facilitate energy production. All of these processes involve chemical reactions that are often summarized under the term *metabolism*. This chapter then concerns additional aspects of metabolism beyond those involved in the direct trapping and releasing of energy.

METABOLISM

FOOD AND CALORIES

The source of the raw materials for energy production is food. Basically, organic foodstuffs are composed of carbohydrates, fats, and proteins; the chemical structures of these were discussed in Chapter 2. Fats are the highest potential energy food because large amounts of hydrogen are contained in fatty acids and glycerol. Recall the important role of hydrogen and its electron in energy production described in Chapter 6.

The foods we consume contain specific numbers of *calories*, a term designating a unit of measurement defined as the amount of heat necessary to raise one milliliter of water one degree Celsius (centigrade). A special closed container called a bomb calorimeter is used to determine caloric content (Figure 7–1). It has been determined that, for example, one gram molecular weight of glucose (180 grams) will yield 680,000 calories when completely oxidized. The sample to be combusted is placed in the inner chamber of the calorimeter. The chamber (or bomb) is then charged with oxygen, sealed, and the contents ignited with an electric current. The amount of heat pro-

duced in the combustion is read directly from the thermometer and converted to calories. A calorie may therefore be further defined as a heat equivalent in calculating the potential energy of foods. Calories are usually expressed as kilocalories (1,000 calories), in which case the term "calories" is capitalized. For example, a slice of bread from a standard white loaf contains 63,000 calories (or 63 Calories) and one fried egg contains 77,000 calories (or 77 Calories).

In Chapter 6 we learned that one gram molecular weight of glucose (1 mole) oxidized through glycolysis and the Krebs cycle yields 38 moles of ATP. If we consider one mole of ATP to contain a potential energy of 10,000 calories, one gram molecular weight of glucose biologically oxidized would yield 380,000 calories. With this information we can now calculate the efficiency of the enzymatic energy production from glucose to be about 380,000/680,000 or approximately 56 percent. But when the high-energy bonds are broken in a mole of ATP, only about 8,000 calories are usable. The remaining energy is released in the form of heat which helps to maintain body temperature. The total energy efficiency is therefore somewhat closer to 40 percent.

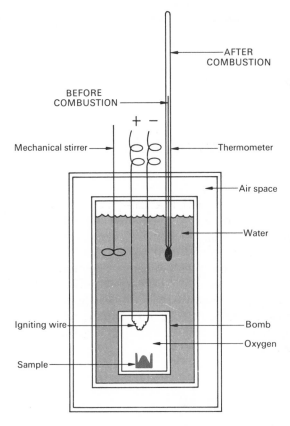

Figure 7–1 Typical components of a bomb calorimeter. The resistance wire between the electrodes ignites the oxygen and combusts the sample in the sealed bomb. The temperature change is read from the thermometer.

CALCULATION OF METABOLIC RATE

The caloric energy requirement may be calculated for any individual. This *basal metabolic rate* or BMR is a measure of the calories utilized by an organism that is awake and completely at rest. The caloric measurement is normally computed according to the amount of oxygen utilized and carbon dioxide released over a specific time interval. The amount of oxygen required and the amount of carbon dioxide released vary with the kinds of foods in an individual's diet. A normal human diet, for example, consists of a mixture of carbohydrates, proteins, and fats with each of these classes of foodstuff requiring a characteristic amount of oxygen when burned. The specific amount of oxygen necessary to oxidize glucose to CO_2 and H_2O is:

$$C_6H_{12}O_6 + 6O_2 \longrightarrow 6CO_2 + 6H_2O + \text{energy}$$
$$\text{(input)} \qquad \text{(output)}$$

Therefore the ratio of carbon-dioxide output to oxygen input is 6/6 or 1.0. This mathematical relationship is called the *respiratory quotient* or R.Q. value. For proteins the value is about 0.9 and for fats, 0.7. The average R.Q. value for a balanced diet is approximately 0.86.

A generalized BMR for humans has been found to be about one Calorie per kilogram of body weight per hour. Significant variation from this normal relationship usually indicates an organic imbalance in hormone or enzyme production. For example, an individual whose BMR Calories are less than one per kilogram of body weight is likely to have a less than normal secretion of the hormone *thyroxin*. Basically, a *hormone* is a substance secreted in one part of an organism which has effects in other parts of the organism. Thyroxin, for instance, is secreted by the thyroid gland and this hormone helps to regulate carbohydrate metabolism.

In addition to weight, several other factors such as age, sex, and body surface area influence the basal metabolic rate. BMRs vary greatly among individuals. The basal metabolic rate for an eighteen-year-old male college student is calculated as follows:

Oxygen consumed in 1 hour = 18 liters

Body weight = 185 pounds ÷ 2.2 = 84 kilograms

It has been determined that one liter of O_2 will produce about 4.8 Calories from a mixed diet—18 liters O_2 × 4.8 Cal = 86.4 Cal.

Therefore the BMR relationship is:

86.4 Cal/84 kilograms/1 hr

or approximately

1 Cal/1 kilogram/1 hr

NUTRITION AND VITAMINS

The chemical balance of foods consumed by an organism is just as important as the energy the foods provide. Although carbohydrates alone might provide enough caloric energy, fats, proteins, mineral ions, and vitamins are essential for the growth and repair of cells, enzyme function, synthesis of molecules, and support of the energy process. Therefore it is important that all organisms obtain the necessary nutritional molecules. With respect to human nutrition, we are aware of the important relationship between a balanced diet and good health.

Vitamins, a large and varied group of compounds, are exceptionally important in nutrition. The study of vitamins began when it was discovered that certain foods could prevent deficiency diseases such as scurvy and beriberi. Later, after analytical techniques were refined, the active substances could be isolated from the foods. Approximately thirty compounds so far have been isolated and classed as vitamins. In many instances it is still not known exactly what a vitamin does in a cell; we merely know what will happen externally if a vitamin is not present. Our knowledge of the roles played by vitamins in cellular functions is rapidly increasing however. For example, it has been clearly established that vitamin B_2 (riboflavin) is the precursor of FAD, a component of the electron-transport system discussed in Chapter 6. In fact, most members of the large vitamin B group seem to be used as raw materials to make coenzymes, which are necessary for catalyzing vital functions. Vitamin D, the only vitamin that humans can synthesize (the synthesis occurs in the skin under the stimulation of UV light), is known to be involved with calcium and phosphorus distribution; a serious lack of this vitamin leads to rickets, a softening of the bones. Again, we know this by the results of a deficiency. The actual molecular role of vitamin D in regulating calcium and phosphorus metabolism is still not known. A list of some of the vitamins with their roles and sources is given in Figure 7–2.

In *autotrophic* forms, most of the essential nutrients are synthesized or brought in with water. But in *heterotrophic* organisms, which cannot synthesize their own food, a mechanism for food procurement and digestion is necessary. *Saprophytes*, organisms which live on dead organic matter, and parasites, which obtain food from a living host, are highly specialized heterotrophs.

ENZYMATIC DIGESTION

The digestion of food is essentially the breakdown of large molecules into smaller molecules that can be absorbed and utilized in the syn-

Vitamin	Deficiency Symptoms	Cell Function	Source
Fat soluble			
Vitamin A	Night blindness; dry, scaly epithelial tissue; susceptibility to infection	Forms part of the molecules involved in the visual process	Yellow and green vegetables, fish oil, liver
Vitamin D	Rickets—abnormal bone development	Metabolism of calcium and phosphorus	Fish-liver oil, eggs, butter
Vitamin E	Muscle and nerve disorders; sterility	H transport in oxidation	Plant products, especially wheat-germ oil
Vitamin K	Slowed blood clotting	H transport in oxidation; synthesis of prothrombin	Most green plants
Water soluble			
Vitamin B_1 (thiamine)	Beriberi, nerve inflammation; muscle paralysis	Coenzyme to remove CO_2; for example, from pyruvic acid	Wheat germ, yeast, pork, eggs
Vitamin B_2 (riboflavin)	Lip lesions and inflamed eyes	Component of FAD, necessary for H transport	Milk products, green vegetables, liver, cereals
Vitamin B_6 (pyridoxine)	Dermatitis and reduced growth	Coenzymes for removal of CO_2 and transanimation	Cereals, eggs, meat
Vitamin B_{12} (cyanocobalamin)	Pernicious anemia—reduced number of red blood cells	Coenzyme necessary for nucleic-acid metabolism	Meat, liver, egg yolk
Nicotinic acid (niacin)	Pellagra—diarrhea, mental disorder, dermatitis	Component of NAD and NADP, necessary for H transport	Meat, liver, milk, yeast
Pantothenic acid	None known in humans	Component of coenzyme A	Most foods
Biotin	Mouth lesions—rarely seen in humans	Part of an enzyme necessary for carboxylation (addition of CO_2)	Vegetables, liver, milk, meat
Folic acid	Anemia—reduced number of red blood cells	Nucleic-acid synthesis	Leafy vegetables and most foods
Vitamin C (ascorbic acid)	Scurvy—inflammation of gums, anemia, and weakness	Aerobic H transport; synthesis of connective tissues	Citrus fruits and tomatoes

Figure 7–2   Summary of some of the important vitamins.

thetic processes, energy metabolism, maintenance, and repair. The splitting of large molecules into smaller units is accomplished by the enzymatic addition of water at certain bonding sites. For digestion to take place water must be added, a process called *hydrolytic cleavage*. This is the reverse of the synthesis of polysaccharides, proteins, and fats through the removal of water (dehydration synthesis).

PROTIST AND ANIMAL EXAMPLES

The process of digestion in some protists and throughout the animal kingdom occurs in many different types of systems, some of which are described and diagrammed in Figure 7–3. In many organisms digestion is entirely *intracellular* (within the cell). The *Amoeba*, a protist, captures its food with a flowing pseudopod, whereas the *Paramecium*

engulfs particles which are carried into a groovelike gullet by beating cilia. In either case the cell membrane surrounds the food which then is pinched off to form a food vacuole within the cell. Intracellular enzymes immediately begin to digest the food and the usable nutrients diffuse into the cytoplasm. In unicellular organisms such as these all of the processes of life must be accomplished in a single cell.

Sponges, considered to be at the cellular

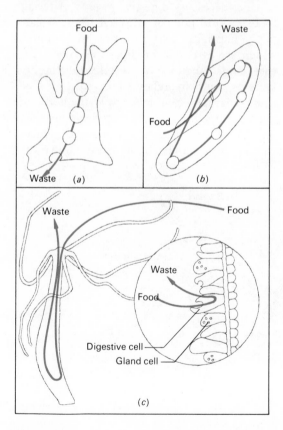

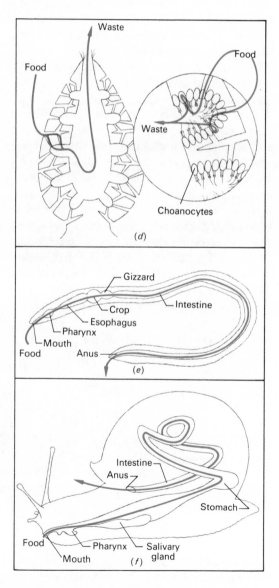

Figure 7–3 Some examples of how digestion occurs among selected protists and animals. (*a*) Amoeba. (*b*) Paramecium. (*c*) Coelenterate (hydra). (*d*) Sponge. (*e*) Earthworm. (*f*) Snail.

207

level of development, have a cavity which is lined with flagellated collar cells (choanocytes). Food particles brought in by the water current produced by the beating flagella are caught and engulfed by the cytoplasm in the collar that surrounds the flagellum. The digestion is again intracellular.

Even in the coelenterates such as hydra, jellyfish, and sea anemones, digestion is almost completely intracellular. Threadlike filaments, however, project from the thin layer of gastric cells lining the gastrovascular cavity and contact the food. These gastric filaments secrete enzymes which can actually initiate the digestive process outside the digestive cells. The one opening to the digestive area (the gastrovascular cavity) serves as both mouth and anus.

In the earthworm, phylum Annelida, a digestive tract with two openings, a mouth and an anus, is present. Along this tract are specialized regions for the digestion and absorption of food. These specialized areas are the crop, a thin-walled portion in which food is stored; the gizzard, a muscular region where food is ground; and the intestine, where digestive enzymes are added from the intestinal walls and digestion takes place. When digestion occurs outside of cells, in a cavity, it is known as extracellular digestion.

A variety of digestive processes are present among the mollusks. Certain aquatic snails digest most of their food within large digestive gland cells, whereas the octopus and the squid possess extracellular digestion almost entirely.

In general, digestive systems become more complex and extracellular digestion more predominant as one investigates the phylogenetic order from the kingdom Monera to the phylum Chordata. The fundamental enzymatic mechanisms of hydrolysis, however, are always similar.

THE VERTEBRATE PLAN

The digestive process as it occurs in man will be presented here as an example of digestion in vertebrates. The vertebrate digestive system, known as the *alimentary canal*, includes the mouth, esophagus, stomach, small intestine, large intestine, rectum, and anus. In addition, the liver, gallbladder, and pancreas serve as accessory digestive organs. Although foodstuffs do not pass through these organs, many hormones and enzymes are produced which are essential for digestion. The structure and function of vertebrate digestive systems vary in relationship to the foods eaten (Figure 7–4). For example, the herbivore digestive tract is generally longer and possesses one or more pouches for storage. During storage, special bacteria break down the

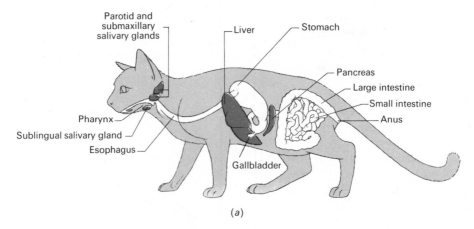

(a)

Figure 7–4 Comparison of digestive systems. (a) Cat. (b) Deer. (c) Man. Note the large storage pouches in the deer, a herbivorous ruminant.

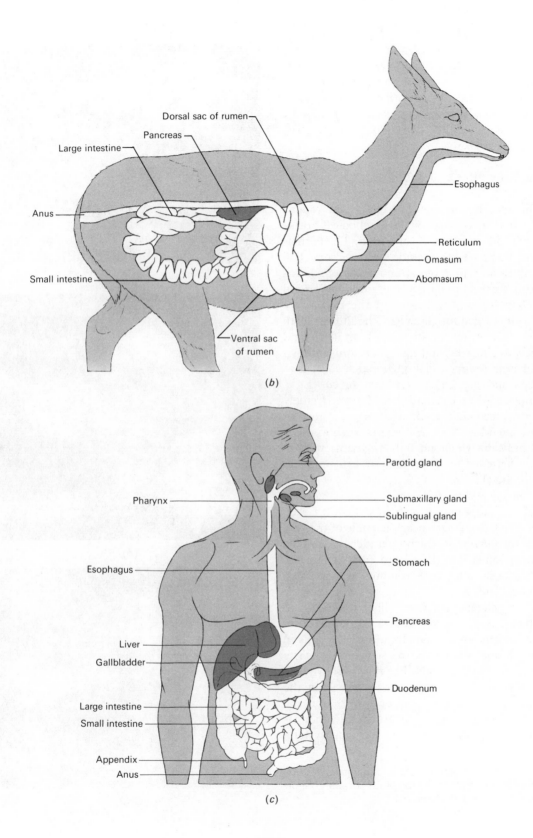

(b)

(c)

209

tough, fibrous cellulose and provide nutrients for the host. The cow and deer have four-part stomachs, and the largest pouch, known as the rumen, is the site of extensive bacterial action.

Functionally, the digestive process may be separated into three phases: salivary, gastric, and intestinal.

SALIVARY PHASE OF DIGESTION

The mouth contains the teeth and tongue which are necessary for the mechanical breakdown and transport of solid food. The permanent human teeth include four incisors, two canine, four premolars, and six molars. Incisors are used in biting, the canines are useful for ripping and tearing, and the molars are broadly ridged for chewing. The human teeth are efficient for masticating both flesh and vegetable matter, and man therefore is classified as an *omnivore* along with such animals as bears and pigs. The meateater or *carnivore*, represented by cats and dogs, have extremely sharp, needlelike teeth necessary for tearing and shredding flesh. *Herbivores*, such as cattle or beavers, which eat only vegetable matter, have flattened tooth surfaces for crushing and grinding (Figure 7–5).

During mastication, three pairs of salivary glands, the *parotid* located just beneath each ear, the *submaxillary* near the angle of the jaw, and the *sublingual* which lie under the tongue, empty saliva into the mouth cavity. Saliva is a viscous liquid that contains water, salts, mucin, and a carbohydrate-splitting enzyme called salivary amylase. The functions of saliva include the breakdown of starches and the lubrication of food. In addition, it aids in speech and allows for the sensation of taste by liquifying dry foods. The flow of saliva may be activated by the presence of food in the mouth, the smell of food, or simply thinking about eating. The control of salivation is directed by the autonomic nervous system.

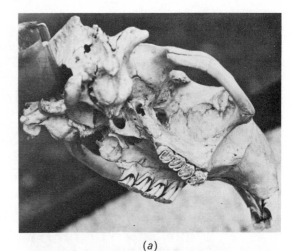

(a)

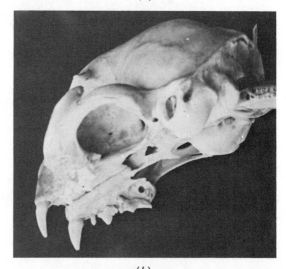

(b)

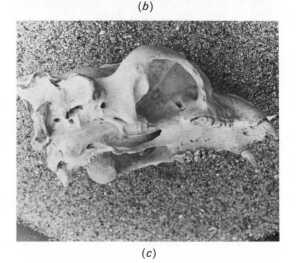

(c)

Figure 7–5 Dentition of the upper jaws of three animals. (*a*) Beaver (herbivore). (*b*) Cat (carnivore. (*c*) Bear (omnivore).

210

This involuntary system will be discussed in the next chapter.

Salivary secretions contain two enzymes, *salivary amylase* or *ptyalin* and *maltase*. Salivary amylase hydrolyzes starches into smaller double-sugar units of maltose ($C_{12}H_{22}O_{11}$). Vertebrate amylases act only on the carbohydrate alpha linkages and have no digestive action on beta-linked cellulose molecules. These linkages were discussed in Chapter 2. Maltase cleaves the maltose into two glucose units through the catalytic addition of water. The pH of the mouth fluids is normally near 7 or neutrality. Experiments with human salivary amylase, using a starch substrate, indicate an optimum activity range of pH 6.5 to 7.5. The term *substrate* indicates a substance that is being acted upon by an enzyme. Glucose, as you learned in the previous chapter, is immediately available for energy metabolism when absorbed into the bloodstream. Total carbohydrate digestion, however, is usually not completed in the mouth. When the ball of food or *bolus* reaches the stomach, the high acid content of that organ ultimately inhibits the action of amylase. The final stages of starch digestion take place in the small intestine.

GASTRIC PHASE OF DIGESTION

The stomach, a muscular, J-shaped organ, lies just below the diaphragm. The esophagus, the tube leading from the mouth, enters the stomach through a constriction called the *cardiac valve*. The stomach is divided into three parts, the upper or *cardiac* portion which includes the saclike *fundus*, the *body*, and the lower region or *pylorus* where it joins with the small intestine. The wall of the stomach is composed of three layers of muscle—an outer longitudinal, a middle oblique, and an internal circular. There is also a lining made up of distinct longitudinal ridges called *rugae*, and these rugae folds allow for expansion. The entrance to the small intestine from the stomach is guarded by a circular muscle called a *sphincter valve*. This valve keeps the food in the stomach for digestion and protects the relatively thin-walled intestine against large, abrasive chunks of food. The bolus to be digested is transported along the entire digestive tract by means of rhythmic waves of muscle contractions. This action, termed *peristalsis*, is controlled by the involuntary nervous system. Carbohydrate digestion has been arrested here because of the extreme acidity of the stomach which ranges from pH 2 to 5.

In invertebrates the stomach functions principally as a storage, grinding, or straining organ. In vertebrates, however, the stomach has a definite secretory role. The *parietal* cells secrete hydrochloric acid (HCl), and the *chief* cells secrete an inactive protein-splitting (proteolytic) enzyme called *pepsinogen*. Pepsinogen is acted on by HCl to form *pepsin* which in turn hydrolyzes protein into polypeptides, dipeptides, and amino acids (Figure 7–6). Hydrochloric acid also serves the important function of killing bacteria and breaking down the intercellular cement of fibrous plant and animal tissues. When food enters through the cardiac valve of the esophagus, the lining of the stomach secretes digestive juices. The presence of the food also activates the lining cells to release the hormone *gastrin* into the bloodstream which stimulates HCl and pepsinogen secretion. Another hormone, *enterogastrone*, produced in the duodenum, inhibits the secretion of gastric juice, thereby preventing overproduction. Due to nervous

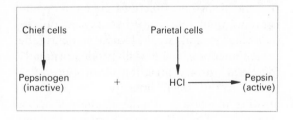

Figure 7–6 Pepsinogen secreted by the chief cells of the stomach is activated by HCl, which is secreted by the parietal cells. Both of these cell types are located in the gastric mucosa.

211

stimulation some gastric secretion may occur when food is taken into the mouth. In young mammals, a special milk-coagulating enzyme, *rennin*, causes the normally soluble casein protein of milk to unite with calcium and fat to form insoluble curds. As the individual matures, rennin production is greatly decreased or lost; the curdling role is adequately accomplished, however, by pepsin and HCl. The curds are finally digested by proteolytic and fat enzymes in the stomach and small intestine.

The occurrence of gastric ulcers illustrates the fact that gastric secretions are controlled primarily by the autonomic nervous system. An ulcer is an area of the alimentary canal that has been eroded away owing to the excessive action of peristalsis, HCl, and digestive enzymes. Anxiety and nervous tension can cause this condition. The stomach normally is lined with a glycoprotein coating, *mucin*, which protects the cells from self-digestion (autolysis). Excessive secretion and peristaltic action in the absence of food removes this protective coating. Ulcers are often painful and may produce internal hemorrhages if the blood vessels lying below the lining are also eroded.

INTESTINAL PHASE OF DIGESTION

Peristaltic contractions force the partially digested food through the *pyloric valve* into the first portion of the small intestine. The first ten inches of the small intestine, called the *duodenum*, is the site of a number of digestive and absorptive functions. The duodenum contains numerous fingerlike projections or *villi* which extend into the lumen (center) of the tube. Functionally, these villi produce a greatly increased surface area for absorption. The fluids in the small intestine are generally alkaline in contrast to the stomach's acidic secretions. The pH ranges between 6.8 and 8.0 in the small intestine.

PANCREATIC ENZYMES

The presence of partially digested food in the duodenum stimulates the intestinal mucosa

cells to secrete the hormone *secretin* which in turn causes the pancreas to secrete large amounts of sodium bicarbonate. It is this substance that maintains the duodenum in an alkaline condition. A second hormone produced by the duodenum, *pancreozymin*, stimulates the pancreas to release its digestive enzymes. Each day the pancreas produces 500 to 800 ml of fluid containing the various enzymes needed for the hydrolysis of all types of food. The specific enzymes produced by the pancreas and the types of food they hydrolyze are (1) *pancreatic amylase*—starch, (2) *pancreatic lipase*—fats, (3) *trypsin*—native protein (albumins, collagen), and (4) *carboxypeptidase*—peptide bonds which are adjacent to a free-COOH group.

The action of pancreatic amylase on starches is very similar to that in the mouth. Pancreatic lipase cleaves fats at the ester bonds to release glycerol and fatty acids. Large globules of fat are emulsified by *bile* which enters the small intestine near the pancreatic duct via the common bile duct from the liver and the gallbladder. The bile lowers the surface tension surrounding the fat molecules and produces smaller droplets which exposes more surface area to the lipase enzyme. Thus bile is only an aid to fat digestion and not an enzyme. The presence of fats in the small intestine stimulates the intestinal lining (mucosa) to secrete the hormone *cholecystokinin* which enters the bloodstream and causes the release of bile from the gallbladder.

Trypsin, a protein-breaking enzyme, is comparable to gastric pepsin. It acts in an alkaline medium, however, and hydrolyzes complex proteins at a slower rate than does pepsin. Trypsin is secreted by the pancreas in an inactive form called *trypsinogen*. The conversion of trypsinogen to trypsin is accomplished by the action of a nondigestive enzyme secreted by the intestinal mucosa called *enterokinase*. It has been demonstrated that enterokinase removes a fragment from the trypsinogen molecule which permits it to become active. Since we know that an enzyme has a very specific geometry with important substrate-contact areas called "active sites," it is probable that the conversion process is

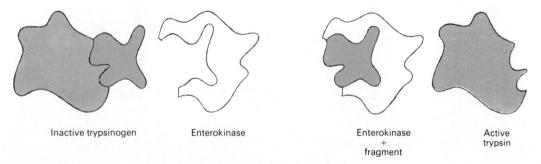

Inactive trypsinogen Enterokinase

Enterokinase
+
fragment

Active
trypsin

Figure 7–7 Model of the unmasking action of enterokinase on trypsinogen. The removal of the fragment frees the active site, and trypsin becomes functional.

simply an unmasking of the active sites (Figure 7–7).

Carboxypeptidase, the remaining proteolytic enzyme supplied by the pancreas, serves a very specific function. It hydrolyzes the peptide linkages which are adjacent to free carboxyl (acid) groups.

INTESTINAL ENZYMES

The small intestine is the site of final digestion and a number of digestive enzymes are secreted here. These enzymes are secreted by individual cells that lie at the base of the villi folds and also by the compound intestinal glands located in the submucosa layer. The flow of intestinal enzymes is initiated by the release of the hormone *enterocrinin* from the intestinal mucosa. All of the digestive hormones included in this discussion are summarized in Figure 7–8.

Intestinal lipase and amylase have functions similar to pancreatic enzymes already described. Dipeptidases split the small units of double amino acids into individual acids which can then be absorbed and utilized. *Aminopeptidase* is similar in action to carboxypeptidase in that it breaks peptide bonds adjacent to free amino groups. Most of the complex carbohydrates have been broken into twelve-carbon sugars by salivary and pancreatic amylases. The intestine produces not only an amylase but also three enzymes commonly classed as *disaccharases* which split disaccharides (twelve-carbon sugars). These three enzymes are: *maltase* (maltose → glucose + glucose), *sucrase* (sucrose → fructose + glucose), and *lactase* (lactose → galactose + glu-

cose). The digestion of foods is thus a stepwise process in which intermediate products are formed on the way to the end products (Figure 7–9).

ABSORPTION OF DIGESTIVE PRODUCTS

The duodenum is the first area of absorption of digested nutrients and absorption occurs along most of the small intestine. The cells lining the intestinal villi display selective absorption —that is, certain substances are absorbed faster than others. For example, the six-

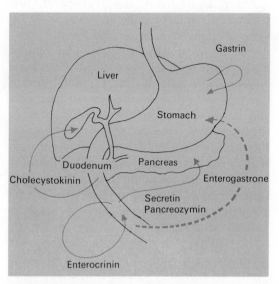

Figure 7–8 Summary of the hormones involved in the digestive process of man. The broken arrow indicates inhibition of gastric secretion by the hormone enterogastrone.

213

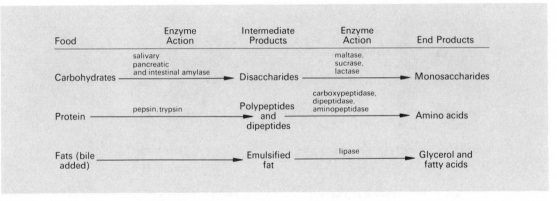

Food	Enzyme Action	Intermediate Products	Enzyme Action	End Products
Carbohydrates	salivary pancreatic and intestinal amylase	Disaccharides	maltase, sucrase, lactase	Monosaccharides
Protein	pepsin, trypsin	Polypeptides and dipeptides	carboxypeptidase, dipeptidase, aminopeptidase	Amino acids
Fats (bile added)		Emulsified fat	lipase	Glycerol and fatty acids

Figure 7–9 Summary showing the intermediate and end products resulting from the digestion of the three classes of foods. Some of the major enzymes that function at each step are noted.

carbon sugar galactose is absorbed faster than glucose, and glucose is absorbed faster than fructose. The cells are also capable of absorbing substances against a *concentration gradient.* In our earlier definition of diffusion we learned that particles tend to diffuse away from the greatest concentration. As absorption continues it is certain that each cell will collect a higher concentration of nutrients than is found in the intestinal juice. The movement of these substances into the cells and bloodstream thus is against the gradient and requires energy in the form of ATP. You might benefit by reviewing the section on active transport in Chapter 3 at this time.

Absorbed nutrients pass through the intestinal cells and enter the bloodstream. Each villus contains an arteriole and a venule connected by a capillary network. The venules finally form a larger vein called the *hepatic portal vein.* As a result of absorption, blood in this vein is highly concentrated with nutrients and passes directly to the capillary beds of the liver. Most veins lead directly to the heart; the term *portal* identifies any venous system that carries blood to an organ other than the heart. In frogs, for example, a special venous system carries blood from the legs to the capillaries of the kidneys, thus this vessel is termed the renal portal vein.

A third type of vessel called a *lacteal* is located in each villus. The lacteal vessels are part of an accessory venous system known as the *lymphatic system.* The lacteals absorb emulsified fats and route them away from the liver and into a larger lymphatic duct or *thoracic duct* which passes upward through the diaphragm and empties into the left subclavian vein above the heart. Perhaps it is now clear to you how excessive fat ingestion can cause fat deposition in the vessels near the heart.

The remaining part of the small intestine is separated into the *jejunum* (about eight feet) and the *ileum* (twelve feet). The junction between the ileum and the ascending colon of the large intestine is controlled by the *ileocecal* valve which keeps nonabsorbed wastes from backing up in the system. The vermiform appendix (a vestigial organ in man) extends from the caecum or blind pouch of the ascending colon. The appendix apparently no longer serves a vital function. The major organs and enzymes involved in digestion in man are summarized in Figure 7–10.

THE ROLE OF THE LARGE INTESTINE

The large intestine or colon functions primarily in water and ion absorption, concentration of feces, and defecation. Bacteria are common in the colon where residual polysaccharides and cellulose may be further broken down through the action of bacterial enzymes. In addition some bacteria produce vitamin K and a few B vitamins. The colon averages about two

214

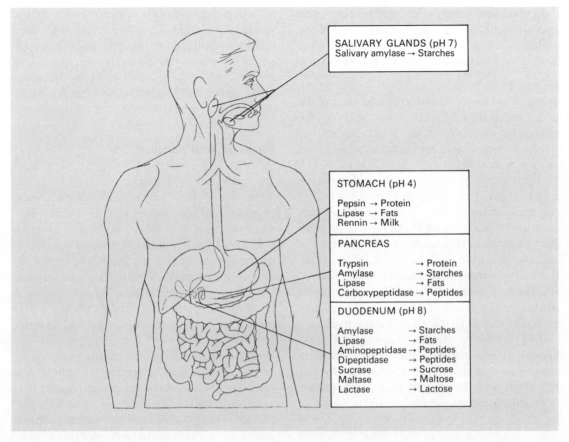

Figure 7–10 Summary of digestion in man. The enzymes and the foods they act on are shown for each area of digestion.

and a half inches in width and is five to six feet long. The descending colon, in a long S shape, is often referred to as the sigmoid colon. The last eight to ten inches of the alimentary tract includes the rectum, anal canal, and anus.

THE LIVER AND METABOLISM

The largest and one of the most important organs for general metabolism in vertebrates is the liver. In adult humans it weighs between three and four pounds and performs a variety of functions. This four-lobed organ lies just below the diaphragm and above the stomach. The liver-tissue cells are all similar, and each one appears to be capable of all functions. Among the most important functions we

should consider are synthesis, storage, regulation, and detoxification.

SYNTHESIS

The liver is the site of many chemical reactions. Some of the glucose molecules brought into the liver spaces from the small intestine are synthesized into the polysaccharide glycogen. The formation of glycogen from glucose molecules is termed *glycogenesis*. It is also possible for the liver cells to convert non-carbohydrate molecules such as amino acids and fats into glycogen, and this more complex process is called *glyconeogenesis*. The "neo" (meaning "new") indicates that glycogen was synthesized from molecules other than carbohydrates.

215

In the liver, amino acids may be converted into *keto* acids by the enzymatic removal of the amino group in a process known as *deamination*. The term *keto* refers to the structural group

$$C—\overset{\overset{\textstyle O}{\|}}{C}—C.$$

Most amino acids can be transformed into different amino acids by the enzymatic exchange of an amino group between an amino acid and a keto or fatty acid in a *transamination* reaction (Figure 7–11). In this manner the liver regulates the amino-acid balance of the body and quickly supplies required amino acids. The body does not store amino acids except in the form of protein. Any amino acid that cannot be synthesized or cannot be synthesized fast enough to satisfy the body demand is termed *essential*, that is, it must be obtained from the food supply. In man, 10 amino acids of a list of approximately 20 have been determined to be essential.

The synthesis of the yellow-green fluid known as bile occurs continuously in liver cells. The secreted fluid is collected by the bile ducts and transported to the gallbladder to be stored. Bile is a complex substance made up chiefly of pigments, salts, cholesterol, and water. Biliverdin (green) and bilirubin (yellow) pigments are derived from the hemoglobin of old red blood cells broken down in the spleen, liver, and bone marrow. Bile is released from the gallbladder into the small intestine where it emulsifies fats. In the process of emulsification, large particles of fat are separated into smaller units which can be easily digested by enzymes.

STORAGE AND REGULATION

The cells and intercellular spaces of the liver, often called the "sugar bin" of the body, provide storage space for glycogen, fats, vitamins, iron, and bile. The liver is also important in maintaining the general balance of many chemical activities. Especially important is its regulation of carbohydrate metabolism. Glycogenesis is accelerated by the hormone *insulin* from specific cells in the pancreas. Hormones from the adrenal cortex and anterior pituitary gland also help in glycogenesis. The breakdown of stored glycogen into blood sugar, called *glycogenolysis* (meaning to split glycogen), is enhanced by a second pancreatic hormone, *glucagon*. The function of insulin and glucagon is a good example of the antagonistic action or check-and-balance system of hormonal control. The control of carbohydrate,

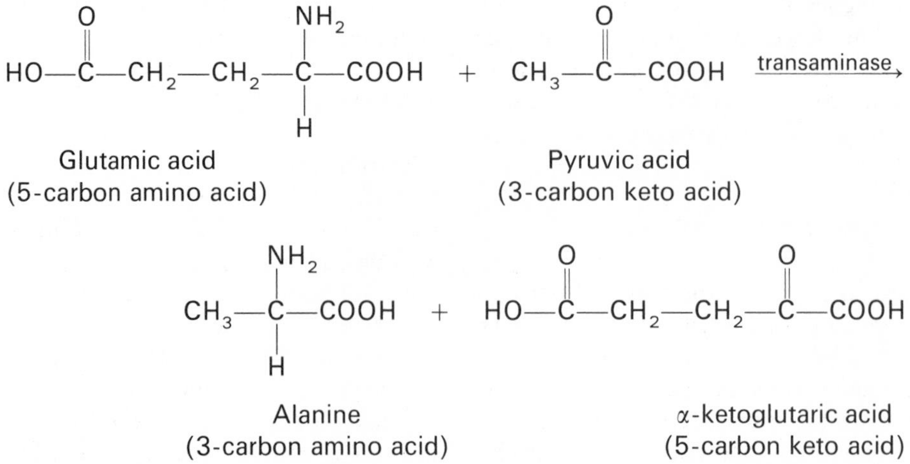

Glutamic acid
(5-carbon amino acid)

Pyruvic acid
(3-carbon keto acid)

transaminase→

Alanine
(3-carbon amino acid)

α-ketoglutaric acid
(5-carbon keto acid)

Figure 7–11 Transamination between glutamic acid and pyruvic acid. This reaction yields alanine and α-ketoglutaric acid.

216

protein, and fat metabolism occurring in the liver is illustrated in Figure 7–12.

DETOXIFICATION

Many organic compounds may be toxic to the organism if they accumulate in large amounts. Nitrogen in the compound ammonia is released in deamination and is extremely toxic. This toxicity results from the reaction of ammonia with water to produce an alkaline pH. We learn later in this chapter how the liver incorporates ammonia into less poisonous urea which may be safely excreted by the kidneys.

Large detoxifying cells (macrophages) located in the liver capillaries actually engulf and digest small particles such as bacteria and parasitic protozoa. These star-shaped cells move somewhat like amoebae in trapping and engulfing foreign material.

CIRCULATION AND TRANSPORTATION

Organisms range in size from single cells of less than a micron to the 100-foot-long, 150-ton great blue whale. The world's largest plants are represented by the 300-foot giant redwoods of California. It is fairly clear to us how compounds enter, circulate, and leave small organisms by diffusion. It is somewhat more difficult, however, to understand the complex mechanism of circulation and transportation of materials in the whale or the giant redwoods.

Perhaps the most basic factor in circulation and transportation problems is the ratio between the volume of the organism to its external surface area. Most multicellular plants and animals which possess a high volume-to-surface-area ratio must also have special systems to facilitate nutrition, gas exchange, and excretion. This is necessary because most of

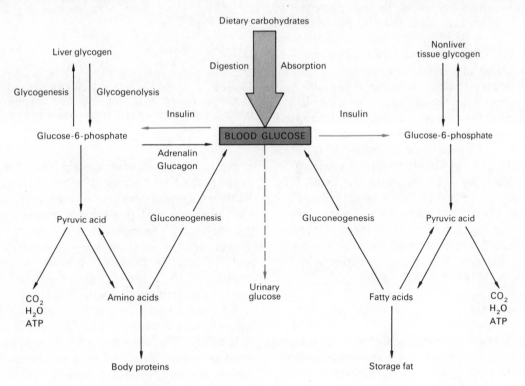

Figure 7–12 Possible fate of blood glucose. When blood glucose is high, insulin promotes the phosphorylation of glucose to produce glycogen. When blood sugar is low, glucagon and adrenalin initiate the conversion of glycogen to glucose.

217

the mass of the body of the organism is not directly exposed to the environment.

IN PLANTS

In Chapter 4 we learned that vascular plants contain special transport tissues. Xylem vessels carry water from the roots to all the branches and leaves. The fact that a redwood tree can effectively "lift" water over 300 feet against gravity is still an intriguing question to scientists. The most accepted theory to explain this has been presented by an English botanist, H. H. Dixon. Dixon demonstrated that molecules of water standing in slender tubes have very high cohesion—that is, they tend to stick together. As water is lost through *transpiration* (evaporation of water from stomates) or utilized in photosynthesis, new water molecules diffuse into the vessels at the root level. Roots generally possess high osmotic pressures owing to the presence of sugar-laden sap. High osmotic pressure permits water to move into the root cells from the soil—that is, from a region of greater concentration to a region of lesser concentration. This pressure alone, however, is not sufficient to account for the lifting of the water in the column. Transpiration creates a pulling effect on the unbroken column of water. These events are summarized in Figure 7–13.

The phloem vessels transport sugars from the leaves to other organs of the plant. The direction of this food flow is principally downward toward the roots. In the winter when food production is reduced, the flow may be upward from the storage areas in the roots. The movement of organic nutrients in the phloem is called *translocation*.

IN ANIMALS

Many small and parasitic forms, such as tapeworms and liver flukes, lack specific circulatory and respiratory systems. In general, however, two types of blood circulatory systems are found in animals—open and closed. In *open circulatory systems* the blood is pumped from

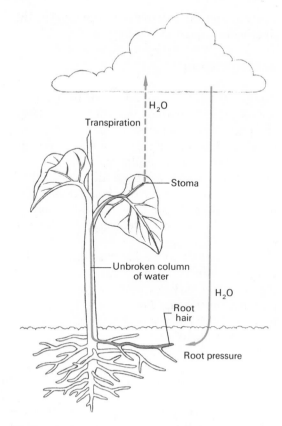

Figure 7–13 Movement of water from the roots to the leaves in trees. An unbroken column of water is essential between root pressure and transpirational pull.

a contractile heart into a main artery that supplies the body tissues. The blood collects in tissue sinuses (spaces), bathing each cell with nutrients and providing a medium for gas exchange. The blood then is collected in a large sinus or *hemocoel* before oxygenation and recirculation through the heart. A good example of the open system is found in the crayfish, an arthropod (Figure 7–14).

A *closed circulatory system* is present in earthworms (Annelida) and all vertebrates (Chordata). The closed system is composed of an artery–capillary bed–vein structure with which you are probably familiar (Figures 7–15 and 7–16). Exchange of gases, uptake of nutrients, and release of waste materials by the cells must occur across the capillary mem-

218

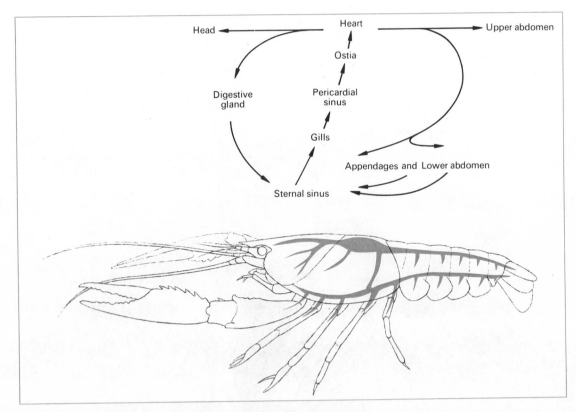

Figure 7-14 Open circulatory system of the crayfish, an arthropod. Note the sternal (hemocoel) and pericardial sinuses.

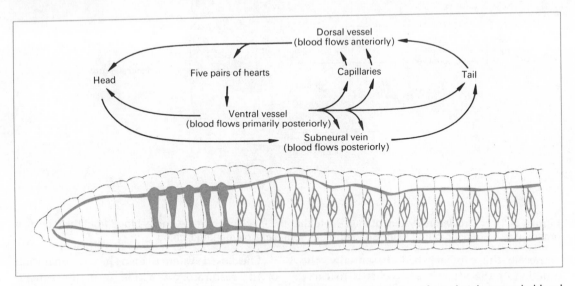

Figure 7-15 Closed blood flow in the earthworm. Each segment has a set of arteries that supply blood to the digestive tract, excretory organs, and muscles. All the arteries and veins are connected by capillary vessels. Oxygenation occurs by diffusion through the skin.

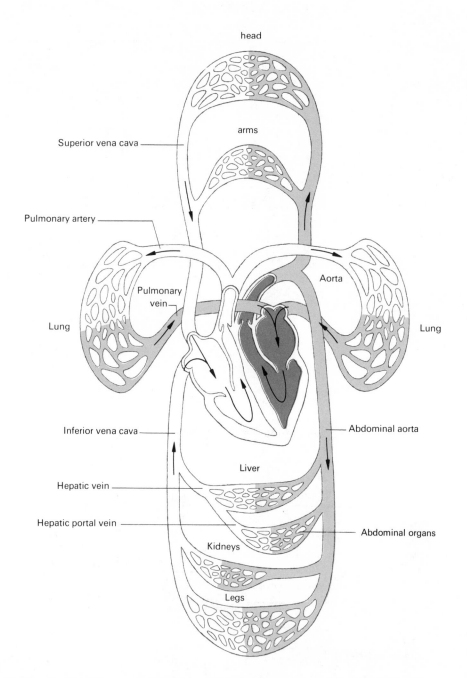

Figure 7–16 Circulatory system of man. Note that the liver collects the venous blood from the digestive organs via the hepatic portal vein. Shaded areas represent oxygenated blood.

branes in the capillary bed. Essentially, the function of the arteries and veins is to carry blood to and from the capillary beds. The higher pressure of the closed system greatly aids this process, as we shall see later.

The closed system in man shows a separation of the respiratory function from the general circulation. All deoxygenated blood is collected in the right atrium, transfered into the right ventricle, and then pumped to the lungs through the pulmonary artery. This is the only artery that carries deoxygenated blood. The oxygenated blood is returned to the left atrium, passed into the left ventricle, and pumped throughout the body. After passing through capillaries, the blood returns to the heart through veins. The flow of blood is maintained by pressure which results from the strength and rate of contraction of the left ventricle and the size and elasticity of the arteries. The pressure resulting from the contraction of the left ventricle, *systolic* pressure, is approximately 120 mm Hg pressure; the pressure remaining when the ventricle relaxes, *diastolic* pressure, is approximately 80 mm Hg. Blood pressures are generally reported as systole/diastole, or 120/80 mm Hg in this example. The average human heart contracts or beats about 72 times per minute. This rate is controlled primarily by the "pacemaker," a node of specialized tissue in the wall of the right atrium, the sinoatrial (SA) node (Figure 7–17). This SA node sends impulses through the atria to another node (the AV or atrioventricular) located in the lower part of the septum between the two atria. The impulse is next relayed down the ventricular septum and out into the muscle of the ventricles. The origin of the heart beat is definitely in the heart muscle, but the beat is normally coordinated by the pacemaker. Heart rate is also under the influence of two sets of involuntary nerves, one which increases heart rate and one which slows it. In addition, the rate of the heart beat is affected by hormones and other chemicals. Impairment of this control-conducting system

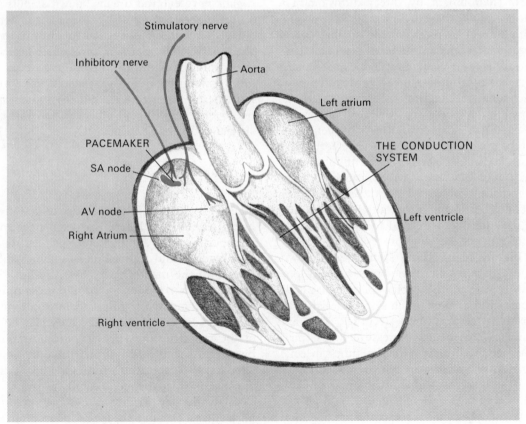

Figure 7–17 Human heart showing the chambers, pacemaker, conduction system, and two sets of involuntary nerves which influence heart rate. (Redrawn from *Pacemaker Patient Booklet—An Informational Guide for the Patient*, 1971, courtesy of Medtronic, Minneapolis, Minnesota.)

can be corrected by an artificial pacemaker. These are essentially fixed-rate, battery generators which send regular impulses to the heart muscle.

When arteries become old and inelastic or narrowed through fatty deposits (arteriosclerosis), blood pressure increases. Extremely high blood pressure can cause a *stroke*, the rupture of blood vessels in the brain. When one of the coronary arteries which supply blood to the heart is blocked by a clot or fat deposits, a heart attack can occur.

GAS EXCHANGE

Small aquatic organisms such as amoebae or even the flatworms can exchange gases with their environment by direct diffusion. The surface area of these organisms is large enough with respect to their volume so that special breathing organs are unnecessary. This large surface-area-to-volume ratio does not exist in vertebrates or most of the larger invertebrates, and some mechanism or organ system for breathing is necessary. Cellular respiration, discussed in Chapter 6, utilizes oxygen in the Krebs cycle and the electron-transport series. Carbon dioxide, which is given off in this process, must be carried away from the cell and eventually transported back to the environment. Keep in mind that although breathing or gas exchange is related to cellular respiration, it is not the same process.

Five basic breathing systems are known: (1) direct diffusion (plants, protists, and some invertebrate animals such as planaria), (2) gills (crustaceans, some mollusks, and fish), (3) positive-pressure lungs (reptiles and amphibians), (4) negative-pressure lungs (birds and mammals), and (5) tracheal tubes (insects). These five systems are illustrated in Figure 7–18 and discussed individually in the following sections. We should note that in all systems other than the direct diffusion of certain single-celled organisms and plants, a thin, moist membrane is necessary for the exchange of gases.

DIRECT DIFFUSION

All aerobic (oxygen-requiring) protists exchange gases through body-surface diffusion. Since most of these organisms are aquatic and essentially unicellular, direct diffusion is an efficient mechanism. Sponges, coelenterates, and flatworms, although being larger and multicellular, require no special breathing organs or systems. In plants the exchange of gases occurs principally through small openings in the leaves called stomata (described in Chapter 4 in the section on plant tissues).

GILLS

Aquatic animals possessing many tissues and organs have evolved organs known as gills to increase surface area for gas exchange. Very sluggish invertebrates such as tubeworms and snails have gills. Starfish have small projections from the skin which function as a type of gill. In more active animals, such as fish, water must be moved across the gills by swimming or, as with crayfish and other crustaceans, by special paddlelike appendages.

POSITIVE-PRESSURE LUNGS

The complications of the vertebrate body require a highly efficient gas-exchange and transport system. Amphibians, such as frogs, salamanders, and reptiles, possess lungs that open into the mouth cavity by a *trachea*. In order to inflate the lungs, these animals must close their mouths tightly and force air into the lungs by compressing the muscular floor of the mouth cavity (Figure 7–19). Amphibians that spend much of their time in moist habitats also "breathe" through their thin, moist skin, since the blood capillaries are very close to the skin surface. Frogs may accomplish at least one-third of their total respiration by this *cutaneous breathing*. Cutaneous diffusion is very important during winter hibernation at the bottom of ponds.

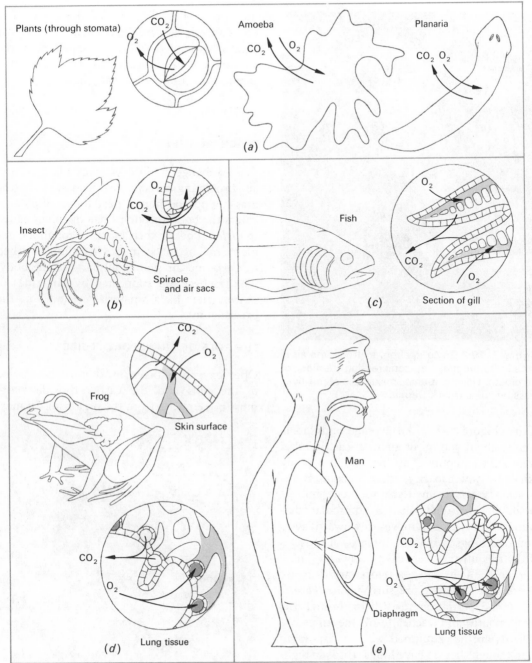

Figure 7–18 Basic breathing systems. Shaded areas represent oxygenated blood. (*a*) Diffusion. (*b*) Tracheal tubes. (*c*) Gills. (*d*) Positive-pressure lungs and cutaneous diffusion. (*e*) Negative-pressure lungs.

NEGATIVE-PRESSURE LUNGS

Mammals, including man, have structurally complex lungs. The tissue of the human lung is a good example of the thin, moist membranes needed for gas exchange. The tiny *alveolar sacs* are composed of extremely thin cells and are continuously bathed by tissue

fluids (Figure 7–20). An average adult male inhales about 500 ml of air with each normal breath. The amount of air that can be forcibly exhaled (vital capacity) after maximum inhalation varies from 4,500 to 7,000 ml. At inhalation the dome-shaped, muscular diaphragm contracts and moves downward, away from the lungs, while the intercostal muscles of the ribs lift the chest cavity upward. These combined efforts cause a temporary decrease in pressure (negative pressure) in the *thoracic cavity* and permit air to rush in through the nose, mouth, and trachea to fill the lungs.

Birds are not equipped with a diaphragm even though they do have lungs. Birds in flight require a lot of energy and maintain very high metabolic rates. Gas exchange then becomes a critical problem, and, since they do not gulp air as amphibians do, they must possess some unique mechanism. Bird lungs are small and compact and lie close to the body wall. Four pairs of lung sacs extend from the main lung

into practically all parts of the body. The lungs and air sacs are filled when the muscular chest is expanded, and the trapped air in the air sacs is forced back into the lungs upon exhalation. Thus the main lung of a bird actually receives air at both inhalation and exhalation.

TRACHEAL TUBES

Gas exchange in insects takes place by the air circulating directly to the tissues. In the grasshopper or honey bee, for example, air enters the body through small openings called *spiracles*. The air then passes through a complex branched system of tiny tubules called *tracheae* and air sacs to all parts of the body. The tracheae are supported by tiny rings of *chitin* (the hard material found in the exoskeleton).

THE ROLE OF TRANSPORT FLUIDS

Once oxygen is taken in, it must be carried to the cells and the carbon-dioxide waste must be removed from the organism. In most

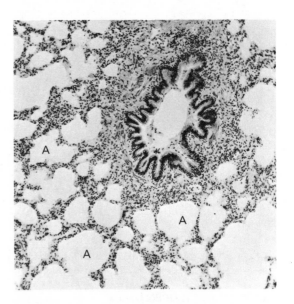

Figure 7–20 Photomicrograph of a cross section of human lung tissue. The alveolar sacs (A) are composed of very thin epithelium. (Courtesy of Eliott Weier.)

224

organisms, this task is accomplished by body fluids. The fluid portion of blood (plasma) can transport oxygen, but this is not sufficient to meet the needs of most animals. Consequently, special molecules capable of transporting oxygen are often present. Since these molecules usually show color, we refer to them as respiratory pigments.

The earthworm has a rather complex circulatory system which contains plasma and small, colorless corpuscles. The blood is red due to the presence of the iron-containing pigment *hemoglobin* dissolved in the plasma. Although this pigment is not found in the corpuscles, it is very similar to the hemoglobin of human red blood cells, and it does transport oxygen. The blood of arthropods is generally colorless but certain crustaceans, such as crayfish, crabs, and lobsters, possess a bluish copper-containing pigment called *hemocyanin*. Hemocyanin is dissolved in the plasma and carries oxygen.

HEMOGLOBIN AND OXYGEN

The respiratory pigment of all vertebrates and some invertebrates is hemoglobin. The tetrapyrrole ring arrangement of hemoglobin (Figure 7–21) is very similar to the basic structure of the cytochromes and chlorophyll (see corresponding figures in Chapter 6). The iron-pyrrole complex is termed the *heme* group and the attached protein is called *globin* (Figure 7–22).

The primary function of hemoglobin is to combine with oxygen in the lungs and to transport this oxygen to the tissues of the organism. When hemoglobin picks up oxygen, a bright red complex known as oxyhemoglobin (often noted as HbO_2) is formed. The oxygenated arterial blood may be easily distinguished from the bluish venous blood which contains much less oxygen.

Chemically, the combination of oxygen with hemoglobin is quite loose since oxygen uptake and release must occur rapidly and easily. The uptake of oxygen in the lungs, or "loading" as it is sometimes called, takes place across the thin, moist alveolar membranes.

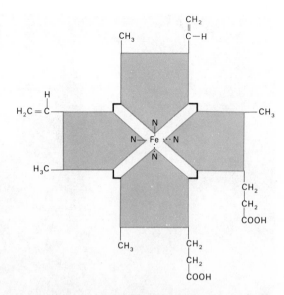

Figure 7–21 Structure of heme, the porphyrin part of the hemoglobin molecule.

The venous blood entering the lungs contains a low partial pressure of oxygen and a high partial pressure of carbon dioxide. In physical terms, the pressure of a mixture of gases is equal to the sum of the pressures of the individual gases. The pressure then of a specific gas in a mixture is known as the partial pressure of that gas. Partial pressures are generally stated in terms of millimeters of mercury (mmHg)—that is, the pressure required to support a column of mercury one centimeter in diameter at that height.

Since the oxygen pressure in the alveolar sacs is higher than in the blood, oxygen diffuses into the blood, whereas the high partial pressure of carbon dioxide in venous blood causes the CO_2 to diffuse into the alveolar air. When the red blood cells reach the tissue capillaries, the reverse occurs. The tissue cells have utilized oxygen and therefore have a low oxygen content. Due to the diffusion gradient across the capillary membrane, the hemoglobin immediately releases its oxygen to the cells. Since carbon dioxide was released to the environment through the lungs, the arterial blood has a comparatively low CO_2 pressure and this allows CO_2 to move from the tissues into the bloodstream (Figure 7–23).

Figure 7–22 Model of the hemoglobin molecule as deduced from X-ray diffraction studies. The light blocks represent α-polypeptide chains, and the dark are β-polypeptide chains. The oxygen-binding sites are marked O_2. (Courtesy of M. F. Perutz.)

CARBONIC ANHYDRASE AND CARBON DIOXIDE

Although a small amount of CO_2 will combine with hemoglobin to form $HbCO_2$, most of the CO_2 is transported in another way. A special enzyme called *carbonic anhydrase* located within the red blood cells catalyzes the combination of CO_2 with H_2O to form carbonic acid, H_2CO_3. Carbonic acid dissociates into H^+ and HCO_3^-, and the bicarbonate ion (HCO_3^-) diffuses into the plasma. Therefore CO_2 is transported primarily to the lungs in the plasma as bicarbonate ions. In the lungs, the reaction in the red blood cells is reversed ($HCO_3^- + H^+ \rightarrow H_2O + CO_2$) and carbon dioxide is released.

When HCO_3^- leaves the red blood cells in the tissues, an imbalance of charges results.

The ionic balance is restored when a chloride ion (Cl^-) moves into the cell. This exchange of negative-charged ions is called the *chloride shift* (Figure 7–24). A reverse exchange must take place in the lungs when HCO_3^- enters the red blood cells to produce CO_2. At this time, chloride ions leave the red blood cells in order to maintain ionic balance.

THE CONTROL OF BREATHING

The coordination centers for breathing are found in the medulla oblongata and pons of the human brain. The medulla contains the expiratory and inspiratory centers. A *pneumotaxic center* located in the pons has nervous connections with the expiratory and inspiratory centers and functions in relaying impulses and coordinating the breathing

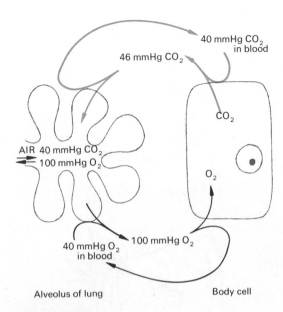

Figure 7–23 Gas exchange between lungs and body cells showing the partial pressures that effect diffusion.

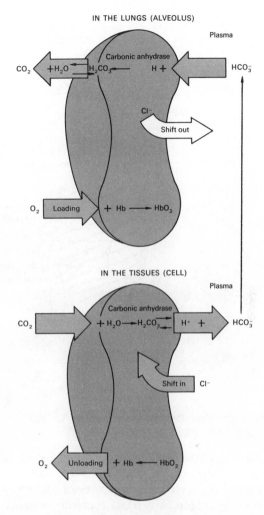

Figure 7–24 Major gas-exchange events occurring in the lungs and tissues. Note that CO_2 is carried in the plasma as the bicarbonate ion.

rhythm especially during labored breathing. The centers in the medulla, however, control the rate and depth of breathing during sleep and normal quiet breathing. Nerve pathways enter the breathing centers from the cerebral cortex and the hypothalamus. Because of these cerebral cortex associations, an individual may consciously regulate his breathing or hold his breath for a short time.

Impulses are issued constantly from the inspiratory center and sent to the rib muscles and diaphragm to cause inspiration. At the same time impulses are sent to the pneumotaxic center, which activates the expiratory center to inhibit the inspiratory impulses. During this cessation of inspiratory impulses, a passive expiration occurs. An additional regulatory mechanism found in the lungs, are the tiny nerve endings, called *stretch receptors,* located in the alveoli. As the air sacs fill and stretch during inspiration, impulses are sent to the expiratory center through the vagus nerve. These impulses sufficiently inhibit the inspiratory center to permit expiration. This feedback mechanism, working with the pneumotaxic center, ensures that expiration will

occur. This reflex mechanism between the alveoli and the expiratory center is known as the *Hering-Breuer reflex* (Figure 7–25).

The inspiratory center is sensitive to the amount of carbon dioxide in the blood. In fact, this is the primary stimulation for inspiration. In addition, oxygen- and CO_2-sensitive nerve receptors called *carotid bodies* are located in the carotid arteries and wall of the aorta. These bodies stimulate the inspiratory center and increase the rate and depth of breathing with any decrease in oxygen or increase in carbon dioxide in the blood.

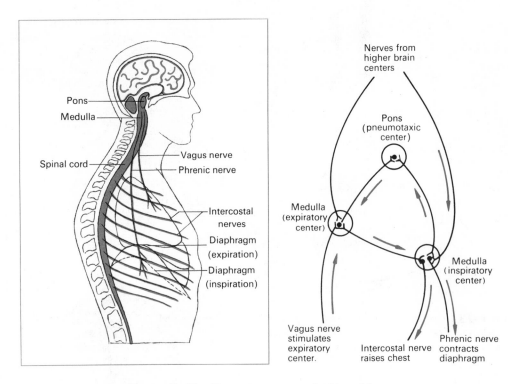

Figure 7–25   The nervous control of breathing.

EXCRETION OF METABOLIC WASTES AND WATER BALANCE

All organisms have the problem of ridding their bodies of metabolic wastes, some of which are extremely toxic even in small amounts. Plants, which lack excretory systems, have evolved a variety of mechanisms for the disposal of metabolic wastes. Some wastes are given off as diffusible gases and others are deposited in certain parts of the cell or on the external parts of the plant. Synthetic processes in plants can actually perform an excretory function when certain toxic nitrogen compounds are synthesized into nontoxic compounds. Caffeine and morphine are examples of these synthetic secretions.

As a result of the metabolism of amino acids and the breakdown of other nitrogen compounds in animal cells, especially in the cells of the liver in vertebrates, large amounts of nitrogen are released into the tissue fluids and blood. The waste nitrogen combines readily with water to form toxic ammonia. Small organisms living in an aqueous environment quickly discharge ammonia by diffusion. Most terrestrial animals, however, must conserve water and thus the nitrogenous wastes are held in the body longer. The cells of most animals have enzyme systems to detoxify the nitrogen compounds. The most common products of nitrogen detoxification are urea and uric acid. Since animals may excrete ammonia, urea, or uric acid as their nitrogenous waste products, they are sometimes classified by these products—that is, as *ammonotelic* (ammonia), *ureotelic* (urea) or *uricotelic* (uric acid). By comparison, ammonia is the most toxic followed by urea and the almost insoluble uric acid.

AMMONOTELIC, UREOTELIC, AND URICOTELIC EXCRETION

Most aquatic invertebrates are ammonotelic. This is easy to understand since they are relatively small and can easily diffuse waste compounds into the water. Freshwater bony

228

fish also excrete ammonia through their gills. Earthworms excrete urea in the air and ammonia in water.

Urea is the major detoxification product of amphibians, sharks, and mammals. It is synthesized in the liver, released to the bloodstream, and filtered into the urine by the kidneys. When the intermediate compounds and enzymes of urea synthesis were worked out, it was learned that the process occurred in a cycle (Figure 7–26). In this cycle ammonia and CO_2 combine with ornithine to produce a series of intermediate compounds which culminates in the production of urea and the regeneration of ornithine. Aspartic acid, an amino acid, is essential to the completion of this cycle. Most of the aspartic-acid molecule is lost, however, and can enter the citric-acid

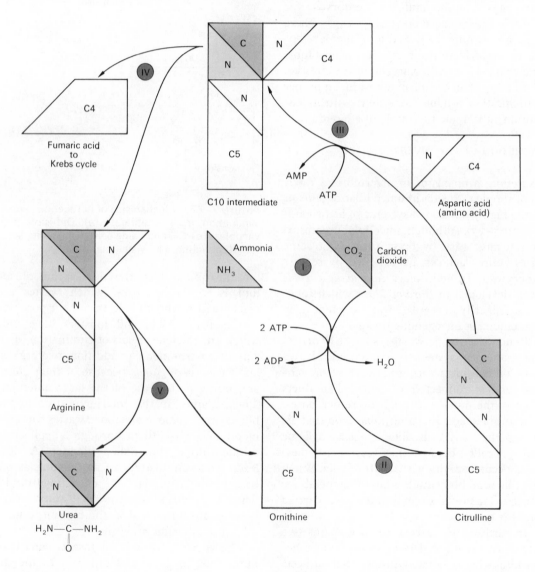

Figure 7–26 The urea or ornithine cycle. The cycle begins at I and continues counterclockwise. Each numbered segment requires a specific enzyme. Excess amounts of nitrogen and carbon dioxide are removed in the liver through the formation of urea. The urea is removed from the blood and excreted by the kidneys.

cycle to be oxidized (Chapter 6). One nitrogen atom from aspartic acid remains and becomes part of the released urea molecule.

Animals producing uric acid include some insects, birds, reptiles, and land snails. The white portion of bird droppings indicates the presence of uric acid. Uric acid, the least toxic compound, is synthesized by animals that must retain body water or produce land-type eggs. Reptile and bird embryos, for example, must develop inside eggs where toxic wastes must be stored with the developing embryo. Here the formation of insoluble uric acid is vital to the survival of the embryo. The ability of an organism to produce a proper detoxification product consistent with its environment is a good example of adaptation.

EXCRETION IN THE INVERTEBRATES

Excretion mechanisms in invertebrates range from simple diffusion in unicellular organisms to the highly developed systems of arthropods (Figure 7–27). Although unicellular organisms excrete most waste by direct diffusion, in some cases entire vacuoles are expelled by reverse pinocytosis. In addition, a *contractile vacuole* (well developed in *Paramecium*), which functions primarily to regulate water content, may also eliminate nitrogenous wastes.

In nonparasitic flatworms, such as *Planaria*, the excretory system is composed of two longitudinal ducts with a network of branching tubules connected to them. The ducts open to the outside through excretory pores. The tubules end in large *flame cells* that lie among the body cells. The specialized flame cells (so called because they resemble flames) have a central cavity with a tuft of cilia. When the cilia beat, body fluids containing metabolic wastes (including excess water) are carried into the tubules.

In earthworms each segment contains two excretory organs called *nephridia*. Each nephridium has a ciliated funnel that projects through the septum of the preceding segment and filters the body fluids into a collecting duct. In addition, a capillary network surrounds the collecting tubules allowing the absorption of waste products from the blood

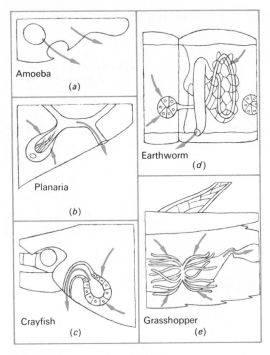

Figure 7–27 Mechanisms of nitrogenous waste elimination in invertebrates. (*a*) Diffusion plus vacuoles. (*b*) Ciliated flame cells. (*c*) Green gland. (*d*) Nephridium. (*e*) Malpighian tubules.

into the tubules. Near the end of each nephridium is a bladder from which wastes are discharged to the outside through a pore.

Crayfish, crabs, and lobsters have gills which are efficient organs of elimination in an aquatic environment. In addition, two organs, known as *green glands* because of their color, are found at the base of the large antennae. These glands, in the anterior portion of the blood sinus, remove metabolic wastes from the blood and pass them through a collecting tubule into a thin-walled bladder. A duct leads from the bladder to an opening at the base of the antenna. The collecting tubule, which is practically absent in saltwater forms, is probably functional in the reabsorption of salts in freshwater crayfish.

The excretory organs of insects consist of numerous, long tubules attached to the digestive tract between the stomach and intestine. These thin-walled tubules project into the body cavity and absorb nitrogenous wastes and salts from the blood. The tubules empty into the intestine. Malpighi, the famed Italian

230

microscopist of the seventeenth century, described these organs and they still bear his name as *Malpighian tubules.*

EXCRETION IN THE VERTEBRATES— THE KIDNEY

The major organs of excretion among vertebrates are the *kidneys.* These paired, bean-shaped organs lie against the dorsal body wall on either side of the vertebral column. A rich supply of blood is received from the abdominal aorta and venous blood is returned to the inferior vena cava (Figure 7–28). The wastes are filtered from the blood in the cortex which, in the human kidney, contains about one million *nephron* units (Figure 7–28c).

Blood enters the capillary network, known as the *glomerulus,* at approximately 75 mmHg pressure. Since local capillary pressure in other tissues is only about 20 mmHg, filtration in the glomerulus is essentially by diffusion under pressure, sometimes termed *ultrafiltration.* The thin membrane of the glomerulus allows the filtration of glucose, vitamins, fatty acids, and amino acids, but normally does not permit serum blood proteins to pass through. In cases of persistent or severe infection, such as pneumonia or middle-ear infection, the glomerular membranes may degenerate to such an extent that they allow large amounts of protein to enter the urine (Bright's disease). The loss of protein from the blood causes a decreased osmotic concentration in the plasma, and the tissues collect water bringing about edema (swelling).

The glomerular filtrate is collected in the *Bowman's capsule* and passed into the *proximal convoluted tubule* where substances required by the body are reabsorbed. For example, under normal conditions all the glucose filtered through the glomerulus is reabsorbed into surrounding capillaries, the *peritubular capillaries,* by diffusion and active transport. When the glucose level of the blood rises above 180 mg per 100 ml of blood, all the glucose cannot be reabsorbed and some glucose appears in the urine. The proximal convoluted tubules reabsorb Na^+, K^+, Cl^-, glucose, water, amino acids, and some urea and uric acid. The reabsorption of mineral ions is controlled, to some degree, by a group of hormones known as mineralocorticoids secreted by the cortex of the adrenal glands. When ions and molecules are transported from the tubules into the surrounding capillaries, an osmotic gradient is formed. Water must then move into the capillaries according to the gradient; this situation is *obligatory water reabsorption.* Osmotic reabsorption of water also occurs in the next segment of the nephron, the loop of Henle. This long tubule bends back upon itself to form a U-shaped loop. Na^+, K^+, and Cl^- may also be reabsorbed in this segment.

In the *distal convoluted tubule* and *collecting tubule,* water reabsorption is controlled by a hormone produced in the posterior lobe of the pituitary gland, the *antidiuretic hormone* (ADH). ADH increases the permeability of the tubule cells to water, thereby increasing water reabsorption. The urine thus is concentrated and body water is conserved. The distal convoluted tubule actively reabsorbs Na^+, K^+, Ca^{++}, and Mg^{++}, but in addition to its role in reabsorption, it can secrete ions from the blood and pass them into the urine. Large amounts of hydrogen ion (H^+) and ammonia (NH_3) are actively removed from the blood which helps to maintain a proper acid-base balance in the body. The distal tubule is more selective in reabsorption than the proximal tubule. The high hydrostatic pressure in the proximal tubule causes the diffusion of many substances into the peritubular capillaries. The composition of urine includes water (95 percent), urea, uric acid, ammonia, and creatinine (a product of amino-acid metabolism). Several ions, pigments, hormones, and vitamins may also be found in this waste product.

Human kidney malfunction is quite common, often reaching the serious stage where the kidneys cannot effectively rid the body of nitrogen wastes. Artificial kidneys have been developed to assist or replace normal kidney function. In these machines a patient's blood is shunted through a series of artificial membranes surrounded by a special fluid. The wastes diffuse across the membrane from the blood to the fluid. Essentially, the blood is routed from the body, cleansed, and returned.

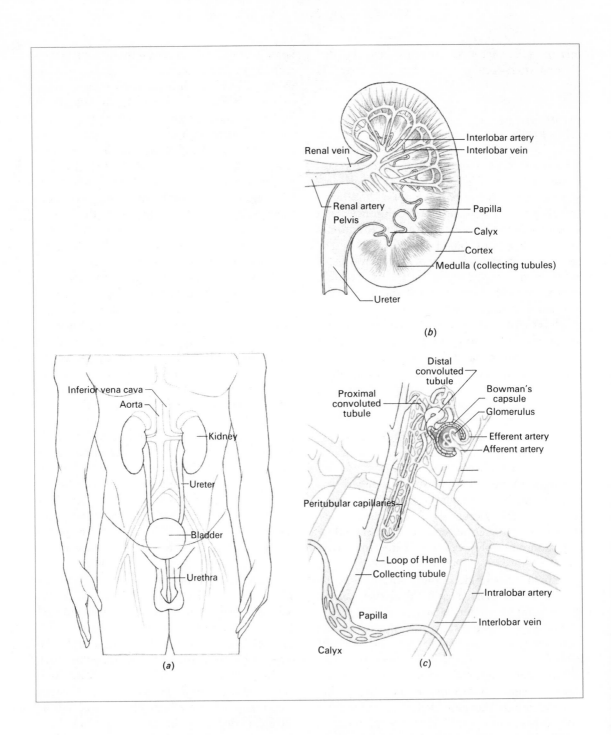

Figure 7–28 (*a*) Urinary system in man. (*b*) Longitudinal section of the kidney showing the location of the major blood vessels. (*c*) Structure of the nephron unit of vertebrate kidneys. The principal functions of the segments are as follows. *Proximal tubule:* reabsorption of glucose, water, Na$^+$, K$^+$, and amino acids. *Loop of Henle:* reabsorption of Na$^+$, K$^+$, and Cl$^-$; obligatory water reabsorption. *Distal tubule:* reabsorption of Na$^+$ and K$^+$; secretion of H$^+$ and NH$_3$. *Collecting tubule:* reabsorption of water.

OSMOREGULATION

It is probably apparent that the kidney is not simply an organ for the elimination of toxic nitrogenous wastes. It is also involved in the balance of water, sugar, and ions within the organism. In fact, throughout the animal kingdom the processes of excretion of nitrogenous wastes and ion and water balance are closely related. The general term used to refer to the ability of an organism to control and regulate the fluid content of its body is *osmoregulation*.

In Terrestrial Animals

The essential problem facing land animals is the conservation of internal water. The most important defense against the dry environment is probably a thick epidermis. The presence of scales, hair, fur, or feathers add varying degrees of insulation. In addition to physical barriers against evaporation, most terrestrial animals also possess well-developed kidneys to provide for water and salt reabsorption. Animals surviving in extremely dry conditions eliminate very dry feces and highly concentrated urine. The small desert kangaroo rat (*Dipodomys*) shows a further adaptation in having no sweat glands. In addition, these tiny rodents live in an underground burrow and forage for food only at night. Under normal conditions, they never require a drink of water since the water from their food is sufficient.

In mammals water loss is most extensive through breathing and perspiration. Man, for instance, must maintain a body temperature of about 37°C and does so primarily through the evaporation of perspiration. Camels, on the other hand, are well adapted to desert conditions with their mat of insulating fur; furthermore, they do not begin to sweat until their body temperature rises to about 41°C.

One of the most interesting adaptations is found in marine birds. These birds feed on fish and apparently drink salt water. All marine birds possess special glands called salt glands above each eye which actively excrete sodium

chloride when the bird's body fluids acquire excess salt (Figure 7–29).

In Aquatic Organisms

In aquatic organisms three conditions may exist (Figure 7–30). (1) The concentration of water and dissolved substances may be the same inside the organism as in the environment, and water is neither gained nor lost from the organism. This condition is called *isosmotic*. (2) The concentration of water may be lower and the concentration of dissolved substances higher inside the organism than in the environment which means water would move into the organism through osmosis. This condition is typical in freshwater organisms and is called *hyposmotic*. (3) The concentration of water may be higher and the concentration of dissolved substances lower inside the organism than in the environment. Consequently, water tends to move from the organism into the

Figure 7–29 Marine birds, such as this sea gull, possess a salt-excreting gland. A highly concentrated salt solution flows into the nasal cavity and drips off the beak. (Courtesy of Henry B. Kane.)

233

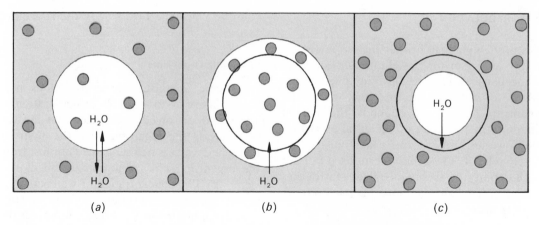

Figure 7–30 Three possible osmotic conditions in aquatic organisms. (*a*) Isosmotic environment in which water moves in equal amounts into and out of the organism, producing no net gain or loss of water. (*b*) Hyposmotic environment in which water is gained by the organism. (*c*) Hyperosmotic environment in which water is lost by the organism.

environment, and this condition is called *hyperosmotic.*

Isosmotic conditions are found in many aquatic invertebrates that live in the sea. A simple example of hyposmotic conditions is displayed by *Paramecium.* The contractile vacuole of this freshwater protist has already been noted as a structure which can "bail out" the excessive amount of water that enters from the environment. Freshwater fish eliminate water by producing large amounts of a very dilute urine, but since salts also tend to be lost in this waste product, special cells in the gills must actively absorb salts from the water. The hyperosmotic condition of saltwater fish presents the opposite problem of freshwater fish—that is, they are constantly losing water. These animals drink large amounts of sea water but produce a small amount of urine. The gills of these fish secrete excess salt back into the sea. Sharks and their relatives, which also live in a marine environment, have solved the balance problem in yet another way. Urea and other organic compounds normally excreted are maintained at higher levels in the blood. This raises the concentration of dissolved substances in the animals to a concentration equal to or greater than that in the sea and produces an almost isosmotic state of equilibrium. The conditions described here for fish and sharks are shown in Figure 7–31.

Most marine invertebrates contain body fluid and salt concentrations equal to that of sea water. If the salt concentration of the water changes, the internal fluid also changes. These marine forms can survive only short-term changes slightly above or below normal. Organisms which cannot maintain their internal fluid concentrations against that of the environment are known as nonosmoregulators. The heavy line in Figure 7–32 indicates the survival range of these marine invertebrates, such as the spider crab, in varying seawater concentrations.

Many marine animals can move from their normal saltwater environment into more dilute or brackish water such as estuaries. Investigations by August Krogh and others on estuarine invertebrates have demonstrated that certain species of crabs can actively regulate their internal fluid and salt concentration by taking up salt through their gills. The green glands (a type of kidney) are also involved in this process and function primarily in the regulation of body water. One example is the shore crab which normally lives in brackish water but can move easily onto shore or even into fresh water in search of food. The shore crabs, however, do not fare as well in higher than normal saltwater concentrations and react similarly to nonregulating forms under these conditions (Figure 7–32).

Perhaps the most outstanding example of osmoregulation is that of the Chinese mitten

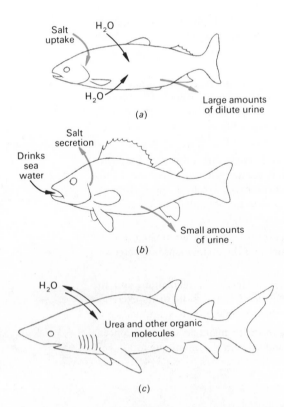

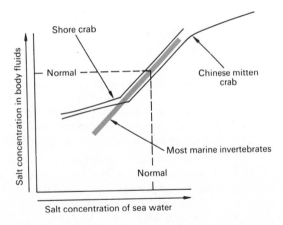

Figure 7–32 Relationships of body fluid and salt concentrations against varying concentrations of sea water. The colored line indicates equal concentrations (isosmotic) found in nonosmoregulating invertebrates.

Figure 7–31 Mechanisms for the maintenance of osmotic balance. (*a*) Freshwater fish. (*b*) Saltwater fish. (*c*) Shark (marine).

crab (*Eriocheir*) which invades the rivers of central Europe. These crabs possess one of the most efficient regulatory mechanisms that

has been studied and can live equally well in fresh and salt water. The mitten crab is capable of actively transporting salt from its blood into the water.

Thus all the materials taken into, or produced within, an organism must somehow be kept in a state of balance. All of the metabolic processes described in this chapter support energy production in some way, but these processes are not the principal regulatory or control mechanisms. We will see these in the next chapter.

SUMMARIZING STATEMENTS

The chemical reactions and physical processes not directly involved in energy production may be called *supporting processes*; they include digestion, absorption, circulation, gas exchange, and excretion. Metabolism is the total of all the chemical reactions occurring in an organism.

The vertebrate liver performs numerous functions essential to life; among these are synthesis, storage, regulation, and detoxification.

Large food molecules must be broken into smaller molecules that can be absorbed into the bloodstream and utilized by the cells; the process by which this is accomplished is enzymatic digestion.

In man and other mammals the digestive process and the enzymes involved can be organized into three phases—salivary, gastric, and intestinal; the pancreas is an important accessory gland that supplies enzymes for all classes of foods to the small intestine. The end products of digestion include simple sugars, fatty acids, glycerol, and amino acids.

The products of digestion are absorbed by the epithelial cells lining the small intestine; most of these nutrients are transported by the blood to the liver. The large intestine functions primarily in the control of water and ion balance.

Nutrients, gases, wastes, and other materials must be circulated and transported from one part of a living system to another; this is particularly important in large, multicellular organisms. In plants this is accomplished principally in vascular tissue—xylem and phloem. In animals a blood system composed of a heart and conducting vessels serves this purpose.

Gas exchange is accomplished in a variety of ways: direct diffusion (in plants, protists, and some invertebrates), gills (crustaceans, some mollusks, and fish), lungs (amphibians, reptiles, birds, and mammals), tracheal tubes (insects). Special gas-transporting pigments are utilized in many animals to increase gas-exchange efficiency.

Toxic substances, especially nitrogenous wastes, must be eliminated from all organisms; the excretion of metabolic wastes and the maintenance of water and ion balance are closely related processes.

The vertebrate organ involved in water balance, ion regulation, and the separation of nitrogenous wastes from the blood is the kidney; its excretion product, urine, contains water, urea and other organic products, and ions.

Osmoregulation is the ability of an organism to maintain constant concentrations of body fluids despite changing conditions in the environment.

REVIEW QUESTIONS

1 Lettuce, carrots, and celery are good sources of vitamins and minerals and are widely used for reducing diets. Why is this so, considering the high carbohydrate content of these vegetables?

2 Taking large dosages of vitamins has become common for the cure of certain illnesses and the promotion of better health. What possible mechanisms might be involved?

3 A person watching his weight is concerned with the number of calories taken into his body in a day. Why do we use heat units, such as calories, as reference units in weight control?

4 Some diets provide mainly proteins; how is it possible for the individual to get sufficient carbohydrates under these conditions?

5 What is the general scheme of carbohydrate metabolism regulation in the mammalian body? What effect does this control have on blood sugar?

6 The general pattern of food digestion in the mammalian body is:

large, nonabsorbable molecules $+ H_2O \rightarrow$ smaller, absorbable molecules

Use this scheme and note the specific molecules produced by carbohydrate, fat, and protein digestion.

7 What is the primary difference between an open and a closed circulatory system? What animals have open systems? Closed systems?

8 Some animals, such as salmon and certain crabs, are capable of moving from salt water to fresh water and vice versa. What are some of the mechanisms that make this osmoregulation possible?

9 Structurally, what do all animal breathing systems have in common? What is the relationship of a circulatory system to the gas-exchange process?

236

10 How does bicarbonate ion (HCO_3^-) function in both uptake and release of CO_2 in the red blood corpuscle?

11 Trace a nerve impulse originating in the pacemaker of the human heart through a complete heartbeat cycle.

12 In diseases such as hardening of the arteries why would you expect a high diastolic pressure?

13 Why does a human continue to breathe rhythmically while sleeping? Why is it impossible to hold one's breath indefinitely?

14 If a human contracted a kidney disease that caused faulty distal tubules in his nephrons, what symptoms might he exhibit?

SUPPLEMENTARY READINGS

Avery, Mary Ellen, Nai-San Wong, and H. W. Taeusch, Jr., "The Lung of the Newborn Infant," *Scientific American*, April, 1973.

Biddulph, S., and O. Biddulph, "The Circulatory System of Plants," *Scientific American*, February, 1959.

Carey, F. G., "Fishes with Warm Bodies," *Scientific American*, February, 1973.

Comroe, Julius H., Jr., "The Lung," *Scientific American*, February, 1966.

Davenport, H. W., "Why the Stomach Does Not Digest Itself," *Scientific American*, January, 1972.

Fenn, W. O., "The Mechanism of Breathing," *Scientific American*, January, 1960.

Hammond, E. Cuyler, "The Effects of Smoking," *Scientific American*, July, 1962.

Kretchmer, Norman, "Lactose and Lactase," *Scientific American*, October, 1972.

Kylstra, J. A., "Experiments in Water-Breathing," *Scientific American*, August, 1968.

Merrill, J. P., "The Artificial Kidney," *Scientific American*, July, 1961.

Perutz, M. F., "The Hemoglobin Molecule," *Scientific American*, November, 1964.

Schmidt-Nielson, Knut, "Salt Glands," *Scientific American*, January, 1959.

Schmidt-Nielson, Knut, "The Physiology of the Camel," *Scientific American*, December, 1959.

Schmidt-Nielson, Knut, *Desert Animals*, Oxford, Oxford University Press, 1964.

Schmidt-Nielson, Knut, "How Birds Breathe," *Scientific American*, December, 1971.

Scholander, P. F., "The Master Switch of Life," *Scientific American*, December, 1963.

Smith, Homer W., "The Kidney," *Scientific American*, January, 1953.

Solomon, A. K., "Pumps in the Living Cell," *Scientific American*, August, 1962.

Wiggers, Carl J., "The Heart," *Scientific American*, May, 1957.

Williams, C. M., "Insect Breathing," *Scientific American*, February, 1953.

Wolf, A. V., "Body Water," *Scientific American*, November, 1958.

Wooldridge, Dean E., *The Machinery of Life*, New York, McGraw-Hill, 1966.

Young, V. R., and N. S. Scrimshaw, "The Physiology of Starvation," *Scientific American*, October, 1971.

Zimmermann, M. H., "How Sap Moves in Trees," *Scientific American*, March, 1963.

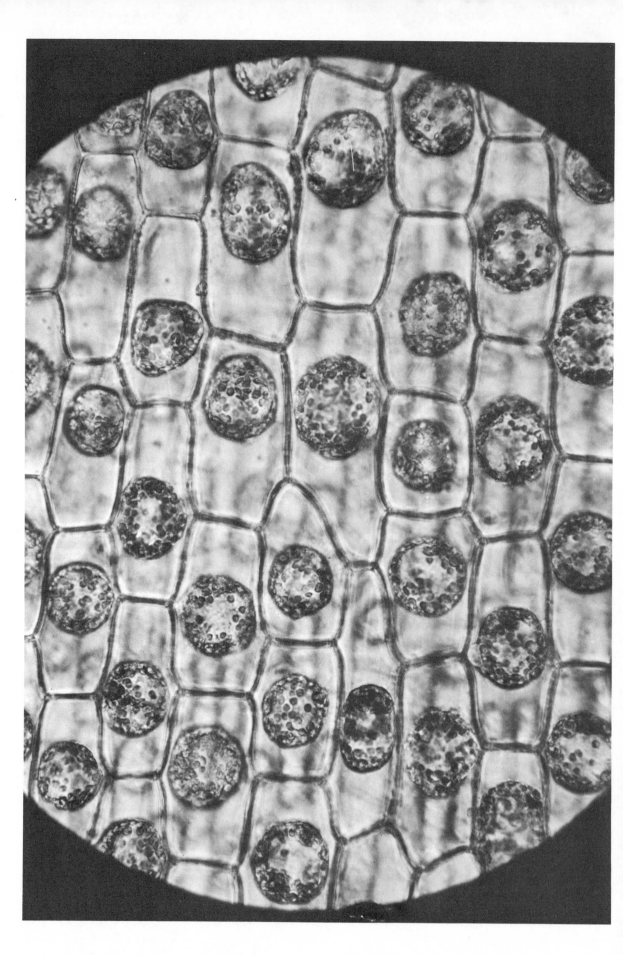

8

Dynamic Equilibrium

Up to this point we have been discussing the many processes and chemical reactions that take place in all organisms. Since we know now that a myriad of chemical reactions must occur each second simply to keep an organism alive, we might wonder how these are coordinated and regulated within the cell and throughout the organism to prevent a state of disorder.

Internal conditions in all living systems are never static since materials are constantly entering and leaving the body of an organism. Moreover, external conditions also change the environment so that it is never exactly the same from minute to minute. Consider for a moment some of the factors that might influence you while you are reading this book. The gas content of the room— that is, the O_2/CO_2 ratio—will vary depending on whether the doors and windows are open or closed or whether you are in the room alone or with others. Your attitude or state of mind also may be determined by the poeple or other organisms in the room. Your ability to comprehend and understand the material you are reading may be influenced by the food you were served at your previous meal (or the thoughts you may be entertaining about the next meal) or a recent encounter with a fellow human being. Certainly the weather conditions can have a profound effect, especially if you are overly cold or warm. An organism must adjust to these and the many other changes that occur in the environment. In this chapter we will explore the more simple and almost automatic regulatory mechanisms. This will lay the foundation for the more complex modes of behavior presented in the next chapter.

When we examine nature closely, we quickly see that the problems faced by organisms are due to change—changes produced internally by physical and chemical processes or externally by changes in the environment. The two phenomena are related since changes in the external environment can and do bring about internal changes. This chapter is concerned with the mechanisms employed by living systems in their constant struggle to prevent harmful internal change. Since the process of change is active and continuous, the internal medium will not always be in perfect equilibrium; we speak, therefore, of a *dynamic equilibrium.* The maintenance of this internal *steady state* is of paramount importance for, if this fails, illness or death results. Another term frequently used for this overall condition is *homeostasis.* Many biologists consider the continuous effort by living organisms to maintain a uniform internal environment to be the central theme of biology.

The human body temperature is usually given as 37°C (98.6°F). We know that exercise, emotions, sleep, the various metabolic activities, cold or hot weather, and so on, influence the body temperature and consequently it varies above and below 37°C. A hypothetical situation which could occur in the normal day of an individual is shown in Figure 8–1. The temperature in most humans fluctuates around 37°C because control mechanisms are attempting to maintain this temperature. What would happen if the temperature continued to rise and did not return to the 37°C base line? This does occur under certain conditions such as heat stroke when the temperature-control mechanisms in the body have ceased to function properly. If the controls cannot be put back into operation when this happens, death will result. Every acceleration must be followed by a deceleration and vice versa.

SOME PHYSICAL MODELS

Physical models can be used to illustrate the problem of maintaining internal stability in organisms. A series of three differently constructed water containers and the corresponding variations in water level that might be expected in each are shown in Figure 8–2. The first model is a closed and sealed container from which the water cannot escape and to which water cannot be added. The water level cannot fluctuate under these conditions and the straight line on the graph to the right of the container indicates this constant condition. If there were a corresponding system in organisms, there would, of course, be no problem in maintaining a homeostatic state. The second model represents an open tank provided with an overflow pipe. The tank can accumulate rain water and it is subject to the process of evaporation. The only control feature that can assist in maintaining a constant level is the overflow pipe, so great fluctuations can be expected as illustrated by the erratic wavy line on the graph. Any living system corresponding to this situation would be in a difficult position, since all the control is outside the system.

Several features could be added to an open tank to provide more uniform control, and

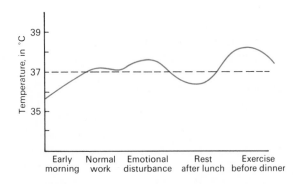

Figure 8–1 Body temperature in a human being plotted against a hypothetical portion of a normal day. Note that while the temperature varies, it always fluctuates about the 37°C line.

240

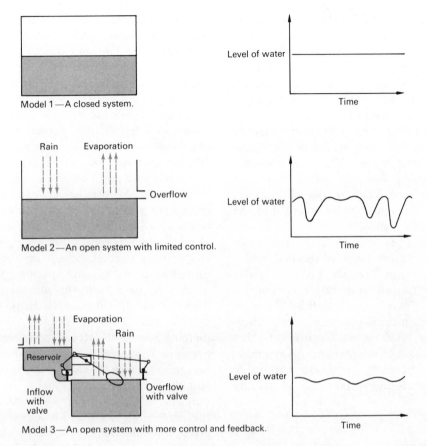

Model 1 — A closed system.

Model 2 — An open system with limited control.

Model 3 — An open system with more control and feedback.

Figure 8–2   Three models to assist in understanding the problem of regulation in control in organisms.

model 3 of Figure 8–2 illustrates the basic mechanisms found in organisms. An inflow pipe connected to a reservoir of water provides a constant supply of water. Valves, attached to both the inflow and overflow pipes, regulate the amount of water entering and leaving the tank. A float, attached to the valves, rises and falls with the water level (similar to the tank of a toilet) to control the valve action. When the water level drops, the float drops, closing the overflow valve and simultaneously opening the inflow valve. The tank thus can fill to its original level, raising the float until both valves are closed. A rise in water would produce the opposite reaction and the water level will fluctuate only slightly over a period of time.

The water in the tank is moving and changing, yet the water level remains fairly stable.

To appreciate the similarities between the last model and a living system, four features of the model should be considered. *First*, it is a self-regulating system since the valves opened and closed automatically when certain limits were exceeded. *Second*, the element of *feedback* is part of the system—that is, both valves close automatically when the original level is reached and inflow and outflow action stop. *Third*, action is immediate when a change occurs in the tank so the water level does not undergo extreme changes in level. This is extremely important to living systems since they cannot withstand great changes from their normal range of operation. *Fourth*, more than one control element is utilized to regulate this process. In living things, most processes are multicontrolled. The value of this is simply that several control mechanisms offer a finer and more uniform level of control than only one mechanism.

Another important point to note is that the water level in the third model is not represented by a straight line. The level is shown as an undulating line which indicates what actually happened. Very soon after the water level drops, the inflow valve opens and the water level rises again. In other words, the inflow valve does not close at the exact moment the proper level is reached and a slight "overshooting" occurs. The outlet valve opens momentarily to drop the level to normal, but it again "overshoots" slightly. Thus an equilibrium is maintained—not a static equilibrium, but a dynamic equilibrium that requires continuous maintenance. Any graph, then, that represents metabolic activity in living organisms must show this variability (see Figure 8–1).

GENERAL SCHEME OF CONTROL

The homeostatic condition is so universal in living organisms that a general scheme is apparent, and all control activities seem to follow this pattern. Once again we can employ a model to explain and describe the general process. Both external and internal changes require regulation and action by an organism (Figure 8–3). Feedback must be built into the regulation to prevent excessive reaction (overshooting)—that is, the regulation machinery must *know* when enough action has been taken. Otherwise, the action might well continue, and this could be just as harmful to the organism as the original change that necessitated the action. In order for this process to work, a constant flow of information is needed along the various routes. For example, specific *receptors* are needed to pick up the stimulus caused by a change, and specific *effectors* are needed to carry out the action. A simple example of this flow may help show the complicated chain of events. A mosquito piercing a human's left arm and sucking blood presents a change to the individual. As the mosquito pierces the skin, touch receptors are stimulated and the individual is aware of the mosquito's presence. Almost simultaneously the person may look at his left arm and, by virtue of information stored in his brain, recognize a mosquito. Through the coordination afforded by another part of the brain and information traveling along nerves, action is taken in the form of a slap by the right arm.

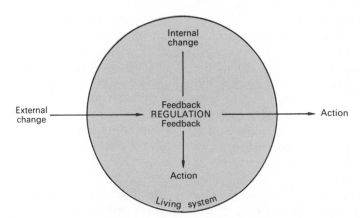

Figure 8–3 Steady-state control. Internal and external changes require regulation before action is accomplished. Feedback is part of the regulatory process which acts to prevent excessive "overshooting" by the process.

242

This either kills the mosquito or drives it away. Feedback prevents the continuation of the slapping since the mosquito is no longer present on the left arm. This sequence of events can be shown in the general scheme diagrammed in Figure 8–4.

The specific receptors and effectors are not always as clear cut as in this example, since receptor and effector activity may occur in the blood or body fluids with no external change. External changes can, of course, set off internal changes and the action that results in the internal medium can be quite complex. External forces, for instance, may cause an emotional disturbance which in turn can cause the heartbeat to increase, the face to flush, or perspiration to flow. We should turn now to some of the interesting specific control mechanisms employed by living forms and attempt to gain an understanding of how some of these work. Actually control mechanisms are encountered throughout this book. Though we are now considering some specific and well-defined mechanisms, regulatory aspects of many functions have already been noted. The regulation and control of energy pathways, digestion, breathing, and water and ion balance may now seem more important. The antigen-antibody reaction is a vertebrate's method of coping with an invader. Cancer is a good example of an apparent complete breakdown of control mechanisms when certain cells continue dividing in an uncontrolled manner.

GENERAL METABOLIC REGULATION

ENZYMES

The role of enzymes in controlling and regulating vital chemical reactions of life was stressed in Chapter 2, so you have some knowledge about the basic and most important control mechanisms in a living system. When we recall that all enzymes are proteins and also recall the pattern of protein synthesis through the DNA-RNA system (Chapter 3), the ultimate role of the gene as a control agent becomes apparent. In Chapter 2 we also showed a model explaining enzyme function on the basis of specific active sites on an enzyme molecule when it entered into loose chemical arrangements with the substrate molecules.

Another problem related to enzyme activity is that of explaining how enzymes are "turned off" or stopped when enough of a particular product has been manufactured by the cell. Two theories, each supported by considerable experimental work, have been suggested to explain how enzyme action can be controlled by a feedback process. One theory holds that

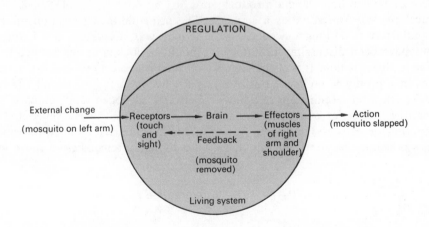

Figure 8–4 Example of regulation where specific receptors and effectors are utilized.

Compound A $\xrightarrow{\text{enzyme a}}$ Compound B $\xrightarrow{\text{enzyme b}}$ Compound C $\xrightarrow{\text{enzyme c}}$ Compound D $\xrightarrow{\text{enzyme d}}$ Product

Figure 8–5 Enzyme repression. The final product interferes with the synthesis of an enzyme which is essential to formation of the product.

the enzyme stops when the manufacture of the product is completed. In other words, the product of the chemical reaction represses further synthesis of the enzyme. The genetic mechanism for this repression will be explained in detail in Chapter 11, where regulator and operator genes are discussed. Such a series of reactions showing enzyme *repression* is illustrated in Figure 8–5. In this example the product interferes with the synthesis of enzyme c, which normally catalyzes the step from compound C to compound D. As the product gradually accumulates in this series of reactions and inhibits the synthesis of enzyme c, less product will be formed.

Another theory of how enzyme activity may be reduced is called *inhibition*. This means that the product interacts with the enzyme to inhibit its action. For instance, numerous experiments with bacteria have shown that the presence of the amino acid lysine can slow the action of an enzyme that is needed for the production of lysine. The pathway by which lysine is produced and the site of enzyme inhibition are shown in Figure 8–6.

Both theories explain how the end product of a chemical reaction can serve as a signal that its manufacture is no longer needed.

So far we have been discussing inhibitory or repressive feedback action. It is also known that some cellular products can have a positive or stimulatory effect on certain steps of a biochemical pathway. A series of reactions that provides energy for cells is familiar to you since it was studied in Chapter 6. We saw that

the ultimate end products that trap the energy are the AMP-ADP-ATP system. These products can control the liberation of energy through glycolysis and the Krebs cycle by inhibitory and stimulatory effects. The places at which these products function and the manner in which they function is shown in the abbreviated diagram of the energy pathway in Figure 8–7. ATP apparently is an inhibitor of the enzyme that catalyzes the reaction to permit acetyl-CoA to enter the Krebs cycle. As long as a high concentration of ATP is available, most of the acetyl-CoA will be used in other biochemical processes. AMP (adenosine monophosphate) exerts a stimulating effect on those enzymes that catalyze glycogen to glucose-6-phosphate and fructose-6-phosphate to fructose diphosphate. Thus when AMP is abundant in cells, energy metabolism is enhanced. The overall control picture is, of course, more complex than described here since other sites of stimulation and inhibition exist in the energy pathway.

MASS ACTION

The principle of mass action in chemical reactions was discussed in Chapter 2, but it should be looked at again since the direction of chemical reactions can be determined, in part, by mass action. Recall the relationship between glycogen and glucose: glucose $\rightleftharpoons$ glycogen. Since this is a reversible reaction, it exists in somewhat of an equilibrium—that is, if a living system takes in more glucose, the

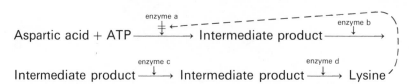

Aspartic acid + ATP $\xrightarrow{\text{enzyme a}}$ Intermediate product $\xrightarrow{\text{enzyme b}}$

Intermediate product $\xrightarrow{\text{enzyme c}}$ Intermediate product $\xrightarrow{\text{enzyme d}}$ Lysine

Figure 8–6 Enzyme inhibition. The final product (lysine) interacts with an enzyme in the biochemical pathway and inhibits its action.

reaction will increase to the right because of the mass-action effect of more glucose. Soon more glycogen is produced and the reaction will tend more to the left. If glucose is used up in an organism and little is being added, the reaction will shift strongly to the left. But mass action is only one control mechanism on this particular reaction; other control agents, to be discussed later in this chapter, also influence the relationship.

pH

Another controlling effect in living cells is the concentration of the hydrogen ion (pH). You have already learned that the rates of chemical reactions often depend on the pH of the medium. For example, the enzyme salivary amylase is very effective in breaking starch down to glucose at certain pH's, but it is almost ineffective at others (Figure 8–8). The chief influence of the pH on a chemical reaction is on the enzyme. We should also note the importance of maintaining an extremely stable acidic and alkaline condition in a living system. The molecular mechanism for this control through a buffer system was described in Chapter 2. The average pH of the human body, for example, is 7.4; in arterial blood it is usually 7.45, whereas in venous blood the pH is around 7.35.

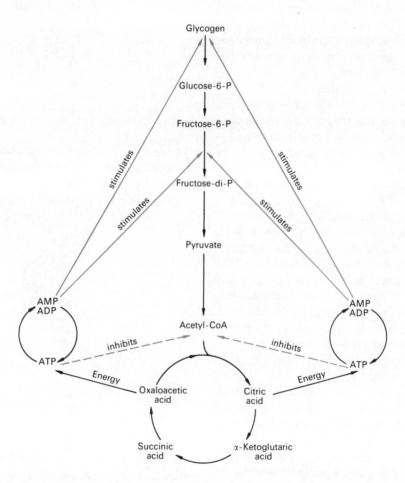

Figure 8–7 Example of feedback in energy metabolism. Some intermediate compounds are omitted from both the glycolytic pathway and the Krebs cycle in order to show a simplified diagram.

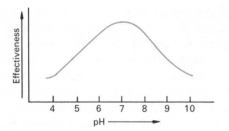

Figure 8–8 Relative function of salivary amylase at varying pH.

HORMONES

IN PLANTS

An extremely interesting and important group of control agents known as *hormones* are found in most organisms. Although a hormone may be concerned with a specific control function, its overall effect on the total organism is usually complex. Plants produce hormones that control growth, bending movements (*tropisms*), and flowering. The growth hormones, or *auxins*, as they are collectively known, are produced in all actively growing regions of plants, but they are especially concentrated in the stem and root tips. Perhaps the following discussion on auxins will clarify hormonal control.

Plant-growth studies were stimulated by observations of plant movements in response to external stimuli such as light (phototropism). Charles Darwin and his son Francis performed some of the first studies on plant movements in the 1870s and thus provided the groundwork and stimulation for further study in this field. Their studies on the coleoptile of grass seedlings, a sheathlike structure of only a few cells in thickness which covers the emerging shoot of grass, showed that when a coleoptile is exposed to light from one side, it will bend toward the light. This bending was prevented either by covering the tip or removing it (Figure 8–9). Since the actual bending occurred along the stem just below the tip, Darwin, in his book *The Power of Movement in Plants* (1881), suggested that the stimulus for growth passed from the tip to the stem.

Researchers have long since confirmed Dar-

win's hypothesis by performing various experiments on other plant-growth regions. One of the most widely used techniques has been to remove the stem tip, place it on an agar (gelatinlike) block and permit the auxins to diffuse onto the agar. Various concentrations of auxins can be accumulated in this manner, and the blocks of agar can then be used in experiments to determine the degree of bending and other variable factors (Figure 8–10).

In addition to these experiments, auxins have been isolated from plants and analyzed. We know that the principal growth hormone is indoleacetic acid and that it is found in most plants. The molecular structure of indoleacetic acid is:

Indole ring   Acetic acid

The indole ring, with its attached acetic-acid molecule, then is another fundamental structure in living systems.

It is also known that, if the uppermost bud,

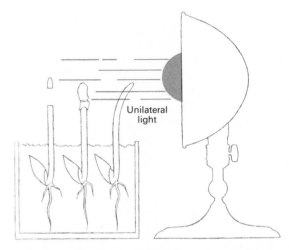

Figure 8–9 Phototropism in grass seedlings. The seedling with covered tip and the one with its tip removed do not bend toward the light.

246

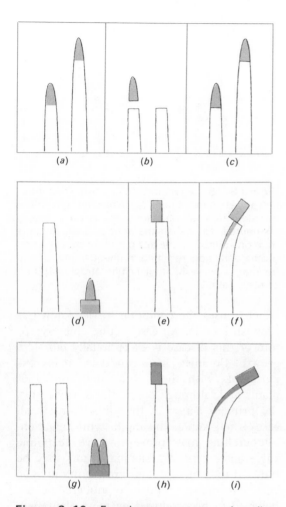

Figure 8–10 Experiments on grass coleoptiles. (a) Tip intact: growth. (b) Tip removed: no growth. (c) Tip replaced: growth. (d) Tip removed and placed on block of agar: auxin diffuses into block. (e) Section placed on tipless coleoptile. (f) Coleoptile bends in response to auxin. (g) Two tips removed: more auxin diffuses into block. (h) Section placed on tipless coleoptile. (i) Coleoptile bends in response to increased auxin.

or apical bud, is pruned, the lateral buds lower on the stem will grow in many plants. This knowledge led to the theory that the apical bud exerts an inhibiting influence on the lower buds via its auxin supply. Some plants show strong apical dominance and grow tall and straight, whereas other plants, those that branch heavily and are bushy, show weak apical dominance (Figure 8–11).

Other interesting aspects of growth-hormone control are the effects that auxins apparently

have in the developing stem and root. When a seed germinates the root bends downward into the soil and the stem bends upward. The control of these behaviors is believed to be differential effects of auxin concentration on the two structures. When the embryonic parts emerge from the germinating seed (Figure 8–12), gravity forces concentration to be on the lower side of the structures. This apparently stimulates the cells of the stem in this region and they undergo a more rapid

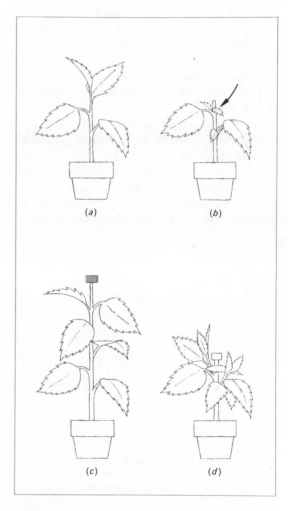

Figure 8–11 Experiments to show apical dominance. (a) Apical bud inhibits lateral growth. (b) Lateral buds develop when apical bud is removed. (c) Lateral buds are inhibited if an agar block containing auxin is applied. (d) Lateral buds continue to grow when agar block containing no auxin is applied.

growth than the cells on the upper side. This uneven growth causes the stem to bend upward. On the other hand, the auxin concentration inhibits the growth of the cells in the lower part of the root and permits the upper cells to grow faster, thus causing the root to turn downward.

Everyone is familiar with the phenomenon of the bending of a whole plant toward the light. This unequal growth of the stem is attributed to an uneven auxin distribution. In other words, the auxin on the side of the stem toward the light migrates to the opposite side and this stimulates the cells away from the light to grow at a faster rate, producing the bending (Figure 8–13).

What does the auxin actually do to the cells to produce growth? At the present time, this is not known for sure, but one hypothesis suggests that auxins affect the cell wall and permit the cell to take in more water, thereby increasing the size of the cell.

Another group of growth compounds are the *gibberellins*, discovered by Japanese botanist E. Kurosawa in 1926. Gibberellins are produced by the fungus *Gibberella fujikuroi*,

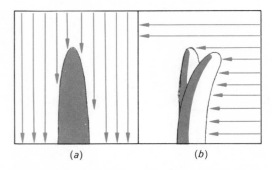

Figure 8–13 Effect of light on auxin concentration and stem movement. (*a*) When the light strikes the stem from all directions, the auxin is evenly distributed. (*b*) When the light is predominantly from one direction, the auxin is more concentrated on the dark side, resulting in unequal growth and bending—thus exhibiting the phototropic response of plant stems.

which causes the condition in rice known as "foolish-seedling disease." The chief symptom of this disease is exceptionally tall stem growth. Botanists have conducted many experiments with these compounds on other plants and, although other effects may result, the primary action of the gibberellins in all cases is to produce this rapid stem elongation. Gibberellins may prove to have economic value since typically biennial plants may be induced to complete their growth in only one year. Hormones similar to gibberellins are believed to be produced by most plants and to possibly interact with other hormones (auxins) in the control of stem growth and development. Recent studies indicate that the action of gibberellins results in increased enzyme synthesis and cell division (Figure 8–14).

Certain chemical compounds which are not normally synthesized in plants have hormone-like growth effects. One of the most familiar is 2,4-dichlorophenoxyacetic acid, commonly known as 2,4-D, a weed killer. At specific concentrations this compound produces abnormal growth and thus kills some broad-leaved plants such as dandelions and ragweed. At the same concentration, 2,4-D has no harmful effect on the narrow-leaf grasses and

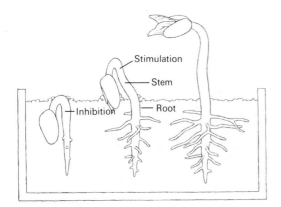

Figure 8–12 In the developing root, auxin is concentrated in the lower side because of gravity. It inhibits the elongation of the lower cells and permits the elongation of the upper cells, thus causing the root to grow downward. The concentration of auxin on the lower side of the stem, however, stimulates elongation of the lower cells and the stem turns upward.

consequently is an effective weed killer on lawns.

The growth and development of ovaries into fruits normally follows the stimulation provided by fertilization. In the absence of fertilization, however, some plant ovaries can be forced into fruit development and made to grow through the use of synthetic hormone-like substances. Thus seedless fruits can be induced in such plants as watermelons, tomatoes, oranges, and cucumbers (Figure 8–15).

Flowering—Photoperiodism

Flowering does not occur in all plants at the same time of the year. Experiments conducted in the early 1900s by government biologists W. Garner and H. Allard have shown that flowering is determined in some plants by the relative periods of light and darkness. For example, some plants, known as "short-day" plants, will not flower unless they are subjected to periods of short illumination normally represented by a period of short days. Others, which will not flower until exposed to long periods of light, are called "long-day" plants. A third group of plants, the "day-neutral" species, are reproductively insensitive to light and can bloom under varying light conditions. Asters, strawberries, cockleburs, and poinsettias are examples of short-day plants; corn, clover, lettuce, and beets represent long-day plants. Some day-neutral species are dandelions, tomatoes, sunflowers, and cucumbers. This effect of varying light periods upon flowering in certain plants is called *photoperiodism* (Figure 8–16).

It is believed that photoperiodism is determined by the presence of the hormone *florigen*, which has never been isolated, however. This theory is supported by the following observations. Since leaves must be present on a plant before it can respond to photoperiods and flower, the hormone is probably produced in the leaf and then transported to the flower bud. The critical period for short-day plants is the length of the dark period—that is, flowering will not occur unless these plants are subjected to dark periods of a specific duration. The critical period for long-day plants, on the other hand, is the length of the

Figure 8–15 Seedless navel oranges grown in Florida. The seedless condition is the result of a natural mutation. (Robert Lamb; National Audubon Society.)

(a)   (b)

Figure 8–16 Photoperiodism in chrysanthemums. (*a*) Plant was subjected to one hour of light
in the middle of the normal dark period; blooming
was therefore delayed. (*b*) Control plant. (Courtesy
of U.S. Department of Agriculture.)

variety of animal groups including insects,
crustaceans, mollusks, worms, and echinoderms. For example, the orderly *metamorphosis*
process in insects is under hormonal control.

Much more is known about mammalian,
especially human, hormonal systems than any
other. Some of the hormones produced in
humans can serve as examples since the intent
here is to acquaint you with hormonal control.
Human hormones are products of specific
glands, known as *endocrine glands*, which have
no ducts and secrete their hormones directly
into the bloodstream. Although we speak of
individual glands, we should keep in mind
that strong interactions exist among the glands
of the endocrine system, and they often
operate together as a unit. A hormone from
one gland may stimulate or inhibit another
gland, or it may reinforce the action of
another hormone. In most cases of endocrine
malfunction, more than one gland is involved.
The locations of the principal endocrine
glands in humans are shown in Figure 8–17.

The Pancreas

Perhaps the best-known example of endocrine
deficiency is *diabetes mellitus*, in which large
amounts of sugar (glucose) are excreted in the
urine. About 1890, two physicians experiment-
ing with dogs discovered that the pancreas
produces a substance that alleviates symptoms
of diabetes. When the pancreas was removed
surgically, an increased amount of sugar appeared in the urine. In 1922, two other
researchers successfully isolated insulin from
excised dog pancreases. It is common knowledge now that insulin injections will counteract
a diabetic condition. It is also interesting to
note that insulin, which is a protein, was the
first protein to have its amino-acid sequence
worked out (Figure 8–18). This was accomplished in 1954 after approximately ten years
of research by Frederick Sanger of Cambridge
University.

You have already studied the pancreas and
therefore know something of its function in
digestion. The pancreas contains two distinct
types of tissue (Figure 8–19). The most

light period; this daylight length must be
sufficient to produce flowering. Perhaps several
intermediate compounds, whose syntheses
depend on light and dark periods, are required
for the production of florigen. In addition,
other chemicals in the plant probably interact
with florigen to produce the photoperiodic
response.

IN ANIMALS

Some of the most remarkable examples of
growth, metabolic control, and coordination
are shown by the hormone systems of animals.
In fact, many growth anomalies, mistakes,
aberrant development, and behavior in humans
are results of malfunctioning hormonal systems. Hormones have been discovered in a

250

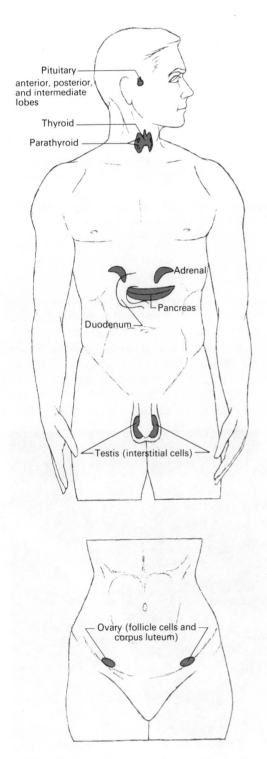

Pituitary
anterior, posterior,
and intermediate
lobes

Thyroid

Parathyroid

Adrenal

Pancreas

Duodenum

Testis (interstitial cells)

Ovary (follicle cells and
corpus luteum)

Figure 8–17 Location of the principal endocrine glands in humans.

abundant of these two tissues are the dark-staining tubule cells which secrete digestive enzymes. Scattered irregularly throughout this tissue are larger, lighter-staining cell groups that secrete hormones. These patches are called *islets of Langerhans*. Two types of cells (beta and alpha) are found in the islets and each produces a different hormone—the beta cells, insulin, and the alpha cells, glucagon.

We should now return to the relationship between insulin and sugar in the urine. You will recall from Chapter 7 that digested carbohydrates in the form of glucose (blood sugar) are carried to the liver by the hepatic portal system. In the liver much of the glucose is converted to glycogen which can be stored. This conversion of glucose to glycogen can also take place in the muscles. Under normal conditions the blood retains about 80 to 120 mg of glucose per 100 ml of blood, and the remainder is converted to glycogen by the liver and muscles. Glycogen, however, can be converted back to glucose as you know and distributed to the blood to be carried to tissues for fuel. When the concentration of blood glucose reaches 180 mg per 100 ml of blood, glucose is excreted in the urine. This is where insulin comes into the picture. We know that glucose must either enter cells to be burned as a fuel or be converted to glycogen in the liver and muscle cells. We know that insulin does facilitate the conversion of glucose to glycogen. It is also believed that insulin increases membrane permeability in liver and muscle cells to permit glucose to enter these cells faster. In addition, insulin probably inhibits the liver from converting glycogen to glucose.

Several other control agents play important roles in maintaining proper levels of blood sugar. Glucagon has already been listed as another hormone produced by the pancreas. It seems to have the opposite effects of insulin —that is, it causes an increase in the blood-sugar level. The pancreas is one of the most interesting equilibrium-producing glands since it produces two hormones with opposite effects. Several other hormones also act as

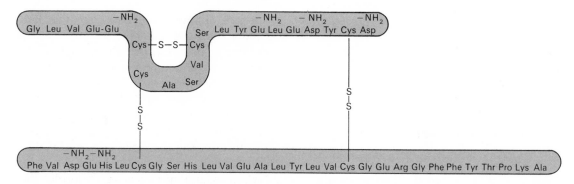

Figure 8–18 Molecular structure of insulin. The two amino-acid chains are connected by disulfide bridges. The amino acids represented are: glycine (Gly), leucine (Leu), valine (Val), glutamine (Glu $-NH_2$), cystine (Cys), alanine (Ala), serine (Ser), tyrosine (Tyr), asparagine (Asp $-NH_2$), phenylalanine (Phe), glutamic acid (Glu), histidine (His), arginine (Arg), threonine (Thr), proline (Pro), and lysine (Lys).

control agents for blood sugar. We know, for instance, that *epinephrine* (adrenalin) can increase blood-sugar level; this will be discussed further under adrenal glands. *ACTH*, a hormone secretion of the pituitary gland, stimulates the adrenal gland's cortex to produce *glucocorticoid* hormone which can also increase the level of blood sugar. One other hormone involved in the glucose-glycogen relationship is thyroxin, secreted by the thyroid gland, which controls the rate at which glucose is burned in glycolysis and the Krebs cycle. When thyroxin is increased in the blood, glucose is burned faster; thus, increasing thyroxin in the blood tends to decrease the blood-sugar level. These hor-

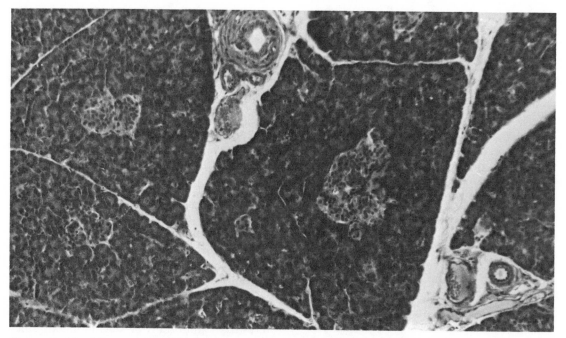

Figure 8–19 Microscopic section of the pancreas (X 450). The lighter stained areas in the lobes are the islets of Langerhans. The more abundant, darkly stained tissue secretes digestive enzymes.

252

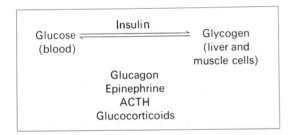

Figure 8–20 The various hormones that influence the glucose-glycogen relationship. If the hormones are present in normal levels, mass action also has an effect.

mones are itemized in Figure 8–20 and glucose-glycogen metabolism is summarized in Figure 8–21.

In diabetes mellitus the harm to the patient is not caused by the sugar in the urine. The essential damage is produced when cells must burn fats and proteins for fuel rather than the number one fuel, glucose. In the oxidation of large amounts of fats, toxic products are given off and the body cannot cope with these. These products alter the body pH and can cause death. When diabetes is diagnosed the patient can supplement his faulty metabolism with insulin from other animals and live a normal life. A condition called *insulin shock* results when an overdose of insulin is administered. In such cases the blood-sugar level drops so low that the brain does not receive enough glucose, and unconsciousness or convulsions can result.

The Pituitary Gland

In any discussion of the human endocrine system considerable time must be devoted to the pituitary gland which lies beneath the midbrain at the base of the skull. The pituitary is a principal initiator of many behavioral patterns, and this role will be stressed in Chapter 9. It is divided into three lobes— posterior, intermediate, and anterior (Figure 8–22) and is connected to the *hypothalamus* of the brain by a stalk which contains both neural and blood connections, the portal vessels. This is important to remember since we know that the nervous system produces hormones also. In fact, the hormones secreted from the posterior lobe apparently are produced in the hypothalamus and transported to the posterior lobe. Since it has been demonstrated that vascular (blood) connections exist between the hypothalamus and the anterior pituitary, hormones secreted from the hypothalamus can stimulate the anterior pituitary to release its

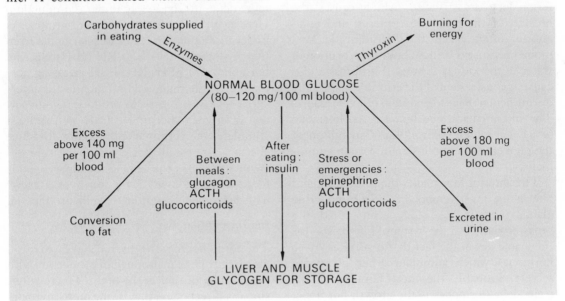

Figure 8–21 Summary of the factors involved in glucose-glycogen metabolism.

253

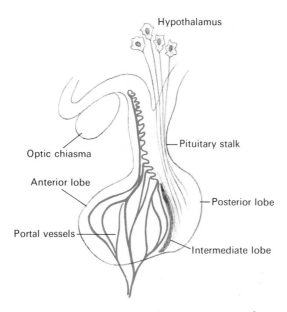

Hypothalamus

Optic chiasma

Pituitary stalk

Anterior lobe

Posterior lobe

Portal vessels

Intermediate lobe

Figure 8–22 Section of the pituitary gland showing nerve fibers to the posterior lobe and portal vessels to the anterior lobe.

hormones. At least nine such "releaser" hormones from the hypothalamus to the pituitary have now been identified, and these hormones apparently regulate the release of most of the anterior pituitary hormones.

The two hormones secreted from the posterior lobe are *oxytocin*, which causes the muscles of the uterus to contract, and *vasopressin*, often called the "antidiuretic hormone" because it brings about reabsorption of water in the kidney tubules. Vasopressin also causes a constriction of the arterioles especially during hemorrhage to maintain blood pressure. The intermediate lobe secretes the hormone *intermedin* which controls the distribution of the pigmentation in the skin of certain amphibians.

The anterior lobe makes the pituitary gland one of the most remarkable of all endocrine glands, and it has often been called the "master gland" of the system. The reason for this name lies in the fact that it secretes *tropic* hormones which stimulate other glands to secrete. Probably the most familiar of anterior-lobe hormones is the growth hormone, *somatotropin*, which, along with thyroxin,

controls the growth of the entire body. Increased amounts of this during the growing stage can lead to *giantism*, and a decreased amount below normal produces *dwarfism*. If oversecretion occurs later in life, only those bones will grow that are still capable of growth, such as some facial bones and the hands and feet. This condition is known as *acromegaly*.

Two very important examples of anterior-lobe hormones controlling other glands in the endocrine system are *thyrotropic* hormone which stimulates the thyroid gland and *ACTH* (adrenocorticotropic hormone) which controls the adrenal gland. Apparently the anterior lobe is stimulated by the hypothalamus of the brain during periods of stress to produce ACTH. The hormone, CRH (corticotropin-releasing hormone), was the first hypothalamic releasing hormone to be demonstrated.

Two other pituitary hormones control the development and function of the gonads (ovaries and testes), and these are called *gonadotropic* (GTH) hormones. Specifically they are FSH (follicle-stimulating hormone) and LH (luteinizing hormone). One of the clearest examples of hormonal control is shown in the female where critical ratios of FSH and LH control ovulation. This will be discussed in more detail in Chapter 10 under reproduction. Here again the secretion of these hormones is under the regulation of releaser hormones from the hypothalamus—LH–RH (LH-releasing hormone) and FSH–RH (FSH-releasing hormone). In the male, LH stimulates the interstitial cells of the testis to produce *testosterone*, the chief male hormone. FSH in the male stimulates the germinal epithelium to produce sperm. *Lactotropin* hormone (LTH) or *prolactin* stimulates the female mammary glands to produce milk after the birth of a baby. This hormone is essential for milk production.

The Thyroid Gland

The hormone from the thyroid gland, *thyroxin*, has already been mentioned in connection with the burning of fuel in the body. The relationship is a direct one—that is, the more thyroxin, the faster the food is oxidized. Thus people

254

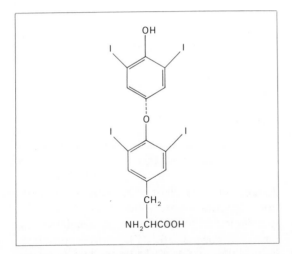

Figure 8–23 Structural formula of thyroxin. Note the four iodine (I) atoms. If only two iodine atoms are present, the molecule exhibits only a fraction of normal activity.

with an overactive thyroid show symptoms of weight loss, nervousness, and irritability. Opposite symptoms such as overweight and sluggishness are associated with an underactive thyroid in the adult. If the thyroid undersecretes in early childhood, *cretinism* results in which the child's growth, sexual maturity, and mental development are retarded.

Chemically, thyroxin is an amino acid containing iodine (Figure 8–23). *Goiter*, which is overdevelopment of the thyroid gland, occurs when the thyroid cells lack enough iodine to make effective thyroxin. Hypothyroid goiter, as this type of goiter is known, is treated by the addition of iodine to the diet to increase the production of thyroxin. The excess thyroid tissue may then be removed by surgery. Hypothyroid goiter was once a common problem in inland areas such as the Alps in Switzerland and the Great Lakes region of the United States, but today iodized salt prevents this type of goiter in most areas. An oversecreting thyroid gland can also produce goiter due to the overactivity of the cells. This latter type of goiter, known as hyperthyroid goiter, is more serious and may increase metabolism by 50 percent above normal.

As we have said, the thyroid gland is stimulated to secrete thyroxin by the thyrotropic hormone, also known as thyroid-stimulating hormone (TSH), from the anterior lobe of the pituitary. The releaser hormone from the hypothalamus which stimulates the anterior pituitary in this case is TRH (thyrotropin-releasing hormone). Some feedback mechanism must exist to signal the anterior lobe when an adequate supply of thyroxin has been produced. This feedback is believed to work as follows: a high concentration of thyroxin inhibits the production of TSH; when the supply of TSH drops off, so does the amount of thyroxin since TSH is no longer stimulating the thyroid gland; when the concentration of thyroxin is reduced, TSH can again be secreted to stimulate the thyroid gland to produce thyroxin once more. This would provide a fairly constant level of thyroxin in the body (Figure 8–24).

In general thyroxin serves to stimulate most body functions. Addition of thyroxin, for example, increases the production of many enzymes, speeds up heart rate and circulation, and increases the excitability of the nervous system. For instance, metamorphic development in frogs is definitely under control of the thyroid gland. If the thyroid gland is removed from tadpoles, they cannot develop into adult frogs. Moreover, if thyroxin is added to the water of developing tadpoles, they metamorphose much earlier than those not receiving additional thyroxin.

Another hormone produced by the thyroid gland, *calcitonin*, is involved in the regulation of calcium balance. Recently it has been

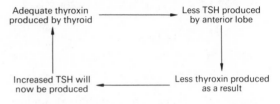

Figure 8–24 Events involved in the control of thyroxin secretion. The feedback principle is evident in this cycle of events.

demonstrated that calcitonin acts to lower the concentration of blood calcium by inhibiting the release of calcium from bone to blood. This hormone has the opposite effect of the parathyroid hormone which we will consider next.

The Parathyroid Glands

When the four parathyroid glands, which are located near or in the thyroid (Figure 8–25), are surgically removed in experimental animals, muscle twitching and convulsions occur. Death results if injections of parathyroid hormone, known as *parathormone*, are not given to the animal. Physiologically, the calcium level in the blood drops when parathormone is not present, and rises when the hormone is added. Essentially, then, this gland is concerned with calcium metabolism and circulation in the blood. An undersecretion of it produces a hyperirritability of these organs with slow reactions.

A second function of these glands is the control of the removal of phosphate from the body by the kidneys. Parathormone increases the concentration of calcium in the blood, but it decreases the concentration of phosphates. An undersecretion of the hormone, then, increases the phosphate level in the blood. Bones are partly composed of a calcium

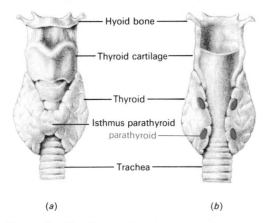

(a)   **(b)**

Figure 8–25 Human thyroid gland. (*a*) Anterior view showing the connecting isthmus over the trachea. (*b*) Posterior view illustrating the parathyroid glands embedded in the thyroid.

phosphate compound, so when calcium is released to the blood, the excess phosphate is removed from the body. Parathyroid hormone, along with the antagonistic action of calcitonin, from the thyroid, controls both of these activities.

The Adrenals and the Gonads

The adrenal glands lie on top of the kidneys and serve a variety of functions, some of which have already been mentioned. Each gland is divided into two distinct parts, each with distinct functions. An inner mass called the *medulla* is surrounded by an outside layer, the *cortex* (Figure 8–26). The cortex produces three different groups of hormones (there are also three layers to the cortex and it is tempting to suppose that each layer secretes a class of hormones). The *glucocorticoids* not only assist in controlling the conversion of glycogen to glucose (the opposite action to insulin) but are also concerned with fat and amino-acid metabolism. Part of the action is to convert these two groups of compounds to glucose. The second class of hormones secreted by the cortex are the *mineralocorticoids* and, as the name implies, these are involved in salt and water balance. If these hormones are decreased for any reason, such as a diseased cortex, the sodium, chloride, and water concentrations of the body fluids drop while the potassium concentration increases. The hormones tend to increase kidney reabsorption of sodium and excretion of potassium. In Addison's disease, which is caused by a degeneration of the cortex, dehydration and changes in skin pigmentation occur and the sodium level decreases while the potassium level rises. Moreover, the patient has difficulty coping with mild disturbances and illnesses which are usually of minor consequence. An intact and normal cortex seems to be important to the organism in meeting stress situations. Here is another place where the connection between the nervous and the endocrine systems seems apparent. *Sex hormones* are also produced by the cortex; although these are predominantly male hormones (*androgens*),

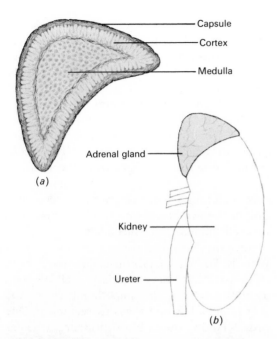

Figure 8–26 Adrenal gland. (a) Cross section showing the cortex and the medulla. (b) Position of the adrenal gland on the superior surface of the kidney.

female hormones (*estrogens* and *progesterone*) are also secreted. Overactivity of the cortex at an early age can, and does on occasion, produce early and abnormal sexual maturity.

Do you remember that ACTH from the pituitary stimulates the cortex to produce its hormones? A faulty pituitary, therefore, can cause the cortex to over- or undersecrete. You should also note the structure of some of the hormones secreted by the cortex. Most of these are the basic steroid configuration with varying side chains (Figure 8–27).

The medulla of the adrenal gland produces the hormones *epinephrine* and *norepinephrine* which are commonly referred to as *adrenalin*. This has often been called the *emergency hormone* since it exerts the following effects: increases the blood-sugar level (the opposite of insulin), increases the heart rate and blood pressure, dilates the blood vessels in heart and skeletal muscle while at the same time constricting those vessels in smooth muscle, and causes erection of skin hairs to produce "goose bumps." You probably quickly recognize these characteristics as those that would enhance an individual's chances if he were faced with an emergency situation. The body resources are mobilized in emergencies and adrenalin seems to be the hormone that does it.

The ovaries in females and the testes in males produce hormones that bring about secondary sex characteristics and maintain the distinctiveness of the sex. In the male these hormones are called *androgens* (which include testosterone) and in the female, *estrogens*. Actually each sex produces both hormones but it is the relative amounts of each which determine sex. In the male therefore, more androgens than estrogens are produced whereas the opposite is true in the female. Remember that these organs are also stimulated by tropic hormones from the anterior lobe of the pituitary.

A summary of the principal endocrine glands and the major hormones they secrete is shown in Figure 8–28.

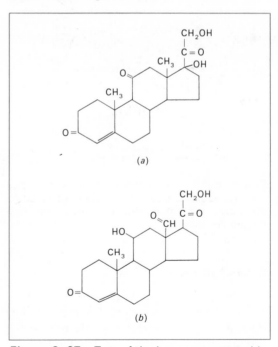

Figure 8–27 Two of the hormones secreted by the adrenal cortex. (a) Cortisone, a glucocorticoid hormone. (b) Aldosterone, a mineralocorticoid hormone.

257

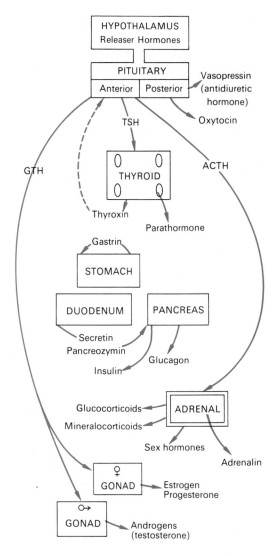

Figure 8–28 Principal endocrine glands and their secretions. One feedback flow is indicated by the broken line; other feedback mechanisms exist but are not shown.

Other Hormones

The hormones of the digestive system have already been discussed in Chapter 7. The thymus gland, in addition to its role in the production of lymphocytes and antibodies, also produces a hormone, *thymosin*. This hormone is believed to be essential for the full development of the antibody-producing ability of lymphocytes. A substance, *histamine*, released from damaged tissues is a questionable hormone at this time. Antigen-antibody reactions such as those which occur in hay fever damage the lining of the nasal passages permitting histamine to escape. Histamine increases the permeability of the blood vessels and increases mucus secretions. Antihistamines are often taken to relieve this condition. The bronchioles, small air passages from the lungs to the trachea, are constricted by histamines also, and breathing is difficult under these conditions (known as *asthma*). Antihistamines can be used to counteract this effect.

Recently, a group of hormonelike compounds known as *prostaglandins* have been demonstrated to have a variety of effects such as contraction of the smooth muscle of the uterus and inhibition of gastric secretions. One prostaglandin lowers blood pressure, whereas another one raises it. These compounds also may function to clear the nasal passages and relax the bronchioles. Many cells show minute amounts of prostaglandins in their membranes, but the richest source is in the seminal fluids. Prostaglandins may be an effective agent in the functioning of cell membranes and in some cases may be associated with the cyclic AMP mechanism.

Hormone Action

One of the primary questions about hormones is how they produce their effects on specific tissues and organs when they flow freely in the circulating fluids of an organism. Researchers in the 1950s and 1960s attempted to find answers to this problem, and some progress was made when it appeared that estrogen exerts some of its effects by uniting with a specific protein in the uterus. But the most exciting research on the mechanism of hormone action to date has come from the work of Earl W. Sutherland who won the Nobel Prize in Physiology or Medicine in 1971 (Figure 8–29). His work centered on the reactions whereby adrenalin increases the breakdown of glycogen to glucose in the liver. Sutherland and his colleagues discovered the series of

Figure 8–29 Earl W. Sutherland of Vanderbilt University, recipient of the Nobel Prize in Physiology or Medicine in 1971 for his research on hormone action. (Courtesy of Dr. Sutherland.)

steps that led from the secretion of the hormone to the final action—the enzymatic breakdown of glycogen by *phosphorylase*. This enzyme must be activated by other enzymes before it can function, and adrenalin must activate these enzymes. This is the basic role of adrenalin in the release of glucose; but exactly how does adrenalin do this?

When adrenalin is released from the adrenal cortex, it stimulates an enzyme, *adenyl cyclase*, in the cell membrane of target cells. Next, activated adenyl cyclase on the inner membrane surface catalyzes the synthesis of cyclic AMP (cAMP) from ATP inside the cell. Cyclic AMP can then have an effect on the rate of various cellular processes (Figure 8–30); in this case, it activates the enzymes capable of converting inactive phosphorylase to an active state. In the active state, phosphorylase catalyzes the breakdown of glycogen to glucose. The hormone is thus called a "first messenger," and it acts on a receptor on the outside of the membrane; cAMP, the "second messenger," produces its effect inside the cell. Thus a "two-messenger" model for the action of this hormone (adrenalin) has now been proposed. Apparently many other hormones behave in this manner and exert their effects through a similar two-messenger pattern. Among them are glucagon, ACTH, TSH, and parathormone. It is interesting to note that insulin, which has the opposite effect of adrenalin, apparently lowers the level of cAMP. Steroid hormones apparently function through a different mechanism.

THE NERVOUS SYSTEM

Although the hormonal system may be slow in responding to change, taking perhaps minutes or days, the nervous system can react quickly and provide for immediate action—an action that may save an animal's life. A fly sitting on a table becomes aware of a sudden change in its environment because of receptors that can detect the change (a *stimulus*). Nerve impulses are then carried to *modulators* (the central nervous system) which in turn direct the impulse message to the appropriate effectors (wing muscles) which permit the animal to fly to safety. It is apparent, then, that special cells exist which provide for a two-way communication system between an animal and its environment and between parts of an animal. Neurons or nerve cells are irritable—that is, they will respond to a stimulus, but some nerve cells show a high degree of irritability and, in addition, conductivity. It is these neurons that provide for the rapid and often complex behavioral activity of animals, which will be studied in the next chapter. Although some plants such as the Venus's-flytrap respond to touch, there is no real counterpart here to neurons or the nervous system. Plants respond to stimuli in the manner described earlier under tropisms.

Most multicelled animals have some type of a nervous system to provide coordination and communication. This system may consist

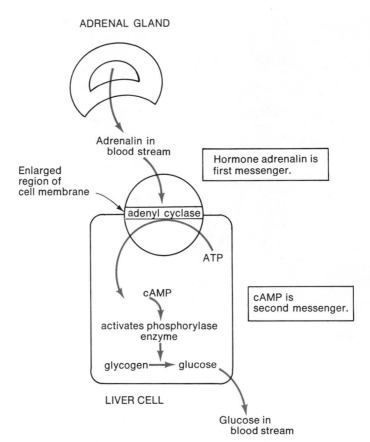

Figure 8-30 The action of adrenalin in stimulating the formation of glucose. Adrenalin is a first messenger, and cAMP is the second messenger. Cyclic AMP (cAMP) converts inactive phosphorylase to its active form. Phosphorylase then catalyzes the breakdown of glycogen to glucose.

of nothing more than a group of connected neurons scattered throughout the animal's body to form a nerve net. In more advanced forms many neurons may come together to form a *ganglion* (a group or collection of nerve cell bodies) which can then act as a coordinating center. A series of connected ganglia may also form a nerve cord, which might be located either ventrally or dorsally, from which lateral nerves can emerge to distant parts of the body. Some of the various nervous systems found in the animal world are illustrated in Figure 8–31.

ANATOMY OF THE HUMAN NERVOUS SYSTEM

The most complex nervous system of all is found in vertebrate animals. We will use the human as our example here, but remember that all vertebrates possess similar structures differing only in size and number of various parts. For example, the cerebrum of the human brain shows considerably more development and complexity than any other vertebrate. The vertebrate nervous system can be considered to consist of two parts: the *central nervous system* (CNS) and the *peripheral nervous system* (PNS). The CNS is composed of the brain and spinal cord which contain the cell bodies, while the cranial and spinal nerves form the PNS. Information in the form of nerve impulses, to be discussed later in this chapter, can be carried to various parts of the body over the peripheral nerves from the brain and spinal cord. In the same manner, information can be transmitted to the CNS from various parts of the body. A nerve leading into the CNS is called a *sensory* or *afferent pathway*. A nerve leading from the CNS is referred to as a *motor* or *efferent pathway*. Of the twelve

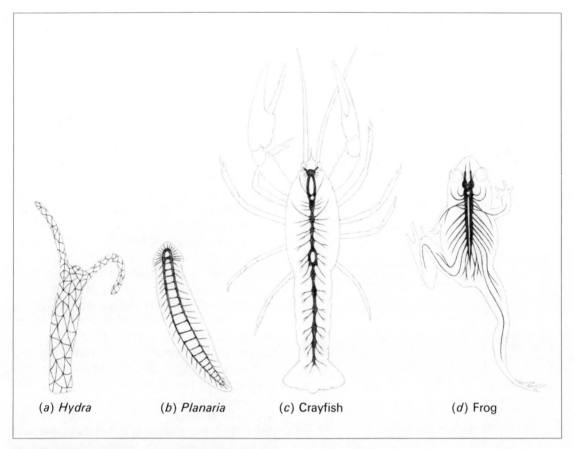

(*a*) *Hydra*	(*b*) *Planaria*	(*c*) Crayfish	(*d*) Frog

Figure 8–31 Various types of nervous systems found in the animal kingdom. (*a*) Nerve net. (*b*) Ladder-type nerve system. (*c*) Ventral nerve cord. (*d*) Dorsal nerve cord.

pairs of cranial nerves emanating from the undersurface of the brain, some are motor, some are sensory, and some are mixed, that is, they contain both sensory and motor nerves. The thirty-one pairs of spinal nerves attached to the spinal cord are all mixed nerves. The cranial nerves serve mainly the head and neck regions, whereas the spinal nerves are distributed to the rest of the body supplying the skeletal muscles, skin, sweat glands, and blood vessels. In addition, from some spinal and cranial nerves, lateral ganglia arise which send nerve fibers to visceral organs. This part of the nervous system is not under voluntary control and is often referred to as the *autonomic nervous system* (ANS). The peripheral nervous system, therefore, consists of two parts: the *voluntary*, serving skeletal muscles, etc., and the *involuntary* (ANS), serving visceral organs. The diagram in Figure 8–32 should assist in

understanding the anatomy of the human nervous system discussed to this point.

Each spinal nerve is connected to the spinal cord by two roots; one is dorsal and one is ventral. All of the nerves leading to the spinal cord (sensory) at this point enter the dorsal root, and those leaving the cord (motor) travel over the ventral root. These are shown more clearly in Figure 8–33 which illustrates reflex action.

Reflexes

A discussion of reflexes helps in understanding the detailed structure of some aspects of the nervous system. Moreover, it provides basic information on how the system functions. In the next chapter, the relationship of reflexes to behavior will be studied. A *reflex* is considered to be a simple form of behavior wherein a stimulus evokes a specific response. One of the

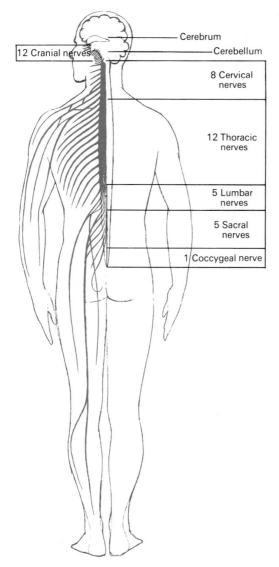

Cerebrum
Cerebellum
12 Cranial nerves
8 Cervical nerves
12 Thoracic nerves
5 Lumbar nerves
5 Sacral nerves
1 Coccygeal nerve

Figure 8–32 Human nervous system showing the twelve pairs of cranial nerves and the thirty-one pairs of spinal nerves.

when the original sensory pathway of the reflex is replaced by a different sensory element. The response or the motor pathway remains the same. The famous experiments of Pavlov are cited in Chapter 9 to explain how conditioning can be effected.

A reflex results when a nerve impulse travels over a *reflex arc*. The spinal cord (or areas of the brain) is part of this reflex arc. The arc may consist of only two neurons or may involve three or more neurons. The neuron that picks up the stimulus and brings the information to the spinal cord is called the sensory or afferent pathway. The information (in the form of a nerve impulse) is then passed to a second neuron that carries the impulse out over a motor or efferent pathway to an effector which produces the response. In many reflexes other neurons called *internuncial* or connecting neurons are involved. These are located in the spinal cord between the two pathways. Both of these examples are diagrammed in Figure 8–33. You should note that where two neurons meet, the axon of one is closely associated with the dendrite of the other. This association is called a synapse and the transmission of the nerve impulse across this region is accomplished by a chemical process.

It should also be noted how well the reflex arc illustrates the processes of control and regulation as described earlier in Figures 8–3 and 8–4. A reflex thus occurs as a result of a change which requires action from the living system; the regulating mechanism here is the nervous system employing sensory and motor neurons and the spinal cord.

The Brain

The CNS is considered to be the controller of nervous activity since it sends messages to all parts of the body through the PNS. The role of the spinal cord in this process was just discussed. The brain is the chief organ in this integration and it receives messages, transmitted upward through the spinal cord, sorts them out and relays the information to the appropriate part of the CNS for action. Many

most familiar examples is the extension of the lower leg upon the stimulation (tapping) of the patellar (knee cap) tendon. The immediate withdrawal of the foot or hand upon touching a hot object is another familiar example. These actions occur instantaneously and involuntarily. A natural reflex can be modified by experience; this is often referred to as conditioning or a *conditioned reflex*. This can arise

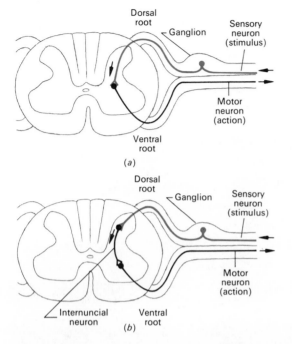

Figure 8–33 Reflex arcs. In the cross sections of the spinal cord, note that the cell body of the sensory neuron is in the ganglion of the dorsal root, whereas the cell body of the motor neuron lies in the spinal cord. The direction of the nerve impulse is indicated by the arrows. The H-shaped area of the spinal cord is the so-called gray region where the cell bodies lie; the white region of the cord is composed only of nerve fibers that carry impulses up and down the spinal cord, to and from the brain. (a) Reflex arc involving two neurons. The knee jerk exemplifies this type. (b) Reflex arc involving three neurons. Removing your hand from a hot stove exemplifies this type.

reflexes, therefore, may be modified as a result of brain action. Certainly all learned and intelligent behavior must involve the brain and certain parts of the brain should be discussed here (Figures 8–34 and 8–35).

The *cerebrum* contains the nerve centers that govern and integrate motor and sensory functions. In addition, the cerebrum is the site of the important functions of reasoning, intelligence, and memory. It is composed of two hemispheres and is by far the largest part of man's brain. The *corpus callosum* connects the two hemispheres of the cerebrum. The function of the *thalamus* can be summarized

in two categories: (1) it relays sensory impulses to the cerebrum; and (2) it provides a low level of conscious recognition of sensations such as pain and temperature. The small area known as the *hypothalamus* is involved essentially with the control of involuntary or autonomic functions such as regulating appetite, sleep and waking states, water balance, body temperature, and stimulation of the pituitary gland through releaser hormones. The *cerebellum* provides, or assists in providing, the coordination of muscular movements and the control of posture. The *medulla* contains many reflex centers for such functions as coughing, sneezing, and swallowing. More important, however, are the vital centers located in the medulla for the control of breathing and heart action.

The Autonomic Nervous System

A division of the nervous system was mentioned earlier that is not under willful control and we called it the *autonomic nervous system* (ANS). Even though this part of the nervous system is "self-controlled," it is still connected to the rest of the nervous system through the spinal and cranial nerves. This connection with the spinal nerves is shown in the diagram in Figure 8–36. The ANS is divided into two divisions on the basis of function and anatomy (Figure 8–37). The *sympathetic* division arises from all of the spinal nerves in the thoracic region and the first three lumbar nerves. This division therefore is sometimes called the *thoracolumbar* portion of the ANS. The *parasympathetic* division is composed of branches of the third, seventh, ninth, and tenth cranial nerves and the second, third, and fourth sacral spinal nerves. This division of the ANS is often referred to as the *craniosacral*.

These two divisions not only come from different regions of the CNS but also function entirely different—in fact, one division is antagonistic toward the other. (Remember that this is an involuntary system.) The sympathetic system accelerates the heartbeat, whereas the parasympathetic slows it down. The sympathetic system can produce dilation

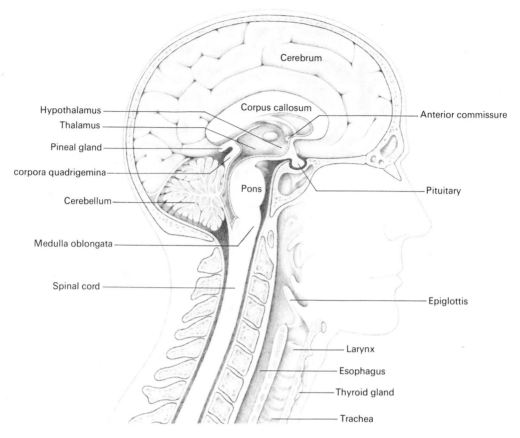

Figure 8–34   Median longitudinal view of the human brain.

of the pupils of the eyes and the parasympathetic can bring about their constriction. The sympathetic system seems to be concerned with the mobilization of body resources for emergencies, whereas the parasympathetic returns the body to a more normal state after an emergency passes. The two divisions usually work together to provide a normal range of operation for the body through their accelerating and decelerating effects. The diagram in Figure 8–37 illustrates some of the effects of each system upon certain parts of the body.

THE NERVE IMPULSE

In preceding paragraphs we mentioned a nerve "message" traveling along a nerve. This message, possibly better termed a *nerve im-*

pulse, occurs along an axon or dendrite when a nerve is stimulated. The process of nerve conduction has been studied by biologists for many years. In 1902, Bernstein, a German biologist, proposed a theory for the transmission of the nerve impulse, and experimental evidence in the 1930s and 1940s, especially by Hodgkin and Huxley, confirmed his theory. In fact, Bernstein's model, with slight modifications, is still used today to explain nerve-impulse transmission. The theory is based on the knowledge that the concentrations of specific ions are different inside the neurons from those outside. It is also known that the concentrations of some of these ions change instantaneously with the passage of the nerve impulse. Therefore the process must be due to changes in ionic concentrations along the cell membrane.

264

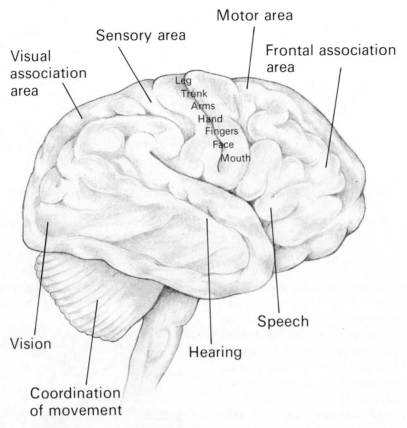

Leg
Trunk
Arms
Hand
Fingers
Face
Mouth

Visual
association
area

Sensory area

Motor area

Frontal association
area

Speech

Vision

Hearing

Coordination
of movement

Figure 8–35 Some functional areas of the cortex in the human brain.

In a nerve that is not conducting, more negative ions, mostly organic, are inside the cell than are outside. This produces a negatively charged region in comparison to the outside. The concentration of sodium ions (Na^+) is much greater outside the cell than inside, and more potassium ions (K^+) are found inside the cell. This uneven distribution of ions (more negative ions inside and more positive ions outside the cell) produces a potential across the membrane of living nerve cells of the magnitude of 50 to 70 millivolts. This is referred to as the *resting potential* and it establishes a definite polarity. When a nerve is stimulated the membrane becomes more permeable to sodium ions and they rush into the cell across the membrane. This reverses the polarity that previously existed and produces a temporary positive charge on

the inside of the cell in relationship to the outside. When this depolarization occurs, we say that an *action potential* has developed. Immediately following the influx of sodium ions the membrane is highly permeable to potassium ions which flow through the membrane to the outside. At this point we must consider the restoration of the nerve cell to the state that existed before stimulation—that is, the original ionic balance with a greater concentration of sodium ions outside the cell and a greater concentration of potassium ions inside. If this should fail to occur, the neuron could not conduct nerve impulses again. It is known that a neuron normally can recover almost instantaneously, within thousandths of a second, and be ready to conduct once more.

For sodium ions to move outside the cell

265

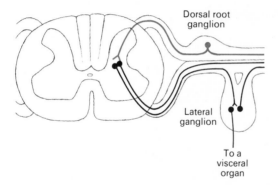

Figure 8–36 Relationship between the autonomic nervous system and the parasympathetic nervous system. A lateral autonomic ganglion is shown arising from a spinal nerve.

again and potassium ions to move inside would require the movement of these ions against a concentration gradient. The only way this can be done is by an active-transport mechanism such as that described in Chapter 3. In other words, sodium is actively transported to the outside while potassium is apparently moved back inside the cell. When this occurs the inside of the cell becomes negative again. The model proposed to account for these activities has been called the "sodium pump" or, more recently, the "sodium-potassium exchange pump." The latter mechanism postulates that the same system which transports sodium out of the cell also moves potassium back into the cell. Perhaps a carrier molecule, similar to that proposed for the transport of glucose in Chapter 3, is operative in this process.

If the events described here account for the transmission of an impulse at one spot on the nerve, it is reasonable to assume this same process occurs for transmission along the entire length of the nerve. But how are the events set off in the region adjacent to the stimulated area and in succeeding regions? It was proposed by Bernstein, and others more recently, that the disturbance in membrane permeability which originally permitted the impulse to start upset the normal membrane permeability in the adjacent area. The impulse would then move to neighboring regions of the nerve until the impulse had traveled the length of the nerve. Thus a wave of depolarization moves along the nerve which is self-propagating and which is "powered" at each step along the way. This movement of the impulse along the nerve has been likened to a burning dynamite fuse that propagates itself by lowering the kindling temperature in the adjacent regions as the fuse burns. The series of events just described is summarized in Figure 8–38.

All nerve impulses are apparently the same whether the stimulus be touch or light or sound waves. That is, the impulse does not differ but receptors are different and they lead to different parts of the brain for interpretation. It should also be noted that a

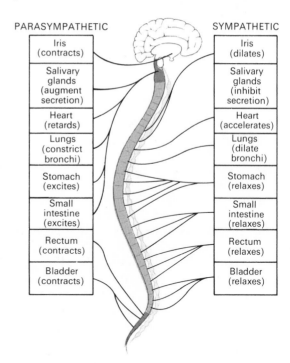

Figure 8–37 The two components of the autonomic nervous system and their action on various organs. Note the opposing effects of the two divisions. Darker shades denote the parasympathetic system; lighter shades denote the sympathetic system.

266

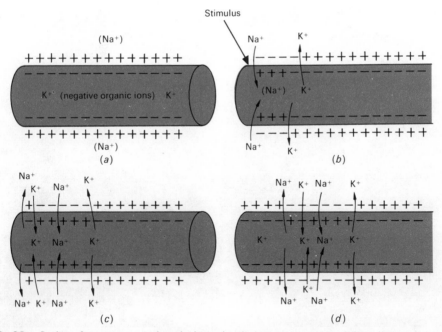

Figure 8–38 Series of events occurring during stimulation of a nerve and the subsequent conduction of the impulse. (*a*) Nonconducting nerve fiber. (*b*) Stimulus applied and Na⁺ flow in; very shortly thereafter, K⁺ move out. (*c*) The adjacent region becomes depolarized and the impulse is conducted along the nerve; note the region of the original stimulus is beginning to recover. Na⁺ is being transported out and K⁺ back in. (*d*) Conduction continues along the nerve to the right as recovery occurs at the left end of the fiber.

stimulus must be of a sufficient strength in order to initiate an impulse. This intensity is often referred to as a *threshold stimulus*.

The basic cause of the nerve impulse is electrochemical—that is, the ionic changes which occur along the membrane produce electrical events. Moreover, these events can be visualized and studied by the use of electronic instrumentation. When a nerve impulse is picked up between two points on a nerve it produces a "spike" (the action potential noted earlier) on an *oscilloscope*, an instrument that records a visual image of an electrical event on a fluorescent screen (Figures 8–39 and 8–40). We often refer to these electrochemical changes as *bioelectricity*, but it is entirely different from conventional electricity which travels through copper wiring. Common electricity results from electron movement along a wire, whereas bioelectricity is due to a separation of charged particles (ions)

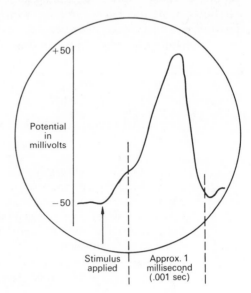

Figure 8–39 Visible part of a nerve impulse (the "spike") as it would appear on an oscilloscope.

267

Figure 8–40 An oscilloscope—a type commonly used in experiments in college laboratory classes.

by a membrane (a process requiring active transport by the membrane). Electricity travels at the rate of 186,000 miles per second and is much faster than the nerve impulse which varies from 1 to 300 meters per second.

In this chapter the basic mechanisms of control were discussed; these often lead to organismic activity commonly called *behavior*. Knowledge of hormonal and nervous systems assists in the study of behavior. In Chapter 9 we will see how behavior also contributes to the control and regulation of organisms.

SUMMARIZING STATEMENTS

All organisms must react to changing conditions in order to maintain a fairly constant internal environment. This internal balance (dynamic equilibrium) is accomplished through the active coordination and regulation of chemical and physical processes in the organism. Some of the factors involved in the maintenance of a steady state in organisms can be demonstrated by physical models. Four features are necessary: self-regulating mechanism, feedback, immediate response, and multicontrols.

General scheme of control: internal and external changes require regulation before action; feedback is necessary to prevent overreaction. These responses to change involve hormonal and nervous systems as well as certain ions, vitamins, and enzymes that may regulate specific chemical reactions.

Hormones produced by plants control growth, movement, and flowering. Animal hormones are usually secreted from endocrine glands and generally produce widespread effects. Examples of animal hormone action are: regulation

268

of growth, development, metabolism, reproduction, digestion, and water and ion balance. Studies show that some hormones act as a "first messenger" to stimulate a "second messenger," cAMP, which produces an effect inside a cell.

The nervous system is composed of neurons and nerve tracts; whereas hormonal control is often slow and generalized, the nervous system provides for fast, specific action. The nervous system of man may be considered in three functional divisions: the central, peripheral, and autonomic systems. CNS—the brain and spinal cord; PNS—the cranial and spinal nerves; ANS—an involuntary system consisting of two antagonistic divisions, the sympathetic and para-sympathetic.

The reflex arc is a nerve pathway involving sensory, motor, and sometimes internuncial neurons. It occurs across the spinal cord from dorsal root to ventral root before the brain can modulate the sensory input. Some reflexes can be conditioned through training.

Nerve cells have the ability to pass a wave of excitation along their full length and transfer this excitation to other nerve cells. Electrochemical events involving ions (especially sodium and potassium) account for this wave of excitation.

REVIEW QUESTIONS

1 In what ways can the external environment of an organism affect its internal environment?

2 Describe the control or regulative reactions that would occur in the following situation: You are stepping from a curb into the street and suddenly you glimpse a fast approaching automobile about 25 feet away.

3 Can you explain the value of having both nervous and hormonal systems in animals? What are the advantages of each?

4 What evidence do we have that enzymes and genes act as control agents?

5 If a potato tuber is grown in a jar, the apical bud develops into a large and vigorous shoot and the lateral buds ("eyes") produce small shoots, if any. However, if the tuber is cut into five or six pieces, all "eyes" will develop sprouts of about the same size. Explain.

6 Land snails in the northwestern United States come into reproductive activity about May and June. What conditions must a researcher modify and control if he wants these snails to reproduce in the months of February and March?

7 What are some of the changes you would expect in a young rabbit that has been given periodic injections of pituitary extract?

8 What are some of the effects of an excessive growth of adrenal cortex tissue (a tumor). Consider the changes that might occur in a 5-year-old male and a 35-year-old male.

9 People with high blood pressure and a history of heart trouble are often advised not to attend exciting athletic contests. Explain.

10 Summarize the control mechanisms that interact to maintain normal blood-glucose metabolism.

11   How are hormones believed to function at the molecular level?

12   Describe the portal connection between the hypothalamus of the brain and the anterior pituitary. What are the possibilities for interaction between these two structures?

13   Why would a physician test several specific reflexes on a patient following an accident that leaves the individual unconscious?

14   What effect would a severed ventral root of a spinal nerve have on a reflex arc?

15   Compare the effects of the sympathetic and parasympathetic divisions of the ANS on: digestion, heart rate, and blood pressure.

16   Explain why it is possible to start a nerve impulse along a nerve by applying electrical stimulation, pressure, or certain chemicals.

SUPPLEMENTARY READINGS

Baker, Peter F., "The Nerve Axon," *Scientific American*, March, 1966.

Bayliss, L. E., *Living Control Systems*, San Francisco, Freeman, 1966.

Benzinger, T. H., "The Human Thermostat," *Scientific American*, January, 1961.

Bonner, John T., "Hormones in Social Amoebae and Mammals," *Scientific American*, June, 1969.

Butler, W. L., and R. J. Downs, "Light and Plant Development," *Scientific American*, April, 1960.

Changeux, J. P., "The Control of Biochemical Reactions," *Scientific American*, April, 1965.

Di Cara, Leo V., "Learning in the Autonomic Nervous System," *Scientific American*, January, 1970.

Evarts, Edward V., "Brain Mechanisms in Movement," *Scientific American*, July, 1973.

Fieser, Louis F., "Steroids," *Scientific American*, January, 1955.

Gardner, Lytt I., "Deprivation Dwarfism," *Scientific American*, July, 1972.

Gillie, R. B., "Endemic Goiter," *Scientific American*, June, 1971.

Gordon, Barbara, "The Superior Solliculus of the Brain," *Scientific American*, December, 1972.

Guillemin, Roger, and R. Burgus, "The Hormones of the Hypothalamus," *Scientific American*, November, 1972.

Heimer, Lennart, "Pathways in the Brain," *Scientific American*, July, 1971.

Katz, Bernhard, "The Nerve Impulse," *Scientific American*, November, 1952.

Keynes, Richard D., "The Nerve Impulse and the Squid," *Scientific American*, December, 1958.

Kimura, Doreen, "The Asymmetry of the Human Brain," *Scientific American*, March, 1973.

Levey, R. H., "The Thymus Hormone," *Scientific American*, July, 1964.

Levine, Rachmiel, and M. S. Goldstein, "The Action of Insulin," *Scientific American*, May, 1958.

Li, Choh Hao, "The ACTH Molecule," *Scientific American*, July, 1963.

"The Life-Giving Balancing Act," Part 5 in series on The Human Body, *Life Magazine*, November 8, 1963.

Loewenstein, Werner R., "Biological Transducers," *Scientific American*, August, 1960.

Mayr, Otto, "The Origins of Feedback Control," *Scientific American*, October, 1970.

McCashland, Benjamin W., *Animal Coordinating Mechanisms*, Dubuque, Iowa, Wm. C. Brown, 1968.

Nathan, Peter, *The Nervous System*, Philadelphia, Lippincott, 1969.

Overbeek, Johannes van, "The Control of Plant Growth," *Scientific American*, July, 1968.

Overmire, Thomas G., *Homeostatic Regulation*, BSCS Pamphlet No. 9, American Institute of Biological Sciences, Boston, Heath, 1963.

Pastan, Ira, "Cyclic AMP," *Scientific American*, August, 1972.

Pike, John E., "Prostaglandins," *Scientific American*, November, 1971.

Rasmussen, Howard, "The Parathyroid Hormone," *Scientific American*, April, 1961.

Rasmussen, Howard, and M. M. Pechet, "Calcitonin," *Scientific American*, October, 1970.

Salisbury, Frank B., "Plant Growth Substances," *Scientific American*, April, 1957.

Salisbury, Frank B., "The Flowering Process," *Scientific American*, April, 1958.

Snider, R. S., "The Cerebellum," *Scientific American*, August, 1958.

Steward, F. C., "The Control of Growth in Plant Cells," *Scientific American*, October, 1963.

Suckling, E. E., *Bioelectricity*, BSCS Pamphlet No. 4, American Institute of Biological Sciences, Boston, Heath, 1962.

Went, Frits W., "Plant Growth and Plant Hormones," in W. Johnson and W. Steere, eds., *This Is Life*, New York, Holt, Rinehart and Winston, 1962.

9

Behavior—What Organisms Do

All organisms show *behavior*. On the facing page, a blue-footed booby of the Galápagos Islands is shown shielding its egg from direct sunlight. The parent's body does not touch the egg. This behavior is essential to the survival of this species since exposure to the direct rays of the tropical sun can destroy the developing young in the egg. Since the parent is exposed to direct sunlight, its body heat increases. Ruffing the back feathers, a component of the shielding behavior, provides ventilation and allows the release of excessive body heat. When the temperature cools down, especially during the evening hours, the booby's behavior changes, and the bird warms its egg with its large, webbed feet. The parents take turns attending the egg and exchange positions about every eighteen hours. In cooler parts of the world most birds use a different behavior pattern to protect their eggs—they must nestle them close to keep the eggs warm. At first sight the behavior pattern is simple: a bird attends its egg. A closer look shows us that, if we want to understand what is happening, we need to describe the function of a behavior pattern, the timing of its expression, and its place in the total life of the animal.

Behavior, usually some action in response to a stimulus, fulfills the needs of an organism to maintain a stable environment, both internal and external. In other words, behavior helps the organism survive and adapt to its environment. In this chapter, our purpose is to bring together

273

principles and ideas derived from the study of behavior, to show the adaptive importance of behavior, and to explain how some behavioral patterns occur.

STUDYING BEHAVIOR

Animal behavior is complex, and it is often very difficult to determine how or why a particular animal acts as it does. For example, how is it possible for certain birds to migrate in predictable pathways each year? Behavior is at the center of our own daily lives, and we frequently ask ourselves, "Why did he act that way?" or "Why did I act as I did?" Most of us are familiar with such varied areas of behavior as politics, learning, buying, selling, competition, and working with others. To study and understand behavior, however, demands the use of the most highly developed scientific tools and methods from the disciplines of biology, psychology, and other fields. In fact the study of behavior has become so interdisciplinary that even a background in chemistry is necessary to understand many facets of behavior.

Some failures in the study of animal behavior have occurred either because scientific procedures were not followed, because all variable factors were not considered, or because researchers used a simple single theory to cover a broad area. Another obstacle to understanding behavior has been the tendency to explain all animal behavior in terms of human behavior, a process called *anthropomorphism*. It is often difficult to avoid anthropomorphic statements when discussing pets. We often say that an animal is happy or sad. These are descriptions of human feelings and are not necessarily appropriate explanations of an animal's response to a stimulus.

SOCIAL BEHAVIOR

Animal behavior studies often require much time and patience from the investigator. A good example of successful patient effort is that of Jane van Lawick-Goodall in her study of wild chimpanzees near Lake Tanganyika in Africa (Figure 9–1). It was over a year before Goodall could get close enough to the animals for actual study; during this time, she was avoided and even threatened. Only after gaining acceptance from the chimpanzees was she able to follow them through the bush and observe their social structure. She could then study and record many aspects of their daily lives and habits. Her work was the first comprehensive study of the social behavior of wild chimpanzees.

Before Goodall's study, there had been a strong tendency to think of all primates, including man's ancestors, as having a social structure somewhat like the rigid society formed by baboon colonies in captivity. But field studies have shown an enormous variation in the life styles of different primates. Chimpanzees interact in a very loose social structure allowing a great deal of individual freedom; a strict social hierarchial structure does not exist. Social bands are essentially nomadic and travel to find food. Consequently, a chimpanzee seldom sleeps two nights in the same tree. Little aggressive behavior is shown among members of a band, and "arguments" are usually short and without physical violence. Mothers devote much time and patience to their young, and the mother-child bond is very strong. Even though nursing ceases after four or five years, the young may remain with their mother for as long as eight years. Another important aspect of the offspring's development is their inclination to play among themselves and with objects.

A surprising observation was the extent of tool making and tool using among chimpanzees. They learn from other chimpanzees how to fashion thin probes from vines or grass and then use these probes for removing termites from underground nests. Chimpanzees were thought to be strict herbivores before they were observed hunting and killing smaller primates—red colobus monkeys and young baboons. The meat may be shared with others, and chimpanzees are the only subhuman primate group known to share their kills.

Chimpanzees are gregarious and often re-

Figure 9–1 Wild chimpanzees in Africa's Gombe Stream Game Reserve may charge and bristle with excitement; yet at times they can be as gentle and affectionate as this one is with Jane van Lawick-Goodall. (Baron Hugo van Lawick; © National Geographic Society.)

late to one another through exaggerated displays such as dancing, hugging, and shrieking. This behavior occurs especially when they find a source of food or when two bands meet. Greeting ceremonies, accompanied by much noise and movement occur frequently when two unfamiliar groups meet.

In all behavioral studies, such field observations must be analyzed and evaluated. Interpretation of recorded data and results is also important.

ANALYSIS AND INTERPRETATION

Since most behavior is complex, especially in the higher animals, researchers must be exceptionally careful in the analysis and interpretation of their experiments. A good illustration of this was supplied by experiments

conducted at the Western Electric Company's Hawthorne Works in Chicago during the 1920s and 1930s. Better lighting and frequent rest periods improved the morale and increased the production of one group of employees. In an attempt to show that productivity and morale increased because of these changes, the working conditions were returned to their previous levels. But morale and production remained high. Apparently, because of the experiments, the employees began to feel that the company cared for them and that they were considered special; therefore they produced more and were more secure in their work. The term *Hawthorne effect* is now used to describe positive results obtained merely because an experiment was conducted.

SIMPLE TYPES OF BEHAVIOR

All organisms have some behavioral responses to stimuli which appear to be automatic. An organism's orientation to its environment often fits this description. Almost all protists and lower animals respond automatically to environmental stimuli such as light, chemicals, gravity, and temperature. *Euglena*, a photosynthetic, flagellated protist, moves toward moderate light; *Paramecium*, a ciliated protist, avoids a strong acid; and *Amoeba*, moving with its pseudopods, follows the chemical stimulus of food (Figure 9–2). When a *Paramecium* bumps into an object, it backs away (by reversing the beat of its cilia), turns about 30 degrees, and moves forward again. If it again encounters an object, the *Paramecium* will again reverse direction, turn another 30 degrees, and go forward again. This activity will continue until the object is cleared and the *Paramecium* can swim by freely (Figure 9–3).

TROPISMS

A type of movement, classified as *tropism*, occurs in vascular plants, and instances of this behavior were discussed in Chapter 8. We saw, for example, that when grass seedlings are exposed to light from one side, the stems bend

275

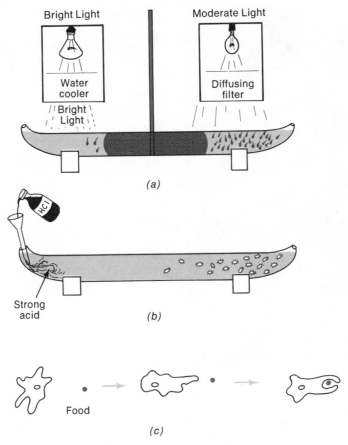

Figure 9-2 Simple orientation responses by some protists to environmental stimuli. (*a*) *Euglena* moving toward moderate light. (*b*) *Paramecium* avoiding strong acid. (*c*) *Amoeba* moving toward food.

toward the light. (Recall the explanation given for this movement—an unequal distribution of plant hormones in the stem.) This example is a relatively simple type of behavior—a single, directed response to a stimulus.

Another interesting example of a tropism is shown by the "sensitive plant," *Mimosa* (Figure 9-4). The leaves of this plant are composed of many pairs of leaflets. When the tip of a leaf is touched, the leaflets fold upward, and the entire leaf droops. These changes are caused by the loss of water from the large cells at the base of the leaflets and leaves; the water pressure in these cells holds them in their normal positions.

TAXES

A behavioral activity, a *taxis*, is an oriented movement of an entire organism. One type of taxis occurs when an animal orients itself to obtain equal intensity of a stimulus on both of its sides. After a period in darkness the drone-fly (*Eristalis*) reacts positively to light by flying or walking directly to a light source. When the light source is turned on, the fly turns until each eye receives an equal amount of light stimulation. Grayling butterflies escape from predators by flying toward the sun. Again, orientation is achieved by moving in a direction in which the eyes are stimulated equally. This taxic behavior has adaptive value since it provides an escape from enemies which are blinded by the sun.

REFLEXES

Reflexes were introduced in Chapter 8 with the discussion of the anatomical relationships of a reflex arc. In this chapter, we are con-

276

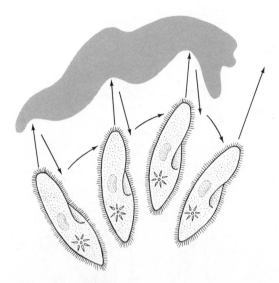

Figure 9–3 Trial-and-error behavior of a *Paramecium*. As a *Paramecium* bumps into an object, it backs off, turns about 30°, and moves forward again. This behavior is continued until the obstacle has been cleared.

cerned with the function of reflexes and what they do for an organism. The adaptive value of a reflex is shown by the stinging apparatus of a bee. The stinger is activated upon the stimulation of touch, and the reflex will operate even if the abdomen is severed from the rest of the body. Our eyes blink in response to the stimulus of an object thrust before them. In each of these examples the reflex produces a prompt response to an emergency.

One reflex often follows another (chain reflexes) in organized behavior. These chain reflexes can be observed in a feeding frog whose tongue extends to catch an insect. The presence of an insect on the tongue stimulates the mouth to close and next provides a stimulus for swallowing reflexes. Reflexes may also occur in coordinated groups. The stimulus of stepping on a tack brings about the response of lifting the foot. Other reflexes, perhaps not so apparent to the person who steps on the tack, occur in other parts of the body; for example, the opposite leg will stiffen in an effort to maintain balance (Figure 9–5). Since the message is transmitted to the brain, other behavior may accompany the initial reflex action. A cry of pain might be uttered, or the injured foot might be lifted for inspection and removal of the tack. Broadly speaking, all behavior might be explained as a series of complicated interactions among reflexes where one stimulus may set off more than one response. However, we would not advance very far in our understanding of more complex behavior if we confined our studies strictly to reflex patterns. We shall see in our study of more

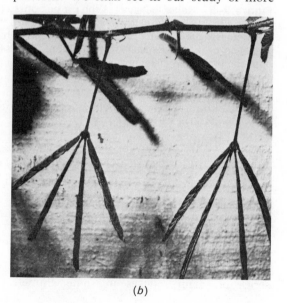

| (a) | (b) |

Figure 9–4 The response to touch by the sensitive plant *Mimosa*. (a) Leaflets in normal position. (b) Leaflets in response to touch. (Edward S. Ross; California Academy of Sciences.)

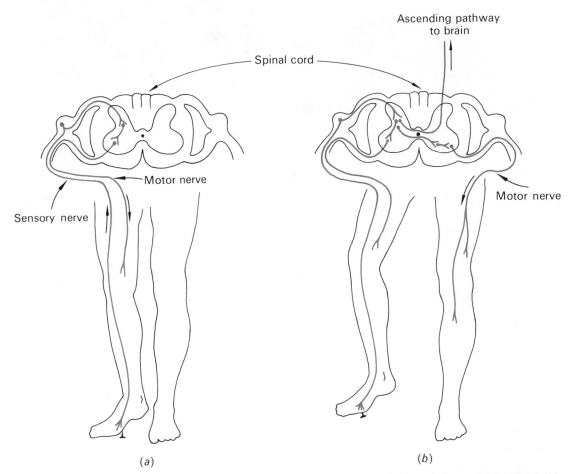

Spinal cord

Ascending pathway
to brain

Motor nerve

Sensory nerve

Motor nerve

(a)

(b)

Figure 9–5 Reflex behavior. When a person steps on a tack (a), the foot is immediately lifted (b). (a) The simple reflex from the receptors in the foot, through the spinal cord, and to the upper leg muscles. (b) Impulses are shown going to the brain through an ascending pathway in the spinal cord, where the sensation of pain is registered. In addition, impulses are sent across the spinal cord to muscles of the opposite leg which maintains balance.

complex behavior that reflexes are often involved, although other principles of organization must also be considered.

COMPLEX SPECIES BEHAVIOR

Some animal behavior, more complicated than taxes and tropisms, is apparently inherited, since the same patterns or responses are usually always followed from one generation to the next. Certain behavior appears to occur as a series of chain reflexes in some animals,

whereas in others these events may be modified by some learning. This stereotyped behavior is often called *instinct* (or *innate* behavior), although instinct is now considered to be an oversimplification. Behavior is what is observed, and as such, it is not possible to fully separate inherited and environmental factors.

The importance of genetic contribution to behavior has been stressed by many European naturalists. Perhaps foremost in these natural behavioral studies are Konrad Lorenz and N. Tinbergen, recipients of the Nobel Prize in Physiology or Medicine in 1973. Today *ethology* is the term commonly applied to the study of species-characteristic behavior, regardless of the degree to which the behavior is learned or innate. Ethologists frequently stress the role of animal behavior in adaptation.

It must be remembered as we study behavior that it is very difficult, and sometimes impossible, to distinguish between what is learned and what occurs as a result of heredity in a specific behavior pattern. Moreover, there is considerable discussion among ethologists over the concept of instinct and the exact neurophysiological basis of such behavior. Behavior in a complex animal is the result of organized output in a given environment; this output depends on heredity (evolutionary relationships) and past experiences (learning). Some behavior seems to involve a larger component of inherited pattern, whereas other behavior results more from learning. Most animal behavior is due to a mixture of both learned and innate responses. We will first consider examples of behavior which have been attributed mainly to instinct and attempt to understand some of the characteristics and the conditions under which the behavior occurs.

SEQUENTIAL BEHAVIOR PATTERNS

The reproductive behavior pattern exhibited by solitary wasps is a good example of an innate sequence of activities involving no apparent previous learning or training. Such behavior occurs in an almost fixed-action pattern in each generation. It begins when a female wasp digs a hole for a nest, seeks out her prey, which is usually a caterpillar, and paralyzes it with a sting. The caterpillar is next dragged to the nest and pushed in; several more caterpillars may be added in a similar manner. The female then lays an egg on the caterpillars and seals the nest (Figure 9–6). When the egg hatches, it has a source of food; the larva matures, spins a cocoon, and remains in the sealed cell until emerging as an adult. An adult female will duplicate the reproductive behavior, even though she never before observed the process. Each response in the series acts as a stimulus

to produce the next response. If the process is interfered with experimentally by removing the caterpillars before egg laying, the wasp will lay an egg anyway and seal the nest. Each step follows the previous step in an automatic manner, and some kinds of interference do not alter the behavioral sequence. In nature the caterpillars are not normally removed; the fixed behavior pattern has adaptive value for the wasp since this precision helps to insure continuation of the species.

The three-spined stickleback, a fish approximately three inches long, is common in both Europe and North America in a variety of habitats including salt water, freshwater streams and ponds, and brackish water. In the spring sticklebacks migrate into shallow fresh water where they perform a very precise mating behavior. A male stickleback first establishes a territory and defends it from other males. Next, he builds a nest by scooping out a pit from the sandy bottom, and then he brings in weeds to form a mound which is held together by sticky kidney secretions. A hole is made through the mound, and the nest is complete. During this time the male changes color from a drab gray or brown to a bright red underside and a bluish back. He is now ready to court any female which enters his territory bulging with eggs. He is equally ready to aggressively ward off any males moving into his established domain. Any red object near his territory will be attacked even though it may not otherwise resemble another male stickleback (Figure 9–7). The important stimulus is apparently the red color and not the shape. If a shiny female, swollen with 50 to 100 eggs, enters a male's territory, he immediately responds with a zigzag movement toward her, he continues this motion until she responds by raising the head end of her body. The male now swims to the nest and makes several pokes toward the nest with his head; the female follows and enters. Inside the tiny nest, with her head and tail protruding, the female is jabbed several times near the base of the tail by the snout of the male, and she

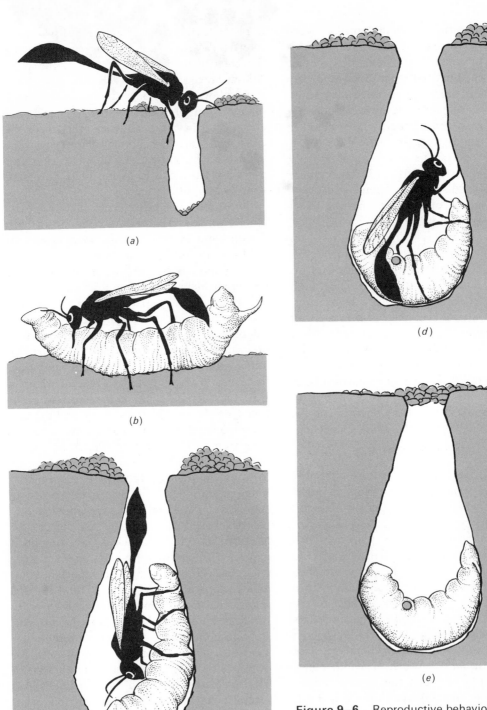

(a)

(b)

(c)

(d)

(e)

Figure 9–6 Reproductive behavior of a solitary, or digger, wasp. (*a*) Digs a nest. (*b*) Captures and stings a caterpillar. (*c*) Drags the prey into the nest. (*d*) Lays an egg on the caterpillar and crawls out of the nest. (*e*) The nest is finally sealed.

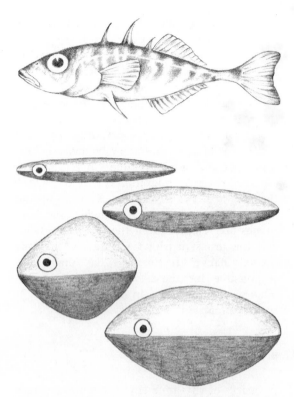

how a series of stimulus-response activities can result in a complex behavior pattern which has adaptive value for the species. The response to one stimulus becomes the stimulus for the next response in the sequence, similar to the events in a chain of reflexes. In complicated behavioral activity each stimulus may not "take," and thus a sequence may not go through to completion. Other factors in the environment may influence the reactions of the fish. The

Figure 9–7 Models of stickleback fish used in experiments with male sticklebacks. The four models with red bellies were attacked much more frequently by male sticklebacks than was the more realistic model, which lacked the red underside. (Redrawn from N. Tinbergen, *The Study of Instinct,* 1951. By permission of The Clarendon Press, Oxford.)

responds by laying eggs. After the eggs are laid, the female slithers out of the nest, and the male quickly moves in to fertilize the eggs (Figure 9–8). One male may court several females and repeat this ritual, but soon after the matings the male must care for the eggs. With his pectoral fins the male fans the water near the nest opening to enhance the supply of oxygen to the developing eggs. This fanning activity gradually increases until the eggs hatch. The details of this mating cycle were described by many biologists, but perhaps the most eloquent report is by N. Tinbergen in his book, *The Study of Instinct.*

Stickleback reproductive behavior shows

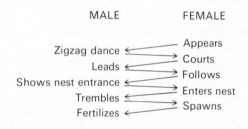

MALE		FEMALE
Zigzag dance	⇄	Appears
Leads	⇄	Courts
Shows nest entrance	⇄	Follows
Trembles	⇄	Enters nest
Fertilizes	⇄	Spawns

Figure 9–8 The usual sequence of events in the mating behavior of the three-spined stickleback. Activity starts as a female enters a male's nesting territory. After this initial stimulus, the reaction sequence proceeds as indicated. (Redrawn from N. Tinbergen, *The Study of Instinct,* 1951. By permission of The Clarendon Press, Oxford.)

281

female may not respond to the initial courtship activity; a male intruder may interrupt; or one member of the mating pair may not completely follow through with one of the specific responses. The description of this behavior then can be expressed in terms of probability—that is, the sequence of events described here is the most probable one after the behavior is initiated.

RELEASERS

Let us take a closer look at some of the stimuli that contribute to the stickleback mating behavior. It was learned that the male stickleback will attack almost any object entering its territory if the object has a red underside. The critical stimulus which causes the response is therefore the red color of the object and not its shape. The characteristic (red color) which produces the behavior is called a *releaser*, a term originated by Konrad Lorenz, the noted Austrian student of behavior. "Releaser" is used more generally to describe a stereotyped object, structure, behavior, or sound which can initiate a fixed-action pattern. For example, a hen will react more strongly to a call from its chick than it will to the chick's actions. In other words, if a chick is in trouble, the releaser which triggers a response from the mother is a sound and not a visible activity. The releaser for egg laying by the female stickleback is the poking of its posterior end by the snout of the male. Egg laying at this stage of the cycle can be released by poking the female's posterior end with a glass rod. Releasers are important in animal behavior since every animal is confronted with many stimuli, and it is definitely of survival value to react to a relevant stimulus with a satisfactory response. The steps of reproductive behavior vary among the various species of sticklebacks, and two members of different species break the sequence when one of them produces an ineffective releaser. Thus, the releaser behavior not only helps to synchronize mating but also protects against mismatches.

One might logically ask how a behavioral sequence begins. What is the primary initiator of the sequence of steps that follow? Much behavior is triggered internally by varying amounts of hormones. In the sticklebacks, for example, the thyroid gland releases an increased amount of hormone in the spring of the year, and the fish move from the salt water into fresh water to begin breeding. In some birds, this kind of migratory behavior is also quite specific. For example, in the white-crowned sparrow, migration is triggered when the length of the day increases in the spring of the year. At this time gonadotropic hormones are released from the pituitary gland, and the testes develop. Apparently environmental changes (in this case, day length) are responsible for these behavioral responses. This will be discussed in more detail later in this chapter.

RHYTHMIC ACTIVITY AND BIOLOGICAL CLOCKS

A variety of rhythmic environmental changes occurs as a result of the relationships between the earth and other bodies in our solar system and because of the earth's tilted rotational axis with respect to the sun. We therefore recognize regular day–night cycles and an orderly progression through the seasons of a year—the yearly cycle. In addition, the moon revolves about the earth producing cyclic effects, often termed *lunar cycles*. As a result, rhythmic changes are observed in light, temperature, and the tides of the ocean. These physical cycles have definite and specific effects upon life's reproduction and other activities. The photoperiodic response of plants in reproduction was discussed in Chapter 8, and examples of rhythmic reproductive activity in animals will be presented in Chapter 10.

Circadian Rhythms

Some biological activity or behavior can take place in response to internal timing mechanisms, often referred to as *biological clocks*, which continue to operate under constant (noncyclical) environmental conditions (Fig-

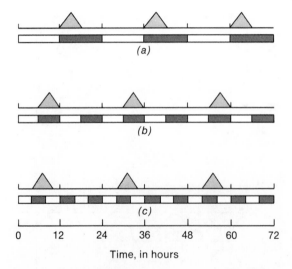

Time, in hours

Figure 9–9 Effects of different photoperiods on activity rhythm of an insect. (*a*) Photoperiod is 12 hrs light, 12 hrs darkness. Activity rhythm (shaded triangle) is on 24-hr cycle, with peak of activity shortly after dark. (*b*) Photoperiod is 6 hrs light, 6 hrs darkness. Thus two photoperiods every 24 hrs, but insect shows only one activity period during each 24-hr period. (*c*) Photoperiod is 4 hrs light, 4 hrs darkness. Activity rhythm still on 24-hr cycle. (From *Animal Photoperiodism* by S. D. Beck. Copyright © 1963 by Holt, Rinehart and Winston, Inc. Redrawn by permission of the publishers, Holt, Rinehart and Winston, Inc.)

ure 9-9). Those behavioral patterns occurring approximately every 24 hours are termed *circadian rhythms* (*circa dies* is Latin for "about a day"). It is known for example that the effect on rats of a specific dosage of amphetamines depends on the time of day the drugs are administered. If the amphetamine is given early in their daily cycle, only 6 percent of the rats die, but the same dosage will kill 77 percent when given during their nighttime period of greatest activity. Fiddler crabs which scurry around the shore with changes in the tide are darker in color during the daytime, but as night falls they become lighter. These animals continue to undergo this daily color variation even when kept in a laboratory under constant light. Circadian rhythms can also be observed in the movement of bean-seedling leaves which are elevated during the day and lowered at

night. These "sleep movements" are characteristic of many plants which continue their normal day–night leaf movements even under constant light and temperature.

A person who ordinarily awakens at 7:00 A.M. each day on the West Coast flies to the East Coast and finds that he can quite easily sleep until 10:00 A.M. After several days on the East Coast his sleeping behavior will have adjusted to the change in time zones, even though his internal clocks for other functions, such as the secretion of certain hormones, may not reset so easily. Since the normal sleeping behavior persists for several days in a new environment, it appears that the individual is not merely responding to the environment but also has some internal timing. Similarly, sheep that are normally fall breeders in the northern hemisphere will continue to breed at the same time of the year when transported to the southern hemisphere where it is spring. Biological clocks thus show a certain amount of stability and support the theory that internal timing mechanisms are well established within organisms. But even though biological clocks are largely internally controlled, they can be reset. The breeding behavior of the sheep just mentioned will switch over and conform to the seasonal conditions of the southern hemisphere after the second season. If fiddler crabs are moved from their normal beach to one where the tides occur at different times, their activity cycles change after a short period of time to match the new tidal cycles. The fact that internal clocks can be reset after some period of time also indicates the adaptability of these mechanisms in assisting organisms to adjust to new environments. Apparently, the mechanisms which determine the timing of biological clocks are complex internal sequences of metabolic events that can closely parallel and be affected by cyclic environmental events. Circadian activity has been demonstrated in humans, and information has come from studies on shift workers, travelers, and subjects in isolation experiments where conditions were held constant. When humans are experimentally kept in a dark environment, they gradually lose track of time. However, certain body functions, such as pulse and temperature, may persist on an approximate 24-hour cycle. Metabolic cycles, secretions of hormones, reactions to medications, the sharpness of the senses, and even susceptibility to infection seem to occur in cyclical patterns.

Circannual Rhythms

Scientists have also investigated biological clocks that are based on yearly cycles—the *circannual rhythms.* Hibernation behavior is one example which suggests that annual cycles are part of nature. A definite circannual cycle in a species of ground squirrel has been reported by Pengelley and Asmundson of the University of California at Riverside. Typically, these ground squirrels lose weight during hibernation. A series of experiments was conducted in which one group of squirrels was kept at room temperature and another group at near freezing temperatures. Both groups showed parallel hibernation times and weight loss (Figure 9-10). The squirrels apparently possess an internal control over hibernation which is principally independent of temperature.

Another example of a yearly cycle is the urinary excretion in human males of the 17-ketosteroid hormones, many of which are secreted by the adrenal cortex. An annual rhythm is indicated with high secretory peaks in September and November followed by a low in May. The best examples of yearly behavior, however, are bird migrations.

MIGRATION

The annual migrations of many species of birds have intrigued man for centuries. Each year birds fill the air over North and South America in four major flyways: the Atlantic, Mississippi, Central, and Pacific.

The Arctic tern migrates each year from the north pole region to Antarctica and back again (nearly 25,000 miles). The golden plover travels the Atlantic flyway from the Arctic to

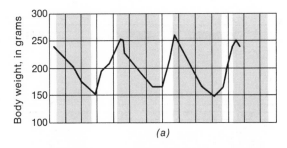

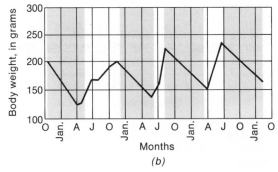

Figure 9–10 Records over four years provide evidence that the circannual rhythm of ground-squirrel hibernation is not influenced by the normal range of temperature. The shaded bands indicate hibernation. (*a*) The room temperature is 12°C (53.6°F). (*b*) The room temperature is just above the freezing point. (Redrawn from "Annual Biological Clocks" by Eric T. Pengelley and Sally J. Asmundson. Copyright © 1971 by Scientific American, Inc. All rights reserved.)

Argentina and back each year (Figure 9-11). One group of northern cliff swallows has gained world-wide attention by consistently returning to the historic mission in San Juan Capistrano, California about March 20th of every year. These swallows build vase-shaped mud nests at the mission, mate, and rear their young. About the middle of September, they leave their nesting territories and wing southward to overwinter in Brazil.

But not all bird migrations are so extensive. Some, such as the jays, juncos, and grosbeaks, simply move to higher altitudes in the summer. The western evening grosbeaks, for example, breed in mountains from Canada to Arizona but winter in adjacent lowlands.

Observation and experimental studies have shown that these seasonal movements are controlled by several stimuli. The fact that all

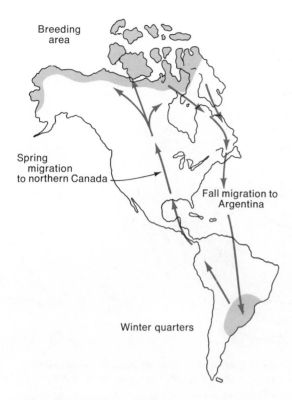

Figure 9–11 The migratory route of the eastern golden plover.

birds do not migrate or that all birds do not go in the same direction or at the same time indicates several variables. In some species migration can be correlated with changes in temperature, food supply, or rainfall, but these correlations do not always hold true even among closely related species. Ornithologists have thus turned to physiological explanations. The most plausible theory offered today involves photoperiodism, a response made to varying periods of light and dark. The perception of relative day-length periods enables some birds to set their internal clocks for breeding and migration. Thus daily photoperiodism can be involved in the control of circannual or yearly cycles.

The white-crowned sparrows which breed and overwinter in temperate latitudes begin gonad development in March under the stimulation of hormones from the pituitary gland. This development coincides with the bird's annual northward migration toward Alaska (Figure 9-12). By the end of May the sparrows are ready for breeding and rearing their young. About the middle of July the gonads begin to regress, the old feathers are molted, and a large amount of body fat is stored. The southward migration begins in mid-September and the winter territory in Mexico or the southeastern United States is reached by November.

Donald Farner of the University of Washington has shown that the development of the gonads, prenuptial molting, and prenorthward migratory fattening are dependent on the long day lengths of spring. Photoreceptors (the eyes or perhaps direct brain stimulation) induce the hypothalamus to release neurohormones which stimulate the pituitary gland to secrete gonadotropins. The primary and secondary sex characteristics are thus stimulated to develop (Figure 9-13). The regression of the gonads in mid-July does not appear to be controlled by day length. Farner believes that the birds become insensitive to long day length (photorefractive) during this time. This photorefractive state is finally broken by the short day lengths of late fall and the preparation for the southward journey is completed.

The migratory activities of birds that winter near the equator are not as easily explained. How do these birds know when to return north? It is suggested that these birds can physiologically accumulate the effects of increments of light. Through this ability to "add up" the light periods of the rather constant day lengths, the northward migration is finally triggered.

ORIENTATION

Perhaps even more astonishing than the timing of migrations is the ability of many organisms to orient themselves in time and space. Green sea turtles return to their native beaches to lay their eggs after years at sea (Figure 9-14); gray whales annually swim from the Arctic to Scammon's Lagoon in Baja, California; salmon return from the sea to spawn on the

285

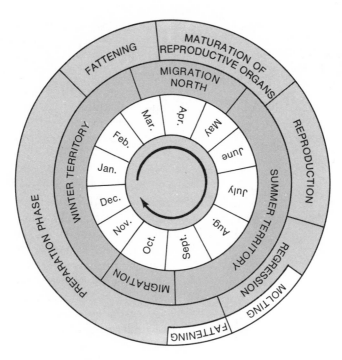

Figure 9-12 Generalized breeding and migratory cycle of birds of the temperate zone. (From *Animal Photoperiodism* by S. D. Beck. Copyright © 1963 by Holt, Rinehart and Winston, Inc. Redrawn by permission of the publishers, Holt, Rinehart and Winston, Inc.)

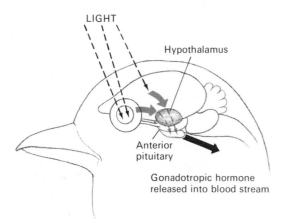

Figure 9-13 Mechanism proposed for photoperiodic stimulation of testes in birds. Photoreceptors in the eyes and brain are stimulated by light. Nerve impulses (colored arrows) activate neurosecretory cells in the hypothalamus which secrete neurohormones into a portal blood system linking the hypothalamus and pituitary gland (broken arrows). The anterior pituitary in turn secretes gonadotropic hormones into the blood stream (black arrow).

gravel-bedded creeks of their birth; and many birds accurately navigate over thousands of miles of earth and sea (Figure 9-15).

Each migrating species must not only have an internal clock which stimulates the migration but must also somehow sense the direction and distance to be traveled. Green turtles that feed for years at sea have a tiny target in the Galápagos Islands nearly 650 miles off the coast of Ecuador. Even a small miscalculation could mean a late arrival at the hatching site with nonviable eggs.

Bird Orientation

The problems of orientation and navigation in birds have been under intense study for the past few years. Some of the factors subjected to experimentation include: (1) visual cues, (2) infra-red sensitivity, (3) rotational force of the turning earth, (4) sun compass, (5) star compass, and (6) magnetic cues.

There is no doubt that diurnal birds which

Figure 9–14 Female green sea turtle returning to land, Wilson Island, Great Barrier Reef. (Courtesy of Keith Gillett, Australia.)

fly over land make use of visual landmarks, but it is impossible to explain navigation on this basis for birds that fly over vast areas of ocean or for young birds that fly their first course alone. Sensitivity to increased infrared radiation at the equator and orientation to the forces produced by the earth's rotation have been difficult to study and are not well accepted.

Orientation through a sense of sun position has been demonstrated. Experiments performed with several species of birds including starlings have demonstrated that some species have an ability to determine a northward direction from the position of the sun. The birds manage to orient themselves at any time of the day, a procedure which requires an internal calculation of the "time-sun position." In order to test the ability of homing pigeons to interpret direction by the apparent movement of the sun, a comparison of homing can be made between regular "sun time" acclimated birds and birds whose internal clocks have been "reset" six hours under artificial illumination. The reset birds will fly away about 90 degrees to the right of the homeward direction—a phenomenon which shows a definite correlation between the internal clock mechanism, the position of the sun, and the sense of direction.

If certain birds then can sense direction according to a sun compass, what about night-

Figure 9–15 Migrating Canada geese. (Gordon Smith; National Audubon Society.)

flying species? Some researchers believe that nocturnal flyers may set their courses on the setting sun, but recent studies by Stephen Emlen at Cornell University have shown that orientation may be based on the position of the stars. When indigo buntings were placed in a planetarium under a fall sky, they oriented in a southerly direction (the normal direction of fall migration). When the planetarium sky was rotated so that "south" was not really south, the buntings maintained their fix on the artificial stars. In most cases, birds lose their orientation when sun, moon, or stars are not available. Under such conditions, the birds are observed to fly restlessly in all directions in their cages. When the proper sky is once again available, however, the birds quickly reorient.

With the increased interest in continental drift and the changing of the earth's magnetic fields, experimentation with magnetic orientation has accelerated. It has been shown that magnets glued onto the backs of homing pigeons caused serious disorientation only when the birds were released under heavy overcast conditions. This suggests that the pigeons use the sun compass as a primary system but perhaps also have the ability to orient to the earth's magnetic fields.

Birds may possess several orientation mechanisms which are used on a preferential basis. This could help explain how ducks and geese navigate on overcast nights or how daylight flyers can leave the land and cross great expanses of ocean without serious disorientation. We must admit little knowledge of the mechanisms which tell the organism the direction in which to orient, the time to begin flight, or how far to travel.

Fish Orientation

The orientation and migration of salmon is a mystery which is gradually being solved. Many studies that involve the tagging, re-

288

lease, and recovery of Pacific salmon have been made under the direction of Lauren Donaldson at the University of Washington. We know that tagged male and female salmon go to sea for as long as four years and later return to their exact spawning area (Figure 9-16). There, the females will lay their eggs; the males will fertilize them; and both sexes die. In European and Atlantic species, the adults may survive and return to spawn several times. How do the salmon recognize their "own" river, tributary, and finally shallow creek bed? Experiments conducted in several laboratories have demonstrated that the returning salmon relies on an exceptionally sensitive sense of smell to detect its home waters. Salmon will choose to swim into streams containing as little as 1 part per billion of its home waters. When the nostrils which allow water to circulate into the olfactory sacs are plugged or when the olfactory lobes of the brain are destroyed, the fish cannot recognize its home water. Orientation is thus determined through acute chemo-perception. Little is known about the factors that send the

fish back to fresh water, but they may be linked with the pituitary hormones and reproductive maturity.

TERRITORIALITY

Populations of most wild animals show distinct behavioral patterns that relate directly to the "ownership" of particular areas. This *territoriality* has been noted among both vertebrate and invertebrate animals, and it is now well established that the claiming and defense of territory plays an important role in animal populations.

The territoriality exhibited by wolves, rabbits, mice, sea lions, and other animals demonstrates that some wild populations regulate their numbers in relationship to space and food. Territories are staked out by animals on both permanent and seasonal bases. Rabbits, for example, construct a permanent burrow-filled warren with established trails and warning signs surrounding the area. Many of the mechanisms utilized by rabbits to mark and protect their territory are known. Roman Mykytowycz, in working with the wild Australian rabbit, has found two glands that produce marking secretions—an anal gland and a chin gland. The anal gland coats fecal pellets with a secretion easily recognized by other rabbits. When a warren is established, the male rabbits excrete pellets in mounds and urinate around the circumference, thereby warning any intruder that the area is occupied. The secretions from the chin gland are utilized in marking twigs and grass for perhaps the same purpose (Figure 9-17).

Song birds establish a temporary territory early in the spring for breeding and nesting. The male flies from tree to tree around his area singing, repulsing males, and attempting to attract a mate. The bird that sings the loudest most often occupies the largest territory, and confrontations over territory seldom involve serious fighting or death. In general, an intruder respects the line drawn by the occupants. If the intruder is larger and stronger than the defender, the defender usually retreats and gives up part of his

Figure 9-16 Steelhead trout migrating upstream to spawn. (Jack Dermid.)

territory. It is thought that the defense of a territory by an individual, pair, or group of animals has the effect of limiting the population density of an area and conserving the availability of food and shelter. If an invader crosses into a territory that is too large for an individual or group to defend, he may settle. If, however, the population density is already high, the invader will often be repulsed and forced to try another area.

Social Hierarchy

In many animals territoriality and *social hierarchy* are closely related. In his study of rabbit territoriality, Mykytowycz also showed a direct correlation between the amount of marker-gland secretion and the position of the individual in the social structure of the warren. The development and secretion of these glands appear to be controlled by the sex hormones. A social structure or ranking can be found in nearly all animal groups. It is very evident among fish, birds, and domestic animals. Some bird species exhibit a rather complex behavior under caged conditions. If the cage is large enough, each bird will settle into a specific territory although eating and drinking facilities may be shared. The addition of more birds will eventually upset this balance and a rigorous *peck order* will result. Each bird will assume his place in the order between those he can peck and those that peck him. Usually the largest and most aggressive bird becomes dominant and is not pecked by any other bird. This social order is maintained in the group, especially in feeding and roosting preferences. Although this social ranking may be regarded as a dictatorship, the result is

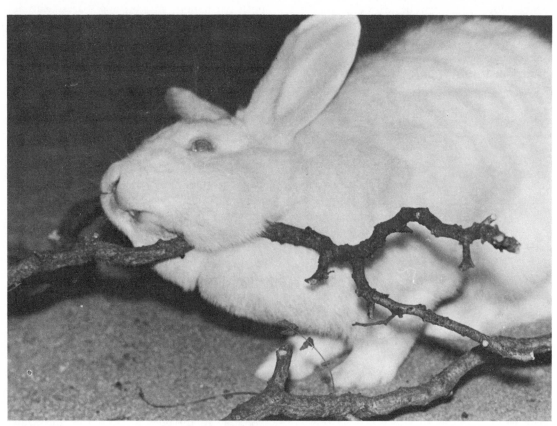

Figure 9–17 Wild rabbit rubbing chin-gland secretions on twig to mark its territory. (Courtesy of Roman Mykytowycz.)

290

generally a stable and efficient society. Perhaps the most well-known example of a peck order is seen in chickens. In a flock of young chickens, aggressive encounters occur between individuals with the winners becoming dominant over the losers. The bird which wins all of its fights becomes the dominant individual. Bird I defeats all the chickens in the flock, and Bird II defeats all other chickens except Bird I. In this manner the hierarchical position of each chicken is established.

COMMUNICATION

The ability to send, receive, and interpret meaningful signals has been observed in most animals. Communication among members of a species has adaptive value in attracting mates, determining territory, securing food, and mutual defense from enemies. It is often convenient to base interpretations of animal communication on human experience, but we must remember that this practice may introduce bias and inaccuracy. In studying animal communication several classes of signals have been formulated: (1) visual displays, (2) chemical signals, (3) audible sounds, (4) tactile systems, and (5) language. Animals may employ several of these signals or a combination to communicate specific messages. For example, a rhesus monkey may scream and pound the ground with his hands when he is threatening another.

Visual Displays

A male magnificent frigate bird makes effective use of its visual sexual display to attract a mate (Figure 9–18). Approximately

Figure 9–18 Male magnificent frigate bird displaying inflated throat pouch. (California Academy of Sciences.)

291

three to four weeks before mating season, a drab pink strip on the breast suddenly becomes bright scarlet. When a female magnificent frigate is spotted, the male pumps air into the scarlet area to form a huge inflated pouch. This inflation is possible because of a connection with the air sacs and the bird's lungs. The male magnificent frigate will court only females of his own species and ignore the closely related great frigate females.

Displays may also be used in territoriality and aggressive behavior. The red-mouthed lava gull of the Galápagos Islands squawks and gapes repeatedly showing its bright red mouth as another bird or a man approaches (Figure 9-19). The green heron shows a more subtle series of visual displays when threatening—first it raises its crown feathers; next the tail feathers are twitched up and down; and finally the beak is opened and the back feathers are ruffed. This series of display activities shows increased intensity in the threat message as an intruder nears.

The blue-footed boobies of the Galápagos Islands make full use of their bright blue feet in both territoriality and courtship. The male blue-foot gains the attention of his intended mate by performing an exaggerated, high-stepping dance (Figure 9-20). The same behavior is displayed as he moves about the boundaries of his territory.

Chemical Messengers—Pheromones

A familiar example of chemical communication occurs when ants follow an "ant trail" to and from their den to obtain food (Figure 9-21). Ants release a chemical onto the ground which other ants of the species recognize and follow. This type of chemical which is released into the environment to cause a certain behavior is called a *pheromone*. The marking ant drags its sting along the ground releasing small quantities of the pheromone which is produced in the hindgut or certain associated glands near the sting. The pheromone dissipates quite rapidly however, and the trails must be continually renewed by ants returning with food. When the food supply is exhausted, the returning ants do not excrete the marker, and the trail is quickly obliterated. Extracts from whole ants or hindguts have been used to make artificial trails for study; ants will follow one of these trails in a circular pattern back to the nest. F. E. Regnier of Purdue University and E. O. Wilson of Harvard University have studied the habits of slave-maker ants, *Formica subintegra*. These ants seek out and attack the nests of other ant species, subdue or kill the defenders, and carry away worker pupae. These ants also use hindgut secretions to mark the trail to the raid. A pheromone from a gland called Dufour's gland has a unique purpose: when the slave makers attack, the chemical is sprayed onto the defending ants causing them to

Figure 9–19 Galápagos lava gull. When an intruder approaches, the gull squawks and shows its red mouth. (David Cavagnaro; California Academy of Sciences.)

Figure 9–20 Male blue-footed booby "parading" in front of a prospective mate.

scatter and leave the nest area. Apparently, the pheromone from the Dufour gland induces an alarm reaction in the other species which produces "fright" and disorganization.

Bert Hölldobler of the University of Frankfurt has worked on a case of interspecific communication between ants and a European beetle known as the rove beetle, a parasite found in the nest of the wood ant *Formica polyctena*. The host ants feed and groom beetle larvae as well or better than their own larvae and accept the adult beetles as equals. How does this happen? How can the defenseless larvae induce the host ants into this behavior even when there are acute food shortages? The answer lies in the ability of the beetle larvae and adults to mimic certain ant communication signals, both pheromonal and mechanical. The larvae are carried into the ants' nest in response to a chemical secreted

from the external surface of the larvae; nourishment is then provided when a larva rears its head and touches the host ant's mouth parts with its own. According to Hölldobler, the beetles perform this "begging" behavior so well and so often that they get more food than the ant larvae (Figure 9–22).

The potent chemical bombykol liberated by female *bombyx* moths attracts male moths from several miles downwind. This is another example of these potent chemical messengers used in activities such as feeding, mating, and complex social behavior.

Audible Sounds

Many kinds of sounds are produced by animals in a variety of ways, and this type of communication is very effective among certain species. Many examples could be selected, but only birds and insects will be mentioned here.

293

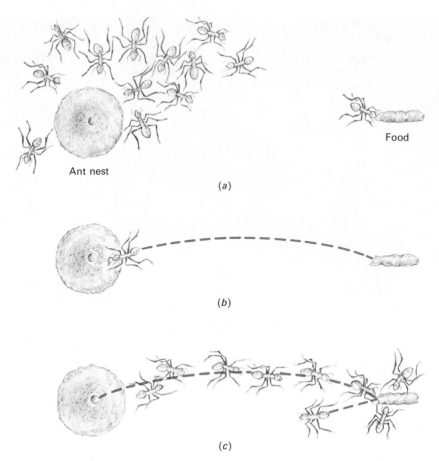

Figure 9–21 Foraging behavior in ants. (*a*) An ant finds a source of food. (*b*) The ant brings a piece back to the nest, laying a pheromone trail between the food and the nest. (*c*) Other ants recognize the trail and make their way to the food. As the food supply dwindles, fewer ants make the return trip and less pheromone is laid down; consequently, the trail disappears.

The familiar songs of birds are useful in the establishment and defense of territories. A bird sings in certain parts of its territory in order to announce ownership to other males of the species. Alarm calls are also used when an intruder comes too near its nest.

Crickets and grasshoppers utilize sounds for species recognition or attracting mates. The cricket sound is produced when the male rubs parts of its wing covers together. The chirping made by one species of cricket is distinct in pitch and frequency from that made by other cricket species.

Tactile Systems

Touch or tactile communication is possible among most animals. The sender of the signals must be in contact with the receiver, and a great variety of messages may be transmitted by varying the frequency, pressure, and time of this contact. Tactile communication is frequently observed in courtship behavior and mating. In bees, touch is utilized for conveying information in the dark hive; the location of food sources is communicated by feeling the pattern of a scout bee's dance, while the spreading of alarm reactions is another type of information that can be conveyed.

Bees and Communication

One instance of communication among animals which has been studied extensively is that of the honeybee. In the late 1940s, the Austrian biologist, Karl von Frisch (Figure 9–23) reported the results of his thorough observations of bees. Von Frisch demonstrated that a

294

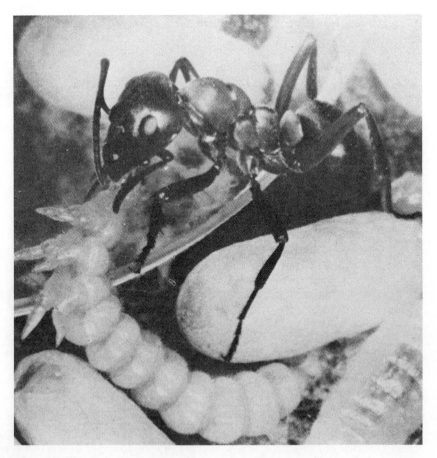

Figure 9–22 A beetle larva is fed a droplet of liquid food by an ant in the brood chamber of an ant nest. (From "Communication between Ants and Their Guests" by Bert Hölldobler. Copyright © 1971 by Scientific American, Inc. All rights reserved. Reproduced by permission of Bert Hölldobler.)

bee returning to its hive was capable of communicating the quality, direction, and distance of a food supply. Bees left the hive after receiving the message and flew directly to the food. Through careful observations, von Frisch learned that the messenger bee performed specific dances on the vertical face of the honeycomb (Figure 9–24). One dance consisted of tracing a circular path and then crossing a diameter in only one direction to form two semicircular paths. As the bee crosses the diameter in a straight line, it waggles its abdomen (represented by the wavy line in Figure 9–24). If the food source is on a line

Figure 9–23 Karl von Frisch, recipient of the Nobel Prize in Physiology or Medicine in 1973 for his studies in the language of the bees. (Courtesy of Ernst Bohm.)

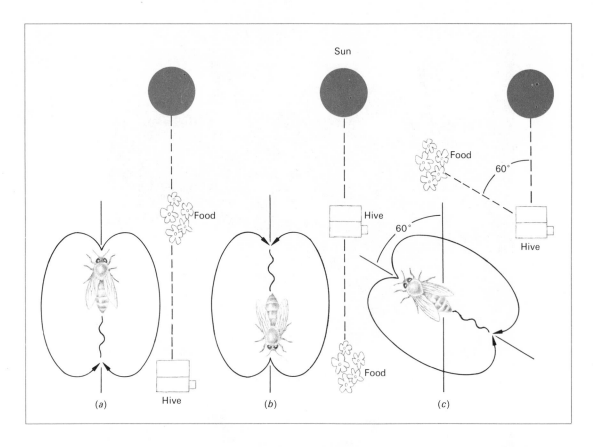

Figure 9-24 Three examples of bee-dance communication. (*a*) The source of food is in a straight path between the hive and the sun. (*b*) The food is directly away from the sun. (*c*) The food is toward the sun, but 60° to the left. (Redrawn from Fig. 355, p. 346, in *Biology* by Karl von Frisch, Harper & Row, 1964.)

directly between the hive and the position of the sun, the straight crossruns are made straight up (↑). If the food is on a line directly away from the sun, the crossruns are straight down (↓). In order to communicate the location of food that is not on a direct line between the hive and the sun, the dancer angles its crossruns to correspond to the direction and angle from the hive (Figure 9–24*c*). For instance, a crossrun angle of 60 degrees to the left of the upward vertical axis means that the food was on a path 60 degrees to the left of the sun-hive line (going toward the sun).

The "bee dance" has since been studied extensively with the aid of modern instrumentation. Harold Esch of the University of Notre Dame discovered that bees also emit sounds during their dance. Furthermore, he learned that "voiceless" bees could not stimu-

late others to leave the hive even though the dance was done repeatedly. Although the exact role of the bee sounds is not yet clear, it is possible that they are essential for interpretation by the bees inside the completely dark hive. In other experiments, Esch proved that the abdominal waggling time is the cue to the distance to the food; the longer the waggling time, the farther away the food. Von Frisch thought that this distance was conveyed by the number of crossruns per minute.

The bee dance borders on the establishment of a *language*. Many components of a language may be inferred from a bee dance. For example, the returning bee is conveying the direction and distance to a food source that none of the bees can see. Furthermore, the dancing bee is using symbolism to denote these characteristics (the angle and waggling time of the straight line). The bee dances, however, appear to be stereotyped and genetically fixed in the species because they apparently cannot create new variations of the dance to convey other meanings.

Learning a Language

We know that language is an important component of almost all human behavior, and we know a great deal about how language is learned. But we don't know as much about the learning of language in lower primates. Can a chimpanzee learn to speak or communicate in a language? Several serious attempts have been made to teach chimpanzees to speak, but they have been able to speak only a few simple words. In a recent experimental program, however, Ann and David Premack at the University of California had remarkable success with a three-year-old chimpanzee named Sarah (Figure 9–25). Sarah not only learned 130 words in the form of colored plastic symbols, but she also learned how to place these words into proper grammar sequences. She also learned to construct questions and to master the difficult "if-then" conditional concept. The Premacks feel that Sarah's language ability approximates that of a two-year-old human child. One must keep in mind, however, that Sarah would have difficulty developing new words on her own or verbalizing. The ability to learn word ideas and the ability to convert these ideas to sounds are apparently separated.

Figure 9–25 Language learning in a chimpanzee. The symbols in the background represent the message given to Sarah the chimpanzee. Reading from the top, the symbols stand for *Sarah, insert, apple, pail, banana,* and *dish*. In order to make the correct interpretation—that she should put the apple in the pail and the banana in the dish—Sarah had to understand sentence structure and not just word order. (From "Teaching Language to an Ape" by Ann James Premack and David Premack. Copyright © 1972 by Scientific American, Inc. All rights reserved.)

BEHAVIOR DEVELOPMENT AND LEARNING

There are many questions as to how behavior develops in an individual, and one question concerns the role of learning. It is difficult to see how learning could be involved in some characteristic behaviors such as the exact construction of spider webs, but other examples clearly show a component of learning. For example, studies in the feeding behavior of young sea gulls suggest that learning is necessary before this trait can fully develop. In the laughing gull, the hungry young chick pecks at the parent's bill, grasps it, and strokes downward (begging peck). This repeated behavior prompts the parent to regurgitate food which the chick pecks at and eats (feeding peck) (Figure 9–26). In order to study how this behavior—which involves the interaction of inherited and learned components—develops, J. P. Hailman of the University of Wisconsin studied newly hatched chicks until they were one-week old, the time when the feeding behavior is well established. The newborn chick is quite inaccurate with its initial begging pecks, but this accuracy improves greatly during the first week. Moreover, a chick often does not see the food when it is dropped by the parent; when the parent picks up the food and the chick strikes it during a begging peck, the chick learns to recognize food. The reward of food also helps the chick to recognize its parent; this recognition of the parent is apparently necessary for accuracy in the begging

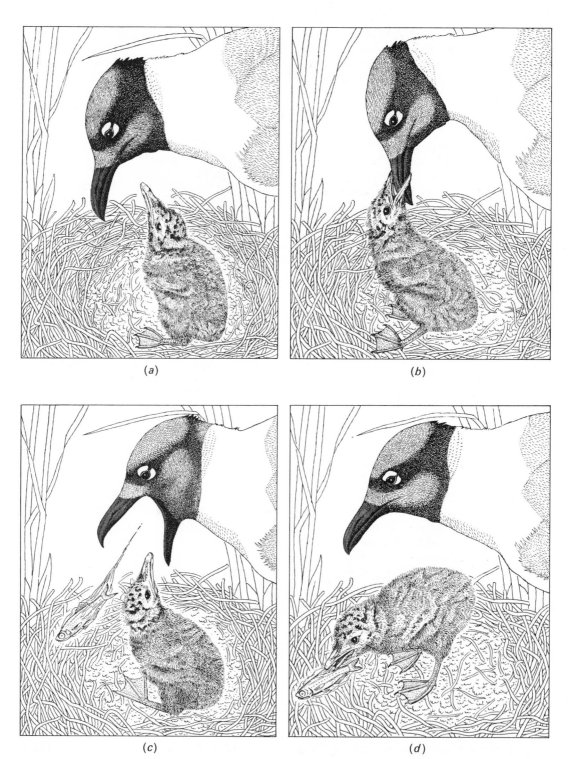

Figure 9–26 Feeding behavior of the laughing-gull chick. (*a*) As the parent lowers its head, a three-day-old chick directs a begging peck at the parent's beak. (*b*) The parent's beak is grasped and stroked. (*c*) The parent then regurgitates partly digested food. (*d*) The chick begins to eat it, using a pecking action known as "the feeding peck." (From "How an Instinct Is Learned" by Jack P. Hailman. Copyright © 1969 by Scientific American, Inc. All rights reserved.)

298

peck and for full development of the total feeding behavior. It has been shown through the use of models that the chick will peck more vigorously at models which resemble the parent's head and which make vertical movements similar to those of the parent. When the chick receives food from the parent, the behavior of pecking is reinforced and a type of conditioning occurs. The young chick thus *learns* to peck at its parent's bill be-cause food is obtained through this behavior.

It should not be surprising that the gull chick uses a combination of behavioral activities in its feeding pattern. Most animals use a variety of modes of behavior (taxes, reflexes, instincts, and learning). But whereas the invertebrate animals tend to utilize simple behaviors, such as taxes and reflexes, vertebrates rely on complex behavior (Figure 9–27). Thus a gradation of behavior from simple to

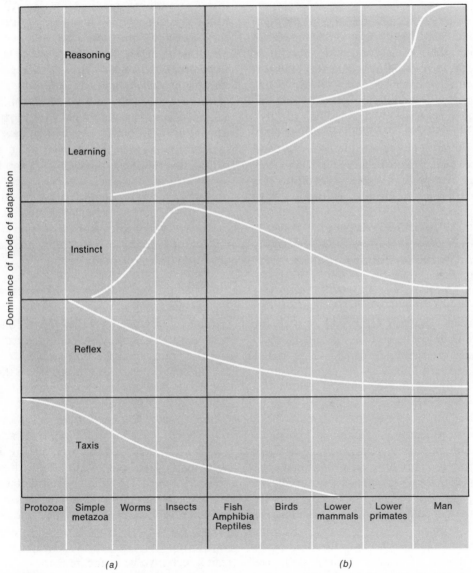

Figure 9–27 Relative use of different modes of behavior in animals. (*a*) Invertebrates rely heavily on taxes, reflexes, and instinctive behavior. (*b*) Vertebrates show more learning and reasoning in their behavior. (Redrawn from V. G. Dethier and Eliot Stellar, *Animal Behavior: Its Evolutionary and Neurological Basis*, Second Edition, © 1964. By permission of Prentice-Hall, Inc., Englewood Cliffs, New Jersey.)

complex forms exists in the animal world. In the primates and man, learning and reasoning dominate behavior.

ASPECTS OF LEARNING— REINFORCEMENT AND MOTIVATION

Learning can be defined as a relatively permanent change in behavior which usually occurs as the result of experience. In the case of the laughing gulls, pecking accuracy increases with practice and maturation; the more the young chicks practice in the first week of their lives, the more accurate they become in their begging pecks. But would this skill improve with age alone? Probably it would improve somewhat, and consequently experience and maturation work together to "fix" the skill in the young animal. A learned skill, such as skiing, requires considerable effort and much practice, but once learned it is not easily forgotten even though a skier stays off his skis for several years. In this skill, maturation plays a role, since some children learn to ski much more quickly after they reach a certain age. It is usually not possible therefore to determine whether improved performance is due to practice or increased maturity.

Another important principle in learning is reinforcement or reward. A performance which is rewarded positively with food or with the removal of an unpleasant sensation is likely to be learned and often learned very rapidly. Praise, as we all know, can be a very positive reinforcer in teaching children. Negative reinforcement in the form of some type of punishment or unpleasant situation can also have an effect on learning. Generally, behavior which leads to positive reinforcement is likely to recur. By providing reinforcement, we actually produce a *motivation* for the animal to perform the same behavioral pattern; in other words, we can motivate the animal to learn. With the example of the skier, it is necessary to be able to turn the skis in order to ski down certain slopes. If simple turning skills are learned, it is possible to ski down gentle slopes; if more difficult turns are mastered, steeper hills can be skied. The capability of skiing more exciting terrain therefore is a reward or reinforcement for perfecting the more difficult turns.

TYPES OF LEARNING

Habituation

In the absence of reinforcement, responses to many stimuli gradually decrease. All organisms are subjected to a variety of stimuli as they develop, and some stimuli are more meaningful or have a greater survival value than others. Animals tend to disregard insignificant stimuli, and this *habituation* is one of the commonest examples of learning. For example, certain noises which are capable of provoking a response but which have little meaning to us may be ignored after a long period of time. It is possible to demonstrate by monitoring the brain waves of a cat that a repeated tone of a certain frequency will soon cease to arouse the cat, whereas changing the frequency will bring about a response. It is important for an animal to learn which stimuli are insignificant or unimportant.

Imprinting

Newly hatched goslings or ducklings respond to the first moving object they see by following it. In nature the object is usually their mother, and the young birds become *imprinted* to her. Under experimental conditions when the eggs are hatched in an incubator, the young will follow a moving ball, a dog, or a human (Figure 9–28). Konrad Lorenz developed this concept of *imprinting* in his work with graylag geese; he showed that the process is relatively permanent and can occur only during a "critical period" of time soon after hatching. If the visual stimulus of a moving object is not presented to the young within the critical period (usually the first few hours), normal imprinting may not occur. Here, then, is a trait which involves some innateness and some learning since the tendency to follow is ap-

Figure 9–28 Konrad Lorenz, recipient of the Nobel Prize in Physiology or Medicine in 1973, and a gaggle of imprinted geese. (Courtesy of Dr. Lorenz.)

parently inherited but the object to be followed is learned. Imprinting is generally used to designate any behavior learned only during critical periods in early life.

Trial and Error

Learning sometimes occurs as a result of *trial and error*, a type of random and often erratic activity. If an act of behavior is positively reinforced (rewarded), it may be tried again. If the behavior meets with negative reinforcement (perhaps punishment) after several trials, it may be dropped. In each case a type of learning has occurred. An example of trial-and-error learning is the running of a maze by rats or other animals (Figure 9–29). After the animal runs the maze successfully and is rewarded with food, it is more apt to repeat the same route in the next trial.

Classical Conditioning

One of the most commonly known types of learning has been labeled *classical conditioning*.

We know what happens when we are presented with a bite of steak or perhaps just the sight and aroma—saliva flows, or as we commonly say, "our mouth waters." Ivan Pavlov, the great Russian physiologist of the early 1900s, observed that a dog might salivate before eating upon hearing the footsteps of his master bringing food. Through experimentation Pavlov was able to show that a dog which ordinarily responded to the stimulus of food by salivating could be conditioned to salivate in response to a neutral stimulus, such as the ringing of a buzzer. This was accomplished by sounding the buzzer at the moment of feeding (blowing meat powder into the dog's mouth) or shortly before (Figure 9–30). After a number of presentations of food and buzzer together, the buzzer alone could elicit the salivation response. Pavlov called this a *conditioned reflex* since it depended on previous training. Much of the training of animals is based on this principle—a response which ordinarily

Figure 9–29 A type of maze used in learning experiments with rats. The rat is rewarded with food when it successfully runs a specific pattern. (Robert J. Smith, from Black Star.)

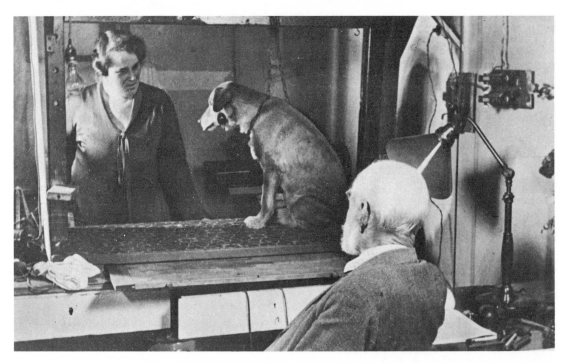

Figure 9–30 Ivan Pavlov (1849–1936), Russian physiologist and Nobel Prize winner in 1904, watching an experiment with a dog (summer 1934). (Fotokhronika Tass; Sovfoto.)

would be made to a natural stimulus is made to a stimulus such as a spoken command or a whistle.

Operant Conditioning

More recently B. F. Skinner of Harvard University has studied another type of conditioning described as *operant conditioning*. In classical conditioning the animal does not control the stimulus, which is followed by reinforcement. In operant conditioning, however, the stimulus which produces a reward is activated or influenced by the behavior of the animal itself. To state the comparison in another way, we could say that under classical conditioning the animal apparently has no real control over its response or behavior, whereas in operant conditioning the animal's behavior determines whether the reward will occur. Let us see how this works. A pigeon is placed in a box with a plastic key which can be pecked and a small food tray which can briefly open and present food. The key is connected to a recording instrument and any pecks on the key can be recorded over a given period of time. The apparatus can be rigged so that a peck on the key will open the food tray, and the pigeon will receive a reward such as a kernel of corn (Figure 9–31). If food is presented with each peck, the pigeon will continue to peck the key at an increasing rate. Such operant conditioning occurs when the pigeon's activity is reinforced at once; in this case, the reinforcer is food. A variety of experiments can be conducted with pigeons or rats using "Skinner boxes" with more elaborate mechanisms such as combinations of keys or levers or other targets to peck or move. For example, a pigeon may be presented with a dozen patterns; if it pecks a matching pair, it will be rewarded with grain. The bird thus learns through experience the combinations which produce the prize. Different reinforcement schedules are also often utilized to determine the most effective "pay" period. Generally the greater responses (such as greater pecking rate) occur when reinforcement occurs at closer intervals of time.

An interesting aspect of this behavior is what happens when a pigeon that is conditioned to

Figure 9–31 Pigeon performing in a "Skinner box" during an operant-conditioning experiment. When the pigeon pecks the key, food is presented in the food box below. (Will Rapport; courtesy of B. F. Skinner.)

peck at a high frequency no longer receives reinforcement. Essentially the conditioning is undone. The pecking rate returns to, or may go below, the original level before reinforcement—a process known as *extinction*. A certain amount of behavior resembling frustration may be associated with extinction. This condition is commonly seen in many deprived animals, including man, who have been conditioned or trained to expect a reward for certain behavior. When the reward is not forthcoming (extinction) varying types of behavior may occur. In humans we may observe puzzlement, random activity, anger, or even rage.

Reasoning

Much learning and learned behavior is very complex and often more difficult to study than the instances cited here. Complicated be-

303

havior patterns can be developed through the use of reinforcement schedules and the use of the various types of learning. It is known that some animals, man included, often use short-cuts in learning when placed in new situations. In solving some problems apparently *insight* is used, and knowledge gained from a former situation is used to solve the immediate problem. Some psychologists refer to this process as *reasoning*, and certainly memory is involved as well.

MEMORY AND CHEMISTRY

What is actually occurring inside an animal during learning? We have already noted the importance of chemistry to an understanding of life's functions. Perhaps we should now seek our explanation of learning in terms of chemistry. Again, we can look at the relationships between the nucleic acids (DNA and RNA) and proteins for some of the answers to our questions.

Recent evidence indicates that interfering with protein synthesis in goldfish and mice very soon after a training period will reduce the performance of a learned behavior. In experiments performed by B. W. Agranoff at the University of Michigan, goldfish were taught to swim from a lighted end of a tank where they received electrical shocks to the darkened end; the task was readily learned by the fish. When a solution of the antibiotic puromycin was injected into the skull and over the brain of the fish immediately after the training period, the performance deteriorated. (Perhaps memory was destroyed.) The same solution injected an hour later, however, did not affect the learned task. Clues as to what was happening at the molecular level during learning came from an understanding of the effect of puromycin. Part of the puromycin molecule resembles part of a transfer RNA molecule and can thus "mimic" the RNA in protein synthesis by entering the polypeptide chain at one point. This action prematurely terminates the growth of the forming protein. But how can a defective protein interfere with the learning or memory process? Proteins are

enzymes or structural components of cells, and probably their normal role along the neuron or at the synapse of neurons is essential to the process of memory. This hypothesis is currently being explored. There have been many attempts to link RNA and learning and even to call RNA the "master molecule" involved in learning, but the evidence has not been established. That RNA is important in the process of learning is probably true, but its exact role has not been determined. Other chemicals can affect the learning process also, and some of these will be discussed later in this chapter.

LOVE AND LEARNING

Love is a concept of great interest to most of us, and we have many questions and feelings about it. Perhaps one of the most important questions about love is: how does it develop? For an answer to this fundamental problem in primate behavior, scientists have turned to studies and experiments with monkeys because of the limitations in working with human subjects. We must recognize that the term love is essentially a human value, and its application to monkeys is anthropomorphic. In this discussion, however, we shall use the term *love* to cover a very diverse group of behavior patterns and mechanisms. For convenience, Harry F. Harlow and his associates at the University of Wisconsin summarized and defined five different kinds of love or affectional systems based on numerous studies of primates over the past forty years. These are: infant, peer, heterosexual, maternal, and paternal. Since these love patterns apparently develop in this sequential order in an individual, it is important that each develops successfully because one type sets the stage for the next. For example, if age-mate or peer affection does not occur, heterosexual love may be abnormal. Let us briefly examine each of these types of love.

In order to study infant love in isolation from maternal love and to determine the extent to which learning is involved, Dr. Harlow utilized imitation monkey mothers (called surrogate mothers). Two types of artificial mothers were constructed—one was composed of a wire mesh with a wooden head while the other was formed from terry cloth with a similar head (Figure 9–32). In some of these experiments, provisions were made for these "mothers" to feed the young. When infant monkeys were placed in a cage with a terry-cloth mother and a wire mother, a much greater preference was shown for the terry-cloth model (Figure 9–33). An infant monkey would spend more time with the terry-cloth mother even though food was coming from the wire mother, an indication of the security derived from this comfortable contact. This led to the conclusion that contact is a most important aspect of the infant-mother relationship. When the young monkeys were frightened in various ways, they invariably ran to the terry-cloth mother. After a period with the artificial mother, they displayed curiosity and investigated the object which produced the fright (Figure 9–34). During this exploratory time, the young monkeys returned periodically to the "security" of their "mother." In other experiments when infants were separated from their mothers before maturation, they at first uttered a vocal protest but soon went into depression. Normal infant behavior could be restored, however, when the infant was returned to its mother.

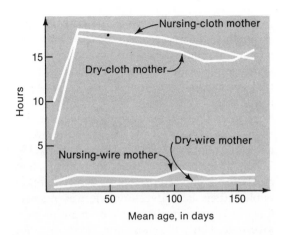

Figure 9–33 Time spent by baby monkey on four different artificial mothers: nursing-cloth, dry-cloth, dry-wire, and nursing-wire. (Redrawn after Harry F. Harlow, *Learning to Love*, 1971. By permission of Albion Publishing Company, San Francisco.)

Figure 9–32 A young monkey and two types of artificial mothers. Greater preference was shown for the terry-cloth mother, even though food came from the wire mother. (Harry F. Harlow, University of Wisconsin Primate Laboratory.)

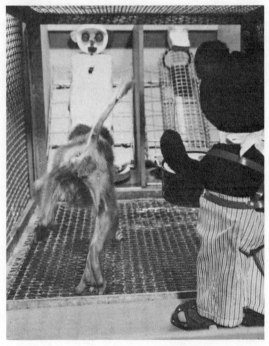

Figure 9–34 When frightened by a toy drummer, the young monkey ran to the terry-cloth mother rather than to the wire mother. (Harry F. Harlow, University of Wisconsin Primate Laboratory.)

Age-mate or peer love follows normal separation from the mother, and the close motherly contact of infant love is now transferred to another individual—a peer. Various types of play are typical of peer love. In a test of the importance of this stage, some monkeys were kept from their peers and raised entirely by their mothers. In later life these monkeys exhibited abnormal social and sexual behavior. When babies were raised with terry-cloth mothers but allowed periods of play with other babies, their later development was normal. The indication is that development of peer love is probably the most important stage for the future social and sexual development of an individual—a concept contrary to the popular belief that the stage of motherly love is the most essential. Close social relationships can occur in peer love, and this prepares the individual for the fourth stage of heterosexual love. This affectional system, which begins at puberty and continues into adulthood, is affected by hormones that also control secondary sex characteristics and the development of eggs and sperm.

Maternal love is the care of a mother for her child, a type of love which can recur with the arrival of each new infant. This behavior is expressed in several stages from meeting the child's basic needs to the final separation from the child. Although the basis of motherly love is not entirely clear, perhaps much of this behavior is learned during the development of the child (stimulus-response mechanisms). A lack of maternal love is exhibited by adult females that were raised in the absence of a mother. These females exhibit serious sexual problems and have difficulty mating. If they do mate and have offspring, the behavior of these "motherless" females toward the baby is often indifferent or abusive and always shows rejection.

Paternal love, the relationship between adult males and infants, is expressed in a protective and a playful way. Experiments utilizing special cages which house several monkey families in separate units have shed some light on paternal love. In these cages only the infants were allowed to move among the units and associate with other families. Under these conditions the fathers accepted all infants, showed a playful attitude, and tolerated more abuseful treatment in play than did adult females.

Finally we might note how rearing baby monkeys in isolation influences the development of affectional systems. We have already mentioned effects on the development of maternal behavior in females raised without a mother. A baby monkey raised in isolation for six months does not learn to relate normally to its mother or to its peers, and later may experience sexual problems. The basic problems here involve social relationships and the ability to interact with others.

SOME FACTORS IN HUMAN BEHAVIOR

MODIFICATION OF BEHAVIOR

That behavior can be modified or changed is well known. In the course of our daily lives, we are constantly influenced by mass media, both consciously and unconsciously. In addition to determining how we spend our money, the media shape in no small part how we react to our environment in general. We are also well aware of the effects of some chemicals on behavior, especially alcohol and tranquilizers. Peter N. Witt of the North Carolina Department of Mental Health used the fairly precise web-spinning ability of a spider to test the effects of certain drugs on behavior. Each species of spider always constructs its web in a definite and exact design. When various drugs are administered, different web patterns will be spun due to the different effects of each drug on the nervous system of the spider (Figure 9–35). In fact, we know that almost any chemical, in amounts varying from those an organism is normally accustomed to, will produce behavioral changes. For example, the effects of changes in CO_2 concentration on breathing and heart rate in humans is well understood by biologists. But behavior can be modified by using methods other than chemicals; some of these methods such as in psychotherapy employ the spoken word.

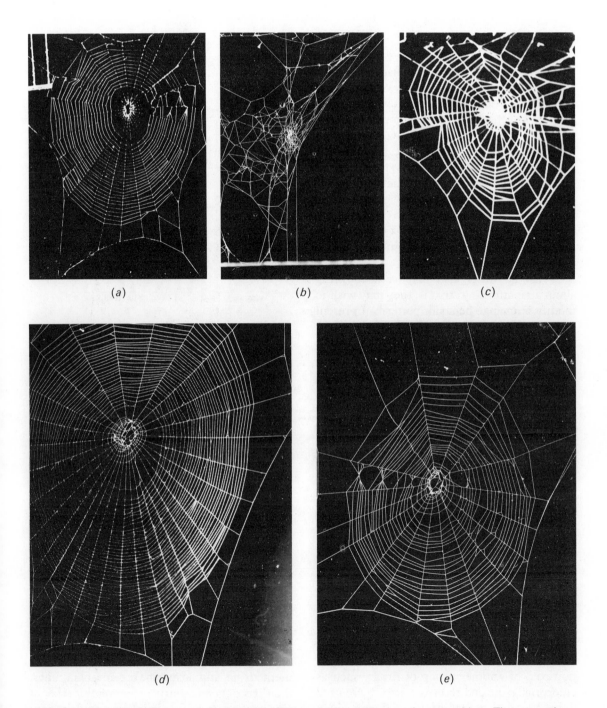

Figure 9–35 The influence of drugs on the web-spinning behavior of cross spiders. The upper three photos (*a, b, c*) show the effects of dextro-amphetamine ("speed"). In the lower photos (*d, e*), the effects of phenobarbital (a sedative) on web-spinning are demonstrated. (*a*) The control web, built on the first day of observation. (*b*) The web constructed by the same spider 12 hours later, after drinking about 0.1 ml of a drop of sugar water which contained 1 mg of dextro-amphetamine; it shows remnants of a hub and erratic radii and strands. (*c*) The web built 24 hours later, showing signs of recovery. (*d*) The web exhibits the normal pattern. (*e*) The web built one and a half days after a high dose of the drug (100 mg/kg); it is smaller and irregular. (Courtesy of Peter N. Witt, North Carolina Department of Mental Health, Division of Research, Raleigh, N.C.)

PSYCHOTHERAPY

In recent years, trained specialists have been able to draw upon a wide variety of techniques to influence behavior. In psychoanalysis (a type of psychotherapy), the psychiatrist attempts to influence present behavior by analyzing the past experiences of the patient. The working hypothesis is that through uncovering some event or experience of the past, better understanding of present behavior will result and may consequently lead to a change in behavior. Primary causes for one's current behavior are therefore sought in experiences from the past.

Psychotherapists also may seek to bring about a repatterning; that is, they may wish to modify or change behavior patterns if present behavior is not satisfactory or simply is not working. Although these types of behavioral changes may be considered the result of free will or choice, in some cases a type of reconditioning may occur which involves reinforcement.

CHEMICAL THERAPY AND DRUGS

The possibilities of chemical therapy in modifying behavior have been widely explored and utilized since the 1950s, and the use of drugs has contributed to advances in the treatment of a variety of mental illnesses (Figure 9–36). Psychiatrists now have at their command a vast arsenal of drugs to combat neuroses, psychoses, depressions, and other problems of behavior. Most people today are well aware of the usefulness of tranquilizers in producing a quiet personality with lowered anxiety and tension; other drugs such as antidepressants serve as mood elevators. Many are not aware, however, of another group of drugs, such as chlorpromazine and reserpine, which are used to treat serious mental disorders. These, along with other chemicals, have been useful in the treatment of *schizophrenia*, a serious mental disorder. The study of schizophrenia as a chemical imbalance has been pursued vigorously, and some insights into the chemical pathways involved and the chemical therapy needed have been gained.

When people use these drugs without medi-

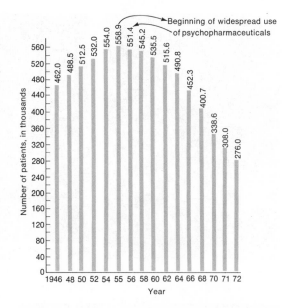

Figure 9–36 The use of drugs in the treatment of mental illness has brought about a drastic reduction in the number of resident patients in government hospitals in the United States. (Courtesy of Nathan S. Kline, M.D., Director, Research Center, Rockland State Hospital, Orangeburg, N.Y.)

cal supervision, it is possible to produce symptoms similar to the mental disorders that the drugs are used to control. The indiscriminate use of drugs can lead to serious behavioral problems. Various schemes for classifying drugs are used, but for our purposes, we will organize drugs into four groups: stimulants, sedatives, opiates, and hallucinogens (Figure 9–37).

Stimulants

These drugs include the *amphetamines* which stimulate the central nervous system and are commonly referred to as pep pills or "speed." Although many drugs such as benzedrine, methedrine, and dexedrine are amphetamines, their basic chemical structure resembles that of epinephrine and norepinephrine, and in general they produce effects similar to these hormones (Figure 9–38). The amphetamines have been prescribed to increase alertness and vigor, but their use in medicine is under careful scrutiny at the present time due to the possibilities of addiction and also because more efficient drugs can now be used to achieve the same purposes. It is interesting to note that amphetamines can also be used in the treatment of overactive children, where their effects are reversed, and they act like sedatives. Cocaine, which is legally classified as a narcotic, produces responses similar to those of the amphetamines.

One of the most common stimulants to the central nervous system is caffeine, a component of the social drinks, coffee, tea, and cola. Whereas the general effects of caffeine are increased alertness and counteraction to fatigue, large amounts can produce nervousness, increased heart rate, blood pressure, and gastric secretion (a serious effect for ulcer patients). Caffeine also causes constriction of blood vessels in the brain and is often used in headache remedies. Experimentally, caffeine, which has a purine structure, has been shown to produce mutations by inhibiting some of the enzymes necessary for nucleic-acid synthesis. Even though these drinks are very important in most social functions and generally have no extremely harmful effects, a psychological dependence can develop.

Sedatives

The most common sedatives are the *barbiturates* (often called "downers") which depress the central nervous system and produce a generally quiet state. Barbiturates are prescribed for high blood pressure, and in some cases for other anxiety symptoms. Again, as in amphetamines, the danger potential is great, and users often become dependent. Many accidental overdoses or usage with other drugs produce numerous deaths each year.

Alcoholism appears to afflict more than 5 percent of the United States population, and many physicians feel that this addiction is our most serious and widespread drug problem. Increasing numbers of deaths are now attributed to alcohol-induced cirrhosis of the liver, automobile accidents resulting from drunken driving, and complex synergistic effects of alcohol in combination with other common drugs such as barbiturates. (A synergistic effect occurs when the combined actions of two substances produce a much greater effect than would be expected from their separate activities.) One side effect of alcohol addiction results from the "empty calories"

that are ingested; an alcoholic may suffer serious protein and vitamin deficiencies simply because he has no interest in food. A recent study of alcoholism reported by Drs. Emanuel Rubin and Charles Lieber of Mount Sinai School of Medicine in New York shows definite damage to the endoplasmic reticulum of the liver cells of rats and humans. Moreover, it was found that ingestion of alcohol inhibits the normal metabolism of other drugs; this may be at least part of the synergistic mechanism.

The tremendous body of knowledge now available from public and private research groups on the effects of nicotine and cigarette smoking is impressive. There is no doubt that smoking tobacco is injurious to an individual's health and may lead to the development of lung cancer, one of the most difficult cancers to treat effectively. In addition, smoking increases susceptibility to emphysema, and many smokers die of this disease. Tobacco smoke contains a mixture of gases, resin tars, and nicotine; of these, the tars and nicotine appear to have the greatest carcinogenic effect.

Nicotine also has many other effects on the body. It produces an increased heart rate, higher blood pressure, and causes constriction of the coronary arterioles. Consequently, with mild usage, nicotine has a slight stimulatory effect on the central nervous system. It mimics the normal synaptic transmitter substance acetylcholine. Over a number of years these effects on body functions may lead to greatly impaired health and vitality.

Hallucinogens

Many drugs are capable of producing hallucinations, but the most well-known are LSD (lysergic acid diethylamide), mescaline (peyote), and psilocybin. This type of drug has been used by man throughout his history, often in his religious rituals. When a drug such as LSD is taken, the user might refer to his "acid trip"—an experience reportedly involving expanded awareness, distorted senses, bright flashing colors, and often a complete loss of reality (for example, believing one can fly). Dizziness and nausea are usually the initial effects which occur before perceptual alterations. Trips are reported as either pleas-

309

Hallucinogenic Drugs

Name	Slang Name	Classification	Medical Use	How Taken	Long-Term Symptoms	Physical Dependence Potential	Psychological Dependence Potential	Organic Damage Potential
Marijuana	Pot, Grass, Hashish, Tea, Gage, Reefers, Mary Jane	Relaxant, mood elevator; in high doses, hallucinogen	None in U.S.	Smoked or swallowed	May lead to decline of energy and motivation	No	Yes	?
LSD	Acid, Big D, Cubes, Trips, Sugar	Hallucinogen	Experimental study of mental function, alcoholism	Swallowed	May intensify existing psychosis, panic reactions	No	Yes	?
Mescaline	Mesc., Cactus	Hallucinogen	None	Swallowed	?	No	Yes	?
Psilocybin		Hallucinogen	None	Swallowed	?	No	Yes	?

Stimulant Drugs

Name	Slang Name	Classification	Medical Use	How Taken	Long-Term Symptoms	Physical Dependence Potential	Psychological Dependence Potential	Organic Damage Potential
Ampheta-mines	Bennies, Dexies, Speed, Wake-Ups, Lid Proppers, Hearts, Pep Pills	Stimulant	Relieve mild depression, control appetite, promote wakefulness	Swallowed or injected	Loss of appetite, delusions, hallucinations, toxic psychosis	?	Yes	?
Cocaine	Corrine, Gold Dust, Coke, Bernice, Flake, Star Dust, Snow	Stimulant	Local (surface) anesthesia	Sniffed, injected, or swallowed	Depression, delusions, hallucinations, toxic psychosis	No	Yes	?

As a result of objective studies such as these, psychiatrists, physicians, and psychologists are better able to diagnose and treat many problems such as impotence and lack of orgasm. Moreover, as many citizens become more knowledgeable about their basic drives, they are willing to seek treatment, if necessary, for sexual malfunctions. This attitude has also helped society to develop more rational views of atypical sexual behavior.

We should now consider some of the more specific details of reproduction and development in all organisms; this will be the subject of the next chapter.

SUMMARIZING STATEMENTS

Behavior is what organisms do, and most behavior has adaptive value. A good example of a social behavioral study in the field was done by Jane van Lawick-Goodall on chimpanzees in Africa.

Some of the simplest types of behavior are tropisms, taxes, and reflexes, which are generally automatic orientations to the environment. Reflexes are principally responses to a stimulus; they usually involve a nervous system; and many serve protective functions. They often occur in chains (the response of one reflex is the stimulus for the next) or in coordinated groups.

All complex species behaviors show evidence of inheritance and learning. Whereas some behavior sequences appear to be instinctive or innate and other behavior patterns seem to be learned, it is becoming more apparent that most behavior is the result of both genetic and environmental contributions. Ethology is the study of species-characteristic behavior. Any object, structure, behavior, or sound which can initiate a fixed-action pattern as a response is known as a releaser.

Certain biological activities are controlled by internal timing mechanisms—biological clocks, which are often affected by environmental conditions such as day length and phases of the moon. Behavioral patterns which are termed *circadian rhythms* occur on a 24-hour cycle; other cycles seem to occur on a yearly basis.

Seasonal migrations in birds are apparently triggered by photoperiodism, a response made to varying periods of light and dark. In some species migration is coupled with photoreception which stimulates the pituitary by way of the hypothalamus. Migration involves orientation, and it is possible that some animals make use of the position of the sun and stars and perhaps the earth's magnetic field to orient themselves.

Territories are claimed and maintained by many animals for the purpose of breeding and feeding, and territoriality has the effect of limiting population density in an area. Peck order is one type of social hierarchy in birds in which the individuals are in a ranked social order.

The various methods of animal communication can be summarized as: visual displays, chemical signals, audible sounds, tactile systems, and language. Visual displays are frequently used by many animals for aggressive purposes, attracting a mate, or defending a territory. Ants release chemicals called *pheromones* onto the ground to mark a trail. Bees often bump against each other for communication in a hive; they also communicate the distance and direction of food by dance movements.

Learning involves changes in behavior which occur as a result of experience. Two important aspects of learning are reinforcement and motivation. The types of learning are: habituation, imprinting, trial and error, classical conditioning, operant conditioning, and reasoning.

The development of love involves learning and apparently proceeds through stages such as: infant, peer, heterosexual, maternal, and paternal.

Behavior can be modified through the use of chemicals. Many drugs are clinically used today to change behavior patterns. Some of these drugs are also used outside of the field of medicine and have produced some problems in our society.

Because of scientific studies, we have arrived at a better understanding of human sexual behavior. This has assisted in the diagnosis and treatment of many sex-oriented problems.

REVIEW QUESTIONS

1   Give examples of tropistic and taxic behavior, and state the adaptive value of such movements to the organisms involved.

2   Outline an example of a chain reflex or a coordinated group of reflexes.

3   Why is it difficult to distinguish in a behavioral pattern between what is learned and what is inherited?

4   Young herring gulls beg for food by pecking at the parent's bill. When models were presented to a group of young gulls, the bill model with a red spot received the most pecks, whereas models with spots of other colors had fewer responses, and models with no spot received fewest pecks. From these experiments what can you conclude about the feeding behavior in young herring gulls?

5   In some birds the color of certain body parts, such as a robin's red breast, may act as a releaser to provoke attack by another bird of the same species. List some examples of other releasers in nature.

6   Organisms can have their biological clocks reset when exposed to new conditions. This resetting generally requires some period of time. Why is this so?

7   Discuss several factors that may influence the annual migrations of birds such as the northern cliff swallows and white-crowned sparrows.

8   Most birds migrate in the daytime, but some migrate at night. What navigational aids are employed by these birds?

9   Most animals display some territoriality in their natural habitats. What are the advantages of this behavior?

10   What are some common examples of conditioned reflexes in humans?

11   Design a simple experiment using a pigeon and a Skinner box that would illustrate positive reinforcement in learning.

12   Recently, much attention has been given to the role of RNA in learning. What are the basic reasons for making this correlation?

13   Why does a barnyard rooster crow from several different perches early in the morning? Why do wolves and dogs urinate on objects all around a general area?

14   How does a language differ from other types of communication among animals? What are some of the essential characteristics of a language?

15 Certain drugs are effective in alleviating the symptoms of epilepsy and schizophrenia. Why can these and other drugs be harmful when used by normal individuals under uncontrolled conditions?

SUPPLEMENTARY READINGS

Agranoff, B. W., "Memory and Protein Synthesis," *Scientific American*, June, 1967.

Allen, Thomas B., ed., *The Marvels of Animal Behavior*, Washington, D.C., National Geographic Society, 1972.

Arbib, Michael A., *The Metaphysical Brain*, New York, Wiley, 1972.

Atkinson, R. C., and R. M. Shiffrin, "The Control of Short-Term Memory," *Scientific American*, August, 1971.

Batra, S. W. T., and Lekh R. Batra, "The Fungus Gardens of Insects," *Scientific American*, November, 1967.

Blum, Richard H., and Associates, *Society and Drugs*, San Francisco, Jossey-Bass, 1969.

Blum, Richard H., and Associates, *Students and Drugs*, San Francisco, Jossey-Bass, 1969.

Bogoch, Samuel, *The Biochemistry of Memory*, New York, Oxford University Press, 1968.

Bower, T. G. R., "The Object in the World of the Infant," *Scientific American*, October, 1971.

Boycott, B. B., "Learning in the Octopus," *Scientific American*, March, 1965.

Brown, Frank A., Jr., "The 'Clocks' Timing Biological Rhythms," *American Scientist*, November-December, 1972.

Camki, Jeffrey M., "Flight Orientation in Locusts," *Scientific American*, August, 1971.

Cloudsley-Thompson, J. L., *Animal Behavior*, New York, Macmillan, 1961.

Collias, Nicholas E., *Animal Language*, New York, Macmillan, 1966.

De Vore, Isven, ed., *Primate Behavior*, New York, Holt, Rinehart and Winston, 1965.

Dethier, V. G., and Eliot Stellar, *Animal Behavior: Its Evolutionary and Neuro-logical Basis* (2nd ed.), Englewood Cliffs, N.J., Prentice-Hall, 1964.

Esch, Harold, "The Evolution of Bee Language," *Scientific American*, April, 1967.

Estes, W. K., "Reinforcement in Human Behavior," *American Scientist*, November-December, 1972.

Farmer, D. S., *Photoperiodism in Animals*, BSCS Pamphlet No. 15, American Institute of Biological Sciences, Boston, Heath, 1964.

Feder, Howard A., "Escape Responses in Marine Invertebrates," *Scientific American*, July, 1972.

Frings, Hubert, and M. Frings, *Animal Communication*, New York, Blaisdell, 1964.

Frisch, Karl von, "Dialects in the Language of the Bees," *Scientific American*, August, 1962.

Geschwind, Norman, "Language and the Brain," *Scientific American*, April, 1972.

317

Grinspoon, L., "Marihuana," *Scientific American*, December, 1969.

Hailman, Jack P., "How an Instinct Is Learned," *Scientific American*, December, 1969.

Harlow, H. F., "Love in Infant Monkeys," *Scientific American*, June, 1959.

Harlow, H. F., *Learning to Love*, San Francisco, Albion, 1971.

Harlow, H. F., and M. K. Harlow, "Learning to Love," *American Scientist*, September, 1966.

Harlow, H. F., and M. K. Harlow, "Social Deprivation in Monkeys," *Scientific American*, November, 1972.

Harlow, H. F., M. K. Harlow, and S. J. Suomi, "From Thought to Therapy: Lessons from a Primate Laboratory," *American Scientist*, September-October, 1971.

Hess, Eckhard H., " 'Imprinting' in a Natural Laboratory," *Scientific American*, August, 1972.

Hölldobler, Bert, "Communication Between Ants and Their Guests," *Scientific American*, March, 1971.

Johnsgard, Paul A., *Animal Behavior*, Dubuque, Wm. C. Brown, 1967.

Jolly, Allison, *The Evolution of Primate Behavior*, New York, Macmillan, 1972.

Kagan, Jerome, "Do Infants Think?" *Scientific American*, March, 1972.

Kandel, Eric R., "Nerve Cells and Behavior," *Scientific American*, July, 1970.

Kinsey, Alfred C., W. B. Pomeroy, and C. E. Martin, *Sexual Behavior in the Human Male*, Philadelphia, Saunders, 1948.

Kinsey, Alfred C., W. B. Pomeroy, C. E. Martin, and P. H. Gebhard, *Sexual Behavior in the Human Female*, Philadelphia, Saunders, 1953.

Klopfer, Peter H., "Mother Love: What Turns It On?" *American Scientist*, July-August, 1971.

Leggett, William C., "The Migration of the Shad," *Scientific American*, March, 1973.

Levine, Seymour, "Stress and Behavior," *Scientific American*, January, 1971.

Longee, Laura B., *The Web of the Spider*, Bloomfield Hills, Mich., Cranbrook Institute of Science, 1964.

Longo, V. G., *Neuropharmacology and Behavior*, San Francisco, Freeman, 1972.

Lorenz, Konrad, *King Solomon's Ring*, New York, Crowell, 1952.

Lorenz, Konrad, "The Evolution of Behavior," *Scientific American*, December, 1958.

Lorenz, Konrad, *On Aggression*, London, Methuen, 1963.

Lorenz, Konrad, *Evolution and Modification of Behavior*, Chicago, University of Chicago Press, 1965.

Luce, G. G., *Biological Rhythms in Human and Animal Behavior*, New York, Dover, 1971.

Masters, William H., and V. E. Johnson, *Human Sexual Response*, Boston, Little, Brown, 1966.

Masters, William H., and V. E. Johnson, *Human Sexual Inadequacy*, Boston, Little, Brown, 1970.

Meyerriecks, Andrew J., *Courtship in Animals*. BSCS Pamphlet No. 3, American Institute of Biological Sciences, Boston, Heath, 1962.

Modell, Walter, *Drugs*, New York, Time, Inc., 1967.

Mykytowycz, T., "Territorial Marking by Rabbits," *Scientific American*, May, 1968.

Pengelley, Eric T., and Sally J. Asmundson, "Annual Biological Clocks," *Scientific American*, April, 1971.

Petrunkevitch, A., "The Spider and the Wasp," *Scientific American*, August, 1952.

Premack, Ann James, and David Premack, "Teaching Language to an Ape," *Scientific American*, October, 1972.

Reynolds, Vernon, *The Apes*, New York, Dutton, 1967.

Rosenblatt, J. S., "Learning in Newborn Kittens," *Scientific American*, December, 1972.

Rosenzweig, Mark R., E. L. Bennett, and M. C. Diamond, "Brain Changes in Response to Experience," *Scientific American*, February, 1972.

Schiller, C. H., ed., *Instinctive Behavior*, New York, International Universities Press, 1957.

Siffre, Michel, *Beyond Time*, New York, McGraw-Hill, 1964.

Skinner, B. F., "The Experimental Analysis of Behavior," *American Scientist*, September, 1957.

Skinner, B. F., *Beyond Freedom and Dignity*, New York, Knopf, 1971.

Tart, Charles T., ed., *Altered States of Consciousness*, New York, Wiley, 1969.

Tavolga, W. N., *Principles of Animal Behavior*, New York, Harper and Row, 1969.

Teale, Edwin W., ed., *The Insect World of J. Henri Fabre*, New York, Dodd, Mead, 1949.

Tinbergen, N., *The Study of Instinct*, New Jersey, Oxford University Press, 1951.

Tinbergen, N., "The Curious Behavior of the Stickleback," *Scientific American*, December, 1952.

Tinbergen, N., *Social Behavior in Animals*, London, Methuen, 1953.

Tinbergen, N., "The Evolution of Behavior in Gulls," *Scientific American*, December, 1960.

Todd, John H., "The Chemical Language of Fishes," *Scientific American*, May, 1971.

Topoff, Howard R., "The Social Behavior of Army Ants," *Scientific American*, November, 1972.

Wallace, R. K., and H. Benson, "The Physiology of Meditation," *Scientific American*, February, 1972.

Watts, C. R., and A. W. Stokes, "The Social Order of Turkeys," *Scientific American*, June, 1971.

Weiss, Jay M., "Psychological Factors in Stress and Disease," *Scientific American*, June, 1972.

Wendt, Herbert, *The Sex Life of the Animals*, New York, Simon and Schuster, 1965.

Willows, A. O. D., "Giant Brain Cells in Mollusks," *Scientific American*, February, 1971.

Wilson, Edward O., "Animal Communication," *Scientific American*, September, 1972.

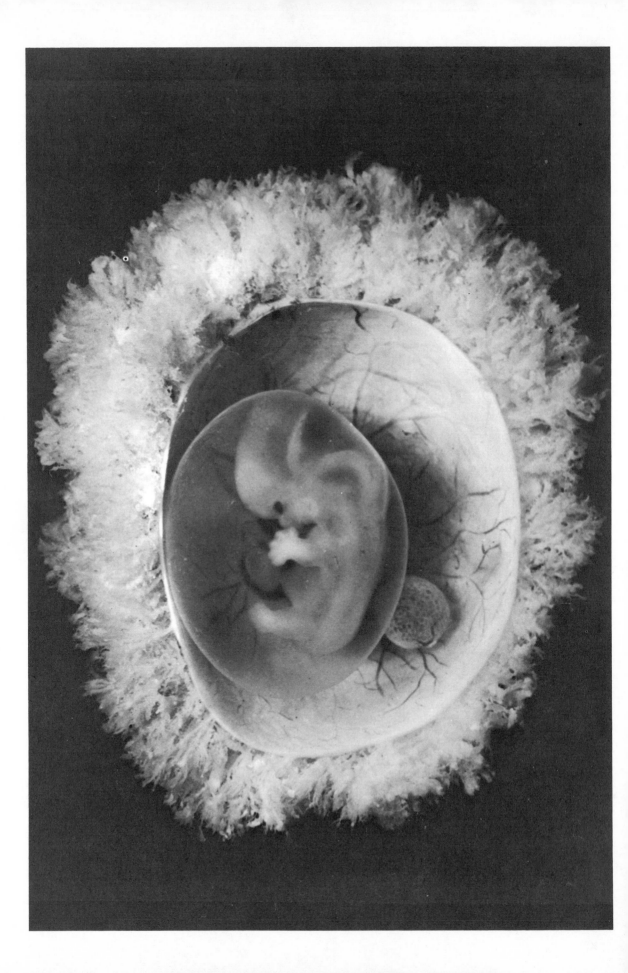

10

Reproduction and Development

The future of all species of plants and animals on this planet depends on their ability to produce offspring which in turn can reproduce. Although we know that some individual organisms can reproduce asexually, it has now been established that most living things are capable of sexual reproduction. Each type of reproduction has distinct characteristics. For example, asexual reproduction produces organisms exactly like the parent, whereas sexual reproduction gives offspring that are always different. Exactly how this variability comes about will be the subject of the next chapter which deals with heredity. The importance of variability to a given species will be stressed in the chapter on evolution. Before organisms can reproduce, cellular reproduction, an orderly series of events, must occur. And before cells can reproduce, molecular duplication must take place. Molecular reproduction in DNA has already been presented in Chapter 2, and now we will discuss the basic reproductive mechanisms at the cellular and organismal levels.

Closely associated with reproduction in organisms is the complicated process of development in which a fertilized egg undergoes a series of changes to produce all the adult tissues and organs. This developmental process must occur in all plants and animals. Perhaps you have wondered just how a tiny fertilized egg can possibly divide and change into a complete, functional, multicellular organism. Certainly one important clue is the code in the DNA molecule (described in Chapter 3) which is essential since specific regions of the molecule direct the development of dividing cells. Development like cellular reproduction is also an orderly series of events. We will first consider the reproductive process and then turn to some examples and studies in development.

CELLULAR REPRODUCTION

The nuclear events that occur during cell division were observed many years before any correlation between chromosomes and cell division was made. Cell division was observed in protozoa as early as 1744 by Trembley, even though he did not recognize them as cells. It was around 1824 that the process of dividing or cleaving frog eggs was finally recognized as multiplication by cell division. In 1888 Thedor Boveri published a classic paper on the division of fertilized *Ascaris* (roundworm) eggs in which he accurately diagrammed the distribution of nuclear material during cleavage.

Two types of cell division occur in most plants and animals: (1) *somatic* or body-cell division and (2) *gametic* or sex-cell division. More specifically the gametes are called *eggs* and *sperms*. Somatic division is known as *mitosis* and gametic division is called *meiosis*. In mitosis both the nucleus and the cytoplasm divide to form two daughter cells which contain the same number and types of chromosomes as the original cell. Meiosis, on the other hand, is a more complex process in which the chromosome number in each gamete is halved in preparation for fertilization. At fertilization each parent contributes, in its gamete, one-half the number of chromosomes characteristic of the species. In humans this number is 23, and this is called the *haploid* number, or simply *n*. The complete chromosome number of a body cell in man is, therefore, 46, and this is the *diploid* or *2n* number.

MITOSIS

The chromosomes of a normal diploid cell occur in pairs, and each member of a chromosome pair is essentially similar in size and shape, and carry inheritance factors which influence similar traits. The term *homologous pairs* is often used to describe chromosomes that have these similar characteristics. In Chapter 11 you will learn more about the role of chromosomal DNA in the transmission of hereditary traits. Since the chromosomes contain DNA, they may be called the physical bearers of heredity, and for this reason the activities of the chromosomes during division are also of great interest to the geneticist.

Before a cell can divide, the chromosomes must duplicate. The DNA of each chromosome duplicates according to the base-pair specificity—adenine to thymine and guanine to cytosine.

The details of mitosis are easier to understand if we study the process in a series of steps or phases. From beginning to end these phases are (1) *interphase*, (2) *prophase*, (3) *metaphase*, (4) *anaphase*, and (5) *telophase* (Figures 10–1 and 10–2).

Mitosis in Animals

Interphase. The chromosomes within the nucleus are long, threadlike, and indistinguishable from one another. Dense-staining areas called *chromomeres* appear at specific points along each chromosome. These thickened regions are concentrations of DNA produced by localized coiling. The nuclear membrane during this stage is intact, and the centrioles are located in the cytoplasm near the nucleus.

For many years after the discovery of mitosis it was thought that the chromosomes duplicated about halfway through the division process (metaphase). When radioisotopes of phosphorus (P^{32}) and hydrogen (H^3, tritium) became available, and tritiated thymidine was added to the medium of dividing cells, it was found that thymidine bases were incorporated

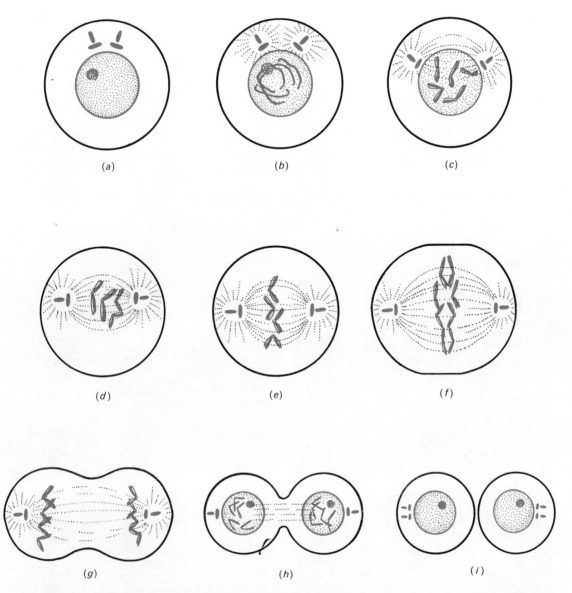

(a) (b) (c)

(d) (e) (f)

(g) (h) (i)

Figure 10–1 Interphase and successive stages of mitosis in an animal cell. (*a*) *Interphase:* chromosomes indistinct, nucleolus visible. (*b*) *Early Prophase:* chromosomes begin coiling, centrioles begin movement to poles. (*c*) *Middle Prophase:* chromosomes very distinct, nucleolus disappears. (*d*) *Late Prophase:* chromosomes shorter and thicker, nuclear membrane disappears, spindle fibers in position, centromeres attach to spindle fibers. (*e*) *Metaphase:* chromosomes line up on equatorial plane. (*f*) *Early Anaphase*: chromatids separate and move to poles. (*g*) *Late Anaphase:* cleavage furrow developing, chromosomes near poles. (*h*) *Telophase:* chromosomes uncoil, nucleoli reappear, nuclear membranes form, cytokinesis nearly complete. (*i*) Two daughter cells result.

into the interphasic chromosomes. Chromosome duplication therefore occurs during interphase.

Prophase. In this early phase of mitosis, the chromosomes which are long and threadlike begin to coil upon themselves much like the

323

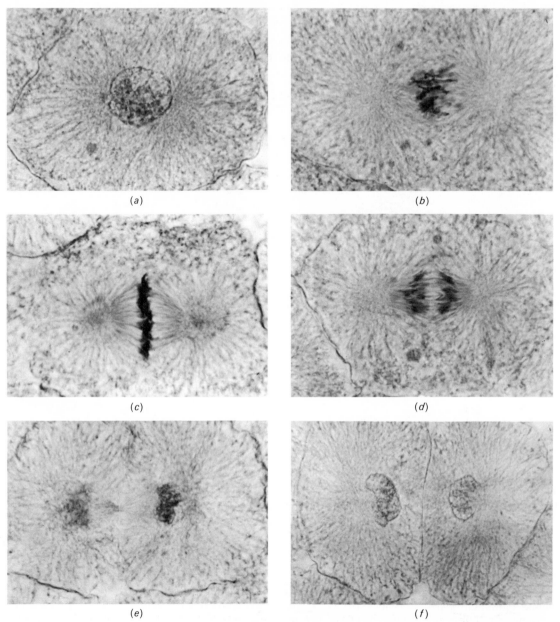

Figure 10–2 Mitotic phases in a developing egg of whitefish. (*a*) Interphase. (*b*) Prophase. (*c*) Metaphase. (*d*) Anaphase. (*e*) Telophase. (*f*) Daughter cells. (Courtesy of CCM: General Biological, Inc., Chicago.)

twisting of a rubber band. During this stage each chromosome becomes shorter, thicker, and more clearly visible. The nucleolus disappears and is not recognized again until the reorganization of the nuclei in the daughter cells. Near the end of prophase the nuclear membrane begins to break down and finally disappears. Radiating protein fibers (microtubules) called *asters* form near each centriole as the centrioles move slowly away from each other around the nucleus to form the opposite poles for the division.

Metaphase. When the centrioles have reached opposite positions across the nuclear area, protein fibers, *spindle fibers*, are synthesized between them. Some spindle fibers attach to specific regions on the chromosomes called *centromeres*. Little is known about the mechanics of spindle-fiber attachment or the molecular structure of the centromere. We do know that each chromosome has one centromere which is always at the same spot on a specific chromosome. Some chromosomes have their centromere in the center and are called *metacentric*, while others have the centromere at the end and are known as *acrocentric*. The metacentric chromosomes typically are V-shaped and the acrocentric, rod-shaped. If the centromere is located between the center and one end, the chromosome is J-shaped and is called *submetacentric*. After the chromosomes have duplicated they appear double and each half is called a *chromatid*. This term will be used extensively in the discussion on meiosis.

During metaphase the chromosomes attached to the spindle fibers move about until they align on an equatorial plane which is oriented perpendicular to the centriole poles. The centrioles, spindle fibers, and chromosomes are collectively known as the *mitotic apparatus*. Daniel Mazia (Figure 10–3) of the University of California has been successful in isolating this mitotic apparatus from dividing cells. By using a chemical to stop division at midpoint and breaking up the cell membranes with detergent, scientists can now remove the entire mitotic apparatus for analytical studies.

Anaphase. The spindle fibers that attach to the chromosomes are called *traction* or *chromosomal fibers*. It is thought that these fibers actually contract and pull the chromosomes to the poles. There are other theories, however, to explain the movement of the chromosomes during anaphase. One such theory is that the chromosomes are pushed apart by the elongation of spindle fibers between the poles. It is also known that a chromosome will not move during anaphase unless its centromere is at-

Figure 10–3 Daniel Mazia of the University of California, outstanding authority on cell division. (Courtesy of Dr. Mazia.)

tached to a spindle fiber. More research is necessary to clearly explain how this movement occurs. The separation of the duplicated chromosomes marks the beginning of nuclear division which is known as *karyokinesis*. By late anaphase, the entire cell begins to divide—that is, a cleavage furrow is formed at the center of the spindle.

Telophase. The last phase of division is marked by the cleavage of the cell into daughter cells, *cytokinesis*. Usually, some of the spindle fibers are still visible between the cells. The tightly coiled chromosomes now begin to relax and uncoil. The nuclear membrane is reconstituted, and the nucleolus is formed. Each cell has received one pair of centrioles in the division process. The aster and spindle fibers disappear, and centrioles are usually duplicated during late telophase. These events complete a normal mitotic cycle, and the two daughter cells thus formed have the characteristics of the interphase condition.

Mitotic cell division in animals usually requires from thirty minutes to several hours. In mammalian cells the time is generally about one hour. In mouse spleen cells in culture, prophase lasts 20–35 minutes, metaphase 6–15 minutes, anaphase 8–14 minutes, and telophase 9–26 minutes (from Hughes, *The Mitotic Cycle*, Academic Press, New York, 1952). Prophase and telophase in general take longer than metaphase or anaphase; in many cases anaphase may be extremely short (less than one minute).

Mitosis in Plants

One significant difference between plant and animal cells is, of course, the rigid plant cell wall. In the animal cell, cleavage of the flexible cell membrane permits the formation of two daughter cells. But how are new cell walls formed in plants? Small cell plates form in the mid-spindle region during anaphase and are believed to originate from the endoplasmic reticulum. These coalesce to form part of the new cell wall separating the daughter cells. Another difference between the mitotic apparatus of plant and animal cells is the absence of astral fibers in plants. Furthermore, most plant cells do not possess centrioles. The question of the formation and function of the spindle fibers in higher plants is still largely unanswered. The mitotic process in an onion-root tip is shown in Figure 10–4.

MEIOSIS

The cell divisions that produce gametes (eggs and sperms) in diploid organisms reduce the chromosome number to one-half that of a normal body cell. This process of meiosis is necessary to maintain a constant chromosome number within a species. Meiosis essentially includes two cell divisions with only one

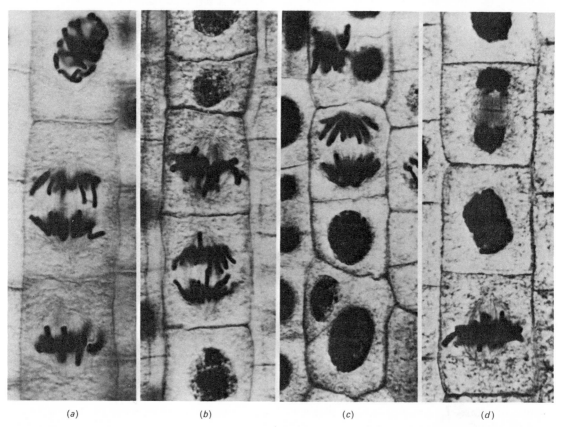

(a)   (b)   (c)   (d)

Figure 10–4   Sections of onion-root tip showing various stages of mitosis. (*a*) From the top: prophase, anaphase, metaphase. (*b*) From the top: two daughter cells, metaphase, anaphase, early prophase. (*c*) Just above center: anaphase. (*d*) Near the top: telophase. (Courtesy of Carolina Biological Supply Company.)

duplication of the chromosomes. In the first division (meiosis I) the duplicated chromosomes are separated into two diploid cells, whereas the second division (meiosis II) separates these two cells into four haploid cells (Figure 10–5). Prophase II and metaphase II are usually very brief. The chromosomes are observed to be double-stranded about midway through a prolonged prophase I. Also at this stage homologous chromosomes pair—that is, each chromosome approaches its homologous partner, and they become attached along their full lengths. This process is called *synapsis* and forms the basis for all subsequent meiotic events. Because one member of each chromosome pair in an individual comes from the mother and the other from the father, we speak of the pairing of maternal and paternal chromosomes. Since each chromosome duplicates itself they appear as double-stranded structures; each strand is a *chromatid*. The synapsed, duplicated chromosomes are called *tetrads* because the four chromatids are together, side by side (Figure 10–6). The centromeres apparently have not duplicated at this point, and each pair of chromatids therefore shares only one centromere. During synapsis, certain segments of the chromatids may *cross over* and exchange genetic information. That is, chromatids can break and recombine with parts of other homologous chromatids. The results of one crossover in one pair of gametic chromosomes are shown in Figure 10–7. In the diagram, the letters represent units of heredity (commonly called *genes*). A comparison of crossover and noncrossover chromosomes illustrates how new combinations of genes may be formed in gametic chromosomes. Though the genetic significance of this process will be discussed in Chapter 11, it should be noted here that this aspect of meiosis allows for the shuffling and recombination of the offspring's grandparental genes. The ability of an organism to adapt to its environment depends in part on crossover of chromosomes and recombination of genes. Crossovers can actually be observed in the chromosomes as they coil and shorten prior

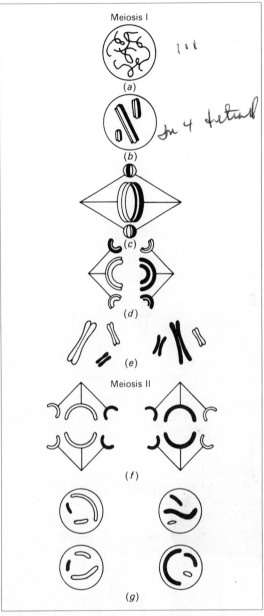

Figure 10–5 Meiosis in a nucleus containing three pairs of chromosomes. (*a*) Early prophase. (*b*) Prophase with duplicated and synapsed homologous chromosomes. (*c*) Metaphase. (*d*) Anaphase—tetrads separate. (*e*) Two diploid nuclei containing one homologous chromosome of each pair and its duplicate. (*f*) Anaphase—chromatids separate. (*g*) Four haploid nuclei each containing three chromosomes. (Redrawn from Fig. 24.11, p. 385, in *Principles of Biology*, Third Edition, by W. Gordon Whaley *et al.*, Harper & Row, 1964.)

327

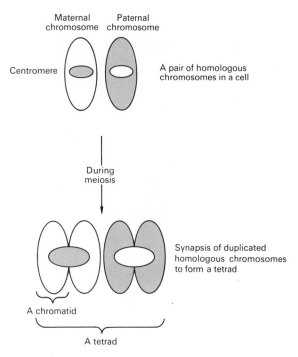

Maternal chromosome   Paternal chromosome

Centromere

A pair of homologous chromosomes in a cell

During meiosis

Synapsis of duplicated homologous chromosomes to form a tetrad

A chromatid

A tetrad

Figure 10–6 A pair of homologous chromosomes in the early stages of meiosis.

to metaphase I. Near the end of prophase, the chromosomes show interesting figures resembling crosses or chains (Figure 10–8). *Chiasmata* are the visible evidence for these crossover events.

At metaphase I the chromosomes are aligned on the equatorial plane and will segregate at random; each half of each tetrad has an equal chance of going to either daughter cell. The segregation possibilities for the chromosomes at anaphase I should be stressed. If two pairs of chromosomes are involved, four possible chromosomal combinations can result (Figure 10–9a). When three pairs of chromosomes are present, eight different combinations are possible (Figure 10–9b). In humans, with their 23 pairs of chromosomes, there are 8,388,608 possible combinations. The segre-

gation possibilities for an organism can be readily computed by raising the base number 2 (the number of chromosomes in a pair) to an exponential power equal to the number of pairs of chromosomes in the species. For example:

$$2^2 = 4 \,;\, 2^3 = 8 \,;\, 2^{23} = 8,388,608$$

Again, it is strictly a matter of chance which half of each tetrad will go to each daughter cell. We must assume, therefore, that each combination has an equal chance or probability of moving to either daughter cell. This point will be stressed again in the chapter on heredity, but it is necessary to understand this random segregation of chromosomes if we are to understand the fundamental principles of heredity.

In anaphase I, the tetrad separates between the synapsed chromosomes (Figures 10–5b and 10–9), and therefore an original chromosome with its duplicate moves to each pole. The chromosome number has essentially been halved at this point since a maternal chromosome and its duplicate went to one daughter cell, and a paternal chromosome and its duplicate went to the other daughter cell. Remember, however, that since crossovers have occurred some parts of the chromosomes have been exchanged. At anaphase II, the centromere of each double-stranded chromosome divides, and the original chromosome and its duplicate are finally separated with each chromatid moving to a separate cell. Each gamete thus receives a chromosome from the original homologous pair. This is important because a fertilized egg then contains a member of each homologous pair—one from the egg and one from the sperm.

The meiotic events that occur in males to produce sperm are called *spermatogenesis* and the production of eggs in females is known as *oögenesis* (Figure 10–10). Each stage of division is labeled in sequence for both meiosis

328

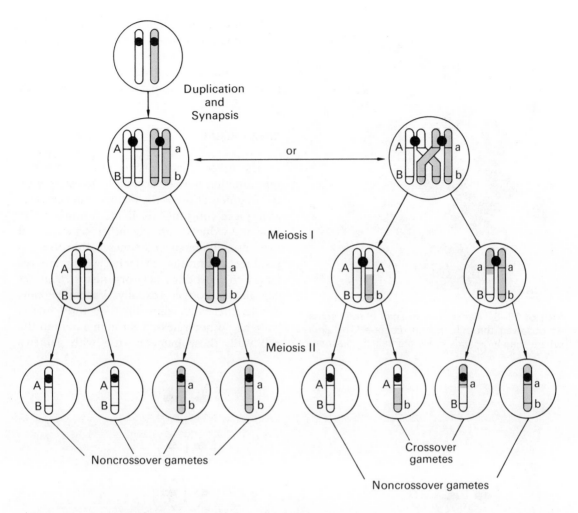

Figure 10-7 Comparison of the chromosomal changes that occur in noncrossover and crossover during synapsis of homologous chromosomes. Crossover occurs in almost all chromosomes.

I and meiosis II. In this diagram the chromosome number for man is used, but the $2n$ and n may represent the specific number for any species. Note that prophase II may be very short or absent entirely. The major difference between spermatogenesis and oögenesis is the production of polar bodies (polocytes) in oögenesis. A *polar body* is simply a packet of chromosomes extruded from the nucleus along with a very small amount of cytoplasm. This process conserves the egg cytoplasm and its

protein-synthesizing ribosomes which will be essential to the developing embryo.

REPRODUCTION IN PROTISTS

A variety of reproductive processes occur in the protists including fragmentation, fission, spore production, and sexuality. Fragmentation reproduction occurs when a portion of an organism becomes separated from the main

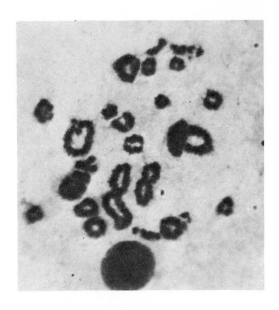

Figure 10–8 Crossovers in snail chromosomes as observed through the microscope. The areas where the chromatids cross are called *chiasmata*.

body and develops into a new organism. Fission, common in one-celled forms, is a process in which an organism splits into nearly equal halves. Spores are cells formed in an asexual process which are capable of giving rise to a new organism.

GREEN ALGAE

In the green alga *Ulothrix* (Figure 10–11), reproduction may be accomplished simply by the fragmentation of the filament; in this case, each piece continues to divide forming many new individuals. On the other hand, a cell may also divide several times within itself to produce swimming *zoöspores* which are released to reproduce new organisms. *Ulothrix* can also reproduce sexually. Vegetative cells divide internally many times to form motile gametes. When released through a pore in the cell wall, these gametes fuse with gametes

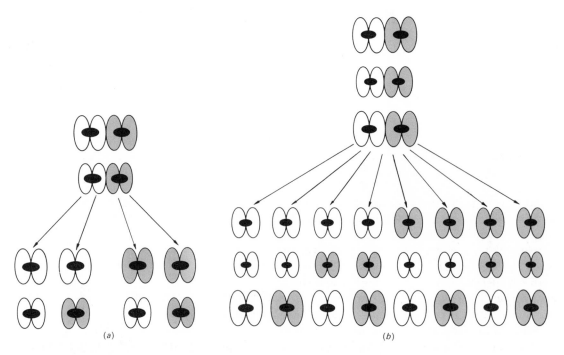

Figure 10–9 The possibilities of chromosomal combinations that can result at anaphase I. (*a*) Organism with two pairs of chromosomes. (*b*) Organism with three pairs of chromosomes.

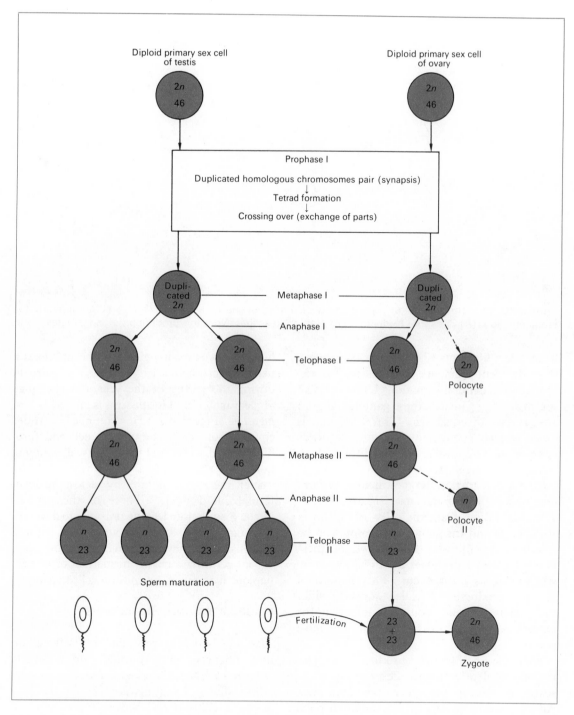

Figure 10–10 Process of meiosis as it occurs in human males (spermatogenesis) and in females (oögenesis). The fertilization of an egg by a sperm to form a zygote is also noted.

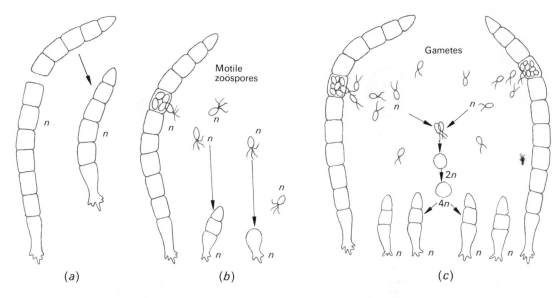

Figure 10–11 Three types of reproduction occurring in the green alga *Ulothrix* (Chlorophyta). (*a*) Fragmentation. (*b*) Zoöspore formation. (*c*) Haplontic sexual. Note the production of isogametes.

from other filaments. The fusion of gametes from different filaments provides for the exchange of genetic information. Unlike typical sperm and egg gametes, these gametes (Figure 10–11c) are of equal size. This condition is called *isogamy* (*iso* meaning *same* or *equal*) as opposed to *heterogamy*, the condition where different-sized gametes are involved. The resulting *zygote* then undergoes meiosis to form four new haploid organisms (Figure 10–11c). The vegetative filament cells of *Ulothrix* are haploid and the gametes therefore can be produced by mitosis. The fusion of these haploid gametes produces a diploid zygote in which meiosis must occur. This pattern of sexual reproduction is called *haplontic* since the alga is haploid. You will note that the pattern is opposite to that of man and most plants.

A discussion of sexual reproduction in algae is not complete without a description of the sexual process in the green alga *Spirogyra*. An outstanding feature of this common pond scum is the spiral chloroplast in each cell and, like *Ulothrix*, the filament cells are normally haploid. Although no morphological distinction can be made as to the sex of a particular filament, two physiologically different "sexes," usually designated as + and −, pair up during the spring of the year and exchange nuclear material. This process is known as *conjugation* (Figure 10–12). Protoplasmic tubes emerge from each conjugating cell and fuse. The walls dissolve and the donor-cell contents flow into the recipient. After fusion of the nuclei, the zygote divides by meiosis to form four haploid nuclei. Three of the haploid nuclei disintegrate leaving only one to develop. A tough shell forms around this haploid nucleus and it may lie dormant for some time. Upon germination the formation of a new haploid filament is by mitotic cell division.

FLAGELLATES AND PROTOZOANS

Euglena divides by reproducing its flagellum and nucleus and splitting longitudinally (Figure 10–13a). The ciliated *Paramecium* may either divide by transverse fission (Figure 10–13b) or undergo a specialized type of sexual reproduction in which nuclear material is exchanged between two individuals. This process is also known as conjugation even though it differs in many respects from that of

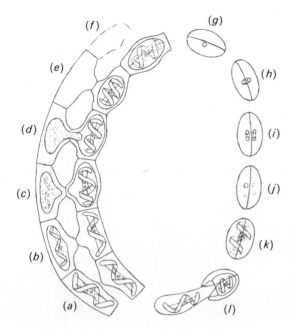

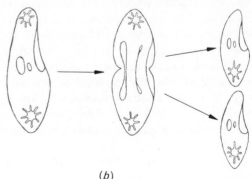

only the micronucleus. The micronucleus next divides twice to produce four nuclei. Three of these disintegrate and the remaining nucleus divides unequally into macro and micro portion. At this point the micro portions (sometimes called male portions) are exchanged across the cell membranes and the micro portions now fuse with the macro portions. This marks the end of the conjugant phase, and the *Paramecia* move apart to complete their reproductive divisions (exconjugant stage). Following this fusion and separation three equal nuclear divisions occur. Of the eight nuclei formed in each *Paramecium*, four will become new macronuclei, three disappear, and one becomes the new micronucleus. In two divisions the macronuclei are distributed into four new individuals; the micronucleus divides each time. Thus two conjugating *Paramecia* produce eight offspring following the exchange of genetic material (Figure 10–14).

Figure 10–12 Sexuality in *Spirogyra*—conjugation. Parts (*a*) through (*f*) show the formation and fusion of protoplasmic tubes between cells of adjacent filaments through which the contents of the donor cell flow into the recipient and form a zygote. Parts (*g*) through (*j*) represent the meiotic divisions that finally produce a single haploid nucleus. Parts (*k*) and (*l*) show the germination and production of a new filament by mitosis.

Spirogyra. Two individuals come together along their oral grooves (Figure 10–14). Each *Paramecium* contains two types of nuclei, a macronucleus and a micronucleus. The macronucleus of each organism disintegrates leaving

REPRODUCTION IN PLANTS

Both asexual and sexual reproduction occur in the plant kingdom. Asexual reproduction is very common in plants, and new individuals frequently arise from bulbs, runners, cuttings, and in some cases even leaves. Sexual reproduction in plants is part of a general life-cycle pattern which can be observed in all members of the plant kingdom. This pattern involves the alternation of a spore-producing (asexual)

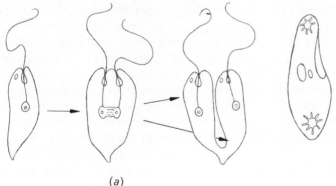

(*a*)   (*b*)

Figure 10–13 Examples of fission in Protozoa. (*a*) Longitudinal fission in *Euglena*. (*b*) Transverse fission in *Paramecium*.

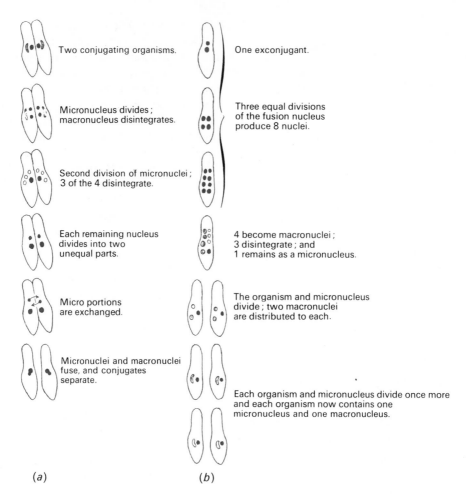

Two conjugating organisms.

One exconjugant.

Micronucleus divides; macronucleus disintegrates.

Three equal divisions of the fusion nucleus produce 8 nuclei.

Second division of micronuclei; 3 of the 4 disintegrate.

4 become macronuclei; 3 disintegrate; and 1 remains as a micronucleus.

Each remaining nucleus divides into two unequal parts.

The organism and micronucleus divide; two macronuclei are distributed to each.

Micro portions are exchanged.

Micronuclei and macronuclei fuse, and conjugates separate.

Each organism and micronucleus divide once more and each organism now contains one micronucleus and one macronucleus.

(a)

(b)

Figure 10–14 Conjugation in *Paramecium*. (*a*) Conjugant stage. (*b*) Exconjugant stage. Note that only one exconjugant is diagrammed.

stage with a gamete-producing (sexual) stage. Thus every plant undergoes a life cycle in which one phase of its existence is devoted to the production of spores and one phase involves the production of gametes. We speak of such a plan as an *alternation of generations*. The stage of the life cycle that produces spores is known as the *sporophyte*, a diploid plant, and that which produces gametes is called the *gametophyte*, a haploid plant (Figure 10–15).

In the progression from simple plants (byrophytes, such as mosses) to more complex plants (seed plants), a greater development of the sporophyte occurs. In the byrophytes the dominant stage of the life cycle is the green, leafy gametophyte. The sporophyte, on the other hand, is usually unable to make its own food and is therefore dependent on the gametophyte. The ferns have a life cycle in which the gametophyte and sporophyte are both capable of making food even though the sporophyte is much larger. In the seed plants, however, the gametophyte generation is reduced to a structure retained on the sporophyte. The gametophyte here is often only a few cells in number. Figure 10–16 shows in a general way the relationships between the gametophyte and sporophyte generations of four of the major plant groups.

It should be noted that the process of alternation of generations between the gametophyte and sporophyte can also be observed in some protists. For example, similar life cycles

334

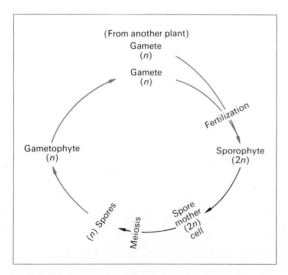

Figure 10–15 Stages in the life history of a plant.

can be found in the green algae but the dominant stage is the gametophyte.

MOSSES (BRYOPHYTES)

When we examine the reproductive patterns of the nonvascular metaphytes such as liverworts and mosses, we find that the life cycle actually involves two plants—the green, leafy gametophyte and the stalklike sporophyte

(Figure 10–17). There are both male and female gametophytes which have sex organs at the tips of their branches. The male sex organ is called the *antheridium* and produces motile sperms, whereas the female structure, an *archegonium*, produces eggs.

During a heavy dew or rain, the sperms move to the archegonium of a female plant and fertilize an egg. The resulting zygote divides to form a new 2n generation, the sporophyte. At the tip of the sporophyte a swollen organ known as the *sporangium* is produced. Usually, part of the old female archegonium is still present at the tip called the *calyptra*; this remnant soon dries out and gives the appearance of a "hairy cap." Certain cells within the sporangium, called *spore mother cells*, divide by meiosis to produce many haploid spores. The spores are released at maturity when the top, or *operculum*, pops off. The spores germinate in the soil and develop into long threads called *protonema*. Buds develop from the protonema and produce new male or female gametophytes. Thus the complete life cycle of the moss requires two interdependent generations. However, the gametophytes may spread by continuous growth or reproduce by asexual buds. The reproductive pattern in mosses is an example of a *diplohaplontic* life

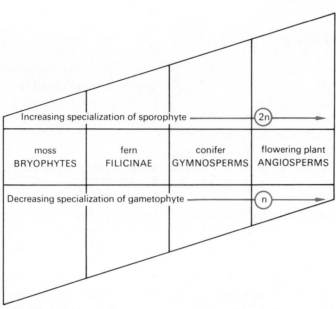

Figure 10–16 Relationships between the gametophyte and the sporophyte generations of four plants.

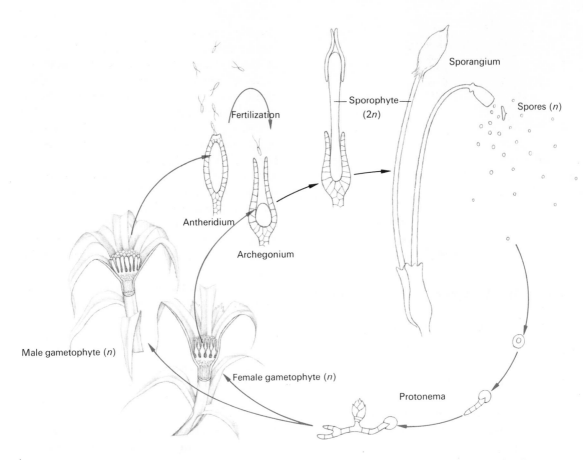

Figure 10–17 Life cycle of a moss. Spores are produced by meiosis in the sporangium and germinate as protonema. Gametes produced by the gametophytes fuse to form a sporophyte (2n). Colored arrows represent haploid stages.

cycle with alternating diploid and haploid generations.

FERNS

The simplest of the vascular metaphytes are the ferns. The basic alternation of generation life cycle is similar to that of the moss (Figure 10–18). The familiar green frond represents the sporophyte generation. Spores are produced by meiosis in small sporangia located in brown clusters called *sori* on the underside of the frond. When the spores are mature, the sporangium dries, opens, and the spores are literally thrown to the winds. Small, heart-shaped gametophyte plants develop from spores and possess both male and female

organs in archegonia and antheridia. Here, as in the moss, water is necessary for the transport of sperms to eggs. Even though the sporophyte stage is more predominant and independent in the fern than in the moss, the life cycle is still diplohaplontic.

SEED PLANTS—GYMNOSPERMS AND ANGIOSPERMS

In gymnosperms such as pine a period of two years is required to complete a reproductive cycle (Figure 10–19). Although the pine cycle described here extends through two seasons, many conifers such as spruce and fir complete their reproductive cycles in one season. The cycle begins with male, or *staminate*, cones and

336

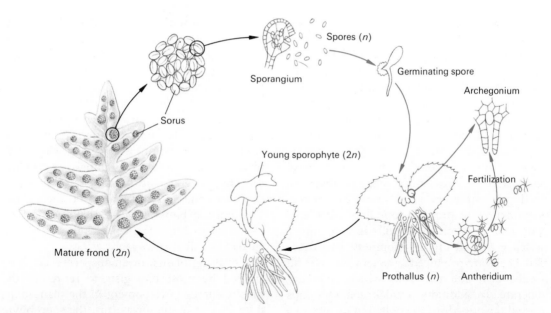

Figure 10–18 Life cycle of a typical fern. The sporophyte (2n) is the predominant generation. In contrast to the moss, the gametophyte is much reduced in size. Colored arrows represent haploid stages.

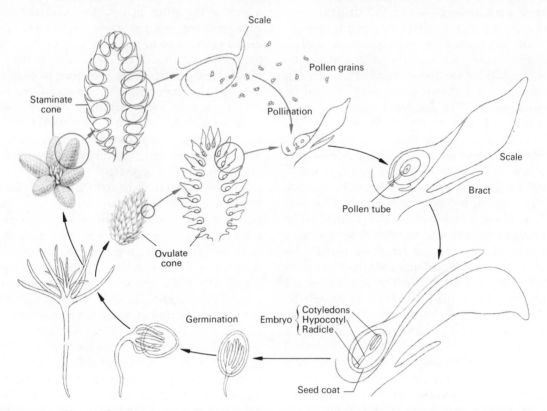

Figure 10–19 Life cycle of a typical conifer. Whereas two years are required to produce a mature seed in pine, in other conifers such as fir and spruce the cycle is completed in one season. Colored arrows represent haploid events.

female, or *ovulate*, cones. The staminate cones produce winged pollen grains that are carried by the wind to the larger, leafy ovulate cones. Each leaflike scale of the female cone develops two *ovules*, each of which contains a *megasporangium*. One megaspore cell divides by meiosis to produce multicelled female gametophytes (*n*) that produce several eggs in archegonia.

Each bractlike structure on the staminate cone, a microsporophyll, bears a pair of *microsporangia*. Each microspore mother cell, produced within the microsporangia, undergoes meiosis to produce four haploid microspores. Each microspore will develop into a pollen grain. In this development two functional cells are produced, a generative cell and a tube cell, and two cells which soon degenerate. In addition, a thick coat develops around the outside of the pollen grain and two winglike structures form. At this point we should note that a pollen grain is actually a male gametophyte—a haploid structure, reduced to only a few cells in most gymnosperms.

In the process of pollination the pollen grains settle between the scales near the central axis of the female cone. The tube cell elongates and slowly grows into the female gametophyte. The generative cell at this time divides into two sperms which enter the tube cell and migrate with the tube to the archegonium. This process may require approximately a year to complete. When an egg is reached, the pollen tube bursts to release the sperms. One sperm fertilizes the egg and a new sporophyte generation (2*n*) is formed. The tissue of the surrounding ovule develops into a hardened coat and the fertilized egg divides to produce a multicellular *embryo*. The developing embryo is nourished by the food stored in the cells of the old female gametophyte. The embryo with its associated food and the hardened coat is known as a *seed* (Figure 10–19). Such a structure has a distinct survival advantage. For example, if it is released from the plant under dry conditions, it can remain dormant until water is available for germination. Furthermore, a newly formed individual

(an embryo) with a source of food and protective seed coat has a definite survival advantage over other plants in most environments. Seed plants are the dominant plants on the earth today.

The female cone dries during the second year and the scales finally open to release the mature seeds. In many conifers, part of the seed coat extends into a thin wing which aids in dispersal. The mature embryo within the seed has several embryonic leaves known as *cotyledons* and an embryonic root, the *radicle*. The portion between these structures which elongates to carry the cotyledons to the soil surface is called the *hypocotyl*.

Flowering plants, or angiosperms, are considered by most biologists to represent the most complex development in the plant kingdom and, as in gymnosperms, the sporophyte generation (diploid) has assumed complete dominance over the gametophyte. The gametes, as in other plants, are produced by gametophytes, but the gametophytes are reduced even more in the angiosperms than in the gymnosperms. Moreover, the gametophytes (and gametes) are produced in highly specialized structures, the *flowers*. Flowers which contain both staminate (male) and pistillate (female) structures are termed *perfect* flowers (Figure 10–20); conversely, if the flower contains only staminate or pistillate organs, it is called *imperfect*.

The small green *sepals* and the fragile, often brightly colored *petals* are attached to the flower base or *receptacle*. The *pistil* which contains the basal ovary may sit above the receptacle (superior ovary) or actually be embedded within it (inferior ovary). The apple is an example of a fruit developed from an inferior ovary. The outer flesh of the apple is formed from the ovary wall. *Stamens* have *anthers* containing microsporangia in which microspores are produced. The microspores then develop into pollen grains, and each pollen grain contains two haploid nuclei or sperms. At maturity, the pollen grains are released from the anther of one plant and carried to the pistil

338

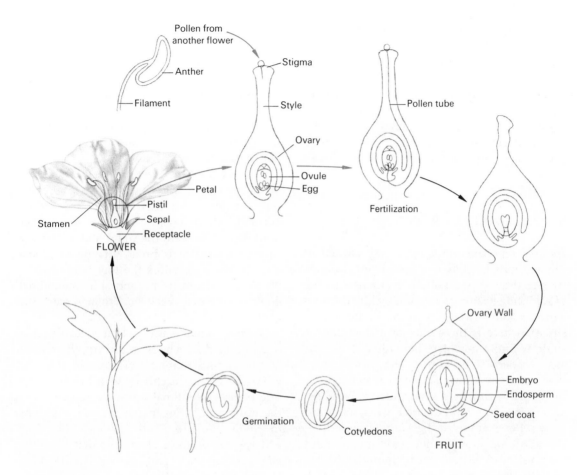

Figure 10–20 Longitudinal section through a typical perfect flower (containing both male and female organs). The fruit develops from the structures indicated. Colored arrows represent haploid events.

of another, usually by wind or insects, where some land on the stigma. Next, a long pollen tube grows down through the style of the pistil to the ovary where fertilization occurs. While pollen formation was occurring in the anthers, megaspores were developing in the ovary. This development results in an ovule containing eight haploid nuclei, three of which are functional—an *egg* and two *polar nuclei*. When the pollen tube reaches the ovule the sperms are released. One sperm unites with the egg to form a diploid zygote, and the other sperm fuses with the polar nuclei to form a $3n$ or triploid nucleus (Figure 10–20). This triploid nucleus is the beginning of the seed *endosperm* which will provide food for the developing

embryo. The resulting embryo, endosperm, and seed coat (formed from the ovule wall) constitute the angiosperm seed. In addition, the ovary wall usually develops into a thickened structure that may be hard or fleshy. The developed ovary wall with the seed or seeds inside is known as a *fruit*. The fruit may assist in dispersal of the seeds, for example, when animals eat fruits or when sticky fruits become attached to fur or clothing. The flower and the fruit, along with the enclosed seeds that contain nourishment for the developing embryo, provide a highly efficient method of reproduction for the angiosperms.

Seeds may remain dormant for long periods; this can be especially advantageous if a seed is in an unfavorable environment. In some plants, chemical or physical changes in the seed or to the seed coat must take place before germination can occur. When a seed germinates, water is taken in and metabolic activity (which remains at a very low level in the dormant condition) greatly increases. This results in cell division and embryonic growth thereby producing a new plant (Figures 10–19 and 10–20).

REPRODUCTION IN ANIMALS

Asexual reproduction is extremely limited in higher animals. It is true that many animals such as the starfish, crab, or lizard are capable of replacing lost or injured body parts through a process known as *regeneration*. An interesting situation here is the ability of a starfish arm to grow into a complete individual if the cut arm contains a portion of the central disc. The common brown *Planaria*, a small, free-living flatworm, may also undergo both regeneration and reproduction when cut into pieces. For example, if the worm is cut in half, the head end grows a new tail and the hind portion forms a new head. Sponges display a high degree of asexual reproduction. If a sponge is cut into very small pieces, each piece will develop into a new individual. Sponges also reproduce by *budding*, a process in which a new individual grows directly as an outgrowth from the parent. In addition, special cells may form gametes to provide sexual reproduction. Throughout the animal kingdom, sexual reproduction is very similar in mechanism—that is, the union of a sperm with a larger egg to form a zygote.

Coelenterates (*Hydra,* jellyfish, and sea anemones) also reproduce by budding as well as sexually. The free-swimming jellyfish *Aurelia* is the sexual stage or *medusa* of an interesting life history. Although the jellyfish shows alternation of sexual and asexual stages,

the body cells of both stages are diploid. After fertilization of gametes in the water, the zygote develops into a flat, ciliated larva called a *planula*. The planula swims about for a time and finally attaches itself to a surface where small buds are produced asexually. These buds, known as *ephyrae*, look like a stack of saucers on the sessile *strobila* and develop into new medusae (Figure 10–21).

The sea anemone, which primarily reproduces sexually, adds a unique type of asexual reproduction to our discussion. The anemones normally are attached to rocks or some other solid objects beneath the water and may move very slowly on their broad attachment pedal disc. In some instances the foot may actually "walk away from itself" and split the animal down the center. Each half then repairs the damage and lives.

In most aquatic invertebrates fertilization occurs outside the body, requiring the release of tremendous numbers of gametes into the water. In the sea urchins which live in ocean tide pools, one animal releasing gametes into the water will "trigger" all the other urchins in the tide pool to release gametes. The eggs and sperms produce chemicals that keep the gametes together and ensure fertilization. Recent evidence indicates that the gelatinous egg coat contains a chemical which reacts with sperms causing them to gather in masses around the egg. Thus we see two mechanisms that aid in the success of external fertilization, synchronous gamete release and the production of chemicals to increase the probability of fertilization.

A few invertebrates and all land vertebrates with the exception of the amphibians utilize methods of direct internal fertilization. The flatworm *Planaria* has a penis through which sperms are transferred into the vagina of another worm (Figure 10–22). *Planaria* is *monoecious* or hermaphroditic, that is, each worm possesses both male and female organs. *Dioecious*, on the other hand, refers to separate

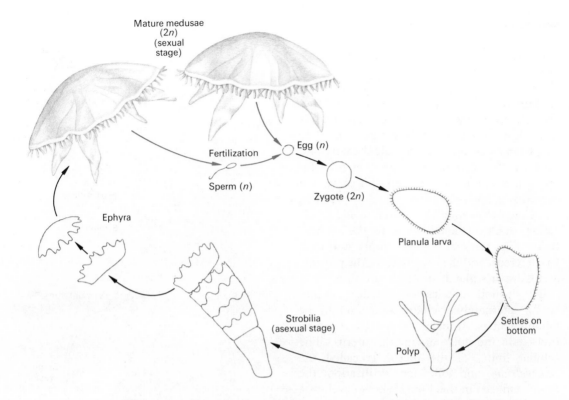

Figure 10–21 Life cycle of the scyphozoan jellyfish *Aurelia*. Colored arrows represent sexual stage.

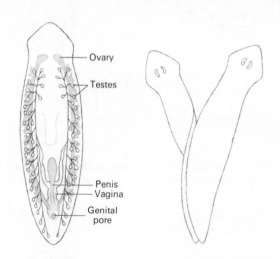

Figure 10–22 Internal fertilization process of *Planaria*. A reciprocal fertilization is accomplished in this manner.

sexes. Although both male and female organs are present in *Planaria*, self-fertilization does not occur.

Amphibians such as frogs and salamanders, which must return to water for reproduction, do not possess a penis. During mating, the male sits astride the back of the female and deposits sperms as the eggs are released. In these animals the urinary, intestinal, and reproductive tracts all come together to form a common canal called the *cloaca* from which the sperms and eggs are released. Birds and lizards also have a cloaca and, since there is no water carrier, fertilization must be accomplished by direct apposition of the cloacal openings of the male and female. In mammals and most reptiles, sperms are introduced through a penis.

The reproductive structures and physiology of the human will be discussed as an example of mammalian reproduction. In the male (Figure 10–23) the sperm-producing tubules of each testis unite to form the epididymis which leaves the testis as the vas deferens. The vas deferens enters the abdominal cavity and unites with the urethra, a common tube for the genital and urinary systems. Three pairs of accessory glands—seminal vesicles, prostate, and Cowper's—enter the system to add lubricating and nutritional fluids to the seminal fluids. The seminal vesicles empty into each vas deferens, and the secretions of the prostate and Cowper's glands enter the urethra.

The paired ovaries of females (Figure 10–24) alternately discharge an ovum into the fallopian tubes. At the junction of the fallopian tubes is a muscular organ, the uterus. The cellular lining of the uterus is called the *endometrium*, and following fertilization, the zygote embeds in this lining which develops a rich blood supply. The females of most species of mammals undergo *estrus*—cyclic periods of egg production and sexual receptivity to the male. Mammals differ in the number of estrus cycles that may occur. The English fox, for example, is monoestrus and breeds only once each year. On the other hand, guinea pigs, rats, and rabbits are polyestrus, with estrus occurring every four to five days until conception occurs.

In the human female the sexual cycle, *menstrual cycle,* differs from estrus in other animals in that there is no distinct period of male receptivity, and at the end of the monthly cycle, the cellular lining of the uterus is shed, accompanied by bleeding. If fertilization occurs the lining and the embyro are maintained for approximately nine months. The normal menstrual cycle, which requires approximately 28 days, is illustrated in Figure 10–25 and is summarized in the following paragraphs. The

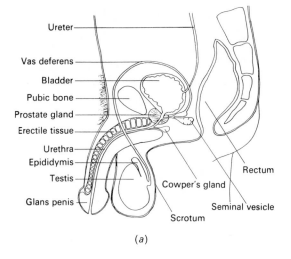

(a)

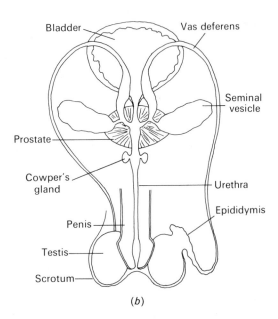

(b)

Figure 10–23 Reproductive system in human male. (a) Side view. (b) Front view.

events that accompany fertilization and interrupt the menstrual cycle are also noted.

1 The ovary is stimulated by a follicle-stimulating hormone (FSH) from the anterior pituitary to produce a follicle which

342

in turn produces an ovum (egg); hormones from the hypothalamus of the brain trigger the release of gonadotropic hormones (FSH and LH).

2   This follicle secretes the female hormone estrogen into the bloodstream which inhibits FSH and stimulates the production of luteinizing hormone (LH).

3   Estrogen also stimulates the lining of the uterus to proliferate and vascularize in preparation for the implanting of the fertilized ovum.

4   After about fourteen days the mature ovum is ejected from the follicle into the fallopian tube. This is called ovulation and occurs as the concentration of FSH is dropping and LH is increasing.

5   The anterior pituitary continues to secrete LH which acts to change the follicle into a yellow body known as the *corpus luteum.* The corpus luteum secretes another hormone, *progesterone,* which continues the development of the uterine lining and maintains it throughout pregnancy. This hormone is also necessary for proper implantation of a fertilized ovum in the uterus. (Estrogen is also secreted by this body but in lesser amounts than those secreted by the follicle.) Progesterone inhibits the production of FSH which usually triggers a new cycle. High levels of progesterone in the absence of fertilization also inhibit LH production.

6   When fertilization does not occur and LH declines, the corpus luteum degenerates, stops secreting progesterone, and the uterine lining is shed—a process known as *menstruation.* This phase of the cycle requires about four or five days.

7   Lowered levels of progesterone permit the stimulating centers in the hypothalamus to again stimulate the pituitary to produce FSH, thereby initiating a new cycle.

8   If fertilization and implantation of the fertilized egg does occur, the corpus luteum continues to secrete progesterone which maintains the uterine lining, inhibits ovulation, and prevents the uterine muscles from contracting.

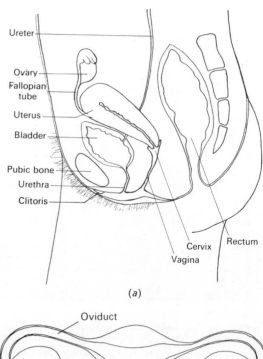

(a)

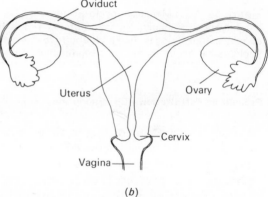

(b)

Figure 10–24   Reproductive system in human female. (*a*) Side view. (*b*) Front view.

The menstrual cycle is apparently controlled by the orderly, successive relationships between four hormones: FSH, estrogen, LH, and progesterone. The first two, FSH and estrogen, function together in the beginning of the cycle, whereas LH and progesterone take over later. Here is an excellent example of a hormonal control system with positive and negative feedback features (Figure 10–26).

343

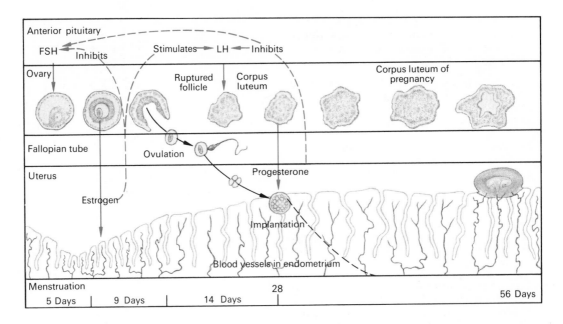

Figure 10–25 Menstrual cycle in humans. The activities of four major areas are correlated: anterior pituitary, ovary, fallopian tube, and uterus. If implantation does not occur, the corpus luteum degenerates and the uterine lining is shed after about 28 days, as shown by the black broken line. When fertilization and implantation occur, the lining is maintained to nourish the embryo until birth.

Preventing Fertilization—Contraception

An awareness of the increasing world population has brought about increased interest in efficient ways to prevent fertilization. Many techniques are now used to prevent conception. Two of the most common are birth-control pills and the intrauterine device (IUD). Perhaps the most widely used and reliable method is "the pill." An understanding of the menstrual cycle and its related hormones allowed for the development of a way to control the ovulation phase of the cycle. The action of birth-control pills inhibits the secretion of FSH and LH (necessary for ovulation) through daily doses of progesterone and estrogen or compounds similar to these sex hormones. Ovulation is thus blocked, and the uterine lining is maintained. In general, pills are taken from the fifth through the twenty-fourth day of the cycle. When they are discontinued, the uterine lining is shed in menstruation. Undesirable side effects from the use of birth-control pills have been noted by some women. As a result, a variety of different pill systems has been developed. Each system is a variant of the basic system described above. Selection and use of hormone contraceptives require the initial supervision of a trained physician.

Various devices, usually a plastic coil or loop, are designed for insertion into the uterus to prevent conception. Although it is not known how the IUD works, it is believed to act as a stimulus to the uterine lining which prevents implantation.

The more common contraceptive techniques before the days of the pill and the IUD were the "rhythm method," rubber condoms, and diaphragms, often used with a vaginal spermicide. The rhythm method is simply the abstinence from intercourse during the time when ovulation is expected to occur. This method, however, is unreliable, since it is based on prediction of the time of ovulation. Ovulation time is not perfectly constant, even

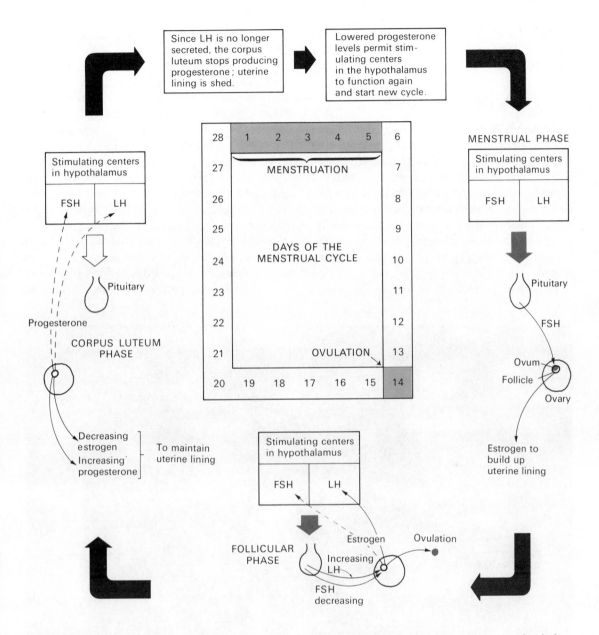

Figure 10–26 Sequence of events in the human menstrual cycle. Solid arrows indicate stimulation, and broken arrows represent inhibition.

in women with regular menstrual cycles, while it generally occurs on about the fourteenth day of the menstrual cycle, it can take place at any time.

Sterilization techniques have now been developed. For men the most common method is vasectomy, or the cutting and tying of the sperm-carrying vas deferens of each testis. Minor surgery operations can also be performed on women in which the fallopian tubes are cut and ligated. These surgical techniques are probably the most effective methods of achieving contraception. Surgical sterilization is not reliably reversible, although progress is being made in improving the restoration of fertility after vasectomy or tubal ligation.

CYCLES AND REPRODUCTION

Most animal (and plant) reproduction occurs in a cyclic pattern—that is, it takes place during a definite breeding season each year. Moreover, a cycle of internal changes associated with the reproduction process occurs in each member of a species. Thus internal changes occur in organisms preparatory to the breeding period or season and these changes often can be correlated with changes in the external environment.

A type of periodicity related to the phases of the moon, lunar cycles, can be observed in the reproduction of several animals. The small grunion fish of the southern California coast swim onto the beaches during the high tides of the spring and summer months to lay their eggs in the sand (Figure 10–27). The females, which are five to eight inches long, bury their tails in the wet sand to deposit their eggs while male grunion lying nearby release sperms that fertilize the eggs. The fish then are carried back to sea by the next waves. The most intriguing aspect of this reproductive behavior is the grunion's unerring sense of the tidal cycle. The tides that bring the fish onto the beach are produced at the new moon and full moon. Since tides are influenced by the gravitational pull of the moon and sun,

Figure 10–27   Grunion spawning on a California beach. (Moody Institute of Science; California Academy of Sciences.)

346

the higher water occurs during conjunction and opposition. Conjunction is when the moon is between the sun and the earth (new moon), whereas in opposition the earth is between the sun and the moon (full moon). In addition to sensing the exact time of the spring tides, the grunion must also deposit their eggs below the highest water. This will ensure that the high water of the next tidal cycle will release the young from the sand and carry them back into the sea. Predictably, the grunion swim onto the sand on the nights following the peak of the spring tides.

Another case of animal reproduction related to lunar phases is that of the annelid Palolo worms of Samoa and the West Indies (Figure 10–28). These segmented worms live in burrows in the coral reefs and consist of two parts, an asexual anterior segment and a postanal, sexual portion. In the Samoan species the posterior sexual segments break away and swim to the surface during the early morning of the first and second days of the last quarter of the October-November moon. The sexual segments swim for several hours on the surface and finally burst, releasing gametes into the sea; by morning, the surface water is soupy with the gametes and the spent segments. The asexual segments remaining in the burrow produce new sexual segments. The Atlantic species on Bermuda, however, release their gametes in May and June. Thus the monthly reproductive cycles of these two species are similar, yet the yearly time is different. Most investigators believe that the phase of the moon is simply one aspect of the reproductive regulatory mechanism; some correlations have also been found with regard to ocean turbidity and wave action.

Many birds and mammals breed either in the spring or the fall of the year. Deer and elk, for example, breed in the late fall while mating occurs in the varying hare in March or April. Charles Lyman of Harvard University has shown that the longer days of spring are responsible for estrus in the female hare and the development of the testes in the male. In certain breeds of sheep in the northern hem-

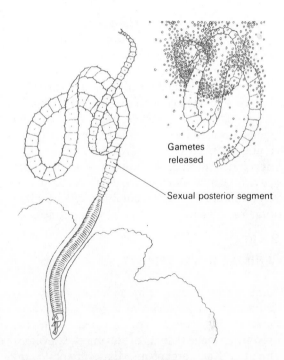

Gametes released

Sexual posterior segment

Figure 10–28 Palolo worm releasing gametes.

isphere, the shorter days of fall produce estrus in the females and increase sperm production in the males. In cases such as the hare and the sheep the length of day must act as a trigger mechanism to bring about internal changes which determine that reproduction will occur at a specific time each year. Apparently these internal clocks "recognize" the duration of individual photoperiods which ultimately produce an accumulative effect—the breeding time.

Finally we might ask why are rhythmic and cyclic activities, especially in reproduction, important to organisms? Certainly when all members of a species are under the control of similar biological clocks and hence are capable of breeding at the same time, the probability of fertilization is greatly increased. For a particular species of plant, pollen and eggs would reach maturation at the same time. Animals such as worms or starfish living in the vast expanses of the ocean must produce their gametes at exactly the same time or the chance of fertilization is greatly reduced. For most vertebrates the cyclic events leading up to mating have a preparatory effect for the vital final event of fertilization. Courtship may even be a part of the reproductive cycles of some animals in which elaborate behavior may be used to attract a mate. Reproductive or breeding cycles therefore must be generally viewed as activities that ensure a greater probability of survival for organisms. The synchronization of internal mechanisms with rhythmic environmental phenomena such as light and temperature provides a common synchronization for all members of a particular species.

ANIMAL DEVELOPMENT

The study of development, embryology, includes two major areas, *descriptive* and *experimental*. Descriptive studies deal with the visible changes that occur during the development of an organism. Experimental embryology, on the other hand, investigates the cellular mechanisms that cause or control these visible changes. For example, what determines the future of a particular cell? Why does one cell become a muscle cell while a nearby cell develops into a connective-tissue cell? Why is a specific number of cells produced in one region of an organism? Why does development of one structure begin only after another structure is produced? Many experiments have been performed in attempts to answer these and other questions of development.

DESCRIPTIVE EMBRYOLOGY

We will first briefly outline the descriptive embryology of the starfish, frog, and human which represent three distinct patterns of development. These will introduce most of the basic principles of embryological development.

The Starfish

A relatively uncomplicated example of the development of a fertilized egg into a multicellular organism is the starfish. The early cleavage of the starfish zygote is complete and equal—that is, the entire egg cleaves at each division. The first stage of development is characterized by a series of rapid mitotic divisions in which 2, 4, 8, 16, and 32 cells are produced (Figure 10–29). Soon a solid ball of cells, the *morula*, is formed. After many more divisions, this ball of ciliated cells develops a central cavity, the *blastocoel*, which is indicative of the "hollow ball" stage or *blastula* (Figure 10–30).

Shortly after this formation, an area of the blastula wall begins to push into the blastocoel, similar to the effect produced when one sticks his finger into a balloon or tennis ball. This invagination of cells is the beginning of the *gastrula* stage. The process of gastrulation produces a new cavity called the *archenteron* or primitive gut and leaves an opening in the wall, the *blastopore*. The old blastocoel is pushed ahead of this advancing invagination and gradually disappears. The two cellular layers produced by gastrulation are the *ectoderm* (outer layer) and *endoderm* (inner layer). A middle layer known as the *mesoderm* is next produced by a proliferation of cells from the ectoderm and endoderm. Animals showing this type of development are termed *triploblastic* and all tissues and organs of the adult animal will arise from these three primary germ layers. In vertebrates, for example, the ectoderm gives rise to the epidermis and nervous system. Mesodermal structures include the skeleton, dermis of the skin, blood, muscles, connective tissues, and most of the excretory and reproductive systems. Endodermal derivatives constitute the lining of the digestive and respiratory tracts and the urinary bladder.

Following gastrulation in starfish, a primitive gut forms which has a mouth, stomach, and anus (the anus is formed in the region of the blastopore). At this point ciliated bands form on three pairs of lateral lobes and transform the embryo into a free-moving, feeding larva called a *bipinnaria*. Later, this bilateral bipinnaria larva develops long, ciliated lobes and

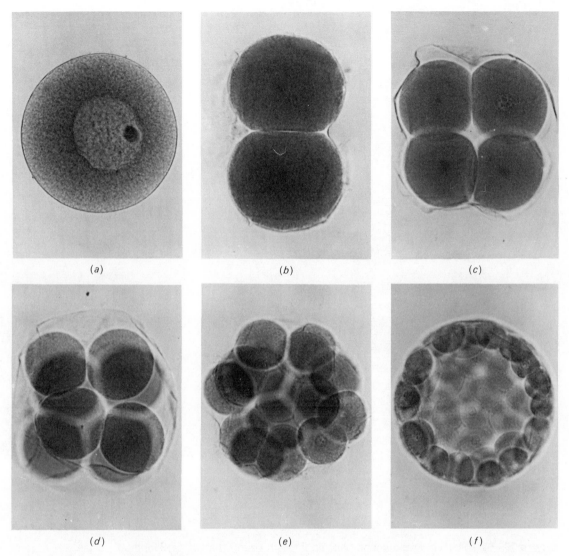

Figure 10–29 Starfish development, early cleavage stages. (*a*) Unfertilized egg. (*b*) Two-cell stage. (*c*) Four-cell stage. (*d*) Eight-cell stage. (*e*) Sixteen-cell stage. (*f*) Sixty-four-cell stage. (Courtesy of Carolina Biological Supply Company.)

becomes a *brachiolaria* larva. The brachiolaria finally develop into very small, radially symmetrical starfish (Figure 10–30).

The Frog

The frog is an *oviparous* animal which means that the fertilized egg develops outside of the parent's body. Upon inspection of a fertilized frog egg, it can be observed that one-half is highly pigmented. This dark hemisphere is called the *animal pole* because the embryo will develop in this area. The white hemisphere, the *vegetal pole*, contains a heavy concentration of yolk nutrients. About one hour after fertilization the egg undergoes a mitotic cell division which constitutes the first cleavage. A second cleavage then occurs in the same plane at 90 degrees to the first (Figure 10–31).

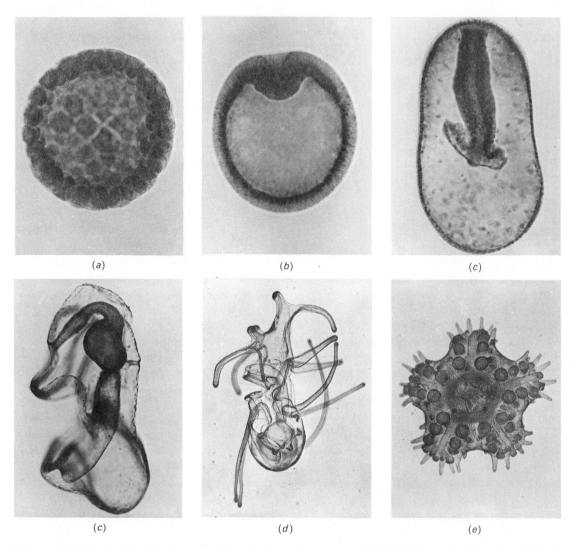

(a) *(b)* *(c)*

(c) *(d)* *(e)*

Figure 10–30 Starfish development, blastula through young starfish. (*a*) Nonmotile blastula. (*b*) Early gastrula. (*c*) Late gastrula. (*d*) Late bipinnaria. (*e*) Brachiolaria. (*f*) Young starfish. (Courtesy of Carolina Biological Supply Company.)

During subsequent cleavages the cells in the animal hemisphere divide more frequently than the yolk cells. It is important to note that this cleavage process has not increased the mass of the original egg.

The frog blastula is similar to that of the starfish except the blastocoel is relatively smaller and displaced toward the animal pole owing to the presence of the yolk and the unequal cleavage. The process of gastrulation, however, is different in the frog. At a point 180 degrees from the entrance of the sperm and the spot where the cells of the animal and vegetal portions merge, the cells of the animal pole turn inward and move into the blastocoel. In this process the animal cells actually overgrow the vegetal or yolk cells and turn inward forming a blastopore. The yolk cells fill the hole produced by gastrulation and form a yolk plug (Figure 10–31*g*). The position of the blastopore and its yolk plug marks the eventual orientation of the embryo since the blastopore

350

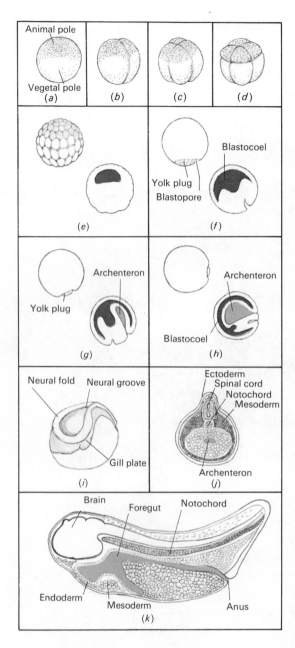

Animal pole

Vegetal pole
(a)   (b)   (c)   (d)

(e)

Blastocoel

Yolk plug
Blastopore
(f)

Archenteron

Yolk plug

Blastocoel
(g)

Archenteron

Blastocoel
(h)

Neural fold   Neural groove

Gill plate
(i)

Ectoderm
Spinal cord
Notochord
Mesoderm

Archenteron
(j)

Brain
Foregut   Notochord

Endoderm
Mesoderm   Anus
(k)

Figure 10–31 Early embryology of the frog. (a) Egg. (b) Two-cell stage. (c) Four-cell stage. (d) Eight-cell stage. (e) Blastula stage. (f), (g), (h) Developing gastrula stages (cross sections are through the yolk plug). (i) Neurula stage. (j) Cross section of late neurula. (k) Longitudinal section of early embryo.

is finally replaced by the anus and the head develops approximately 180 degrees from this spot.

Following gastrulation, the differentiation of primary germ layers into various organs begins and the first of these is the neural tube. The dorsal ectoderm sinks down to form a groove which closes at the top to form a single, hollow tube. The anterior portion of this tube will develop into the brain, and the remainder will form the spinal cord (Figure 10–31*i*). This stage of development is called the *neurula*.

In frogs and other chordates one of the most definitive structures that develops at this time is the mid-dorsal, elastic rod known as the *notochord* which is formed primarily of large, vacuolated mesodermal cells. In later development the notochord is replaced by the vertebrae of the spinal column. In the frog, the body cavity (the coelom) is formed by the splitting of two mesodermal sheets which have developed from the endodermal cells roofing the archenteron. One-half is attached to the external wall as a body lining and the other half surrounds the visceral organs (Figure 10–31*j*). By this time the embryo has elongated and a segmental series of paired mesodermal blocks, known as *somites*, have formed along the length of the organism. Three regions exist in each somite: an outer part that will form the dermis of the skin, an inner region from which the skeletal muscles will develop, and an upper part that will give rise to the vertebrae of the vertebral column. Internal organs and external gills develop next and, in ten to twelve days, depending on the particular kind of frog, the tadpole can be recognized. Limb buds and internal lungs develop, and the tail is reabsorbed so that in approximately ninety days after fertilization a young frog is produced.

Man

Fertilization and development is internal in mammals, and the female gives birth to well-developed young, a condition described as *viviparous*. In humans, cleavage is complete

351

and equal-sized cells are produced with each division because of the lack of large amounts of yolk material. With the formation of a solid ball of cells (morula stage), a distinction between the outer layer of cells (the *trophectoderm*) and the inner cell mass can be made (Figure 10–32*a*). The trophectoderm cells flatten and enlarge to produce a blastocoel along one edge of the morula. As the trophectoderm cells divide, the blastocoel becomes larger and the inner cell mass remains at the animal pole (Figure 10–32*b*). The inner

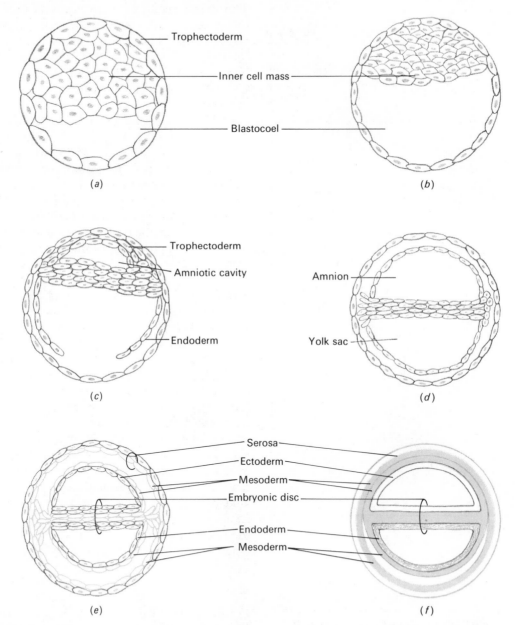

Figure 10–32 Early embryonic development of the human embryo. (*a*), (*b*) Development of the inner cell mass. (*c*), (*d*) Formation of the amnion and yolk sac. (*e*), (*f*) Embryonic disc stage showing position of the primary germ layers.

cell mass soon delaminates (the layers separate) to form a cavity which becomes the *amnion* (the fluid-filled sac which will surround the embryo). Cells from the lower edges of the inner cell mass proliferate and move along the inner wall of the blastocoel to form the yolk sac (Figure 10–32c and d). The layer of the inner cell mass between these two cavities, the embryonic disc, will develop into the embryo. At this point, mesoderm begins forming in several areas, which corresponds to gastrulation in other animals. Ectoderm lines the amnionic cavity and forms the upper layers of the embryonic disc; endoderm lines the yolk sac and the lower layers of the disc; mesoderm differentiates from the center of the embryonic disc and also forms sheets of cells covering the outside of the amnion, the yolk sac, and the

inside of the trophectoderm (Figure 10–32e and f). The outer membrane composed of trophectoderm and mesoderm, the *serosa*, completely envelops the developing embryo.

Another sac, the *allantois*, next pouches from the gut of the embryo near the yolk sac and pushes close to the serosa. The allantoic mesoderm is rich in blood vessels, and the area of its contact with the serosa is called the *chorion*. Small fingerlike villi from the chorion interdigitate with the endometrium of the uterus to form a *placenta* for exchange of gases and the uptake of nutrients from the mother's blood (Figure 10–33). The allantoic sac with its blood vessels, two arteries and a vein, and the yolk sac form the umbilical cord. Under normal conditions the mother's blood is never mixed with the baby's blood and exchange of

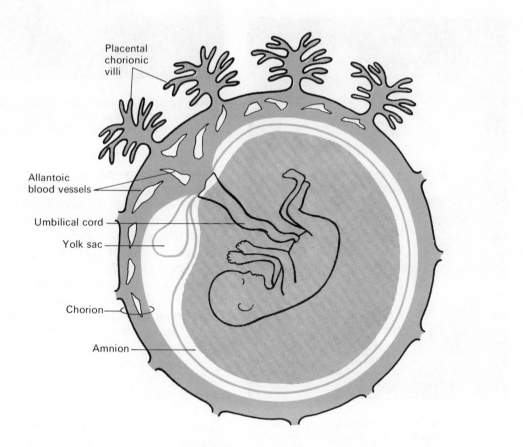

Figure 10–33   Relationship of the extraembryonic membranes to the placenta in the human embryo.

353

products occurs across the thin membranes of the placental villi. Development proceeds in an orderly, sequential manner and after about a month the heart is functional, limb buds are showing, eyes are forming, and remnants of pharyngeal gill clefts may be seen (Figure 10–34).

After about two months the developing embryo looks definitely human (Figure 10–35), and by the twelfth week the *fetus* is about three inches long, weighs nearly an ounce, and some hair is present. By this time all of the organ systems have begun to develop. In the next six months the fetus will continue to grow in size with further development of organs in all systems (Figure 10–36). In the fetus, blood is shunted away from the lungs. This is accomplished through an opening between the right

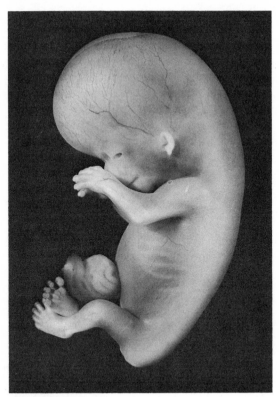

Figure 10–35   Human embryo at 56 days shows definite human characteristics. (Chester F. Reather, RBP, FBPA; Carnegie Institution of Washington.)

and left atria and also a duct between the pulmonary artery and the great aorta. At birth these openings close and a full pulmonary circulation is produced. In some newborn babies, one or both of these openings fail to close completely, and the blood is therefore poorly oxygenated, since it continues to be shunted from the lungs. This condition, known as "blue baby," can usually be corrected through surgery. Generally, birth can be expected to occur about 280 days from the mother's last menstruation, although this time may vary by several days or weeks.

In reptiles and birds, all of the extra-embryonic sacs are essential since the young must develop inside a shelled egg (Figure 10–37). The highly vascularized chorion and allantois act as respiratory membranes and are pressed close to the egg shell. The allantois also serves as a depository for nitrogenous wastes. The yolk sac contains the nutritive

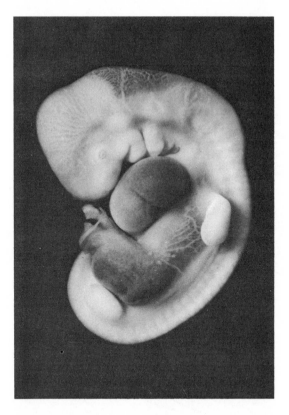

Figure 10–34   Human embryo at 31 days. The eyes and limb buds are developing, and the heart is functional. Note the gill-cleft remnants in the pharyngeal region. (Chester F. Reather, RBP, FBPA; Carnegie Institution of Washington.)

Month	Approximate Size	General Developmental Events
1	1/8 in.	Implantation by 12th day after fertilization; nervous system begins development and eyes, ears, nose begin to form; 32 pairs of somites (blocks of mesoderm which form muscles); pharyngeal arches and clefts; heart becomes functional; small tail-like growth; primitive type of kidneys form (pronephros); major systems start to develop; limb buds show.
2	1 in.	Gill clefts incorporated into developing face and neck; vestigial tail-like structure resorbed; skeleton begins to form; ovaries or testes form; arms and legs assume characteristic shape; all major skeletal muscles developed; brain equals about one-half total length of embryo; completely bathed by amniotic fluid which can be taken into the gut and lungs.
3	3 in. 3/4 oz.	Facial hair produced; further skeletal development; brain equals less than one-third total length.
4	7 in. 5 oz.	Fingerprints develop; complex development of brain surface; eyes and ears assume characteristic shapes; reflexes develop; hair appears on head and body.
5	10 in. 1/2 lb.	Fingernails and toenails form; fetal movements (kicking); loss and replacement of cells of tissues such as the skin; digestive system well developed; blood being formed in bone marrow.
6	12 in. 1½ lbs.	Increased skeletal formation (ossification); development of many sweat and oil glands in skin; fetus now looks like small human.
7	15 in. 2½ lbs.	Fetus could live outside of uterus but would require hospital care; respiratory system functional; testes descend into scrotal sac.
8	16 in. 4 lbs.	Fat tissues accumulate and body fills out; roots of teeth begin to grow; intensive calcium deposition.
9	20 in. 6–8 lbs.	Most of hair coat has disappeared; brain equals one-fourth total length; growth and development slow down; kidneys reach full development; maturation of nervous system and reflex patterns.

Figure 10–36 Summary of the developmental events in human embryo.

yolk material and is much more prominent than in mammals. Upon hatching, all the extraembryonic membranes dry up and are lost.

EXPERIMENTAL EMBRYOLOGY

Differentiation and Induction

One of the most fascinating and interesting areas of modern biology is the field of embryology that deals with the formation of different cell types in a developing organism. This process, in which unspecialized cells become specialized, is known as *differentiation* and represents a permanent change in cells during the course of development. Moreover, we can say that these changes result from an interaction with other cells or chemicals produced by cells or, sometimes, external influences.

Cell differentiation has been compared by C. H. Waddington of England, through the use of a "landscape" model, to a ball rolling down an inclined surface toward a series of valleys (Figure 10–38). As the ball rolls it commits itself to a particular region and, as it continues to roll, fewer opportunities are available. At certain stages there are alternative valleys but these become fewer and fewer until the ball ends up at the bottom of one valley. A developing cell also becomes committed along its course of development and, just as the ball cannot roll back uphill, neither can the cell reverse its differentiation.

In 1891, Hans Driesch, a German embryologist, demonstrated that the cells resulting from the first and second cleavages in sea-urchin eggs could be separated and each would develop into a complete miniature

355

embryo. It was learned, however, that complete development was impossible after the third cleavage. Evidently the cells had differentiated or lost their equal potential after two divisions. This gave rise to the idea that each cell in a developing embryo contained the information necessary to become a specific part of the organism and as development proceeded, each cell became more and more specialized.

Later in the 1920s, Hans Spemann performed a very significant series of experiments with frog embryos. Working with the late gastrula stage, Spemann was able to reciprocally transplant a small piece of dorsal ectoderm (from the area of the presumptive neural tube) with a piece of potential belly ectoderm. The transplanted neural tube ectoderm differentiated into belly skin, and the graft from the belly region became part of the neural tube. Carrying his experiment one step further, Spemann transplanted a piece of the underlying notochord (beneath the neural

tube) into the belly region. The result of this experiment was a double embryo attached belly to belly (Figure 10–39). Obviously, something had been produced by the notochordal cells which altered the normal development of the embryonic tissues in the belly region. This information coupled with the fact that the ectodermal cells did not develop into self-determined structures gave support to the theory of *induction*, which implies that certain cells in an embryo can induce or control the development of other cells. In other words, the fate of a developing cell depends on the influence of neighboring cells or, simply, its position in the embryo. The exact molecular mechanism of induction and the formation of "organizer areas" in the embryo is not completely understood, but many experiments have been performed in attempts to understand the process. Such experiments usually involve moving tissues from one region of an organism to another. In the formation of the vertebrate eye, for example, the optic vesicle

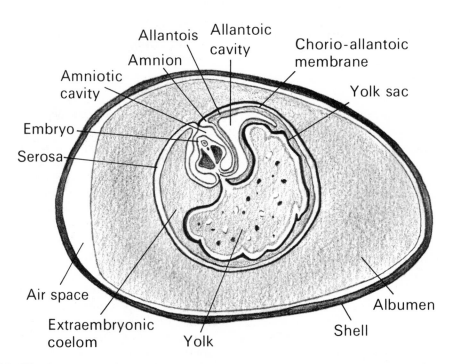

Figure 10–37 Extraembryonic membranes of a chicken embryo at 5 days. Longitudinal section of the egg; cross section of the embryo.

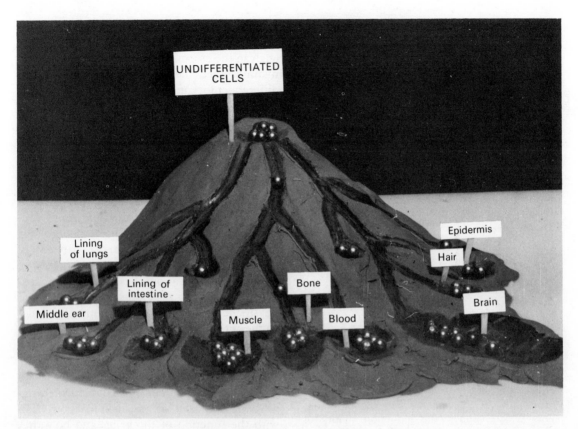

Figure 10–38 "Landscape model" proposed by Waddington which compares cellular differentiation to balls rolling down branched channels. Once a ball has entered a specific channel, it is committed to that line of differentiation. (Richard F. Trump.)

that grows from the midbrain induces the ectoderm in the head region to form a lens. Other eye tissues are then formed and an eye results (Figure 10–40). If the optic vesicle is removed from a chicken embryo, a lens is not formed in the region of the ectoderm where it normally develops. Thus the optic vesicle can be considered an inducer for the development of a lens from the ectoderm.

THE ROLE OF THE NUCLEUS AND CHROMOSOMES

In 1963, a German cytologist named Hammerling performed a number of simple experiments with the green alga *Acetabularia* which is unique in several respects. It is composed of a base that contains the nucleus, a two-inch erect stalk, and a flaring umbrellalike cap

(Figure 10–41). Hammerling noted that these algae possessed a high degree of regeneration, and if the cap was clipped off near the tip, a new cap was quickly reformed.

Closely related species of *Acetabularia* usually have characteristically different caps. By cutting a section of stalk out of two algae having different caps and transplanting them onto the opposite bases, Hammerling observed that the regenerated caps always resembled the nuclear type of the base to which it was transplanted. The cytoplasm, although essential to regeneration, appeared to be under the control of the new nucleus. Experiments with *Amoeba* and amphibians by other researchers have confirmed this theory of nuclear control.

We are already familiar with the controlling influence that nuclear DNA exerts in the

357

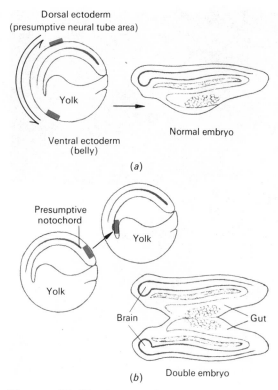

Dorsal ectoderm
(presumptive neural tube area)

Yolk

Normal embryo

Ventral ectoderm
(belly)

(a)

Presumptive
notochord

Yolk

Yolk

Brain

Gut

(b)   Double embryo

Figure 10–39 Spemann's germ-layer transplants which support the induction theory of embryonic differentiation. (*a*) Reciprocal transplant between dorsal ectoderm and ventral ectoderm (belly) at the gastrula stage results in a normal tadpole. (*b*) Transplant of section of notochord to the belly region results in a double embryo.

cytoplasmic synthesis of cellular protein. It is likely, therefore, that the nucleus could produce specific enzymes at certain times during development which in turn could synthesize "organizer substances." Support for this hypothesis was given by Wolfgang Beermann in 1959 in a paper reporting the activities of giant chromosomes in differentiating cells of chironomid fly larvae (small flies related to the fruit fly, *Drosophila*). These chromosomes are over 10,000 times the size of regular chromosomes, because the DNA has duplicated many times without chromosome division (Figure 10–42). Beermann discovered that the giant chromosomes produce large puffs of thready DNA material which facilitates the synthesis of messenger RNA. Beer-

mann and a coworker, Edstrom, were actually able to cut out several of these puffs and analyze the associated messenger RNA. Beermann studied the puffing patterns in several different embryonic tissues and discovered that puffs form at certain locations and appear to parallel developmental changes in these tissues. This evidence suggests that puffing is an expression of genetic action in the chromosome which could be directly related to protein synthesis and cellular differentiation.

Since the time of von Baer, the eminent German embryologist of the nineteenth century, much information has been accumulated which helps to explain many aspects of development. The use of new techniques in experimental situations has opened the door to understanding development as a directed physiochemical process. Certainly the genes on the chromosomes must control the developmental processes even though the exact mechanisms may not be understood at this time. In recent years, the correlation between DNA (the genes) and protein synthesis has been significant, and part of the next chapter deals with the function of the genes and how they control the development of an individual.

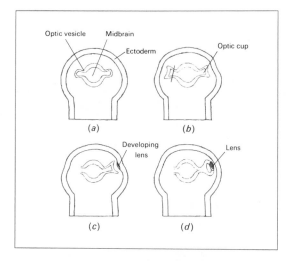

Optic vesicle   Midbrain

Ectoderm

Optic cup

(a)   (b)

Developing
lens

Lens

(c)   (d)

Figure 10–40 Sequence of events in the development of the lens of the eye from the ectoderm. If the optic vesicle is removed, as in (*b*) and (*c*), the lens does not form.

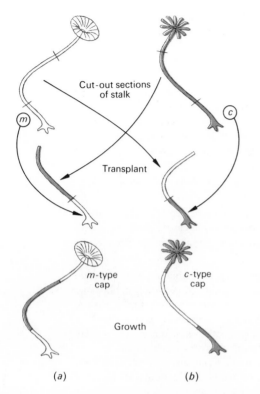

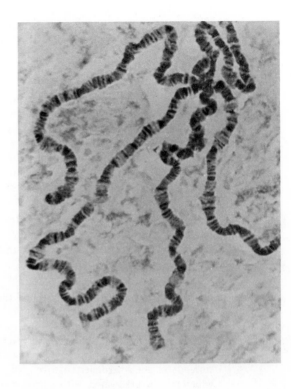

Figure 10–41 Nuclear control of cap development in the unicellular alga *Acetabularia.* (*a*) *A. mediterrania* (smooth cap). (*b*) *A. crenulata* (lobed cap).

Figure 10–42 Giant chromosomes from the salivary gland of the fruit-fly larva (X 1,000). The bands represent the sites of specific gene action. (Courtesy of Dr. B. P. Kaufmann.)

SUMMARIZING STATEMENTS

Reproduction is essential to the success of all organisms. This includes, in addition to reproduction of the total organism, reproduction of molecules, cell parts, and cells. Moreover, multicellular organisms undergo a developmental process in which cells differentiate into specialized structures.

Mitosis is the process in which two daughter cells, identical to the parent cell, are produced. The orderly sequence of nuclear and cytoplasmic events are described in the following phases:

1 Interphase—chromosomes are extended and uncoiled; DNA is replicated.
2 Prophase—chromosomes shorten by coiling, centrioles move to the poles, asters form, nucleoli disappear, nuclear membrane breaks down.
3 Metaphase—spindle fibers are attached to chromosomes; chromosomes align on an equatorial plane.
4 Anaphase—chromosomes move to opposite poles; they appear to be pulled by spindle fibers.

5   Telophase—cell membrane constricts in animals, or cell wall develops in plants; daughter cells are formed; chromosomes and nucleus return to inter-phasic condition.

Meiosis, the process that reduces diploid cells to the haploid chromosome number, consists of two cell divisions with the chromosomes duplicated only once. The chromosomal events provide for the recombination of hereditary information between the maternal and paternal chromosomes; this occurs during prophase of meiosis I when the replicated homologous chromosomes synapse and undergo crossover. Meiotic production of gametes provides the basis for variation among sexually reproducing organisms and, consequently, successful adaptation.

Reproduction in protists includes the asexual processes of fragmentation, budding, fission, and spore production; sexuality involves the production and fusion of gametes. Examples of this sexuality are conjugation in *Paramecium* and *Spirogyra*.

In plants, reproduction involves life histories that include two separate phases, the gametophyte (haploid) and the sporophyte (diploid); generally one stage depends on the other for reproduction. In mosses, the gametophyte is the dominant phase, whereas in ferns, the sporophyte is dominant (diplohaplontic). In seed plants, gymnosperms, and angiosperms, the gametophyte is greatly reduced. A seed, which results from fertilization, consists of a dormant embryo, stored food, and a hardened coat. In addition to seeds, angiosperms produce fruit which are mature ovaries with enclosed seeds; fruits can be fleshy or dry.

Although some animals can reproduce asexually, most reproduce by sexual means. In mammals, sexual reproduction involves an estrus period of female sexual receptivity and egg production. In humans the cyclic production of eggs and preparation of the uterus is termed the menstrual cycle.

In many plants and animals reproductive cycles appear to be triggered by specific environmental conditions such as periods of light and dark, changes in temperature, seasons of the year, and phases of the moon. The reproductive success of a particular species depends on the synchronization of the production of gametes within the species.

Development is the complex series of stages from a fertilized egg to a multi-cellular organism in which certain cells differentiate into primary germ tissues (ectoderm, endoderm, mesoderm). These tissues give rise to the various organs and structures of the adult. The early developmental patterns among animals are strikingly similar—that is, from fertilized egg through gastrulation. The starfish, frog, and human represent three variations of development.

During development embryonic cells become more and more specialized until eventually they differentiate into specific tissues. In this process the course of development of these cells may be induced by neighboring cells.

The control of development is apparently under the direct influence of the chromosomes; they exert this control through the DNA-RNA protein-synthesis mechanism.

1 List at least one significant event involving each of the following structures at each stage of mitosis: (*a*) centrioles and spindle fibers, (*b*) chromosomes, (*c*) nuclear membrane.

2 What is the adaptive significance of synapsis and crossing over which occur in the first meiotic prophase?

3 Compare spermatogenesis with oögenesis. List the differences and similarities for each of the following stages: prophase I, anaphase I, telophase I, anaphase II, telophase II.

4 What does *Spirogyra* have in common with the gametophyte generation of mosses? How do the reproductive patterns differ?

5 Reptiles, birds, and mammals all possess four extraembryonic membranes—amnion, allantois, yolk sac, and chorion. Distinguish the functions of these membranes in each of these groups.

6 Consider the events of the menstrual cycle and correlate these with the general scheme of control presented in Chapter 8. Make specific references to feedback mechanisms.

7 There have been many examples of animals that have developed a third eye. From your knowledge of induction and differentiation, explain how this could occur.

8 List four birth-control methods in the order of their effectiveness. Describe some shortcomings of each method.

9 Distinguish among the processes of gastrulation in the starfish, frog, and man.

10 Briefly outline the physiological effects of the progesterone-estrogen birth-control pill. Why is it nearly 100 percent effective?

11 Correlate the recent model of protein synthesis with the fact that giant salivary chromosomes of *Drosophila* show definite patterns of puffing at specific stages of development.

12 Many flowering plants may be propagated by either cuttings or seeds. What are the particular advantages of each method?

13 Explain why conjugation in *Paramecium* and *Spirogyra* is called a sexual process.

14 Compare the similarities and differences in the reproductive patterns of mosses and ferns.

15 List the advantages that seed-producing plants have over nonseed plants. Compare the seeds of angiosperms and gymnosperms.

16 It is possible to remove the nucleus from a frog egg and replace it with another nucleus. If an egg nucleus is replaced with a nucleus from a blastula cell, the egg will develop normally. If, however, an egg nucleus is replaced with a nucleus from a late gastrula cell, the egg will develop abnormally. Can you offer an explanation for these events?

SUPPLEMENTARY READINGS

Allen, R. D., "The Moment of Fertilization," *Scientific American*, July, 1959.

Balinski, B. I., *An Introduction to Embryology*, 2nd ed., Philadelphia, Saunders, 1965.

Barth, L. J., *Development*, Reading, Mass., Addison-Wesley, 1964.

Beermann, Wolfgang, and Ulrich Clever, "Chromosome Puffs," *Scientific American*, April, 1964.

Bell, Eugene, ed., *Molecular and Cellular Aspects of Development*, New York, Harper & Row, 1965.

Berrill, N. J., *Growth, Development, and Patterns*, San Francisco, Freeman, 1961.

Chase, H. B., *Sex: The Universal Fact*, New York, Dell, 1965.

Csapo, Arpad, "Progesterone," *Scientific American*, April, 1958.

Dreisch, Hans, "The Potency of the First Two Cleavage Cells in the Development of Echinoderms," in M. Gabriel and S. Fogel, eds., *Great Experiments in Biology*, Englewood Cliffs, N.J., Prentice-Hall, 1955.

Ebert, James D., "The First Heartbeats," *Scientific American*, March, 1959.

Etkin, William, "How a Tadpole Becomes a Frog," *Scientific American*, May, 1966.

Fischberg, M., and A. W. Blackler, "How Cells Specialize," *Scientific American*, September, 1961.

Gibor, Aharon, "Acetabularia: A Useful Giant Cell," *Scientific American*, November, 1966.

Gilbert, Margaret S., *Biography of the Unborn*, New York, Hafner, 1962.

Gray, George W., "The Organizer," *Scientific American*, November, 1957.

Gurdon, J. B., "Transplanted Nuclei and Cell Differentiation," *Scientific American*, December, 1968.

Jacobson, Marcus, and R. K. Hunt, "The Origins of Nerve-Cell Specificity," *Scientific American*, February, 1973.

Jaffe, Frederick S., "Public Policy on Fertility Control," *Scientific American*, July, 1973.

Konigsberg, I. R., "The Embryological Origin of Muscle," *Scientific American*, August, 1964.

Manner, Harold W., *Elements of Comparative Vertebrate Embryology*, New York, Macmillan, 1964.

Mazia, Daniel, "How Cells Divide," *Scientific American*, September, 1961.

Meeuse, B. J. D., *The Story of Pollination*, New York, Ronald Press, 1961.

Moscona, A. A., "How Cells Associate," *Scientific American*, September, 1961.

Puck, T. T., "Single Human Cells in Vitro," *Scientific American*, August, 1957.

Spemann, H., *Embryonic Development and Induction*, New Haven, Conn., Yale University Press, 1938.

Spratt, Jr., Nelson, T., *Introduction to Cell Differentiation*, New York, Reinhold, 1964.

Waddington, C. H., "How Do Cells Differentiate?," *Scientific American*, September, 1953.

Waddington, C. H., *How Animals Develop*, New York, Harper Torchbooks, 1962.

Wessels, Norman K., and William J. Rutter, "Phases in Cell Differentiation," *Scientific American*, March, 1969.

11

Similarity and Variation Through Heredity

Through the process of reproduction offspring are produced which, in multicellular organisms, follow a definite pattern of development. Although this developmental sequence of events is quite similar for closely related organisms, it is very specific for members of an individual species, and consequently all members of a given species resemble one another. Yet the offspring within a species, and even from the same parents, are always different. We can assume then that an information system which has a great amount of stability but which still permits some variation and change must be involved. We have already discussed DNA as the principal part of this information system; now the question of how the hereditary material is transmitted from generation to generation arises. Studies in peas, fruit flies, bacteria, and other organisms have revealed the existence of specific patterns in the distribution of hereditary characteristics, but just how is it that the hereditary substance (DNA) functions to produce these characteristics? We know that the fundamental unit of heredity is the *gene*, a small segment of a chromosome, and the study of the transmission and function of the hereditary material is known as *genetics*.

365

THE PHYSICAL BASIS
OF HEREDITY

In the previous chapter the importance of chromosomes in cellular reproduction was pointed out and it was stressed that through sexuality chromosome complements could be changed and mixed. Fertilization provides for parts of two different chromosome groups to unite and form an individual with an entirely new chromosome makeup different from either parent. Meiosis is the process which allows new combinations of chromosomes and genes through random assortment and crossing over. Chromosomal and gene changes can also contribute toward variation in offspring. The chromosome then is the structural unit associated with reproduction, sexuality, heredity, and adaptation; it is the physical carrier of heredity. This relationship was only realized about the turn of the century following considerable experimentation. The question we should concern ourselves with is "How do we really know that heredity is carried in the chromosomes?"

Historical records indicate that early civilized cultures conducted breeding experiments to improve plants and animals. Man has continued these practices down through the ages as he attempts to obtain better domestic organisms. Although these were conscious efforts on the part of the breeders, they certainly did not understand the cellular mechanisms involved. The results obtained were often attributed to a process in which the characteristics of each parent blended together to produce observed effects in the offspring. In fact, many of the early explanations of heredity seem quite absurd and humorous today. For example, there were those who believed that all heredity was carried in either the sperm or the egg, and two schools of thought arose from this controversy—the spermists and the ovists. Others believed at one time that a camel and sparrow could cross and their characteristics would blend to produce an ostrich. Still others believed that heredity was carried by the blood. The

pangenesis theory was a popular one held by some of the Greeks and later by Charles Darwin. This theory proposed that each structure in the body had tiny pangenes that moved into the gametes prior to fertilization. Thus each structure was represented by a pangene and if the structure changed, so would the pangene. This was obviously a mechanism that could explain the inheritance of acquired characteristics, another misconception of heredity. The theory of the inheritance of acquired characteristics is explained in Chapter 12.

Some experimental studies were attempted but usually these were too ambitious since they involved many factors in one experiment or accurate reports were not kept. The first notable experiments in inheritance were conducted by Gregor Mendel and reported in 1866. Later, in the 1890s, Correns of Germany, DeVries of Holland, von Tschermak of Austria, and Spillman of the United States, working on several different organisms, obtained results similar to Mendel's. These studies provided a logical explanation of how traits might be passed from generation to generation and stimulated intense interest in genetics. Some of the most important cellular studies, as far as genetics was concerned, came about in the 1880s and 1890s. Chromosomes were discovered and the details of mitosis and meiosis were worked out by some of the early German cytologists. So, at the same time as explanations were being sought for breeding and heredity experiments, cytological studies were advancing to the stage where they could supply some of the answers.

Perhaps it was only natural that sooner or later several investigators would see relationships between these two fields. At any rate, about 1902, Sutton from the United States and Boveri from Germany, in two notable works, stated the relationship between the fields of heredity and cytology. In effect they pointed out that the results of the inheritance experiments of Mendel and others could be explained by the behavior of the chromosomes in cells. The new field of modern genetics was thus born from this splendid synthesis and the "chromosome theory of heredity" was proposed.

At first this theory was not accepted by all biologists and many sought more definite proof. This involved associating a specific trait with the visible chromosome makeup in the cells. Or, to state it another way, a definite chromosome change must be demonstrated for a physical change in an individual. This was made possible in the early 1900s by improved microscopy and a newly discovered experimental organism, the fruit fly (*Drosophila*). T. H. Morgan (1866–1945), an American geneticist (Figure 11–1), realized the possibilities for genetic studies that this small fly afforded. Populations can be kept in small bottles on a nutrient medium, and a new generation can be produced in approximately ten days. The fruit fly has four pairs of chromosomes (Figure 11–2), and these can be readily studied under the microscope. Furthermore, considerable body variation exists which allows for various genetic crosses. The crucial evi-

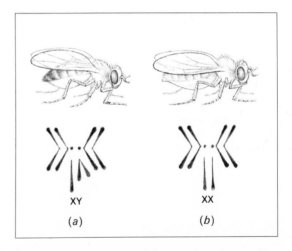

Figure 11–2 Male and female fruit flies (*Drosophila*) and their chromosomes. (*a*) The male sex chromosomes, *XY*. (*b*) The female sex chromosomes, *XX*.

Figure 11–1 T. H. Morgan (1866–1945), the American geneticist who realized the advantages of fruit flies for genetic studies. (Courtesy of National Library of Medicine.)

dence for the chromosome theory of heredity was provided by studies on *Drosophila* about 1914—this will be discussed later in this chapter after the basic laws of heredity have been presented. For now it will be sufficient to say that it is possible to correlate a specific trait with a change in chromosome composition not only in the fruit fly but also in other organisms, including man.

Included in the chromosome theory of heredity is the concept that each chromosome is composed of many genes. Each gene is now believed to determine or influence several traits and, furthermore, most traits are probably influenced by many genes. As you recall from the previous chapter, chromosomes occur in pairs in most organisms. Genes therefore must also occur in pairs and a specific trait may be affected by a specific pair of genes. It has been possible in *Drosophila*, where giant chromosomes occur in the larvae, to correlate a specific characteristic with a specific band or region on a chromosome. If we assume that these bands are genes, or groups of genes, then we can show that a specific characteristic is produced by genes distributed in the same pattern as chromosomes during meiosis.

367

One aspect of genetics is the transmission of the physical material of heredity from generation to generation. This area of genetics, often called *transmission genetics*, seeks to explain how the chromosomes accomplish this process. These details must be understood before we can study the function of the genetic material. Any discussion of the principles of genetic transmission must begin with the work of the Austrian monk, Gregor Mendel (Figure 11–3).

MENDELIAN PRINCIPLES

Mendel, whose experiments extended over an eight-year period and were published in 1866, selected the garden pea as his experimental subject. This was a fortunate selection because this organism has many characteristics produced primarily by single pairs of genes. Also, owing to the structure of the pea flower, self-fertilization usually occurs, and this process

Figure 11–3 Gregor Mendel (1822–1844), Austrian monk whose experiments with peas led to the basic principles of genetics. (Courtesy of American Museum of Natural History.)

had produced many pure breeding plants. Pollen from another plant can be introduced, however, by an experimenter to produce cross-fertilization. Mendel realized that simple experiments that contrasted only one of several characteristics at a time were necessary if the principles of inheritance were to be understood; he also realized the importance of keeping accurate records. Mendel selected seven pairs of contrasting characteristics on which he experimented, and his original paper is still available. Two characteristics that Mendel observed in the pea were the shape of the seeds —they were either round or wrinkled—and the color of the embryonic leaf of the seed (the cotyledon), which was either yellow or green.

MONOHYBRID CROSS

Mendel noted that when pea plants that produced round seeds were self-pollinated, only round seeds resulted from the cross, and that plants producing wrinkled seeds always bred true for wrinkled seeds. When a variety producing round seeds was crossed with a variety producing wrinkled seeds, all of the seeds were round (Figure 11–4). When the plants resulting from this cross were self-pollinated (constituting a self-cross), however, some of the plants produced round seeds while others produced wrinkled seeds. The wrinkled character therefore was not lost in the original cross, and the ratio was approximately three round to one wrinkled. In this particular experiment, out of 7,324 seeds obtained from 253 self-pollinated plants, 5,474 were round and 1,850 were wrinkled.

In considering Mendel's explanation of this experiment you should remember that Mendel was not aware of the process of meiosis. Since you studied meiosis in Chapter 10, you can see how closely his explanation of the events of this cross follows the details of meiosis. Mendel explained this cross as follows and the explanation is summarized in Figure 11–5. Each parent plant has two "units" for a given character. When gametes are produced, each gamete gets one unit and, therefore, indi-

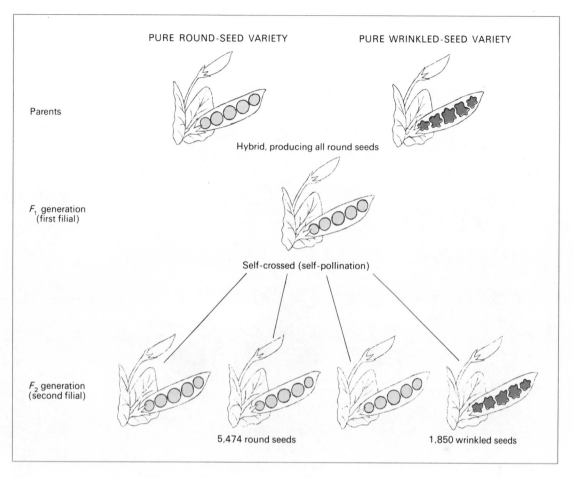

Parents

Hybrid, producing all round seeds

F_1 generation
(first filial)

Self-crossed (self-pollination)

F_2 generation
(second filial)

5,474 round seeds   1,850 wrinkled seeds

Figure 11—4 Results of Mendel's experimental cross of round-seed pea plants with wrinkled-seed pea plants. The exact ratio obtained here was 2.96 :1.

viduals produced from a round-seed plant and a wrinkled-seed plant would contain one unit of each character due to fertilization. Two kinds of gametes can be formed from these parents and, when these plants are crossed, four fertilization combinations are possible. Approximately three-fourths of the resulting offspring would have received at least one unit for round seed (three-fourths also would have received at least a unit for wrinkled seed). We say that round seed is a *dominant* character, and wrinkled seed is *recessive.* Individuals receiving a unit for round seed always produce round seeds, even though they also contain a unit for wrinkled seed. The similarity between Mendel's "units" and "genes," which were mentioned earlier, is quite obvious. In fact, if we were to place chromosomes in the scheme in Figure 11–5 and show the units or genes on the chromosomes, the illustration would then represent our modern explanation of the inheritance of this trait. Mendel pointed out that the units carrying these traits do segregate as discrete factors at meiosis. This is known as *Mendel's Law of Segregation.*

It is important to remember here that chromosomes occur as homologous pairs. Since the genes are located on the chromosomes, there are two genes for each trait. We call these genes *alleles* and we define alleles as alternative or contrasting forms of genes which affect the same trait (R and r) and are located at the same

369

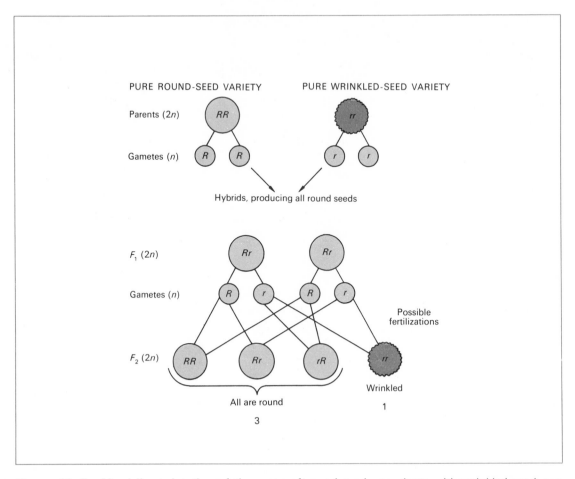

Figure 11–5 Mendel's explanation of the cross of round-seed pea plants with wrinkled-seed pea plants. *R* = a unit (gene) for round seed; *r* = a unit (gene) for wrinkled seed. This would explain the approximate 3:1 ratio that was obtained.

position on homologous chromosomes. Alleles always line up beside each other at synapsis of meiosis. Individuals of the pure round-seed variety have the *RR* makeup and, since both genes are the same, the term *homozygous* (meaning "same in the zygote") is used to describe the gene constitution with regard to round-wrinkled seed condition. Each gamete, however, carries only one-half of the chromosome complement, in this case *R*. When one of these gametes unites with a gamete from a pure wrinkled variety (carrying the allele *r*) in fertilization, a *hybrid, Rr,* is formed and we say that this hybrid is *heterozygous* (meaning "different in the zygote") with respect to the

round-wrinkled seed condition. It appears round, however, due to the presence of the dominant gene *R*. The appearance of the individual is referred to as the *phenotype* and the genetic makeup as the *genotype*. Thus the genotypes *RR* and *Rr* have the same phenotype, round seed. Although an *Rr* individual is round, the wrinkled gene *r* has not changed and it will probably show up in the next generation if two hybrids are crossed. In fact, you may have noted already that it has a 1 to 4 or 25 percent chance of showing up when two hybrids are crossed.

When the heterozygous or hybrid individual, *Rr*, undergoes meiosis, two kinds of

370

gametes may be produced: *R* or *r*. If two hybrids are crossed, then we have the following possibilities for fertilization combinations which correspond to the F_2 zygotes in Figure 11–5:

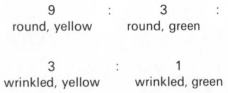

	♂ gametes	
	R	*r*
R	*RR*	*Rr*
r	*rR*	*rr*

(♀ gametes)

Note that the phenotype ratio (actual appearance) would be three round to one wrinkled, whereas the genotype ratio would be one *RR* to two *Rr* to one *rr*.

DIHYBRID CROSS

Mendel also made crosses involving two traits carried on separate chromosomes. One such cross was round-seed, yellow-seed coat plants with wrinkled-seed, green-seed coat plants (hereafter referred to as round, yellow seeds and wrinkled, green seeds). The results of this cross are shown in Figure 11–6, and the explanation for the results is given in Figure 11–7. The phenotype ratio resulting from this cross is:

9	:	3	:
round, yellow		round, green	

3	:	1
wrinkled, yellow		wrinkled, green

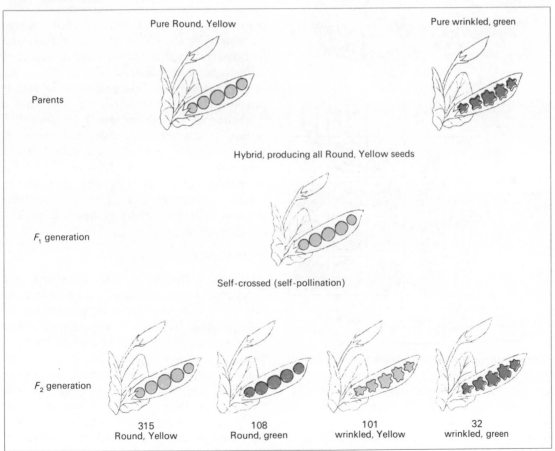

Figure 11–6 One of Mendel's experimental crosses involving two characteristics.

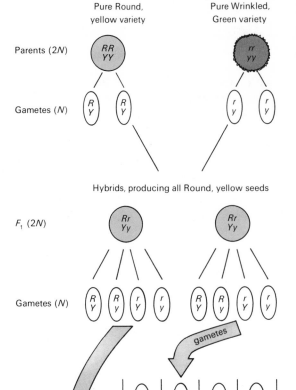

Pure Round, yellow variety

Pure Wrinkled, Green variety

Parents (2N)

RR YY

rr yy

Gametes (N)

R Y R Y r y r y

Hybrids, producing all Round, yellow seeds

F_1 (2N)

Rr Yy Rr Yy

Gametes (N)

R Y R y r Y r y R Y R y r Y r y

gametes

gametes

F_2 (2N)

	R Y	R y	r Y	r y
R Y	RR YY	RR Yy	Rr YY	Rr Yy
R y	RR yY	RR yy	Rr yY	Rr yy
r Y	rR YY	rR Yy	rr YY	rr Yy
r y	rR yY	rR yy	rr yY	rr yy

Figure 11–7 Explanation of Mendel's dihybrid cross.

Thus both dominant characteristics are present in $\frac{9}{16}$ of the offspring, one dominant trait in $\frac{3}{16}$, the other dominant trait in $\frac{3}{16}$, and both recessive traits appear in only $\frac{1}{16}$ of the offspring.

It should be stressed that the members of one pair of genes segregated independently of the other pair since they were on separate

chromosomes. This is often known as *Mendel's Law of Independent Assortment*. Also note that when we are dealing with two pairs of genes on separate chromosomes, four kinds of gametes are possible. A review of the principles of meiosis at this point would show why this is true. Furthermore members of a pair of homologous chromosomes normally never go to the same gamete (an unusual exception will be given later). It should also be noted that whether the chromosome carrying R or the chromosome carrying r will segregate with the chromosome carrying Y or with the chromosome y is purely a matter of chance (Figure 11–8). If a large number of gametes is produced we would expect a 1:1:1:1 ratio of RY, Ry, rY, ry gametes.

At fertilization it is a matter of chance whether a male gamete carrying the RY constitution will unite with a female gamete carrying RY, Ry, rY, or ry. It is also chance that determines if one of the other three types of male gametes will unite with an RY or Ry or rY or ry gamete. When all the fertilization possibilities are considered, we note that a $\frac{9}{16}$ chance or probability exists for getting a round, yellow offspring from this cross. A probability of $\frac{3}{16}$ prevails for a round, green offspring; $\frac{3}{16}$ for a wrinkled, yellow, and $\frac{1}{16}$ for a wrinkled, green. It is possible therefore in certain genetic crosses to state a specific, theoretical probability for obtaining a particular phenotype.

PROBABILITY

The role of chance has been stressed in the independent assortment of chromosomes in producing different classes of gametes and in the union of gametes in fertilization. Since these events are a matter of chance, they are based on the laws of *probability*. In fact, many natural phenomena of chance occurrence (such as electron positions and even the weather) are often stated in terms of probability. Good examples of probability can also be found in dice, cards, and other games of chance from which the laws of probability were first derived many years ago.

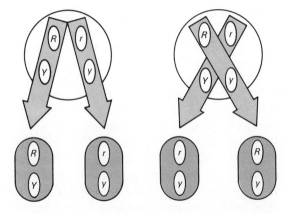

Figure 11–8 Independent assortment of two pairs of chromosomes at meiosis to produce four classes of gametes.

Mathematical probability can be defined as the chance of the occurrence of any particular form of an event, stated as the ratio of the number of ways that form might occur to the total number of ways the event might occur in any form. Thus the probability of X event occurring is:

$$P(X) = \frac{f}{n}$$

where f equals the *number* of events in which X is found and n equals the total number of events that can occur.

Returning to Mendel's cross between round-seed and wrinkled-seed plants we note that the offspring would all be round-seeded but would be heterozygous (Rr). When crossing these F_1 hybrids (or allowing them to self-cross) we might inquire about the probability of obtaining a round-seeded offspring. Recalling the cross (Figure 11–5) we remember that the gametes could have united at fertilization as follows:

		♂ gametes	
		R	r
♀ gametes	R	RR	Rr
	r	rR	rr

The probability of a round-seeded offspring could then be computed as:

$$P \text{ (round seed)} = \frac{f}{n} = \frac{3}{4} = 75\%$$

where f = the number of events that will produce round seeds = RR, Rr, Rr

n = the total number of events that can occur = RR, Rr, Rr, rr

Albinism (a condition in which the hair and skin lack pigment) is produced in man by a recessive gene and, if two normal parents have an albino child, we could outline the series of events as:

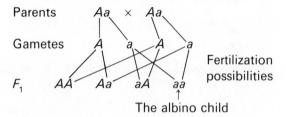

where A = normal pigmentation gene
a = albino gene

If the parents desire another child, they will be concerned about the pigmentation of future offspring. Someone with a knowledge of genetics and probability could compute for them the probability of having an albino child.

$$P \text{ (albino child)} = \frac{f}{n} = \frac{1}{4} = 25\%$$

It should be noted that *all* of the probabilities for any event should always add up to 1. That is, the probability for having a normal child from these parents is:

$$P \text{ (normal pigmented child)} = \frac{f}{n} = \frac{3}{4} = 75\%$$

In sum, 75 percent and 25 percent equal 1.

The parents may also wish to know the probability of having two albino children in a row. This could be calculated for them by applying another principle of probability, the principle governing two events occurring jointly or one directly after the other. This principle states: *the probability of two independent events occurring jointly is the product of the individual probabilities.* Therefore the probability of having two albino children in a row would be:

P (2 albino children) =

$$\frac{f}{n} \times \frac{f}{n} = \frac{1}{4} \times \frac{1}{4} = \frac{1}{16}$$

Again, if we consider all of the possible combinations that might occur if this family had two children, these must add up to one.

P (albino and normal) $= \frac{1}{4} \times \frac{3}{4} = 3/16$

P (normal and albino) $= \frac{3}{4} \times \frac{1}{4} = 3/16$

P (normal and normal) $= \frac{3}{4} \times \frac{3}{4} = 9/16$

P (albino and albino) $= \frac{1}{4} \times \frac{1}{4} = \underline{1/16}$

$$16/16 = 1$$

It should be stressed that the probability of an albino child born to these parents is still $\frac{1}{4}$ for each occurrence. When we consider more than one birth in the family, however, the probability of the two similar events occurring in a row reduces the chance to $\frac{1}{16}$. This is like attempting to roll two 7s in a row in a game of dice and since there are six ways of making a seven with dice, the chance on a single roll is $\frac{6}{36}$ or $\frac{1}{6}$. The chance of rolling two 7s in a row, however, is $\frac{1}{6} \times \frac{1}{6}$ or only $\frac{1}{36}$.

The principles of probability are certainly of importance to plant and animal breeders. Whether or not to conduct a particular breeding program may be decided on the basis of the probability of obtaining the desired offspring.

TEST CROSS

In the cross between round (R) and wrinkled (r) seeds, you probably noted that the genotypes RR and Rr produced the same phenotype. In breeding experiments it is often important to know the exact genotype for a particular trait—that is, whether an individual is homozygous or heterozygous for the trait.

This can be accomplished by a *test cross* (sometimes called a *back cross*), in which the organism under question is crossed with a pure recessive since the genotype of the pure recessive is known. The unknown genotype can then be determined by examining the resulting ratios. When RR is crossed with rr, all the offspring will show the dominant characteristic, that is, all offspring will be Rr. In a cross between Rr and rr, however, one-half of the progeny should show the recessive trait, rr (Figure 11–9). Therefore, if all offspring are round, the plant being tested is RR; if half the offspring are round and half wrinkled, the plant is Rr.

INCOMPLETE DOMINANCE

Up to this point we have considered only genes that are dominant or recessive; this has been done to explain the fundamental laws of

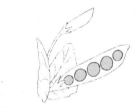

This pea plant produces round seeds. Is it homozygous (RR) or heterozygous (Rr)?

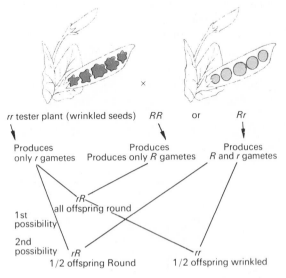

Figure 11–9 Process of making a test cross and examining the results.

heredity. It is extremely important, however, to realize that many pairs of genes (alleles) exist in which dominance does not occur. In these situations, since neither gene is dominant, an intermediate effect is produced in the hybrid. It should be understood that this effect is not produced by a "blending of the genes," since further crosses of these intermediate hybrids will produce offspring showing the original parental types. This principle of inheritance has been demonstrated by several classic experiments on flower color in a plant family commonly called the "four-o'clock" family. In one experiment a white flowering plant crossed with a red flowering plant produces all plants with pink flowers. When two pink-flowered plants are crossed, the result is a ratio of one red, two pink, and one white (1:2:1) (Figure 11–10). We will return to this principle of nondominance of genes to explain the inheritance of characteristics such as intelligence in man.

INTERACTION OF GENES

In some cases a pair of genes may be incapable of producing their effect because of the influence of another pair of genes. When a gene at one position on a chromosome suppresses the action of a gene at another position, it is called *epistasis* (meaning "standing above"). The example of coat color in mice illustrates this principle. The gray color (agouti) in mice is due to a dominant gene (*B*). The homozygous recessive condition (*bb*) produces a black coat. Another gene (*A*) is necessary, however, for any pigment to be produced, and in the homozygous recessive condition (*aa*) no pigment is present and an albino results. This is true regardless of whether the mouse is *BB* or *Bb* or *bb*. Since two genes are involved here we might expect a typical dihybrid ratio from a cross of two *F*₁ hybrids. Because of the epistatic action of one gene pair on another, however, a modified ratio of 9:3:4 results (Figure 11–11).

A good example of epistasis in man is the albino condition in blacks, where, even though dark pigmentation genes are present, they can-

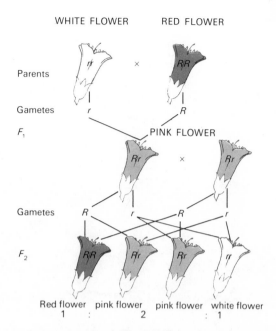

Figure 11–10 Inheritance of color in the four-o'clock flower family. This illustrates the principle of incomplete dominance of genes.

not function due to the lack of a dominant gene that permits their expression.

TRANSMISSION GENETICS II

In most organisms the members of one pair of chromosomes are different in the male than in the female. In the fruit fly, for example, the two homologous chromosomes labeled X are similar in the female, but the corresponding chromosomes in the male show only one X and a shorter homologue labeled Y (Figure 11–2). These chromosomes are called the *sex chromosomes*, whereas other chromosomes in the cells are referred to as the *autosomes*. So far the traits we have been discussing in this chapter have been carried by genes on the autosomes. Genes on certain parts of the sex chromosomes may exhibit a different pattern of inheritance than those on the autosomes. This is true since all regions of the X and Y chromosomes are not homologous and an individual receiving only one X chromosome will receive only one allele of some genes. This changes the pattern of inheritance and we will see how in a few pages.

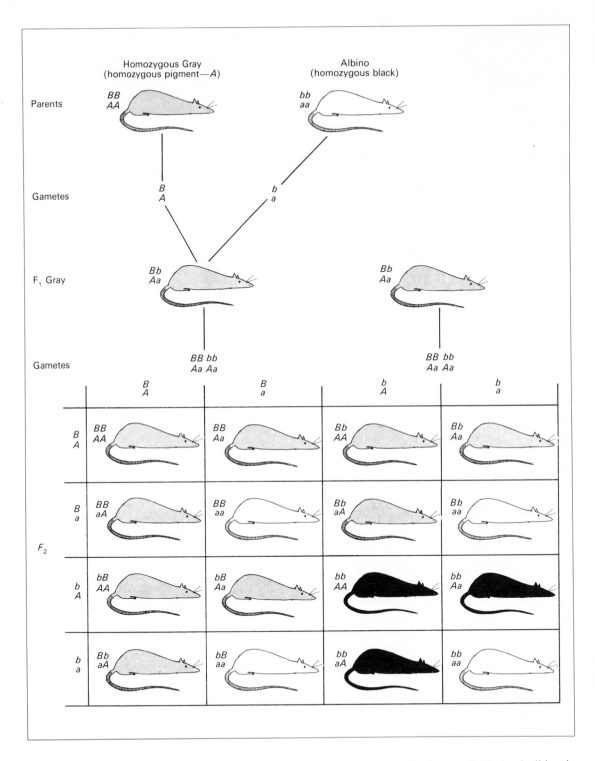

Figure 11–11 Gene interaction (epistasis) in mice-coat color. The ratio 9 gray : 3 black : 4 albino is produced.

The many differences between the sexes in all organisms are ultimately due to chromosomal differences although, in some species, there is no visible difference in the chromosome makeup of the two sexes. In others, however, such as the fruit fly, the chromosome difference between the sexes is quite apparent. In the early 1900s it was noted that in many species of insects the female had one more chromosome than the male, and for a while some people thought that this was the universal difference between sexes. Soon, however, the smaller Y chromosome was detected in the cells of the fruit fly and in many other organisms, including man. At first it was believed that the X chromosome carried genes for determining femaleness and the Y carried genes for maleness. This generalization was found to be untrue, and in many organisms, such as the fruit fly, the Y chromosome has very little to do with sex determination. From experiments on the fruit fly it is apparent that sex is determined by the ratio of autosomes to sex chromosomes, and this seems to be the situation generally in most organisms. In humans and presumably all mammals, however, the Y chromosome is necessary to produce the male characteristics.

It should be added here that the correlation between visible differences in organisms and chromosomal differences would certainly suggest proof for the "chromosome theory of heredity." If all individuals of a particular species with 22 chromosomes were females and all individuals with 21 chromosomes were males, the differences in sex would appear to be due to the chromosome composition. Various means of sex determination have evolved among the organisms and Figure 11-12 lists some of these mechanisms.

SEX-LINKED HEREDITY

In the late 1700s two examples of what we now know to be sex-linked heredity in humans were recorded—red-green color blindness and *hemophilia* (a disorder in which the blood-clotting mechanism functions improperly). In each case the trait is produced by a recessive gene carried on the X chromosome. Since females have two X chromosomes and males have only one, we would expect these traits to occur more often in males because it requires only one recessive gene to produce the disorder (Figure 11-13). For example, a homozygous, normal female (X^c, X^c) and her color-blind husband (X^c, y) will produce normal-visioned sons and carrier (X^c, X^c) daughters. When a carrier daughter has children by a non-color-blind male, one-half of the sons may be color-blind and one-half of the daughters may be carriers (Figure 11-14). This pattern is often referred to as "crisscross" inheritance since an affected father can pass the gene to his daughter and the daughter can then transmit it to her sons.

Experiments with *Drosophila* have provided many explanations about the mechanisms of genetic transfer and we can turn to this organism again for another example of sex-linked heredity. The case of red–white eye color is diagrammed in Figure 11–15. You should note

Organism	Male	Female
Human	44 autosomes + *XY*	44 autosomes + *XX*
Fruit fly	6 autosomes + *XY*	6 autosomes + *XX*
Grasshopper	20 autosomes + *X*	20 autosomes + *XX*
Fowl	16 autosomes + *ZZ*	16 autosomes + *ZW*
Honeybee	16 chromosomes (*N*)	32 chromosomes (*2N*)

Figure 11–12 Different mechanisms of sex determination. Note that in fowl the sex chromosomes are

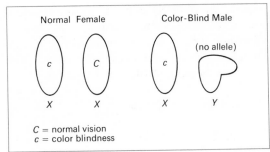

Figure 11–13 Red-green color blindness as carried by the sex chromosomes. The female has the gene for color blindness, but she has another X chromosome with the dominant normal gene. The male has the gene for color blindness, but does not have another X chromosome on which a normal dominant could be present.

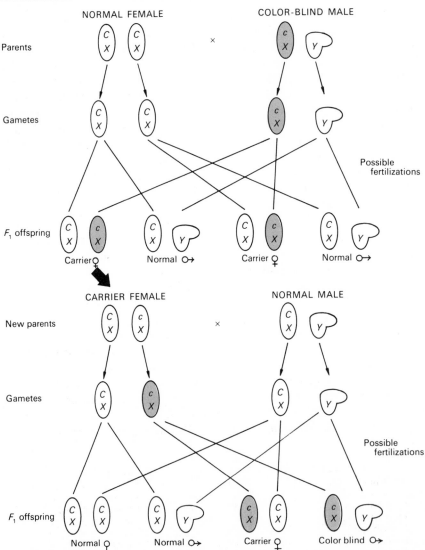

Figure 11–14 Sex-linked heredity in humans: the inheritance of red-green color blindness. Note how the daughter of a color-blind man can be a carrier. It can also be seen how she could pass this to her sons. Color blindness in females, thought not impossible, is less likely to occur since both recessives are required.

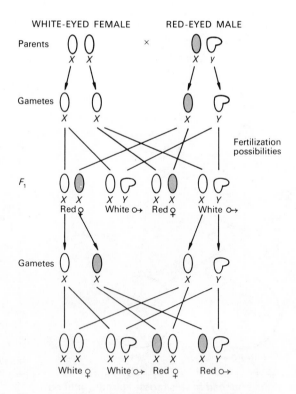

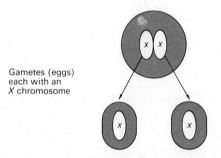

WHITE-EYED FEMALE   RED-EYED MALE

Parents

Gametes

Fertilization
possibilities

F_1

X X   X Y   X X   X Y
Red ♀   White ♂→ Red ♀   White ♂→

Gametes

X X   X Y   X X   X Y
White ♀   White ♂→ Red ♀   Red ♂→

Figure 11–15 Sex-linked heredity in *Drosophila*: the inheritance of red–white eye color. Shaded *X* chromosomes indicate the presence of the gene for red eye; clear *X* chromosomes, the gene for white eye.

that red-eyed daughters of the F_1 generation were produced by a red-eyed father and, in the F_2 generation, the red-eyed females transmit the trait to one-half of their sons.

NONDISJUNCTION

The pattern of inheritance for red–white eye color in the fruit fly had been worked out early in the 1900s by T. H. Morgan and his students. However, one of his students, Calvin Bridges, noted some exceptions to the F_1 pattern (Figure 11–15). On very rare occasions white-eyed females and red-eyed males were produced from a cross between a white-eyed female and a red-eyed male. Such a cross normally produces only red-eyed females and white-eyed males. In order to explain this, Bridges postulated a phenomenon known as

nondisjunction of chromosomes. Normally, homologous chromosomes will separate at meiosis with one member of each pair going to a gamete as illustrated below:

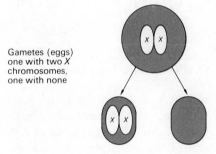

Gametes (eggs)
each with an
X chromosome

If the chromosomes failed to separate (nondisjunction), then the gametes appear as below:

Gametes (eggs)
one with two *X*
chromosomes,
one with none

A cross between a white-eyed female in which nondisjunction occurred and a red-eyed male is shown in Figure 11–16. Bridges looked at cells of the offspring from this cross under the microscope and verified the chromosome compositions he had predicted in these offspring. This was the proof that was needed for the chromosome theory of heredity.

Recently the occurrence of nondisjunction in the chromosomes of humans has also been observed and several developmental anomalies such as *Turner's syndrome* and *Klinefelter's syndrome* have been traced to nondisjunction of the *X* chromosomes. Turner's syndrome results from the union of an *O* egg with an *X*-carrying sperm to form *XO*. This individual is a sterile female and possesses many male characteristics such as heavy neck muscles and narrow hips. In the Klinefelter syndrome,

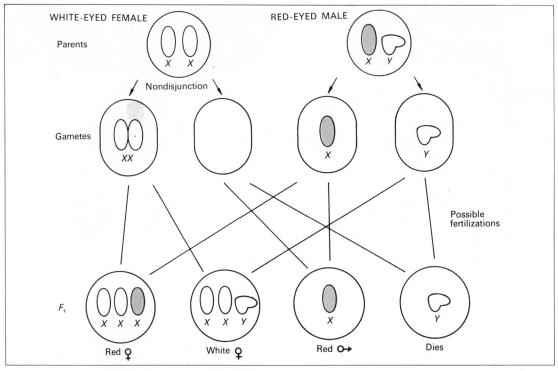

Parents

Nondisjunction

Gametes

XX

X   Y

Possible fertilizations

F₁

X X X   X X Y   X   Y

Red ♀   White ♀   Red ♂→   Dies

Figure 11–16 Bridges' explanation of the rare results obtained in this cross—nondisjunction.

the nondisjunct *XX* unites with a *Y*-carrying sperm to produce a fundamentally male (*XXY*) individual due to the presence of the *Y* chromosome. The male, however, possesses many female characteristics and, as in Turner's syndrome, the sex organs do not reach maturity. Another anomaly, the mongoloid or *Down's syndrome*, is produced by the presence of an extra chromosome (number 21) in the cells of mongoloid individuals. An extra chromosome 21 may appear in human cells by three different mechanisms, and these are illustrated in Figure 11–17.

The most common abnormality in Down's syndrome is *trisomy* (Figure 11–17*a*), where the child has three number 21 chromosomes instead of the normal pair. This occurs when chromosome pair 21 fails to separate during gametogenesis in the mother; the offspring, therefore, has a total chromosome count of 47 instead of the normal 46. *Translocation* (Figure 11–17*b*) is a second mechanism resulting in

Down's syndrome. In this case, the actual chromosome count is the normal 46, but, as in trisomy, the individual has an overdose of chromosome 21 originating from a carrier parent with a 45 chromosome count and a translocation between chromosomes 15 and 21. In other words, one chromosome 15 of the carrier parent also contains chromosome 21 material as illustrated below:

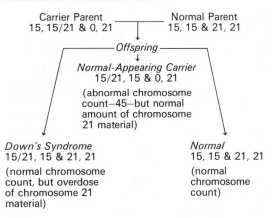

Carrier Parent _____ Normal Parent
15, 15/21 & 0, 21   15, 15 & 21, 21

Offspring

↓

Normal-Appearing Carrier
15/21, 15 & 0, 21

(abnormal chromosome count—45—but normal amount of chromosome 21 material)

Down's Syndrome
15/21, 15 & 21, 21

(normal chromosome count, but overdose of chromosome 21 material)

Normal
15, 15 & 21, 21

(normal chromosome count)

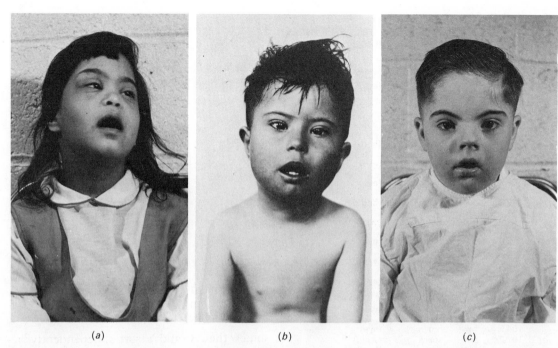

(a)   (b)   (c)

Figure 11–17 The three types of Down's syndrome. (a) Standard trisomy, 1 : 600 births/rarely familial. (b) Translocation, rare/familial. (c) Mosaicism, very rare/not familial. (From *Chromosome 21*; courtesy of The National Foundation—March of Dimes.)

Mosaicism (Figure 11–17c), the third mechanism resulting in Down's syndrome, occurs when cells with different chromosome counts coexist in one individual. Skin cells, for example, may show 46 chromosomes while blood cells show 47. This abnormality is the result of an error in division of an early embryonic cell and is not passed to the individual from a parent.

LINKAGE AND CROSSING OVER

It is believed that each species has thousands of genes controlling the numerous chemical processes and structures necessary for life. However, organisms do not have thousands of chromosomes, and it follows then that each chromosome must contain many genes. We can further state that the genes on a particular chromosome are linked together in a group. For example, all of the known genes in the fruit fly fall into four *linkage groups*, a

fact that Morgan and his students recognized early in their studies. If Mendel had chosen traits other than the seven he experimented with, perhaps he would have noted this principle in peas. Figure 11–18 illustrates the number 2 chromosome of the fruit fly showing the locations of some of the genes. The numbers on the left side of the diagram refer to the relative distances between genes. This type of diagram is called a *chromosome map* and fairly complete maps have now been made for all four of the fruit fly's chromosomes. Such maps have also been made for the chromosomes of corn, some bacteria and viruses, and, to some degree, for a few chromosomes of mice and humans. Perhaps the following discussion will help you understand how these maps are constructed.

In Figure 11–18 note the two recessive genes, *b* for black body and *vg* for vestigial wings (arrows point to these). The normal allele for black body is gray body and is usually

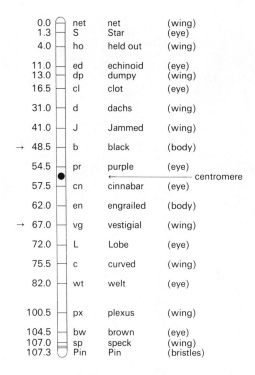

0.0	net	net	(wing)
1.3	S	Star	(eye)
4.0	ho	held out	(wing)
11.0	ed	echinoid	(eye)
13.0	dp	dumpy	(wing)
16.5	cl	clot	(eye)
31.0	d	dachs	(wing)
41.0	J	Jammed	(wing)
→ 48.5	b	black	(body)
54.5	pr	purple	(eye)
		← centromere	
57.5	cn	cinnabar	(eye)
62.0	en	engrailed	(body)
→ 67.0	vg	vestigial	(wing)
72.0	L	Lobe	(eye)
75.5	c	curved	(wing)
82.0	wt	welt	(eye)
100.5	px	plexus	(wing)
104.5	bw	brown	(eye)
107.0	sp	speck	(wing)
107.3	Pin	Pin	(bristles)

Figure 11–18 Chromosome map for the second chromosome of *Drosophila*.

represented by *B*, whereas the normal allele for vestigial wing is long wing, represented by *Vg*. Thus gray body and long wings are dominant over black body and vestigial wings, a condition in which the wings are greatly reduced in size (Figure 11–19). If we were to cross flies homozygous for gray bodies and normal wings with black-bodied, vestigial-winged flies, the *F*₁ generation would all have gray bodies and long wings but would be heterozygous (Figure 11–20).

If these genes were on separate chromo-

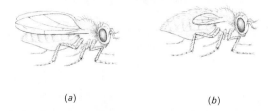

(a)   (b)

Figure 11–19 Comparison of wings in *Drosophila*. (a) Normal. (b) Vestigial.

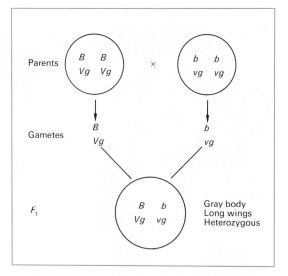

Figure 11–20 Cross in *Drosophila* between gray-body, long-wing flies and black-body, vestigial-wing flies.

somes they would assort independently according to Mendel's second law. (You may remember in the earlier discussion of the dihybrid cross the point was made that the two traits considered were carried on separate chromosomes.) But since the genes are linked they should not assort at meiosis. Let us look at the results of an experimental cross between parents heterozygous for both of these traits (the F_1 of Figure 11–20). It is possible to test-cross individuals from the F_1 generation with individuals homozygous for black body and vestigial wings (double recessive). The "tester" flies can produce only one type of gamete, *b vg*, whether the genes for these traits are linked on one chromosome or are on separate chromosomes. If the genes are inseparably linked, the F_1 individuals would produce two types of gametes, *B Vg* and *b vg*, and offspring from the test cross would be produced in a 1:1 ratio (Figure 11–21a). However, if the genes are not linked but are on separate chromosomes, four classes of gametes would be formed with equal frequencies: *B Vg*, *B vg*, *b Vg*, *b vg*. Four kinds of offspring would therefore be produced in a 1:1:1:1 ratio (Figure 11–21b).

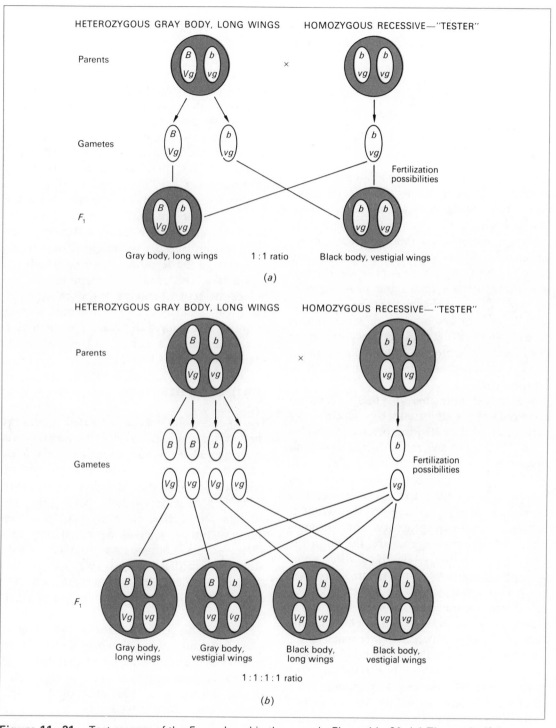

Figure 11–21 Test crosses of the F_1 produced in the cross in Figure 11–20. (*a*) The results if the genes are linked on the same chromosome. (*b*) The results if the genes are on separate chromosomes.

As it turns out neither possibility provides the true answer. The results of the actual experiment are:*

Gray body, long wings	965
Black body, vestigial wings	944
Gray body, vestigial wings	185
Black body, long wings	206
	2,300

All four types of offspring postulated in Figure 11–21b are present but *not* in a 1:1:1:1 ratio. Gray body, long wings and black body, vestigial wings, the two parental types, are present in almost a 1:1 ratio, but how can we account for the low numbers of the other two types of offspring? The answer lies in the fact that the genes are linked but crossing over occurred which exchanged the genes on the homologous chromosomes. The details of this process from a cytological viewpoint were discussed in Chapter 10 and an experimental cross, showing crossover, is diagrammed in Figure 11–22.

We further note that 391 total crossovers occurred (185 + 206), and this is about 17 percent of all the offspring produced (391 ÷ 2,300). If this cross were conducted again and again (and it has been), the same percentage of crossovers, 17 percent, would occur. This has significance since the crossing-over frequency is directly related to the distance between these two genes on the chromosome. The closer two genes are, the lower the percent of crossing over; the farther apart they are, the greater the percent of crossing over. This principle will be more evident to you if you examine the chromosome map in Figure 11–18 again. One unit of chromosome maps represents 1 percent of crossing over.

From Figure 11–18 you should also note that the distance between the black-body gene and the vestigial-wing gene is 18.5 units (18.5 percent). We have stated the crossover frequency here as only 17 percent and the discrepancy should be explained. Crossing over

*A. M. Winchester, *Genetics* (3rd ed.; Boston: Houghton Mifflin, 1966).

occurs all along the chromosome and a *double crossover* between these two genes would return them to the original chromosome. Consequently, the actual percentage of crossing over between the two genes would be obscured. In comparing the crossover rates of the two genes discussed with other genes between the two, we note that the true distance is closer to 18.5 than 17, the difference accounted for by the double crossovers (Figure 11–23).

The actual mechanical processes that occur during crossing over are not completely understood. We can observe the chiasmata between the chromatids under the microscope, and we can observe the resulting offspring which are products of the gametes. Recombination involves the actual breaking and exchanging of parts of homologous chromosomes during meiosis. (See figures in Chapter 10 depicting crossover during synapsis and crossovers in snail chromosomes.)

MULTIPLE ALLELES

Up to this point we have treated a gene as though it could exist in only two forms—that is, as two alleles. Thus we spoke of the gene for body color on the second chromosome of the fruit fly as producing either a gray-body color (*B*) or a black-body color (*b*). The vestigial-wing gene, however, may have five different forms, whereas we noted only two alleles—normal wings and vestigial. Three other intermediate alleles seem to exist—nicked, notched, and strap—but any individual fruit fly can have only two of these alleles.

There is no particular reason why a gene must have only two varieties or forms. If we assume that the normal gene changed once we can also assume that it could change again. If the altered gene was successful in the environment, then it would be present in a definite frequency in the population. Some inheritance patterns can be explained only on the basis of several forms of a specific gene, *multiple alleles*.

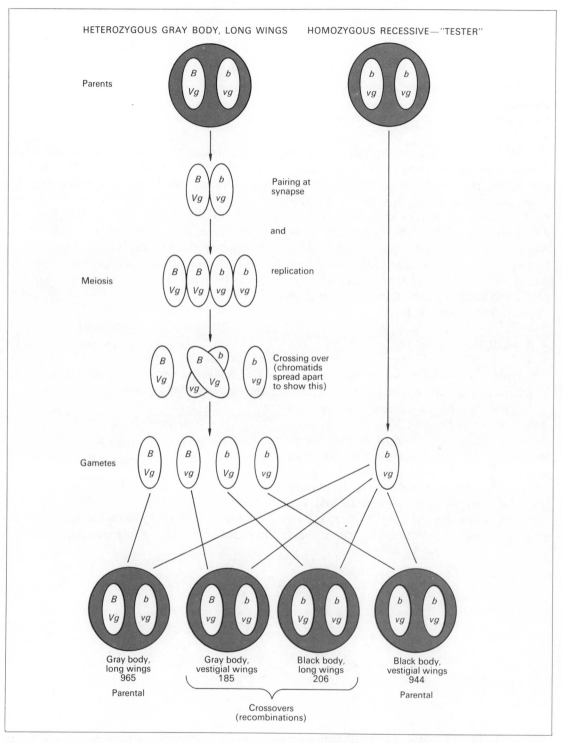

Figure 11—22 Explanation of the results of a test cross in *Drosophila* to determine if the black, vestigial genes are linked and, if so, the amount of crossing over that occurs.

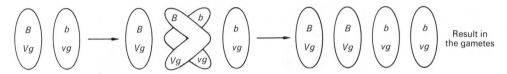

Figure 11–23 How double crossovers can return two genes to the same chromosome. The fact that crossing over occurred between these two genes could then be missed.

Coat color in rabbits apparently is due to various combinations of any two of four different alleles at one position (locus) on the chromosome. The wild-gray color (C) is dominant to all the others; chinchilla (c^{ch}) is dominant to the other two; himalayan (c^{h}) is dominant to albino; and albino (c^{a}) is recessive to all the other alleles. Any individual rabbit would have only two of these alleles and his coat color would be determined according to the hierarchical scheme listed.

A, B, AB, O Blood Types

The only way blood types in humans can be adequately explained is on the basis of multiple alleles (in this case, three). Humans are placed in one of the four blood groups, A, B, AB, or O, on the basis of *agglutination* (clumping of the red corpuscles) tests. This clumping occurs because of a reaction between *antigens* on the corpuscles and *antibodies* in the plasma. Two different antigens, A and B, and two different antibodies, a and b, are known (Figure 11–24). A person with type A blood

has antibodies (b) capable of agglutinating the red blood corpuscles of type B blood. In transfusions, therefore, care must be taken not to administer any blood that can be agglutinated by the antibodies of the recipient. Compatible and incompatible types can be recognized from Figure 11–24.

The following three alleles can account for the inheritance of blood type:

$$I^{O} - \text{no antigen produced}$$
$$I^{A} - \text{antigen } A \text{ produced}$$
$$I^{B} - \text{antigen } B \text{ produced}$$

The following genotypes would then explain the various blood groups:

$$I^{A} \, I^{A} \text{ or } I^{A} \, I^{O} - \text{type A}$$
$$I^{B} \, I^{B} \text{ or } I^{B} \, I^{O} - \text{type B}$$
$$I^{A} \, I^{B} \qquad\quad - \text{type AB}$$
$$I^{O} \, I^{O} \qquad\quad - \text{type O}$$

This information can be useful but not always conclusive in cases of disputed parenthood. It

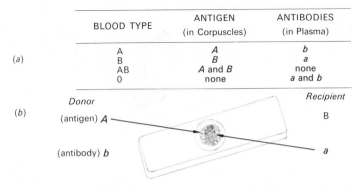

	BLOOD TYPE	ANTIGEN (in Corpuscles)	ANTIBODIES (in Plasma)
(a)	A	A	b
	B	B	a
	AB	A and B	none
	0	none	a and b

(b)   Donor   Recipient

(antigen) *A*   B

(antibody) *b*   a

Figure 11–24 (*a*) Human blood types showing distributions of antigens and antibodies. (*b*) The result of transfusing incompatible blood types. The antigen *A* in blood type A reacts with the antibody *a* in blood type B to produce clumping of the red blood corpuscles.

would be possible, for example, to state only that a man could not possibly be the father of a specific baby, or that he possibly could be, on the basis of blood types.

Rh Blood Factors

When red blood cells from a rhesus monkey are injected into a rabbit, the rabbit makes antibodies against an antigen contained in the cells. These antibodies will cause a clumping reaction when added to rhesus monkey blood. Using these rabbit antibodies, Karl Landsteiner and A. S. Wiener tested 448 persons in New York City and found that about 85 percent of those tested possessed this antigen; they were designated as Rh-positive (Rh$^+$) since the antigen was originally discovered in the rhesus monkey. The remaining 15 percent has no antigen and were therefore termed Rh-negative (Rh$^-$). In addition, Rh$^-$ individuals normally carry no Rh antibodies. Later it was learned that there are at least twelve types of positive antigens.

Two theories have been proposed to explain the inheritance of Rh antigens: (1) a series of three closely linked genes on a single chromosome, and (2) at least eight variations of one gene (multiple alleles). Whichever theory is correct, it is possible to deal with the situation by assuming that Rh$^+$ is dominant to Rh$^-$. Therefore, in this simplified explanation Rh$^+$ Rh$^+$ = Rh$^+$; Rh$^+$ Rh$^-$ = Rh$^+$; and Rh$^-$ Rh$^-$ = Rh$^-$.

The most common problems encountered with Rh factor occur in blood transfusions and child bearing. An Rh$^-$ person may be transfused with Rh$^+$ blood with no adverse effects. However, his blood has become "sensitized" due to the production of antibodies, and a second transfusion of Rh$^+$ blood may be fatal because of extensive agglutination. If an Rh$^-$ mother bears an Rh$^-$ child, no blood complications will arise. Furthermore, no problems are usually encountered when an Rh$^-$ mother bears her first Rh$^+$ child. A slight leak in the placenta, however, may allow some of the Rh$^+$ red blood cells from the fetus to enter the mother's blood and "sensitize" her. A sub-sequent Rh$^+$ child is in serious danger of having its blood clumped by the antibodies produced in this manner. This condition is known as *erythroblastosis fetalis* and may be fatal. It should be emphasized here that there is usually no problem if both the mother and father are Rh$^-$ or if the mother is Rh$^+$.

Today we are able to detect Rh factor complications before birth and make a complete transfusion of the infant's blood. An Rh factor serum has also been developed which if given to an Rh$^-$ mother immediately after each childbirth protects the next child. This serum contains Rh antibodies which destroy fetal Rh antigens before they can cause the mother to produce Rh antibodies.

QUANTITATIVE INHERITANCE

In previous examples we spoke of characteristics in a qualitative sense—that is, whether or not a given trait was present. Moreover, we have been attributing most of these traits to one gene. For example, Mendel's peas were considered to have either round seeds or wrinkled seeds and the trait was due to two alleles. Two groups therefore would be present in the population, round and wrinkled seeded varieties. There are characteristics in organisms, however, that do not fit into discrete, contrasting groups. These characteristics show a continuous distribution in the population and are usually represented by the well-known normal distribution curve (Figure 11–25). Some of these traits are intelligence and body

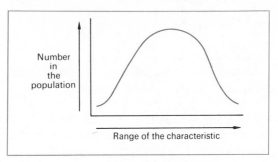

Figure 11–25 Normal distribution curve in the population for traits such as intelligence and body stature in humans.

387

stature in humans, height in corn plants, and seed-coat color in wheat. Characteristics such as these can be explained only on the basis of several to many nondominant genes sorting independently but exerting a cumulative or additive effect on the particular trait. We have already considered the effect of one pair of nondominant alleles on a characteristic such as flower color (Figure 11–10). When two pink hybrids were crossed, the resulting phenotypic ratio was 1:2:1 (1 red: 2 pink: 1 white).

Let us now consider a trait that results when two pairs of alleles lacking dominance have a cumulative effect on that trait; the phenotypic ratio under these conditions would be 1:4:6:4:1 (Figure 11–26). If a trait were produced by three pairs of nondominant alleles, the ratio would be 1:6:15:20:15:6:1. Such a ratio would produce a much smoother curve than one for only two alleles. In humans it is estimated that skin color is produced by four to seven pairs of alleles.

EFFECT OF ENVIRONMENT

It must be remembered that we inherit genes not traits. When we say that a boy got his brown eyes from his dad, what we really mean is that he got the genes for brown eyes from his dad. Every gene must develop in an environment, and the environment determines to some extent how that gene will develop. In the case of vestigial wings in fruit flies (Figure 11–19), the vestigial-wing characteristic will develop if the flies are raised at room temperature. If the flies are reared at about 92° F (33° C), however, the wings will be almost normal.

Identical twins reared apart will often show striking differences when compared later in life. The question, "Which is more important, heredity or environment?" can be a moot question since both factors are necessary in the development of an individual organism. First, it is essential that we understand the genetic mechanism for a specific trait. Furthermore, we must be able to determine how much effect the environment can have on the development of any given genetic system. In a few cases,

such as Down's syndrome (described earlier in this chapter), we do not know that the presence of an extra number 21 chromosome sets genetic limits which are impossible to overcome completely in any environment. In general, any trait is the outcome of a varying interaction between genetic factors and the environment. As yet, the exact relationship between genetics and environment is poorly understood.

GENE-ACTION GENETICS

While transmission genetics is concerned with the mechanical details of genes passed from generation to generation, gene action attempts to explain what the genes are actually doing to produce their effects. One of the most active studies going on in modern biology is concerned with what happens between the gene on the chromosome and the visible phenotype expressed by that gene. There are still problems to be answered in transmission genetics, but the greatest interest and activity in genetics today is in the field of gene action. How a gene produces its effect has already been indicated in Chapter 3 under the concept of protein synthesis. This basic scheme of DNA → RNA → protein forms the foundation for our discussion on gene action.

INBORN ERRORS OF METABOLISM

Perhaps the first notable discussion on gene action was published in 1908 by an English physician, Sir Archibald Garrod. In a book entitled *Inborn Errors of Metabolism*, he dealt with a group of congenital metabolic disorders. In tracing the inheritance pattern of these diseases, Garrod noted that they were apparently produced by the action of one gene. One of these "inborn errors" he studied was *alcaptonuria*, which has the symptoms of blackening of the urine upon exposure to air and the darkening of certain cartilages. The substance responsible for this is homogentisic acid, a carbon-ring compound that is normally split in the metabolism of an individual. Garrod believed that alcaptonuria was caused by the inability of afflicted individuals to split

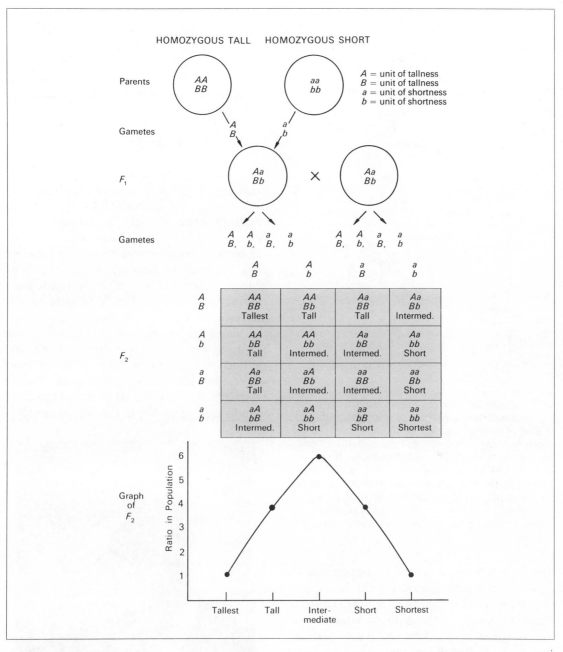

HOMOZYGOUS TALL   HOMOZYGOUS SHORT

A = unit of tallness
B = unit of tallness
a = unit of shortness
b = unit of shortness

Figure 11—26 Quantitative inheritance of the trait of height in some organism assuming that the trait is produced by two pairs of cumulative, nondominant alleles. The graph of the F_2 generation shows a normal curve.

this ring compound due to the absence or inactivity of an enzyme. He further hypothesized that the lack of an effective enzyme was due to the absence of the normal form of a particular gene. Garrod was actually suggesting that a gene is responsible for the production of a specific enzyme and this idea was later developed as the *one gene—one enzyme* theory. It is interesting to note that in the 1930s it was discovered that individuals afflicted with alcaptonuria do lack the liver enzyme homogentisate oxidase which is essential for catalyz-

389

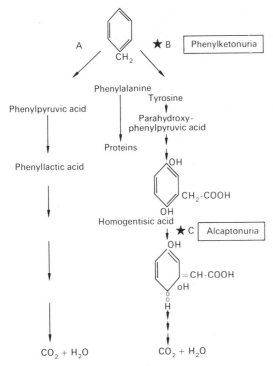

Phenylketonuria

A   ★ B

CH$_2$

Phenylalanine

Tyrosine

Phenylpyruvic acid

Parahydroxy-
phenylpyruvic acid

Proteins

Phenyllactic acid

OH

CH$_2$-COOH

OH

Homogentisic acid   ★ C   Alcaptonuria

OH

=CH-COOH

OH

CO$_2$ + H$_2$O   CO$_2$ + H$_2$O

Figure 11–27 Partial metabolism of phenylalanine. It can be incorporated into proteins in the cell or converted to tyrosine or phenylpyruvic acid. If the enzyme is lacking at B, then most of the phenylalanine converts to phenylpyruvic acid, producing the disease phenylketonuria. If the enzyme is lacking (or is defective) at C, alcaptonuria results. Note that normally the ultimate products in these pathways are burned to CO$_2$ + H$_2$O in the Krebs cycle. Many intermediate products are omitted here; thus the series of arrows in some places.

ing the reaction that splits the ring compound, homogentisic acid (Figure 11–27).

A more serious "inborn error" is the disease *phenylketonuria*, which produces extreme mental retardation in children. This disorder results when phenylalanine cannot be converted to tyrosine, also due to the lack of an enzyme (Figure 11–27). When this occurs, phenylpyruvic acid accumulates and apparently affects brain development. It has been shown that this disease is the result of homozygosity for a recessive gene and only about one birth in 25,000 in the United States results in phenylketonuria (known also as PKU).

Urine tests can determine at birth whether an individual is phenylketonuric and these tests are mandatory in some states. If affected individuals are then placed on phenylalanine-free diets in the early years of their lives, most of the damage can be prevented.

NEUROSPORA STUDIES

If we want to know what a gene is doing in an organism, it is better to study haploid organisms (one set of chromosomes) than diploid organisms (two sets of chromosomes). The reason for this is that a mutant recessive gene can be masked by a dominant allele in a diploid form, whereas in a haploid organism the single gene, whether it is normal or mutated, must express itself. George Beadle (Figure 11–28) and Edward Tatum (who were later awarded the Nobel Prize along with Joshua Lederberg for their work in genetics) realized this and utilized the red mold *Neurospora* in their studies of gene action. This mold (Figure 11–29) displays a life cycle in which the mold spends most of its life in the haploid state.

Figure 11–28 George Beadle, recipient of the Nobel Prize in 1958 for his studies in gene action. (Courtesy of Dr. Beadle.)

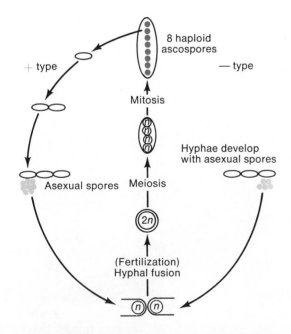

Figure 11–29 Life cycle of the red mold *Neurospora*. The events in the cycle start at hyphal-fusion stage (a hypha is a filamentous strand). The situation is similar to that in *Spirogyra*, where conjugation occurs. The combining forms are represented as + and − types. Note that *Neurospora* can produce asexual spores also.

To summarize, *Neurospora* is well suited to genetic experiments for the following reasons:

1 It can be easily grown in the laboratory on a simple (called *minimal*) medium of sugar, inorganic salts, and biotin (a vitamin B).
2 The spores produced by meiosis are in a linear order (Figure 11–30) in a spore case and can be analyzed readily.
3 It can reproduce asexually (as well as sexually) so that different types can be propagated without genetic change.
4 It is haploid throughout most of its life cycle so that recessive genes cannot be masked by dominant alleles.

Beadle and Tatum knew that it was difficult to determine what a gene was doing if only the normal gene was available to study. However, they felt that if a gene could be changed so that it no longer performed normally then it should be possible to determine what the gene was doing. An analogous situation in an as-

sembly line is described in Figure 11–31. Their objective then was to produce *mutations* in the genes and determine what related chemical changes occurred in the organism. By noting the specific chemical difference between the mutant and the normal molds, it should be possible to associate the normal chemical function with the normal gene.

The procedure used by Beadle and Tatum can be simply outlined as follows:

1 Asexually produced spores were x-rayed to produce mutations.
2 These growing spores were crossed with another strain and eight haploid spores (ascospores) were produced.
3 The ascospores then were transferred to a complete medium that included minimal medium plus all the vitamins and amino

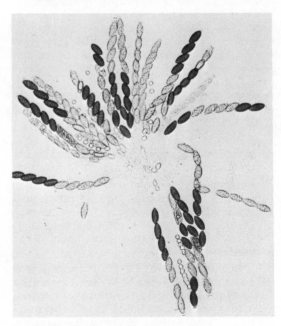

Figure 11–30 Appearance of the spore-containing structures (asci) produced when a wild-type strain of *Neurospora* is crossed with a mutant that exhibits delayed maturation. The dark spores are the wild type, while the lighter ones are mutant. Eight spores are produced in each ascus. When the spores are aligned with four dark and four light in an ascus, crossing over does not occur at meiosis. Other spore distributions indicate crossing over at meiosis. (Courtesy of Dr. David R. Stadler.)

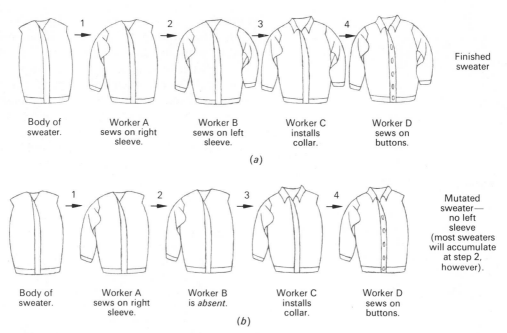

Figure 11–31 Hypothetical sweater factory. (*a*) Normal assembly-line procedure. (*b*) Changed or interrupted assembly-line procedure. When the normal assembly operation is changed or interrupted, the finished product is changed. If worker B is absent, the factory piles up sweaters with no left sleeve, no collar, and no buttons. If worker C is absent, sweaters accumulate having no collar and no buttons. Thus, by observing the factory on a day when B is missing and on another day when C is missing, we can deduce that B puts on left sleeves and that C puts on either collars or buttons, and that B handles the sweater before C does.

acids; here they grew and produced colonies.

4 Portions of these colonies next were transferred to minimal medium and some could not grow here (remember that all normal *Neurospora* can grow on minimal medium); those that could not grow here were evidently mutated.

5 Since Beadle and Tatum theorized that these mutated forms had lost the ability to synthesize necessary vitamins or amino acids, the next step was to transfer portions of colonies unable to grow on minimal medium to two different kinds of media: (*a*) minimal plus vitamins and (*b*) minimal plus amino acids. In this way it could be determined whether the mutation produced the inability to make a necessary vitamin or a necessary amino acid.

6 Those spores that grew on the minimal-plus-vitamin medium and died on the minimal-plus-amino-acid medium evidently had lost the ability to produce a particular vitamin; those that displayed opposite results on the two media could not make certain amino acids.

7 The next step was to determine which specific vitamin or amino acid the mold was unable to synthesize. This could be tested by placing portions of the colony of the mutant that lacked necessary vitamins on individual cultures which contained minimal medium plus one vitamin. If the mutant would then grow, for example, only on minimal medium plus vitamin B_1, the mutant had evidently lost the ability through a mutation to produce vitamin B_1. These steps are summarized in Figure 11–32.

Beadle and Tatum concluded that the mutant was unable to make vitamin B_1 because of the inability to produce a specific enzyme necessary for its synthesis. They further theorized that the inability to make the enzyme was due to a mutated gene. They were able to show through genetic crosses of the

392

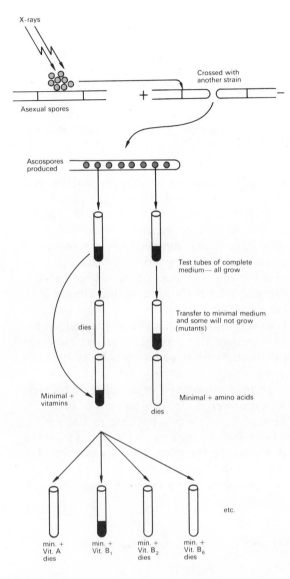

X-rays

Asexual spores

Crossed with
another strain

+ −

Ascospores
produced

Test tubes of complete
medium— all grow

dies

Transfer to minimal medium
and some will not grow
(mutants)

Minimal +
vitamins

Minimal + amino acids

dies

etc.

min. +
Vit. A
dies

min. +
Vit. B₁

min. +
Vit. B₂
dies

min. +
Vit. B₆
dies

Figure 11–32 *Neurospora* experiment of Beadle and Tatum. Note the mutant ultimately grows on minimal medium plus vitamin B₁ only.

mutant strain with a normal strain that the inheritance of the mutant trait followed the pattern of Mendel's monohybrid cross. Beadle and Tatum's work thus strengthened the one gene–one enzyme theory of gene action held at that time. The current concept is "one gene –one polypeptide."

Studies on *Neurospora* have been extremely helpful in the tracing of biochemical pathways in the synthesis of certain products, such as vitamins. Through the method of deductive reasoning, as noted in Figure 11–31, specific intermediate steps can be determined. As a result of these studies it has been possible to correlate many of the steps in these pathways with specific genes. Through these correlations we arrive at a better understanding of how genes act. For example, many of the steps in the synthesis of niacin (another B vitamin) from anthranilic acid in *Neurospora* are known, as well as the enzymes that control these steps. That specific genes are responsible for the production of specific enzymes in this sequence of events is also known (determined from genetic crosses). These general events are illustrated in Figure 11–33.

HEMOGLOBIN STUDIES

Another approach to the understanding of gene action was made by Vernon Ingram at the University of Cambridge. He reasoned that if genes do determine the synthesis of specific proteins, an examination of two different proteins, one produced by a normal gene and one produced by a mutant gene, should reveal how the genes produced these different proteins. Of the several deviant forms of human hemoglobin known, perhaps the best known is the sickle-cell type, which produces sickle-cell anemia, a hereditary disease transmitted by a single gene. Two closely related proteins—normal hemoglobin and sickle-cell hemoglobin—can be studied and compared.

Ingram and his coworkers proceeded to analyze these two proteins (a complex chemical analysis which need not be presented here). Each protein was separated into twenty-eight peptide groups and studied for differences. The peptides were exactly alike in the two proteins except for the number 4 peptide unit. In this peptide group, where normal hemoglobin has a glutamic-acid molecule, sickle-cell hemoglobin has a valine molecule. Thus the two proteins differ in only one amino acid out of 300. This may seem like an insignificant

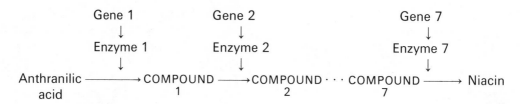

Figure 11-33 General scheme for the synthesis of niacin from anthranilic acid. The relationship between genes, enzymes, and intermediate compounds is shown.

variation in the two molecules but the shape of red blood cells containing sickle-cell hemoglobin can be radically changed and the circulation to tissues greatly reduced.

In looking for the mechanism that produced these structural changes in the proteins, Ingram utilized the concept presented in Chapter 3 of DNA providing a code for the construction of specific proteins. The gene would therefore be a segment of the DNA molecule with the nucleotide sequence instructing the cell which protein to make (Figure 11-34).

BACTERIAL AND VIRAL GENETICS

It is extremely important to select organisms for experimental studies which are well suited for the investigation of a particular problem. We have seen how valuable the fruit fly has

been to the field of transmission genetics, and that *Neurospora* had distinct advantages for gene-action studies. In studies on the fundamental hereditary material, viruses (noncellular structures composed only of protein and nucleic acids) and bacteria, which have all their genes in one chromosome, have been helpful. Genetic studies on bacteria and viruses have suggested that the gene is far more complex than we originally thought. For example, it is now evident that crossing over and mutation can occur within genes as well as between genes.

In 1946 *conjugation*, or sexuality, in bacteria was discovered. In this process a bridge is formed between two bacteria of compatible strains and genetic material is passed from the donor to the recipient. It is also known that the amount of genetic material transferred can be controlled by varying the length of conjugation time.

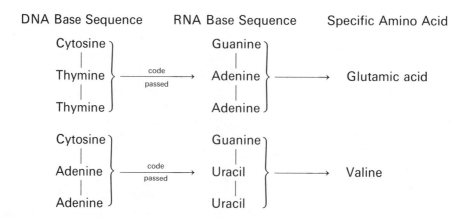

Figure 11-34 Proposed scheme for the coding of glutamic acid and valine into proteins. A slight change in one segment of the DNA base sequence could change the code in the RNA; hence a different amino acid would be incorporated into the protein.

Another interesting and informative genetic-transfer mechanism in bacteria is *transformation*, the process wherein extracted DNA from one strain of bacteria is taken up by another strain of bacteria. This mechanism was one of the first strong indications that DNA is the chief substance of heredity. For example, pneumococcus bacteria (producers of bacterial pneumonia) are typically enclosed in smooth capsules, but a mutation may produce bacteria that cannot make a capsule and consequently appear irregular and rough. DNA can be extracted from a colony of smooth, encapsulated bacteria and introduced into the culture medium of rough-coated bacteria. When this is done a low percentage (much higher than the mutation rate, however) of smooth colonies will appear among the rough colonies (Figure 11–35). It is believed that the DNA from the smooth bacteria is actually incorporated into the DNA of the rough strains. If the protein from encapsulated bacteria is placed in the culture, transformation does not occur. Since DNA is required to bring about transformation, it appears that DNA is the carrier of heredity.

A third type of genetic transfer in bacteria is *transduction*, in which *bacteriophages* (viruses which infect bacteria) act as vectors and transport DNA from one bacterium to another. After a virus enters a bacterial cell, the virus DNA can combine with the DNA of the host

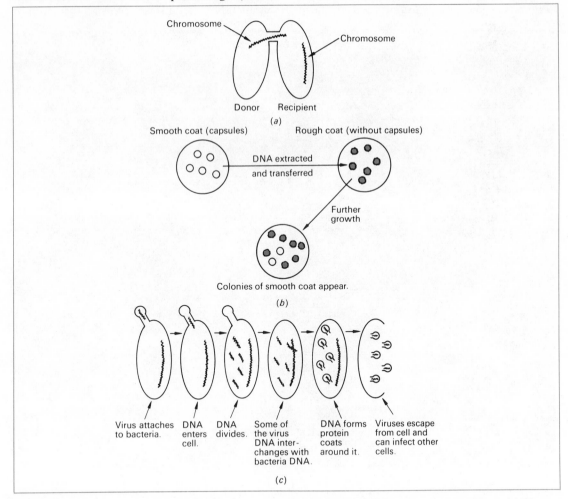

Figure 11–35 Types of genetic transfer in bacteria. (*a*) Conjugation. (*b*) Transformation. (*c*) Transduction.

395

under certain conditions, and the viral DNA utilizes the protein-synthesis mechanism of the bacterium to reproduce itself. After the viruses reproduce and leave a bacterium, they can transfer part of that bacterium's DNA to another bacterium. Evidence from several studies indicates that only the DNA enters the bacterium cell while the protein jacket stays outside. This is one more bit of evidence that DNA is the genetic substance.

While some viruses contain DNA as their nucleic acid, others have RNA, and genetic studies have been conducted on both types. We will only discuss here the DNA containing T2 and T4 viruses which infect *Escherichia coli*, the bacterium found in the colon of man (Figure 11–36). They are composed of a head,

tail base or end plate with spikes, and tail fibers. The effects of bacteriophages (often shortened to *phage*) can be studied rather easily since they leave a clear area, known as a *plaque*, in a bacterial culture where they have destroyed the bacterial cells. Many mutant forms of phages are known and these can be studied, and often identified, by the plaque, or type of plaque, that develops when they infect their hosts.

A T4 virus attaches itself to the bacterial surface of an *E. coli* cell by the tail fibers and spikes of the end plate. The tail then penetrates the cell wall and permits the DNA to pass into the cell from the head of the virus (Figure 11–37). Upon entering the cell the viral DNA begins to control the protein-

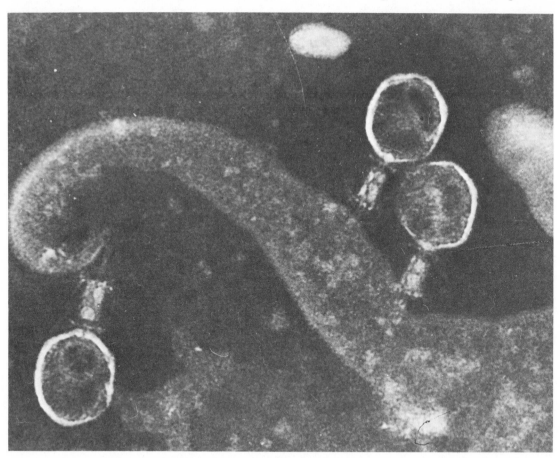

Figure 11–36 Electron micrograph of T2 bacteriophages attached to a fragment of a bacterial cell wall (× 200,000). (Courtesy of Dr. R. W. Horne.)

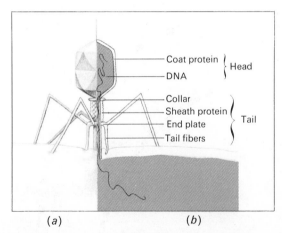

Coat protein } Head
DNA

Collar
Sheath protein } Tail
End plate
Tail fibers

(a)   (b)

Figure 11–37 (a) Bacteriophage particle showing the six-sided "head" containing the strands of DNA, the "tail" with its central core, the "tail" plate and fibers. (b) The same bacteriophage particle showing the movement of DNA into the bacterial cell. The central core has penetrated the wall of the bacterium, and the DNA has passed down into the cell. (Redrawn from K. M. Smith, *Viruses*, 1963. By permission of Cambridge University Press, New York.)

synthesis mechanism of the bacterial cell and viral DNA and protein are made. About one-half hour after infection, approximately 200 new viruses have been produced and these are released from the destroyed bacterial cell in a process known as *lysis*. (Plaques thus form where lysis occurs.) A normal virus must be complete if it is to be infective—that is, the head, tail, end plate, etc. must be put together in an orderly manner. Over 40 genes are known in the T4 virus which control the normal development and construction of an individual phage, and more than 75 mutations are known which can interfere with normal development.

W. B. Wood and R. S. Edgar have recently studied the sequential steps involved in the normal assemblage of a T4 virus. They infected bacteria with various mutants, determined which parts of the virus had been constructed, and analyzed electron micrographs of the viral structures at various stages. One of their experiments is diagrammed in Figure 11–38. A partial genetic map of the T4 virus chromosome is shown in Figure 11–39 along with the way in which each

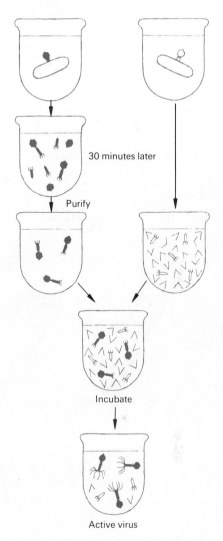

Mutant defective in genes 34, 35, 37, 38   Mutant defective in gene 23

30 minutes later

Purify

Incubate

Active virus

Figure 11–38 Experiment of tail fibers attached to fiberless particles. Cells are infected with a virus (black) bearing defective tail-fiber genes. The progeny particles are isolated with a centrifuge. A virus with a head-gene mutation (white) infects a second bacterial culture, providing an extract containing free tails and tail fibers. When the two preparations are mixed and incubated at 30°C, the fiberless particles are converted to infectious virus particles by the attachment of the free fibers. (From "Building a Bacterial Virus" by William B. Wood and R. S. Edgar. Copyright © 1967 by Scientific American, Inc. All rights reserved.)

397

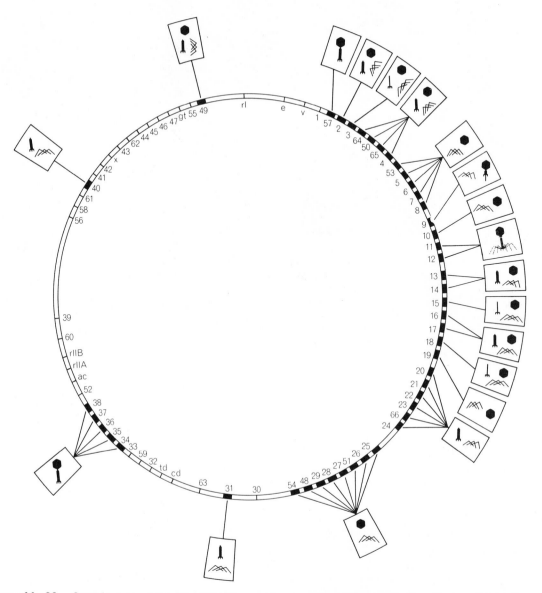

Figure 11–39 Genetic map of the T4 virus. The numbers represent the genes identified so far on the basis of mutations. The small diagrams radiating from each blackened gene area show the effect of that mutation. A mutation in gene 19, for example, would produce an incomplete virus, one without a collar and most of the tail. (From "Building a Bacterial Virus" by William B. Wood and R. S. Edgar. Copyright © 1967 by Scientific American, Inc. All rights reserved.)

mutant interferes with normal development. This study represents an attempt to discover how each gene functions in the development of a virus.

MUTATIONS

Mutations have already been introduced in this chapter and they were described as essentially permanent changes in the genetic material. The concept and term were first proposed by Hugo De Vries in 1901 to account for some sudden changes he observed in his experiments on the evening primrose. When we speak of a mutation we generally mean a gene mutation, although chromosomal mutations certainly do occur. Chromosomal mutations are structural alterations known as *deletions*, *translocations*, and *inversions*, and involve segments of one or more chromosomes (Figure 11–40).

Deletion occurs when any part of a chromosome breaks away during division and is lost in the cytoplasm. The result of deletion is usually the production of gametes which are nonviable because of the loss of genetic information. A deletion may occur at the end of a chromatid (one break) or in the middle of the arm (two breaks). In the second case, the broken ends may fuse to save the remainder of the chromosome. *Translocation* implies that some segment of a chromosome is shifted from its normal position and the broken piece may fuse with its homologue or even with a non-homologue.

Inversion is the 180-degree reversal of a section of a chromosome and may occur in a terminal segment or involve two simultaneous breaks (Figures 11–40 and 11–41). When a chromosome with an inversion pairs with its homologue in prophase of meiosis, it must form a loop (inversion loop) to facilitate the gene-to-gene pairing. If a crossover occurs within the loop, serious genetic consequences result (Figure 11–41). Not only are certain genes repeated or deleted, but dicentric (having two centromeres) and acentric (without a centromere) chromosomes are produced. The dicentric chromosome is broken during division and the acentric is lost completely.

Gene mutations, on the other hand, are often called *point* mutations (or just mutations) and probably involve only one or a few nucleotides in the chromosome. We can also differentiate between spontaneous and induced mutations. Spontaneous mutations occur at random without known cause, and their rates vary considerably among organisms and among specific genes. It is difficult, therefore, to state a general spontaneous mutation rate although one in 100,000 to one in 1,000,000 cells is often given as the general frequency of occurrence. The mutation rate for the gene that produces hemophilia is rather high, one in approximately every 40,000 gametes, whereas the gene that produces aniridia in man (absence of an iris in the eye) mutates with a frequency of about one in every 200,000

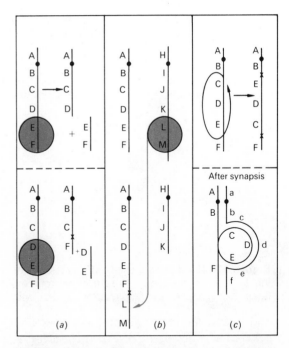

Figure 11–40 Three common types of chromosome aberrations. (*a*) Deletion, two types. (*b*) Nonhomologous translocation. (*c*) Inversion. Note the formation of the inversion loop during synapsis in the inversion. Refer to Figure 11–41 for the meiotic results.

gametes. Induced mutations, on the other hand, are the result of exposure to radiation and certain chemicals.

Mutations are certainly important to the evolutionary process, for they offer the only real source of raw material on which natural selection can work. New chromosome and gene combinations can be produced through meiosis, crossing over, and random fertilizations, but only mutations (chromosomal or gene) really offer new raw material to the process. Most mutations that we observe today are considered harmful. Since well-adapted organisms are the result of a long selection process, any change in their evolutionary development is more likely to be harmful than helpful. We should therefore expect useful mutations to the well-adapted organism to be quite rare. Whether a mutation is beneficial or detrimental may depend on the specific environment at the time it occurs. Moreover, if a mutation is to be passed on to the offspring, it must occur in the gametes. Mutations in the

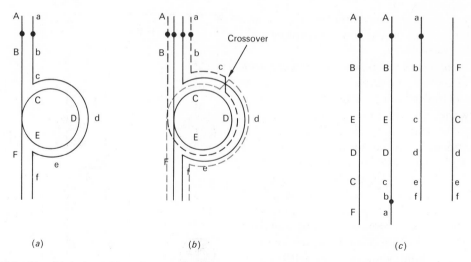

Figure 11–41 Meiotic results of a crossover occurring in a paracentric inversion (the centromeres are located outside the loop). Note that one chromosome contains two centromeres and that another has none. (*a*) Synapsis. (*b*) Duplication (tetrad) with crossover. (*c*) Final gametic distribution.

body cells are not transmitted to the next generation but often reveal themselves as patches of abnormal tissue, often forming mosaic patterns.

Mutations that may be harmful to a particular species are often selected by man for his benefit. A seedless orange obviously can only be harmful to the species that produced it, but to man it represents a fruit that can be eaten conveniently. The Ancon breed of sheep, characterized by extremely short legs, arose from a single gene mutation that was first noted in 1791 in Massachusetts. For the sheep this is definitely a detrimental condition since it restricts their movement, but for man it is advantageous since lower fences are required to contain the sheep.

Some of the earliest experiments on the induction of mutations were performed with x-rays on *Drosophila* in 1927 by Herman J. Muller, who later won the Nobel Prize for his contributions. Since that time numerous experiments have shown many chemicals and radiations to be mutagenic. A variety of chemical agents such as formaldehyde, peroxide, caffeine, nicotine, nitrous oxide, 5-bromouracil, 2-aminopurine, and mustard gas can produce mutations. Furthermore heat, ultraviolet light, high-energy radiation such

as x-rays, gamma rays, alpha and beta particles, and cosmic rays can all be mutagenic. Just how these many agents bring about mutations is the subject of much discussion among biologists. The ultimate result must be a change in the DNA molecule, and this must involve a change in one or more base pairs in the normal sequence of nucleotides. Any mechanism that could open the DNA molecule or make it unstable, or substitute for some of the normal bases, could conceivably produce this effect. A group of compounds known as base analogues, represented by 5-bromouracil and 2-aminopurine mentioned above, are similar in structure to the normal purines and pyrimidines contained in DNA. These are highly mutagenic and it could be that these replace normal bases in certain positions and then pair with a different normal base, thereby bringing about a change in the original nucleotide sequence. Such a process could bring about base-pair changes from thymine-adenine to cytosine-guanine, for example. When such a change occurs, T–A to C–G (or A–T to C–G or T–A to C–G, etc.), the coded message has been changed (Figure 11–42). This is the kind of change which produces the slight differences between proteins such as normal and sickle-cell hemoglobins where they differ

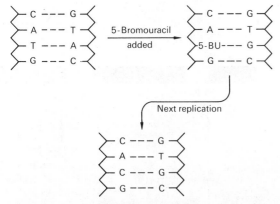

Figure 11–42 Hypothetical events that might produce a change in the code of the DNA molecule. 5-Bromouracil replaces thymine; during replication, 5-BU pairs with guanine. In the next replication, cytosine replaces 5-BU and combines with guanine. The ultimate effect is a change in a T-A base pair to C-G.

in only one amino acid out of 300. Modern medicine utilizes base analogues, as well as x-rays and other radiation, to interfere with the mechanism of certain cells that are growing abnormally.

WHAT IS A GENE?

The word *gene* was first used in 1909 to indicate a single unit of heredity that occupied a specific position in a chromosome. Experiments on *Drosophila* (fruit fly) added to an understanding of the gene in terms of recombinational (crossing over) and mutational units. *Neurospora* studies certainly shed much light on the gene as a functional unit—that is, what it actually does in the cell. The contribution of microbial genetics (bacteria and viruses) was really twofold: first, transformation and transduction experiments confirmed the fact that DNA is the hereditary substance and showed that a gene is a segment of the DNA molecule; second, studies on these simple forms which contain less complex genetic material have provided new concepts of the recombinational and mutational aspects of the gene. Moreover, research in microbial genetics has shown that crossing over and mutation can occur within a gene.

In 1953, when geneticists working with bacteria and *Neurospora* were making significant contributions, a model that could account for the duplication, coding, and mutational features of DNA was proposed. Known as the Watson-Crick model, it suggested that the hereditary substance was composed of base pairs of nucleotides and that these bases spelled out a code to the cell's machinery. Since the one gene–one enzyme theory was strongly held, it seemed that the code was directing the cell to manufacture specific enzymes or proteins. Studies on the specific protein, hemoglobin, showed that the normal form differed from a mutant form by only one amino acid. A change in the code, perhaps in only one nucleotide, could account for the substitution of the wrong amino acid. This was how we defined a mutation, a change in the coded message of the DNA molecule.

So we see that our concept of a gene has been modified considerably from the factors of Mendel to the nucleotides of the modern geneticist. In this modern concept, a gene is considered to be a segment of DNA coding for a complete polypeptide (which may be an enzyme or structural protein or a subunit of an enzyme or structural protein). It is useful, however, to consider a gene in ways other than its functional role; it can be regarded as a unit of recombination (crossing over) and as a unit of mutation. In all three roles (a unit of function, a unit of recombination, and a unit of mutation), it is still considered as a series of nucleotides along the DNA molecule. As it was pointed out earlier, however, microbial genetics show that these three activities can occur within sites formerly called genes and may have different boundaries. To account for this, three terms were designated and defined: *recon*—the smallest unit of recombination and perhaps only one nucleotide in size; *muton*—the smallest unit of mutation and composed of one nucleotide; *cistron*—the smallest unit of function and probably many nucleotides in length. Most geneticists however accept the general definition of a gene as a sequence of nucleotides that code for a specific polypeptide.

We have been following this one gene–one polypeptide principle (the cistron) throughout our discussions and explanations of gene action.

Finally, in our consideration of the nature of the gene, we must remember that each gene is part of a functioning system. A certain gene that produces an enzyme to catalyze one step in the production of the vitamin thiamine could not really do its job if it were not for other genes producing other enzymes necessary for the total synthetic pathway. In fact, experimental evidence suggests that even the position of the gene on the chromosome is vital to its function.

That genes function together has been well demonstrated. Recent studies by the French microbiologists Jacob and Monod (1961) have shown that three different types of genes influence the synthesis of enzymes in the colon bacteria, *E. coli*. In their work they were able to demonstrate the presence of *structural genes*, *operator genes*, and *regulator genes* (Figure 11–43). These can be summarized as follows:

1 *Structural genes*—These genes code messenger RNA for the synthesis of a specific polypeptide (enzyme) on the ribosomes. This is the gene discussed in Chapter 3 under protein synthesis.

2 *Operator gene*—This gene controls the function of a specific series of structural genes. It is always located adjacent to the genes it controls and turns the structural genes on and off. The operator gene and its related structural genes are termed an *operon*.

3 *Regulator genes*—In combination with chemical compounds from the cytoplasm (often the substrate or the metabolic end product of a synthesis pathway), these genes control the operator genes. A regulator gene, which may be located some distance from the operator gene it controls, produces a *repressor* substance capable of combining with the operator gene to repress its action. Apparently the repressor must combine with a *corepressor*, a cytoplasmic substance (in some systems, the metabolic end product catalyzed by the last structural gene of that operon), to "shut off" the operator gene. In other cases, *inducers* from the cytoplasm can unite with repressor molecules, thereby preventing

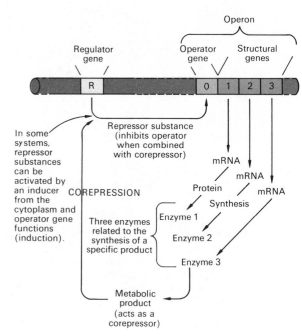

Figure 11–43 Functional relationships among structural, operator, and regulator genes. In this case the metabolic product apparently combines with the repressor substance produced by the regulator gene to inhibit the action of the operator gene.

the repressor from inactivating the operator gene. Inducer substances can be the substrate on which the enzymes produced by that operon will act. The process by which these enzymes are initiated is known as *enzyme induction*. Some insight into enzyme induction came from the discovery that certain enzymes are only produced in the presence of the substrate which they act upon. For example, the presence of lactose in a culture of *E. coli* can induce the production of the enzymes which hydrolyze lactose. Thus, in different situations, repressor substances may be inactive when combined with inducers or active when associated with corepressors. When a repressor is inactive, the operon works; when a repressor is activated, the operon is shut off.

POPULATION GENETICS

In most organisms one gene affects several to many traits, and each trait in turn is produced by the action of many genes. Therefore all of the genes in an individual contribute to its

402

development and welfare through a process of interaction. This is also true for a population of individuals. That is, all of the genes in a population, known as the *gene pool*, are involved in the adaptation and survival of the total species. *Population genetics* is the discipline that deals with the heredity of a reproducing group of organisms (a population).

In 1908, Hardy, an English mathematician, and Weinberg, a physician from Germany, formulated a concept about the frequencies of genes in a population under certain conditions. This is now known as the *Hardy-Weinberg principle* and provides the basis for the study of population genetics. The principle essentially states that genotype frequencies will remain in a state of equilibrium (will not change) from generation to generation provided the population is large; mutations do not occur, or are in equilibrium; migration in and out of the population is minimal; and mating is random. In other words, if one form

of a gene does not have a selective advantage over another form of the gene in a population, the genotype frequencies will remain the same from generation to generation.

We must hasten to add that the Hardy-Weinberg principle is essentially a theoretical concept and the conditions proposed by the principle are in reality never met in a natural breeding population. Breeding populations are often small, mutations do occur, migration occurs, and mating is never really random. But the Hardy-Weinberg principle is of value since it provides a theoretical basis with which we can compare the actual process occurring in nature.

We can use a specific example, *sickle-cell anemia*, to illustrate how the Hardy-Weinberg principle can be applied. As was noted earlier in this chapter, sickle-cell anemia, a hereditary disease caused by a defective type of hemoglobin, is characterized by sickle- or crescent-shaped red blood cells produced under low oxygen conditions (Figure 11–44). It is be-

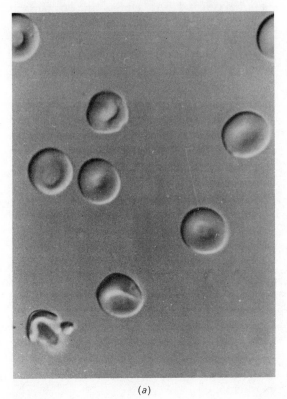

(a)

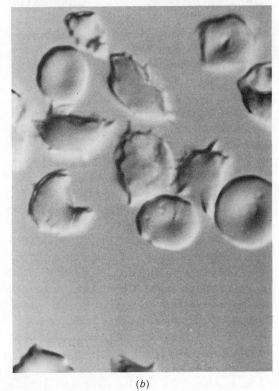

(b)

Figure 11–44 Human red blood cells. (*a*) Normal (oxygenated). (*b*) Sickle- or crescent-shaped (deoxygenated). (Courtesy of The National Foundation—March of Dimes.)

lieved that a rigid crystalline structure forms in some of the cells containing hemoglobin S (sickle-cell hemoglobin), and because of this inflexibility in structure, the red blood cells can't easily pass through small capillaries. This can obstruct blood flow to the tissues, deprive them of oxygen, and cause a variety of problems—pain, fever, swelling, jaundice, susceptibility to infection, kidney trouble, and other symptoms. Sickle-cell anemia is essentially a disease affecting blacks (although whites have it in some parts of the world), at a rate of approximately 1 in 500 members of the black population in the United States. Sickle-cell hemoglobin is produced in individuals who carry a gene different from the gene that produces normal hemoglobin (hemoglobin A); when an individual carries both alleles for sickle-cell hemoglobin (HbS, HbS) sickle-cell anemia will result. *Sickle-cell trait*, on the other hand, is the condition which results when an individual has only one gene for sickle cell and one gene for normal hemoglobin (HbS, HbA). Although sickle-cell anemia kills many victims by age 20 and most others by age 40, individuals having sickle-cell trait can survive provided they avoid certain conditions such as unpressurized aircraft or severe physical strain to which they are unaccustomed. Approximately one out of every ten blacks in the United States carry sickle-cell trait, but in Africa the incidence is much higher—one out of two. The question arises: Why is the sickle-cell gene more prevalent in Africa than in the United States? The Hardy-Weinberg principle helps explain the answer. The incidence of sickle-cell trait is highest in Africa where malaria is most common. Apparently the organism causing malaria, a red blood cell disease, can not grow and develop as well in sickle-cell hemoglobin as in normal hemoglobin. Thus individuals possessing sickle-cell hemoglobin will have a greater resistance to malaria, and as a result of the selective effects of malaria, the frequency of the HbS gene in the population will be increased. The situation in Africa and in parts of India and Greece where the sickle-cell gene shows a greater frequency in the population can be explained as follows: since there is selection against the sickle-cell homozygous condition (HbS, HbS) through death, and selection against normal homozygous individuals (HbA, HbA) due to malaria, the heterozgote (HbS, HbA), which is resistant to malaria and shows anemia only under great physical stress, is selected; thus the heterozygote genotype (HbS, HbA) increases in the population. The selection pressure against sickle-cell anemia, however, is much greater than against malaria; that is, more individuals die from sickle-cell anemia than from malaria. This means that the HbA gene has a higher selection advantage than HbS; and, therefore, the frequency of HbA gene is higher in the population than the frequency of HbS gene.

In parts of Africa where the frequency of the HbS gene reaches approximately 30 percent, an equilibrium is established. In the population the percent of phenotypes will be about 49 percent normal (HbA, HbA), 42 percent heterozygous (HbA, HbS), and 9 percent sickle cell (HbS, HbS) (Figure 11–45).

In the United States, where there is less malaria, the gene frequencies are much different, and the HbA gene is more frequent in the black population. The HbS gene no longer has a selective advantage in the heterozygote (due to the lowered incidence of malaria), and its frequency is less than in Africa, about 10 percent. The sickle-cell story, in addition to illustrating the effects of selection pressure on a gene, also shows how a gene can be disadvantageous in one environment but advantageous in another area under different conditions. Using the Hardy-Weinberg principle, we should be able to predict what the frequency of this gene (HbS) would be if malaria did not exist.

As we have just seen, gene frequencies can change in a population, and this is known as evolution. The next chapter will deal with evolution—the gradual replacement of one genotype by another genotype as natural selection operates on the total gene pool of a population.

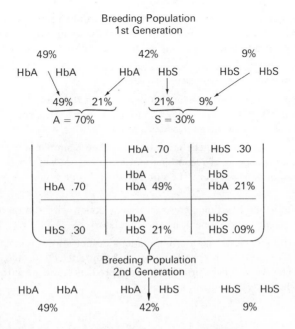

Breeding Population
1st Generation

Figure 11–45   How gene frequencies will remain the same under the same selection pressure. This is the situation in Africa, where malaria is acting as a selection agent for the HbS gene. The genotype HbA, HbA has a 49 percent frequency in the population, while the genotype HbA, HbS has a 42 percent frequency and the genotype HbS, HbS has a 9 percent frequency. This means that the frequency of the HbA gene is 70 percent (HbA, HbA = 49% and one-half of the HbA, HbS genotype is HbA; therefore, one-half of 42% = 21%; 49% and 21% = 70%). Calculating in a similar manner, we see that the frequency of the HbS gene is 30 percent. This gene frequency will remain the same in future generations as long as malaria continues to exert the same selection pressure.

SUMMARIZING STATEMENTS

Heredity and cytological studies laid the foundation for the science of modern genetics. It has been established that the chromosomes are the physical bearers of heredity.

Transmission genetics deals with the transfer and recombination of the genetic material from generation to generation. It involves Mendel's Law of Segregation and Law of Independent Assortment in monohybrid and dihybrid crosses and his concepts of dominance and recessiveness. Further aspects of transmission genetics are: sex-linked heredity, linkage and crossing over, multiple alleles, and quantitative inheritance.

Sex determination in most organisms can be correlated with a specific pair of chromosomes, the sex chromosomes.

The chance of the occurrence of a genetic event can be predicted through the use of the laws of probability. Therefore, if parental genotypes are known, the probability of certain traits occurring in the progeny may be determined.

Every gene must develop in a specific environment, and varying environmental factors can often affect the expression of a gene.

Various experiments have shown that genes direct the synthesis of enzymes. They apparently perform this action by serving as a code for protein synthesis. An alteration of a specific genetic code is a mutation.

Today the definition of a gene must be more than a simple unit of heredity; it can include the aspects of recombination, mutation, and function. The most accepted definition, however, can be summarized as a one gene–one polypeptide relationship.

The operon is one functional concept of gene action with several interacting types of genes: structural, operator, and regulator.

Genotype frequencies in natural populations do not always remain the same from one generation to another because mutations, selection, and migration occur. The Hardy-Weinberg principle, which predicts stable gene frequencies, is useful in the study of population genetics.

REVIEW QUESTIONS

1 Why is a knowledge of heredity and cell biology necessary in order to understand genetics?

2 What would be the distribution pattern of two different pairs of genes if: (a) they are on separate pairs of chromosomes or (b) they are on the same pair of chromosomes?

3 In any given roll of a pair of dice, what is the probability that one will throw a seven?

A systematic approach should be used in solving genetic problems. Dominant traits are usually indicated by a capital letter and recessive traits by the lower-case letter of the dominant. For example, R is used to indicate the dominant trait, round seeds in peas, and r is used for the recessive condition, wrinkled seeds. Use this notation to list the genotypes of the parents in the following problems. Next, note the types of gametes produced by each parent. Then match the gametes of each parent against the gametes of the other parent, in a checkerboard pattern (similar to the ones used in this chapter to explain Mendel's work). The resulting genotypes of the cross can then be analyzed to determine the possible phenotypes produced from the cross; similar phenotypes can be tallied and a ratio stated. Often the probability of a specific genotype or phenotype is requested in a problem, and this can be computed by using the approach just described. In each problem you should determine exactly what the problem asks you to do. The procedure may be modified according to the specific problem.

4 In tomatoes, red fruit color (R) is dominant over yellow (r). List the genotypes and phenotypes that could result from the following crosses:
(a) Rr × rr (b) Rr × RR (c) rr × RR (d) Rr × Rr

5 Some species of plants have flowers that are red, pink, or white. Flower color in these species is due to a single pair of genes. In one experiment in

which pink was crossed with pink, the following ratio was obtained: 25 % red, 49 % pink, and 26 % white. How can you explain this ratio?

6 Glossy leaves in broccoli results from a recessive mutation and are susceptible to insects. Normally broccoli has dull leaves. A farmer desires to eliminate the glossy trait from his crops. In this process he would need to determine which plants were heterozygous and which were homozygous. How should he proceed?

7 In humans, free earlobe (F) is dominant over attached (f) earlobe, and the ability to taste phenylthiocarbamide, PTC (T) is dominant over the inability to taste PTC (t). A woman with free earlobes who cannot taste PTC whose mother had attached lobes marries a man with attached lobes who can taste PTC but whose mother could not. What are the possible phenotypes of their children?

8 The polled or hornless (P) variety of cattle is dominant over horned (p). The heterozygous condition between red coat (R) and white coat (r) is roan. A polled, roan cow is mated to a horned, red bull. A horned, red offspring results. Show the genotypes of the parents and the offspring of this cross.

9 In fruit flies, long wings (V) are dominant to vestigial wings (v) and gray body color (B) is dominant over black body (b). A fly homozygous for both dominant traits is crossed with a fly showing both recessive traits. Diagram this cross, the F_1, and show the resulting genotypes. Now cross two of these and show all the genotypes and phenotypes of the F_2 generation.

10 A color-blind man marries a woman who has normal vision but whose father was color blind. Describe the possible genotypes and phenotypes of their children.

11 Summarize the evidence supporting the concept that DNA is the physical hereditary material.

12 What was the significance of Beadle's research on *Neurospora* for the field of genetics?

13 How does the modern concept of a gene correspond to the earlier notion that a gene was a structure on the chromosome?

14 What information from Chapter 3 supports the discussion in this chapter on how a gene functions?

15 How does the Jacob-Monod model indicate that most genes function in concert with other genes?

16 If man continues to reduce malaria around the world, what effect could this have on the frequency of the gene for sickle cell?

17 Many characteristics in a natural, sexually breeding population have been observed to change over a long period of time. How does the Hardy-Weinberg principle explain these changes?

SUPPLEMENTARY READINGS

Auerbach, Charlotte, *The Science of Genetics*, New York, Harper & Row, 1961.

Barry, J. M., *Molecular Biology: Genes and the Chemical Control of Living Cells*, Englewood Cliffs, N.J., Prentice-Hall, 1964.

Beadle, George W., "The Genes of Men and Molds," *Scientific American*, September, 1948.

Beadle, George W., "Structure of the Genetic Material and the Concept of the Gene," in W. Johnson and W. Steere, eds., *This Is Life*, New York, Holt, Rinehart and Winston, 1962.

Beadle, George, and Muriel Beadle, *The Language of Life*, Garden City, N.Y., Doubleday, 1966.

Bearn, A. G., and J. L. German, III, "Chromosomes and Disease," *Scientific American*, November, 1961.

Benzer, Seymour, "The Fine Structure of the Gene," *Scientific American*, January, 1962.

Borek, Ernest, *The Code of Life*, New York, Columbia University Press, 1965.

Brady, Roscoe O., "Heredity Fat-Metabolism Diseases," *Scientific American*, August, 1973.

Brown, Donald D., "The Isolation of Genes," *Scientific American*, August, 1973.

Clarke, C. W., "The Prevention of 'Rhesus' Babies," *Scientific American*, November, 1968.

Clowes, Royston C., "The Molecule of Infectious Drug Resistance," *Scientific American*, April, 1973.

Davidson, E. H., "Hormones and Genes," *Scientific American*, June, 1965.

Eckhardt, R. B., "Population Genetics and Human Origins," *Scientific American*, January, 1972.

Fraser, Alex, *Heredity: Genes and Chromosomes*, New York, McGraw-Hill, 1966.

Fried, John J., *The Mystery of Heredity*, New York, John Day, 1971.

Friedmann, Theodore, "Prenatal Diagnosis of Genetic Disease," *Scientific American*, November, 1971.

Hartman, P. E., and S. R. Suskind, *Gene Action*, Englewood Cliffs, N.J., Prentice-Hall, 1965.

Hotchkiss, R. D., and E. Weiss, "Transformed Bacteria," *Scientific American*, November, 1956.

Ingram, Vernon M., "How Do Genes Act?" *Scientific American*, November, 1957.

Losick, Richard, and Phillips W. Robbins, "The Receptor Site for a Bacterial Virus," *Scientific American*, November, 1969.

Macalpine, Ida, and Richard Hunter, "Porphyria and King George III," *Scientific American*, July, 1969.

McKusick, Victor A., "The Mapping of Human Chromosomes," *Scientific American*, April, 1971.

Medvedev, Z. A., *The Rise and Fall of T. D. Lysenko*, New York, Columbia University Press, 1969.

Mendel, G., *Experiments in Plant Hybridization*, Cambridge, Mass., Harvard University Press, 1948 (a description of his original work; translated from his paper of 1866).

Miller, O. L., Jr., "The Visualization of Genes in Action," *Scientific American*, March, 1973.

Moody, Paul Amos, *Genetics of Man,* New York, Norton, 1967.

Muller, H. J., "Radiation and Human Mutation," *Scientific American,* November, 1955.

Peters, J. A., ed., *Classic Papers in Genetics,* Englewood Cliffs, N.J., Prentice-Hall, 1959.

Sager, Ruth, "Genes Outside the Chromosomes," *Scientific American,* January, 1965.

Sigurbjörnson, Björn, "Induced Mutations in Plants," *Scientific American,* January, 1971.

Sutton, H. Eldon, *Genes, Enzymes, and Inherited Diseases,* New York, Holt, Rinehart and Winston, 1962.

Tomasz, Alexander, "Cellular Factors in Genetic Transformation," *Scientific American,* January, 1969.

Whittinghill, Maurice, *Human Genetics and Its Foundations,* New York, Reinhold, 1965.

Wollman, E. L., and F. Jacob, "Sexuality in Bacteria," *Scientific American,* July, 1956.

Wood, William B., and R. S. Edgar, "Building a Bacterial Virus," *Scientific American,* July, 1967.

Yanofsky, Charles, "Gene Structure and Protein Structure," *Scientific American,* May, 1967.

Zinder, Norton D., "Transduction in Bacteria," *Scientific American,* November, 1958.

12

Evolution and Natural Selection

Overwhelming evidence indicates that during the course of time all species of organisms have changed. This can be demonstrated not only from the fossil record but with living populations under experimental and natural conditions. Evolution is often defined as the theory or concept dealing with the changes that occur in living organisms as a result of slight genetic variations through successive generations. This implies that present-day organisms have developed from preexisting forms and that the visible changes were produced by changes in genes and gene frequencies. Evolution, therefore, can be defined as a change in gene frequencies. The Hardy-Weinberg principle, discussed at the conclusion of the previous chapter, suggested how gene frequencies might change in a population under the influence of natural selection. Evolution is a generally accepted concept in society today and modern biology recognizes its foundation in genetic mechanisms. Moreover, evolution unifies the entire field of biology and helps to clarify the fundamental structural and functional relationships that exist among all organisms.

EVIDENCES OF EVOLUTION

FOSSILS

An excellent opportunity for reviewing the history of the development of life exists in the fossil record, and the *fossilization* process permits us to see the living forms that existed at various times in the history of the earth. Most fossils are formed when organisms containing hard, mineralized parts are buried in mud or sand before they have decayed. After burial, decay stops and fossilization can occur in several ways. One type of fossil is the impression or mold that forms in the developing rock layers as the organismic parts are dissolved. Another type is formed when the original chemical compounds composing the hard parts of the organism, such as calcium carbonate, are preserved. A more common fossil, however, is formed by the replacement or recrystalization of the original minerals by another mineral. Silicates and other minerals are present in the water associated with the sand or mud and can enter porous materials such as bone marrow or spaces left by the decay of softer parts.

If fossil-bearing rocks of approximate known dates are exposed, scientists can gain some knowledge of the plants and animals that existed in those times. Such a source is the Grand Canyon (Figure 12–1) where the Colorado River has exposed a series of rock layers a mile deep representing a two-billion-year period of time. Here we have a virtual storybook of our earth and a record of some of the organisms that lived in the various eras over this period of time. The oldest rock is found at the bottom of the canyon, whereas the youngest rock occurs at the top. A diagrammatic cross section (Figure 12–2) shows the geologic eras and periods represented by the various layers. Representatives of each period are listed next to the layers in which they are found. As we might expect, the fossils of the most simple living forms are found near the bottom of the canyon and the fossils of more complex organisms are found progressively nearer the top of the canyon. From these observations it may be generalized that this represents the developmental pattern of life.

Another way in which the fossil record can be utilized is to trace the development of a specific family of plants or animals. From such studies general patterns of evolution can be determined. The excellent fossils produced by vertebrate animals make this group a good subject for such study, and perhaps the most well-known group is the horse family. Because of the extensive assemblage of fossils available, the horse family has been traced back approximately 55 million years although the early members of this family were far different from the horses we know today.

The family tree of the horse has been reconstructed by paleontologists (Figure 12–3). In this reconstruction one should note the increase in overall size, the increase in the length of legs, the increase in the size of the skull (the brain also increased in size and complexity), and the changes in the forefoot from four toes to one toe. We should not visualize a straightline lineage beginning with *Eohippus*, changing to *Miohippus* and then to *Merychippus* and ultimately culminating in the modern horse, *Equus*. There were many lines, many experiments in nature, and *Eohippus* did not completely "die out" when *Miohippus* appeared, but its frequency in the population probably decreased. Thus the frequency of the genotype producing *Eohippus* became less in the population as the genotype that produced the horse *Miohippus* increased. This process of the gradual replacement of some genotypes for others in the populations occurred over the past 55 million years until the most successful genotype for our present environment, *Equus*, remained.

Considerable genetic variation exists within the modern horse family, and breeders have reported particularly great variations in size and foot structure. It is possible, therefore, through "backward breeding," or selection for primitive characteristics, to produce horses that resemble the forerunners of the modern horse. Through this process varieties have been developed that reach less than thirty inches in height and possess multiple toes.

EMBRYOLOGY

If we become more than a casual student of nature we feel compelled to go beyond the observational state and inquire about relationships. In fact, if we look closely at the natural environment, it is difficult to ignore some of the relationships and developmental patterns.

412

Figure 12–1 The Grand Canyon from the south rim. (M. W. Williams ; courtesy of National Park Service, U.S. Department of the Interior.)

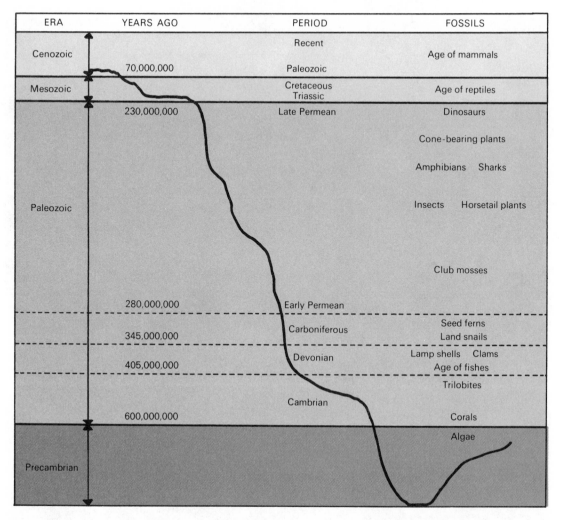

ERA	YEARS AGO	PERIOD	FOSSILS
Cenozoic		Recent	Age of mammals
	70,000,000	Paleozoic	
Mesozoic		Cretaceous Triassic	Age of reptiles
	230,000,000	Late Permean	Dinosaurs
			Cone-bearing plants
			Amphibians Sharks
Paleozoic			Insects Horsetail plants
			Club mosses
	280,000,000	Early Permean	
		Carboniferous	Seed ferns
	345,000,000		Land snails
		Devonian	Lamp shells Clams
	405,000,000		Age of fishes
			Trilobites
		Cambrian	
	600,000,000		Corals
			Algae
Precambrian			

Figure 12–2 Section through the Grand Canyon and vicinity showing the geologic eras, selected periods, and the common names for some of the fossils.

For example, an observation of the developing embryos of vertebrate organisms reveals a remarkable similarity during early stages (Figure 12–4). A closer examination shows *pharyngeal gill clefts* in all vertebrate embryos (in fact, in all members of the phylum chordata). The clefts are similar in structure and appearance in the throat region of early vertebrate embryos. As development progresses in the various vertebrates, however, these clefts assume different functions. In the fish and fish-like animals, some of the gill clefts develop into gill slits which are associated with respiratory organs. Birds and mammals, however, occupy a different habitat where gills are unnecessary, but they face other problems such as transmission and detection of sound (sound is transmitted more readily in water than in air). Portions of the original gill cleft and arch arrangement have been modified in birds and mammals into parts of the sound-producing and sound-detecting mechanisms. In man the auditory canal and the eustachian tube which connects the middle ear and the throat are remnants of gill clefts. Here is an example of the opportunistic nature of the evolutionary process—a process that can take existing structures and modify them for a new environ-

414

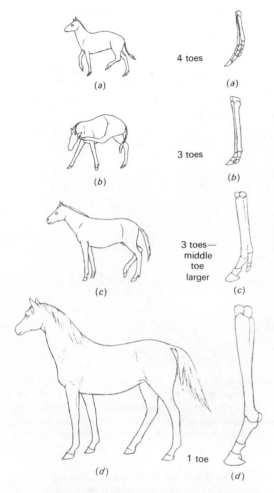

similarity of bone structure that apparently comes from similar embryonic development. Thus it would appear that the same basic plan was utilized for all vertebrate forelimbs, but modifications that occur are correlated with the different habits and habitats of these animals. This phenomenon of similarity in structure based on inheritance from a common ancestor is known as *homology* and the structures so derived are called *homologous*. Some of the comparative anatomists as early as the eighteenth and nineteenth centuries clearly saw these relationships in nature. Several variations from the generalized or ancestral-type vertebrate forelimb are shown in Figure 12–6. Functional comparisons between certain structures can also be made; for example, the wings of birds and insects have different origins although they serve the same function. Structures that are similar in function but different in evolutionary origin are termed *analogous*.

INTERMEDIATE FORMS AND "LIVING FOSSILS"

Classification schemes are simply attempts to group organisms according to similar charac-

Figure 12–3 Part of the family tree of the horse. The forelegs are shown on the right. (*a*) Eohippus. (*b*) Miohippus. (*c*) Merychippus. (*d*) Equus. (Redrawn from Fig. 52.4, p. 571, "Horse Family Tree," in *Introduction to Zoology* by H. W. Manter and D. D. Miller [Based largely on G. G. Simpson, *The Meaning of Evolution*, Yale University Press, 1949], Harper & Row, 1959.)

ment. Modifications of some of the clefts and arches in various vertebrates are illustrated in Figure 12–5.

HOMOLOGY

Another observation on vertebrates reveals a basic similarity in the structure of the forelimbs. Although the forelimbs of man, whales, and birds appear to be different, there is a

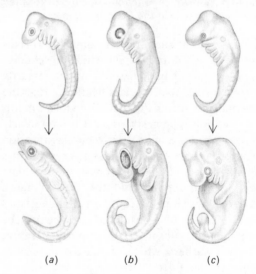

Figure 12–4 Sketches of the developing embryos of three vertebrates. (*a*) Fish. (*b*) Chick. (*c*) Human. Note how the embryos are quite similar in the early stage, but change as development proceeds. Also note the gill arches and clefts in all three embryos.

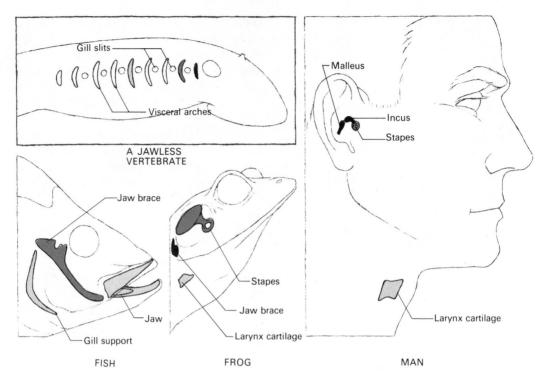

Figure 12–5 Modification of pharyngeal slits and arches in selected vertebrates. (*a*) Fish. (*b*) Frog. (*c*) Man. Note that the first visceral arch forms the jaws in the adult fish, the jaw braces in the frog, and two of the middle-ear bones—incus and malleus—in man (for sound conduction). The second arch serves as the jaw brace in the fish; in the frog and in man, it forms the stapes (bone for sound conduction). The fifth arch, which functions as support for the gills in the fish, develops into part of the cartilage support for the larynx in the frog and in man.

teristics and, as such, reflect man's interpretation of nature. (Actually classification schemes do vary and all biologists do not necessarily agree on one plan of classification.) Existing intermediate forms that actually violate man's classification schemes represent the popularly known "missing links" between classification groups. Perhaps the most classic example of a missing link is *Archaeopteryx*, an intermediate between the reptiles and the birds (Figure 12–7). It has so many reptilian characteristics that it could be considered as one of the flying reptiles except for one important feature —it had feathers, which can clearly be seen in some of the fossils. *Archaeopteryx*, then, is probably an intermediate form between these two large groups of animals.

An interesting little animal resembling a caterpillar is found in Africa, New Zealand, Australia, Central America, and other similar environments. *Peripatus*, which is about two inches long, lives an obscure life in damp places under bark and leaves (Figure 12–8). Its present discontinuous distribution indicates that it may have been more widespread in earlier times but is now nearing extinction. The importance of this group of animals (about seventy species) is that it has many characteristics of the Annelida (segmented worms) and the Arthropoda (insects, crustaceans, etc.). The respiratory system, blood system, and mouth parts are distinctly insect-like, whereas the excretory system, reproductive ducts, and body wall resemble the earthworm group. Where should this organism be classified—in the Annelida or the Arthropoda? Most zoologists place it with the arthropods since this is a diverse phylum

416

anyway, but it does have characteristics of another phylum. These missing links suggest strongly that organisms developed in a continuous fashion and were not "created" in large, discrete, and immutable groups.

On occasion living organisms have been found that were once known only as fossils. These "living fossils" provide biologists with a link to the past. An interesting example is that of *Metasequoia*, a deciduous, cone-bearing tree, commonly known as the *dawn redwood* and closely related to the familiar redwood of the genus *Sequoia* (Figure 12–9). In 1941, a Japanese botanist proposed the genus name *Metasequoia* for fossil specimens of this tree which had been studied for some time. Then in the same year, after the Chinese had retreated from the Japanese armies into the interior of China, a forest survey disclosed the living *Metasequoia*. Later in the 1940s, after the close of World War II, United States botanists studied the plants in their natural

habitat and shipped seeds all over the world. Today the tree has been moved back into areas such as the West Coast of the United States where fossils show that it once thrived.

One of the more exciting discoveries of a "living fossil" came in 1938 when a prehistoric-looking fish with lobed fins was taken by commercial fishermen in deep water off the coast of South Africa (Figure 12–10). This fish, which was about five feet long, proved to be a coelacanth (the genus *Latimeria*) which was known widely in the fossil record from the Devonian period (about 400,000,000 years ago) through the Cretaceous (about 75,000,000 years ago). It had been considered extinct since the Cretaceous period. Since 1952 more coelacanths have been taken off the coast of Madagascar near the Comoro Islands and subsequent studies of its anatomy have provided important information to students of animal evolutionary development. This animal is a direct relative of the group of

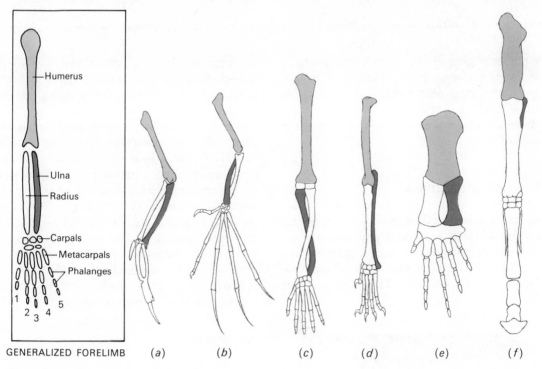

GENERALIZED FORELIMB   (*a*)   (*b*)   (*c*)   (*d*)   (*e*)   (*f*)

Figure 12–6 Homologous development of vertebrate forelimbs. The basic plan of organization is shown in the inset as a generalized forelimb. Variations of the plan can clearly be seen in the six examples of vertebrate forelimbs. (*a*) Pigeon. (*b*) Bat. (*c*) Man. (*d*) Cat. (*e*) Whale. (*f*) Horse.

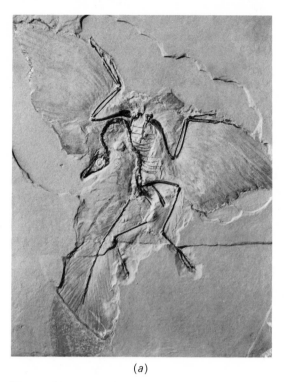

(a)

(b)

Figure 12–7 *Archaeopteryx.* (*a*) Cast of the fossil. (*b*) Photo of a restoration. (American Museum of Natural History.)

fishes belonging to the order Crossopterygii, which gave rise to the amphibians. Thus the coelacanth is closely related to a group of organisms that lies in the direct line of descent of animals who made the transition from water to land.

VESTIGIAL STRUCTURES

In many plants and animals, structures are present which have no apparent function but are often homologous to specific parts of close relatives. Such apparently useless parts are called *vestigial structures.* The most probable

Figure 12–8 *Peripatus,* an intermediate form which shows characteristics of two phyla, the Annelida and the Arthropoda. (Courtesy of Carolina Biological Supply Company.)

explanation for these structures is that, although they are no longer needed in some species, they are still carried along in the heredity of the entire group. They also represent a visible testimony to the relationships of the organisms possessing similar vestigial features. In some snakes, for example, bones resembling a pelvic girdle (hip bones) are present, indicating a relationship to four-legged vertebrates. The small splint bones on the horse foreleg are interpreted as reduced toes homologous to the two outer toes of some of its three-toed fossil relatives. Man possesses many vestigial organs such as the appendix, the last several vertebrae (the coccyx), ear lobes, and "wisdom" teeth.

MOLECULAR

One of the most complete relationships among all eucaryotic cells has been demonstrated by the study of the structure of cytochrome c molecules (see Figure 6–8). All organisms with

418

(a)   (b)

Figure 12–9 *Metasequoia*, the dawn redwood. (*a*) Full view. (*b*) Close-up of a branch. (Lola B. Graham; National Audubon Society.)

eucaryotic cells have cytochrome c as one of the important molecules for the release of energy, and the sequence of amino acids in this molecule has been worked out for over 40 species ranging from molds to humans. The most important functional aspect of a cytochrome c molecule is its folded pattern; differences in amino-acid sequence are not as important to its biological role of electron transport. Although the molecules are remarkably similar in folded structure and in a large portion of their amino-acid molecules (35 out of 104), differences do exist in the amino-acid sequence along certain parts of the molecule. The greatest difference is found between *Neurospora* (red bread mold) and humans— 44 out of 104 amino acids. Cytochrome c molecules are exactly alike in humans and chimpanzees and differ by only one amino acid in rhesus monkey. Human cytochrome c differs from that of *Drosophila* (fruit fly) in 29 amino acids out of the 104. To summarize, the evolutionary relationships shown by cytochrome c structures throughout the eucaryotic forms closely parallel the classical evolutionary tree. The greater the difference in the amino-acid sequence of cytochrome c, the less relation there is between two organisms.

THE MECHANISM OF EVOLUTION

HISTORICAL DEVELOPMENT OF THE CONCEPT

In the preceding paragraphs the term *evolution* was defined and some evidence was presented to show that such a process does occur. We should now attempt to understand

Figure 12–10 *Latimeria*, the lobe-finned coelacanth.

419

the mechanism that governs or controls this process. Man has attempted to do this in the past—in fact, long before conclusive evidence of evolution was available. In this discussion we will follow the sequence of man's thoughts and efforts leading to the development of a meaningful concept of evolution. Any suggestion of change to an established system usually meets resistance from certain segments of society and the theory of evolution is no exception. We will see, however, that man has been aware of relationships and development (even if he did not always use the word *evolution*) among living forms for some time. We should not be too critical of the investigators and observers of the past even though today their explanations and theories sound highly improbable (if not impossible). We must remember that we have the benefit of their contributions, whereas they often had very little information on the subject to assist them.

As soon as primitive man could care for his immediate needs he probably began to ponder his relationship to the natural world, his origin, and, no doubt, the "why" for his existence. Modern man is still thinking about these problems. We do not know exactly when man began this search or how the very early cultures considered these problems, but we do know something of Greek thought concerning evolution. Anaximander, one of the Ionian philosophers who lived around 600 B.C., believed that life sprang from mud which had covered the earth. He thought that plants, animals, and human beings arose in that order, with the land-dwelling animals living first in water and then moving onto land. It was Aristotle who noted a consistent pattern in the living world and who organized the known living organisms into a "ladder of life" (*scala naturae*, Figure 1–4), beginning with simple forms and ending in more complex forms. Two of his statements are quite descriptive of his thought: "nature proceeds little by little from things lifeless to animal life" and "nature passes from lifeless objects to animals in such unbroken sequences, inter-

posing between them beings which live and yet are not animals." In the works of Anaximander and Aristotle we see a recognition of the evolutionary process although there is little specific attempt at explaining the mechanism responsible for it. Aristotle, however, proposed a "perfecting principle" which was inherent in the organism and which could produce change.

After Aristotle there was little discussion of change or development in the world. The concept of a static world without alterations, not only in the living forms but also in the physical world, became predominate. Several theories have been advanced to account for this, among them being the rise of Christianity and the indifference of the Romans to any pure scientific work. All of nature was considered to be inert; the mountains would never change, climates were forever true, and living forms were immutable. This was the prevailing attitude as mankind entered the seventeenth century—a time often designated as "The Intellectual Revolution" or the "Age of Enlightenment." Societal changes occurred in the 1600s and 1700s and existing political systems were challenged. The rights of the individual were stressed and the infallibility of the church was questioned. Along with changes in social structures came changes in the conceptual schemes in the physical sciences under the stimulation of such memorable scientists as Galileo and Sir Isaac Newton. It was this background that established the groundwork for changes in the geological and biological sciences.

The classification work of Linnaeus in the 1700s established a static and fixed concept about species. Although such a system of classification was desirable and necessary for the biological sciences, this particular system tended to reinforce the church's position on the static nature of the world. The idea of change and a dynamic environment had to be introduced if man were to understand and develop relationships about his natural world. The immutability of species was challenged almost immediately by the French natural historian Buffon (1707–1788), who believed, contrary to theological doctrine, that animals did change. He was impressed with similarity in structure in some organisms and how a "basic plan" often occurred in the structure of organs such as the vertebrate forelimb. It was evident to Buffon that "nature" had produced many organisms over long periods of time and that some forms had become extinct.

It was not only important to establish that the living world was in a process of change—if we were to know the mechanics, the relationships between time and change and development on our earth were also needed. It was long believed that the changes in the landscape of the earth were due to catastrophes—sudden disturbances. But geologist James Hutton, in his *Theory of the Earth*, published in 1788, proposed that the continuous processes of erosion, mountain building, and vulcanism have changed the earth's features and that these same forces are active today. He recognized the importance of time as a factor in the development of the earth, and this had not been appreciated before. Hutton appeared to understand the role of cyclical events in the history of the world and concluded the first chapter of his treatise with the phrase, "we find no vestige of a beginning—no prospect of an end."

Another geologist, William Smith (about 1790), through a bit of deductive reasoning, arrived at the simple conclusion that in beds of deposition, the older layers were on the bottom and the overlying strata were younger. Hence the fossils found in lower strata were older than those found in strata above, and that a comparison of these fossils would indicate the developmental pattern of life on our planet. Since a particular stratum had its own characteristic fossils and if the age of that stratum were known, any other layer bearing these fossils must be of the same relative age. Thus certain fossils could be used to determine the age of various strata. Smith had tied the fossil record to the development of life on earth in relationship to time. Somewhat later Charles Lyell published a revolutionary textbook, *Principles of Geology* (1830), in which he clearly presented the dynamic effect of physical forces, working through time, in shaping our planet. He actually paved the way for Charles Darwin's great work and probably influenced Darwin more than any other person. Lyell mentioned the creation of new species in his book and came very close to stating Darwin's theory. He had actually recognized natural selection but failed to see how it could be a creative force. Perhaps the most significant factor is that people were gradually becoming accustomed to the concept of change.

One of the most familiar (and sometimes considered the first) evolutionist was Jean Baptiste Lamarck (1744–1829). Although Lamarck recognized an evolutionary process in nature, his explanation of the mechanisms that produced this change and development was not correct, and is incompatible with modern biological knowledge. Lamarck's theory is often stated as "the theory of the *inheritance of acquired characteristics*," and it shows that, although he recognized the importance of the environment in evolution, Lamarck did not completely understand its role. He proposed that organisms moving to a new environment would require certain structural modifications. Because of this need, changes in structure would result and the more a specific structure was used, the more highly it would be developed. As a result of this modification, other structures might not be used and these would tend to disappear. This part of Lamarck's theory is often referred to as the "use and disuse of parts." Thus a Lamarckian (one who accepts Lamarck's theory of evolution) would explain the reduction of the horse's lateral toes on the foreleg by stating that only the middle toe was used for running. Furthermore, Lamarck believed that a change in one generation, produced by the environment, would be passed on to the next generation through inheritance. An absurd example, if this theory were carried to its ultimate, would be the transmission of bulging biceps to his son by a father who had lifted weights during his

421

lifetime. A more sophisticated example of the employment of Lamarckism would be a case of white-skinned humans moving to tropical islands where the sun might not only tan their skins, but would cause the next generation to be born darker. We now know that this inheritance of acquired characteristics does not occur from changes in the body or somatic cells; only alterations in germinal or sex cells can be transmitted to the next generation.

CHARLES DARWIN'S CONTRIBUTIONS

The most important figure in the development of the theory of evolution was Charles Darwin (Figure 12–11). He was able to add to the concept of an evolutionary process and to propose a mechanism to account for it which was to gain almost universal acceptance. Born in 1809 in England, Darwin was the son of a physician and the grandson of a famous natural philosopher, Erasmus Darwin. His grandfather was

Figure 12–11 Charles Darwin (1809–1882). (American Museum of Natural History.)

also concerned with changes in living organisms and he accepted Lamarck's viewpoint of the inheritance of acquired characteristics to explain these changes. Young Darwin was interested in pursuing a medical career but soon dropped this program at Edinburgh and turned to theology at Cambridge. His real interests, however, were in geology and natural history and he was strongly influenced by the geologist Lyell. Another influence on Darwin was the *Essay on Population* written by Malthus, which stated the now well-known concept that populations increase at a geometric rate although resources for living are generally limited. Malthus believed that populations must be held in check or they would soon run out of subsistence, and this suggested to Darwin the idea of competition and a struggle for existence in populations.

That species could and did in fact change was a certainty to Darwin. The production of new varieties of domestic animals seemed to illustrate this point very well, and Darwin became extremely interested in animal breeding. In addition to familiarizing himself with many animal-breeding programs, Darwin conducted breeding experiments with various races of pigeons. He was acutely aware of the possibilities of obtaining desired traits in the offspring through the selection of characteristics in the parents. If man could produce varieties through controlled breeding experiments, why, wondered Darwin, cannot nature modify species in a similar manner through a selection process?

Perhaps the most important biological background for Charles Darwin was provided by a trip on *H.M.S. Beagle* during the years 1831 to 1836 (Figure 12–12). Although the expedition was essentially for mapping and charting purposes, the value of having a naturalist was recognized and Darwin was selected for this job. As a result he was able to spend considerable time in the southern hemisphere, especially South America and the Galápagos Islands. Here Darwin observed native tribes and wild animals in an almost undisturbed state, and the results of this trip

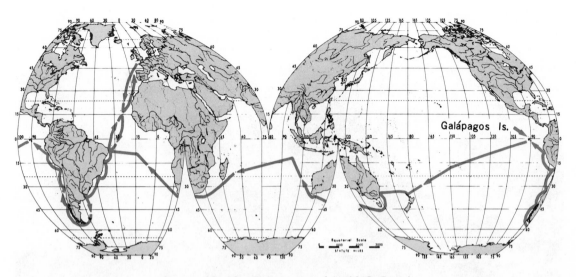

Figure 12–12 The voyage of *H. M. S. Beagle*.

were described in a widely read publication entitled *The Voyage of the Beagle*. Darwin regarded this trip as the most important aspect of his education and preparation for the formulation of the theory of evolution.

The Galápagos Islands (Figure 12–13), located 650 miles west of Ecuador, are composed of volcanic peaks. Since some of the peaks are high enough to produce local climatic differences, a variety of habitats exists, ranging from lava cliffs to cactus forests to moist, lush forests (Figure 12–14). Although located very near the equator, the small group of islands is washed by cool antarctic currents as well as tropical currents, and the islands are separated from each other by great expanses (up to 60 miles) of deep water. All of these factors add up to a unique place, and it is no wonder that this archipelago has been called a "living laboratory." Geologically the islands are considered to be rather young and the animal and plant life is American—that is, the inhabiting species probably came from the coast of South America. Seeds and spores, and possibly insects, could have been blown in by the wind. Additional plants and animals could have arrived on "rafts" from the mainland, while some birds could have flown the distance. Equally important, however, is the fact that the invading organisms had to find a suitable

habitat if they were to survive in this environment. Here on these islands a unique and interesting fauna developed, numbering among its members the giant 400-pound tortoises, the prehistoric-looking iguana lizards, a small penguin species, flightless cormorants, boobies, and a variety of finches (Figures 12–15 and 12–16). Darwin studied all of these animals and particularly noted that the iguanas differed from island to island. But the animals in which he was most interested from the standpoint of the development of new species was the finch group. Through a detailed study of the fourteen species of

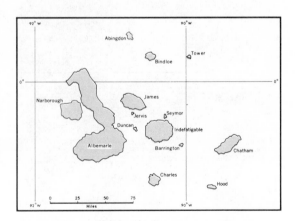

Figure 12–13 The Galápagos Islands.

423

Figure 12–14 Sullivan Bay in the Galápagos Islands showing James Island in the distance. (Courtesy of James Murray.)

finches in the Galápagos Islands, Darwin arrived at a theory to explain the evolution of new species.

He reasoned that a single finch species arriving from the mainland found a variety of habitats available to it. Since variation existed

Figure 12–15 Land iguana from the Galápagos Islands. (Los Angeles County Museum of Natural History.)

among the individual members of the species (and Darwin did not understand the source of this variability), it was possible for the species to exploit all of these available habitats which included barren ground, grasslands, shrubs, and trees. The fourteen species show a great variation in bill structure, and perhaps it was this anatomical feature more than any other that permitted the habitation of the various niches. In Darwin's words, this is "a most singular group of finches, related to each other in the structure of their beaks, short tails, form of body, and plumage." He further summarized his feelings about this group by stating: "seeing this gradation and diversity of structure in one small, intimately related group of birds, one might really fancy that from an original paucity of birds in this archipelago, one species had been taken and modified for different ends." Actually this group of finches had filled the ecological roles of birds not found in this environment such as warblers, grosbeaks, blackbirds, woodpeckers, and nuthatches.

We can sense the value of these islands to science and to an understanding of the evolutionary process when we read Darwin's thoughts on this environment:

Both in space and time, we seem to be brought somewhat near to that great fact—that mystery of mysteries—the first appearance of new beings on this earth. Reviewing the facts here given, one is astonished at the amount of creative force, if such an expression may be used, displayed on these small, barren, and rocky islands; and still more so, at its diverse yet analogous action on points so near each other. I have said that the Galápagos Archipelago might be called a satellite attached to America, but it should rather be called a group of satellites, physically similar, organically distinct, yet intimately related to each other, and all related in a marked, though much lesser degree, to the great American continent.

After assimilation of the material from the voyage of the Beagle and other studies, Darwin proposed his theory of evolution in 1859 in the now famous book entitled *On the Origin of Species by Means of Natural Selection.* The first printing was sold out almost instantly and its contents threw the world into a controversy over the mechanism of the develop-

Figure 12–16 Flightless cormorant. (Courtesy of California Academy of Sciences.)

ment of life. The church and many biologists violently opposed it while many other biologists and some laymen applauded it. It is necessary to note here that another biologist, Alfred Wallace, had arrived at conclusions identical to Darwin's and had in fact sent Darwin a copy of his theory in 1858. Wallace had arrived at his concept independently of Darwin through his studies of the flora and fauna of Malaya. It was decided that they should publish their works simultaneously and thus most biologists speak of the *Darwin-Wallace theory.* Since Darwin's thesis was much better documented, the theory is often referred to as Darwinism. The Darwin-Wallace theory of how life has evolved to its present diversity can be briefly summarized as:

1 Variation exists among the members of a particular species (look about you at your fellow human beings).

2 Overproduction usually occurs in a population and more individuals are produced than can be supported in a particular environment (the species population remains relatively constant, however, because of the following factors).

3 Competition results from the population pressure on the environmental resources (a struggle for existence).

4 Certain individuals with favorable characteristics for the particular environment survive (*natural selection*).

5 A preservation of favored individuals occurs and these characteristics are passed on to their offspring (survival of the fittest).

As we have said, Darwin failed to recognize the source of the variation in organisms, and he looked to a modification of Lamarckism for the answer. He used a theory called "pangenesis" in which it was supposed that tiny units called "pangenes" pass from each part of the body into the gametes to determine what the offspring will inherit in the next generation. This was clearly a type of inheritance of acquired characteristics. But the essence of the Darwin-Wallace theory was the concept of natural selection—that is, the selective force of the environment.

THE MODERN CONCEPT—NEO-DARWINISM

Since the time of the Darwin-Wallace theory, discoveries in biology have contributed greatly to our knowledge of the process of evolution. Studies in sexuality, chromosomes, mutations, and genetics (the work of Mendel) have added to the basic theory proposed by Darwin. Therefore we cannot really credit the modern concept of evolution to any one man and must recognize that, as in most modern scientific theories, the labors and research of many are utilized in the formulation of a workable and probable concept to explain the development of life.

Modern biology attributes variation in living organisms to inheritable chromosomal units, called *genes*. Since the genes are on the chromosomes, variations are produced in the events of meiosis (crossovers and recombination) and mutation and are transmitted through fertilization. The role of the environment then is not to *produce* the variations but to *select* the variations. A particular environment acts as a "screen" permitting certain genotypes to inhabit it and "selecting out" other genotypes. Natural selection, as used by Darwin and most modern biologists, refers to the selecting role and function of the environment upon genotypes living in it. We speak of those organisms selected by a particular environment as being adapted to that habitat, and those characteristics they display, which are of value in that environment, as *adaptations*. Because heritable adaptations increase the probable success of a species, adaptive changes are beneficial. Many changes can occur in a species and all of these are evolutionary; all changes, however, are not necessarily adaptive.

Since better-adapted organisms in a particular environment reproduce at a higher rate than the less adapted, biologists currently use the term *differential reproduction* to denote the success of favored forms rather than the term "survival of the fittest." As a result of differential reproduction, the frequency of certain genotypes increases in the population while the frequency of others decreases. If the environment should change, the overall frequency of genotypes could change and organisms of different appearance and function might result. It is quite correct then to treat evolution as a change in gene frequencies. Returning momentarily to the example of the horse used earlier, we see that horses with characteristics of the modern horse could better escape their predators, reproduce and increase their frequency in the horse population. A comparison of the Lamarckian, Darwinian, and *neo-Darwinian* concept of evolution is shown in Figure 12-17.

ADAPTATIONS

Adaptations have been described as those traits of an organism (or a species) that enhance its chances for survival and reproduction in a specific environment. Although the obvious adaptations to most of us are the variations in body structure, adaptive characteristics can also be physiological or behavioral. Some adaptations are for physical offensive and defensive purposes (such as claws, strong muscles, and teeth); others, such as *mimicry* and camouflage, are less physical but frequently a more effective means of protection (Figure 12-18). Many outdoorsmen are familiar with the adaptive coloration provided by the spots on fawns and many recognize the "broken wing" behavior of the female grouse as she limps through the brush diverting the intruder's attention from her brood hidden nearby. Everyone is also familiar with the pungent odor released by the skunk to deter his enemies. The whitish uric acid excreted by birds and reptiles is a physiological adaptation which provides for the release of nitrogenous wastes with little loss of water. And we could go on and on discussing adaptations, for these are essentially the story of biology—how organisms live, reproduce, and survive in their environments. Although the subject of adaptation has filled entire books, it is more important for us to understand the process, and for this we will consider an example of a particular adaptation in a species over a definite period of time.

Most species of butterflies and moths dis-

426

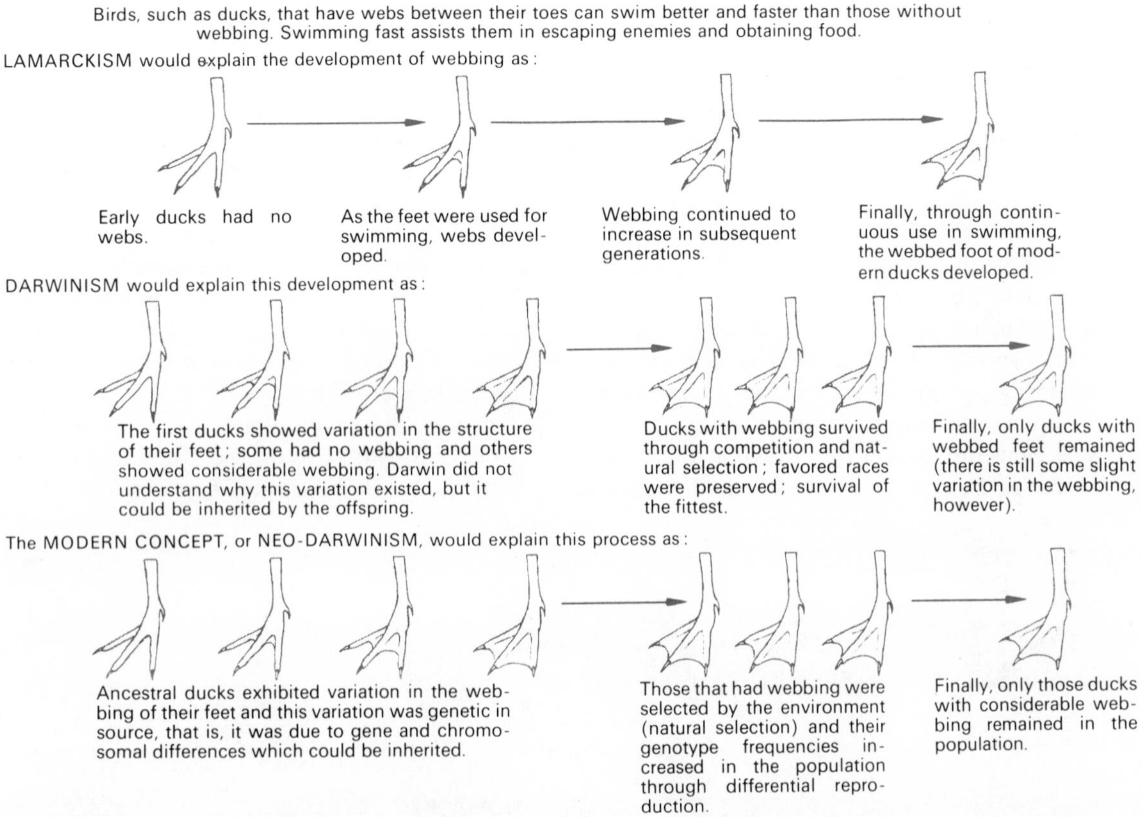

Birds, such as ducks, that have webs between their toes can swim better and faster than those without webbing. Swimming fast assists them in escaping enemies and obtaining food.

LAMARCKISM would explain the development of webbing as:

Early ducks had no webs.

As the feet were used for swimming, webs developed.

Webbing continued to increase in subsequent generations.

Finally, through continuous use in swimming, the webbed foot of modern ducks developed.

DARWINISM would explain this development as:

The first ducks showed variation in the structure of their feet; some had no webbing and others showed considerable webbing. Darwin did not understand why this variation existed, but it could be inherited by the offspring.

Ducks with webbing survived through competition and natural selection; favored races were preserved; survival of the fittest.

Finally, only ducks with webbed feet remained (there is still some slight variation in the webbing, however).

The MODERN CONCEPT, or NEO-DARWINISM, would explain this process as:

Ancestral ducks exhibited variation in the webbing of their feet and this variation was genetic in source, that is, it was due to gene and chromosomal differences which could be inherited.

Those that had webbing were selected by the environment (natural selection) and their genotype frequencies increased in the population through differential reproduction.

Finally, only those ducks with considerable webbing remained in the population.

Figure 12–17 Comparison among Lamarckism, Darwinism, and neo-Darwinism. Note the similarity between Darwin's concept and the modern interpretation, or neo-Darwinism.

Figure 12–18 Examples of mimicry, a type of adaptation in which an animal blends with its surroundings. Here the insects resemble the leaves on which they are resting. (Courtesy of Dr. Asa C. Thoresen.)

427

play some variation in their coloration. In the British Isles many of the light-colored moth species have naturally occurring black mutants which represent a definite percentage of the population. About 1850, in the area of Manchester, England (Figure 12–19), the black form of the peppered moth, *Biston betularia*, represented only about 1 percent of the population (Figure 12–20). This rural area was characterized by a clear atmosphere and white, lichen-covered tree trunks. Thus the white variety of the moth blended into and could be camouflaged by the environment. The dark variety, however, was under heavy selection pressure from preying birds who could easily spot them and pick them off as

they rested on trees in the daytime. As the Manchester area became industrialized, the environment changed, air pollution resulted, and the tree trunks were darkened from soot and the death of the lichen growth. By 1900 it was estimated that the black form made up over 99 percent of the population (Figure 12–19). To test the hypothesis that predation accounted for the change in gene frequencies in the population of *Biston betularia*, researchers released equal numbers of black and light forms in a polluted area and in a natural area. Approximately twice as many black forms were recovered in the industrialized, polluted environment, whereas in the unpolluted area, many more of the lighter forms survived. It

Figure 12–19 Map of the British Isles showing the relative distribution of the light and dark forms of *Biston betularia*. Industrial areas are designated by black dots. Large colored circles represent moth populations composed largely of light forms, whereas the shaded areas represent populations of predominantly dark forms.

(a)   (b)

Figure 12–20 The peppered moth and its black form, *carboneria*. (*a*) On a soot-covered oak trunk near Birmingham, England. (*b*) On a lichen-covered tree in an unpolluted area. (From the experiments of Dr. H. B. D. Kettlewell, University of Oxford.)

should be noted that the environmental changes did not produce the black mutant; it was always present in the population, and its frequency would have remained fairly constant had certain environmental changes not occurred. (Remember the Hardy-Weinberg principle.) When conditions in the environment which favored the light form changed, the black mutant was merely selected by the new environment. In other words, the light moth was adapted for one environment and the black moth for another. Variation is of definite survival value to a species since, as we have just noted, if the environment changes, certain variant members of the species may continue to exist.

With the enforcement of antipollution laws in the past decade tree trunks in England are returning to their lighter, natural state. It is significant that recent studies indicate an increase of the lighter form in the population. Thus it is apparent that the ratio of light to dark forms is again changing due to natural selection.

SPECIATION

Some biologists criticized Darwin and his theory of natural selection because they could not understand how the process could produce anything new. They frequently saw it acting in a destructive manner and, like Darwin himself, could not understand its creative possibilities. In the following discussion, emphasis will be placed on the creative aspects of natural selection.

It is interesting to speculate what might happen if some members of a species were isolated from the others for a long period of time. Could the two populations change enough to produce two separate species?

Within a large breeding population, smaller breeding groups exist known as *demes* or gene pools. Demes are simply local breeding groups in which members are more likely to mate because they are closer together. The field mice in one field may form one deme and those a half mile away another. Figure 12–21 illustrates the breeding pattern among demes of a

429

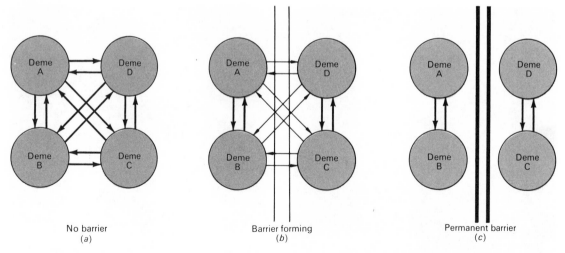

Figure 12–21 The splitting of a population by a barrier. (*a*) Free mating among all demes occurs. (*b*) Barrier is forming. (*c*) The barrier has become permanent, restricting mating, so that two separate breeding groups are formed.

population; the arrows indicate that a free flow of genes is possible in the population. This population is also referred to as a "total gene pool." This figure also shows what will happen to the mating pattern if the population is split —that is, demes A and B can still mate and exchange hereditary material but they cannot mate with demes C and D. By splitting the population, we simply mean that the gene flow has been interrupted. Essentially, two new populations result.

Two questions need to be answered at this point: (1) what will happen under this new mating pattern to each of the new populations and (2) what kinds of barriers can bring about situations such as this? In answer to the first question, gene and chromosomal mutations will continue on each side of the barrier, perhaps at the same rate and of the same kind or perhaps not. The environments on either side may be different or may change as a result of the barrier. Certain hereditary features may be incorporated into one population and not in the other through natural selection or through chance. If the two populations remain separated long enough, selection may incorporate different gene and chromosome mutations into the separate populations. If organisms from either population come together

again, they may not be compatible; that is, they may not be able to produce fertile offspring. When this happens, two species exist where only one was present before and we say that speciation has taken place. The time required for this to occur has been estimated to be between 10,000 and 1,000,000 years. This large variation in time is due to the different rates of effective mutations and natural selection. The effect of a barrier on a population and the ultimate result are summarized in Figure 12–22.

Most barriers between populations are geographical, such as bodies of water or land masses. Barriers could be produced when a river cuts through land or when an earthquake dams up a river to change its course or form a lake. Mountain-building forces or earthquakes causing land slides could impose a land mass to separate a population. Any extensive, unsuitable habitat within the territory of a population will tend to isolate parts of that population. But before new species can be formed, a *biological barrier* or a biological isolating mechanism must occur which prevents the two groups from producing fertile offspring should they come together again. Such biological barriers can include the incompatibility of gametes, a difference in be-

430

havior, or a variation in breeding season. A type of biological isolation occurs between two closely related species of pine trees in California where interbreeding is prevented because the pollen of one species is mature in February and the pollen of the other is not ready until April. Differences in behavior may isolate two closely related species of fish that occupy the same stream. The male of one species of stickleback fish may construct its nest slightly different from the male of another species and the females of each species can recognize the difference. In the fiddler crab several species may occupy the same shore, but the courtship dance performed by the male differs in each species so that only the female of his species is attracted to him. The donkey and the horse came from similar ancestral stock and can be mated to produce a sterile mule. The isolating mechanism here is known as "hybrid inviability" and results from incompatible chromosomes that cannot synapse at meiosis. The mule cannot produce functional viable gametes and is therefore a sterile organism.

Both geographical and biological isolating mechanisms play a role in speciation. Most biologists believe that geographical or spatial isolation must occur first and after that some type of biological barrier develops to reproductively isolate the two groups of the original population. To summarize the speciation process we should note that two factors are important, namely: (1) genetic variability must exist in the population; and (2) the population must be split by isolating mechanisms known as barriers.

Earlier in this chapter we mentioned the Grand Canyon and its geologic time table. This area also provides us with a notable example of speciation. The Grand Canyon could certainly have acted as a geographical barrier to isolate two parts of any population that once occupied the entire area. This is believed to have happened in the case of the Kaibab squirrel on the north rim and the Abert squirrel of the south rim (Figure 12–23). These two squirrels have tufted ears and bushy tails and are very similar in appearance, yet they are generally considered to be two distinct species because they

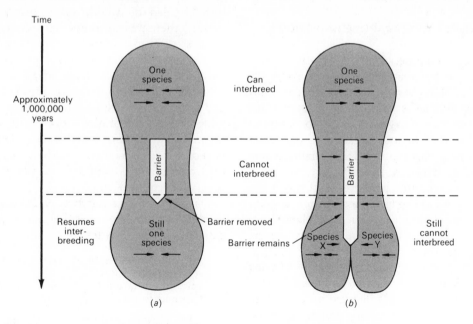

Figure 12–22 (a) A barrier occurs in a population of a species, but it does not persist long enough to effect speciation. (b) The barrier lasts longer, and two species result.

431

(a)   (b)

Figure 12-23 Closely related squirrels of the Grand Canyon. (*a*) The Kaibab, from the north rim, has a distinctly larger and whiter tail. (Courtesy of Grand Canyon National Park, U.S. Department of the Interior.) (*b*) The Abert, on the other hand, has a white underside. (Courtesy of National Park Service, U.S. Department of the Interior.)

are effectively isolated by the canyon. Several other species apparently have undergone similar isolation and speciation in this area—for example, the pocket mouse, the antelope squirrel, and several plants.

DIVERGENCE AND ADAPTIVE RADIATION

The speciation process is an explanation of how species can be created and diverge from one another. Moreover, each new species may undergo further speciation at a later time. This further *divergence* leads to *adaptive radiation* wherein individuals of a particular species may move into different habitats and speciation continues. Eventually, a variety of organisms would be produced and this is the condition we see today. Classification systems reflect this divergence; when we denote the members of a classification category we are recognizing the subgroups that have diverged from a common ancestral group (Figure 12-24). Many major radiations have occurred in some of the large familiar groups of animals such as placental mammals, marsupial mammals, and the phylum Mollusca. But we will return to a group we have already discussed

for our example, Darwin's finches (Figure 12-25). An ancestral finch arriving in the Galápagos Islands could have radiated into all of the habitats and ecological niches available to it. In fact, finches could even fill niches usually filled by woodpeckers and warblers because there was no competition. Some of the finches eat seeds whereas others feed on insects. Of the seed eaters, some eat cactus seeds specifically and others have adapted to large or small seeds of other plants. This speciation and subsequent adaptive radiation was possible because the original species was able to disperse throughout the widely separated islands. Through this isolation, hereditary dissimilarities developed to a point where speciation could occur.

Darwin's finches can be divided into four categories based on their habitat and food-gathering characteristics:

1 *Ground finches*—six species that feed on seeds of varying sizes. The size of the seed eaten is related to the size of the bill. Competition for food therefore is avoided.

2 *Tree finches*—six species that live in moist forests and feed on insects in the trees. One tree finch, *C. pallidus*, uses a cactus

432

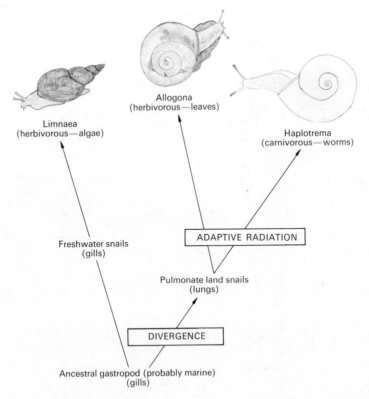

Limnaea
(herbivorous—algae)

Allogona
(herbivorous—leaves)

Haplotrema
(carnivorous—worms)

Freshwater snails
(gills)

ADAPTIVE RADIATION

Pulmonate land snails
(lungs)

DIVERGENCE

Ancestral gastropod (probably marine)
(gills)

Figure 12–24 Evolutionary divergence in snails. Gills developed in the freshwater snails, whereas lungs evolved in the land snails. Note that adaptive radiation occurred between the two closely related pulmonates.

spine to probe insects from crevices. This represents a typical woodpecker niche. The use of tools by animals other than humans is quite rare and the spine-using finch is unique among birds.

3 *Warblerlike finch*—a single species that has found a habitat in the low bushes and feeds on insects.

4 *Cocos Island finch*—a single species that lives in a moist forest and feeds on insects. This bird is isolated from all the others since Cocos Island is several hundred miles to the northeast of the main group. It is thought that the Cocos Island species came directly from the mainland and is only indirectly related to the others.

CONVERGENCE AND PARALLELISM

Another evolutionary pattern occurs when two organisms (or groups) of different ancestry develop similar characteristics. Such a process

is known as *convergence* and this pattern has occurred in marsupial and placental mammals (Figure 12–26). In placental mammals the embryo develops before birth inside the mother's uterus, attached by a placenta; marsupial embryos complete their development after an immature birth in an abdominal pouch on the mother. Placental mammals live extensively in all parts of the world. Although marsupial representatives are dispersed throughout various parts of the world, their primary development has been in Australia, and they have radiated into almost every available niche. The principal reason for their extensive evolution on the continent of Australia was probably the absence of competition from placental mammals. When convergence occurs among fairly closely related organisms such as these, it is often termed *parallelism*. It is interesting that no marsupial has adapted to the flying

433

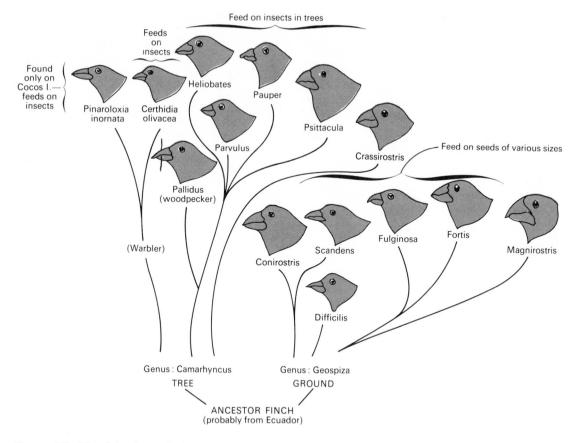

Found
only on
Cocos I.—
feeds on
insects

Feeds
on
insects

Feed on insects in trees

Pinaroloxia
inornata

Certhidia
olivacea

Heliobates

Pauper

Psittacula

Feed on seeds of various sizes

Parvulus

Crassirostris

Pallidus
(woodpecker)

(Warbler)

Conirostris

Scandens

Fulginosa

Fortis

Magnirostris

Difficilis

Genus: Camarhyncus
TREE

Genus: Geospiza
GROUND

ANCESTOR FINCH
(probably from Ecuador)

Figure 12–25 Adaptive radiation as shown by Darwin's finches. The first radiation was one of habitat: between ground and trees. Subsequent radiations were primarily on the basis of food.

niche represented by the bat in placentals. Some ecologists have proposed that the only reason this is true is that the flying niche in Australia may have been filled by bats from Asia and marsupials could not compete successfully. The principles of divergence and convergence are diagrammed in Figure 12–27.

EVOLUTION OF THE PRIMATES

The order Primates includes such mammals as tree shrews, lemurs, tarsiers, monkeys, gibbons, chimpanzees, and man. Some of the common characteristics for this group include five fingers or toes on each limb, grasping hands or feet, front-facing eyes, and highly developed cerebral hemispheres in the brain.

Most of the primates, with the notable exceptions of man, the gorilla, and the baboon, live much of their lives in trees (arboreal habitat). The branch of the primate evolutionary tree which gave rise to anthropoids (monkeys, apes, and man) is believed to have separated from the prosimian line (pre-ape) of modern tree shrews, lemurs, and tarsiers about 30 million years ago. Living lemurs may be found today only on the island of Madagascar off the east coast of Africa, and tarsiers are limited to Southeast Asia (Figure 12–28).

Many attempts have been made to show the evolutionary relationships among the primates, especially those involving man. A generalized scheme shows that man has the closest ancestory with gorillas and chimpanzees and is

434

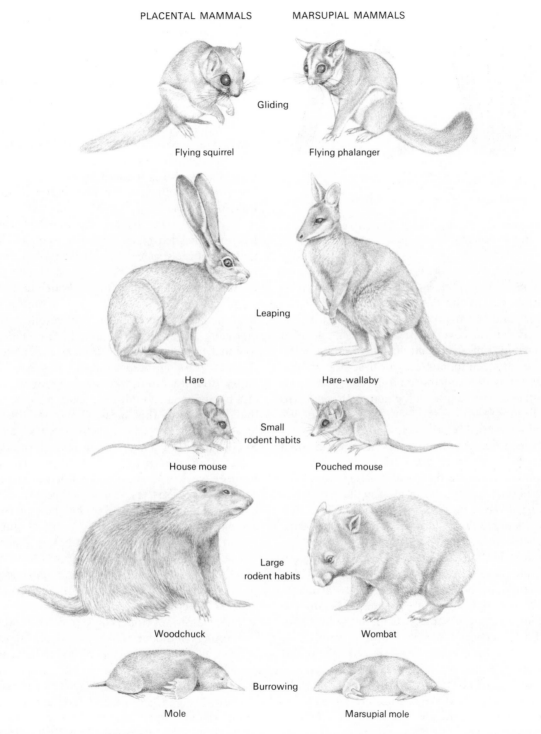

PLACENTAL MAMMALS   MARSUPIAL MAMMALS

Gliding

Flying squirrel   Flying phalanger

Leaping

Hare   Hare-wallaby

Small
rodent habits

House mouse   Pouched mouse

Large
rodent habits

Woodchuck   Wombat

Burrowing

Mole   Marsupial mole

Figure 12–26   Convergent evolution in placental and marsupial mammals. (Redrawn from E. L. Cock-rum and J. E. McCauley, *Zoology*, Philadelphia, W. B. Saunders Co., 1965.)

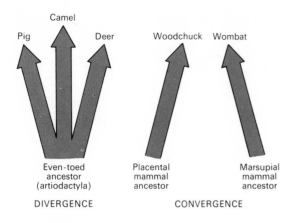

| DIVERGENCE | CONVERGENCE |

Figure 12–27 Examples of divergence and convergence among mammals.

least related to Old World monkeys and gibbons (Figure 12–29). This relationship is supported by comparisons of anatomical structure and blood proteins (Figure 12–30).

Recent discoveries in East Africa and Asia have lead most paleontologists to support the idea that chimpanzees, gorillas, orangutans, and man descended from different species of a small Miocene ape of the genus *Dryopithecus* (Figure 12–31). A few teeth and jaw fragments of a presumably pre-Australopithecine species named *Ramapithecus* have been found in India and Africa. It is generally agreed that this genus, considered to have arisen about 14 million years ago, is an intermediate between *Dryopithecus* and *Australopithecus*. Very little evidence is available for the pre-Pleistocene ancestors of the gibbon and orangutan of Asia, but it is thought that they split off the stem group in the late Oligocene and early Miocene. Somewhat more information is now available on the development of hominids in the Pleistocene era some two million years ago. The discoveries of the southern apes, *Australopithecus* (Figure 12–32), by Raymond Dart in South Africa in 1924, and *Zinjanthropus* (Figure 12–33), in East Africa by L. S. B. Leakey in 1959, have filled some of the evolutionary gaps in the fossil record. *Zinjanthropus*, now considered to be a species of *Australopithecus*, has been estimated to be nearly two million years old by radioactive dating.

In general, these "ape-men" (or perhaps more appropriately, "near-men") had large faces with small brains not much larger than 600 cubic centimeters. (Modern man's brain averages about 1,400 cubic centimeters.) The skeletal structure of *Australopithecus* indicates that they were short in stature (about four feet), walked upright, had stereoscopic vision, and had teeth with human characteristics. Dart and Leakey have both found stone tools in their digs, and it is thought by many that this group could represent the beginnings of the human species.

A study of the fossil remains of African near-men has led many scientists to conclude that one of the species of *Australopithecus* now renamed as *Homo transvaalensis* began to manufacture chip-edged tools about one and a half million years ago. *Homo transvaalensis*, who appears to have been omniverous, was gradually replaced by a more highly skilled tool maker and omnivore, *Homo erectus*, about 700,000 years ago. *Homo erectus* possessed a larger brain (about 1,300 cubic centimeters), and his living sites indicate a societal mode of life. Remains of this species have now been located in Java, China, and Central and South Africa. Java and Peking man (formerly called *Pithecanthropus*) and Leakey's *Homo habilis* from Kenya are now included in *Homo erectus* (Figure 12–34). A new find reported in late 1972 by Richard Leakey has been dated at two and one-half million years (Figure 12–35). This new evidence indicates that a larger-brained, truly upright hominid lived at the same time as *Australopithecus* and casts serious doubts on the theory that modern man evolved directly from *Australopithecus*.

The transition from *Homo erectus* to the forerunners of modern *Homo sapiens* is still not entirely clear, but we can cite Neanderthal man as a representative who lived 70,000 to 100,000 years ago. *Homo sapiens neanderthalensis* lived in Europe and Asia and had a brain volume equal to that of the average modern human. The skeletal bones were thick and heavy, especially those of the limbs. Neanderthal man had a low, sloping forehead

Figure 12–28 (*a*) Common tree shrew. (*b*) White-fronted lemur: male at left, female at right. (*c*) Mindanao tarsier. (Ron Garrison; San Diego Zoo.)

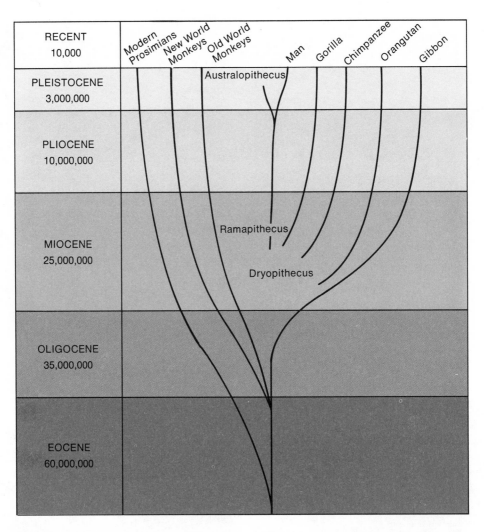

RECENT 10,000	Modern Prosimians	New World Monkeys	Old World Monkeys		Man	Gorilla	Chimpanzee	Orangutan	Gibbon
PLEISTOCENE 3,000,000				Australopithecus					
PLIOCENE 10,000,000									
MIOCENE 25,000,000				Ramapithecus Dryopithecus					
OLIGOCENE 35,000,000									
EOCENE 60,000,000									

Figure 12–29 Generalized family tree of the primates. Time in years is shown at the left as approximate times from the beginning of each geologic period.

and heavy brow ridges (Figure 12–36).

The fossil record leads finally to the European forms known as Cro-Magnon, originally found in caves in southern France in 1868. In this type we see a well-developed chin, moderate brow ridges, and a high and full forehead very similar to modern European men (Figure 12–37). In addition, Cro-Magnon possessed longer, thinner shin bones than did Neanderthal. It is suspected that Neanderthal became extinct about 30,000 to 35,000 years ago and was superceded by Cro-Magnon, who gave rise to the modern races of man. Several theories have been advanced for the disappearance of Neanderthal man. Extermination by rival humans and gradual incorporation by interbreeding have been proposed, but the fossil record has not yet supplied an answer.

Thus we see another example of evolution within a related group, the primates. The exact nature of the evolutionary tree leading to modern higher primates is clouded by the

438

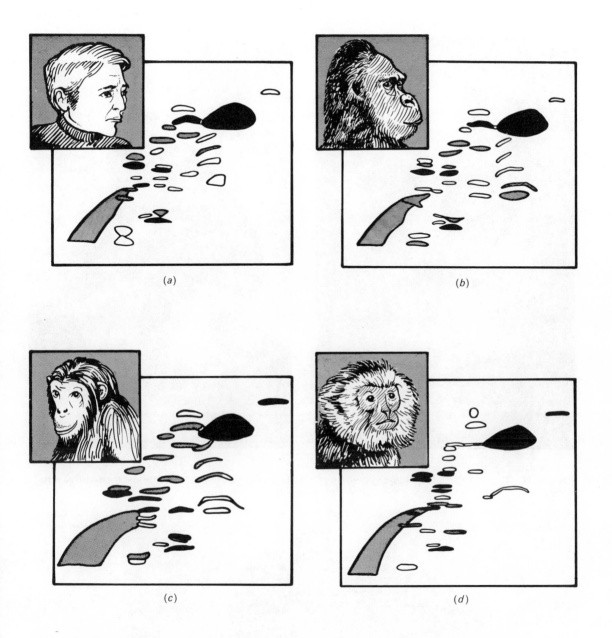

Figure 12–30 Comparison of blood proteins showing evolutionary relationships. (*a*) Man. (*b*) Gorilla. (*c*) Chimpanzee. (*d*) Gibbon. These patterns are produced when blood-serum samples are exposed to an electrical field on a carrier substance such as filter paper or starch gel. Since proteins vary in size and electrical charge, they move at different rates along the carrier. The patterns of man, gorilla, and chimpanzee are similar; whereas the pattern of the gibbon is considerably different. This evidence supports the theory that the African chimpanzee and gorilla are more closely related to man than is the Asian gibbon. (Redrawn from Sherwood L. Washburn, editor, *Classification and Human Evolution*, Chicago: Aldine Publishing Company, 1963; copyright © 1963 by Wenner-Gren Foundation for Anthropological Research, Inc. by permission of the author and Aldine Publishing Company.)

(a)   (b)

Figure 12–31   (a) Partial skull of *Dryopithecus*. (b) Drawing of the probable appearance of this short-armed Miocene ape. (Trustees of the British Museum [Natural History].)

Figure 12–32   *Australopithecus* restoration. (Courtesy of the American Museum of Natural History.)

440

Figure 12–33 Olduvai Gorge in Tanzania contains one of the richest deposits of prehistoric fossils ever discovered. Here the late British anthropologist Louis S. B. Leakey discovered the remains and tools of creatures who lived two million years ago. (Robert F. Sisson; © National Geographic Society.)

Figure 12–34 *Pithecanthropus* restoration. (Courtesy of the American Museum of Natural History.)

occurrence of many contemporary and diverse types. With the existence of many possible interbreeding genotypes, some were more successful than others, and the frequencies of these genotypes increased in the population. The most successful genotypes persisted and led to the assemblage of primates we see today.

MODERN MAN AND EVOLUTION

With the appearance of man a new type of evolution developed—cultural evolution—which is exclusive and unique to the human species. Through this process, man can transmit his knowledge and culture to future generations. Cultural evolution is possible because of man's large brain and his capacity for abstract thought and learning. Greater progress is thus possible when one generation can profit from the advances and mistakes of past generations. With the advent of man's large brain also came the ability to perceive ethics, moral relationships, concepts about the environment, and religions. All races of human beings therefore can concern themselves with more than simply acquiring food and shelter.

It is increasingly apparent that man has

Figure 12–35 Richard Leakey holding the skull and upper jaw of the fossil man found near Lake Rudolf in Kenya. It is believed to be 2.5 million years old, which would make it the oldest complete skull of early man ever found. (Bob Campbell; © National Geographic Society.)

Figure 12–36 Reconstruction of a Neanderthal family group. (Field Museum of Natural History, Chicago.)

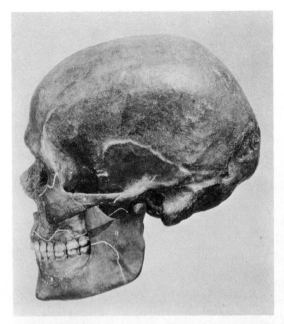

Figure 12–37 Cro-Magnon man. (*a*) Skull. (*b*) Restoration. (Courtesy of the American Museum of Natural History.)

become an evolutionary agent who can modify, create, and destroy species through his interference with the normal environment. Practically every domestic plant or animal providing for man's subsistence has been artificially selected and bred for that role with man acting as the selective force. Human beings can also bring a species to extinction or near extinction as in the case of the passenger pigeon and the buffalo. Populations of wild animals such as deer can be regulated through game-management policies. In other words, nature is not the same since the human organism evolved and man can now control the evolutionary development of other species if he chooses. But can man control his own development and evolution? It seems that this could be possible since he understands the selective process and is learning more and more about the hereditary mechanism. The chief problem lies in the answer to the questions, how can man establish the principles to be used in the selection process in the human species, and which characteristics will be selected? At the present time there are certain traits that many people would agree are harm-

ful to the human species, but the legal processes necessary to bring about selection against these traits would be too difficult to achieve. Many people fear the legal control of human heredity and behavior since its use obviously depends on who is in power. There are others, though, who believe that man will be forced to apply his knowledge of genetics and evolution to the human species if he is to survive and develop to his fullest capacities.

Many students of evolution have speculated on the appearance of the man of the future. These speculations range from very little change to a considerably different-appearing organism. Proponents of the "great change" hypothesis believe that, since man has changed so much in the short time that he has been on this planet (less than a million years), we can look for continued change in the future. One concept of change is in the direction of a larger cranium, to accommodate a slightly larger brain, and finer facial features. Another hypothesis holds that in the next 5,000 years man will be slightly taller, have a skull that is more globular with the sensory organs more developed, have a more refined face with

443

Figure 12–38 Theodosius Dobzhansky, outstanding investigator of the genetic basis of evolution. (Courtesy of Dr. Dobzhansky and The Rockefeller Foundation.)

smaller and fewer teeth (the wisdom teeth missing), have less hair on his body, and have a slightly reduced appendix. That some changes will occur is almost certain, since we know that all species are mutable.

Perhaps of greater importance than man's future appearance is the problem of how an evolutionary concept is accepted by society. Conflicts between the modern concept of evolution and literal biblical interpretation have been frequent. However, this conflict is avoided by many religions today and evolution is accepted as the actual means for accom-

plishing the changes recorded in Genesis. As Theodosius Dobzhansky (Figure 12–38) has stated: "Evolution is the method whereby Creation is accomplished." The general feeling today is that a concept of evolution leads to a better understanding of our world and should be applied to other facets of our society, such as religion. Probably the greatest effect of the concept of evolution is that it provides a unifying framework for all of biology, and the great synthesis by Charles Darwin in 1859 provided all fields of biology with a central theme.

SUMMARIZING STATEMENTS

Evolution is the concept that changes occurring in organisms result from slight genetic variations that are transmitted through successive generations. This orderly succession of change from preexisting species is a result of changes in genes and genotype frequencies.

Direct evidence for the existence of earlier forms of life may be obtained through the collection and dating of fossils. The well-preserved fossils of horses have provided an excellent reconstruction of the changes that have occurred in this family.

Numerous examples for illustrating evolution can be found in the development and structure of species living today, and many similarities exist in the embryology of closely related species. Several forms with characteristics intermediate between classification categories are known which strengthen the concept of gradual change.

The concept of organic evolution followed the realization that geological changes have occurred over periods of time. The statement of the theory of evolution and its probable mechanism through natural selection was made by Darwin and Wallace in 1858. Although Darwin accepted the Lamarckian theory of the inheritance of acquired characteristics, we now know that changes in species and subsequent natural selection are due to genetic changes with environmental selection for characteristics of adaptive value.

In order for new species to develop, it is generally accepted that an isolating mechanism must separate two parts of a population long enough for genotypes to become incompatible. In time further selection upon these two gene pools may give rise to other new species.

The history of primate evolution indicates that the anthropoids (monkeys, apes, and man) diverged from prosimian stock (tree shrews, lemurs, and tarsiers) about 30 million years ago. Chimpanzees, gorillas, orangutans, and man descended from several species of a small ape, *Dryopithecus*. About one and one-half million years ago the genus *Homo* emerged, possessing a larger brain and a societal mode of life. The forerunners of modern *Homo sapiens* were Neanderthal and Cro-Magnon man.

REVIEW QUESTIONS

1   What sources of genetic variation are necessary for the evolutionary process to occur?

2   Compare how Lamarck, Darwin, and modern biologists would explain the development of the long neck in giraffes.

3   Summarize the contribution of the Galápagos finches to Darwin's theory of natural selection.

4   How does the study of the molecular structure of cytochrome c assist in the understanding of evolutionary relationships?

5   A naturalist made the following observation: A species of field mice living in a wooded hillside and a field were studied; those in the forests had dark coats whereas those living in the field had light coats. What is the probable explanation for this?

6   Two marine organisms, the lampshell and horseshoe crab, appear relatively unchanged from their fossil ancestors dating back over 300,000,000 years, whereas the horse has changed radically in only 60,000,000 years. How can you account for these differences in rates of evolution?

7 Bacteria exposed to penicillin over a number of generations have been found to develop an immunity to this antibiotic. What is the probable explanation of this?

8 List as many examples as you can of convergent, divergent, and parallel evolution.

9 Show the relationship between the Hardy-Weinberg principle and the concept of natural selection.

10 If you were a researcher and desired a race of rats smaller than the normal, average size, how would you set up a breeding program to accomplish this? What problems might you encounter?

11 How has the concept of evolution influenced our thought in fields other than the biological sciences, such as political science, sociology, economics, and theology?

12 From what you now understand about genetics and evolution, describe events which could have led from *Dryopithecus* to modern man.

SUPPLEMENTARY READINGS

Allison, Anthony C., "Sickle Cells and Evolution," *Scientific American*, August, 1956.

Barghoorn, Elso S., "The Oldest Fossils," *Scientific American*, May, 1971.

Bell, P. R., ed., *Darwin's Biological Work*, New York, Wiley, 1964.

Bitterman, M. E., "The Evolution of Intelligence," *Scientific American*, January, 1965.

Crow, James F., "Ionizing Radiation and Evolution," *Scientific American*, September, 1959.

Dart, Raymond A., *Adventures with the Missing Link*, Philadelphia, The Institutes Press, 1967.

Dayhoff, Margaret O., "Computer Analysis of Protein Evolution," *Scientific American*, July, 1969.

De Beer, Sir Gavin, *Charles Darwin*, Garden City, N.Y., Doubleday, 1967.

Dickerson, Richard E., "The Structure and History of an Ancient Protein," *Scientific American*, April, 1972.

Dobzhansky, Theodosius, "The Genetic Basis of Evolution," *Scientific American*, January, 1950.

Dobzhansky, Theodosius, "The Present Evolution of Man," *Scientific American*, September, 1960.

Eaton, T. H., *Evolution*, New York, Norton, 1970.

Eiseley, Loren C., "Charles Darwin," *Scientific American*, February, 1956.

Eiseley, Loren C., "Charles Lyell," *Scientific American*, August, 1959.

Glass, Bentley, O. Temkin, and W. L. Straus, Jr., *Forerunners of Darwin: 1745-1859*, Baltimore, Johns Hopkins Press, 1968.

Goldsby, Richard A., *Race and Races*, New York, Macmillan, 1971.

Hallan, A., "Continental Drift and the Fossil Record," *Scientific American*, November, 1972.

Hardin, G., *Nature and Man's Fate*, New York, New American Library (Mentor Books), 1961.

Howells, William W., "Homo Erectus," *Scientific American*, November, 1966.

Huxley, Julian, *The Living Thoughts of Darwin*, Greenwich, Fawcett, 1939.

Kerkut, G. A., *The Implications of Evolution*, New York, Pergamon, 1960.

Kettlewell, H. B. D., "Darwin's Missing Evidence," *Scientific American*, March, 1959.

Lack, David, "Darwin's Finches," *Scientific American*, April, 1953.

Lasker, G. W., *The Evolution of Man*, New York, Holt, Rinehart and Winston, 1961.

Livingston, John, and Lister Sinclair, *Darwin and the Galápagos*, Canadian Broadcasting Corp., 1966.

MacNeish, Richard S., "Early Man in the Andes," *Scientific American*, April, 1971.

Margulis, Lynn, "Symbiosis and Evolution," *Scientific American*, August, 1971.

Mayr, Ernst, *Populations, Species, and Evolution*, Cambridge, Harvard University Press, 1970.

Millot, Jacques, "The Coelacanth," *Scientific American*, December, 1955.

Napier, J., "The Evolution of the Hand," *Scientific American*, December, 1962.

Nelson, Bryan, *Galápagos: Islands of Birds*, New York, Morrow, 1968.

Pfeiffer, John E., *The Emergence of Man*, New York, Harper and Row, 1972.

Portmann, A., *Animal Camouflage*, Ann Arbor, University of Michigan Press, 1959.

Rensch, Bernhard, *Homo Sapiens: From Man to Demigod*, New York, Columbia University Press, 1972.

Simons, Elwyn L., "The Early Relatives of Man," *Scientific American*, July, 1964.

Stebbins, G. L., *Processes of Organic Evolution*, Englewood Cliffs, N.J., Prentice-Hall, 1966.

Teleki, Geza, "The Omnivorous Chimpanzee," *Scientific American*, January, 1973.

Thornton, Ian, *Darwin's Islands: A Natural History of the Galápagos*, New York, Natural History Press, 1971.

Van Lawick-Goodall, Jane, *In the Shadow of Man*, Boston, Houghton Mifflin, 1971.

Volpe, E. Peter, *Understanding Evolution*, Dubuque, Iowa, Wm. C. Brown, 1967.

Wallace, Alfred Russel, *The Malay Archipelago*, New York, Dover, 1962.

Washburn, Sherwood L., "Tools and Human Evolution," *Scientific American*, September, 1960.

Appendix

Classification of the Living World

The hierarchical levels of classification generally used are applied below to three different organisms.

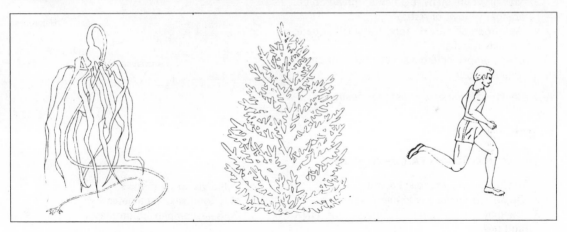

	Organism I	*Organism II*	*Organism III*
Kingdom	Protista	Metaphyta	Metazoa
Phylum	Phaeophyta	Tracheophyta	Chordata
Subphylum		Pteropsida	Vertebrata
Class	Heterogeneratae	Gymnospermae	Mammalia
Subclass	Polystichineae		
Order	Laminariales	Coniferales	Primates
Family	Lessoniaceae	Pinaceae	Hominidae
Genus	*Nereocystis*	*Pseudotsuga*	*Homo*
Species	*luetkeana*	*menziesii*	*sapiens*
Common name	Kelp	Douglas fir	Man

Kingdom MONERA

Phylum SCHIZOPHYTA (bacteria):

1. Microscopic in size.
2. Chromosomes composed of DNA only; no organized nucleus.
3. Autotrophic by photosynthesis or chemosynthesis.
4. Simple chromatophores similar to individual grana of a chloroplast.
5. Many produce toxins pathogenic to higher organisms.

Representative genera: *Bacillus, Streptococcus, Spirillum*

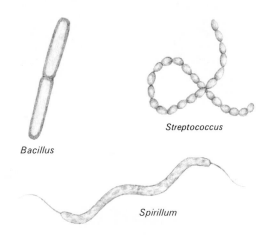

Streptococcus

Bacillus

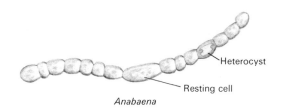

Spirillum

Phylum CYANOPHYTA (blue-green algae):

1. Mostly aquatic and filamentous.
2. No organized nucleus.
3. May contain many pigments: green, blue, orange, yellow, or red.
4. Autotrophic; provide food for small aquatic animals and fish.
5. Large, empty heterocyst cells burst to cause fragmentation.

Representative genera: *Oscillatoria, Anabaena*

Heterocyst

Resting cell

Anabaena

Kingdom PROTISTA

Phylum CHLOROPHYTA (green algae):

1. Mostly aquatic or moist habitats.
2. Organized nucleus with membrane.
3. Distinct chromosomes composed of DNA and protein.
4. Cell division by mitosis.
5. May form sexual gametes.
6. Possess complex chloroplasts.

Representative genera: *Pleurococcus, Ulothrix, Spirogyra*

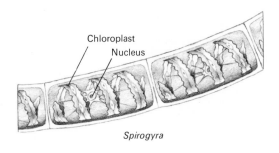

Chloroplast
Nucleus

Spirogyra

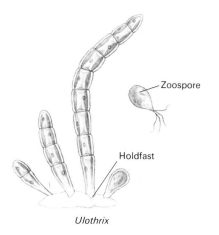

Zoospore

Holdfast

Ulothrix

450

Phylum CHRYSOPHYTA (diatoms):

1. Occur in both fresh water and marine.
2. Possess complex silicon—aluminum two-part "shells" or tests.
3. Contain yellow or brown pigments in addition to chlorophyll.

Representative genera: *Pinnularia, Staurastrum, Tabellaria*

4. Diatomaceous earth is important as a commercial abrasive.
5. Store oil as an energy source rather than starch.
6. First link in most aquatic food chains.

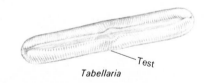

Tabellaria

Phylum PHAEOPHYTA (brown algae):

1. Contain chlorophyll and yellow or brown pigments.
2. Generally large, marine, leaflike forms.

3. Alternation of generation with diploid sporophytes.
4. Body differentiated into specific parts—holdfast, stipe, blade.

Representative genera: *Fucus, Laminaria, Macrocystis, Nereocystis*

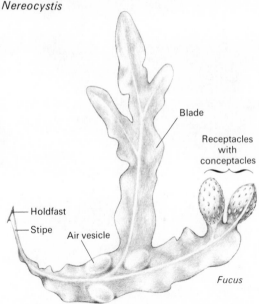

Blade

Receptacles with conceptacles

Holdfast

Stipe

Air vesicle

Fucus

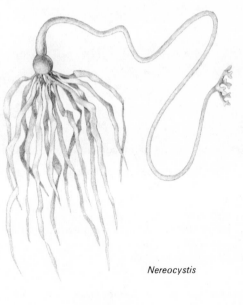

Nereocystis

Phylum RHODOPHYTA (red algae):

1. Contain chlorophyll and a red pigment, phycoerythrin.
2. Generally marine.
3. Alternation of generation with diploid sporophyte (some have three generations).
4. Feathery, filamentous, or leaflike.
5. Some deposit calcium on their cell walls.

Representative genera: *Polysiphonia, Corallina* (red-encrusting alga), *Grinnellia* (leafy red alga)

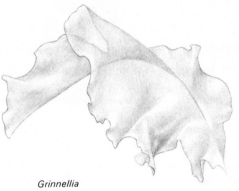

Grinnellia

451

Phylum MASTIGOPHORA (flagellates):

Class: Phytomastigina (autotrophic flagellates):

1. One to several flagella for locomotion.
2. Contain chloroplasts.
3. Store starch as food reserve.
4. Occur solitary or in colonies.

Representative genera: *Euglena, Volvox*

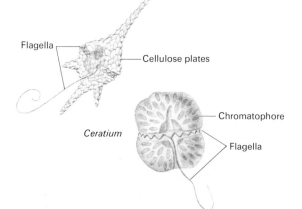

Euglena

Volvox

Class: Dinoflagellata (dinoflagellates or fire algae):

1. Two flagella; one longitudinal and one transverse as a girdle.
2. May be armored with hard cellulose plates or naked.
3. Large blooms of these organisms in the sea are called *red tides*.
4. Contain chlorophyll.

Representative genera: *Ceratium, Gymnodinium, Gonyaulax*

Ceratium

Gymnodinium

Class: Zoömastigina (heterotrophic flagellates):

1. Possess one to many flagella for locomotion.
2. Many are parasitic in the blood of animals and humans, such as sleeping sickness (*Trypanosoma*).
3. Some are commensal in the gut of termites where they digest cellulose (*Trichonympha*).

Representative genera: *Trypanosoma, Trichonympha*

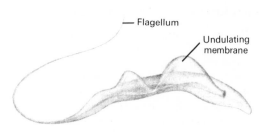

Trypanosoma

452

Phylum MYXOMYCETES (slime molds):

1. Two stages in the life cycle: a multinucleate ameboid plasmodium and a stalked fruiting body which produces haploid spores.
2. Spores germinate into flagellated gametes. Two fuse to produce a new plasmodium stage.
3. Nutrition is phagotrophic. Ingest bacteria and decaying particles of organic matter.

Representative genera: *Physarum, Stemonitis*

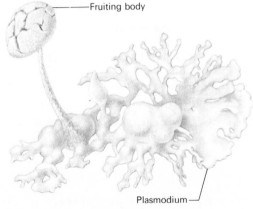

Fruiting body

Plasmodium

Slime mold

Phylum EUMYCOPHYTA (fungi):

1. Most of body is made up of filaments called *hyphae*; a mass of hyphae is a *mycelium*.
2. Contain no photosynthetic pigments.
3. Nutrition is saprophytic on decaying organic matter.

Class: Phycomycetes (algal fungi):

1. Mostly aquatic fungi.
2. Long hyphae filaments.
3. Hyphae lack transverse walls.

Representative genus: *Rhizopus* (black bread mold)

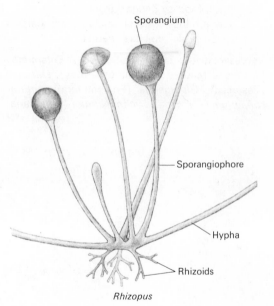

Sporangium

Sporangiophore

Hypha

Rhizoids

Rhizopus

Class: Ascomycetes (cup fungi):

1. Possess septate (transverse walls) hyphae.
2. Fruiting body is generally cup-shaped and called an *ascocarp*.
3. Includes the yeasts, molds, and mildews.
4. Many are pathogenic to plants.

Representative genera: *Saccharomyces, Penicillium, Aspergillus, Peziza*

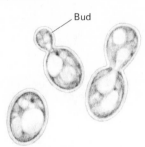

Bud

Yeast cells
Saccaromyces

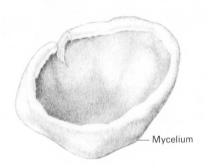

Mycelium

Peziza (cup fungus)

453

Class: Basidiomycetes (club fungi) :

1. Have septate hyphae.
2. Fruiting body of mycelium is large and characteristic (mushrooms, bracket fungi, and puffballs).
3. Spores are produced as buds from a club-shaped hyphal tip called a *basidium*.

Representative genera : *Amanita* (poisonous mushroom), *Fomes* (bracket fungus)

Phylum SARCODINA (amoebae):

1. Move by extending pseudopods.
2. Ingest food by phagocytosis.
3. May produce tests of calcium carbonate or silicon or pick up bits of debris.

Representative genera : *Amoeba*, *Entamoeba histolytica* (causes amoebic dysentery), *Difflugia* (Testacea), *Globigerina* (Foraminifera), *Actinosphaerium* (Heliozoa), *Lychnocanium* (Radiolaria)

Mycelium

Amanita

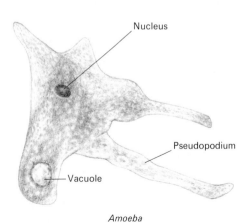

Nucleus

Pseudopodium

Vacuole

Amoeba

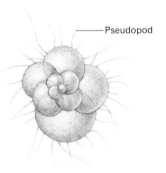

Pseudopod

Globigerina

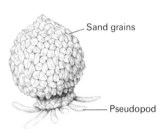

Sand grains

Pseudopod

Difflugia

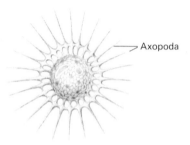

Axopoda

Actinosphaerium

454

Phylum SPOROZOA (sporozoans):

1. All species are parasitic and bear spores at some stage of the life cycle.
2. Life cycle may involve a vector carrier such as the mosquito.
3. Possess no specialized organelles for locomotion.
4. Alternate stages of sexual and asexual reproduction.
5. Infest blood and tissues of animals and man.

Representative genera: *Plasmodium* (causes malaria), *Eimeria* (causes coccidiosis)

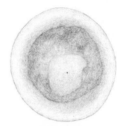

Plasmodium
(ring stage of malaria parasite in red blood cell)

Phylum CILIOPHORA:

1. Have cilia or sucking tentacles.
2. Possess two types of nuclei.

Class: Ciliata (ciliates or infusoria) :

1. Move by means of cilia throughout life.
2. Have definite body shape and a cell mouth and anus.
3. Possess stinging organelles (trichocysts) for protection and food capture.

Representative genera: *Paramecium* (slipper animal), *Stentor* (trumpet animal)

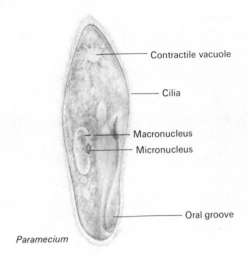

Paramecium

- Contractile vacuole
- Cilia
- Macronucleus
- Micronucleus
- Oral groove

Class: Suctoria (suctorians) :

1. Cilia present only in motile young stages.
2. Mature adults lose cilia and generally become stalked and sessile.
3. Feed on protistans by piercing them with a sharp tentacle and sucking out the protoplasm.

Representative genera: *Podyphyra* (stalked), *Anarma* (no stalk)

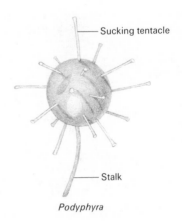

- Sucking tentacle
- Stalk

Podyphyra

Kingdom METAPHYTA

Phylum BRYOPHYTA:

1. Lack true roots, stems or leaves.
2. Possess multicellular reproductive organs.
3. Zygote develops within female gametophyte.
4. Produce multicellular embryos.
5. Undergo definite alternation of generation.
6. Gametophyte (haploid) generation is dominant.

455

Class: Hepaticae (liverworts) :

1. Flat leaflike gametophyte.
2. Produce stalked sex organs.
3. Form asexual buds called *gemmae*.

Representative genus : *Marchantia*

Class: Musci (mosses) :

1. Erect or trailing leafy gametophyte.
2. Produce asexual buds in "leaf" axils or stem bases.

Representative genera : *Polytrichum* (hairy cap), *Sphagnum* (peat bog moss)

Class: Anthocerotae (hornworts) :

1. Sex organs lie in cavities in the gametophyte thallus.
2. An erect sporophyte grows out of gametophyte.

Representative genus : *Anthoceros*

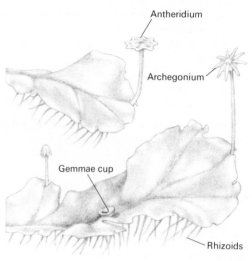

Marchantia

Polytrichum

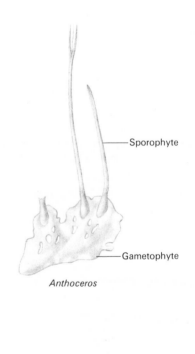

Anthoceros

456

Phylum TRACHEOPHYTA:

1. Possess conducting tissues, xylem, and phloem.
2. Have true roots, stems, and leaves.
3. Sporophyte is dominant generation.

Subphylum PSILOPSIDA:

1. Have small, scalelike leaves.
2. Stems produce capsulelike sporangia that form spores.
3. Tropical or subtropical distribution.
4. Only two living genera.

Representative genus: *Psilotum*

Subphylum LYCOPSIDA (club mosses):

1. Sporangia develop in conelike structures in leaf axils.
2. Asexual reproduction by buds called *bulbils*.

Representative genera: *Selaginella*, *Lycopodium* (ground pine)

Subphylum SPHENOPSIDA (horsetails):

1. Sporophytes are of two types, large sexual stalks bearing a conelike strobilus and a smaller, leafy vegetative stalk.
2. Narrow leaves are arranged in whorls or jointed stalks.
3. Strobilus is not composed of leaves but is a "new" structure—produces spores.

Representative genus: *Equisetum* (scouring rush or horsetail)

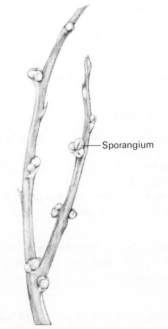

Psilotum

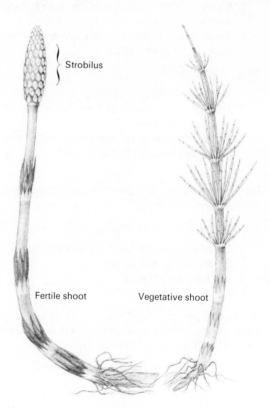

Equisetum

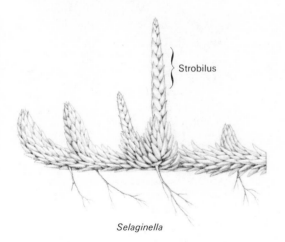

Selaginella

457

Subphylum PTEROPSIDA:

1. Sporophyte generation dominant.
2. Possess large, complex leaves.
3. Produce seeds (except the ferns).
4. Conducting tissues are prominent.

Class: Filicinae (ferns):

1. Fronds arise from a long underground stem called a *rhizome*.
2. Fronds bear clusters of sporangia called *sori* on underside.
3. Gametophyte known as a *prothallus* develops from a spore in the soil.

Representative genera: *Pteridium* (bracken), *Polypodium* (licorice), *Polystichum* (sword fern), *Adiantum* (maidenhair)

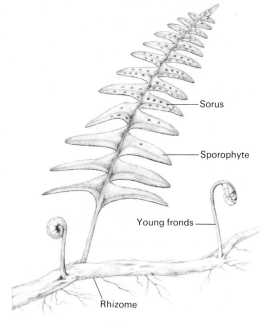

Polypodium

Class: Gymnospermae (cone-bearing seed plants):

1. Seeds are exposed on scales of cones.
2. Seeds contain endosperm as starch food reserve.
3. Seeds develop on the sporophyte and are released for germination.

Order: Cycadales:

1. Mostly fossil plants—9 living genera.
2. Tropical and subtropical distribution—South America and Africa.
3. Many are known as tree ferns—grow over 50 feet tall and look like palm trees.

Representative genera: *Encephalartos* (large tree fern), *Dioon* (low plant)

Order: Coniferales (conifers):

1. Usually trees with large branched stems.
2. Small, needle-like leaves.
3. Produce woody stem.

Representative genera: *Pinus* (pine), *Abies* (fir), *Larix* (larch), *Thuja* (western red cedar), *Tsuga* (hemlock), *Sequoia* (giant redwood)

Class: Angiospermae (covered-seed plants):

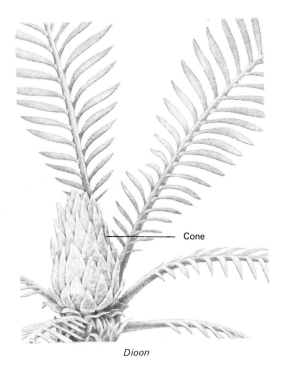

Dioon

1. Seeds enclosed in a fleshy or dry fruit derived from ovary.
2. Produce flowers.
3. Produce herbaceous or woody stems.

Subclass: Monocotyledonae :

1. One embryonic leaf at germination.
2. Parallel veined leaves.
3. No cambium rings.
4. Vascular bundles scattered.
5. Flower parts in threes or multiples of three.

Representative genera : *Zea* (corn), *Lilium* (lily), *Triticum* (wheat)

Subclass: Dicotyledonae :

1. Two embryonic leaves at germination.
2. Net-veined leaves.
3. Distinct cambium present.
4. Vascular bundles in rings.
5. Flower parts in fours or fives or multiples.

Representative genera : *Acer* (maple tree), *Ranunculus* (buttercup)

Kingdom METAZOA

Phylum PORIFERA (sponges—porebearers) :

1. Cellular level of organization.
2. Collect food by passing water currents through a porous body. There is usually a large internal cavity.
3. Water passages are lined with flagellate collar cells called choanocytes which produce water currents and digest food.
4. Body possesses skeletal spines called spicules among the cells.
5. Reproduction by asexual budding or sexual gametic fusion.

Class: Hexactinellida (glass sponges) :

1. Silicon dioxide spicules.
2. Fine, lacelike structure.

Representative genus : *Euplectella* (Venus' flower-basket sponge)

Class: Calcarea (calcareous sponges) :

1. Calcium carbonate spicules.

Representative genus : *Scypha* (the vase sponge)

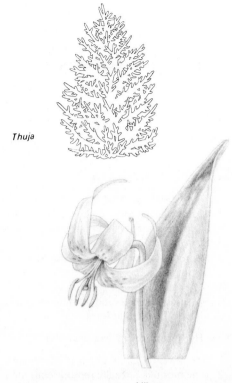

Thuja

Lilium

Ranunculus

Euplectella

459

Class: Demospongiae (bath sponges) :

1. Silicon dioxide spicules.
2. Contain a fibrous protein called *spongin*.
3. Have very complex water passages.

Representative genus : *Spongia* (bath sponge)

Phylum COELENTERATA :

1. Tissue level of development (nerve tissue).
2. Mouth surrounded by tentacles containing stinging cells called *cnidocytes* (formerly called nematocysts).
3. Reproduction by asexual budding and sexual gamete fusion.
4. No anus.
5. Sessile polyp often alternating with a sexual medusa or jellyfish form.

Class: Hydrozoa (hydra-like animals) :

1. Solitary or colonial polyp predominant.
2. May produce sexually reproducing medusae.
3. Polyps may float on gas-filled bladders.

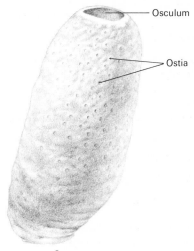

Sponge

Representative genera : *Hydra* (solitary—no medusa stage), *Obelia* (colonial, medusa stage), *Gonionemus* (conspicuous medusa stage), *Physalia* (Portuguese man-of-war ; colonial polyps on gas float)

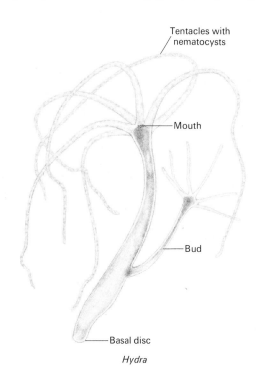

Hydra

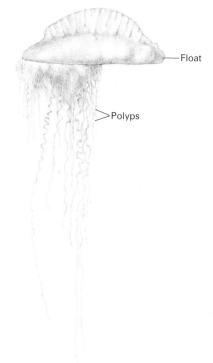

Physalia

460

Class: Scyphozoa (true jellyfish) :

1. Sexual medusa stage predominant.
2. Polyp produces asexual buds that develop into medusae.
3. Medusae possess balance organs at the edge of the bell.

Representative genera : *Aurelia, Cyanea*

Class: Anthozoa (flowerlike animals) :

1. Polyp stage predominant : solitary or colonial.
2. Reproduction by budding and gamete fusion.
3. Fairly well-developed nerve-net system with giant fibers for quick reactions.

Representative genera: *Metridium* and *Anthopleura* (sea anemones), *Lophelia* (coral)

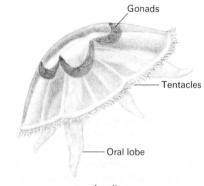

Aurelia

Phylum PLATYHELMINTHES (flatworms):

1. Organ level of development.
2. Flattened dorsoventrally.
3. Incomplete digestive system or none.
4. Development of a head with "brain" and sense organs (cephalization) in free-living forms.
5. Most species are parasitic and follow complex life cycle.
6. No body cavity (acoelomate).

Class: Turbellaria (free-living flatworms) :

1. Digestive system with mouth but no anus.
2. Cellular epidermis.
3. High degree of regeneration.
4. Monoecious (possessing both male and female organs).

Representative genus : *Planaria*

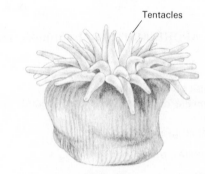

Anthopleura

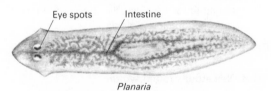

Planaria

Class: Trematoda (flukes) :

1. All parasitic.
2. Highly developed reproductive system—monoecious.
3. No digestive, respiratory, or circulatory systems.
4. Life cycle usually involves an intermediate host such as a snail.
5. Anterior and ventral suckers.
6. Body covered by protective cuticle.

Representative genera : *Fasciola* (sheep liver fluke), *Clonorchis* (human liver fluke), *Paragonimus* (lung fluke), *Schistosoma* (blood fluke)

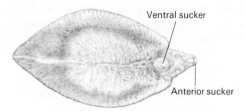

Fasciola

461

Class: Cestoda (tapeworms) :

1. All parasitic.
2. Highly developed reproductive system—monoecious.
3. No digestive, respiratory, or circulatory systems.
4. Life cycle may involve intermediate host such as pig, dog, fish, or a copepod.
5. Body composed of head, neck, and proglottids (individual reproductive units).
6. Head (or scolex) may be armed with hooks or suckers for attachment to intestinal wall.

Representative genera: *Taenia saginata* (in beef), *Dibothrocephalus* (in fish)

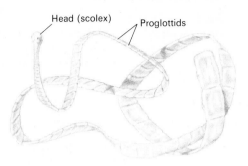

Head (scolex)   Proglottids

Taenia

Phylum ASCHELMINTHES (wormlike animals):

1. Organ-system level of development.
2. A false body cavity (pseudocoelom).
3. Complete digestive system with mouth and anus.
4. A varied group.

Class: Rotifera (wheel animals) :

1. Aquatic.
2. Small—up to 1 mm.
3. Possess two ciliated food-collecting discs called a *corona*.
4. Elongated trunk usually has attachment "toes" with cement gland.

Representative genera: *Rotaria, Philodina, Keratella*

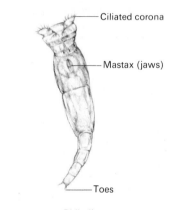

Ciliated corona

Mastax (jaws)

Toes

Philodina

Class: Nematoda (round worms) :

1. Many are parasitic.
2. Cylindrical worms covered with a cuticle.
3. Well-developed nerve tracts.

Representative genera: *Turbatrix* (vinegar eels), *Ascaris* (in pig or horse intestine), *Trichinella* (in pig muscle), *Wuchereria* (filarial worm—elephantiasis)

Class: Nematomorpha (horsehair worms) :

1. Larval stage is parasitic in an arthropod such as a grasshopper.
2. Free-living adults possess only a reproductive system and live only a short time.
3. Long, threadlike body.

Representative genus: *Gordius* (horsehair worm)

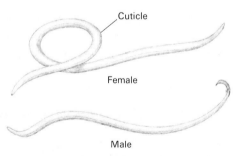

Cuticle

Female

Male

Ascaris

Phylum ECTOPROCTA (moss animals; sometimes called Bryozoa):

1. Mostly marine.
2. Live in colonies that resemble patches of moss.
3. Each animal lives in a shell-like cuticle.
4. Have a true body cavity, a coelom (lined on both sides with mesoderm).
5. Complete U-shaped digestive tract.
6. No respiratory or circulatory systems.
7. Possess a horseshoe-shaped band called a *lophophore* for food collection; the lophophore contains many ciliated tentacles.

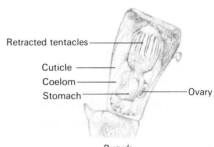

Bugula

Representative genera: *Bugula* (fuzzy ectoproct found on pilings), *Membranipora* (encrusting ectoproct)

Phylum BRACHIOPODA (lamp shells):

1. Possess a true coelom.
2. All species marine.
3. Reside in hinged calcium carbonate shells. (Unlike a clam, the animal is oriented in a dorsoventral position; clams are laterally compressed.)
4. Collect food with a lophophore.
5. Have a complete circulatory system, heart, and blood vessels.
6. Attach to substratum by a fleshy stalk called a *peduncle.*

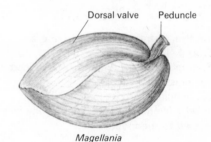

Magellania

Representative genera: *Terebratulina, Magellania* (lamp shells)

Phylum MOLLUSCA (soft-bodied animals):

1. Possess a true coelom.
2. Freshwater, marine, or terrestrial.
3. All produce a fleshy mantle which may secrete a hard shell.
4. Possess all organ systems, respiration by gills, lungs, or mantle; open circulatory system.
5. Many have a highly developed ventral muscular foot.

Class: Amphineura (chitons):

1. Marine.
2. Large muscular foot.
3. Eight dorsal calcium carbonate plates.
4. Reduced head.
5. Possess a radula for scraping up algae.

Tonicella

Representative genera: *Katharina* (black leather chitons), *Tonicella* (lined chiton), *Cryptochiton* (gum boot)

463

Class: Scaphopoda (tooth shells) :

1. Marine.
2. Small foot.
3. Live in open cylindrical shell.
4. No definite head.
5. Possess a radula and six grasping tentacles.

Representative genus : *Dentalium* (tooth shell)

Foot

Dentalium

Class: Gastropoda (stomach foot, snail-like) :

1. Freshwater, marine, and terrestrial types.
2. Large creeping foot.
3. Shell simple, coiled, or absent.
4. Well-developed head.

Representative genera : *Helix* (land snail), *Tegula* (turban snail), *Anisodoris* (sea lemon—nudibranch), *Hermissenda* (opalescent nudibranch)

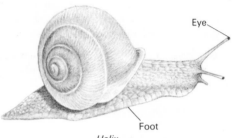

Eye

Foot

Helix

Class: Pelecypoda (hatchet foot) :

1. Bivalve, laterally compressed shells.
2. Dorsal hinge.
3. Foot modified for digging (or reduced as in sea mussels).
4. No definite head or radula.
5. Food is filtered from the water by the gills and passed to the mouth.

Representative genera : *Anodonta* (freshwater clam), *Siliqua* (razor clam), *Mytilus* (sea mussel), *Teredo* (ship borer), *Mya* (soft-shelled clam)

Hermissenda

Class: Cephalopoda (head foot) :

1. Shell reduced or absent.
2. Conspicuous head with well-developed camera-type eyes.
3. Foot represented by arms or tentacles.
4. Well-developed brain and nervous system.
5. Possess a radula and a horny beak.

Representative genera : *Loligo* (squid), *Octopus*, *Sepia* (cuttlefish), *Nautilus* (chambered nautilus)

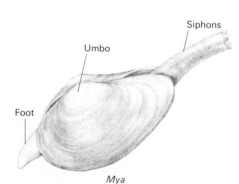

Siphons

Umbo

Foot

Mya

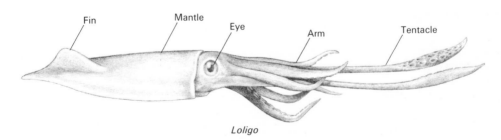

Fin   Mantle   Eye   Arm   Tentacle

Loligo

Phylum ANNELIDA (segmented worms):

1. Freshwater, marine, and terrestrial.
2. Body separated into segments.
3. High degree of cephalization in some species.
4. True coelom.
5. Respiration primarily through body surface.
6. Closed circulatory system with arteries, capillaries, and veins.
7. Special excretory organs called nephridia.

Class: Oligochaeta (worms with few hairs):

1. Reduced head with few sense organs.
2. Small bristles or setae on each segment.
3. Monoecious.

Representative genus: *Lumbricus* (earthworm)

Class: Polychaeta (many-haired worms):

1. Highly cephalized with eyes, sensory palps, and tentacles.
2. Each segment possesses a pair of flaplike appendages having long bristles.
3. Usually dioecious.

Representative genera: *Nereis* (marine clam worm), *Aphrodite* (sea mouse)

Class: Hirudinea (leeches):

1. Reduced head.
2. No bristles present.
3. Anterior and posterior suckers.
4. Blood-sucking forms possess three chitinous teeth.
5. All species are monoecious.

Representative genus: *Hirudo* (medicinal leech)

Phylum ARTHROPODA (joint-footed animals):

1. Segmented body has paired jointed appendages.
2. High degree of cephalization with many sense organs.
3. Possess a chitinous exoskeleton.
4. Body divided into head, thorax, and abdomen.
5. Circulatory system is open—has no capillaries.
6. Live in practically every world habitat.

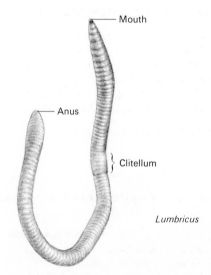

Lumbricus

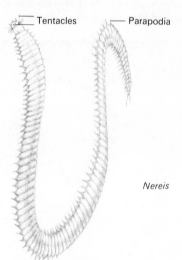

Nereis

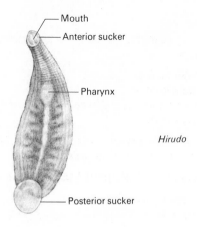

Hirudo

465

Subphylum: ONYCHOPHORA (claw bearers):

1. Internally segmented like annelid worms.
2. Possess nephridia like annelids.
3. Have small, clawed jointed appendages.
4. Respiration by tracheal tubes.
5. Characteristics place it phylogenetically between Annelida and Arthropoda.

Representative genus: *Peripatus*

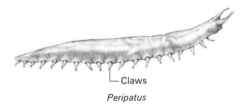

Claws

Peripatus

Subphylum: CHELICERATA (hard claws):

1. No jaws.
2. First pair of appendages have pincer claws for gathering food.
3. Head and thorax fused.
4. Respiration by book gills at base of abdominal appendages or gills or tracheae.

Representative genus: *Limulus* (horseshoe "crab")

Class: Merostomata:

1. Cephalothorax conspicuous.
2. Possess gills.
3. Two lateral compound eyes.

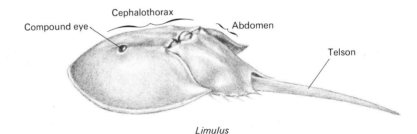

Compound eye — Cephalothorax — Abdomen — Telson

Limulus

Class: Arachnida (spiders, ticks, mites, and scorpions):

1. Four pairs of legs.
2. No antennae.
3. Respiration by tracheae, gills, or book lungs (spiders).

Representative genera: *Argiope* (garden spider), *Dermacentor* (tick), *Centrurus* (scorpion)

Subphylum: MANDIBULATA (possess jaws):

1. Possess mandibles (jaws).
2. Have antennae.

Mite   Dermacentor (atick)

Class: Crustacea (shelled) :

1. Mostly aquatic species, although some live in moist soil.
2. Respiration by gills.
3. Two pairs of antennae.

Representative genera : *Cambarus* (crayfish), *Homarus* (lobster), *Daphnia* (water flea), *Cyclops* (copepod), *Cancer* (edible crab), *Porcellio* (terrestrial sow bug)

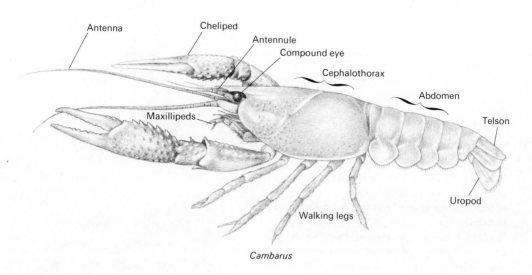

Cambarus

Class: Diplopoda :

1. Generally, two pairs of jointed appendages on each segment.
2. Cylindrical body.

Representative genus : *Spirobolus* (millipede)

Class: Chilopoda :

1. One pair of jointed appendages on each segment.
2. Dorsoventrally flattened.

Representative genus : *Scolopendra* (centipede)

Class: Insecta or Hexapoda (six-legged) :

1. Body divided into three distinct regions : head, thorax, and abdomen.
2. Three pairs of appendages on the thorax.
3. Thorax may possess one or two pairs of wings or none.
4. Respiration by tracheal tubes.
5. Open circulatory system.
6. High degree of cephalization, one pair of antennae, and compound and simple eyes.
7. As many as 700,000 species have been identified.

Scolopendra

Representative genera: *Dynastes* (rhinoceros beetle), *Musca* (housefly), *Speyeria* (fritillary butterfly), *Apis* (honeybee), *Romalea* (grasshopper)

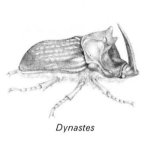

Dynastes

Apis

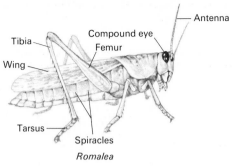

Romalea

Phylum ECHINODERMATA (spiny-skinned animals):

1. Endoskeleton of separate or fused calcareous plates (covered by epidermis).
2. Move by means of a water vascular system with tube feet.
3. Possess a true coelom derived from the same embryonic region as that of vertebrates.
4. Head absent.
5. Radial symmetry as adults; bilateral symmetry as larvae.

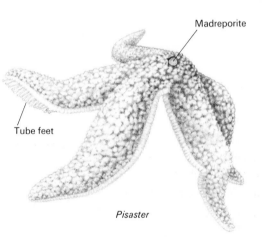

Pisaster

Class: Asteroidea (sea stars):

1. Oral, aboral flattening.
2. Five, six, twenty, or more radiating arms.
3. Two rows of tube feet in open groove under each arm.
4. Respiration by small dermal branchiae (gills) on aboral surface.

Representative genera: *Pisaster* (purple star), *Henricia* (blood star), *Leptasterias* (6-rayed star), *Solaster* (sun star)

Class: Ophiuroidea (serpent or brittle stars):

1. Small oral disc with no anus.
2. Long, slender arms.
3. Arm grooves closed or absent.

Representative genera: *Ophioderma* (brittle star), *Gorgonocephalus* (basket star)

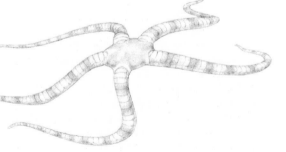

Ophioderma

Class: Echinoidea (sea urchins, sand dollars, and sea biscuits) :

1. Calcareous plates fused to form a hollow test.
2. Possess movable calcareous spines.
3. Tube feet extend from small pores in the test.
4. Oral opening has a five-toothed structure for feeding (Aristotle's lantern).
5. Respire by dermal branchiae.

Representative genera: *Strongylocentrotus* (sea urchin), *Dendraster* (sand dollar), *Clypeaster* (sea biscuit)

Clypeaster

Class: Holothuroidea (sea cucumbers) :

1. Muscular body has extremely reduced plates.
2. Tube feet occur in five double rows along the soft cylindrical body.
3. Retractile tentacles surround the mouth.
4. Respire by internal, branching, anal trees.

Representative genus: *Cucumaria* (red sea cucumber)

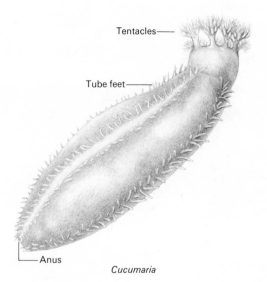

Tentacles

Tube feet

Anus

Cucumaria

Phylum CHORDATA:

1. Possess a notochord.
2. Pharyngeal gill slits or clefts at some stage of development.
3. Have a single, dorsal hollow nerve tube.

Subphylum: UROCHORDATA (tunicates):

1. Free-swimming larva possesses a notochord and segmental muscle.
2. Adult is solitary or colonial and sessile. Notochord is lost.
3. Surrounded by a tough cellulose tunic which contains incurrent and excurrent siphons.
4. All marine species.

Representative genera: *Molgula*, *Ciona* (sea squirts)

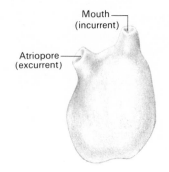

Mouth
(incurrent)

Atriopore
(excurrent)

Molgula

Subphylum: CEPHALOCHORDATA:

1. Fishlike animal with a head.
2. Notochord remains throughout life.
3. Segmental muscle and postanal tail.

Representative genus: *Branchiostoma* (lancelet or amphioxus)

Subphylum: **VERTEBRATA**:

1. Notochord replaced by cartilage or bone vertebral column.
2. Usually have paired appendages.

Class: Agnatha (jawless fishes):
Representative genus: *Entosphenus* (lamprey eel)

Class: Chondrichthyes (cartilagenous fishes):
Representative genus: *Squalus* (dogfish shark)

Class: Osteichthyes (bony fishes):
Representative genus: *Perca* (perch), *Salmo* (trout).

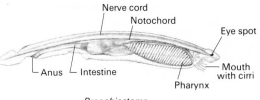

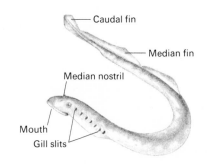

Branchiostoma

Entosphenus

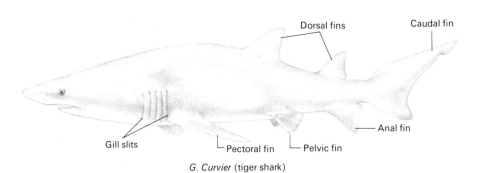

G. Curvier (tiger shark)

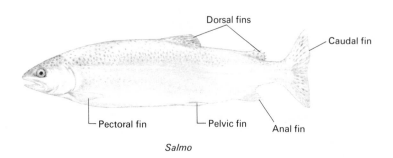

Salmo

Class: Amphibia (frogs, toads, and salamanders) :

1. Thin, moist skin.
2. Most have four fleshy, jointed limbs.
3. Possess lungs.
4. Three-chambered heart.

Representative genera: *Hyla* (tree frog), *Taricha* (rough-skinned newt), *Ensatina, Bufo* (common toad)

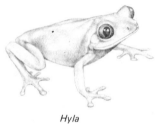

Hyla

Ensatina

Bufo

Class: Reptilia (snakes, lizards, turtles, alligators, and crocodiles) :

1. Possess clawed appendages (except snakes).
2. Body protected by scales.
3. Lay hard-shelled or leathery land-type eggs with functional allantois and yolk sac.
4. Three-chambered heart except crocodile which has four.

Lampropeltis

Representative genera : *Lampropeltis* (king snake), *Sceloporus* (Pacific swift lizard), *Caretta* (loggerhead turtle)

Caretta

Crocodylidac (American alligator)

Class: Aves (birds) :

1. Possess feathers.
2. May have wings with bone structure homologous to forelimb of tetrapods.
3. Four-chambered heart.
4. Warm-blooded (homeothermic).
5. Lay hard-shelled, land-type eggs.

Representative genera: *Turdus* (robin), *Larus*
(herring gull), *Struthio* (ostrich)

Class: Mammalia (milk producers) :

1. Possess mammary glands.
2. Have external body hair.
3. Warm-blooded (homeothermic).
4. Four-chambered heart.
5. Embryo develops internally, attached to a
   placenta except in the egg-laying monotremes
   (*Platypus*).

Subclass: Prototheria :

Order: Monotremata (egg-laying mammals) :

1. Possess a horny beak as adults.
2. Lay small, leathery eggs.
3. Young nurse from small mammary glands
   distributed on the abdomen.

Representative genera: *Ornithorhynchus* (duck-
billed platypus), *Echidna* (spiny anteater)

Subclass: Metatheria :

Order: Marsupialia (pouched mammals) :

1. Possess an abdominal pouch which contains
   mammary glands.
2. Immature young leave uterus, migrate to the
   pouch, and attach to nipples with their
   mouths.

Representative genera : *Didelphis* (American opos-
sum), *Macropus* (kangaroo)

Larus

Ornithorhynchus

Didelphis

472

Subclass: Eutheria (placental mammals):

Representative orders:

Insectivora—small; insect eating; live in underground burrows; shrews, moles, and hedgehogs.

Sorex (shrew)

Chiroptera—possess membranous wings, enlarged ears, and sharp teeth; most feed on flying insects; bats.

Myotis (bat)

Lagomorpha—rabbitlike mammals; herbivorous; continuously growing incisors, no canine teeth, hind legs elongated for jumping; rabbits, hares, and pikas.

Sylvilagus

473

Rodentia—gnawing mammals; herbivorous; incisor
teeth grow continuously, no canine teeth; rats,
mice, beavers, squirrels, and porcupines.

Sciurus

Cetacea—aquatic; possess flippers, and dorsal nostrils or blow hole; whales, dolphins, and porpoises.

Tursiops (bottlenosed dolphin)

Carnivora—flesh eating; well-developed canine teeth, and sense organs; cats, dogs, foxes, raccoons,
bears, and aquatic forms such as seals and sea lions.

Vulpes (red fox)

Proboscidea—herbivorous ; large head and ears, elongated proboscis or trunk, upper incisors produce tusks ; pachyderms ; largest land mammals : African and Indian elephants.

Elephas

Perissodactyla—hoofed with odd number of toes; herbivorous; teeth with grinding ridges; horses, rhinoceroses, and tapirs.

Tapirus (Malayan tapir)

Artiodactyla—hoofed with even number of toes; herbivorous; four-part stomach; pigs, hippopotamuses, camels, cattle, moose, deer, and giraffes.

Alces

476

Primates—five digits on hands and feet, thumbs opposable to innermost digits permit grasping, head rotates on spine, well-developed brain, especially cerebrum; lemurs, monkeys, apes, and man.

Cercopithecus (grass monkey)

Glossary

abiotic: denotes the nonliving aspects of the community.

acid: a compound that produces hydrogen ions in a solution.

acrocentric: describes the chromosome in which the centromere occurs at one end; the chromosome is rod-shaped at anaphase.

ACTH: *see* adrenocorticotropic hormone

action potential: the bioelectric potential that changes along a nerve membrane as a result of the propagation of an impulse.

activation energy: the amount of energy necessary to initiate a chemical reaction.

active sites: specific structural areas in the enzyme molecule which combine with specific reactant molecules.

active transport: the movement of materials across cell membranes against a concentration gradient, thus requiring the expenditure of energy.

adaptive radiation: the divergence of organisms into separate ecological niches where further adaptation and speciation occur.

adenosine triphosphate (ATP): an organic molecule composed of an adenine nucleotide that has three phosphate ester groups attached to the ribose; this molecule is the principal source of energy for all living organisms.

ADH: *see* vasopressin.

adrenocorticotropic hormone (ACTH): a hormone secreted by the anterior lobe of the pituitary which stimulates the adrenal cortex.

adrenalin: *see* epinephrine.

agglutination: the clumping or massing together of red blood cells under the influence of specific antibodies during incompatible transfusion.

albinism: a recessive genetic condition (*aa*) in which the organism cannot produce pigments.

alcaptonuria: a metabolic disease evidenced by the absence of homogentisate oxidase in the liver; apparently caused by the action of one gene.

alchemy: the early study of chemistry; alchemists frequently were preoccupied with the changing of iron or lead into gold.

alkali: *see* base.

allantois: an extraembryonic membrane with varying functions; in birds and reptiles it has a respiratory and excretory function, whereas in mammals it forms part of the blood vessel connection between embryo and mother.

alleles: alternative forms of a gene for a particular trait (for example, tall or dwarf are alleles for tallness in peas).

allergy: the result of an antigen-antibody reaction which requires specific capability within an organism.

alveoli: the small air sacs of the lungs where gas exchange occurs.

amino acid: an organic acid containing a carboxyl and an amino group on the same carbon; there are approximately 23 amino acids.

aminopeptidase: an enzyme secreted by the intestine which breaks peptide bonds adjacent to free amino groups.

ammonotelic: describes the excretion of ammonia as the principal form of nitrogenous waste.

amnion: the fluid-filled sac surrounding the embryo.

analogous structures: structures having similar functions but different evolutionary origins.

anaphase: a stage of mitosis in which the chromosomes move to opposite poles; they appear to be pulled by spindle fibers.

androgen: a general term for male hormones (testosterone).

anther: the part of a flower that produces pollen; often called the male part.

antheridium: the sperm-producing organ of a gametophyte.

anthropomorphism: the explanation of animal behavior in terms of human behavior.

antibody: a specific substance produced by cells which reacts with a specific antigen.

anticodon: three unpaired nitrogen bases in transfer RNA which are complimentary to three nitrogen bases of a messenger RNA codon.

antigen: a substance, usually a protein, foreign to an organism which stimulates the formation of specific antibodies in the organism.

archegonium: the egg-producing organ of a gametophyte.

archenteron: the cavity in the gastrula which later becomes the intestinal tract.

atom: the modern term for the basic unit of any element, proposed by John Dalton in 1808.

atomic number: a number equal to the number of protons in an atomic nucleus.

atomic weight: the sum of the number of protons and neutrons in an atomic nucleus.

atomos: the fundamental unit of all matter, unique and indivisible for each element, which was proposed by Democritus.

ATP: *see* adenosine triphosphate.

autonomic nervous system: an involuntary system closely associated with, but not under direct control of, the central nervous system; it controls secretions of various glands and smooth muscle contractions; it consists of two antagonistic divisions, the sympathetic and the parasympathetic.

autosomes: chromosomes other than the sex chromosomes.

autotrophic: describing an organism that can produce its own food from inorganic materials.

auxins: hormones that regulate the growth of roots and stems.

back cross: *see* test cross.

bacteriophage: a virus that parasitizes bacteria.

basal metabolic rate (BMR): the metabolic rate of an organism theoretically in a state of complete rest; usually expressed as Calories produced per kilogram of body weight per hour.

base (or alkali): in general, a compound in solution which can take up or accept hydrogen ions; often a substance that dissociates to release hydroxyl ions (OH^-).

base analogues: certain chemicals that can incorporate into nucleic acids, but are nonfunctional; they can cause mutation or death of the cell.

behavior: activity of organisms, usually a response to a stimulus.

bilateral symmetry: a body plan that can be halved in only one plane so that each half is a mirror image of the other.

bile: a substance secreted by the liver which emulsifies fats for digestion.

biomes: the major terrestrial regions of the earth which are characterized by the dominant plant and animal life; these include tundra, northern coniferous forest, deciduous forest, tropical forest, grassland, and desert.

blastula: the stage in animal development when a single layered ball of cells is formed; it is usually hollow, containing a blastocoel or blastula cavity.

blood: the fluid that circulates in the principal vascular system of man and other vertebrates, in man consisting of colloidal plasma in which cells and cell fragments are suspended; blood components function in gas exchange, ingestion of foreign substances, and blood clotting.

BMR: *see* basal metabolic rate

bolus: a swallowed ball of chewed food.

Bowman's capsule: the structure of a nephron in which the glomerulus or capillary network is contained; filtration products are collected here.

Brownian motion: the random movement of particles in liquid or gas due to molecular bombardment.

budding: a type of asexual reproduction whereby a complete, new individual grows from an organism.

buffer: a substance that moderates the hydrogen-ion concentration of a solution, thereby preventing excessive pH changes.

calorie: the amount of heat necessary to raise one gram of pure water by one degree Celsius (centigrade).

capillary: the smallest vessel of the closed circulatory system which connects the arteries and veins.

carbohydrates: compounds composed primarily of carbon, oxygen, and hydrogen, such as sugars, starches, glycogen, and cellulose.

carbonic anhydrase: an enzyme found in the red blood cell which catalyzes the formation of H_2CO_3 and its breakdown into H_2O and CO_2.

carboxypeptidase: an enzyme that breaks peptide bonds adjacent to free carboxyl (acid) groups.

cardiac stomach: the upper portion of the stomach which receives the food from the esophagus and includes the fundus.

carnivore: an animal that eats a primarily meat diet; for example, cats and dogs.

carotenes: generally orange-red colored pigments closely associated with chlorophyll in the chloroplast.

carotid bodies: nerve receptors in the carotid arteries that are sensitive to increased levels of CO_2 and decreased levels of O_2; this causes an increase in respiratory rate.

carrying capacity: the number of species that a specific ecosystem can support; involves availability of food and shelter.

cell: all living organisms are composed of individual units called cells, which are divided into two main regions—the cytoplasm and the nucleus; the cytoplasm includes the cell membrane, centrioles, Golgi apparatus, mitochondria, endoplasmic reticulum, lysosomes, and ribosomes; nuclear cell parts are the nuclear membrane, chromosomes, and nucleolus.

cell membrane: the fat-protein structure between the cell and its environment.

cell wall: the outer, nonliving structure of a plant cell composed of cellulose, lignin, and pectin.

central nervous system (CNS): the brain and spinal cord.

centrioles: self-replicating bodies that form the spindle for cell division in animals and some protists.

centromere: the area of a chromosome to which the spindle fiber attaches at cell division.

cerebellum: connected hemispheres between the cerebrum and brain stem; functions in equilibrium and coordination of voluntary muscles.

cerebrum: the largest hemispheres of the brain; concerned with conscious, sensory, and motor functions.

chief cells: cells located in the stomach lining which secrete pepsinogen (inactive pepsin).

chitin: a tough carbohydrate-nitrogen substance found in the exoskeleton of insects and crustaceans.

chloride shift: the exchange of Cl^- for HCO_3^- and vice versa in the red blood cell in the transport of carbon dioxide; the shift maintains electrical balance.

cholecystokinin: a hormone released by the intestinal lining which activates the release of bile from the gallbladder.

cholinesterase: an enzyme which breaks down acetylcholine at nerve synapses.

chorion: the outermost extraembryonic membrane which forms part of the placenta in some mammals.

chromatid: each half of a duplicated chromosome.

chromomeres: areas of localized coiling on interphasic chromosomes; they stain heavily with nuclear dyes.

chromosome map: a diagram of the positions of genes along a chromosome based on the percent of crossover occurring among the genes.

chromosomes: long filaments in the cell nucleus composed primarily of DNA and protein.

cilia: short, whiplike structures specialized for locomotion in some protists; cilia also occur on certain tissues of higher animals.

circadian rhythms: cyclic behavior patterns which occur approximately every 24 hours.

circannual rhythms: annual behavioral cycles.

cistron: the individual functional units of a gene locus; perhaps involving many nucleotides.

classical conditioning: a process in which a neutral stimulus can replace a natural stimulus and bring about a response.

climax: the final successional stage in an area which is stable and self-reproducing.

cloaca: the canal in some vertebrates where the digestive, excretory, and reproductive tracts come together.

closed circulatory system: a blood system composed of a continuous system of vessels—arteries, capillaries, and veins.

CNS: *see* central nervous system.

codon: a series of three nucleotides which code the position of a specific amino acid in a protein.

coelom: a body cavity in animals between the visceral organs and the body wall which is completely lined with mesoderm (this lining is called a peritoneum).

coenzyme A: a complex molecule containing the vitamin pantothenic acid which combines with pyruvic acid as it enters the Krebs cycle.

coenzymes: small organic molecules which activate enzymes and can transport intermediate products such as hydrogen in specific enzyme reactions.

cohesion: the attraction of like molecules for each other.

collenchyma: thick-walled cells that provide support in the stem region of plants.

colloid: the suspension of small particles (usually larger than molecules) in a medium; it can exist as a sol or a gel; in a cell the particles are protein and the medium is mainly water.

commensalism: two organisms living together in which one organism is benefited and the other is not harmed.

community: all the organisms living and interacting within a particular area.

complement: a substance found in blood plasma which in the presence of antibodies causes the rupture and destruction of foreign cells.

compound: the chemical combination of two or more elements.

conditioned reflex: behavior in which a response is made to a specific stimulus which is different from the stimulus that naturally illicits the response; acquired through experience.

conjugation: the process in which genetic material is exchanged between two protists.

connective tissue: provides intercellular support and cohesion among all types of tissues; cartilage and bone are dense connective tissues specially adapted for support.

consumers: organisms that feed on other species, either producers or other consumers.

contractile vacuole: a specialized organelle in some protozoans which functions in water balance and excretion.

convergence: the development of similar characteristics in two or more groups of organisms which are not closely related.

corepressor: a metabolic end product which unites with a repressor substance to inhibit an operator gene.

corpus callosum: a band of nerve fibers that interconnects the two cerebral hemispheres.

coupled reactions: two interrelated chemical reactions that occur simultaneously.

covalent bond: the bond formed when two atoms share a pair of electrons, such as the bond between carbon and hydrogen.

cretinism: a condition caused by lack of thyroxin during development; characterized by low mentality, retarded growth, and impish face.

crossover: the breaking and exchange between homologous chromatids during meiotic prophase (observed at tetrad stage); the microscopical observations are termed chiasmata.

cutaneous breathing: gas exchange that occurs across moist skin such as found in amphibians.

cytochrome: a tetrapyrrole ring molecule containing an atom of iron; the iron functions in the transport of electrons through alternate oxidation and reduction.

cytokinesis: division of the cell cytoplasm to form daughter cells.

cytology: study of cells.

Darwin-Wallace theory: the theory of evolution based on changes in species due to natural selection.

deamination: the removal of an amino group (NH_2) from an amino acid.

decomposers: bacteria and fungi that break large organic molecules of dead organisms into smaller reusable molecules.

deletions: parts of chromosomes that are lost.

deme: small breeding group within a population.

denaturation: a permanent structural change in a protein which alters its function in the cell.

denitrifying bacteria: bacteria that convert ammonia, nitrites, and nitrates into free nitrogen.

deoxyribonucleic acid (DNA): a nucleic acid containing deoxyribose, found chiefly in the nucleus of cells, that functions in the transference of genetic characteristics and in the synthesis of protein.

diaphragm: the muscular separation between the chest and abdominal cavities; functions in respiration and elimination.

diastolic pressure: the blood pressure resulting from relaxation of the atria and ventricles of the heart during a heartbeat cycle.

differential reproduction: organisms better suited to their environment give rise to more and better adapted offspring than those less suited.

differentiation: a process of change in the developing organism in which nonspecialized cells become specialized.

diffusion: the movement of gas or solid particles from a region of high concentration to a region of low concentration.

dihybrid cross: a genetic cross involving two characteristics; for example, tallness and seed color in peas.

dioecious: the condition in which male and female or staminate and pistillate structures are in separate individuals.

dipeptidase: an enzyme that splits double amino acids into single amino acids.

diplohaplontic: describes an organism with alternating haploid and diploid generations; haploid spores are produced by meiosis.

diploid: the number of chromosomes formed by the union of two gametes ($2n$); 46 in humans.

diplontic: describes a life cycle with diploid adults; gametes produced by meiosis.

disaccharases: enzymes that split double sugars into simple sugars.

disaccharides: twelve-carbon sugars such as maltose.

distal convoluted tubule: the region of the nephron where further reabsorption occurs, especially of water and some ions.

divergence: the development of different characteristics in two or more groups of closely related organisms.

DNA: *see* deoxyribonucleic acid.

dominant gene: a gene that always produces its characteristic when it is present.

double covalent bond: the sharing of two pairs of electrons between two atoms such as $C = C$ in benzene.

Down's syndrome: often called mongolism; evidenced by a third chromosome in pair 21.

duodenum: the first ten inches of the small intestine.

dynamic equilibrium: a balance due to the active coordination and regulation of all the chemical and physical interactions occurring in an organism.

ecology: the study of the relationships of organisms to one another and to the environment.

ecosystem: the living community and the physical environment associated with it.

ectoderm: the outside germ layer in the developing embryo; the skin and nervous system develop from this layer.

effectors: structures that react to stimuli to bring about a counterchange.

electrolytes: ionically bonded compounds that dissociate into charged particles in water and will conduct an electric current; for example, sodium chloride.

electron: a tiny particle located outside the atomic nucleus which possesses a negative charge.

electron-transport series: a series of reactions among electron-transfer compounds which serves to produce ATP and water; occurs in the mitochondrion; NAD, FAD, and cytochromes are important members of the series.

electrovalent (or ionic) bond: a bond formed by the transfer of one or more electrons from one atom to another; for example, sodium chloride.

element: a substance that contains atoms of only one type.

embryo: the multicellular beginnings of an organism before germination, hatching, or birth.

endergonic: describing chemical reactions that require energy.

endocrine glands: ductless glands that secrete hormones directly into the bloodstream.

482

endoderm: the inside germ layer (formed during gastrulation) in the developing embryo; forms the lining of the intestinal tract and the lining of several other internal organs.

endoplasmic reticulum: the membranous structure in the cytoplasm.

endosperm: the food material in the seeds of flowering plants.

energy: energy may be defined as the ability to do work; in living organisms, energy is required to perform the chemical reactions necessary for life.

enterocoelom: a coelom formed in some animals by the outpouching of mesoderm from the developing gut.

enterocrinin: the hormone secreted by the intestinal lining that initiates the flow of intestinal enzymes.

enterokinase: a nondigestive enzyme secreted by the intestinal mucosa which activates trypsinogen to trypsin.

entropy: a measurement of the degree of disorganization in a chemical system.

environmental biology: a branch of biology dealing with the quality of environment, particularly as it affects man.

enzyme: a protein molecule capable of bringing specific reactants together to speed up a biochemical reaction.

enzyme induction: the synthesis of an enzyme due to the presence of a specific inducer substance.

epidermal tissue: the protective tissue covering many plant parts; in the leaf, special guard cells surround openings (stomata) to permit gas exchange.

epigenesis: the concept that new structures arise during embryonic development.

epilimnion: the region of a body of water above the thermocline.

epinephrine (adrenalin): a hormone secreted by the adrenal medulla which increases respiration, heartbeat, and blood sugar.

epistasis: the effect of one gene influencing the expression of another nonallelic gene.

epithelial tissue: tissue that covers or lines the organs of the animal body and sometimes forms glandular tissue; generally specialized for protection, absorption, or secretion; specific types include squamous, cuboidal, and columnar.

erepsin: a general term for a group of intestinal enzymes that hydrolyze polypeptides into amino acids.

estrogen: the female hormone produced by the egg follicle; responsible for female secondary sex characteristics.

estrus: a cycle of events in most female mammals in which the female is receptive to the male; the egg is released at this time.

ethology: the study of behavior under natural conditions.

eucaryotic: describes cells possessing a nuclear membrane, DNA-protein chromosomes, and cytoplasmic organelles.

eutrophic: describing a body of water that contains a large number of organisms and organic products.

evolution: the theory that all existing plants and animals were derived from preexisting forms; also includes the concept that the changes occurring in organisms are due to slight genetic variations through successive generations.

excretion: generally the release of waste products from a cell or an organism.

exergonic: describing chemical reactions that release energy.

experimental control: the standard or normal situation to which a test situation is compared in an experiment.

extracellular digestion: digestion that takes place outside the cells in a cavity such as the stomach or intestine.

extraembryonic membranes: a group of membranous sacs associated with the embryos of most reptiles, birds, and mammals; these membranes are the chorion, amnion, and allantois, and they function in protection, respiration, nutrition, and waste disposal.

FAD: *see* flavine adenine dinucleotide.

fats: compounds composed of glycerine and fatty acids.

feedback: a mechanism by which the output of a reaction may act to modify that reaction.

ferredoxin: an iron-containing protein that acts as an electron acceptor in system I of photosynthesis.

fetus: a stage of early development in man and other mammals; generally, in humans, from the third month of pregnancy until birth.

flagella: whiplike appendages similar to cilia in structure and function but much longer; flagella also occur as the locomotor organelles of sperm.

flame cells: specialized ciliated cells which function in excretion and water balance; for example, in flatworms.

flavine adenine dinucleotide (FAD): a hydrogen-transporting coenzyme.

follicle-stimulating hormone (FSH): a hormone secreted by the anterior lobe of the pituitary; it stimulates the production of an egg in the ovary.

food chain: the flow of energy from one trophic level to another based on which organisms eat other organisms.

food web: a complex of food chains involving many different species.

fossilization: the process of preserving the form or actual structures of an organism.

free energy: the energy in a biological system that is available to perform useful work.

fruit: a mature ovary with seeds enclosed.

FSH: *see* follicle-stimulating hormone.

fundamental tissue: various kinds of cells which function in support, food making, or food storage; the three types are parenchyma, collenchyma, and sclerenchyma.

galaxy: a group of stars such as our own Milky Way.

gametophyte: the haploid generation of a plant which produces gametes.

ganglion: a collection of nerve cell bodies; for example, dorsal root ganglia.

gastrin: a hormone secreted by the stomach lining which causes the secretion of pepsin.

gastrovascular cavity: a cavity in some lower animals which serves the functions of both digestion and circulation (coelenterates).

gastrula: the stage in animal development when a two-layered (and later, three) structure is formed; a new cavity, which will become the intestinal tract, forms and replaces the blastocoel.

gene: the fundamental unit of heredity; a small segment of a chromosome defined according to its functional characteristics.

gene pool: the total possible genotypes in an interbreeding population.

genotype: the actual genetic composition of the alleles resulting from a cross.

gills: small membranous structures found in many aquatic animals which function in gas exchange.

glomerulus: the blood capillary network of a nephron.

glucagon: a hormone produced by the alpha cells of the islets of Langerhans which stimulates the conversion of glycogen into blood glucose.

glucocorticoids: a group of hormones secreted by the adrenal cortex which tend to increase blood glucose.

glycogenesis: the synthesis of glycogen from glucose.

glycogenolysis: the enzymatic hydrolysis of glycogen to glucose.

glycolysis: the breakdown of glucose or glycogen to pyruvic acid; this series of reactions occurs in the cell cytoplasm and involves the removal of hydrogen and the synthesis of ATP.

glyconeogenesis: the conversion of non-carbohydrate molecules into glycogen (amino acids and fats).

goiter: an overgrowth of thyroid gland tissue sometimes caused by inactive thyroxin due to iodine deficiency.

Golgi apparatus: smooth, membranous sacs in the cytoplasm which seem to function in the storage and transport of cellular secretions.

gonads: the male and female sex glands.

gram-atomic weight: the atomic weight of a substance expressed in grams.

granum: a structure composed of alternate layers of protein-lipid membrane in the chloroplast and containing all the pigments and enzymes necessary for photosynthesis.

green glands: excretory organs found in the head region of crayfish.

group: the vertical rows of the periodic chart in which all elements have the same number of electrons in their outer shell.

habitat: the specific physical area in which an organism lives.

habituation: the decreased response to stimuli

which are not associated with positive reinforcement.

haploid: the basic chromosome number for an organism abbreviated as (n); generally the number of chromosomes in gametic cells; 23 in humans.

haplontic: having only one set of chromosomes per cell in the adult organism; meiosis follows gamete fusion.

Hardy-Weinberg principle: in a biparental, sexually reproducing population, genotype frequencies will remain constant if the following conditions are met: no mutations, random mating, and a relatively large and isolated population.

hemocoel: a part of a body cavity which collects blood in open circulatory systems.

hemocyanin: a blue, copper-containing pigment found in the blood of some arthropods and molluscs.

hemoglobin: the respiratory pigment of man, other vertebrates, and some invertebrates; a complex of iron porphyrin and protein.

hemophilia: a sex-linked genetic disease in which the blood does not clot normally; commonly known as bleeder's disease.

hepatic portal vein: an accessory venous system which carries nutrient-laden blood from the intestines to the liver.

herbivore: an animal that eats a diet of only plant material; examples of herbivores are cow, sheep, and rabbit.

Hering-Breuer reflex: a nerve reflex that inhibits inspiration when the alveoli are filled with air.

heterogamy: gametes of different size, usually micro (male) and macro (female); gametic union occurs only between the two different forms; includes sperm and egg.

heterotrophs: organisms that cannot synthesize their own food (consumers).

heterozygous: describes the situation in which the alleles for a particular trait are different on homologous chromosomes (R,r).

histology: the study of tissues.

homeostasis (steady state): the concept that all processes in an organism must be controlled within certain limits or death will result.

homologous chromosomes: chromosomes occur as pairs following fertilization, one member of each pair coming from the mother and the other from the father; homologous chromosomes are similar in size, shape, and genetic content.

homologous structures: structures that have similar origins; for example, the forelimb bone structure of bird and man.

homozygous: describes the situation in which both alleles on homologous chromosomes are the same (RR or rr).

hormone: a chemical substance secreted by specific cells in one part of an organism and capable of stimulating cells in other regions.

hybrid: the offspring resulting from the crossing of two genetically different parents.

hydrogen bond: the attraction of the hydrogen proton for negatively charged chemical groups.

hydrogen ion: the positive ion produced when hydrogen is separated from its electron.

hydrolysis: a chemical process in which large molecules are split into smaller molecules; this usually involves the addition of water (hydrolytic cleavage).

hydroxyl ion: when a hydrogen ion is removed from water, the resulting charged radical is called a hydroxyl ion (OH^-).

hyperosmotic: a solution on one side of a membrane which has more dissolved particles (therefore a lesser water concentration) than the solution on the other side.

hypha: an individual, threadlike structure composing the body of a fungus.

hypolimnion: the region of a body of water below the thermocline.

hyposmotic: a solution on one side of a membrane which has fewer dissolved particles (therefore a higher water concentration) than the solution on the other side.

hypothalamus: the area of the brain beneath the thalamus; it is connected to the pituitary gland and regulates body temperature and some hormone secretion from the posterior pituitary.

hypothesis: an educated guess as to the explanation of an observed event.

iliocecal valve: the muscular constriction between the small and large intestine.

immunity: resistance to infection.

imprinting: a type of learning, occurring early

in life, in which an individual learns to recognize an object and becomes attached to it.

incomplete dominance: describes the situation in which one member of a pair of alleles is not dominant; each allele expresses itself and contributes to the phenotype.

independent assortment: genes on different chromosomes separate independently of one another during gamete formation; Mendel's second law.

induction: the developmental process in which a group of cells or tissues brings about the differentiation of neighboring cells; thus the position of cells in a developing organ is an important determiner of what they will become.

ingestion: the intake of materials into a cell or organism.

inhibition: a situation in which the product of an enzymatic reaction restrains or checks the action of an enzyme necessary for the formation of that product.

innate: describes a type or a component of behavior in which the pattern is essentially inherited.

instinct: a series or pattern of successive reflexes producing an often elaborate type of behavior which appears to be mainly inherited.

insulin: a hormone produced by the beta cells of the islets of Langerhans in the pancreas which converts glucose into glycogen.

interferon: a protein substance released by animal cells upon stimulation by certain viruses; this substance produces resistance to viruses in neighboring cells.

intermedin: a hormone secreted by the intermediate lobe of the pituitary which controls pigmentation in some animals.

internuncial neuron: the intermediate neuron located in the gray matter of the spinal cord which shunts the impulse from the sensory to the motor tracts.

interphase: a stage of mitosis in which the chromosomes are extended and uncoiled; DNA is replicated.

intracellular digestion: digestion that occurs inside the cell.

inversion: an event in which a portion of a chromosome breaks and reunites on the same chromosome in such a way that the genetic order is reversed.

ion: a charged atom or group of atoms resulting from the gain or loss of electrons.

ionic bond: *see* electrovalent bond.

islets of Langerhans: isolated patches of endocrine tissue found throughout the pancreas.

isogamy: the fusion of gametes of similar size and shape to form a diploid cell.

isosmotic: refers to equal concentrations of water and dissolved substances on either side of a membrane.

isotope: any atom of an element which has a different number of neutrons and consequently a different atomic weight.

karyokinesis: division of the nuclear material; in some cases nuclear division occurs without cellular division.

kinetic theory: the theory that all matter is in constant motion in the universe.

kingdom: the most fundamental category for classification of the living world; examples of kingdoms are Monera, Protista, Metaphyta, and Metazoa.

Klinefelter's syndrome: a condition in humans in which the offspring receives a double X and a single Y chromosome because of nondisjunction.

Krebs cycle: a cyclic series of chemical reactions that occurs in the mitochondrion; pyruvic acid is oxidized to produce ATP, carbon dioxide, and water.

lactase: an enzyme that hydrolyzes lactose into glucose and galactose.

lacteals: small vessels found in the intestinal villi which absorb emulsified fat.

law: a theory which has a high degree of probability based on experimentation.

law of mass action: the rate of a chemical reaction is directly proportional to the concentration of the reactants.

learning: a modification of behavior as a result of experience.

LH: *see* luteinizing hormone.

linkage groups: genes on the same chromosome which are inherited as a group.

luteinizing hormone (LH): a hormone of the

anterior pituitary which causes the formation of corpus luteum from the egg follicle after ovulation.

lymphatic system: a network of vessels that carries emulsified fat and lymph to the veins near the heart.

lysis: the dissolution or destruction of cells; a breaking down or decomposition.

lysosomes: membranous bags containing enzymes which digest proteins, fats, and nucleic acids.

Malpighian tubules: long, thin excretory structures connected to the digestive tract of insects.

maltase: an enzyme specifically for the hydrolysis of the double sugar maltose to two molecules of glucose.

mechanism: the concept that all natural phenomena can be explained in terms of physics and chemistry.

medulla oblongata: the anterior portion of the spinal cord which controls heartbeat and respiration; it is the origin of many spinal nerves.

medusa: the sexual jellyfish stage of certain coelenterates.

megasporangium: the structure that produces megaspores which will develop into female gametophytes.

meiosis: the process of gamete production in which the chromosome number is reduced from diploid to haploid.

meristematic tissue: cells responsible for growth in plants; these cells can form other tissue later.

mesentery: thin sheets of tissue which hold the internal organs together and to the body wall; composed primarily of connective tissue.

mesoderm: the middle germ layer (between ectoderm and endoderm) in the developing embryo; most parts of the animal body come from this layer—for example, muscles, bone, excretory system, and reproductive system.

messenger RNA (mRNA): soluble RNA synthesized by DNA in the nucleus into specific nucleotide sequences which convey information for protein synthesis to the cytoplasmic ribosomes.

metabolism: the total of all the chemical reactions occurring in an organism; the breakdown of food to produce the fuel molecules for energy is an important part of metabolism.

metacentric: describes the situation in which the centromere occurs at the center of a chromosome, producing arms of equal length; V-shaped at anaphase.

metamorphosis: the change in body form following embryonic development; often the changes from larva to adult.

metaphase: the stage of mitosis in which the chromosomes align on the equatorial plate prior to division.

Metaphyta: the kingdom name for plants.

Metazoa: the kingdom name for animals.

microsporangium: the structure that produces microspores which will develop into male gametophytes.

migration: the movement of species from one area into another.

mimicry: the imitation of one organism by another which serves for protection.

mineralocorticoids: steroid hormones secreted by the adrenal cortex which regulate the reabsorption of mineral ions by the kidneys.

mitochondria: membranous organelles in the cell cytoplasm that contain enzyme systems for energy production (Krebs cycle and the electron-transport series).

mitosis: an orderly sequence of nuclear and cytoplasmic events which produce two daughter cells exactly like the parent cell.

models: generally synonymous with the term theory; models are formulated from existing evidence and subjected to more experimentation.

mole: the amount of a substance that is equal to its molecular weight in grams.

molecule: a group of atoms held together by mutual attractions called chemical bonds.

Monera: the kingdom name of the procaryotic bacteria and blue-green algae which have no true nuclei, no cytoplasmic organelles, and no protein in their chromosomes.

monoecious: the condition in which male and female or staminate and pistillate structures are present in the same individual.

monohybrid cross: a genetic cross involving only one characteristic—for example, tallness in peas.

monosaccharides: simple sugars such as glucose which may unite to form more complex carbohydrates.

motor (efferent) pathway: nerve tracts carrying impulses from the spinal cord to effect a response (muscle contraction).

mRNA: *see* messenger RNA.

mucin: a complex polysaccharide protein which is the major constituent of mucus secreted along the digestive tract.

multiple alleles: describes the situation in which more than one set of alleles contribute to the expression of a particular trait.

mutation: any stable change in the genetic constitution of an organism.

muton: the smallest unit of genetic mutation; may correspond to a change in a single DNA nucleotide pair.

mutualism: two organisms living together in which both are mutually benefited.

mycelium: a collective mass of hyphae which forms the body of a fungus.

NAD: *see* nicotinamide adenine dinucleotide.

NADP: *see* nicotinamide adenine dinucleotide phosphate.

natural selection: the effect of different reproductive rates in a population due to the influence of the environment upon the different genetic types in that population. A more classical definition is: a process in nature resulting in the survival and perpetuation of only those forms of plant and animal life having certain favorable characteristics that enable them to adapt to a specific environment.

neo-Darwinism: the modern development of Darwin's theory of evolution which incorporates the theories of mutation and gene action.

nephridium: a tubular excretory organ found in some invertebrates such as the earthworm.

nephron: the individual, minute excretory unit of the vertebrate kidney.

nerve tissue: a tissue composed of cells specialized for the functions of irritability and conductivity; the fundamental nerve cell is called the neuron.

neutron: a component of the atomic nucleus which contributes one unit of mass but has no charge.

niche: the functional place of an organism in the community; sometimes called its "occupation."

nicotinamide adenine dinucleotide (NAD): a coenzyme that transports hydrogen.

nicotinamide adenine dinucleotide phosphate (NADP): a coenzyme that transports hydrogen.

nitrogen fixing: the production of usable nitrate from atmospheric nitrogen by certain bacteria; $N_2 \rightarrow NO_2 \rightarrow NO_3$.

nondisjunction: a situation in which homologous chromosomes do not separate during meiosis II; one gamete receives an extra chromosome and one receives none.

nonelectrolytes: compounds that do not dissociate in water and do not conduct electricity; for example, covalent compounds like sucrose.

notochord: a supporting rodlike structure occurring at some stage of development in all chordates.

nucleic acids: macromolecules composed of long chains of nucleotides; the two types are RNA and DNA.

nucleotide: the basic unit of nucleic acids composed of a nitrogen base, a five-carbon sugar, and phosphoric acid.

nucleus: the structure in most cells that contains the chromosomes (carriers of heredity) and the nucleoli (storage centers for ribosomal RNA).

oligotrophic: a body of water that contains little organic material in ratio to the volume of water.

omnivore: an animal that eats both plant and animal material; for example, man, pig, and bear.

oögenesis: the meiotic process in the ovary which produces eggs.

open circulatory system: a blood system composed of a heart and main arteries (no veins or capillaries) found in arthropods and some mollusks.

operant conditioning: learning through a program of reinforcement, such as a reward of food, for a certain behavior; the animal's behavior is instrumental in producing the learning.

operator gene: a gene that controls the function of a series of structural genes by turning the structural genes off or on.

operon: an operator gene and the associated structural genes that it controls.

organ: a group of tissues, united structurally,

that performs a specific function in a multicellular organism.

organism: a living unit in nature.

ornithine cycle: *see* urea cycle.

oscilloscope: an electronic instrument somewhat similar to a television set which allows visualization of electrical events such as the movement of a nerve impulse.

osmoregulation: the ability to maintain constant concentrations of body fluids despite changing conditions in the environment.

osmosis: the movement of water across a semipermeable membrane from a region of high concentration of water to a region of low concentration of water.

oviparous: describes the development of an organism within an egg that has been laid outside the mother's body.

ovule: the structure of the seed plant in which the egg or ovum is contained.

oxidation: the addition of oxygen to a compound or the loss of electrons (removal of hydrogen).

oxytocin: a hormone secreted by the posterior lobe of the pituitary which stimulates contraction of smooth muscle.

pancreatic amylase: an enzyme produced in the pancreas which hydrolyzes complex carbohydrates in the small intestine.

pancreatic lipase: a pancreatic enzyme that hydrolyzes fats to glycerol and fatty acids in the small intestine.

pancreozymin: a hormone secreted by the intestinal lining which initiates the flow of pancreatic enzymes.

pangenesis: the theory that small "pangenes" were collected into the gametes from all parts of the body.

parallelism: the evolutionary development of similar characteristics in two groups of organisms that are closely related.

parasitism: two organisms living together in which one is benefited but the other is harmed.

parathormone: the hormone secreted by the parathyroid glands which regulates the metabolism of calcium and phosphorus in the blood.

parenchyma: thin-walled cells that often contain chlorophyll and hence are sites of food making; they may also be sites for food storage in the stem or root.

parietal cells: cells in the stomach lining which secrete hydrochloric acid.

peck order: a social ranking system by which a definite hierarchy is established within a group; commonly observed in birds.

pepsin: an enzyme released into the stomach which breaks down complex proteins.

period: the horizontal rows of the periodic chart organized according to increasing atomic weight.

periodic chart: a table of all the known elements in which the elements are organized according to their chemical properties.

peripheral nervous system (PNS): a nerve network that includes the 12 pairs of cranial nerves and the 31 pairs of spinal nerves.

peristalsis: the rhythmic muscular contractions that move food along the digestive tract.

petals: the generally thin, leaflike, colored structures of the flower.

pH: *see* pH scale.

phagocytosis: the engulfment of solid particles into the cell.

pharyngeal gill slits: slitlike openings that appear in the pharynx of the embryonic stages of all chordates.

phenotype: the visible characteristics resulting from a genetic cross.

phenylketonuria (PKU): a metabolic disease that produces mental retardation and is caused by the inability of the organism to convert phenylalanine to tyrosine; phenylpyruvic acid is accumulated due to the absence of an enzyme.

pheromone: chemicals secreted by an organism which influence the behavior of other members of the same species.

phloem: food-conducting tissue of the plant that consists of sieve tubes and companion cells; it composes much of the bark of a tree.

photolysis: the separation of water into $[H^+ + e^- + OH]$ through the action of light and chlorophyll; sometimes called the light reaction of photosynthesis.

photosynthesis: the process of trapping light energy with the aid of chlorophyll to combine water and carbon dioxide to form carbohydrate.

pH scale: a numerical scale that indicates the relative amount of hydrogen ion in a solution; a pH value between 0 and 7 is acidic and between 7 and 14 is alkaline (7 represents neutral).

phylum: a major classification category of organisms with similar characteristics; phyla are subcategories within each kingdom.

pinocytosis: the engulfment of water into the cell.

pistil: the egg-producing portion of a flower, consisting of a stigma, style, and ovary; often called the female part.

pistillate: having a pistil or pistils, the egg- or ovule-producing structures in seed plants.

pituitary gland: the "master" endocrine gland attached by a short stalk to the hypothalamus of the brain; it is composed of three parts—a large anterior lobe, an intermediate lobe, and a posterior lobe.

PKU: *see* phenylketonuria.

placenta: the structural and functional connection between the mother and the embryo in most mammals; it is formed from parts of the chorion membrane and the lining of the uterus.

planet: a solid body of matter that orbits about a star and reflects light.

plankton: organisms that characteristically float with wind and tide; they provide food for larger consumers.

plasma cells: cells developed from lymphocytes capable of producing antibodies.

plasma membrane: the outermost living membrane of a cell.

plastids: bodies found in the cytoplasm of plant and some protist cells; the three kinds are leucoplasts, chromoplasts, and chloroplasts.

plastoquinone: an organic compound that contains a carbon-ring structure which can take up and release electrons; it is important in photolysis of photosynthesis.

pneumotaxic center: the area in the medulla oblongata of the brain that functions in the nervous control of breathing.

PNS: *see* peripheral nervous system.

pollination: the process in which the pollen grain comes in contact with an ovule and, ultimately, the egg.

polyribosome: a complex in the cytoplasm of a cell consisting of functional ribosomes and messenger RNA.

polysaccharides: long chains of monosaccharide units; for example, starch, glycogen, and cellulose.

population: a group of one species of organisms.

population genetics: the genetics of a breeding group or population.

porphyrins: a class of compounds composed of four pyrrole rings and a metallic ion; the fundamental structure of chlorophyll, hemoglobin, and cytochromes.

predation: a relation between animals in which one species (predator) hunts down and kills another species (prey) for food.

probability: the chance, often expressed as a percentage, that a specific event will occur; a probability of 1 (or 100 percent) represents certainty.

procaryotic: cells lacking a nuclear membrane, DNA-protein chromosomes, Golgi, mitochondria, lysosomes, and chloroplasts (bacteria and blue-green algae).

producers: primarily the photosynthetic members of the ecosystem.

productivity: generally the amount of carbon (as glucose or starch) made available by producers.

progesterone: a hormone secreted by the corpus luteum which promotes the vascularization of the uterine lining prior to the implantation of the fertilized egg.

prophase: a stage of mitosis in which chromosomes shorten, centrioles move to poles, asters form, nucleoli disappear, and the nuclear membrane breaks down; in meiosis, homologous chromosomes synapse.

proteins: complex compounds composed of amino acids connected by peptide linkages.

Protista: the kingdom name for organisms that cannot be classified as either true plants or animals.

proton: a component of the nucleus of an atom which has one unit of mass and a positive charge.

protonema: the "first thread" or filament of a germinating moss spore.

proximal convoluted tubule: the region of the nephron near the glomerulus where reabsorption of glucose, water, and some ions occurs.

pseudocoelom: a body cavity incompletely lined with mesoderm.

ptyalin: *see* salivary amylase.

pyloric valve: the muscular constriction between the pyloric stomach and the small intestine.

pylorus: the lower portion of the stomach which passes digesting food into the small intestine.

quantitative inheritance: when more than one set of alleles appear to influence the expression of a trait; sometimes called additive inheritance.

radial symmetry: a circular body plan that can be halved in two or more planes so that each half is a mirror image of the other.

reasoning: application of prior learning to new situations.

receptors: structures, often specialized, for the detection of chemical or physical changes both internal and external.

recessive gene: a gene that produces its characteristic only when two of the same type are present, that is, in the absence of a dominant gene.

recon: the unit of recombination; the distance between adjacent nucleotides in DNA.

reduction: the addition of electrons (or hydrogen) to a compound.

reflex: an involuntary response to a stimulus.

reflex arc: the reflex pathway that commonly involves sensory (afferent), internuncial, and motor (efferent) neurons; occurs across the spinal cord from dorsal root to ventral root.

regeneration: the process of producing a new structure to replace a lost part.

regulator gene: a gene that exerts a controlling action on other genes; acts on the operator gene.

releaser: a structure, chemical, sound, or action which acts as a stimulus to trigger specific behavior patterns.

rennin: an enzyme present in the stomach of young mammals which causes the curdling of milk.

repression: a situation in which the product of an enzymatic reaction interferes with the synthesis of an enzyme necessary for the formation of that product.

repressor: a protein which inhibits the synthesis of messenger RNA when combined with an operator gene.

respiration: the release of energy in the form of ATP from organic fuel molecules which can be used by cells; hydrogen atoms are removed in a sequence of reactions with the liberation of carbon dioxide and water.

respiratory quotient (R.Q.): the ratio of carbon dioxide produced to oxygen used in the oxidation of foods ($R.Q. = CO_2/O_2$).

resting potential: the electrical potential between ions inside and outside a nonconducting nerve cell membrane.

Rh factor: a group of antigens found in the red corpuscles of many humans that react with antibodies formed against rhesus monkey cells.

ribonucleic acid (RNA): a nucleic acid that contains ribose, found chiefly in the cytoplasm of cells; in comparison to DNA, it is generally single stranded and contains the pyrimidine uracil; the genetic material of many viruses.

ribulose diphosphate: a five-carbon sugar ($C_5H_8O_7P_2$) that combines with carbon dioxide in the first step of the dark reaction (carbon fixation) of photosynthesis.

RNA: *see* ribonucleic acid.

root pressure: the pressure produced by water moving into root hair cells which helps move water upward in the plant.

RQ: *see* respiratory quotient.

rugae: the ridgelike folds of the interior stomach wall.

salivary amylase (ptyalin): a salivary enzyme that hydrolyzes carbohydrate to double sugars.

salt: the product formed in the reaction between a strong acid and a strong base.

saprophyte: an organism which obtains its nutrition from dead organic material.

schizocoelom: a coelom formed in some animals by the splitting of a mesodermal sheet.

science: an organized study of the material universe; scientific methods involve procedures that provide an orderly and systematic approach to problems dealing with matter.

sclerenchyma: cells with thick, hardened walls which provide support and rigidity to plant stems.

secretin: a hormone secreted by the intestinal lining which stimulates the flow of sodium bicarbonate from the pancreas.

seed: an embryo with associated food and a hardened coat.

segregation: the random separation of genes during meiosis when each gamete receives a complete set of alleles; Mendel's first law.

sensory (afferent) pathway: the nerve tract bringing sensory impulses into the spinal cord.

sepals: the green, leaflike structures that protect the flower bud and are located at the base of an open flower.

serosa: the extraembryonic membrane formed by the apposition of the chorion and allantois.

sex chromosomes: a pair of chromosomes distinguishable from other chromosomes in the cell which are often different in male and female.

sickle-cell anemia: an anemia (impaired oxygen transport) caused by the production of an inefficient hemoglobin and deformed sickle-shaped red blood cells.

somatotropin: a hormone secreted by the anterior lobe of the pituitary which stimulates growth and metabolism.

speciation: the process by which new species are formed; when sufficient changes have occurred in the genotypes of certain populations due to physical or biological barriers so that the organisms cannot interbreed, a new species is formed.

spermatogenesis: the meiotic process in the testes which produces sperm cells.

spindle: the mitotic spindle consists of long protein fibers between the two centrioles; each chromosome is attached to a spindle fiber.

spiracles: the small outside openings of the tracheal tube respiratory system in insects.

sporangium: the spore-producing structure of the sporophyte.

sporophyte: the diploid generation of a plant which produces spores.

stamen: the organ of a flower consisting of a pollen-producing anther and a supporting filament.

staminate: having a stamen or stamens, the pollen-producing structures in seed plants.

star: a self-luminescent collection of matter in the universe.

steady state: *see* homeostasis.

stimulus: any internal or external change that can cause a biological reaction.

stroke: a loss of blood supply or hemorrhage in the brain often causing paralysis and loss of sensation.

structural gene: the gene that codes messenger RNA for the production of a specific protein.

submetacentric: describes the situation in which the centromere occurs nearer one end of a chromosome to produce a long and a short arm; J-shaped at anaphase.

succession: the progressive changes in vegetation in an area.

sucrase: an enzyme that hydrolyzes sucrose into glucose and fructose.

symbiosis: the living together of two dissimilar organisms, especially when the association is mutually beneficial.

synapse: the junction between two neurons.

synapsis: the pairing of homologous chromosomes in the first prophase of meiosis.

synthesis: a chemical process in which small molecules are joined to form larger molecules; this usually involves the loss of water (dehydration).

systolic pressure: the blood pressure resulting from contraction of the atria and ventricles of the heart during a heartbeat cycle.

taxis: movement of an organism in response to a stimulus.

teleology: a philosophy which states that all things exist for a predestined purpose; events occurring under this philosophy are sometimes referred to as the "divine plan."

telophase: a stage of mitosis in which the cell membrane constricts (in animals) or cell wall develops (in plants) and daughter cells are formed; chromosomes and nucleus return to interphasic condition.

territoriality: the phenomenon whereby a specific number of animals mark and defend a particular area against intruding species.

test cross (back cross): a test for determining whether a parent is homozygous or heterozygous dominant; the doubtful genotype is crossed back to the recessive character.

testosterone: the male hormone secreted by the interstitial cells of the testis which is responsible for male secondary sex characteristics.

tetrad: the result of duplicated homologous chromosomes following synapsis; it is thought that crossover occurs at this stage of meiosis.

thalamus: a portion of the forebrain beneath and posterior to each cerebral hemisphere; provides relay connections between spinal cord and cerebrum.

theory: an explanation of an observed event based on extensive experimentation or testing.

thermocline: a zone in a lake or ocean in which there is a rapid drop in temperature related to depth.

thoracic cavity: the chest cavity containing the heart and lungs.

thoracic duct: the large duct of the lymphatic system in mammals which transports fats and lymph from the lacteals to the superior vena cava.

thyroid gland: a bilobed endocrine gland located on each side of the trachea, the secretion of which regulates the rates of metabolism and body growth.

thyrotropic hormone (TSH): also called thyroid-stimulating hormone; a hormone secreted by the anterior lobe of the pituitary which stimulates the thyroid gland to produce thyroxin.

thyroxin: the hormone secreted by the thyroid gland which contains iodine and increases metabolism.

trachea: the windpipe leading to the lungs.

tracheal tubes: a system of small tubules in insects which supply air directly to the tissues.

transamination: the exchange of an amino (NH_2) group between an amino acid and a keto acid or between two amino acids.

transduction: the result of the transfer of DNA from one bacterium into another through the agency of a bacterial virus.

transfer RNA (tRNA): RNA synthesized by DNA in the nucleus which has two areas of unpaired bases—one area attaches to a specific amino acid and the other recognizes the mRNA code on the ribosomes.

transformation: the result of the direct transfer of DNA from one bacterium into another.

translocation: the movement of food materials in plants from the leaves to other areas for storage or respiration; also the breaking off of a segment of a chromosome followed by a reunion of that segment with a homologous or nonhomologous chromosome.

transmission genetics: the part of genetics that deals with the transfer and recombination of genetic traits between organisms.

transpiration: the release of water to the atmosphere from the leaves and stems of plants.

tRNA: *see* transfer RNA.

trophectoderm: the outer layer of cells surrounding the inner cell mass of developing primate eggs.

trophic levels: the various energy levels in an ecosystem beginning with the producers and ending with the decomposers.

tropism: a movement in plants caused by a growth response to a stimulus.

trypsin: a pancreatic enzyme that hydrolyzes proteins into amino acids in the intestine.

TSH: *see* thyrotropic hormone.

Turner's syndrome: a human condition in which the offspring receives only a single X chromosome because of nondisjunction in the female; the single X chromosome comes from the male.

umbilical cord: the cord that contains blood vessels and connects the embryo to the placenta; the navel is the point of attachment on the embryo.

urea cycle (ornithine cycle): a cyclic series of chemical reactions that combine carbon dioxide and ammonia into urea.

ureotelic: describes the excretion of urea as the principal form of nitrogenous waste.

uricotelic: denotes the excretion of uric acid as the principal form of nitrogenous waste.

valence: the bonding potential of an atom; valence is determined by the number of electrons in the outer shell.

vasopressin (ADH): an antidiuretic hormone (ADH) secreted by the posterior lobe of the pituitary which causes constriction of blood vessels and reabsorption of water in the kidney tubules.

vestigial: describes anatomical structures that have been retained in an organism but are no longer of functional significance.

villi: fingerlike projections of the lining of the intestine; they greatly increase the absorptive surface area.

vitalism: a philosophy which holds that events of unknown cause are produced by supernatural forces.

vitamins: organic compounds necessary for the proper functioning of specific enzymes, usually forming a vital part of a coenzyme.

viviparous: indicates the development of an organism within the mother's body.

xylem: plant tissue that conducts water upward in the plant and consists mainly of tracheid and vessel cells and fibers; it forms the woody part of a tree.

yolk sac: the food source for embryos of reptiles and birds but practically nonfunctional in most mammals.

zoöspores: flagellated, motile spores that develop directly into new plants.

zygote: the result of the union of two gametes; a fertilized egg ($2n$).

Index